Bears' Guide to Earning College Degrees Nontraditionally
12th Edition for 1996

John Bear, Ph.D.
Mariah Bear, M.A.

C & B PUBLISHING
BENICIA, CALIFORNIA

ALSO DISTRIBUTED BY
TEN SPEED PRESS
BERKELEY, CALIFORNIA

Published by
C & B PUBLISHING
P.O. Box 826 • Benicia, California 94510
(707) 747-5950

Library of Congress Catalog Number: 95-67362 • ISBN 0-9629312-3-3

Also by John Bear and Mariah Bear:
Finding Money for College (Ten Speed Press, 1993; annual editions starting with 1996)

Some Other Books by John Bear:
(Ten Speed Press books can be purchased at most bookstores, or by calling 1-800-841-BOOK)
The #1 New York Times Bestseller (Ten Speed Press, 1993)
Computer Wimp No More: The Intelligent Beginner's Guide to Computers (Ten Speed Press, 1992)
Morning Food: Breakfast Cooking at the Cafe Beaujolais (with Margaret Fox, Ten Speed Press, 1989)
How to Repair Food (with Marina Bear, Ten Speed Press, 1988)
Cafe Beaujolais Cookbook (with Margaret Fox, Ten Speed Press, 1984)
Computer Wimp: 166 things I wish I had known before I bought my first computer (Ten Speed Press, 1983)
The Alternative Guide to Higher Education (Grosset & Dunlap, 1980)
Communication (Time-Life Books, 1976)
The United States of America: The Land and Its People (Time-Life Books, 1974)

Library of Congress Catloging-in-Publication Data
(prepared by Quality Books, Inc.)

Bear, John 1938-
Bears' guide to earning college degrees nontraditionally/ John B. Bear, Mariah P. Bear. -- 12th ed.
p. cm.
Includes bibliographic references and indexes.
Preassigned LCCN: 95-67362
ISBN 0-9629312-3-3

1. Universities and colleges--United States--Directories. 2. Non-formal education--United States--Directories. 3. Correspondence schools and courses--United States--Directories. 4. Degrees, Academic--United States--Directories. I. Bear, Mariah P. II. Title. III Title: Guide to earning college degrees nontraditionally.

L901.B37 1995   378.2'025'73
                       QBI95-20011

Disclaimer
While the authors believe that the information in this book is correct as of the time of publication,
it is possible we may have made errors, which we will correct at the first available opportunity.
Neither we, the publisher, nor the distributor can be responsible for any problems that may
arise in readers' interactions with any schools described in the book.

Printed in the United States of America

CONTENTS

DEDICATIONS

Mariah's

To Joe,
who survived months of book-related abandonment with equanimity,
and only got into trouble once or twice.

John's

To Marina,
for the twelfth consecutive time, with undiminished love,
thanks, and gratitude for all you have done.

ACKNOWLEDGEMENTS

We do not have a staff. We do not have platoons of graduate students whom we can send to the library to do research for us. Like Blanche Dubois, we are dependent upon the kindness of strangers: those many hundreds of readers who regularly write, fax, and email to tell us of errors, changes, new schools and new programs in old schools. There are far too many such kind people for us to list individually. We are especially grateful for the assistance, over the years, of Lal Balkaran in Canada, Jim Delmont in Nebraska, Allen Ezell in Florida, Lili Garrett in Florida, Bob Giovatti in California, Lyndon Jones in England, Louis Luyt in South Africa, Peter Proehl in California, Reg Sheldrick in Louisiana, William Sloane in Pennsylvania, Werner Stiewe in Germany, and Josh Walston in Washington. Some of the early research for this twelfth edition was done by John's other daughters (and Mariah's sisters), Susannah Lujan-Bear and Tanya Zeryck. Thank you both.

Long-time readers of this book will note that for the first time in its more-than-twenty-year life span, it has been professionally designed and produced. We are especially pleased with the initial design concept from Alexandra Chappell, the further design work and the meticulous and skillful rendering of the text into PageMaker by Felipe Lujan-Bear, and the splendid cover by Cale Burr. Thank you one and all.

About the Authors:
Their Lives, Their Biases,
and a Request for Help

Sharp-eyed regular readers may have noted a small but very significant change in the title of this edition. The apostrophe has moved one notch to the right. No longer *Bear's Guide*, it is now *Bears' Guide*, signifying more than one Bear involved. Here is some of the background of the two Bears who produced this 12th edition.

John Bear attended school at a time when nontraditional education was virtually nonexistent in the United States. Still, he *was* able to create his own alternative program within the traditional framework. He started working full-time during his junior year at Reed College, and continued to hold a variety of demanding off-campus jobs while earning his Master's at Berkeley and Ph.D. from Michigan State University. He was generally able to integrate these jobs—which included working as a newspaper reporter, prison psychologist, advertising writer, and researcher at a school for the deaf—into his academic studies, but received little support or encouragement from faculty or administration.

Dr. Bear has taught at major universities (Iowa, Berkeley, Michigan State) and small schools (City College of San Francisco, College of the Redwoods), been a business executive (research director for Bell & Howell's educational division, director of communications for the Midas Muffler Shop chain), director of the Center for the Gifted Child in San Francisco, and consultant to a wide range of organizations, including General Motors, Xerox, *Encyclopaedia Britannica*, and the Grateful Dead. Since 1974, he has devoted much of his time to investigating and writing about nontraditional higher education.

In 1977, he established Degree Consulting Services, to offer detailed consulting to people seeking more personal advice than a book can provide. While he no longer counsels individual clients, the service is still available (see Appendix C for further information).

He is currently the North American agent for the MBA by distance learning offered by Heriot-Watt University of Edinburgh, Scotland.

John's daughter Mariah joins him as a coauthor with this edition. She can honestly claim a lifelong involvement with nontraditional education, beginning around the age of seven when she earned allowance money working in her father's office. She took six years to get her Bachelor's degree at Berkeley (Phi Beta Kappa), scheduling classes around a flex-time job with a major book publisher. (Well-intentioned admissions counselors discourage this sort of thing; they often seem to feel a challenging job is incompatible with academic success.) In graduate school, Mariah managed to schedule all but one of her required classes in the evenings, allowing her to freelance at *New York* magazine, the *Village Voice*, and other publications while earning a Master's in journalism from New York University.

The rest of the family pursued similarly nontraditional paths to higher education. Twenty years after completing her traditional B.A., Marina (wife of John, mother of Mariah) earned the nonresident M.A. in humanities at California State University, Dominguez Hills, followed by a Ph.D. at Vanderbilt University. The other two children, twin daughters, both left high school at age 15, midway through 10th grade, and passed the state high school equivalency exam. Susannah went on to college at that early age; Tanya worked for three years, then entered college at the "traditional" age of 18.

BIASES

As you read this book, you will note that it is biased. The authors have strong opinions about which schools and programs are good and which are not, and do not hesitate to say so. Bear has been sued three times for millions of dollars by people who operate what he called (and continues to call) illegal diploma mills. None has ever won a cent. While the research and experiences are largely John's, the opinions are shared by both authors.

Over the years, John has done consulting or advisory work for various schools in return for money, goods (generally the use of their mailing lists to help sell this book), and, in two cases, stock:

♦ In return for consulting work in the mid 1970s, Columbia Pacific University paid him with a small amount of its stock, which he sold more than a decade ago.

♦ Bear was one of four founders of Fairfax University, a not-for-profit nontraditional school. Once it was launched, he resigned, and had no further connection whatsoever.

♦ In 1987, eager to experience nontraditional education from the other side of the desk, as it were, he accepted the presidency of the International Institute for Advanced Studies, a small, older (in this field, being founded in 1972 makes one a true pioneer) nonprofit school. That school evolved into Greenwich University.

♦ For 18 months in 1990-1991, he served as full-time president of Greenwich University in Hawaii.

♦ In late 1991, he and his wife were appointed the U.S. agents for the Heriot-Watt University Distance Learning M.B.A. Heriot-Watt is a large Scottish university that was founded in 1821. They have opened an office in California, for North Americans interested in this splendid program, the world's only accredited home-study MBA that does not require a Bachelor's degree. You will find it described on page 99.

We are confident that these activities have had, and will continue to have, no bearing on the opinions expressed in this book. Hundreds of excellent schools have never even taken us to lunch, yet we recommend them highly. (We will probably accept if they ever do offer lunch.) On the other side of the ledger, there is no way in the world we can be persuaded to say good things about bad, or questionable, schools. While individual evaluations may change (schools do get better or worse, new information comes to light), the basic judgment criteria are not subject to outside influence. And contrary to what some operators of sleazy schools claim, no one has ever paid a cent to be listed in this book.

HELP

Over the years, readers have provided great amounts of immensely valuable feedback. If you are aware of schools or programs we have overlooked, please let us know. If your experience with a school is at odds with what we've written, please don't hesitate to tell us about it. This book may be biased, but the authors like to think they are open-minded, and many schools' evaluations have changed (both up and down) in the past 20 years.

Please communicate in writing, and if you'd like a reply (we can't guarantee it, but we'll do our best), please enclose a stamped self-addressed envelope or, outside the U.S., two international reply coupons, available at your post office. You can reach us at this address:

John and Mariah Bear
P.O. Box 7070
Berkeley, CA 94707

Thank you.

6

"It is my wish that this be the most educated country in the world, and toward that end I hereby ordain that each and every one of my people be given a diploma."

*You're never too old to begin home study.
This woman is 137 years old, and she is
halfway through her volleyball textbook.*

What Nontraditional Education Is All About

In times of great change, learners inherit the earth, while the learned find themselves beautifully equipped for a world that no longer exists.
MICHAEL PORTER

The man on the telephone was so distraught, he was almost in tears. For more than 20 years, he had been in charge of sawing off dead tree branches for a large midwestern city. But a new personnel policy in that city decreed that henceforth, all department heads would have to have Bachelor's degrees. If this man could not earn a degree within two years, he would no longer be permitted to continue in the job he had been performing satisfactorily for over two decades.

It is an unfortunate but very real aspect of life today that a college or university degree is often more important (or at least more useful) than a good education or substantial knowledge in your field, whether that field involves nuclear physics or sawing off branches. It doesn't matter if you've been reading, studying, and learning all your life. It doesn't matter how good you are at what you do. In many situations, if you don't have a piece of (usually imitation) parchment that certifies you as a Bachelor, Master, or Doctor, you are perceived as somehow less worthy, and are often denied the better jobs and higher salaries that go to degree-holders.

In fact, as more and more degree-holders, from space scientists to philosophers, are unable to find employment in their specific chosen fields and move elsewhere in the job market, degrees become more important than ever. Consider, for instance, a job opening for a high-school English teacher. Five applicants with comparable skills apply, but one has a Doctorate while the other four have Bachelor's degrees. Who do you think would probably get the job?

Never mind that you don't need a Ph.D. to teach high-school English any more than you need a B.A. to chop down trees. The simple fact is that degrees are extremely valuable commodities in the job market.

Happily, as the need for degrees increases, availability has kept pace. Since the mid 1970s, there has been a virtual explosion in what is now commonly called "alternative" or "nontraditional" and "external" or "off-campus" education—ways and means of getting an education or a degree (or both, if you wish) without sitting in classrooms day after day, year after year.

The rallying cry was, in fact, sounded in 1973 by Ewald B. Nyquist, then president of the wonderfully innovative University of the State of New York. He said:

> There are thousands of people . . . who contribute in important ways to the life of the communities in which they live, even though they do not have a college degree. Through native intelligence, hard work and sacrifice, many have gained in knowledge and understanding. And yet, the social and economic advancement of these people has been thwarted in part by the emphasis that is put on the possession of credentials . . . As long as we remain a strongly credentialed society . . . employers will not be disposed to hire people on the basis of what they know, rather than on what degrees and diplomas they hold. If attendance at a college is the only road to these credentials, those who cannot or have not availed themselves of this route but have acquired knowledge and skills through other sources, will be denied the recognition and advancement to which they are entitled. Such inequity should not be tolerated.

Nontraditional education takes many forms, including the following:

♦ credit (and degrees) for life-experience learning, even if the learning took place long before you entered school;

♦ credit (and degrees) for passing examinations;

♦ credit (and degrees) for independent study, whether or not you were enrolled in a school at the time;

♦ credit (and degrees) through intensive study (for instance, 10 hours a day for a month instead of one hour a day for a year);

♦ credit (and degrees) through guided private study at your own pace, from your own home or office, under the supervision of a faculty member with whom you communicate on a regular basis;

♦ credit (and degrees) for work done on your home or office computer, linked to your school's computer, wherever in the world it may be;

♦ credit (and degrees) from weekend schools, evening schools, and summer-only schools;

♦ credit (and degrees) entirely by correspondence;

♦ credit (and degrees) through the use of audio- and videotaped courses that you can review at your convenience.

This book endeavors to cover all these areas, and more, as completely as possible. Yet this is truly an impossible task. New programs are introduced literally every day. In recent years, an average of one new college or university has opened for business every *week*, while old, established universities are disappearing at the rate of two or three per month.

So, although this book is as current and correct as we can possibly make it, some recent changes probably won't be covered, and, inevitably, there will be errors and omissions. For all of these, we apologize now, and invite your suggestions and criticisms for the next edition. Thank you.

Perhaps the best way to make clear, in a short space, the differences between the traditional (dare one say old-fashioned) approaches to education and degrees and the nontraditional (or modern) approach is to offer the following dozen comparisons:

Traditional education awards degrees on the basis of time served and credit earned.
Nontraditional education awards degrees on the basis of competencies and performance skills.

Traditional education bases degree requirements on a medieval formula that calls for some generalized education and some specialized education.
Nontraditional education bases degree requirements on an agreement between the student and the faculty, aimed at helping the student achieve his or her career, personal, or professional goals.

Traditional education awards the degree when the student has taken the required number of credits in the required order.
Nontraditional education awards the degree when the student's actual work and learning reach certain previously agreed-upon levels.

Traditional education considers the years from age 18 to age 22 the appropriate time to earn a first degree.
Nontraditional education assumes learning is desirable at any age, and that degrees should be available to people of all ages.

Traditional education considers the classroom to be the primary source of information and the campus the center of learning.
Nontraditional education believes that some sort of learning can and does occur in any part of the world.

Traditional education believes that printed texts should be the principal learning resource.
Nontraditional education believes the range of learning resources is limitless, from the daily newspaper to personal interviews; from videotapes to computers to world travel.

Traditional faculty must have appropriate credentials and degrees.
Nontraditional faculty are selected for competency and personal qualities in *addition* to credentials and degrees.

Traditional credits and degrees are based primarily on mastery of course content.
Nontraditional credits and degrees add a consideration of learning *how to learn*, and the integration of diverse fields of knowledge.

Traditional education cultivates dependence on authority through prescribed curricula, required campus residence, and required classes.
Nontraditional education cultivates self-direction and independence through planned independent study, both on and off campus.

Traditional curricula are generally oriented toward traditional disciplines and well-established professions.
Nontraditional curricula reflect a range of individual students' needs and goals, and are likely to be problem-oriented, issue-oriented, and world-oriented.

Traditional education aims at producing "finished products"—students who are done with their education and ready for the job market.
Nontraditional education aims at producing lifelong learners, capable of responding to their own evolving needs and those of society over an entire lifetime.

Traditional education, to adapt the old saying, gives you a fish and feeds you for a day.
Nontraditional education teaches you how to fish, and feeds you for life.

Traditional education had nothing to offer the dead-tree-limb expert.
Nontraditional education made it possible for him to complete a good Bachelor's degree in less than a year, entirely by correspondence and at a modest cost. His job is now secure.

♦2♦
What Are Colleges and Universities, and How Do They Work?

A college is a machine that transfers information from the notes of the professor to the notes of the student without it passing through the mind of either.
TRADITIONAL

The question posed by this chapter's title may sound trivial or inconsequential, but it turns out to be quite a complex issue for which there is no simple answer at all.

Many state legislatures have struggled with the problem of producing precise definitions of words like *college* and *university*. (One school even tried to sue its state's department of education to force them to define "educational process." The state managed to evade the suit.)

Some states have simply given up the problem as unsolvable, which is why they either have virtually no laws governing higher education, or laws that are incredibly restrictive. Needless to say, the former policy encourages the proliferation of degree mills and other bad schools, and the latter policy discourages the establishment of any creative new nontraditional schools or programs.

Other states have, from time to time, produced rather ingenious definitions, such as Ohio's (later repealed), stating that a "university" was anything that (a) said it was a university, and (b) had an endowment or facilities worth $1 million. The assumption, of course, was that no degree mill could be so well endowed. California once had a similar law under which the sum was only $50,000. In the 1980s, much tougher requirements were instituted and, although California still has more unaccredited schools than any other state, the number is declining rapidly. Hawaii is fast becoming the next home for many of these schools—some good, some awful.

Many people remember a famous CBS *60 Minutes* episode in 1978, in which the proprietor of a flagrant diploma mill was actually arrested while being interviewed by Mike Wallace. At the time, his school, California Pacifica University, was licensed by the state of California. The owner had bought some used books and office furniture, declared this property to be worth $50,000, and consequently received state authorization to grant degrees, up to and including Doctorates.

History repeated itself in 1990 when the proprietor of yet another degree mill, North American University, was enjoined from operating by the state of Utah on the very day that *Inside Edition*'s television crew arrived to film his nefarious operation.

The problem of definition is made even more complicated by the inconsistent way in which the words "college" and "university" are used.

In the United States, the two words are used almost interchangeably. Before long, they will probably mean exactly the same thing. Historically, a college has been a subdivision of a university. For instance, the University of California is divided into a College of Arts and Sciences, a College of Education, a College of Law, and so on. The University of Oxford is comprised of Balliol College, Exeter College, Magdalen College, and about three dozen others.

Today, however, many degree-granting colleges exist independent of any university, and many universities have no colleges. There is also an ever-growing trend for colleges to rename themselves as universities, either to reflect their growth or enhance their image, or both. In recent years, dozens of colleges, from Antioch in Ohio to San Francisco State in California, have turned themselves into universities. While many British traditionalists sneered at the U.S. for doing this, the same thing happened in the United Kingdom in the early and mid 1990s: dozens of technical schools, colleges, and institutes overnight became universities, at least in name.

The situation outside the United States makes all this even more complex. In most countries, the word "college" rarely refers to a degree-granting institution, and often is used for what Americans call a high school. American personnel managers and admissions officers have been fooled by this fact. An Englishman, for instance, who states on his job application, "Graduate of Eton College," means, simply, that he has completed the high school of that name.

Many readers have told us that they simply will not go to a "college," no matter how good it may be, because the word just doesn't sound *real* enough to them.

Finally, some degree-granting institutions choose a name other than "college" or "university." The most common are "school" (e.g., the New School for Social Research; California School of Professional Psychology, etc.) and "institute" (e.g., Fielding Institute, Union Institute, etc.).

HOW COLLEGES AND UNIVERSITIES WORK

The Calendar

There is no uniform pattern to the calendar, or scheduling of classes, from one school to the next. However, most schools tend to follow one of four basic patterns:

1. **The semester plan.** A semester is 16 to 18 weeks long and there are usually two semesters per year, plus a shorter summer session. Many classes are one semester long, but some extend over two or more semesters (e.g., Algebra I in the fall semester and Algebra II in the spring).

A class that meets three hours a week for one semester is likely to be worth three semester hours of credit. The *actual* amount of credit could be anywhere from two to six semester hours for such a class, depending on the amount of homework, additional reading, laboratory time, etc.

2. **The quarter plan.** Many universities divide the year into four quarters of equal length, usually 11 or 12 weeks each. Many courses require two or more quarters to complete. A course that meets three hours a week for a quarter will probably be worth three quarter hours, or quarter units, but can range from two to six. One semester unit is equal to one-and-a-half quarter units.

3. **The trimester plan.** A much smaller number of schools divide the year into three equal trimesters of 15 or 16 weeks each. A trimester unit is usually equal to one-and-a-quarter semester units.

4. **Weekend colleges.** An innovative and increasingly common system that allows schools to make more efficient use of their facilities, and working students to earn a conventional degree. All courses are taught intensively on Friday nights, Saturdays, and/or Sundays. Hundreds of traditional residential schools in the U.S. offer some weekend programs, many of which are described in chapters 18 and 21. For additional programs in your area, check with nearby community colleges, colleges, and universities.

Other alternatives: National University, the University of Phoenix, and other relatively new schools have popularized a system in which students take one course per month, and can begin their degree program on the first day of any month. The school offers one or more complete, intensive course each month.

Many nonresident programs have no calendar at all. Students can begin their independent-study program as soon as they have been admitted.

How Credit Is Earned

In a traditional school, most credit is earned by taking classes. Nontraditional units may be earned in other ways. There are four common methods:

1. **Life experience learning.** Credit is given for what you have learned, regardless of how or where it was learned. For example, a given university might offer six courses in German worth four semester units each. If you can show them that you speak and write German just as well as someone who has taken and passed those six courses, they will award you 24 semester units of German, whether you learned the language from your grandmother, from living in Germany, or from Berlitz tapes. The same philosophy applies to business experience, learning to fly an airplane, military training, and dozens of other nonclassroom learning experiences.

2. **Equivalency examinations.** Many schools say that anyone who can pass an examination in a subject should get credit for knowing that subject, without having to sit in a classroom month after month to "learn" what they already know. More than 100 standard equivalency exams are offered, worth anywhere from two to 30 semester units each. In general, each hour of examination is worth from two to six semester units, but different schools may award significantly different amounts of credit for the same examinations. Some schools will design examinations in fields in which there are no standard exams.

3. **Correspondence courses.** More than 100 universities offer thousands of home-study courses, most of which can be taken by people living anywhere in the world. These courses are generally worth two to six semester units each and can take anywhere from a month or two to a year or more to complete.

4. **Learning contracts.** Quite a few schools negotiate learning contracts with their students. A learning contract is a formal, negotiated agreement between the student and the school, stating that if the student successfully completes certain tasks (for instance, reads these books, writes a paper of this length, does the following laboratory experiments, etc.), the school will award an agreed-upon number of credits.

Learning contracts can be written for a few units, an entire degree program, or anything in between. Often the school will provide a faculty member to guide the course of study.

All four of these alternative ways to earn credit will be discussed in some detail in later chapters.

Grading and Evaluation Systems

Most schools, traditional and nontraditional, use one of four common grading systems. Grades are generally given for each separate course taken. Some schools assign grades to equivalency examinations, learning-contract work, and correspondence courses as well. Life-experience credit is rarely graded; schools usually assign it a certain number of units without further evaluation.

The four common systems are:

1. **Letter grades.** An "A" is the highest grade; "B" means "good," "C" means "average," "D" stands for "barely passing" (or, in some cases, "failing"), and "F" is a failing grade. Some schools add pluses and minuses—a B+ is better than a B, but not quite as good as an A-. Some schools use "AB" instead of B+ or A-. And some give an "A+" for superior work.

2. **Number grades.** Many schools grade on a scale of 0 (worst grade) to 4 (highest grade). The best students receive grades of 3.9 or 4.0; other outstanding students might get a 3.7 or 3.8. To pass, students usually must score at least 1.0 (or a 1.5). Just to make it even more confusing, some schools use a 0 to 3 or 0 to 5 scale, but 4 is the most common top grade. A small number of schools give the numerical equivalent of A+, a 4.5, which means that even on a four-point scale, it is possible to have a grade point average higher than four.

3. **Percentage grades.** A smaller number of schools follow the European system of grading each student in each class on a percentage score, from 0 to 100 percent. In most (but not all) schools, a grade of 90 to 100 percent is considered excellent, 80 to 90 is good, 70 to 80 is fair, 60 to 70 is either failure or barely passing, and below 60 percent is failing.

4. **Pass/fail.** Quite a few universities offer a pass/fail option, either for some classes or, more rarely, for all classes.

In such a system, the teacher does not evaluate the student's performance beyond stating whether each student has passed or failed the course. At many schools students may choose the pass/fail option for one or two out of the four or five courses they are expected to take each semester or quarter. In some pass/fail situations, a numerical or letter grade is actually given, but not revealed to the student or used to calculate grade point average. And in a few schools, the actual grade will be revealed only if the student asks and, sometimes, pays an additional fee.

Grade Point Average

Most schools report a student's overall performance in terms of the G.P.A., or grade point average. This is the average of all grades received, weighted by the number of semester or quarter units each course is worth.

For example, if a student gets a 4.0 (or an A) in a course worth 3 semester units, and a 3.0 (or a B) in a course worth 2 semester units, his or her G.P.A. would be calculated like this: 3 x 4.0 = 12. And 2 x 3.0 = 6. So, 12 + 6 = 18, divided by a total of 5 semester units, results in a G.P.A. of 3.6.

Pass/fail courses are generally not taken into account when calculating a grade point average.

One's G.P.A. can be very important. Often it is necessary to maintain a certain average in order to earn a degree—typically a 2.0 (in a four-point system) for a Bachelor's degree, and a 3.0 for a Master's degree or Doctorate. Honors degrees (*magna cum laude*, etc.), scholarships, and even permission to play on the football team are dependent on the G.P.A. (No, nonresident schools do not have football teams. Some of us are waiting for a chess-by-mail or computer-game league to spring up, however.)

COPPERFIELD University Home Study Course in Child Care. Lesson 17: Raise this baby to the age of 3. Teach it to speak and read. Then mail it back in for evaluation.

Degrees, Degree Requirements, and Transcripts

It is not titles that honor men, but men that honor titles.
NICCOLÓ MACHIAVELLI

A degree is a title conferred by a school to show that a certain course of study has been successfully completed. A diploma is the actual document or certificate that is given to the student as evidence of the awarding of the degree.

Diplomas are also awarded for courses of study that do *not* result in a degree such as, for example, on completion of a program in real-estate management, air-conditioning repair, or military leadership. This can lead to confusion, often intentionally, as in the case of someone who says, "I earned my diploma at Harvard," meaning that he or she attended a weekend seminar there, and received some sort of diploma of completion.

The following six kinds of degrees are awarded by colleges and universities in the United States:

The Associate's Degree

The Associate's degree is a relatively recent development, reflecting the tremendous growth of two-year community colleges (which is the new and presumably more respectable name for what used to be known as junior colleges).

Since many of the students who attend these schools do not continue on to another school to complete a Bachelor's degree, a need was felt for a degree to be awarded at the end of these two years of full-time study (or their equivalent by nontraditional means). More than 2,000 two-year schools now award the Associate's degree, and a small but growing number of four-year schools also award it, to students who leave after two years.

The two most common Associate's degrees are the A.A. (Associate of Arts) and the A.S. (Associate of Science), but more than 100 other titles have been devised, ranging from the A.M.E. (Associate of Mechanical Engineering) to the A.D.T. (Associate of Dance Therapy).

An Associate's degree typically requires 60 to 64 semester hours of credit (or 90 to 96 quarter hours), which, in a traditional program, normally takes two academic years (four semesters, or six quarters) to complete.

The Bachelor's Degree

The Bachelor's degree has been around for hundreds of years. In virtually every nation worldwide, it is the first university degree earned. (The Associate's is little used outside the United States.) In America, the Bachelor's is traditionally considered to be a four-year degree (120 to 128 semester units, or 180 to 192 quarter units, of full-time study), although a rather surprising report in 1990 revealed that the average Bachelor's takes closer to six years. In most of the rest of the world, it is expected to take three years. Through nontraditional approaches, some people with a good deal of prior learning can earn their Bachelor's degrees in as little as two or three months.

The Bachelor's degree is supposed to signify that the holder has accumulated a "batch" of knowledge; that he or she has learned a considerable amount in a particular field of study (the "major"), and gained some broad general knowledge of the world as well (history, literature, art, social science, mathematics). This broad approach to the degree is peculiar to traditional American programs. In most other countries, and in nontraditional American programs, the Bachelor's degree involves much more intensive study in a given field. When someone educated in England says, "I read history at Oxford," it means that for the better part of three years he or she did, in fact, read history and not much else. This is one reason traditional American degrees take longer to acquire than most foreign ones.

More than 300 different Bachelor's degree titles have been used in the last hundred years, but the great majority of the million-plus Bachelor's degrees awarded in the United States each year are either the B.A. (Bachelor of Arts) or the B.S. (Bachelor of Science), sometimes with additional letters to indicate the field (B.S.E.E. for electrical engineering, B.A.B.A. for business administration, and so on). Other common Bachelor's degree titles include the B.B.A. (Bachelor of Business Administration), B.Mus. (Music), B.Ed. (Education), and B.Eng. (Engineering). Some nontraditional schools and programs award the B.G.S. (Bachelor of General Studies), B.I.S. (Independent Studies), or B.L.S. (Liberal Studies).

In the late 19th century, educators felt that the title of "Bachelor" was inappropriate for young ladies, so some schools awarded female graduates titles such as Mistress of Arts or Maid of Science.

The Master's Degree

Until the 20th century, the "Master's" and "Doctor's" titles were used somewhat interchangeably, and considered appropriate for anyone who had completed work of significance beyond the Bachelor's degree. Today, however, the Master's is almost always the first degree earned after the Bachelor's, and is always considered to be a lower degree than the Doctorate.

The traditional Master's degree requires from one to two years of on-campus work after the Bachelor's. Some nontraditional Master's degrees may be earned entirely through nonresident study, while others require anywhere from a few days to a few weeks on campus.

There are several philosophical approaches to the Master's degree. Some schools (or departments within schools) regard it as a sort of advanced Bachelor's, requiring only the completion of one to two years of advanced-level studies and courses. Others see it as more of a junior Doctorate, requiring at least *some* creative, original research, culminating in the writing of a thesis, or original research paper. Some programs let students choose their approach, requiring, for example, either 10 courses and a thesis or 13 courses with no thesis.

And in a few world-famous schools, including Oxford and Cambridge, the Master's degree is an almost meaningless award, given automatically to all holders of the school's Bachelor's degree who have managed, as the saying goes, to stay out of jail for four years, and can afford the small fee. (Most American schools had a similar practice at one time, but Harvard abolished it more than a century ago and the rest followed suit soon after. However, some ivy league schools—Harvard, Yale, etc.—do maintain the quaint practice of awarding a Master's degree to new professors who do not happen to have a degree from that school, even if they have a doctorate from one of equal renown. It is a sort of housewarming gift, so that all senior faculty will have at least one degree from the school at which they are teaching.)

Master's degree titles are very similar to Bachelors'—the M.A. (Master of Arts) and M.S. (Master of Science) are by far the most common, along with that staple of American business, the M.B.A. (Master of Business Administration). Other common Master's degrees include the M.Ed., M.Eng., M.L.S. (Library Science), and M.J. (either Journalism or Jurisprudence).

The Doctorate

The term "Doctor" has been a title of respect for a learned person since biblical times. Moses, in Deuteronomy 31:28 (Douay version), says, "Gather unto me all the ancients of your tribes and your doctors, and I will speak these words in their hearing."

About 800 years ago, in the mid 12th century, outstanding scholars at the University of Bologna and the University of Paris began to be called either "Doctor" or "Professor," the first recorded academic use of the term.

The first American use came in the late 17th century, under, as the story has it, rather amusing circumstances. There had long been a tradition (and, to a large extent, there still is) that "it takes a Doctor to make a Doctor." In other words, only a person with a Doctorate can confer a Doctorate on someone else.

But in all of America, no one had a Doctorate, least of all Harvard's president, Increase Mather, who, as a Dissenter, was ineligible for a Doctorate from any English university, all of which were controlled by the Church.

Still, Harvard was eager to get into the Doctorate business, so their entire faculty (that is to say, a Mr. Leverett and a Mr. Brattle) got together and unanimously agreed to award an honorary Doctorate to Mr. Mather, whereupon Mather was then able to confer Doctorates upon his faculty who, subsequently, were able to doctor their students.

This, in essence, was the start of graduate education in America, and there are those who say things have gone downhill ever since.

America's next Doctorate, incidentally, was also awarded under rather odd circumstances. In this case, a British physician named Daniel Turner was eager to get into the Royal Society of Physicians and Surgeons, but needed an M.D. to do so. In England, then as now, most doctors have a *Bachelor* of Medicine; the *Doctor* of Medicine is an advanced degree. No English university would give Turner a Doctorate because he did not belong to the Church of England. Scottish universities turned him down because he had published some unkind remarks about the quality of Scottish education. And of course no European university would give a degree to an Englishman. So Mr. Turner made a deal with Yale University.

Yale agreed to award Turner the Doctorate in absentia (he never set foot in America), and he, in turn, gave Yale a gift of 50 valuable medical books. Wags at the time remarked that the M.D. he got must stand for the Latin *multum donavit*, "he gave a lot."

Nowadays the academic title of "Doctor" (as distinguished from the professional and honorary titles, to be discussed shortly) has come to be awarded for completion of an advanced course of study, culminating in a piece of original research in one's field, known as the doctoral thesis or dissertation.

While traditional Doctorates used to require at least two years of on-campus study after the Master's degree, followed by a period of dissertation research and writing, the trend lately has been to require little more than the dissertation. More and more schools are letting people without a Master's into their doctoral programs, and awarding the Master's along the way, on completion of the coursework (and any qualifying exams).

The total elapsed time can be anywhere from three years on up. Indeed, the trend in the 1980s and '90s has been for Doctorates to take longer and longer. In his splendid book, *Winning the Ph.D. Game*, Richard Moore offers evidence that a typical Ph.D. now takes six or seven years, with a range from three to 10 (not all of it necessarily spent in residence on campus, however).

Many nontraditional doctoral programs waive the on-campus study, on the assumption that a mature candidate already knows a great deal about his or her field. Such programs require little or no coursework, focusing instead on the dissertation, with the emphasis on demonstrating creativity.

Some nontraditional doctoral programs permit the use of work already done (books written, symphonies composed, business plans created, etc.) as partial (or, in a few cases, full) satisfaction of the dissertation requirement. But many schools insist on all, or almost all, new work.

The most frequently awarded (and, many people feel, the most prestigious) Doctorate is the Doctor of Philosophy (known as the Ph.D. in North America, and the D.Phil. in many other countries). The Doctor of Philosophy does not necessarily have anything to do with the study of philosophy. It is awarded for studies in dozens of fields, ranging from chemistry to communication, from agriculture to aviation management.

> Until well into the 20th century, the Ph.D. was also given as an honorary degree. But in the late 1930s, Gonzaga University in Spokane, Washington, spoiled the whole thing by handing out an honorary Ph.D. to one Harry Lillis "Bing" Crosby, to thank him for donating some equipment to the football team. Crosby made great sport about being a Doctor on his popular radio program that week. The academic world rose in distressed anger and that, effectively, was the end of the honorary Ph.D.

More than 500 other types of Doctorate have been identified in the English language alone. After the Ph.D., the most common include the Ed.D. (Education), D.B.A. (Business Administration), D.P.A. (Public Administration), D.A. (Art or Administration), Eng.D. (Engineering), Psy.D. (Psychology), D.Sc. (Science), and D.Hum. (Humanities). The latter two are often, but not always, awarded as honorary degrees in the U.S.; in the rest of the world, they are earned like any other Doctorate.

A Bachelor's degree is almost always required for admission to a Doctoral program, and many traditional schools require a Master's as well. However, more and more Doctoral programs are admitting otherwise qualified applicants without a Master's degree. Most nontraditional programs will accept equivalent career experience in lieu of a Master's, and, in rare instances, in lieu of a Bachelor's as well.

> In the late 1950s, someone submitted what was essentially Eleanor Roosevelt's resumé (changing the name and disguising some of her more obvious remarkable achievements) as part of an application to various doctoral programs. Mrs. Roosevelt had never attended college. All 12 schools turned her down, most suggesting that she reapply after completing a Bachelor's and a Master's, presumably six to eight years later.

In Europe, but very rarely in America, a so-called "higher Doctorate" (typically the D.Litt., Doctor of Letters) is awarded solely on the basis of one's life work, with no further studies required. The great majority of those receiving a D.Litt. already have one Doctorate, but it is not essential. In most quarters, the D.Litt. is considered to be an earned, not an honorary degree, but there are those who disagree.

Finally, it should be mentioned that several American schools, concerned with what one called the "doctoral glut," are reported to be seriously considering instituting a new degree, *higher* than the Doctorate, presumably requiring more years of study and a more extensive dissertation. The name "Chancellorate" has been bandied about. Indeed, the prestigious *Chronicle of Higher Education* devoted a major article to this possibility a few years ago. It may well be that holders of a Chancellorate (Ph.C.?) would not appreciably affect the job market, since most of them would be drawing their old age pensions by the time they completed this degree.

Professional Degrees

Professional degrees are earned by people who intend to enter what are often called "the professions"—medicine, dentistry, law, the ministry, and so forth. In the United States, these degrees are almost always earned *after* completing a Bachelor's degree, and almost always carry the title of "Doctor" (e.g., Doctor of Medicine, Doctor of Divinity).

In many other countries, it is common to enter professional school directly from high school, in which case the first professional degree earned is a Bachelor's. (For instance, there is the British Bachelor of Medicine, whose holders are invariably called "Doctor," unless they have earned the more advanced Doctor of Medicine degree, in which case they insist on being called "Mister." No one ever said the British were easy to understand.)

One exception in the United States is the D.C. (Doctor of Chiropractic), a program that students used to be able to enter right from high school. It now requires two years of college, but still no Bachelor's degree. This may be one reason so many medical doctors look down their noses at chiropractors.

Another exception used to be the law degree which, until the mid 1960s, was an LL.B., or Bachelor of Laws. Many lawyers objected to working three or four years beyond their Bachelor's degree simply to end up with yet another Bachelor's degree, while optometrists, podiatrists, and others were becoming doctors in the same length of time.

Nowadays, virtually every American law school awards a Doctorate as the first law degree, usually the J.D., which stands for either Doctor of Jurisprudence or Juris Doctor.

Almost all law schools offered their graduates with Bachelor of Law degrees the option of turning in their old LL.B. diplomas and, in effect, being retroactively Doctored with a J.D. A fair number of lawyers accepted this unprecedented offer, although few actually call themselves "Doctor."

The LL.D., known as both Doctor of Law and Doctor of Laws, is now used almost exclusively as an honorary title in the U.S.; elsewhere in the world, it is an earned, advanced law degree.

The traditional law degree requires three years of study beyond the Bachelor's degree. Some nontraditional approaches will be discussed in chapter 23.

The only widely accepted medical degree in America is the M.D. (Doctor of Medicine), which requires four years of study beyond the Bachelor's degree, although some shorter approaches, and some alternative ones, will be discussed in chapter 24.

A number of other medical or health specialties have their own professional Doctorates. These include, for instance, D.O. (Osteopathy), D.P. (Podiatry), and O.D. (Optometry).

There are no accelerated approaches to the dental degree, and few of us would really want to go to a dentist who *had* taken shortcuts. The traditional dental degree for many years has been the D.D.S. (Doctor of Dental Surgery), although there has recently been a strong trend toward the D.M.D. (Doctor of Medical Dentistry). Both programs require four years of study beyond the Bachelor's degree.

More than 100 different professional degree titles have been awarded in the area of religion. None can be said to be *the* standard one. They include the S.T.D. (Sacred Theology), D.Min. (Ministry), Th.D. (Theology), D.D. (Divinity), D.Rel. (Religion), D.R.E. (Religious Education), D.S.R. (Science of Religion), and so forth, as well as the Ph.D. in religion.

> The Canadian mathematician and humorist Stephen Leacock writes that shortly after he received his Ph.D., he was on board a cruise ship. When a lovely young lady fainted, the call went out, "Is there a doctor on board?" Leacock says he rushed to the Captain's cabin, but he was too late. Two D.D.'s and an S.T.D. had gotten there before him.

Quite a few other degrees are deemed honest professional titles by those who hold them, but are regarded with vigorously raised eyebrows by many others. These include, for example, the N.D. (Naturopathy, Naprapathy, or Napropathy), D.Hyp. (Hypnotism), H.M.D. or M.D.(H.) (Homeopathic Medicine), D.M.S. (Military Science), Met.D. (Metaphysics), Graph.D. (Graphoanalysis), and so forth.

Honorary Degrees

The honorary degree is truly the stepchild of the academic world, and a most curious one at that. In fact, it is a reflection of academic achievement to the same degree that former basketball star Doctor J's title reflected his medical skills. It is simply a title that some institutions (and some scoundrels) have chosen to bestow, from time to time, and for a wide variety of reasons, upon certain people. These reasons often have to do with the donation of money, or with attracting celebrities to a commencement ceremony.

The honorary Doctorate has no academic standing whatsoever, and yet, because it carries the same title, "Doctor," as the earned degree, it has become an extremely desirable commodity for those who covet titles and the prestige they bring. For respectable universities to award the title of "Doctor" via an honorary Doctorate is as peculiar as if the Army awarded civilians the honorary title of "General"—a title the civilians could then use in their everyday life.

More than 1,000 traditional colleges and universities award honorary Doctorates (anywhere from one to 50 per year each), and a great many Bible schools, spurious schools, and degree mills hand them out with wild abandon to almost anyone willing to pay the price. The situation is discussed in detail in chapter 26.

TRANSCRIPTS

A transcript is, quite simply, an official record of all the work one has done at a given university. While the diploma is the piece of paper (or parchment) that shows that a given degree has been earned, the transcript is the detailed description of all the work done to earn that degree.

The traditional transcript is a computer printout listing all the courses taken, when they were taken, and the grade received. The overall G.P.A. (grade point average) is calculated as of the end of each semester or quarter.

Nearly all nontraditional schools and programs issue transcripts as well. Sometimes they try to make the transcripts look as traditional as possible, listing, for instance, life-experience learning credit for aviation as "Aviation 100, 4 units," "Aviation 101, 3 units," etc. Other programs offer a *narrative transcript*, which describes the procedures used by the school to evaluate various types of experience.

The original copy of a transcript is always kept by the school. Official copies, bearing an official raised seal or, sometimes, printed on special paper that cannot easily be tampered with, can be made for the student, other schools, or employers, at the student's request.

Unfortunately, there is a great deal of traffic in forged transcripts. Students have been known to change a few grades to improve the G.P.A., or even add entire classes. Of course such changes would normally only affect the copy, which is why most schools and many employers will only accept transcripts that are sent directly from the office of the school's registrar. Beginning in the late 1980s, however, and continuing into the 1990s, there have been more than a few fake transcript scandals. Some involved creative use of color copiers and laser printers. Others involved tampering with a university's computer, either by hackers having fun or by dishonest employees selling their services. Such unfortunate behaviors raise questions about the validity of *any* university-produced document.

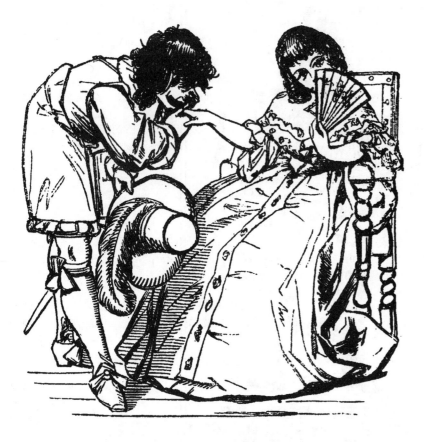

*"Marry me, Yolanda. I have a fine home, a Ford Mustang, and
a diploma from the Milwaukee School of Meatcutting."*

◆4◆
Is a Degree Worth the Effort?

Question: I'm 38 years old, and thinking about pursuing a
Bachelor's degree, but I'm not sure I should, because
if I do, I'll be 42 years old when I'm done.
Answer: And how old will you be in four years if you don't do it?
PARAPHRASED FROM THE DEAR ABBY COLUMN

The simple answer to the question in the chapter title is *yes* for nontraditional degrees; very likely *no* for traditional degrees.

Let us first elaborate on why the nontraditional degree is worth the effort, and then offer arguments as to why the old-fashioned way may not be worth it
.

WHY THE NONTRADITIONAL DEGREE MAKES SENSE

Much depends on the degree itself, and on the reasons for wanting it. If, for instance, you need to have a Bachelor's degree to get a job, promotion, or salary increase, then an accredited degree from the University of the State of New York, earned entirely by correspondence courses, is exactly as good as any Bachelor's degree earned by sitting in classrooms for four or five or six years at a state university, and it would be about 95 percent cheaper (not to mention that one can continue earning a living while pursuing the nontraditional degree).

As another example, a nonresident Doctorate, earned through a combination of life-experience credit and new work, from one of the better unaccredited state-licensed universities may be of minimal value in getting a faculty position at Harvard. But such degrees have proved useful in many cases for advancement in business, government, and industry, not to mention doing wonders for self-image and gaining the respect of others.

Finally, a Doctorate purchased for a hundred bucks from a no-questions-asked degree mill may ultimately bring shame, public embarrassment, loss of a job, and even a fine and imprisonment.

Many nontraditional degrees are good for most people in most situations. But there can be major exceptions, which is why it pays to check out the school in advance (this book is a good place to start) and to make as sure as you can that the degree you seek will satisfy any gatekeepers who may appear in your path.

A word of warning: Please do not be misled by the results of a study on the acceptance of nontraditional degrees, sponsored by the National Institute of Education in the late 1970s. This study, by Sosdian and Sharp, has been misquoted and misinterpreted in the literature of dozens of nontraditional universities, in a most misleading effort to convince prospective students that their degrees will be accepted in the academic, professional, or business world.

Sosdian and Sharp did indeed determine that there was a high level of acceptance—*but their research was based entirely on the acceptance level of Associate's and Bachelor's degrees that either were regionally accredited or, in a very few cases, state-run schools that were candidates for regional accreditation.* It is totally misleading to imply, as many have done, that results would be comparable for unaccredited degrees, much less Master's and Doctorates. It just isn't so, and those schools should be ashamed of themselves.

Now, let's look at the six main reasons why people choose to pursue nontraditional degrees, and the kinds of degrees that may be most appropriate.

1. Job or salary advancement in business, industry, or civil service. Many job descriptions specify that a certain degree is required, or that additional salary will be paid, if a certain degree is held. In many of these situations, a good unaccredited degree will suffice.

It is crucial to find out in advance, whenever possible, if a given degree will be accepted. While many businesses, large and small, will recognize good unaccredited degrees, many will not. We have heard dozens of tragic stories from people who spent many thousands of dollars on degree programs, only to find that the degree they earned was not acceptable to their employer or potential employer.

2. Job or salary advancement in education. The academic world has been more reluctant to accept unaccredited degrees than has the world of business or government. Even some excellent accredited, nontraditional degrees have occasionally caused problems. However, the situation remains extremely variable. It is almost impossible to draw general rules or conclusions. Many universities refuse to consider hiring a faculty member with an unaccredited degree, or to admit people with such degrees into their graduate programs. Others welcome them. And the most enlightened schools consider each case on its own merits.

John once asked a group of school-board presidents for their boards' policies on salary incentives for district teachers who completed Master's degrees or Doctorates. The results were pretty evenly divided into four categories. About one fourth said the degrees had to be accredited. Another quarter said they could be unaccredited. Twenty-five percent said they judge each case individually. And the remainder either didn't understand the difference between accredited and unaccredited degrees, or said that no one had ever asked the question so there was no policy.

Once again, the watchword is to check in advance before spending any money with any school.

3. Job or salary advancement in the professions. When a profession must be licensed by the state or a trade organization, that body often has certain degree requirements. Depending on the state, this may apply to psychologists, marriage counselors, engineers, accountants, real-estate brokers, social workers, hypnotists, massage practitioners, and others. There is absolutely no pattern here in the acceptability of nontraditional degrees, other than a small trend in favor of their increased acceptance.

In one state, for example, a psychologist must have a traditionally accredited Doctorate while a civil engineer with sufficient career experience may have an unaccredited degree or no degree at all. In another state, it may be just the opposite. Many regulations are exceedingly unclear on this subject, so a judgment is made in each individual case. Once again, it is crucial to determine in advance if a given degree will meet a given need.

4. Admission to traditional graduate schools. The trend is strongly in the direction of increased acceptance of alternative degrees, including the better unaccredited degrees, for admission to Master's and doctoral programs at traditional universities. For example, one highly regarded unaccredited program reported that its students have transferred to more than 30 traditional universities, getting credit for their work at the unaccredited school. Another unaccredited university has received letters from Harvard, Yale, and Princeton, among others, indicating a willingness to consider their students for admission to graduate school.

5. Self-satisfaction. This is a perfectly good reason for wanting a degree, and no one should ever feel embarrassed about it. Many degree-counseling clients (see Appendix C) seek a degree (generally a Doctorate) for self-satisfaction, to gain respect from others, to feel more comfortable with colleagues, or to "validate" a long and worthwhile career. Such people are generally well satisfied with a degree from one of the more respectable unaccredited schools. One of the main criteria to consider here is avoidance of potential embarrassment. More than one holder of a degree from a legitimate, but not especially good, nontraditional school has suffered extreme discomfort or embarrassment when newspaper articles or television stories on the school made big local waves.

One of John's favorite consulting clients wrote to him that his doctoral dissertation had been rejected by Columbia University in 1910, and now he'd like to finish the degree. John wrote back offering suggestions, and mentioned what he thought was an amusing typographical error in the letter; he said 1910. No, the man wrote back, that's correct. He was now 96 years old, and these events had happened 70 years earlier. He was accepted by a good nontraditional external program, and completed his Ph.D. shortly before his 100th birthday.

6. Fooling people. An alarming number of people want fake degrees for all manner of devious purposes. After CBS broadcast its degree-mill report on *60 Minutes*, they received a huge number of telephone calls from people wanting to know the addresses and phone numbers of the fake schools they had just seen exposed.

Almost every week we hear from people who would like "a Doctorate from Harvard University, please, with no work required, and can it be back-dated to 1974, and I need it by next Tuesday." The best one can do is warn these people that they are endangering their reputations (and possibly their freedom) by considering such a course. Then we usually suggest that if they must have a degree by return mail, they consider a degree from a far-less-dangerous, second-rate Bible college. Nothing to be especially proud of, but less hazardous to one's health.

WHY A TRADITIONAL DEGREE MAKES LESS SENSE

People attend traditional colleges for a great many different reasons, as Caroline Bird writes in her fascinating book, *The Case Against College*:

A great majority of our nine million post-secondary students who are "in college" are there because it has become the thing to do, or because college is a pleasant place to be . . . because it's the only way they can get parents or taxpayers to support them without working at a job they don't like; because Mother wanted them to go; or for some reasons utterly irrelevant to the course of studies for which the college is supposedly organized.

There seem to be two basic reasons people go to college: to get an education or to get a degree. The two can be quite independent. Some people only care about the training, others only want the degree, and some want or need both.

Sadly, there is a strong trend in America toward what David Hapgood calls "diplomaism" in his book of that title. He writes:

> We are well on our way to repealing the American dream of individual accomplishment and replacing it with a system in which the diploma is the measure of a man, a diploma which bears no relation to performance. The career market is closing its doors to those without degrees. . . . Diplomaism zones people into a set of categories that tends to eliminate the variety and surprise of human experience. In a system run by diplomas, all avenues to personal advancement are blocked except one: the school that gives the diploma. . . . When we leave the institution, like carcasses coming off a packing plant's assembly line, an anonymous hand affixes an indelible stamp . . . which thereafter determines what we can do, and how we shall be rewarded. And that stamp, unlike the imprint on a side of beef, reflects neither our personal value to the society, nor the needs of the economic system.

There are, in fact, three major problems with traditional schools and traditional degree programs:

1. There is often little connection between degrees earned traditionally and on-the-job performance.
2. There is much evidence that vast numbers of students are spending huge amounts of time being trained for jobs that simply do not exist.
3. The cash investment in a traditional college education is frequently an extremely poor investment indeed.

Let us consider each of these three problems in greater depth.

Traditional College Training and On-the-Job Performance

Many studies have found little or no relationship between college coursework and "real life" performance, and in some cases that relationship was a negative one. One extensive study, by Ivar Berg of Columbia University, published under the delightful title, *Education and Jobs: The Great Training Robbery*, looked at various jobs in which people with degrees and people without were doing identical work. In many situations, there was no difference in performance between the two groups, and in a few jobs (including air traffic controllers and pants makers), the people without degrees were doing a better job.

Sadly, Berg also found that many bosses either ignored or refused to believe the evidence that had been collected in their own offices and factories. For instance, in one big chemical firm where the laboratory workers without degrees were outperforming those with degrees, the management steadfastly maintained its policy of promoting only those employees with degrees.

Hapgood believes that personnel practices at such firms are not likely to be changed in the foreseeable future, because "employers made it clear they were demanding diplomas for reasons that had little to do with job performance." The real reasons, he thinks, had to do with conformity to the dominant culture and with the "ability" to stay in school for four or more years. "It proves that he was docile enough (or good or patient or stupid enough; choose your own adjective) to stay out of trouble for 13 or 17 or 20 years in a series of institutions that demand a high degree of unthinking conformity."

John was given similar responses when he surveyed the personnel managers of major airlines. Almost all require pilots to have an accredited Bachelor's degree, but they don't care whether the degree is in aviation or Chinese history. The important thing, they say, is that an employee is disciplined enough to complete a degree program. You may have been flying for 10 years for the navy or the air force. But that doesn't count. And if the hypocrisy needs to be underlined, consider the fact that when pilot trainees are in short supply, the degree requirement mysteriously disappears.

Whatever the reasons, the system is a confused and disarrayed one, with the one strongly positive note being the increasing acceptance of nontraditional degrees, whose holders often have far more practical knowledge and experience through on-the-job training than those who learned about the subject in the college classroom.

There is an ever-growing number of employers who will say, for instance, that you learn more about practical journalism in your first two weeks working on a daily newspaper than in four years of journalism school. (The same goes for law, advertising, and dozens of other fields.) And the person who has both the experience and the nontraditional degree based, at least in part, on that experience may be in the best situation of all.

It used to be the case that many employers denied jobs to people without degrees, even if the degree had nothing to do with the ability to perform the job. But following a key Supreme Court decision (*Griggs* v. *Duke Power Company, 1971*), employers must now prove that a degree is required to do a certain job, or they cannot discriminate against those without them. This is equally true for high school diplomas, Doctorates, and everything in between.

Is a Traditional College Degree Useful in Today's Marketplace?

A certain large state prison used to take great pride in its vocational training program. It operated a large cotton mill, where the inmates learned how to run the equipment and, in fact, made their own prison uniforms. When they got out of prison, however, they learned that not only was the equipment they had learned to operate hopelessly out-of-date, but the nearest large cotton mill was 2,000 miles away. No wonder many of them returned to a life of crime.

Much the same sort of thing goes on in traditional colleges and universities. As an example, throughout the 1960s hundreds of thousands of students were told about the great teacher shortages that were coming, so they graduated with degrees in education. But, as Alexander Mood wrote in a report for the Carnegie Commission:

It has been evident for some time to professors of education that they were training far more teachers than would ever find jobs teaching school, but few of them bothered to mention that fact to their students. That is understandable, of course, since their incomes depend on having students.

Much the same thing happened with the study of space science and astrophysics in the 1970s, and again with computer science in the 1980s and early '90s.

And so we find thousands of people with Doctorates teaching high school, people with Master's degrees teaching first grade, and an awful lot of people with Bachelor's degrees in education waiting on tables and doing clerical work.

The business world is not exempt. A survey by the *Wall Street Journal* found copious numbers of highly disillusioned M.B.A. students and recent graduates. "I wouldn't have come here and spent all that money if I had known it would be this tight," said one jobless M.B.A. "Graduate school was a waste of time," said another, after 10 months of fruitless searching for a business job. But cheer up. The president of the Association of MBA Executives, Inc., says things have gotten much better later in the 1990s, at least for MBAs.

These problems are by no means confined to education and business. In virtually any field you look at, from psychology to civil engineering, you find lots of well-trained and unemployed practitioners. In one recent year, for instance, there were over 100,000 graduates in the field of communications, and about 14,000 new jobs in the communications industries. Five thousand anthropology graduates are finding about 400 job openings in their field. And so it goes. Or doesn't go.

According to Bird, "Law schools are already graduating twice as many new lawyers every year as the Department of Labor thinks will be needed," and Mood says that

in the past, the investment in higher education did at least pay off for most students; that is, they did get access to higher-status jobs; now for the first time in history, a college degree is being judged by many parents and students as not worth the price. They see too many of last year's graduates unable to find work, or taking jobs ordinarily regarded as suitable for high school graduates.... Moreover, this is not a temporary phenomenon.

The Bureau of Labor Statistics says that about 25 percent of college graduates entering the labor market are getting jobs previously held by people without degrees. That doesn't mean the degrees are needed to perform those jobs, of course, but only that there are millions of job-seekers with degrees who cannot find jobs requiring their degrees.

So the outlook for the traditional degree is rather bleak. People will continue to pursue them for the wrong reasons, and industry will continue to require them for the wrong reasons. And enlightened people of all ages will, more and more, come to realize that a nontraditional degree can do just about anything a traditional one can—with a much smaller expenditure of time, effort, and money.

Is a Traditional Degree Worth the Cost?

Just what is the cost? Anything we write today will be out of date tomorrow, because traditional college costs are escalating so fast. In 1995, the average cost of attending a private college for four years in the United States was in excess of $70,000, including tuition, room and board, books, etc. At public colleges, the average cost is "only" around $40,000 to $45,000.

Based on a highly conservative 6 percent rate of academic inflation (most schools do try to hold the line, but there are limits to how much they can do), here is how things may look in years to come with regard to college costs:

YEAR	4 YRS. PRIVATE COLLEGE	4 YRS. PUBLIC COLLEGE
1995	$72,000	$42,000
2000	$93,000	$56,000
2005	$125,000	$75,000

It seems more than likely that a child who was born in 1990, who will enter college in 2008, can expect to pay well over $100,000 for a traditional college education.

Even today, many people simply cannot afford to

pursue a traditional degree. Yet a degree can almost always mean a higher salary, increased likelihood of getting better jobs, and personal satisfaction. For a while, the gap seemed to be narrowing. In the early 1980s, the average Bachelor's degree–holder was earning about 35 percent more than the average high-school graduate (down from 53 percent in the '70s). In recent years, however, that trend has dramatically reversed—one recent survey showed the average Bachelor's degree–holder earning a whopping 76 percent more than a high-school graduate.

Here are average lifetime earnings based on levels of education. The amount shown is total lifetime earnings, from the year of entering the job market (at the age of 18 for high-school graduates, 22 for Bachelor's degree–holders, etc.) until age 65:

Attended high school, did not graduate:	$407,000
High-school graduate, did not go to college:	$589,000
Attended college for 1 to 3 years:	$645,000
Bachelor's degree:	$950,000
Master's degree:	$1,126,000
Doctorate:	$1,449,000
Professional degree:	$1,625,820

Here are some enlightening differences in earnings between sexes and races. These figures are all for people with Master's degrees, where the most data were available:

	PER YEAR	LIFETIME
All persons with Master's	$37,575	$1,503,000
Men with Master's	$40,332	$1,613,000
Women with Master's	$30,245	$1,209,000
Whites with Master's	$45,103	$1,804,000
Blacks with Master's	$36,457	$1,458,000

(Who says that the Equal Rights Amendment and other civil rights legislation is unnecessary?)

From the above numbers, it may look, to an 18-year-old on the brink of either college or a job, as if taking four years off to earn a Bachelor's degree is going to be worth more than $360,000 in the long run. However, Caroline Bird thinks that if the only reason people go to college is to make more money, then higher education is a truly dumb financial investment.

She argues this way (we have adapted her 1976 figures to the reality of the different interest rates of the mid 1990s): The average Princeton graduate will have spent about $70,000 to get a degree, including tuition, room and board, books, travel, etc. If you put that sum of money into certificates of deposit earning 6 percent interest, you could have over $5 million by the age of 65, without ever having done a day's work. That, needless to say, is about 15 times more than the "mere" $360,000 additional that the average Bachelor's degree–holder makes in a lifetime.

Of course, most people wouldn't have the $70,000 to invest at age 18. But Bird argues that if one enters the job market at 18, the earnings over the next four years, plus, perhaps, some advance from parents on what they would otherwise have spent on college tuition, wisely invested, would produce a similar result.

A study by Drs. J. H. Hollomon of the Massachusetts Institute of Technology and Richard Freeman of Harvard University concludes that "in the brief span of about five years, the college job market has gone from a major boom to a major bust. Large numbers of young people, for the first time, are likely to obtain less schooling and potentially lower occupational status than their parents."

All very well and good, but none of these people takes nontraditional education and degrees into account. Bird and others have produced some powerful reasons not to pursue a *traditional* degree. But it is now possible, and will become increasingly easier, to earn degrees at a low cost while remaining fully employed, thereby having the best of both worlds.

Whether pursuing a degree for the learning, the diploma, or both, the alternative student seems far more likely:

♦ to be motivated to complete his or her program;

♦ to select courses and programs that are appropriate and relevant to his or her needs;

♦ to avoid cluttering up campuses and dormitories (which, in the words of former Columbia University president William McGill, are in danger of becoming "storage houses for bored young people");

♦ to save years over the time of traditional programs (or, alternatively, to pursue educational objectives without giving up job or family), and, perhaps most importantly for most people, to save a tremendous amount of time and money, compared with the demands and costs of a traditional degree program.

Many nontraditional programs, in fact, come very close to John Holt's ideal educational system, which he describes by analogy with a public library: you go whenever you want something it has to offer, no one checks your credentials at the door, you leave when you have gotten what you wanted, and it is you, not the librarian, who decides if it has been a worthwhile experience.

WHERE, THEN, ARE THINGS GOING?

One message of Charles Reich's fascinating book, *The Greening of America*, is that things are happening now that have never happened before; that for the first time, the standards and lessons of the past may have no relevance for the future.

Things are indeed changing almost amazingly fast in higher education. The direction in which they are changing is away from traditional education and degrees toward alternative higher education and nontraditional degrees.

It is always difficult—and challenging—to live in a

time of great change. On one hand, we have universities that have refused (or were unable, by law) to invite people like Eleanor Roosevelt, Buckminster Fuller, Andrew Wyeth, or Eric Hoffer to lecture, because they never earned a college degree. On the other hand, we have people earning higher degrees entirely by correspondence, entering prestigious doctoral programs without even a high-school diploma, and earning law degrees without ever seeing the inside of a law school.

Thirty years ago, if you wanted to earn a degree without sitting in classrooms for three or four years, and wanted to remain in North America, you had exactly two legal alternatives: the University of London and the University of South Africa, both of which offered (and still offer) nonresident programs from the Bachelor's level through the Doctorate, as well as various professional degrees.

At the same time, predictably, many traditional universities and colleges are suffering the financial impact of decreased enrollments and rising costs. Unprecedented numbers of traditional schools are simply going out of business, and many others are almost frantically implementing nontraditional programs as a last resort to stay afloat. Things are likely to get worse for traditional schools, as the "baby bust" generation of the late 1960s and 1970s has reached college age.

Alternative education and the nontraditional degree seem, indeed, to be the wave of the educational future.

The Great Diploma of Cheops

♦5♦
Using Titles

Question: What do you call the person who finishes last in his or her medical school class?
Answer: Doctor.
TRADITIONAL

One question that arose regularly in the degree consulting practice John used to operate was this: "If I earn a degree, especially an alternative or nontraditional degree, in what way am I entitled to use the degree, and the title that comes with it (in the case of Doctorates), in my life and career?"

There is no simple answer to this question, since rules and regulations vary from state to state, and from profession to profession. The basic philosophy behind these laws is, essentially, this: You can probably do almost anything you want in the way of titles, as long as you do not do it with the intent of deceiving anyone—except in the state of Florida. (Florida has a new law that prohibits people with unaccredited degrees, even from long-established, state-approved schools, from even mentioning those degrees in any way, in writing or orally, whether on a business card, letterhead, advertisement, etc. One wonders if Billy Graham would be arrested upon crossing the Florida border.)

No one ever had Colonel Sanders arrested for pretending to be a military officer, nor is Doc Severinsen in danger of prosecution for impersonating a physician. However, when a man who has never earned a Doctorate gets a job as a meteorologist for a New York television station using the title of "Doctor," there *is* a major problem, because it can be reasonably assumed that the title helped him get the job—even if he was performing his duties satisfactorily without benefit of doctoral training. (The meteorologist lost his job after his lack of a degree was exposed.)

In general, as long as the degree comes from an unquestionably legal and legitimate school, there is usually no problem in using that degree in public life, as long as all local and licensing requirements are met.

In some states, a "quickie" Doctorate from a one-room Bible school is sufficient to set up practice as a marriage counselor and psychotherapist. In other states with stiffer licensing requirements, this same behavior could result in major legal problems.

The use of degree titles varies considerably from profession to profession, and from nation to nation. Most people in the United States do not append a Bachelor's degree notation to their letterhead or signature, while in most of the rest of the world, it is quite common to see, for instance, "Maxwell Zeryck, B.A." The name or abbreviation of the school is often appended, as well: "Felipe Lujan, B.A. (Oxon)" or "B.A. (Cantab)," indicating that the degree is from Oxford or Cambridge.

Master's degrees are more commonly used in print in the United States, especially the M.B.A. (e.g., "Joseph Judd, M.B.A.")

Holders of a Doctorate almost always use it in their public or professional lives—with the curious exception of politicians. (Most prominent politicians with earned Doctorates, from Woodrow Wilson to George McGovern, seem to have gone to great lengths to avoid public disclosure of the degree. Perhaps there is merit to columnist Herb Caen's belief that people will never vote for anyone they think is more intelligent than they are.)

There are, and probably always will be, educational conservatives who decry the use of nontraditional (and particularly unaccredited nontraditional) titles. A typical situation has occurred in the field of electrical engineering, where a gentleman in New York formed the "Committee of Concerned E.E.'s" for the purpose of carrying on a vigorous campaign against the right of electrical engineers with unaccredited Doctorates to use the title of "Doctor." The journals in this field often carry articles and letters from people on various aspects of this issue.

Thomas Carlyle's observation regarding the "peculiar ambition of Americans to hobble down to posterity on crutches of capital letters," notwithstanding, Americans are far less likely than Europeans and Asians to use all the letters at their command. Whereas a typical Englishman will list all his degrees, and perhaps a few fellowships besides (e.g., "Lowell James Hicks, B.A., M.A., Ph.D., F.R.S., L.C.P."), most Americans would only use their highest degree (e.g., "Heather Bourne, Ph.D."), unless they have more than one Doctorate, in which case both would be listed (e.g., "Howard Siegel, M.D., Ph.D.")

Not everyone agrees with this. The former president of a California religious school, for instance, regularly used all nine of his claimed Doctorates, with his civil-service rank (G.S.9) thrown in between Doctorates number four and five, for good measure. And then there was the chap who wrote to us from Massachusetts, using these letters after his name: L.R.A., M.N.G.S., B.S.A. When asked, he explained that the letters stood for Licensed Real Estate Agent, Member of the National Geographic Society, and Boy Scouts of America.

Holders of honorary Doctorates are treading on far more dangerous ground when they use their degrees in public, especially if such degrees were purchased "over the counter," no matter how legally. Still, public figures from Billy Graham to the late Edward Land, founder of Polaroid, regularly use (or used) the title "Doctor" based on honorary degrees from major universities.

Nonetheless, if an insurance agent makes a sale, if a clergyman makes a convert, or if a teacher makes a salary increase that can be attributed, even in part, to the prestige of being called "Doctor," and if that Doctorate is unearned, then the claim can always be made that that person is acting, at least in part, on false pretenses.

There is also the matter of whether a Doctorate-holder chooses to call himself, for example, Roger Williams, Ph.D. or Dr. Roger Williams. Although either form would appear to be acceptable in many circumstances, a New York audiologist (someone who fits hearing aids) suffered legal repercussions for calling himself Dr. So-and-so rather than So-and-so, Ph.D. The prosecution's claim was that the use of the word "Doctor" in such a near-medical field was done to deceive clients into thinking he was a medical doctor.

Another category of title abusers are those people who use degrees they never earned, and there are a surprising number of them. When the head of a major motion picture studio got into legal troubles a few years back, a side-light of the case was that the degree he said he had from Yale University turned out to be nonexistent. At the same time, Yale revealed that they keep files on all cases of publicly claimed Yale degrees that were never actually awarded, and that to date they had logged more than 7,000 such fraudulent claims.

It seems reasonable to hypothesize that these 7,000 are just the tip of the iceberg. Untold thousands of others are going about free, only because so few people ever bother to check up on anyone's degrees. Most exposures happen in connection with other events, often when something good happens to a person. Let us give a number of examples, in the hopes of dissuading some readers from considering this course of action.

♦ The Arizona "Teacher of the Year" for 1987, after he entered the public eye, was discovered to have falsified his claim to a Doctorate. He forfeited the $10,000 prize that came with this honor, and his career was in jeopardy.

♦ Two of the 1988 presidential hopefuls, Biden and Robertson, got a lot of press coverage when it turned out their academic credentials were not as they had represented.

♦ The chairman of the board of a major university in the South resigned when it became known his Doctorate was from a "school" whose founder was in federal prison for selling degrees.

♦ The young woman whose 1981 Pulitzer Prize was taken away when it turned out she had falsified her story about a young drug addict also turned out to have two fake degrees listed on her *Washington Post* job application.

♦ A finalist for fire chief in a major midwestern city in 1994 was found (by one of his opponents) to have a Bachelor's degree that he purchased for $45 from a Texas degree mill.

♦ The chief engineer of San Francisco's transit system lost his $81,000-a-year job when his employer discovered that he did not have the degree he claimed.

♦ The superintendent of one of California's largest school districts lost his $98,000-a-year job and faced criminal charges when a reporter learned he did not have the Stanford doctorate he claimed.

♦ A prominent Florida university professor of surgery resigned when someone checked up and found he didn't have the Master's degree he had listed on his resume.

♦ A controversial member of the Canadian parliament got huge page one headlines in Toronto when it was learned that he was signing letters "LL.B." even though he did not have a law degree.

♦ During the 1994 elections, candidates in five states were discovered to be claiming degrees they did not earn. After the ensuing publicity, four out of five lost.

♦ The London *Daily Telegraph* revealed gleefully that Italian neo-fascist MP Alessandra Mussolini, granddaughter of Il Duce, had allegedly purchased her degree in history and moral philosophy from Rome's Sapienza University for about $500, utilizing professor's signatures forged by a porter. (The newspaper suggested that the porter might have been just as good a judge of moral philosophy as the professor.)

♦ A large midwestern county went to court to obtain a summary judgment to remove its health commissioner, after learning that the source of his graduate degree was less than reputable.

And so it goes. Do you know where your own doctor, lawyer, and accountant earned their degrees? Have you checked with the schools just to be sure? A diploma on the wall is not sufficient evidence. We know of three different places that have sold fake diplomas from any school, printed to order for a modest sum. John has two fake Harvard diplomas hanging on his wall, alongside his real ones. His medical degree cost $50 from a "lost diploma replacement service" in Oregon. What if your family doctor had their catalog? His Harvard law degree, purchased just before this edition of our book went to press, cost just over $50 from a "service" in Florida. (No, we are not going to give out names and addresses; these businesses do enough damage in the world as it is.)

This topic moves very rapidly from the abstract to the concrete when something happens nearby. It was clearly brought home some years ago when a locally prominent "certified public accountant" who lived just down the road from us hurriedly packed his shingle and left town. One of his clients had decided to check, and found out that he simply did not have the credentials he said he had.

So then, common sense should be sufficient to make your decision on how to use a degree in almost any situation that may arise. Where there is any doubt at all about using a given degree or title, it may be wise to seek legal advice, or at the very least to check with the relevant state agencies—generally the state education department (see chapter 6), or the appropriate licensing agencies.

And, in general, it isn't a bad idea to worry just a little about other people's degrees and titles. A lot of fakes and frauds are out there right now, practicing medicine, teaching classes, practicing law, counseling troubled families, building bridges, pulling teeth, and keeping books, without benefit of a degree, a license, or proper training. If more people would ask a few more questions about the title before the name, or the document on the wall, these dangerous phonies would be stopped before they do more harm to us all. Almost every school will confirm, either by mail or by telephone, whether or not a given person has indeed earned a degree from them. This is not an invasion of privacy, since the facts are known as "directory information," available to the public through printed directories or publicly accessible university information files.

(Glad you asked. John Bear's Ph.D. was awarded by Michigan State University, East Lansing, Michigan, on March 19, 1966, and you are most welcome to check it out with them.)

NONACADEMIC TITLES

There are two kinds of things people do, other than earning (or buying) degrees that result in letters after their names and/or titles before them. These "designations" and "titles" are not the main province of this book, but they are closely allied, which is why we address them briefly.

Designations

Designations are, typically, titles or credentials awarded by various professional and trade organizations and associations upon completion of a course of study and, often,

examinations. Perhaps most common are the designations of C.P.A. (Certified Public Accountant) in the U.S. and C.A. (Chartered Accountant) in Canada. The designation is earned upon completing certain courses and passing examinations.

Other popular designations are those of C.L.U. (Certified Life Underwriter), C.F.P. (Certified Financial Planner), and Realtor. But there are many hundreds of others, some easy to gain, others requiring arduous examinations, and most permitting the holder to add letters following his or her name.

Some organizations, especially those in Europe, have several levels of designation, depending on which series of examinations one has passed. For instance, one can be an M.A.B.E. (Member of the Association of Business Executives) or, following additional exams, an F.A.B.E. (Fellow of the (etc.)).

Some designations are clearly academic, and are regarded as such by many institutions. For instance, an American C.P.A. will often not have to take either an accounting or a quantitative methods course if he or she enrolls in certain M.B.A. programs.

One thing the world needs is a comprehensive guide to designations, making clear just what was done to earn it. At presstime we were shown a draft manuscript of a massive compendium of U.S. designations, prepared by a business executive in Texas. We hope he will add non-U.S. designations, and find a publisher. It will be a valuable resource.

Titles

People often ask, "Well, if I can't become a Doctor overnight, what about becoming a baron or a knight or something?" Indeed, it has been suggested that one reason honorary Doctorates are so popular in America is that we don't have titles of nobility. This topic is really not within the scope of the book, but here are a few opportunities of which we have become aware over the years. Please understand that we know nothing about any of this stuff, and are simply passing along other peoples' information. Don't blame us if you are arrested for impersonating a Baron or are drafted into the Byzantine army.

Baron of Bosnia

The Royal and Imperial House of Serbia and Bosnia, represented by His Royal Highness, King Marcijan II, is willing to grant the "fully inheritable" noble titles of Baron, Viscount, or Count of Serbia and Bosnia upon a contribution of from $10,000 to $20,000. Since the king insists that recipients be able to "represent this honour," a resumé is required as well, to be sure one is suitable. Information from The Cultural Counsel for the Royal and Imperial House of Serbia and Bosnia, Winfried Heffner, Ralf Count Huber, Schloss Wiedergrun, D7601 Durbach, Germany.

Ambassador of the Byzantine Empire

According to the Permanent Diplomatic Delegation of the Byzantine Empire, the last recognized heir, Prince Pietro III, Paleologo, is interested in granting various titles of nobility, upon proper remuneration. The Empire claims to have "diplomatic relations with more than 70 governments." Details from Joseph Baier, Director for External Relations and International Cooperation of the Byzantine Empire, POB 8, A-9500 Villach, Austria.

Knight of Malta

At least 19 separate organizations call themselves Knights of Malta. Some of them offer knighthood in return for a donation. The original order was established in the year 1113, and is officially called the Sovereign Military Hospitaller Order of St. John of Jerusalem of Rhodes and Malta. Catholics may be nominated by their bishop, and if the top people in Rome approve, nominees pay $1,500 and are entitled to put the letters K.M. after their names, but no title before the name. See your bishop. Then there is the Sovereign Military and Hospitaller Order of Saint John of Jerusalem, Knights of Malta, which may be an offshoot of the original, established for non-Catholics by the czar of Russia in 1798. This order will seriously consider knighthood to appropriate people, many of whom are said to have made non-tax-deductible donations of $10,000 and up. Further information from Grand Sovereign Master Prince Khimchiachvili, Duke de l'Eliseni, Knights of Malta Chancellery, 116 Central Park South, New York, NY 10019.

Please note that we have received angry letters from people representing one or another Maltese organization, claiming that theirs is the real thing and all the others are phonies. As E. B. White used to write, in response to all critical letters, "You may be right."

Knight Templar

The equally historic and venerable Order of the Knights Templar offers a more reasonably priced knighthood, some $1,000 for the title. For more information, write to the Commander of Cyprus, in care of the Cyprus Center of Medeivalism and Heraldry, P.O. Box 3355, Nicosia, Cyprus.

Patriarchate of Antioch

This church offers appointments to the Patriarchal Nobility and Diplomatic Corps and Orders of Chivalry in exchange for donations. They range from $375 for the Order of the Star of the Nile to $1,000 for Prince, Baron, or Knight to $5,000 for creation of a Grand Dukedom with qualification to $10,000 for "recognition of claims to thrones (by treaty)." An Ambassadorship ($5,000) comes with diplomatic ID cards and Lettres de Chancellerie. Full details from The Church Coadjutor, Patriarchate of Antioch, BM3254, 27A Old Gloucester Street, London WC1N 3XX, England. (The address is a mail-forwarding service, so be cautious about sending money.)

If these aren't enough, you will find many more opportunities in a little book called *$tatu$ for Sale: the complete guide to instant prestige,* by Wayne Yeager, published by Charter Publications, 3119 Isabel Drive, Los Angeles, California 90065.

Listings include many that the purveyors take seriously (yet more Knights of Malta organizations, the German Order of the Griffin, the Scottish Order of St. Andrew, the Polish Order of the White Eagle, etc.); and many from people out to make money and/or have fun (The Church of the Sub-Genius will elect you Pope for $10, the same price the Universal Life Church charges to declare you a saint).

Yeager reports, among much else, that the Council of Westphalia (c/o The Roman Forum, 13 Oakleigh Road, Stratford-upon-Avon, Warwickshire CV37 0DW England) is in the business of finding extinct British titles, unlikely ever to be reclaimed, and bestowing them on people who support their archaeological research.

Yeager also describes four European services that specialize in getting their clients either married into or adopted into the royal houses of Europe at fees ranging from $20,000 to more than $300,000. (Please, no catty remarks wondering which one Princess What's-her-name used.)

Finally, in this vein, *Parade Magazine* reported that Zsa Zsa Gabor's eighth husband, Prince Frederick von Anhalt, Duke of Saxony, Count of Ascania, is the son of a German policeman, who was adopted by an impoverished German princess, after which he sold 68 knighthoods at $50,000 each.

♦ 6 ♦

How to Evaluate a School

Some people spend more time deciding which soda to buy from a soft drink machine than they do in choosing the school where they will earn their degree.
PROSECUTOR AT THE TRIAL OF A STATE PSYCHOLOGIST WITH A PHONY PH.D.

An investigative reporter for a large newspaper once told John that he could go into any building on the street, "that office, that hospital, that laundromat, that factory—and given enough time and money, I would find a story there that would probably make page one."

The same is very likely true of virtually every school in this book, from Harvard on down. Some simply have a lot more skeletons in a lot more closets than others.

It would be wonderful to have an army of trained investigators and detectives at our disposal. With our very limited resources and manpower, we cannot do a detailed and intensive investigation of every single school. Happily, we have received a great deal of assistance from readers of this book, who have followed our advice on checking out schools and have reported their findings to us.

Here, then, is the four-step procedure we recommend for investigating schools that are not covered in this book, or looking further into those that are. And please, if you do this, share your research with us at P. O. Box 7070, Berkeley, California 94707. (Thank you.)

Step One: Check It Out in This Book
If a school isn't here, it may be because it is very new, or because we didn't consider it sufficiently nontraditional for inclusion—or quite possibly because we simply missed it. And even if it *is* listed here, don't take our opinions as the gospel truth. Hardly a day passes that we don't get a letter challenging our opinions. Sometimes they begin, "You idiot, don't you know that . . ." and sometimes they begin, "I beg to differ with you in regard to . . ." Whatever the tone, we are always glad to have these opinions. There have been quite a few instances where such a letter spurred us to look more closely at a school, resulting in a revised opinion, either upward or downward.

Step Two: Check It Out with Friends, Colleagues, or Employers
If you need the degree for a new job, a salary increase, or a state license, be sure to find out specifically if this degree will suffice before investing any money in any school. Many

schools will gladly enter into correspondence with employers, state agencies, or others you may designate, to explain their programs and establish their credentials.

People regularly tell the consulting practice horror stories about losing thousands of dollars and wasting incredible amounts of time completing a degree that was useless to them. "But the school said it was accredited," they lament.

Step Three: Check It Out with the Proper Government Agency
Every state and every nation has an agency that oversees higher education. Check the school out with the agency in your state or in the state or country in which the school is located. A list of these agencies is given at the end of the chapter. Some correspondence schools are well known (positively or negatively) to the Better Business Bureau as well. And all nations have a department, bureau, or ministry of education that may be able to supply information on a school. They also all have embassies in Washington, DC, and United Nations delegations in New York to which questions may be addressed. You may get bogged down in voice mail, but it is worth the effort.

Step Four: Check Out the School Itself
Visit the campus or the offices if at all possible, especially if you have any doubts. If the school's literature does not make clear its precise legal or accreditation status, or if you still have any questions, check with the appropriate accrediting agency. They are all listed in chapter 7. If the accreditor is not listed in chapter 7, be careful. There are a lot of phony accrediting agencies in operation.

Here are some of the questions you may wish to ask. Do *not* just make up a form letter and send it to 50 or more schools, as more than a few readers have done. Being more selective, both about schools and questions, will save you and the schools time and money. Also, match the question to the school. If you are inquiring of an obscure unaccredited school, it may be most appropriate to ask where the president earned his or her degrees, but there is no need to ask that of, say, the University of Wisconsin.

♦ How many students are currently enrolled? (Curiously, quite a few schools seem reluctant to reveal these numbers. Sometimes it is because they are embarrassed about how large they are, as, for instance, in the case of one alternative school that at one time had more than 3,000 students and a faculty of five! Sometimes it is because they are embarrassed about how small they are, as is the case with one heavily advertised school that has impressive literature, extremely high tuition, and fewer than 50 students.)

♦ How many degrees have been awarded in the last year?

♦ What is the size of the faculty? How many of these are full-time and how many are part-time or adjunct faculty? If the catalog doesn't make it clear, from which schools did the faculty earn their degrees?

♦ From which school(s) did the president, the dean, and other administrators earn their own degrees? (There is nothing inherently wrong with staff members earning degrees from their own school, but when the number doing so is 25 percent or more, as is the case at some institutions, it starts sounding a little suspicious.)

♦ May I have the names and addresses of some recent graduates in my field of study, and/or in my geographical area?

♦ May I look at the work done by students? (Inspection of Master's theses and doctoral dissertations can often give a good idea of the quality of work expected, and the caliber of the students. But you may either have to visit the school [not a bad idea] or offer to pay for making and sending copies.)

♦ Will your degree be acceptable for my intended needs (state licensing, certification, graduate school admission, salary advance, new job, whatever)?

♦ What exactly is your legal status, with regard to state agencies and to accrediting associations? If accreditation (or candidacy for accreditation) is claimed, is it with an agency that is approved either by the U.S. Department of Education or the Council on Postsecondary Accreditation? If not accredited, are there any plans to seek accreditation?

No legitimate school should refuse to answer questions like these. Remember, you are shopping for something that may cost you several thousand dollars or more. It is definitely a buyer's market, and the schools all know this. If they see that you are an informed customer, they will know that they must satisfy you or you will take your business elsewhere.

Remember too that alternative education does not require all the trappings of a traditional school. Don't expect to find a big campus with spacious lawns, an extensive library, or a football team. Some outstanding nontraditional schools are run from relatively small suites of rented offices.

You definitely cannot go by the catalog or other school literature alone. Some really bad schools and some outrageous degree mills have hired good writers and designers, and produced very attractive catalogs that are full of lies and misleading statements. A common trick, for instance, is to show a photograph of a large and impressive building, which may or may not be the building in which the school rents a room or two. Another common device is to list a large number of names of faculty and staff, sometimes with photographs of their smiling faces. Our files are full of certified, deliver-to-addressee-only letters sent to these people that have been returned as undeliverable.

Finally, be very suspicious of schools with no telephones, or, perhaps even more of a red flag, schools where you can't call them, they have to call you. For instance, in 1989, we attempted to check out a new and heavily advertised school called North American University. The people who answered their toll-free phone line were cheerful, but after many calls, we were never put through to anyone. It was always, "Dr. Peters will call you back." "Dr. Peters" turned out to be an alias for the school's owner, a convicted felon, who would return calls from his home in another state.

On the other side of the ledger, some good, sincere, legitimate schools have issued typewritten and photocopied catalogs, either to save money or to go along with their low-key images, and a few sincere, very low-budget schools have even operated without a telephone for a while.

STATE AND FOREIGN AGENCIES FOR HIGHER EDUCATION

There is at least one agency in each state, and one in the District of Columbia, that oversees higher education. If you have any concerns about the legality of an institution, or its right to award degrees, these are the places to ask.

State Agencies

For each state, and the District of Columbia, we have listed first the principal higher education agency in that state. This is followed by a new listing: the SPRE, or State Postsecondary Review Entity, and in few cases, by a third relevant agency.

What Is a SPRE?

When Congress passed a massive series of new education laws in 1992, known as the "1992 revision of the Higher Education Act," they attempted to bring some uniformity to the diverse systems of the fifty states by requiring each state to establish a SPRE, or State Postsecondary Review Entity. The main purpose of a SPRE is to monitor compliance of colleges and universities in its state with various federal laws, most especially those related to student loans.

But SPREs can go further: they can investigate schools in their state for any reason, either on their own initiative, or because they have been requested to do so by Washington.

Some states established a brand new agency to comply with the SPRE law; others pretty much ignored the intent and said "We will do SPRE within an existing agency," and yet others fell somewhere in between, typically by assigning SPRE duties to a sub-office of an existing agency. This is a dynamic situation, since some states are still mulling over what to do about their SPREs, and in late 1995, the Republicans in Congress decided to do away with the whole SPRE concept. Stay tuned.

Whom Do You Ask First?

No simple answer, so be prepared to spend a bit of time on the phone or writing letters if you wish to learn the exact status of a school in a given state. Starting with the main higher education agency makes sense, although in some states a SPRE or indeed a third agency (as with California or Hawaii) may be the best place.

We have found, as we call various state agencies fairly often, that the basic answers are generally correct, but often incomplete. A lot depends on who happens to answer the phone. For instance, one time when we called Alabama to check on an unaccredited school operating there, we were told, "Oh, we've been trying to close them down for years. At least we got them to agree not to accept students from the state of Alabama." But on another call to the same office, we were told, "The state of Alabama has no official position with regard to this school."

In another example, we called the proper California agency to ask about a school which we had heard had just lost its State Approval. The helpful person on the phone confirmed this, and gave us the exact date it had happened. But then we found out, a few days later, that the school had gone to court and secured a Writ, which prohibited the state from enforcing its decision until further hearings were held, and thus the school continued legitimately in business.

The inconsistency from state to state, the level of knowledge of state personnel, and the volatile situation with regard to many schools and many laws, makes our job a harder one, and yours as well.

Alabama

Main higher education agency
Commission on Higher Education
3465 Norman Bridge Road
Montgomery 36105
(334) 242-1998
Fax (334) 281-6711
Henry J. Hector, Executive Director

SPRE (State Postsecondary Review Entity)
Same
William O. Blow, Deputy Executive Director

Alaska

Main higher education agency
Alaska Commission on Postsecondary Education
3030 Vintage Blvd.
Juneau 99801
(907) 465-2962
Fax (907) 465-5316
Joe L. McCormick, Executive Director

SPRE (State Postsecondary Review Entity)
Same

Arizona

Main higher education agency
Arizona Board of Regents
2020 North Central Ave., Suite 230
Phoenix 85004
(602) 229-2500
Fax (602) 229-2555
Frank H. Besnette, Executive Director

SPRE (State Postsecondary Review Entity)
Arizona Commission for Postsecondary Education
2020 North Central Ave.
Suite 275
Phoenix 85004
(602) 229-2591
Fax (602) 229-2555
Edward A. Johnson, Executive Director

Arkansas

Main higher education agency
Arkansas Department of Higher Education
114 East Capitol Ave.
Little Rock 72201
(501) 324-9300
Fax (501) 324-9310
Diane S. Gilleland, Director

SPRE (State Postsecondary Review Entity)
Same
Mary Beth Sudduth

California

Main higher education agency
California Postsecondary Education Commission
1303 J St., Suite 500
Sacramento 95814
(916) 445-7933
Fax (916) 327-4417
Warren Fox, Executive Director

SPRE (State Postsecondary Review Entity)
Same
(916) 332-7982
Karl M. Engelbach, SPRE Coordinator

Other Relevant Agency
Council on Private, Postsecondary and Vocational
Education
1027 10th St., Fourth Floor
Sacramento 95814
(916) 445-3427
(They are charged with evaluating unaccredited schools,
to determine if they should be granted State Approval.)

Colorado
Main higher education agency
Colorado Commission on Higher Education
1300 Broadway, 2nd floor
Denver 80203
Dwayne C. Nuzum, Executive Director
(303) 866-2723
Fax (303) 860-9750

SPRE (State Postsecondary Review Entity)
Same

Connecticut
Main higher education agency
Board of Governors for Higher Education
61 Woodland St.
Hartford 06105
(203) 566-5766
Fax (203) 566-7856
Andrew G. De Rocco, Commissioner of Higher
Education

SPRE (State Postsecondary Review Entity)
Connecticut Department of Higher Education
61 Woodland St.
Hartford 06105
(203) 566-4645
Joseph Zikmund, Senior Associate

Delaware
Main higher education agency
Delaware Higher Education Commission
820 North French St.
Wilmington 19801
(302) 577-3240
Fax (302) 571-3862
John F. Corrozi, Executive Director

SPRE (State Postsecondary Review Entity)
Same

District of Columbia
Main higher education agency
Office of Postsecondary Education Research and
Assistance
2100 Martin Luther King, Jr. Ave. S.E., Suite 401
Washington 20020

(202) 727-3685
Fax (202) 727-2739
Sheila Drews, Acting Chief

SPRE (State Postsecondary Review Entity)
Office of Education
441 Fourth St. N.W., Rm. 370-N
Washington 20001
(202) 727-0248
David Ray, Education Consultant

Florida
Main higher education agency
Postsecondary Education Planning Commission
Florida Education Center
Tallahassee 32399
(904) 488-7894
Fax (904) 922-5388
William B. Proctor, Executive Director

SPRE (State Postsecondary Review Entity)
Florida Department of Education
1701 The Capitol
Tallahassee 32399
(904) 488-1812
Fax (904) 922-9620
Lewis Wagar, Director

Georgia
Main higher education agency
Board of Regents
244 Washington St. S.W.
Atlanta 30334
(404) 656-2202
Fax (404) 651-9301
H. D. Propst, Chancellor

SPRE (State Postsecondary Review Entity)
Georgia Nonpublic Postsecondary Education
Commission
2100 East Exchange Place, Suite 203
Tucker 30084
(404) 414-3307
Ross Miller, SPRE Administrator

Hawaii
Main higher education agency
University of Hawaii Board of Regents
2444 Dole St., Room 209
Honolulu 96822
(808) 956-8213
Fax (808) 956-5286
Kenneth P. Mortimer, Executive Officer

SPRE (State Postsecondary Review Entity)
State Postsecondary Education Commission

2444 Dole St., Room 209
Honolulu 96822
(808) 956-6862
Patrick Naughton, SPRE Coordinator

Other Relevant Agency
Department of Consumer Protection
Philip Doi, Director
(808) 587-3222
(If Hawaii ever decides to enforce the unaccredited school registration law passed by the legislature in 1990, it would probably be administered through this office.)

Idaho
Main higher education agency
State Board of Education
650 W. State St.
Room 307
Boise 83720
(208) 334-2270
Fax (208) 334-2632
Rayburn Barton, Executive Director

SPRE (State Postsecondary Review Entity)
Same
Robin Dodson, Chief Academic Officer

Illinois
Main higher education agency
Board of Higher Education
4 West Old Capitol Plaza, Room 500
Springfield 62701
(217) 782-2551
Fax (217) 782-8548
Richard D. Wagner, Executive Director

SPRE (State Postsecondary Review Entity)
Illinois Student Assistance Commission
1755 Lake Cook Road
Deerfield 60015
(708) 948-8500, ext. 3302
Wendy M. Rothenbach, Compliance Administrator

Indiana
Main higher education agency
Commission for Higher Education
101 West Ohio St.
Suite 550
Indianapolis 46204
(317) 232-1900
Fax (317) 232-1899
Clyde R. Ingle, Commissioner

SPRE (State Postsecondary Review Entity)
Same
 H. Kent Weldon, Deputy Commissioner

Iowa
Main higher education agency
State Board of Regents
East 12th St. and Grand Ave.
Des Moines 50319
(515) 281-3934
(515) 281-6420
R. Wayne Richey, Executive Director

SPRE (State Postsecondary Review Entity)
Iowa Coordinating Council for Post High School Education
East 12th St. and Grand Ave.
Des Moines 50319
(515) 281-3934
Robert J. Barak, Permanent Secretary

Kansas
Main higher education agency
Kansas Board of Regents
700 Southwest Harrison
Suite 1410
Topeka 66603
(913) 296-3421
Fax (913) 296-0983
Stephen M. Jordan, Executive Director

SPRE (State Postsecondary Review Entity)
Kansas State Board of Education
120 Southeast 10th Ave.
Topeka 66612
(913) 296-3204
Rodney J. Bieker, General Counsel

Kentucky
Main higher education agency
Council on Higher Education
1050 U.S. 127 South, Suite 101
Frankfort 40601
(502) 564-3553
Fax (502) 564-2063
Gary S. Cox, Executive Director

SPRE (State Postsecondary Review Entity)
Same
Charles Wade, SPRE Coordinator

Louisiana
Main higher education agency
Board of Regents
150 Third St.
Suite 129
Baton Rouge 90801
(504) 342-4253
Fax (504) 342-9318
Sammie W. Cosper, Commissioner

SPRE (State Postsecondary Review Entity)
Louisiana Postsecondary Review Commission
P. O. Box 94004
Baton Rouge 70804
(504) 342-0998
Sally Clausen, Education Advisor

Maine
Main higher education agency
Department of Education
Division of Higher Education Services
State House Station #23
Augusta 04333
(207) 287-5803
Fax (207) 287-5900
Fred Douglas, Director

SPRE (State Postsecondary Review Entity)
Finance Authority of Maine
State House, Station 119
Augusta 04333
(207) 287-2183
Mia Purcell, Director of Education-Assistance Division

Maryland
Main higher education agency
Higher Education Commission
16 Francis St.
Annapolis 21401
(410) 974-2971
Fax (410) 974-3513
Shaila R. Aery, Secretary of Higher Education

SPRE (State Postsecondary Review Entity)
Same
Mary Bowde, Assistant Secretary

Massachusetts
Main higher education agency
Higher Education Coordinating Council
One Ashburton Place, Room 1401
Boston 02108
(617) 727-7785
Fax (617) 727-6397
Stanley Z. Koplik, Chancellor

SPRE (State Postsecondary Review Entity)
Same
Michael S. Noetzel, Executive Assistant

Michigan
Main higher education agency
State Department of Education
P. O. Box 30008
Lansing 48909
(517) 335-4933

Fax (517) 335-4602
C. Danford Austin, Associate Superintendent

SPRE (State Postsecondary Review Entity)
Same

Minnesota
Main higher education agency
Higher Education Coordinating Board
550 Cedar St., Suite 400
St. Paul 55101
(612) 296-9665
(612) 297-8880
David R. Powers, Executive Director

SPRE (State Postsecondary Review Entity)
Same
(612) 296-9693
Paul F. Thomas Senior Policy Advisor

Mississippi
Main higher education agency
Board of Trustees of State Institutions of
Higher Learning
3825 Ridgewood Road
Jackson 39211
(601) 982-6623
Fax (601) 987-4172
W. Ray Cleere, Commissioner

SPRE (State Postsecondary Review Entity)
Same
(601) 982-6296
Milton Baxter, Assistant Commissioner

Missouri
Main higher education agency
Coordinating Board for Higher Education
3515 Amazonas Drive
Jefferson City 65109
(314) 751-2361
Fax (314) 751-6635
Charles J. McClain, Commissioner

SPRE (State Postsecondary Review Entity)
Same
Michael A. McMannis, Association Commissioner

Montana
Main higher education agency
Montana University System
2500 Broadway
Helena 59620
(406) 444-0351
Jeffrey D. Baker, Commissioner of Higher Education

SPRE (State Postsecondary Review Entity)
Board of Regents for Higher Education
2500 Broadway
Helena 59620
(406) 444-0351
Bill Lannan, Director, Guaranteed Student Loan Program

Nebraska
Main higher education agency
Coordinating Commission for Postsecondary Education
P. O. Box 95005
Lincoln 68509
(402) 471-2847
Fax (402) 471-2886
Bruce G. Stahl, Executive Director

SPRE (State Postsecondary Review Entity)
Same
(402) 471-2847
Christine E. Denicola, Coordinator

Nevada
Main higher education agency
University and Community College Systems of Nevada
2601 Enterprise Road
Reno 89512
(702) 784-4905
Fax (702) 784-1127
John A. Richardson, Chancellor

SPRE (State Postsecondary Review Entity)
Same

New Hampshire
Main higher education agency
Postsecondary Education Commission
2 Industrial Park Drive
Concord 03301
(603) 271-2555
Fax (603) 271-2696
James A. Busselle, Executive Director

SPRE (State Postsecondary Review Entity)
Same

New Jersey
Main higher education agency
Commission on Higher Education
20 West State St., CN542
Trenton 08625
(609) 292-4310
Fax (609) 292-7225
Edward D. Goldberg, Chancellor

SPRE (State Postsecondary Review Entity)
Same

(609) 292-2955
Amorita Suarez

New Mexico
Main higher education agency
Commission on Higher Education
1068 Cerrillos Road
Santa Fe 87501
(505) 827-7383
Fax (505) 827-7392
Bruce D. Hamlett, Executive Director

SPRE (State Postsecondary Review Entity)
Same
Bill Simpson, Senior Research and Policy Analyst

New York
Main higher education agency
State Education Department
Cultural Education Center, Room 5B28
Albany 12230
(518) 474-5851
Fax (518) 486-2175
Donald J. Nolan, Deputy Commissioner

SPRE (State Postsecondary Review Entity)
Same
(518) 474-3896
Mike Van Ryn, Assistant Commissioner

North Carolina
Main higher education agency
Commission on Higher Education Facilities
UNC General Administration
910 Raleigh Rd., Box 2688
Chapel Hill 27515
(919) 962-1000
Fax (919) 96200488
Charles L. Wheeler, Associate Vice President

SPRE (State Postsecondary Review Entity)
Postsecondary Eligibility Review Commission
130 Penmarc Drive
Suite 109
Raleigh 27603
(919) 733-7535
Bernell C. Dickinson, Interim Director

North Dakota
Main higher education agency
North Dakota University System
600 East Blvd.
Bismarck 58505
(701) 224-2960
Fax (701) 224-2961
Douglas M. Treadway, Chancellor

SPRE (State Postsecondary Review Entity)
Same
(701) 224-4114
Gene Kemper, Vice-Chancellor

Ohio
Main higher education agency
Board of Regents
30 E. Broad St., 36th floor
Columbus 43266
(614) 466-6000
Fax (614) 466-5866
Elaine H. Hairston, Chancellor

SPRE (State Postsecondary Review Entity)
Same
(614) 466-6000
Charles Corbato, SPRE Director

Oklahoma
Main higher education agency
State Regents for Higher Education
500 Education Building
Oklahoma City 73105
(405) 524-9100
Fax (405) 524-9235
Hans Brisch, Chancellor

SPRE (State Postsecondary Review Entity)
Same
(405) 524-9154
Joe Hagy, Director of Special Programs

Oregon
Main higher education agency
State Board of Higher Education
1263 University of Oregon
Eugene 97403
(503) 346-5795
Fax (503) 346-5764
Virginia L. Thompson, Secretary of the Board

SPRE (State Postsecondary Review Entity)
Office of Education Policy and Planning
255 Capitol St. N.E., Suite 126
Salem 97310
(503) 378-3921
David Young, Administrator of SPRE Program

Pennsylvania
Main higher education agency
Department of Education
333 Market St., 12th Floor
Harrisburg 17126
(717) 787-5041

Fax (717) 783-5420
Charles R. Fuget, Commissioner

SPRE (State Postsecondary Review Entity)
Same
(717) 787-2414
Jane Stockdale, Chief, Division of Veterans and Military Education

Rhode Island
Main higher education agency
Office of Higher Education
301 Promenade St.
Providence 02908
(401) 277-6561
Fax (401) 277-2545
Americo W. Petrocelli, Commissioner

SPRE (State Postsecondary Review Entity)
Same
(401) 277-6560, Ext. 134
Diane Reedy, SPRE Coordinator

South Carolina
Main higher education agency
Commission on Higher Education
1333 Main St., Suite 200
Columbia 29201
(803) 737-2276
Fax (803) 737-2297
Fred R. Sheheen, Commissioner

SPRE (State Postsecondary Review Entity)
Same
(803) 737-2265
Lynn Metcalf, SPRE Coordinator

South Dakota
Main higher education agency
Board of Regents
207 E. Capitol Ave.
Pierre 57501
(605) 773-3455
Fax (605) 773-5320
James Shekleton, Interim Executive Director

SPRE (State Postsecondary Review Entity)
Same

Tennessee
Main higher education agency
Higher Education Commission
404 James Robertson Parkway
Suite 1900
Nashville 37219
(615) 741-3605

Fax (615) 741-6230
Arliss L. Roaden, Executive Director

SPRE (State Postsecondary Review Entity)
Same
Alan R. Cullum, SPRE Director

Texas
Main higher education agency
Higher Education Coordinating Board
P. O. Box 12788, Capitol Station
Austin 78711
(512) 483-6101
Fax (512) 483-6127
Kenneth H. Ashworth, Commissioner

SPRE (State Postsecondary Review Entity)
Same
(512) 483-6200
William H. Sanford, Assistant Commissioner

Utah
Main higher education agency
Utah System of Higher Education
355 West North Temple, Suite 550
Salt Lake City 84180
(801) 321-7100
Cecelia H. Foxley, Commissioner

SPRE (State Postsecondary Review Entity)
Same
(801) 321-7110
Don A. Carpenter, Associate Commissioner

Vermont
Main higher education agency
Vermont State Colleges
P. O. Box 359
Waterbury 05676
(802) 241-2520
Thomas P. Salmon, President

SPRE (State Postsecondary Review Entity)
Vermont Higher Education Council
P. O. Box 47
Essex Junction 05453
(802) 878-7466
Robert Stanfield, VSPRE Coordinator

Virginia
Main higher education agency
State Council of Higher Education for Virginia
101 North 14th St., 9th Floor
Richmond 23219
(804) 225-2137
Fax (804) 225-2604

Gordon K. Davies, Director

SPRE (State Postsecondary Review Entity)
Same
(804) 225-2610
J. Michael Mullen, Deputy Director

Washington
Main higher education agency
Higher Education Coordinating Board
917 Lakeridge Way
Olympia 98504
(206) 753-2210
Fax (206) 753-1784
Elson S. Floyd, Executive Director

SPRE (State Postsecondary Review Entity)
Same
(206) 586-5701
Cedric Page, Associate Director

West Virginia
Main higher education agency
State College System of West Virginia
1018 Kanawha Blvd. East
Suite 700
Charleston 25301
(304) 558-0699
Fax (304) 558-1011
James W. Rowley, Interim Chancellor

SPRE (State Postsecondary Review Entity)
State College and University System
1018 Kanawha Blvd. East
Charleston 25301
(304) 588-0263
Joseph W. Corder, Jr.

Wisconsin
Main higher education agency
University of Wisconsin System
1220 Linden Drive
Room 1720
Madison 53706
(608) 262-2321
Katharine C. Lyall, President Higher
Educational Aids Board

SPRE (State Postsecondary Review Entity)
Higher Educational Aids Board
131 W. Wilson St.
Room 902
Madison 53703
(608) 267-2208
Fax (608) 267-2808
Ms. Valorie T. Olson, Executive Secretary

Wyoming
Main higher education agency
Postsecondary Education Planning and Coordinating Council
Office of the Governor
Cheyenne 82002
(307) 777-7434
Gov. Michael J. Sullivan, Chairman

SPRE (State Postsecondary Review Entity)
Department of Education
2300 Capitol Ave., 2nd Floor
Cheyenne 82002
(307) 777-6265
D. Leeds Pickering, SPRE Coordinator

Guam
Main higher education agency
Pacific Post-Secondary Education Council
P. O. Box 23067
G M F Guam 96921
(617) 734-2962
William A. Kinder, Executive Director

Puerto Rico
Main higher education agency
Council on Higher Education
University of Puerto Rico Station, Box 23305
San Juan 00931
(809) 758-3350
Fax (809) 763-8394
Ismael Ramirez-Soto, Executive Secretary

AGENCIES OUTSIDE THE U.S.

Australia
Department of Education
MLC Tower, Keltie St.
Phillip, ACT 2606
(062) 891333
Minister for Education

Belgium
Ministry of National Education
Centre Arts Lux, 4th and 5th Floors
58 Ave. des Arts, BP5
1040 Brussels
(02) 512-66-60
Minister of Education

Brazil
Ministry of Education and Culture
Esplanada dos Ministerios, Bloco L
74.047 Brasilia, DF
(061) 214-8432
Minister of Education

Bulgaria
Ministry of Education
Blvd. A, Stamboliski 18
Sofia 1000
84-81
Minister of Education

Canada

Alberta
Department of Advanced Education
Devonian Building, East Tower
11160 Jasper Ave.
Edmonton T5K 0L3
(403) 427-2781
Fax (403) 427-4185

British Columbia
Ministry of Skills, Training and Labour
Parliament Buildings
Room 109
Victoria V8V 1X4
(604) 387-1986
Fax (604) 387-3200

Manitoba
Department of Education and Training
Postsecondary Adult & Continuing Education Division
Legislative Building
Winnipeg R3C 0V8
(204) 945-2211
Fax (204) 945-8692

New Brunswick
Department of Advanced Education and Labour
P. O. Box 6000
470 York St.
Fredericton E3B 5H1
(506) 453-2597

Newfoundland
Department of Education
Postsecondary Education Division
Confederation Building
P. O. Box 8700
St. John's A1B 4J6
(709) 729-5097
Fax (709) 729-5896

Nova Scotia
Department of Education
P. O. Box 2065
Station "M"
Halifax B3J 3B7
(902) 424-5168
Fax (902) 424-5168

Ontario
Ministry of Education and Training
900 Bay St., 6th Floor
Mowat Block
Toronto M7A 1L2
(416) 325-2929
Fax (416) 325-2934

Prince Edward Island
Department of Education and Human Resources
4th Floor, Shaw Building
95 Rochford St.
P. O. Box 2000
Charlottetown C1A 7N8
(902) 368-4620
Fax (902) 368-4663

Quebec
Ministère de l'ènseignement supérior et de la science
Direction de communications
1033 rue de La Chevrotière
Edifice Marie-Guyart, 19e étage
Québec G1R 5K9
(418) 643-6788

Saskatchewan
Ministry of Education, Training and Employment
Post-Secondary and Adult Education
2220 College Ave.
Regina S4P 3V7
(306) 787-5626
Fax (306) 787-7392

Cuba
Ministry of Higher Education
Calle 23y F, Vedado
Havana
3-6655
Minister of Education

Denmark
Ministry of Education
Federiksholms Kanal 21-25
1220 Copenhagen K.
(01) 92-50-00
Minister of Education

Egypt
Ministry of Education
Sharia El Fellaky
Cairo
(02) 27363
Minister of National Education

Finland
Ministry of Education

Kirkkokat U3
00170 Helsinki
(90) 171636
First Minister of Education for Veterans' Education and Proprietary Schools

France
Ministry of National Education
110 Rue De Grenelle
75700 Paris
(1) 45-50-10-10

Germany
Ministry of Education and Science
Heinemannstr. 2
5300 Bonn 2
(0228) 571
Minister of Education

Greece
Ministry of Education and Religion
Odos Mihalakopoulou 80
Athens
(21) 3230461; telex 216059
Minister of Education and Religion

Hungary
Ministry of Culture and National Education
Szalay u. 10/14
1055 Budapest
530-600
Minister of Culture and National Education

India
Ministry of Education
Shastri Bhavan, New Delhi   110011
(11) 3012380
Minister of Education

Indonesia
Ministry of Education and Culture
Jalan Jenderal Sudirman
Senayan
Jakarta Pusat
(021) 581618
Minister of Education and Culture

Ireland
Ministry of Education
Marlborough St.
Dublin 1
(01) 717101; telex 31136
Minister of Education

Israel
Ministry of Education and Culture

Hakirya, 14 Klausner St.
Tel Aviv
414155
Minister of Education

Italy
Ministry of Education
Viale Trastevere 76A
00100 Rome
Telex 4759841
Minister of Education

Japan
Ministry of Education
3-2, Kasumigaseki
Chiyoda–Ku
Tokyo
(3) 581-4211
Minister of Education

Mexico
Secretariat of State for Public Education
Republica de Argentina y Gonzales
Obregon 28, 06029 Mexico, DF
5103029
Secretary of Public Education

Netherlands
Ministry of Education and Science
Europaweg 4, POB 25000
2700 LZ Zoetermeer
(079) 531911; telex 32636
Minister of Education and Science

New Zealand
Department of Education
Private Bag Wellington
(04) 735499
Minister of Education

Norway
Ministry of Church and Education
POB 8119, Dep., 0520 1
Oslo
(2) 11-90-90
Minister of Church and Education

Philippines
Ministry of Education, Culture, and Sports
Palacio del Gobernador
Gen. Luna St.

Cnr Aduana St.
Intramuros, Manila
(02) 402949
Minister of Education

Portugal
Ministry of Education
Av. 5 de Outubro 107
1000 Lisbon
731291
Minister of Education and Culture

Republic of Korea (South Korea)
Ministry of Education
77-6 Sejong–no
Chongno–Ku, Seoul
720-3315; telex 24758
Minister of Education

South Africa
Ministry of National Education
Civitas BLDG, Struben St, Private Bag X114
Pretoria
282551
Minister of National Education

Spain
Ministerios de Educacion y Ciencia
Alcala 34, Madrid 14
2321300
Minister of Education and Science

Sweden
Ministry of Education and Cultural Affairs
Mynttorget 1, 103 33 Stockholm
(8) 736-10-00; telex 13284
Minister of Education and Cultural Affairs

Turkey
Ministry of Education, Youth, and Sports
Milli Egitim, Genclik ve Spor
Bakanligi, Ankara
(41) 231160

United Kingdom
Department of Education and Science
Elizabeth House, York Rd.
London SE1 7PH
(171) 928-9222; telex 23171
Secretary of State for Education and Science

◆7◆
Accreditation

The comfortable world of accreditation seems to be unraveling.
OPENING SENTENCE, CHRONICLE OF HIGHER EDUCATION ARTICLE ON
THE STATE OF ACCREDITATION, JUNE 9, 1993

*The credibility of voluntary accreditation has sunk so low that we have to do
something dramatic if it's going to survive.*
DR. ROBERT E. ATWELL, PRESIDENT, AMERICAN COUNCIL ON EDUCATION, JANUARY 28, 1994

ACCREDITATION "LITE"
*(This is a complex chapter. If you read
nothing else, read this small section.)*

1. Generally, you can't go wrong by choosing a school accredited by a recognized accrediting agency.
2. There are some legitimate and useful unaccredited schools.
3. There are a very few legitimate but unrecognized accrediting agencies.
4. There are a great many phony accrediting agencies.
5. The world of accreditation is changing, generally in the direction of dealing more with outcomes: how schools teach or train their students and how well the students perform.

ACCREDITATION "REGULAR"

Accreditation is perhaps the most complex, confusing, and important issue in higher education. It is surely the most misunderstood and the most misused concept—both intentionally and unintentionally.

In selecting a school, there are four important things to know about accreditation:

1. What it is;
2. Why it is important in certain situations;
3. What are the many kinds of accreditors, and
4. What's all the fuss and bother that led to those two quotations at the top of this chapter?

We will address these matters more or less in this order.

WHAT IS ACCREDITATION?

Quite simply, it is a validation—a statement by a group of persons who are, theoretically, impartial experts in higher education, that a given school, or department within a school, has been thoroughly investigated and found worthy of approval.

Accreditation is a peculiarly American concept. In every other country in the world, all colleges and universities either are operated by the government, or gain the full right to grant degrees directly from the government, so there is no need for a separate, independent agency to say that a given school is OK.

In the United States, accreditation is an *entirely voluntary process*, done by private, nongovernmental agencies. As a result of this lack of central control or authority, there have evolved good accrediting agencies and bad ones, recognized ones and unrecognized ones, legitimate ones and phony ones.

So when a school says, "we are accredited," that statement alone means nothing. You must always ask, "Accredited by whom?" Unfortunately, many consumer-oriented articles and bulletins simply say that one is much safer dealing only with accredited schools, but they do not attempt to unravel the complex situation. We hear regularly from distressed people who say, about the degrees they have just learned are worthless, "But the school was accredited; I even checked with the accrediting agency." The agency, needless to say, turned out to be as phony as the school. The wrong kind of accreditation can be a lot worse than none at all.

Normally, a school wishing to be accredited will make application to the appropriate accrediting agency. After a substantial preliminary investigation to determine that the school is probably operating legally and run legitimately, it may be granted correspondent or provisional status. Typically this step will take anywhere from several months to several years or more, and when completed does not imply any kind of endorsement or recommendation, but is merely an indication that the first steps on a long path have been taken.

Next, teams from the accrediting agency, often composed of faculty of already accredited institutions, will visit the school. These "visitations," conducted at regular intervals throughout the year, are to observe the school in action, and to study the copious amounts of information

43

that the school must prepare, relating to its legal and academic structure, educational philosophy, curriculum, financial status, planning, and so forth.

After these investigations and, normally, following at least two years of successful operation (sometimes a great deal more), the school may be advanced to the status of "candidate for accreditation." Being a candidate means, in effect, "Yes, you are probably worthy of accreditation, but we want to watch your operation for a while longer."

This "while" can range from a year or two to six years or more. The great majority of schools that reach candidacy status eventually achieve full accreditation. Some accreditors do not have a candidacy status; with them it is an all-or-nothing situation. (The terms "accredited" and "fully accredited" are used interchangeably. There is no such thing as "partly accredited.")

Once a school is accredited, it is visited by inspection teams at infrequent intervals (every five to 10 years is common) to see if it is still worthy of its accreditation. The status is always subject to review at any time, should new programs be developed or should there be any significant new developments, positive or negative.

THE IMPORTANCE OF ACCREDITATION

Although accreditation is undeniably important to both schools and students (and would-be students), this importance is undermined and confused by these three factors:

1. There are no significant national standards for accreditation. What is accreditable in New York may not be accreditable in California, and vice versa. The demands and standards of the group that accredits schools of chemistry may be very different from the people who accredit schools of forestry. And so on.

2. Many very good schools (or departments within schools) are not accredited, either by their own choice (since accreditation is a totally voluntary and often very expensive procedure), or because they are too new (all schools were unaccredited at one time in their lives) or too experimental (many would say too innovative) for the generally conservative accreditors.

3. Many very bad schools claim to be accredited—but it is always by unrecognized, sometimes nonexistent accrediting associations, often of their own creation.

Still, accreditation is the only widespread system of school evaluation that we have. A school's accreditation status can be helpful to the potential student in this way: while many good schools are not accredited, it is very unlikely that any very bad or illegal school is authentically accredited. (There have been exceptions, but they are quite rare.)

In other words, *authentic* accreditation is a pretty good sign that a given school is legitimate. But it is important to remember that *lack of accreditation need not mean that a school is either inferior or illegal.* All schools are, of necessity, unaccredited when they open for business, since accreditation is based on their performance, not their proposed performance.

We stress the term *authentic* accreditation, since there are very few laws or regulations anywhere governing the establishment of an accrediting association. Anyone can start a degree mill, then turn around and open an accrediting agency next door, give his school its blessing, and begin advertising "fully accredited degrees." Indeed, this has happened many times.

The crucial question, then, is this: Who accredits the accreditors?

WHO ACCREDITS THE ACCREDITORS?

The situation is confusing, unsettled, and still undergoing change and redefinition as we head toward the third millennium. To get some sort of a handle on the situation, it will be helpful to have a bit of a historical perspective. In this instance, it makes some sense to begin in 1980, when the Republican party platform echoed Ronald Reagan's belief that the Department of Education should be closed down, since it was inappropriate for the federal government to meddle in matters better left to the states and to private enterprise.

At that time, there were two agencies, one private and one governmental, that had responsibility for evaluating and approving or recognizing accrediting agencies:

1. The U.S. Department of Education's Eligibility and Agency Evaluation Staff (EAES), which is required by law to "publish a list of nationally recognized accrediting agencies which [are determined] to be reliable . . . as to the quality of training offered." This is done as one measure of eligibility for federal financial aid programs for students. EAES also had the job of deciding whether unaccredited schools could qualify for federal aid programs, or their students for veterans' benefits. This was done primarily by what was called the "four-by-three" rule: Proof that credits from at least four students were accepted by at least three accredited schools (12 total acceptances). If they were, then the unaccredited school was recognized by the Department of Education for that purpose. Schools qualifying under the four-by-three rule had to submit evidence of continued acceptance of their credits by accredited schools in order to maintain their status.

2. COPA, the Council on Postsecondary Accreditation. COPA was a nationwide nonprofit corporation, formed in 1975 to evaluate accrediting associations and award recognition to those found worthy.

President Reagan was unable to dismantle the Department of Education during his administration, although key people in the Department strongly suggested that they should get out of the business of recognizing accrediting agencies, and leave that to the states. "Education President" Bush apparently did not share this view; at least no significant changes were made during his administration.

One of the frequent complaints levied against the recognized accrediting agencies (and not just by Republicans) is that they have, in general, been slow to acknowledge the major trend toward alternative or nontraditional education.

Some years ago, the Carnegie Commission on Higher Education conducted research on the relationship between accreditation and nontraditional approaches. Their report, written by Alexander Mood, confirmed that a serious disadvantage of accreditation is "in the suppression of innovation. Schools cannot get far out of line without risking loss of their accreditation—a penalty which they cannot afford." "Also," the report continued, "loss of accreditation implies that the curriculum is somewhat inferior and hence that the degree is inferior. Such a large penalty . . . tends to prevent colleges from striking out in new directions. . . As we look toward the future, it appears likely that accrediting organizations will lose their usefulness and slowly disappear. Colleges will be judged not by what some educational bureaucracy declares but by what they can do for their students. Of much greater relevance would be statistics on student satisfaction, career advancement of graduates, and other such data."

Faced with high-powered criticism of this sort, some accrediting agencies sponsored (with a major grant from the Kellogg Foundation) a large-scale study of how the agencies should deal with nontraditional education.

The four-volume report of the findings of this investigation said very much what the Carnegie report had to say. The accreditors were advised, in effect, not to look at the easy quantitative factors (percentage of Doctorate-holders on the faculty, books in the library, student-faculty ratio, acres of campus, etc.), but rather to evaluate the far more elusive qualitative factors, of which student satisfaction and student performance are the most crucial.

In other words, if the students at a nontraditional, nonresident university regularly produce research and dissertations that are as good as those produced at traditional schools, or if graduates of nontraditional schools are as likely to gain admission to graduate school or high-level employment and perform satisfactorily there—then the nontraditional school may be just as worthy of accreditation as the traditional school.

The response of the accrediting agencies was pretty much to say, "But we already are doing just those things. No changes are needed."

But, with the Carnegie and Kellogg reports, the handwriting was on the wall, if still in small and hard-to-read letters. Things would be changing, however.

In 1987, then Secretary of Education William Bennett (later to become "Drug Czar," and then a bestselling author-philosopher) voiced similar complaints about the failure of accrediting agencies to deal with matters such as student competency and satisfaction. "Historically," he said, "accrediting agencies have examined institutions in terms of the resources they have, such as the number of faculty with earned Doctorates and the number of books in the library. Now [we] are considering the ways agencies take account of student achievement and development."

In 1990, Bennett's successor, Lauro F. Cavazos, while splitting an infinitive or two, said almost exactly the same thing: "Despite increasing evidence that many of our schools are failing to adequately prepare our children, either for further study or for productive careers, the accreditation process still focuses on inputs, such as the number of volumes in libraries or percentage of faculty with appropriate training. It does not examine outcomes—how much students learn."

Around the same time, John W. Harris, chairman of the National Advisory Committee on Accreditation, echoed these concerns: "It is not enough to know that teachers have certain degrees and that students have spent so much time in the classroom. The question is, can institutions document the achievement of students for the degrees awarded?"

The accrediting agencies continued to assure us that they *do* deal with such matters.

In 1992, Secretary of Education Lamar Alexander went further still, issuing an open invitation for new accrediting agencies to come forward and seek his department's blessing, strongly implying that the existing ones were not doing a satisfactory job. And around the same time, high administrators at at least three major universities seriously questioned whether accreditation was necessary for their school. "Why should we spend upwards of $100,000 in staff time and real money to prepare a self-study for the accreditors?" said one administrator. "It is quite likely that the University of Wisconsin would still be taken seriously even if it did not have accreditation."

In 1992, Secretary Alexander flung down an unignorable gauntlet by denying the usual "automatic" reapproval of the powerful Middle States accrediting association, because he maintained that their standards for accreditation did not meet the Department's. (Middle States had previously denied reaccreditation to a major school because it did not meet certain standards of diversity, including 'appropriate' numbers of minority students and faculty. Alexander suggested that Middle States was paying attention to the wrong things. Middle States finally backed down, and made its diversity standards optional.)

When Bill Clinton took office in 1993, the accreditation situation was no less murky, and his choice for Secretary of Education, Richard Riley of South Carolina, seemed more interested in primary and secondary education than in postsecondary. Into this already murky area came two bombshells.

Bombshell #1: First, in early 1993, the six regional accrediting associations, claiming that "the concept of self-regulation as embodied in regional accreditation is being seriously questioned and potentially threatened," announced that they planned to drop out of the Council on Postsecondary Accreditation, and start their own new group by July, 1993, to represent them in Washington. The *Chronicle of Higher Education* reported that "some higher-education observers said they questioned the significance of the action [while] others called it disturbing." The president of the American Council on Education said that "Their pulling out is tantamount to the destruction of COPA."

Bombshell #2: He was right. In April 1993, at their annual meeting in San Francisco, COPA voted itself out of existence as of year-end, by a vote of 14 to two, one abstention. One board member, C. Peter Magrath, president of the National Association of State Universities and Land-Grand Colleges, said that he thought COPA "focused too much on the minutiae of accreditation and not enough on the big issues of improving the quality of undergraduate education."

And so, in April 1993, things were indeed unsettled. The six regional associations were apparently planning to start a new organization to govern themselves, without the participation of the dozens of professional accreditors who were part of COPA. COPA was going about its business, but planning to turn off the lights and shut the door by the end of 1993. And the Clinton Department of Education was busily drawing up proposals that would turn the world of accreditation and school licensing on its ear.

The early thrust of the Clinton/Riley thinking echoed much that had been discussed during the Bush/Bennett/Cavazos/Alexander era: giving increased power to the states to decide what can and cannot be done in the way of higher education within their borders. The big stick wielded by the federal folks, of course, was student aid: loans and grants. The prospect of each state having different standards by which a student could get a Pell Grant, for instance, was daunting.

Around this time, a man named Ralph A. Wolff, an executive with one of the regional accrediting associations, wrote an important 'think piece' for the influential *Chronicle of Higher Education*: "Restoring the Credibility of Accreditation." (June 9, 1993, page B1) Wolff wrote that

> We have constructed a Potemkin Village in which there is less behind the façade of accreditation than we might like to acknowledge. . . . The accreditation process has not held colleges and universities accountable for issues such as the writing ability of graduates or the effectiveness of general-education requirements. . . If accreditation is to regain some of its lost credibility, everyone involved in the process needs to refocus on standards and criteria for demonstrating educational effectiveness. Even the most prestigious institutions will need to address

how much students are learning and the quality of student life at the institution.

Right around the time Wolff was writing, the Department of Education was sending out a limited number of "secret" (not for publication or circulation) drafts of its proposed new regulations. And the six regional accreditors apparently rose up as one to say, in effect, "Hey, wait a minute. You, the feds, are telling us how to run our agencies, and we don't like that."

For instance, the draft regulations would have required accreditors to look at the length of various programs, and their cost vis-a-vis the subject being taught.

A response by James T. Rogers, head of the college division of the Southern Association (a regional accreditor) was typical:

> If final regulations follow the pattern in this latest draft, the Department of Education will have co-opted, in very profound ways, members of the private, voluntary accrediting community to serve as enforcement for the department. . . . This is an extremely disturbing abdication of the department's responsibility to police its own operation.

The *Chronicle* reported (August 4, 1993) that "many of the accrediting groups have sent notices to their member colleges urging them to be prepared to battle the department if the draft is not significantly altered."

And David Longanecker, Assistant Secretary for postsecondary education, was quoted in the *Chronicle* as saying "Many people in higher education say 'You can't measure what it is that we do, it's too valuable.' I don't buy that, and I don't think most people in America buy that today, either."

The battle lines were drawn (or, as the more polite *Chronicle* put it on August 11, 1993), "Accreditors and the Education Department [are] locked in a philosophical disagreement over the role of accreditation." At this point, the six regional accreditors announced they would be joining with seven higher-education groups to form an organization to represent their interests in Washington. This lobbying group was to be called the National Policy Board on Higher Education Institutional Accreditation, or NPBHEIA. And various subsets of the by-now lame duck COPA were making plans to start as many as three replacement organizations to take over some or most or all of COPA's functions.

During the rest of 1993, the Department of Education was busily rewriting its accreditation guidelines, taking into account the unexpectedly fierce "leave us alone" response from the regional and professional accreditors. Meanwhile, Congress, not wishing to be left out of the mix entirely, passed, on November 23, 1993, the Higher Education Technical Amendments of 1993, which, among much, much else, decreed that the Department of Education was to cause each of the 50 states to establish a new State postsecondary review 'entity' (SPRE) to evaluate schools within each state, both for compliance with various federal aid programs and, unexpectedly, to evaluate those colleges and universities that have "been subject to a pattern of complaints from students, faculty, or others, including...misleading or inappropriate advertising and promotion of the institution's educational programs...." If that wasn't an invitation for the states to go into the accreditation business, it was certainly in that direction.

GOODBYE COPA, HELLO CORPA

And while this was going on, the COPA-ending clock was ticking away. Ten days before COPA was to disappear forever, the formation of a single new entity to replace it was announced. COPA was to be replaced with (small fanfare, please) CORPA, the Commission on Recognition of Postsecondary Accreditation. All members of COPA were automatically recognized by CORPA. All COPA provisions for recognition of schools were adopted by CORPA, with the understanding that they might be refined and modified over time. And CORPA's initial Committee on Recognition was composed of the members of COPA's Committee on Recognition. All of this appears to be the academic equivalent of saying that *The Odyssey* was not written by Homer, but by another Greek with the same name. The only apparent difference between COPA and CORPA is the addition of the "R" and the fact that the six regionals are no longer members.

The Department of Education's guidelines were finally published in the *Federal Register* on January 24, 1994: 24 small-type pages on accreditors, and 20 more on the establishing SPREs, the State Postsecondary Review Entities. Once the regulations were published, the public and the higher education establishment had 45 days in which to respond. And respond they did. The headline in the next week's *Chronicle of Higher Education* read: "Accreditors Fight Back."

In turned out that the six regional accreditors, the American Council on Education, and other groups had been meeting privately in Arizona to formulate a battle plan. They considered abandoning the regional approach entirely, in favor of a single national accreditor, but scrapped that in favor of four still-quite-radical ideas (among others):

1. Establishment of minimum uniform national standards for accreditation;

2. Setting of higher standards for schools, focusing on teaching and learning (what a novel concept!);

3. Making public their reports on individual colleges and schools; and

4. Moving toward ceasing to cooperate with the federal government in certifying the eligibility of colleges for federal financial aid.

During the 45-day response period following publishing of the draft guidelines, hundreds of long and serious responses were received from college and university presidents opposing some, most, or all of the regulations that had been proposed by the Department of Education.

The issue of diversity and political correctness in accreditation remained just as controversial as before. While the Western Association (a regional accreditor) for instance, believes that academic quality and ethnic diversity are "profoundly connected," many colleges, large and small, apparently agree with Stanford president Gerhard Casper, who said, "No institution should be required to demonstrate its commitment to diversity to the satisfaction of an external review panel. The [Western Association] is attempting to insert itself in an area in which it has no legitimate standing." Other schools, including the University of California at Berkeley, defended the diversity policy.

By early May, 1994, the Department of Education backed away from some of the more controversial rules, both in terms of telling the accreditors what to look for, and in the powers given to the SPREs. They did this by continuing to say what things an accrediting agency must evaluate, but only suggesting, not demanding, the ways and means by which they might do it. In addition, SPREs would now be limited to dealing with matters of fraud and abuse, and could not initiate an inquiry for other reasons.

Under the now-final guidelines, accrediting agencies are required to evaluate these twelve matters, but the way they do it can be individually determined:

1. Curricula
2. Faculty
3. Facilities, equipment, and supplies
4. Fiscal and administrative capacity
5. Student support services
6. Program length, tuition, and fees in relation to academic objectives
7. Program length, tuition, and fees in relation to credit received
8. Student achievement (job placement, state licensing exams, etc.)
9. Student loan repayments
10. Student complaints received by or available to the accreditor
11. Compliance with student aid rules and regulations
12. Everything else, including recruiting, admissions practices, calendars, catalogues and other publications, grading practices, advertising and publicity, and so on.

And that is where we are. Or, more accurately, were when the foregoing was written in late 1994. It seems apparent that many beasties have escaped from this Pandora's box called "Accreditation," and they will be flying, creeping, and crawling about for many years to come. After decades of minimal interest and attention, the always fascinating world of accreditation is clearly getting more than its fifteen minutes of fame.

One of the next really interesting things that will

happen (for us accreditation-watchers, anyway) will be when the first brand-new accrediting agency applies to the Department of Education (or to CORPA) for recognition as an accreditor. It may happen with one of the long-established but unrecognized agencies such as the National Association for Private Nontraditional Schools and Colleges, or it may be someone brand new. It should be interesting, indeed, to see how the new standards are interpreted and applied, with the Secretary of Education looking over one shoulder and the six regional accreditors over the other.

The Approved Accrediting Agencies

The six regional associations each has responsibility for schools in one region of the United States and its territories. Each one has the authority to accredit an entire college or university. And there are also about 80 professional associations, each with authority to accredit either specialized schools or specific departments or programs within a school.

Thus, it may be the case, for instance, that the North Central Association (one of the six regional associations) will accredit Dolas University. When this happens, the entire school is accredited, and all its degrees may be called accredited degrees, or more accurately, degrees from an accredited institution.

Or it may be the case that just the art department of Dolas University has been accredited by the relevant professional association, in this case the National Association of Schools of Art. If this happens, then only the art majors at Dolas can claim to have accredited degrees.

So if an accredited degree is important for your needs, the first question to ask is, "Has the school been accredited by one of the six regional associations?" If the answer is no, then the next question is, "Has the department in which I am interested been accredited by its relevant professional association?"

There are those jobs (psychology and nursing are two examples) in which professional accreditation is often at least as important as regional accreditation, sometimes more so. In other words, even if a school is accredited by its regional association, unless its psychology department is also accredited by the American Psychology Association, its degree will be less useful for psychology majors.

One of the legends about accreditation has arisen because of these matters: the widespread belief that Harvard is not accredited. Harvard University *is* duly accredited by its regional agency, but its psychology department, and many others, are not accredited by the relevant professional agencies.

In Great Britain, however, the 'legend' that Oxford and Cambridge Universities are not accredited turns out to be true. While all the other British universities are accredited through the granting of a Royal Charter or by a special act of Parliament, it turns out that the two oldest universities have no Royal Charter, no act of Parliament,

nothing that gives them the right to exist and grant degrees other than the fact that they have been around for eight or more centuries.

Totally unrecognized accrediting agencies may still be quite legitimate, or they may be quite phony. Some of the unrecognized ones will be discussed after the following listing of the recognized ones. Each of the approved accreditors will gladly supply lists of all the schools (or departments within schools) they have accredited, and those that are candidates for accreditation and in correspondent status. They will also answer any questions pertaining to any school's status (or lack of status) with them.

The Agencies That Recognize Accrediting Agencies

Department of Education, Division of Eligibility and Agency Evaluation, Bureau of Postsecondary Education, Washington, DC 20202, (202) 245-9875

CORPA, the Commission on Recognition of Postsecondary Accreditation, One Dupont Circle NW, Suite 305, Washington, DC 20036, (202) 452-1433.

RECOGNIZED ACCREDITING AGENCIES

Regional Accrediting Agencies

Middle States Association of Colleges and Schools
Commission on Higher Education
3624 Market St.
Philadelphia, PA 19104 (215) 662-5606
Delaware, District of Columbia, Maryland, New Jersey, New York, Pennsylvania, Puerto Rico, Virgin Islands

New England Association of Schools and Colleges
209 Burlington Road
Bedford, MA 01730 (617) 271-0022
Connecticut, Maine, Massachusetts, New Hampshire, Rhode Island, Vermont

North Central Association of Colleges and Schools
30 N. LaSalle St., Suite 2400
Chicago, IL 60602 (800) 621-7440
Arizona, Arkansas, Colorado, Illinois, Indiana, Iowa, Kansas, Michigan, Minnesota, Missouri, Nebraska, New Mexico, North Dakota, Ohio, Oklahoma, South Dakota, West Virginia, Wisconsin, Wyoming

Northwest Association of Schools and Colleges
3700B University Way N.E.
Seattle, WA 98105 (206) 543-0195
Alaska, Idaho, Montana, Nevada, Oregon, Utah, Washington

Southern Association of Colleges and Schools
1866 Southern Lane

Decatur, GA 30033
(404) 329-6500 or (800) 248-7701
Alabama, Florida, Georgia, Kentucky, Louisiana, Mississippi, North Carolina, South Carolina, Tennessee, Texas, Virginia

Western Association of Schools and Colleges
Box 9990, Mills College
Oakland, CA 94613   (510) 632-5000
California, Hawaii, Guam, Trust Territory of the Pacific

Professional Accrediting Agencies

The Arts and Architecture
Architecture
National Architectural Accrediting Board
1735 New York Ave. NW
Washington, DC 20006 (202) 783-2007

Art
National Association of Schools of Art and Design
11250 Roger Bacon Drive, Suite 21
Reston, VA 22090   (703) 437-0700

Dance
National Association of Schools of Dance
11250 Roger Bacon Drive
Suite 21
Reston, VA 22090   (703) 437-0700

Landscape Architecture
American Society of Landscape Architects
4401 Connecticut Ave. NW, 5th Floor
Washington, DC 20008 (202) 686-2752

Music
National Association of Schools of Music
11250 Roger Bacon Drive
Suite 21
Reston, VA 22090   (703) 437-0700

Theater
National Association of Schools of Theater
11250 Roger Bacon Drive
Suite 21
Reston, VA 22090   (703) 437-0700

Business
Accrediting Council for Independent
Colleges and Schools
750 First St. N.E., Suite 980
Washington, DC 20002   (202) 336-6780

American Assembly of Collegiate Schools of Business
600 Emerson Road, Suite 300
St. Louis, MO 63141   (314) 872-8481

Association of Collegiate Business Schools and Programs
7007 College Blvd., Suite 420
Overland Park, KS 66211   (913) 339-9356

Education
Blind and Visually Handicapped Education
National Accreditation Council for Agencies Serving
Blind and Visually Handicapped
15 East 40th St., Suite 1004
New York, NY 10016   (212) 779-8080

Continuing Education
Accrediting Council for Continuing Education and
Training
600 E. Main St., Suite 1425
Richmond, VA 23219   (804) 648-6742

Teacher Education
National Council for Accreditation of Teacher Education
2010 Massachusetts Ave. N.W.
Suite 202
Washington, DC 20036   (202) 466-7496

Home Study Education
Distance Education and Training Council
1601 18th St. NW
Washington, DC 20009 (202) 234-5100

Occupational, Trade, and Technical Education
Accrediting Commission of Career Schools/Colleges of
Technology
750 First St. NE, Suite 905
Washington, DC 20002 (202) 336-6850

Law
American Bar Association
Indiana University, 550 West North St.
Indianapolis, IN 46202   (317) 264-8340

Medicine and Health
Acupuncture and Oriental Medicine
National Accreditation Commission for Schools and
Colleges of Acupuncture and Oriental Medicine
8403 Colesville Road
Suite 370
Silver Spring, MD 20910   (301) 608-9680

Chiropractic
The Council on Chiropractic Education
7975 North Hayden Road
Suite A-210
Scottsdale, AZ 85258   (602) 443-8877

Straight Chiropractic Academic Standards Assoc.
642 Broad St.
Clifton, NJ 07013   (201) 777-7645

Dentistry
American Dental Association
211 E. Chicago Ave.
Chicago, IL 60611 (312) 440-2500

Dietetics
American Dietetic Association
216 W. Jackson Blvd., Suite 800
Chicago, IL 60606 (312) 899-4870

Health Education
Accrediting Bureau of Health Education Schools
Oak Manor Office, 29089 U.S. 20
West Elkhart, IN 46514 (219) 293-0124

Health Services Administration
Accrediting Commission on Education for
Health Services Administration
1911 N. Fort Myer Dr., Suite 503
Arlington, VA 22209 (703) 524-0511

Medical Schools
American Medical Association
515 N. State St.
Chicago, IL 60610 (312) 464-4657
They are the accreditor for medical schools only in odd-numbered years, beginning on July 1.

Association of American Medical Colleges
2450 N Street NW
Washington, DC 20037 (202) 828-0596
They are the accreditor for medical schools only in even-numbered years, beginning on July 1.

Naturopathy
Council on Naturopathic Medical Education
P.O. Box 11426
Eugene, OR 97440 (503) 484-6028

Nursing
American Association of Nurse Anesthetists
222 Prospect Ave.
Park Ridge, IL 60068 (708) 692-7050

American College of Nurse-Midwives
818 Connecticut Ave. N.W., Suite 900
Washington, DC 20006 (202) 728-9877

National League for Nursing
350 Hudson St.
New York, NY 10014 (800) 669-1656

Optometry and Opticianry
American Optometric Association
243 N. Lindbergh Blvd.
St. Louis, MO 63141 (314) 991-4100

Commission on Opticianry Accreditation
10111 Martin Luther King Jr. Hwy.
Suite 100
Bowie, MD 20720 (301) 459-8075

Osteopathy
American Osteopathic Association
142 E. Ontario St.
Chicago, IL 60611 (312) 280-5800

Paramedical Fields
The American Medical Association
515 N. State St.
Chicago, IL 60610 (312) 464-4657
The American Medical Association has separate accreditation programs for each of 16 paramedical areas. Write to: Programs for the Blood Bank Technologist, Programs for the Cytotechnologist, Programs for the Histologic Technician, Medical Assistant Programs, Medical Laboratory Technician Programs, Programs for the Medical Record Administrator and Medical Record Technician, Programs for the Medical Technologist, Programs for the Nuclear Medicine Technologist, Programs for the Occupational Therapist, Programs for the Physical Therapist, Programs for the Assistant to the Primary Care Physician, Programs for the Radiation Therapist/Technologist, Programs for the Radiographer, Programs for the Respiratory Therapist, Programs for the Surgeon's Assistant, Programs for the Surgical Technologist.

Pharmacy
American Council on Pharmaceutical Education
311 W. Superior
Chicago, IL 60610 (312) 664-3575

Physical Therapy
American Physical Therapy Association
1111 N. Fairfax St.
Alexandria, VA 22314 (703) 684-2782
See also: Paramedical Fields

Podiatry
American Podiatric Medical Association
9312 Old Georgetown Rd.
Bethesda, MD 20814 (301) 571-9200

Public Health
Council on Education for Public Health
1015 15th St. NW
Suite 403
Washington, DC 20005 (202) 789-1050

Veterinary Medicine
American Veterinary Medical Association
930 N. Meacham Road
Schaumburg, IL 60196 (708) 925-8070

Religion
American Association of Bible Colleges
P.O. Box 1523
Fayetteville, AR 72701   (501) 521-8164

Association of Advanced Rabbinical and
Talmudic Schools
175 Fifth Avenue, Room 711
New York, NY 10010   (212) 477-0950

Association for Clinical Pastoral Education, Inc.
1549 Claremont Rd
Suite 103
Decatur, GA 30033   (404) 320-1472

Association of Theological Schools in the U.S. and Canada
10 Summit Park Drive
Pittsburgh, PA 15275 (412) 788-6505

Transnational Association of Christian Colleges & Schools
2114 Arrow Court
Murfreesboro, TN 37130 (615) 890-8384

United States Catholic Conference
4455 Woodson Rd.
St. Louis, MO 63134   (314) 428-2000

Science and Engineering
Computer Science
Computing Science Accreditation Board
2 Landmark Square, Suite 209
Stamford, CT 06901 (203) 975-1117

Engineering
Accrediting Board for Engineering & Technology
111 Market Place, Suite 1050
Baltimore, MD 21202   (410) 347-7700

Forestry
Society of American Foresters
5400 Grosvenor Lane
Bethesda, MD 20814   (301) 897-8720

Industrial Technology
National Association of Industrial Technology
3157 Packard Rd.
Suite A
Ann Arbor, MI 48108   (313) 677-0720

Microbiology
American Academy of Microbiology
1325 Massachusetts Ave. N.W.
Washington, DC 20005 (202) 942-9225

Social sciences
Marriage and Family Therapy

American Assoc. for Marriage and Family Therapy
1100 17th St. N.W., 10th Floor
Washington, DC 20036 (202) 452-0109

Occupational Therapy
American Occupational Therapy Association
1383 Picard Dr.
Suite 300
Rockville, MD 20849   (301) 948-9626

Psychology
American Psychological Association
750 1st St. N.E.
Washington, DC 20002   (202) 336-5979

Social Work
Council on Social Work Education
1600 Duke St.
Alexandria, VA 22314   (703) 683-8080

Speech Pathology
American Speech-Language-Hearing Association
10801 Rockville Pike
Rockville, MD 20852   (301) 897-5700

Vocational and Practical Fields
Construction Education
American Council for Construction Education,
901 Hudson Lane
Monroe, LA 71201   (318) 323-2413

Cosmetology
National Accrediting Commission of Cosmetology Arts
and Sciences
901 N. Stuart St.
Suite 900
Arlington, VA 22203   (703) 527-7600

Culinary Arts
American Culinary Federation Education Institute
959 Melvin Road
Annapolis, MD 21403   (410) 268-5659

Funeral Service Education
American Board of Funeral Service Education
14 Crestwood Rd.
Cumberland, ME 04201   (207) 829-5715

Interior Design Education
Foundation for Interior Design Education Research
60 Monroe Center NW
Grand Rapids, MI 49503   (616) 458-0400

Journalism and Mass Communications
Accrediting Council on Education in Journalism and Mass
Communications

University of Kansas School of Journalism
Stauffer-Flint Hall
Lawrence, KS 66045 (913) 864-3986

Librarianship
American Library Association
50 E. Huron St.
Chicago, IL 60611 (312) 944-6780

Occupational, Trade, and Technical Education
Accrediting Commission of Career
Schools/Colleges of Technology
750 1st St. N.E.
Suite 905
Washington, DC 20002 (202) 336-6850

Recognized State-Run Accrediting Agencies
New York State Board of Regents
State Department of Education
University of the State of New York
Albany, NY 12224 (518) 474-5844

UNRECOGNIZED ACCREDITING AGENCIES
There are a great many so-called accrediting agencies that are not approved or recognized by the Department of Education or CORPA. A small number are clearly sincere and legitimate; many others are not.

Accrediting Commission for Specialized Colleges
Gas City, Indiana. Established by "Bishop" Gordon Da Costa and associates (one of whom was Dr. George Reuter, who left to help establish the International Accrediting Commission, described in this section), from the address of Da Costa's Indiana Northern Graduate School (a dairy farm in Gas City). According to their literature, the accrediting procedures of ACSC seem superficial at best. The only requirement for becoming a candidate for accreditation was to mail in a check for $110.

Accrediting Commissional International for Schools, Colleges and Theological Seminaries
Beebe, Arkansas. See "International Accrediting Commission for Schools, Colleges and Theological Seminaries," in this section. After the IAC was fined and closed down by authorities in Missouri in 1989, Dr. Reuter retired, turning the work over to a colleague, who juggled the words in the name and opened up one state over. All IAC schools were offered automatic accreditation by the ACI. I am not aware of any that turned it down.

Alternative Institution Accrediting Association
Allegedly in Washington, DC, and the accreditor of several phony schools.

American Association of Accredited Colleges and Universities
Another unlocatable agency, the claimed accreditor of Ben Franklin Academy.

American Education Association for the Accreditation of Schools, Colleges and Universities
The accreditor claimed at one time by the University of America. Could not be located.

American Pyscotherapy [sic] Association
Board of Psycotherapy [sic] Examiners, Katy, Texas, originally chartered in Florida, they say, while apologizing for but not correcting the misspellings.

Arizona Commission of Non-Traditional Private Postsecondary Education
Established in the late 1970s by the proprietors of Southland University, which claimed to be a candidate for their accreditation. The name was changed after a complaint by the real state agency, the Arizona Commission on Postsecondary Education (see Western Council, below).

Association of Career Training Schools
A slick booklet sent to schools says, "Have your school accredited with the Association. Why? The Association Seal…could be worth many $ $ $ to you! It lowers sales resistance, sales costs, [and] improves image." Nuff said.

Commission for the Accreditation of European Non-Traditional Universities
The University de la Romande, in England, used to claim accreditation from this agency, which we could never locate.

Council for the Accreditation of Correspondence Colleges
Several curious schools claimed their accreditation; the agency is supposed to be in Louisiana.

Council on Postsecondary Alternative Accreditation
An accreditor claimed in the literature of Western States University. Western States never responded to requests for the address of their accreditor. The name seems to have been chosen to cause confusion with the reputable organization originally known as the Council on Postsecondary Accreditation.

Council on Postsecondary Christian Education
Established by the people who operate LaSalle University and Kent College in Louisiana.

International Accreditation Association
The literature of the University of North America claims that they are accredited by this association. No address is provided, nor could one be located.

International Accrediting Association
The address in Modesto, California is the same as that of the Universal Life Church, an organization that awards Doctorates of all kinds, including the Ph.D., to anyone making a "donation" of $5 to $100.

International Accrediting Commission for Schools, Colleges and Theological Seminaries
Holden, Missouri. More than 150 schools, many of them Bible schools, were accredited by this organization. In 1989, the Attorney General of Missouri conducted a clever "sting" operation, in which he created a fictitious school, the "East Missouri Business College," which rented a one-room office in St. Louis, and issued a type-written catalog with such school executives as "Peelsburi Doughboy" and "Wonarmmd Mann." The Three Stooges were all on the faculty. Their marine biology text was *The Little Golden Book of Fishes*. Nonetheless, Dr. George Reuter, Director of the IAC, visited the school, accepted their money, and duly accredited them. Soon after, the IAC was enjoined from operating, slapped with a sub-stantial fine, and the good Dr. Reuter decided to retire. (But the almost identical "Accrediting Commission In-ternational" immediately arose in Arkansas, offering in-stant accreditation to all IACSCTS members. See above.)

   Before he was apprehended, when someone wrote to Dr. Reuter to ask why this book had less-than-good things to say about his Association, Dr. Reuter replied, "Some of us do not rate Dr. John Bear very high. We think he is really a traditionalist and really favors those colleges and universities, and, at the same time, strives to plant dissent with others." Oh dear, oh dear.

International Association of Non-Traditional Schools
The claimed accreditor of several British degree mills; al-legedly located in England.

International Commission for the Accreditation of Colleges and Universities
Established in Gaithersburg, Maryland, by a diploma mill called the United States University of America (now de-funct) primarily for the purpose of accrediting themselves.

Middle States Accrediting Board
A nonexistent accreditor, made up by Thomas Univer-sity and other degree mills, for the purpose of self-ac-creditation. The name was chosen, of course, to cause confusion with the Middle States Association of Col-leges and Schools, in Philadelphia, one of the six regional associations.

National Accreditation Association
Established in Riverdale, Maryland, by Dr. Glenn Larsen, whose Doctorate is from a diploma mill called the Sussex College of Technology. His associate is Dr. Clarence Franklin, former president and chancellor of American

International University (described in the chapter on di-ploma mills). In a mailing to presidents of unaccredited schools, the NAA offered full accreditation by mail, with no on-site inspection required.

National Association for Private Post-Secondary Education
Washington, DC. Mentioned, in 1990, in the literature of Kennedy-Western University. They say they are not an accrediting agency but a private association of schools.

National Association of Alternative Schools and Colleges
Western States University claimed in their literature that they had been accredited by this organization, which we have never been able to locate.

National Association of Open Campus Colleges
Southwestern University of Arizona and Utah (which closed after its proprietor was sent to prison as a result of the FBI's diploma mill investigations) claimed accredi-tation from this agency. The address in Springfield, Mis-souri, was the same as that of Disciples of Truth, an or-ganization that has in the past operated a chain of diploma mills.

National Association for Private Nontraditional Schools and Colleges
182 Thompson Rd., Grand Junction, CO 81503, (303) 243-5441
The National Association for Private Nontraditional Schools and Colleges (formerly the National Association for Schools and Colleges) is a serious effort to establish an accrediting agency specifically concerned with alterna-tive schools and programs. It was established in the 1970s by a group of educators associated with Western Colo-rado University, a nontraditional school that has since gone out of business. Although NAPNSC's standards for ac-creditation have grown stiffer and stiffer over the years, they are still not recognized by the Department of Edu-cation, but they keep trying.

National Council of Schools and Colleges
Accreditation by this agency was claimed by International University, formerly of New Orleans, later of Pasadena, California, and now out of existence. Despite many in-quiries, the proprietors of the school never provided infor-mation on their accreditor.

Pacific Association of Schools and Colleges
745 Via Concepcion, Riverside, CA 92506.
Established in 1993, this organization is operated by a man who had previously been a senior official in the Cali-fornia Department of Education (and who has a doctor-ate from an unaccredited school). PASC appears to be a serious attempt to create an accreditor that would be bet-

ter able to deal with nontraditional schools. A plan to apply for recognition in early 1994 was deferred pending analysis of the new guidelines issued by the Department of Education.

West European Accrediting Society
Established from a mail-forwarding service in Liederbach, Germany by the proprietors of a chain of diploma mills such as Loyola, Roosevelt, Lafayette, Southern California, and Oliver Cromwell universities, for the purpose of accrediting themselves.

Western Association of Private Alternative Schools
One of several accrediting agencies claimed in the literature of Western States University. No address or phone number has ever been provided, despite many requests.

Western Association of Schools and Colleges
This is the name of the legitimate regional accreditor for California and points west. However it is also the name used by the aforementioned proprietors of Loyola, Roosevelt, etc., from a Los Angeles address, to give accreditation to their own diploma mills.

Western Council on Non-Traditional Private Post Secondary Education
An accrediting agency started by the founders of Southland University, presumably for the purpose of accrediting themselves and others (see Arizona Commission, above).

World Association of Universities and Colleges
6655 West Sahara Blvd., #B-200, Las Vegas, NV 89102, (702) 221-2004
Established in 1992 by Drs. Maxine Asher and Franklin T. Burroughs. The World Association declines to supply us with a list of schools they have accredited. It is safe to assume the list includes American World University (operated by Drs. Asher and Burroughs), and schools owned by Dr. Lloyd Clayton (Chadwick University, the American Institute of Computer Science, etc.), who has had an active role in the operation of WAUC. In February 1995, the national investigative publication *Spy Magazine* ran a most unflattering article on WAUC and subsequently ignored Dr. Asher's request for a retraction.

Worldwide Accrediting Commission
Operated from a mail-forwarding service in Cannes, France, for the purpose of accrediting the fake Loyola University (Paris), Lafayette University, and other American-run degree mills.

BIBLE SCHOOL ACCREDITING AGENCIES
There are six recognized accreditors of religious schools, previously listed, covering everything from evangelical Christian schools to rabbinical seminaries. Religious schools often claim they have not sought accreditation since there are no relevant accreditors. They are not exactly accurate. There are also a great many unrecognized accreditors. Since many Bible schools readily acknowledge that their degrees are not academic in nature, accreditation of them has quite a different meaning. Some of these associations may well be quite legitimate, but their accreditation has no academic relevance. Some accreditors are apparently concerned primarily with doctrinal soundness; others may have other motivations. Among the Bible school accreditors are:

Accreditation Association of Christian Colleges and Seminaries, Morgantown, KY
Accrediting Association of Christian Colleges and Seminaries, Sarasota, FL
AF Sep (we don't know what this means, but Beta International University claims it is the name of their accrediting association), address unknown
American Association of Accredited Colleges and Universities, address unknown
American Association of Theological Institutions, address unknown
American Educational Accrediting Association of Christian Schools, address unknown
Association of Fundamental Institutes of Religious Education (AFIRE), address unknown
International Accrediting Commission, Kenosha, WI
International Accrediting Association of Church Colleges, address unknown
National Educational Accrediting Association, Columbus, OH
Southeast Accrediting Association of Christian Schools, Colleges and Seminaries, Milton, FL

WORDS THAT DO NOT MEAN "ACCREDITED"
Some unaccredited schools use terminology in their catalogs or advertising that might have the effect of misleading unknowledgeable readers. Here are six common phrases:

1. Pursuing accreditation. A school may state that it is "pursuing accreditation," or that it "intends to pursue accreditation." But that says nothing whatever about its chances for achieving same. It's like saying that you are practicing your tennis game, with the intention of playing in the finals at Wimbledon. Don't hold your breath.

2. Chartered. In some places, a charter is the necessary document that a school needs to grant degrees. A common ploy by diploma mill operators is to form a corporation, and state in the articles of incorporation that one of the purposes of the corporation is to grant degrees. This is like forming a corporation whose charter says that it has the right to appoint the Pope. You can *say* it, but that doesn't make it so.

3. **Licensed or registered.** This usually refers to nothing more than a business license, granted by the city or county in which the school is located, but which has nothing to do with the legality of the school, or the usefulness of its degrees.

4. **Recognized.** This can have many possible meanings, ranging from some level of genuine official recognition at the state level, to having been listed in some directory often unrelated to education, perhaps published by the school itself. Two ambitious degree mills (Columbia State University and American International University) have published entire books that look at first glance like this one, solely for the purpose of being able to devote lengthy sections in them to describing their phony schools as "the best in America."

5. **Authorized.** In California, this has had a specific meaning (see below). Elsewhere, the term can be used to mean almost anything the school wants it to—sometimes legitimate, sometimes not. A Canadian degree mill once claimed to be "authorized to grant degrees." It turned out that the owner had authorized his wife to go ahead and print the diplomas.

6. **Approved.** In California, this has a specific meaning (see below). In other locations, it is important to know who is doing the approving. Some not-for-profit schools call themselves "approved by the U.S. Government," which means only that the Internal Revenue Service has approved their nonprofit status for income taxes—and nothing more. At one time, some British schools called themselves "Government Approved," when the approval related only to the school-lunch program.

THE CHANGING SITUATION REGARDING STATE LAWS AND REGULATIONS

Things used to be relatively stable. Some states militantly forbade any nontraditional schools or programs, others allowed anyone to do anything, and most were somewhere in between. Since the passage of the Education Reform Act of 1989 in California, that state, and a handful of others popular with unaccredited schools, have been doing more and more to regulate schools and degrees. More than ever, it is wise to check with a state's Department of Education (or other relevant agency; see p. 33–40) before investing money with any unaccredited school. Here is the situation in the four states with the greatest number of nontraditional schools, both good and bad:

California

In 1992, California's Superintendent of Public Instruction was indicted, and in 1993 convicted of several counts of felony conflict of interest and removed from office. He never was replaced and so, in many respects, higher education in the state was adrift for three years, with few new developments in what had previously been a fairly volatile

situation. What the new Superintendent (who took office early in 1995) will do, if anything, remains to be seen.

Until 1990, California had a three-tiered system: authorized schools, approved schools, and accredited schools. The new legislation does away with the "authorized" status over a period of time, and restricts the amount of credit an approved school can give for prior learning. All authorized schools were automatically awarded "provisionally approved" status, and given a fixed period of time to meet the standards for an approved school, or cease operating in the state. Some formerly-authorized schools promptly moved to other states (Kennedy-Western to Idaho, Century to New Mexico, etc.), while others opened offices in other states (Pacific Western in Louisiana and Hawaii) just in case.

California authorization status was for many years a joke. The primary requirement was owning $50,000 in assets, and even this was not strictly enforced. By the early 1980s, there were over 200 "authorized" schools, many of them less than wonderful. As things got tougher, more than 100 schools either closed, merged, or moved.

"Approval" (or "full institutional approval") these days means the state has inspected a school's academic programs and found them worthy. Until 1984, "approval" was granted for individual programs within a school, not for the entire school. An authorized school might have some approved programs. Then, by mandate of the state senate, and over some vigorous objections from people on the Postsecondary Education Commission, the commission was ordered to approve entire institutions rather than individual programs. The senate directed the superintendent of public instruction to determine that the curriculum of an approved institution "is consistent in quality with curricula offered by appropriate established accredited institutions." Thus until 1990, the state senate required the superintendent to declare that approval is comparable to accreditation, but the Department of Education did not wish to do this. Indeed, a Postsecondary Education Commission report says that "while existing statute states that the curricula of approved institutions is consistent in quality with the curricula of accredited institutions, questions remain about the rigor and thoroughness of the state approval process and its ability to permit the licensure of only quality institutions." Translation: The senate may have ordered us to say certain things, but we're not sure we're ready to do so.

Another confusion in California is that the senate said that holders of approved degrees should be permitted to take relevant state licensing exams, such as those in marriage, family, and child counseling. But the state board of professional licensing refused to go along with this automatic permission, saying that the standards for approval and the standards for certain exams were not at all the same. They now permit degree-holders from some schools, but not others, to take the exams. Be sure to check on this if state licensing is part of your goal.

In late 1994, the California system unexpectedly grew volatile again, amidst charges and counter charges of mismanagement and misappropriation of funds within various higher education agencies in Sacramento. As some of the venerable (that means they have been around for ten years or more) California unaccredited schools came up for renewal of their permission to operate, the state's Council on Private Postsecondary and Vocational Education surprised them, and longtime Sacramento-watchers, by denying licenses to schools like Kensington University and Pacific Western University.

Both of these schools went to court, and secured writs which, in effect, prevent the state from implementing their revocation of license unless and until further hearings are held. At our presstime, the state had not yet decided whether to pursue the matter.

Florida

Florida is a classic case of what can happen when legislation gets out of hand. A 1988 Florida statute (Sections 817.566 and .567, Florida Statutes, 1988 Supplement) made it a crime to use an unaccredited degree in any way in that state, even if it is from a school approved or licensed in another state. It was a "misdemeanor of the first degree" [sic] for a person with, say, a California-approved or a Minnesota-approved degree, to reveal, within the boundaries of Florida, that he or she has that degree.

This rather extraordinary statute was challenged in court, and in July 1995, the State Supreme Court found it to be unconstitutional. However, the judge strongly suggested that if the legislature were to rewrite the law a bit more carefully, it could achieve the same intent and be within the bounds of the constitution. So at the present time, it would appear that holders of legitimate degrees from other states can use them in Florida, but it is clear the situation is far from over.

Hawaii

Until recently, Hawaii did not regulate higher education at all. In 1990, however, a law was passed requiring the state Department of Consumer Affairs to register all unaccredited schools in the state. Five years later, the department had not yet managed to produce the simple, but necessary, forms for schools to fill out, thus thwarting the will and intent of the legislature. Small wonder that America's most notorious degree-mill operator chose to move his phony schools to Hawaii, where neither the state attorney general nor the Department of Consumer Affairs showed any interest. Fortunately, federal authorities *did* care, and those phony schools were closed by the action of postal inspectors.

But as other states grow tougher and tougher in their regulation of unaccredited schools, Hawaii increasingly has become the preferred destination. By early 1995, more than a dozen schools had relocated to Hawaii from Louisiana, California, and elsewhere, and at least another dozen had taken out incorporation papers as a 'safety valve,' should things get too hot for them in their present location. Both of the schools California attempted to delicense in late 1994 had long-established Hawaii arrangements in place.

Despite urgent warnings from some educators in the state that Hawaii was fast becoming known as the "state of last resort" for the unaccredited (or not legitimately accredited) schools of America, authorities in the state have shown no interest in enforcing the existing legislation, much less passing new rules. A school regulating bill was defeated in the 1995 legislature; it may be reintroduced in a later year. Some important politicians in the state have vowed that they will keep the pressure on until Hawaii has a tough school regulating law. It remains to be seen.

Louisiana

For many years, Louisiana's Board of Regents would register any school that filled out a short form, with no evaluation whatsoever. This permitted some completely phony schools to advertise that they were "Appropriately registered with the Board of Regents," or even (improperly) that they were "Recognized by the Board of Regents." In 1991, Louisiana passed a new educational law, which gave more power to the Board of Regents, although nonprofit schools were exempted from increased regulation (a situation that may be rectified within a year or two). In 1992, the Board of Regents decided that only schools with an actual physical presence in the state could be registered. Since dozens of "Louisiana" schools operate either from mail forwarding services or "executive suite" office-rental-by-the-hour establishments, quite a few schools using Louisiana addresses have now moved their addresses elsewhere, mostly to Hawaii.

In 1993 and 1994, Louisiana got even tougher. More than a dozen universities that had small or no physical presence in the state were ordered to close down or leave. And in 1994, the Attorney General of Louisiana determined that schools claiming an exemption from the law because they offer only religious degrees could no longer use that loophole. LaSalle University, for instance, perhaps the largest unaccredited school in the country, all of whose degrees (even their Ph.D.'s in physics or political science) are self-determined to be "religious" degrees, was notified that they could no longer engage in that practice, and would have to apply for licensing as an academic rather than as a religious school. As we go to press, this matter is in the hands of the Attorney General of the state.

The next item on the Louisiana docket may well be those not-for-profit schools that ostensibly operate from within Louisiana but, in fact, have nothing more than a convenience address and telephone answering service there. Such institutions have so far been untouched by the admirable changes sweeping across Louisiana, but they may well change.

The Rest of the United States

Often, legislation arises in response to behavior. If legislators don't like the behavior, they pass laws against it. Commonly, it is only after unaccredited schools (good, bad, or in between) become so numerous or so visible they cannot be ignored, that states consider and even pass legislation to restrict or regulate them. Sometimes legislators are jarred into action by a responsibly-behaving press. At a time when Arizona was the U.S. center for sleazy schools, the Arizona *Republic* newspaper ran a four-day page-one series headlined, "Diploma Mills: a festering sore on the state of Arizona." Within weeks, legislation was introduced to deal with these "schools."

For some years, New Mexico had only one visible unaccredited school, Century University. But after the number reached two, then three, then four, with other schools looking in that direction and writing to the state agency in Santa Fe for information, New Mexico's Commission on Higher Education issued "Rule 730," a 21-page set of rules and guidelines for proprietary schools which either operate within the state, or recruit citizens of New Mexico from outside the state. This rule took effect on July 1, 1994, and makes it much harder to operate an unaccredited school in that state.

Clearly the operators of unaccredited schools are shopping around, perhaps against the day when Hawaii changes. At least once a month, we hear from the proprietor of one school or another, looking for advice on where he might move. And we also hear from the education departments of various states—typically the sparsely populated ones, like Wyoming—who want us

to be sure not to encourage any schools to move in on their territory.

Unless and until there is more international cooperation, it may be that schools will be run like puppets: operators in one country pulling the strings that make the school work in another country. As an example, two of the apparently-large "Louisiana" universities (Fairfax and Somerset) are actually operated by men living in England who apparently do not often come to the U.S. Even the mail goes to England. But England apparently looks on them as "American" schools and doesn't try to regulate them. And the U.S. may consider them to be British schools, since they have neither offices nor personnel, only convenience address in the U.S.

THE LAST WORD ON ACCREDITATION

Don't believe everything anyone says. It seems extraordinary that any school would lie about something so easily checked as accreditation, but it is done. For instance, a degree mill once unabashedly sent out thousands of bulletins announcing their accreditation by a recognized agency. The announcement was totally untrue.

Salespeople trying to recruit students sometimes make accreditation claims that are patently false. Quite a few schools ballyhoo their "fully accredited" status but never mention that the accrediting agency is unrecognized, and so the accreditation is of little or (in most cases) no value.

One accrediting agency (the aforementioned International Accrediting Association for Schools, Colleges and Theological Seminaries) boasted that two copies of every accreditation report they issue are "deposited in the Library of Congress." That sounds impressive, until you learn that for $20, anyone can copyright anything and be able to make the identical claim.

*"I hereby take pen in hand to make application for the Marie Curie
Scholarship in Nuclear Radionics. Alternatively,
I wish also to be considered for the Babe Didrickson Zaharias
Scholarship in shotputting."*

♦8♦
Scholarships and Other Financial Aid

If you think education is expensive, try ignorance.
DEREK BOK, FORMER PRESIDENT OF HARVARD UNIVERSITY

Financial assistance comes in four forms:

Outside scholarships. An outright gift of money paid to you or the school by an outside source (government, foundation, corporation, etc.).

Inside scholarships. The school itself reduces your tuition and/or other expenses. No money changes hands.

Fellowships. Money either from the school or an outside source, usually but not always in return for certain work or services to be performed at the school (generally teaching or research).

Loans. From outside lenders, or from the school itself, to be paid back over a period of anywhere from one to 10 years, generally at interest lower than the current prime rate.

Sadly, as college costs continue to rise substantially, the amount of money available for financial aid is diminishing dramatically. Many loan and scholarship programs were either funded or guaranteed by the federal government, and much of this money was eliminated as part of the Reagan administration's cutbacks and has not been restored. After all, 300,000 cancelled full-tuition scholarships can buy one nuclear-powered aircraft carrier. And already have. (This remark in previous editions has resulted in three stern letters from veterans asking, in effect, if we would rather be protected from a commie invasion by a nuclear battleship or by 300,000 scholars.)

Still, billions of dollars are available to help pay the college costs of people who need help. The vast majority of it goes to full-time students under age 25, pursuing residential degrees at traditional schools.

Tapping into that particular fount is outside the scope of this book. There are several very useful books on this subject, which are described in the reference section, including our own book, *Finding Money for College*, published by Ten Speed Press. With the 1996 edition, this book has now become an annual.

That book is the only one we know of that is specifically oriented to the nontraditional student, the older student, and the graduate student. It covers a wide range of nontraditional strategies, such as bartering skills (gardening, athletic coaching, etc.) for tuition, recruiting new students on a commission basis, and exploiting real estate and tax angles.

Some computerized services collect data on tens of thousands of individual scholarships, and can match their clients' needs and interests with donors for a modest fee. All but a few of these services are licensees, and tap into the same database, so there is no point in getting more than one report. If you'd like to see what they have to offer, you might wish to get the literature from the pioneer in this field, the National Scholarship Research Service, at 2280 Airport Road, Santa Rosa, CA 95403, (707) 546-6777.

If you'd like to do your own research, Dan Cassidy, founder of National Scholarship Research Service, has made it easy for you. Their complete database of available scholarships has been published in a series of three books, for undergraduates, graduates, and people who wish to study abroad. Details are in the Bibliography section.

Some of the scholarships available are, admittedly, awfully peculiar: for rodeo riders with high grades, for Canadian petunia fanciers, for reformed prostitutes from Seattle, for people named Baxendale or Murphy, for people born on certain dates and/or in certain towns, and so on. And many are quite small and/or highly competitive. But many, too, are quite general, and a fair number do not depend on financial need or net worth.

Many colleges and universities subscribe to a service called CASHE (College Aid Sources for Higher Education), a data base of nearly 200,000 scholarships, grants, loans, fellowships, and work study programs. Some schools offer the service free to students or potential students; others make a nominal charge.

Many students enrolled in nontraditional, even nonresidential programs have their expenses paid, all or in part, by their employer. Thousands of large corporations, including nearly all of the Fortune 500, have tuition plans for their employees, and so do a great many small ones. But *billions* of dollars in corporate funds go unclaimed each year, simply because people don't ask for them, or because neither employers nor employees realize that there are significant tax advantages to both in setting up an employee tuition-paying plan.

The tax laws governing such things are what drive the corporate funding. But the tax laws are not etched in stone. In parts of the years 1992-1994, for instance, companies were allowed to deduct up to $5,500 per employee per year for educational expenses, and the employees didn't have to pay tax on the employers' donations. This law expired, then was reenacted, and made retroactive to the expired time, but was then in jeopardy of expiring again. This is the sort of thing that keeps tax accountants solvent.

At times when the law is in place, it is quite a persuasive thing for an employee of any size company to go to his or her boss and say, in effect, "If you pay up to $5,500 of my school expenses, it is all tax deductible for you, and the benefit is not taxable to me."

Some, but not too many, corporations will pay for unaccredited programs. Some unaccredited schools list in their literature the names of hundreds of corporations as well as U.S. and foreign government agencies where their graduates are employed, but this does not necessarily mean the company paid or reimbursed them.

Most nontraditional schools, accredited and unaccredited, offer inside scholarships to their students who need them. In other words, they will award a partial scholarship, in the form of tuition reduction (10 to 30 percent is the usual range), rather than lose a student altogether.

Quite a few schools also offer an extended payment plan, in which the tuition can be paid in a series of smaller monthly installments, or even charged to a major credit card.

There are schools, traditional and nontraditional, that offer tuition reduction in the form of commissions, or finders' fees, for bringing in other students. This quite ethical procedure can result in a tuition reduction of from $50 to several hundred dollars for each referral, when the referred student enrolls.

But the biggest factors, by far, in financial aid for students at nontraditional schools are the speed of their education and the possibility of remaining fully employed while pursuing the degree. If even one year can be cut from a traditional four-year Bachelor's degree program, the savings (including revenue from a year of working for pay) are greater than 99 percent of all scholarship grants. And, as mentioned earlier, the average "four year" Bachelor's degree now takes six years, which should be taken into account in figuring time lost from jobs.

So, while it is nice to "win" money from another source, it is surely the case that to be able to complete an entire degree program for an out-of-pocket cost of from $3,000 to $7,000 (the typical range at nontraditional schools) is one of the great financial bargains of these difficult times.

"I do enjoy studying at home. But why can't the school just mail me the damn books."

♦9♦
Applying to Schools

When any Scholar is able to read Tully or such like classical Latin Author ex tempore, and to make and speak true Latin in verse and prose . . . and decline perfectly the paradigms of Nouns and verbs in the Greek tongue, then may he be admitted into the College, nor shall any claim admission before such qualifications.
ADMISSIONS STANDARDS, HARVARD COLLEGE, C. 1650

HOW MANY SCHOOLS SHOULD YOU APPLY TO?

No single answer to this question is right for everyone. Each person will have to determine his or her own best answer. The decision should be based on the following four factors:

Likelihood of Admission

Some schools are extremely competitive or popular and admit fewer than 10 percent of qualified applicants. Some have an "open admissions" policy and admit literally everyone who applies. Most are somewhere in between.

If your goal is to be admitted to one of the highly competitive schools (for instance, Harvard, Yale, Princeton, Stanford), where your chances of being accepted are not high, then it is wise to apply to at least four or five schools that would be among your top choices, and to at least one "safety valve"—an easier one, in case all else fails.

If your interest is in one of the good, but not world-famous, nonresident programs, your chances for acceptance are probably better than nine in ten, so you might decide to apply only to one or two.

Cost

There is a tremendous range of possible costs for any given degree. For instance, a respectable Ph.D. could cost around $3,000 at a good nonresident school, or more than $50,000 at a well-known university—not even taking into account the lost salary. In general, we think it makes sense to apply to no more than two or three schools in any given price category.

What They Offer You

Shopping around for a school is a little like shopping for a new car. Many schools either have money problems, or operate as profit-making businesses, and in either case, they are most eager to enroll new students. Thus it is not unreasonable to ask the schools what they can do for you. Let them know that you are a knowledgeable "shopper," and that you have read this book. Do they have courses or faculty advisors in your specific field? If not, will they get one for you? How much credit will they give for prior life-experience learning? How long will it take to earn the degree? Are there any scholarship or tuition reduction plans available? Does tuition have to be paid all at once, or can it be spread out over time? If factors like these are important for you, then it could pay to shop around for the best deal.

You might consider investigating at least two or three schools that appear somewhat similar, because there will surely be differences.

> **Caution:** Remember that academic quality and reputation are probably the most important factors—so don't let a small financial saving be a reason to switch from a good school to a less-good school.

Your Own Time and Money

Applying to a school can be a time-consuming process—and it costs money, too. Many schools have application fees ranging from $25 to $100. Some people get so carried away with the process of applying to school after school that they never get around to earning their degree.

Of course once you have prepared a good detailed resume, curriculum vita, or life-experience portfolio, you can use it to apply to more than one school.

Another time factor is how much of a hurry you are in. If you apply to several schools at once, the chances are good that at least one will admit you, and you can begin work promptly. If you apply to only one, and it turns you down, or you get into long delays, then it can take a month or two to go through the admissions process elsewhere.

SPEEDING UP
THE ADMISSIONS PROCESS

The admissions process at most traditional schools is very slow; most people apply nearly a year in advance and do not learn if their application has been accepted for four to six months. Nontraditional programs vary immensely in their policies in this regard. Some will grant conditional acceptance within a few weeks after receiving the application. ("Conditional" means that they must later verify the prior learning experiences you claim.) Others take just as long as traditional programs.

The following three factors can result in a much faster admissions process:

Selecting Schools by Policy

A school's admissions policy should be stated in its catalog. Since you will find a range among schools of a few weeks to six months for a decision, the simple solution is to ask, and then apply to schools with a fast procedure.

Asking for Speedy Decisions

Some schools have formal procedures whereby you can request an early decision on your acceptance. Others do the same thing informally, for those who ask. In effect, what this does is put you at the top of the pile in the admissions office, so you will have the decision in, perhaps, half the usual time. Other schools use what they call a "rolling admissions" procedure, which means, in effect, that each application is considered soon after it is received instead of being held several months and considered with a large batch of others.

Applying Pressure

As previously indicated, many schools are eager to have new students. If you make it clear to a school that you are in a hurry and that you may consider going elsewhere if you don't hear from them promptly, they will usually speed up the process. It is not unreasonable to specify a timeframe. If, for instance, you are mailing in your application on September 1, you might enclose a note saying that you would like to have their decision mailed or phoned to you by October 1. (Some schools routinely telephone their acceptances, others do so if asked, some will only do so by collect call, and others will not, no matter what.)

HOW TO APPLY TO A SCHOOL

The basic procedure is essentially the same at all schools, traditional or nontraditional:

1. You write (or telephone) for the school's catalog, bulletin, or other literature, and admissions forms.
2. You complete the admissions forms and return them to the school, with application fee, if any.
3. You complete any other requirements the school may have (exams, transcripts, letters of recommendation, etc.).
4. The school notifies you of its decision.

It is step three that can vary tremendously from school to school. At some schools all that is required is the admissions application. Others will require various entrance examinations to test your aptitude or knowledge level, transcripts, three or more letters of reference, a statement of financial condition, and possibly a personal interview, either on the campus or with a local representative in your area.

Happily, the majority of nontraditional schools have relatively simple entrance requirements. And all schools supply the materials that tell you exactly what they expect you to do in order to apply. If it is not clear, ask. If the school does not supply prompt, helpful answers, then you probably don't want to deal with them anyway. It's a buyer's market.

It is advisable, in general, *not* to send a whole bunch of stuff to a school the very first time you write to them. A short note asking for their catalog should suffice. You may wish to indicate your field and degree goal ("I am interested in a Master's and possibly a Doctorate in psychology . . .") in case they have different sets of literature for different programs. It probably can do no harm to mention that you are a reader of this book; it might get you slightly prompter or more personal responses. (On the other hand, more than a few grouchy readers have written saying, "I told them I was a personal friend of yours, and it still took six months for an answer." Oh dear. Well, if they hadn't said that, it might have been even longer. Or perhaps shorter. Who knows?)

ENTRANCE EXAMINATIONS

Many nonresident degree programs, even at the Master's and Doctoral levels, do not require any entrance examinations. On the other hand, the majority of residential programs *do* require them. The main reason for this appears to be that nontraditional schools do not have to worry about overcrowding on the campus, so they can admit more students. A second reason is that they tend to deal with more mature students who have the ability to decide which program is best for them.

There are, needless to say, exceptions to both reasons. If you have particular feelings about examinations—positive or negative—you will be able to find schools that meet your requirements. Do not hesitate to ask any school about their exam requirements if it is not clear from the catalog.

Bachelor's Admission Examinations

Most residential universities require applicants to take part or all of the "ATP" or Admissions Testing Program, run by a private agency, the College Entrance Examination Board (888 7th Ave., New York, NY 10019). The main component of the ATP is the SAT, or Scholastic Aptitude Test, which measures verbal and mathematical abilities. There are also achievement tests, testing knowledge levels in specific subject areas such as biology, European history, Latin, etc. These examinations are given at centers all over North America several times each year for modest fees, and by special arrangement in many foreign locations.

A competing private organization, ACT (American College Testing Program, P.O. Box 168, Iowa City, IA 52240) offers a similar range of entrance examinations.

The important point is that very few schools have their own exams; virtually all rely on either the ACT or the ATP.

Graduate Degrees

Again, many nonresidential schools do not require any entrance examinations. Many, but by no means all, residential Master's and Doctoral programs ask their applicants to take the GRE, or Graduate Record Examination, administered by the Educational Testing Service (P.O. Box 955, Princeton, NJ 08541). The basic GRE consists of a three-and-a-half-hour aptitude test (of verbal, quantitative, and analytical abilities). Some schools also require GRE subject-area exams, which are available in a variety of specific fields (chemistry, computer science, music, etc.)

Professional Schools

Most law, business, and medical schools also require a standard examination, rather than having one of their own. The MCAT (Medical College Admission Test) is given several times a year by ACT while the LSAT (Law School Admission Test) and the GMAT (Graduate Management Admissions Test) are given five times a year by ETS.

There are many excellent books available at most libraries and larger bookstores on how to prepare for these various exams, complete with sample questions and answers. Some of these are listed in the bibliography of this book. Also, the testing agencies themselves sell literature on their tests as well as copies of previous years' examinations.

The testing agencies used to deny vigorously that either cramming or coaching could affect one's scores. In the face of overwhelming evidence to the contrary, they no longer make those claims. Some coaching services have documented score increases of 25 to 30 percent. Check the Yellow Pages or the bulletin boards on high school or college campuses for test-preparation workshops in your area.

"For my final exam at the Dolittle Correspondence Veterinary Institute, they mailed me these two sick animals. I have one week to cure them and mail them back."

♦ 10 ♦
Equivalency Examinations

In an examination, those who do not wish to know
ask questions of those who cannot tell.
WALTER RALEIGH

The nontraditional approach to higher education says that if you have knowledge of an academic field, then you should get credit for that knowledge, regardless of how or where you acquired the knowledge. The simplest and fairest way of assessing that knowledge is through an examination.

More than 2,000 colleges and universities in the United States and Canada, many of whom would deny vigorously that there is anything "nontraditional" about them, award students credit toward their Bachelor's degrees (and, in a few cases, Master's and Doctorates) solely on the basis of passing examinations.

Many of the exams are designed to be equivalent to the final exam in a typical college class, and the assumption is that if you score high enough, you get the same amount of credit you would have gotten by taking the class—or, in some cases, a good deal more.

While there are many sources of equivalency exams, including a trend toward schools developing their own, two independent national agencies are dominant in this field. They offer exams known as CLEP and PEP.

CLEP and PEP

CLEP (the College-Level Examination Program) and PEP (the Proficiency Examination Program) administer more than 75 exams. They are given at hundreds of testing centers all over North America and, by special arrangement, many of them can be administered almost anywhere in the world.

CLEP is offered by the College Entrance Examination Board, known as "the College Board" (CN 6600, Princeton, NJ 08541-6600). Military personnel who want to take CLEP should see their education officer or write DANTES, CN, Princeton, NJ 08541.

PEP is offered in the state of New York by the Regents College Proficiency Programs (7 Columbia Circle, Albany, NY 12203), and everywhere else by the American College Testing Program (P.O. Box 4014, Iowa City, IA 52243).

Many of the tests offered by CLEP are available in two versions: entirely multiple-choice questions, or multiple choice plus an essay. Some colleges require applicants to take both parts, others just the multiple choice. There are five general exams, each 90 minutes long, which are multiple choice, except English, which has the option of a 45-minute multiple choice and a 45-minute composition.

CLEP offers 30 subject-area exams, each of them 90 minutes of multiple-choice questions, with the option of an additional 90 minutes for writing an essay. The cost is around $30 per test.

PEP offers 43 subject-area exams, most of them three hours long, but a few are four hours. The fees range from $40 to $125 per exam.

Each college or university sets its own standards for passing grades, and also decides for itself how much credit to give for each exam. Both of these factors can vary substantially from school to school. For instance, the PEP test in anatomy and physiology is a three-hour multiple-choice test. Hundreds of schools give credit for passing this exam. Here are examples:

♦ Central Virginia Community College requires a score of 45 (out of 80), and awards nine credit hours for passing.

♦ Edinboro University in Pennsylvania requires a score of 50 to pass, and awards six credit hours for the same exam.

♦ Concordia College in New York requires a score of 47, but awards only three credit hours.

Similar situations prevail on most of the exams. There is no predictability or consistency, even within a given school. For instance, at the University of South Florida, a three-hour multiple-choice test in maternal nursing is worth 18 units while a three-hour multiple-choice test in psychiatric nursing is worth only nine.

So, with dozens of standard exams available, and more than 2,000 schools offering credit, it pays to shop around a little and select both the school and the exams where you will get the most credit.

CLEP exams are offered in five general subject areas: Social Science and History, English Composition, Humanities, Mathematics, and Natural Science.

Specific subject-area exams are offered in the following fields:

American Government
American History I & II
Educational Psychology
General Psychology
Human Growth & Development
Introductory Marketing
Introductory Macroeconomics
Introductory Sociology
Western Civilization I & II
French I & II
German I & II
Spanish I & II
American Literature
Analysis & Interpretation
College Composition
English Literature
Freshman English
Trigonometry
Algebra & Trigonometry
General Biology
General Chemistry
Computers & Data Processing
Introduction to Management
Introductory Accounting
Introductory Business Law
Calculus & Elementary Functions
College Algebra

PEP exams are offered in these fields:

Abnormal Psychology
Anatomy & Physiology
Earth Science
Foundations of Gerontology
Microbiology
Physical Geology
Statistics
Accounting I & II
Cost Accounting
Auditing
Advanced Accounting
Intermediate Business Law
Federal Income Taxation
Business Policy
Corporate Finance
Principles of Management
Organizational Behavior
Personnel Administration
Labor Relations
Marketing
Management, Human Resources
Statistics
Production/Operations Management

Educational Psychology
Reading Instruction
Fundamentals of Nursing
Remedial Reading and
15 more nursing exams

How Exams Are Scored

CLEP exams are scored on a scale of either 20 to 80 or 200 to 800. This is done to maintain the fiction that no score can have any intrinsic meaning. It is not obvious, for example, whether a score of 514 is either good or bad. But any college-bound high-school senior in America can tell you that 400 is pretty bad, 500 is okay, 600 is good, and 700 is great. Still, each college sets its own minimum score for which it will give credit, and in many cases all that is necessary is to be in the upper half of those taking the test.

PEP gives standard numerical or letter grades for its tests.

Anywhere from one-and-two-thirds to six credits may be earned for each hour of testing. For example, the five basic CLEP tests (90 minutes of multiple choice questions each) are worth anywhere from eight to 30 semester units, depending on the school. Thus it is possible to complete the equivalent of an entire year of college—30 semester units—in two days, by taking and passing these five tests.

CLEP tests are given over a two-day period once each month at more than 1,000 centers, most of them on college or university campuses. PEP tests are given for two consecutive days on a variable schedule in about 100 locations, nationwide.

Persons living more than 150 miles from a test center may make special arrangements for the test to be given nearer home. There is a modest charge for this service. And for those in a big hurry, the CLEP tests are given twice each week in Washington, DC.

There is no stigma attached to poor performance on these tests. In fact, if you wish, you may have the scores reported only to you, so that no one but you and the computer will know how you did. Then, if your scores are high enough, you can have them sent on to the schools of your choice. CLEP allows exams to be taken every six months; you can take the same PEP exam twice in any 12-month period.

How Hard Are These Exams?

This is, of course, an extremely subjective question. However, We have heard from a great many readers who have attempted CLEP and PEP exams, and the most common response is "Gee, that was a lot easier than I had expected." This is especially true with more mature students. The tests are designed for 18-to-20-year-olds, and there appears to be a certain amount of factual knowledge, as well as experience in dealing with testing situations, that people acquire in ordinary life situations as they grow older.

Preparing (and Cramming) for Exams

The testing agencies issue detailed syllabuses describing each test and the specific content area it covers. CLEP also sells a book that gives sample questions and answers from each examination.

At least four educational publishers have produced series of books on how to prepare for such exams, often with full-length sample tests. These can be found in the education or reference section of any good bookstore or library.

For years, the testing agencies vigorously fought the idea of letting test-takers take copies of the test home with them. But consumer legislation in New York has made at least some of the tests available, and a good thing, too. Every so often, someone discovers an incorrect answer or a poorly-phrased question that can have more than one correct answer, necessitating a recalculation and reissuance of scores to all the thousands of people who took that test.

In recent years, there has been much controversy over the value of cramming for examinations. Many counseling clients report having been able to pass four or five CLEP exams in a row by spending an intensive few days (or weeks) cramming for them. Although the various testing agencies used to deny that cramming can be of any value, in the last few years there have been some extremely persuasive research studies that demonstrate the short-term effectiveness of intensive studying. These data have vindicated the claims made by people and agencies that assist students in preparing for examinations. Such services are offered in a great many places, usually in the vicinity of college campuses, by graduate students and moonlighting faculty. The best place to find them is through the classified ads in campus newspapers, on bulletin boards around the campus, and through on-campus extension programs. Prices vary widely, so shop around.

The Princeton Review testing service claims that their preparation materials, in classes or through their book, increase scores by an average of 150 points. (Princeton Review, 2315 Broadway, New York, NY 10024, (800) 2-REVIEW.) Princeton has offices in all 50 states and worldwide. They help prepare for GRE, GMAT, GED, LSAT, MCAT, and TOEFL, but *not* for CLEP and PEP.

The Stanley H. Kaplan Educational Centers offer intensive preparation for dozens of different tests, from college admissions to national medical boards. Although the main method of preparation involves a good deal of classroom attendance at a center (from 20 to over 100 hours), most materials can be rented for home study. Residential tuition for most examination preparation courses is in the range of $150 to $300, but the cost goes as high as $850 for some medical exams. Rental of most sets of materials for home study costs from $100 to $200. Kaplan Centers operate in 40 states, the District of Columbia, Puerto Rico, and in Canada. (Stanley H. Kaplan Educational Center, Ltd., 131 West 56th St., New York, NY 10019, (212) 977-8200; outside New York, (800) 223-1782.)

Often the best strategy is to take a self-scoring test from one of the guidebooks. If you do well, you may wish to take the real exam right away. If you do badly, you may conclude that credit by examination is not your cup of hemlock. And if you score in between, consider cramming on your own, or with the help of a paid tutor or tutoring service.

OTHER EXAMINATIONS

Here are some other examinations that can be used to earn substantial credit toward many nontraditional degree programs:

Graduate Record Examination

The GRE is administered by the Educational Testing Service (P.O. Box 955, Princeton, NJ 08541, (212) 966-5853) and is given at nationwide locations four times each year. The GRE Advanced Test is a three-hour multiple-choice test, designed to test knowledge that would ordinarily be gained by a Bachelor's degree–holder in that given field. The exams are available in the fields of biology, chemistry, computer science, economics, education, engineering, French, geography, geology, German, history, English literature, mathematics, music, philosophy, physics, political science, psychology, sociology, and Spanish.

Schools vary widely in how much credit they will give for each GRE. The range is from none at all to 30 semester units (in the case of Regents College of the University of the State of New York).

A National Guard sergeant once crammed for, took, and passed three GRE exams in a row, thereby earning 90 semester units in nine hours of testing. Then he took the five basic CLEP exams in two days, and earned 30 more units, which was enough to earn an accredited Bachelor's degree, start to finish, in 16 1/2 hours, starting absolutely from scratch with no college credit.

DANTES

The Defense Activity for Non-Traditional Education Support tests, or DANTES, were developed for the Department of Defense, but are available to civilians as well. The tests were developed by the Educational Testing Service, and are offered by hundreds of colleges and universities nationwide. While there is some overlap with PEP and CLEP, there are also many unique subjects. DANTES information is available from the DANTES Program, Mail Stop 3/X, Educational Testing Service, Princeton, NJ 08541. Tests include:

Introductory College Algebra
Principles of Statistics
Art of the Western World
Geography
General Anthropology
Criminal Justice
Principles of Finance
Principles of Financial Accounting
Personnel/Human Resource Management

Organizational Behavior
Business Law II
Basic Marketing
Astronomy
Principles of Physical Science I
Physical Geology
Beginning German I
Beginning German II
Beginning Spanish I
Beginning Spanish II
Beginning Italian I
Technical Writing
Ethics in America
Introduction to World Religions

University End-of-Course Exams

Several schools offer the opportunity to earn credit for a correspondence course solely by taking (and passing) the final exam for that course. One need not be enrolled as a student in the school to do this. Two schools with especially large programs of this kind are Ohio University (Course Credit by Examination, Tupper Hall, Athens, OH 45701) and the University of North Carolina (Independent Study, Abernethy Hall 002A, Chapel Hill, NC 27514).

Advanced Placement Examinations

The College Board offers exams specifically for high school students who wish to earn college credit while still in high school. Exams in 13 subject areas are offered. (College Board Advanced Placement Program, 888 7th Ave., New York, NY 10106)

Special Assessments

For people whose knowledge is both extensive and in an obscure field (or at least one for which no exams have been developed), some schools are willing to develop special exams for a single student. At the University of the State of New York, both for its students and for Regents Credit Bank depositors (see chapter 15), this takes the form of an oral exam. They will find at least two experts in your field, be it Persian military history, paleontology, French poetry, or whatever. Following a three-hour oral exam, conducted at everyone's mutual convenience in Albany, New York, the examiners decide how many credits to award for that particular knowledge area.

♦11♦
Correspondence Courses

The postman is the agent of impolite surprises. Every week, we
ought to have an hour for receiving letters—
and then go and take a bath.
FRIEDRICH NIETZSCHE

There are two kinds of correspondence study, or home-study, courses—vocational and academic. Vocational courses (meat-cutting, locksmithing, appliance repair, etc.) often offer useful training, but rarely lead to degrees, so they are not relevant for this book. The Distance Education and Training Council (formerly known as the National Home Study Council) (1601 18th St. NW, Washington, DC 20009) offers excellent free information on the sources of vocational home-study courses in many fields.

One hundred and eight major universities and teaching institutions in the United States offer academic correspondence (or e-mail) courses—more than 12,000 courses in hundreds of subjects, from accounting to zoology. Virtually all of these courses can be counted toward a degree at almost any college or university. However, most schools have a limit on the amount of correspondence credit they will apply to a degree. This limit is typically around 50 percent, but the range is from zero to 100 percent.

That means that it is indeed possible to earn an accredited Bachelor's degree entirely through correspondence study. This may be done, for instance, through the University of the State of New York, Thomas Edison State College of New Jersey, and Western Illinois University. Courses taken at any of the 108 schools can be applied to a degree at these schools.

Each of the 108 institutions publishes a catalog or bulletin listing their available courses—some offer just a few, others have hundreds. All of the schools accept students living anywhere in the United States, although some charge more for out-of-state students. About 80 percent accept foreign students, but all courses are offered in English only.

A helpful directory called *The Independent Study Catalog* is, in effect, a master catalog, listing all course titles for each of the schools, with surprisingly informative one-line course descriptions: "Hist & phil of phys ed," "Fac career dev in schools," and 12,000 more. Popular subjects

like psychology, business, and education will be offered at a number of schools, but some of the more esoteric topics may only be available at one or two, and the directory points you to them. It is revised approximately every three years by the publisher, Peterson's Guides (P.O. Box 3601, Princeton, NJ 08540). A second Peterson's Guide, *The Electronic University*, lists only those schools that offer courses by computer. Of course you can also write directly to the schools; nearly all of them send out free catalogs.

Correspondence courses range from one to six semester hours worth of credit, and can cost anywhere from less than $40 to more than $150 per semester hour. The average is just over $80, so that a typical three-unit course would cost about $250. Because of the wide range in costs, it pays to shop around.

A typical correspondence course will consist of from five to 20 lessons, each one requiring a short written paper, answers to questions, or an unsupervised test graded by the instructor. There is almost always a supervised final examination. These can usually be taken anywhere in the world that a suitable proctor can be found (usually a high school or college teacher).

People who cannot go to a testing center because, for instance, they are handicapped, live too far away, or are in prison, can usually arrange to have a test supervisor come to them. Schools can be extremely flexible. One correspondence program administrator told us he had two students—a husband and wife—working as missionaries on a remote island where they were the only people who could read and write. He allowed them to supervise each other.

Many schools set limits on how fast and how slow you can complete a correspondence course. The shortest time is generally three to six weeks, while the upper limit ranges from three months to two years. Some schools limit the number of courses you can take at one time, but most do not. Even those with limits are concerned only with courses taken from their own institution. There is no cross-checking, so in theory one could take simultaneous courses from all 108 institutions.

A sidelight: we would have thought that correspondence programs would remain quite stable, since so much time and effort is required to establish one. However in the three years between editions of *Peterson's Guide*s, it's not unusual for up to 10 percent of the list to change— five or six schools will drop their programs, and a similar number start new ones.

Students who want an even wider range of correspondence courses might consider taking one or more from a foreign university (see list below). While these courses are generally intended for citizens who cannot, for whatever reason, attend residential classes, Americans, Canadians, (and others) are often welcome to enroll. Although there's greater potential for problems (with the mails, deadlines, etc.), it's worth it for students who are interested in unusual fields or specific countries (studying Kiswahili with the University of Nairobi as part of an African-American Studies program, for instance). Unless otherwise specified, the programs are taught in the country's native language.

AMERICAN SCHOOLS
Coding as follows:
★ = one of the dozen schools with the most college-level courses
■ = school that offers electronic courses
♥ = school that welcomes students from outside the U.S.
◆ = school that prefers not to deal with foreign students but treats each case on its own merits
✗ = school that will not accept foreign students

Adams State College ♥
Extension Division
Alamosa, CO 81102
(303) 589-7671
Approximately 7 college-level math courses

Arizona State University ♥ ■
Correspondence Study Office, ASB 112
Tempe, AZ 85287
(602) 965-6563
Approximately 90 college-level courses

Atlantic Union College ■
Electronic Distance Learning
Box 1000
South Lancaster, MA 01561
(508) 368-2394
One course offered, by e-mail, in liberal arts/ general studies

Auburn University ♥
Independent Study Program, Mell Hall
Auburn, AL 36849

(205) 826-5103
Approximately 45 college-level courses

Ball State University ✗ ■
School of Continuing Education
Carmichael Hall
Muncie, IN 47306
(317) 285-1581
Approximately 80 college-level courses

Bastyr College ■
Director of Continuing Education
Distance Learning
144 NE 54th St.
Seattle, WA 98105
(206) 527-4763
Courses in allied health management

Boise State University ■
Instructional and Performance Technology
1910 University Drive
Boise, ID 83725
(208) 385-1899

Brigham Young University ♥ ★
Independent Study
206 Harmon Continuing
Education Building
Provo, UT 84604
(801) 378-2868
Approximately 280 college-level courses

California Institute of Integral Studies ■
School for Transformative Learning
765 Ashbury St.
San Francisco, CA 94117
(415) 753-6100, ext. 263

California State University, Chico ■
Regional and Continuing Education
Chico, CA 95929-0250
(916) 898-6105
Graduate and undergraduate courses

California State University,
    Dominguez Hills ■
Dean, Extended Education
1000 East Victoria Street
Carson, CA 90747
(310) 516-3737
Approximately 32 college-level courses

California State University,
    Los Angeles ■
Distance Education Program
State University Drive

Los Angeles, CA 90032
(213) 343-4550
Undergraduate and graduate courses in engineering, fire science, teacher education

California State University, Sacramento ♥
Office of Water Programs
6000 J Street, Sacramento, CA 95819
(916) 454-6142
Approximately 6 college-level courses
All courses deal with wastewater management

Central Michigan University ♥
Office of Independent Study
Rowe Hall 125
Mt. Pleasant, MI 48859
(517) 774-7140
Approximately 70 college-level courses

Colorado State University ♥ ■
Correspondence Program Coordinator
C102 Rockwell Hall, Fort Collins, CO 80523
(303) 491-5288
Approximately 40 college-level courses
Graduate courses in accounting adult and teacher education, business, computer science, engineering, and grantsmanship

Department of Agriculture Graduate School ♥
U. S. Department of Agriculture, 1404 South Bldg.
14th and Independence Ave. SW
Washington, DC 20250
(202) 447-7123
Approximately 80 college-level courses
Many fields are covered, but not agriculture

Eastern Kentucky University ♥
Dean of Extended Programs
Perkins 217
Richmond, KY 40475
(606) 622-2001
Approximately 45 college-level courses

Eastern Michigan University ♦
Coordinator of Independent Study
329 Goodison Hall
Ypsilanti, MI 48197
(313) 487-1081
Approximately 12 college-level courses

Eastern Oregon State College ✗ ■
Zabel, Room 22
1410 L Avenue
La Grande, OR 97850-2899
800-452-8639
Approximately 78 college-level courses

Embry-Riddle Aeronautical University ■
Dept. of Independent Studies
600 S. Clyde Morris Blvd.
Daytona Beach, FL 32114-3900
(904) 226-6397
Approximately 20 college-level courses
Mainly aeronautical fields

Ferris State University
Gerholtz Institute for Lifelong Learning
Alumni 226, 901 South State Street
Big Rapids, MI 49307
(616) 592-2340
Approximately 12 college-level courses
One graduate course, in computers for teachers

George Washington University ■
Continuing Education
Washington, DC 20052
(202) 994-1000
Graduate courses in business/management, computer science, engineering, teacher education

Georgia Institute of Technology ■
Continuing Education
Atlanta, GA 30332
(404) 894-8572
One graduate-level course, in engineering

Governors State University ♥ ■
Independent Correspondence Study, Stuendel Road University Park, IL 60466
(312) 534-5000, Ext. 2121
Approximately 20 college-level courses
Graduate courses in ethnic studies, urban politics, allied health, liberal arts/general studies, teacher education

Home Study International ♥
6940 Carroll Ave.
Takoma Park, MD 20912
(202) 722-6572
Approximately 70 college-level courses

Indiana State University ♥ ■
Director of Independent Study
Alumni Center 124
Terre Haute, IN 47809
(812) 237-2555
Approximately 60 college-level courses
Graduate courses in environmental health and safety, human resource development, industrial technical education, teacher education

Indiana University ♥
Independent Study Program

Owen Hall
Bloomington, IN 47405
(812) 335-3693
Approximately 90 college-level courses

Iowa State University of Science & Technology ■
240 Engineering Annex
Ames, IA 50011
(515) 294-4962
Undergraduate and graduate courses in engineering

Kansas State University ♥ ■
Distance Learning Program, Continuing Education
227 College Court
Manhattan, KS 66506
(913) 532-5686
Approximately 18 college-level courses
Graduate courses in agriculture, business/management, liberal arts/general studies

Loyola University ■
Off-Campus Learning
Box 14, 6363 St. Charles Avenue
New Orleans, LA 70118
(800) 488-6257
One course in nursing, for RN's only

Louisiana State University ★ ♥
Office of Independent Study
Baton Rouge, LA 70803
(504) 388-3171
Approximately 160 college-level courses

Mesa State College
Continuing Education
Elm Hall, Room 205
P.O. Box 2647
Grand Junction, CO 81502
(803) 248-1476
One college-level course, in criminal justice

Mississippi State University ♥
Continuing Education, P. O. Drawer 5247
Mississippi State, MS 39762
(601) 325-3473
Approximately 75 college-level courses

Murray State University ◆ ■
Center for Continuing Education
15th at Main
Murray, KY 42071
(502) 762-4159
Approximately 35 college-level courses
Graduate courses in accounting, allied health, business, nursing, teacher education

New Jersey Institute of Technology ■
University Heights
Newark, NJ 07102
(201) 596-3000
Includes graduate courses in business, chemistry, computer science, engineering, environmental health and safety, mathematics, physics

New York Institute of Technology ♥ ■
American Open University
211 Carlton Avenue, Bldg. #66
Central Islip, NY 11722
(516) 348-3300
Approximately 130 college-level courses

New York University ■
Information Technologies, 48 Cooper Square
New York, NY 10003
(212) 998-7190
Graduate courses in business, computer science

Northern State University ♥
Continuing Education
1200 South Jay Street, NU Box 870
Aberdeen, SD 57401
Approximately 34 college-level courses

Ohio University ♥ ★
Director of Independent Study, 303 Tupper Hall
Athens, OH 45701
(614) 594-6721
Approximately 185 college-level courses

Oklahoma State University ♥
Correspondence Study Dept.
001P Classroom Bldg.
Stillwater, OK 74078
(405) 624-6390
Approximately 120 college-level courses

Oregon State System of Higher Education ♥
Office of Independent Study, P. O. Box 1491
Portland, OR 97207
(800) 547-8887, ext. 4865
Approximately 100 college-level courses

Pennsylvania State University ♥ ★
Independent Learning, 128 Mitchell Building
University Park, PA 16802
(814) 865-5403
Approximately 150 college-level courses

Purdue University ♥ ■
Media-Based Programs
116 Stewart Center
West Lafayette, IN 47907

(317) 494-7231
Approximately 8 college-level courses
Courses in food service, pest control, pharmacology. One graduate course in engineering

Regent University ■
1000 Centerville Turnpike
Virginia Beach, VA 23464
(804) 523-7400
Graduate courses in accounting, bible studies, business

Rochester Institute of Technology ■
Distance Learning
P.O. Box 9887
Rochester, NY 14623
(800) CALL-RIT
Includes a graduate course in computer science

Roosevelt University ♥
College of Continuing Education
430 S. Michigan Avenue
Chicago, IL 60605
(312) 341-3866
Approximately 60 college-level courses
Includes three graduate courses in psychology

Saint Joseph's College ♥ ■
Continuing Education, White's Bridge Road
North Windham, ME 04062-1198
(207) 892-6766
Approximately 50 college-level courses
Graduate course in health-care administration

Salve Regina University ■
Newport, RI 02840-4192
(800) 321-7124
Graduate courses only, in accounting, business/
management, criminal justice, international relations, liberal arts

Savannah State College ♥
Correspondence Study Office, P. O. Box 20372
Savannah, GA 31404
(912) 356-2243
Approximately 25 college-level courses

Southeastern College of the Assemblies of God ♥
Correspondence Study, 1000 Longfellow Blvd.
Lakeland, FL 33801-6099
(813) 665-4404
Approximately 45 college-level courses
Courses include theology, Hebrew, Greek

Southern Illinois University ♥
Division of Continuing Education

Washington Square C
Carbondale, IL 62901
(618) 536-7751
Approximately 14 college-level courses

Southern Methodist University ■
School of Engineering & Applied Science
Dallas, TX 75275
(214) 768-3051
One graduate engineering course

Southwest Texas State University ♥
Correspondence and Extension Studies
P. O. Box 4110, 118 Medina Hall
San Marcos, TX 78666
(512) 245-2322
Approximately 75 college-level courses

Southwest Assemblies of God College ■
Adult & Continuing Education
Waxahachie, TX 75165
(214) 937-4010

SUNY, Empire State College ♥ ■
Center for Distance Learning, 2 Union Ave.
Saratoga Springs, NY 12866
Approximately 90 college-level courses
Program in fire-service administration, much more

Stephens College Without Walls ♥
Campus Box 2083
Columbia, MO 65215
(314) 876-7125
Approximately 120 college-level courses

Syracuse University ♥ ■
Independent Study Programs
301 Reid Hall
Syracuse, NY 13244-6020
(315) 443-3284
Approximately 150 college-level courses
Over 50 graduate-level courses

Texas Tech University ♥ ■
Continuing Education, P. O. Box 4110
Lubbock, TX 79409
(806) 742-1513
Approximately 90 college-level courses
Graduate courses in higher and teacher education

Thomas Edison State College ✗ ■
Directed Independent Learning
101 W. State Street
Trenton, NJ 08608
(609) 984-8448
Approximately 40 college-level courses

University of Alabama ♥ ■ ★
Independent Study Department
P. O. Box 2967
University, AL 35486
(205) 348-7642
Approximately 175 college-level courses
Graduate courses in business, communications,
computer science, engineering

University of Alaska ♥ ■
Correspondence Study
115 Eielson Bldg.
403 Salcha St.
Fairbanks, AK 99701
(907) 474-7222
Approximately 65 college-level courses

University of Arizona ♥ ■
Continuing Education
Babcock Bldg.
Suite 1201
1717 E. Speedway
Tucson, AZ 85719
(602) 621-3021
Approximately 110 college-level courses

University of Arkansas ♥
Department of Independent Study
2 University Ctr.
Fayetteville, AR 72701
(501) 575-3647
Approximately 120 college-level courses

University of California ♥ ★
Independent Study
2223 Fulton St.
Berkeley, CA 94720
(415) 642-4124
Approximately 200 college-level courses

University of Colorado, Boulder ♥ ■
Division of Continuing Education
Campus Box 178
Boulder, CO 80309
(303) 492-5145
Approximately 85 college-level courses
Graduate courses in business, computer science, en-
gineering, environment health & safety, telecom-
munications

University of Colorado, Colorado Springs ■
CU-Net, P.O. Box 7150
Colorado Springs, CO 80933-7150
(719) 593-3597
Includes graduate courses in accounting, engineer-
ing, space studies, teacher education

University of Florida ♥
Department of Independent Correspondence
Study
1938 W. University Ave., Room 1
Gainesville, FL 32603
(904) 392-1711
Approximately 115 college-level courses

University of Georgia ♥
Center for Continuing Education
1197 S. Lumpkin St.
Athens, GA 30602
(404) 542-3243
Approximately 130 college-level courses

University of Idaho ♥ ■
Correspondence Study in Idaho
Continuing Education Building, Room 116
Moscow, ID 83843
(208) 885-6641
Approximately 100 college-level courses
Graduate courses in computer science & engineer-
ing

University of Illinois ◆ ■
Guided Individual Study
1046 Illini Hall
725 S. Wright St.
Champaign, IL 61820
(217) 333-1321
Approximately 140 college-level courses
One graduate course, in engineering

University of Iowa ♥ ■ ★
Center for Credit Programs
W400 Seashore Hall
Iowa City, IA 52242
(319) 353-4963
Approximately 140 college-level courses
Graduate courses in computer science, liberal arts/
general studies, nursing, social work, teacher edu-
cation

University of Kansas ♥
Independent Study, Continuing
Education Building
Lawrence, KS 66045
(913) 864-4792
Approximately 120 college-level courses

University of Kentucky ◆ ■
Independent Studies
Frazee Hall, Room 1
Lexington, KY 40506
(606) 257-3466
Approximately 125 college-level courses

University of Maryland University College
University Blvd. at Adelphi Rd.
College Park, MD 20742-1628
(301) 314-9560
Includes course in paralegal studies

University of Massachusetts at Amherst ■
Distance Education
Amherst, MA 01003
(413) 545-0111
Graduate courses in business, computer science, engineering, environmental health and safety, nursing

University of Michigan ♥
Department of Independent Study
200 Hill St.
Ann Arbor, MI 48104
(313) 764-5306
Approximately 30 college-level courses

University of Minnesota ♥ ★
Independent Study
45 Wesbrook Hall
77 Pleasant St. SE
Minneapolis, MN 55455
(612) 373-3803
Approximately 265 college-level courses

University of Mississippi ♥
Department of Independent Study
Division of Continuing Education
University, MS 38677
(601) 232-7313
Approximately 135 college-level courses
Offers noncredit French and German for Ph.D. candidates.

University of Missouri ♥
Center for Independent Study, 400 Hitt St.
Columbia, MO 65211
(314) 882-6431
Approximately 120 college-level courses

University of Nebraska ♥ ■
269 Nebraska Center for Continuing Education
33rd and Holdrege
Lincoln, NE 68583
(402) 472-1926
Approximately 75 college-level courses

University of Nevada ♥
Independent Study Department, Room 333
College Inn, 1001 S. Virginia St.
Reno, NV 89557
(702) 784-4652
Approximately 65 college-level courses

University of New Mexico ♥
Independent Study Through Correspondence
1634 University Blvd. NE
Albuquerque, NM 87131
(505) 277-2931
Approximately 52 college-level courses

University of North Carolina ♥ ★
Independent Study, 201 Abernethy Hall 002A
Chapel Hill, NC 27514
(919) 962-1106
Approximately 160 college-level courses

University of North Dakota ✗
Department of Correspondence Study
Box 8277, University Station
Grand Forks, ND 58202
(701) 777-3044
Approximately 90 college-level courses

University of Northern Colorado ♥
Frasier Hall, Room 11
Greeley, CO 80639
(303) 351-2944
Approximately 16 college-level courses

University of Northern Iowa ♥
Coordinator of Credit Programs
144 Gilchrist
Cedar Falls, IA 50614
(319) 273-2121
Approximately 55 college-level courses

University of Oklahoma ♥ ★
Independent Study Department
1700 Asp Ave., Room B-1
Norman, OK 73037
(405) 325-1921
Approximately 200 college-level courses

University of South Carolina ♥ ■
Correspondence Study, 915 Gregg St.
Columbia, SC 29208
(803) 777-2188
Approximately 130 college-level courses

University of South Carolina, Aiken ✗
Records Office, 171 Unversity Pkwy..
Aiken, SC 29801
(803) 648-6851
Approximately 110 college-level courses

University of South Dakota ♥
126 Center for Continuing Education
414 E. Clark
Vermillion, SD 57069

(605) 677-5281
Approximately 95 college-level courses

University of Southern Colorado ♥
Office of Continuing Education
2200 Bonforte Blvd.
Pueblo, CO 81001
(719) 549-2316
Nine college-level courses
One graduate course in education; all others in nursing

University of Southern Mississippi ♥
Department of Independent Study
P. O. Box 5056, Southern Station
Hattiesburg, MS 39406
(601) 266-4860
Approximately 90 college-level courses

University of Tennessee ♥ ★ ■
Extended Learning Ctr.
420 Communications Bldg.
Knoxville, TN 37996
(615) 974-5134
Approximately 180 college-level courses
Many noncredit courses in pharmacology, creative writing, Bible study

University of Texas ♥
Correspondence Study
Education Annex F38
P. O. Box 7700
Austin, TX 78713
(512) 471-5616
Approximately 100 college-level courses

University of Utah ♥
Continuing Education
1152 Annex Bldg.
Salt Lake City, UT 84112
(801) 581-6485
Approximately 140 college-level courses

University of Virginia ■
Distance Education
Charlottesville, VA 22903
(804) 924-0311
One graduate course, in teacher education

University of Washington ♥
University Extension—Distance Learning
GH-23, 5001 25th Ave. NE, Room 109
Seattle, WA 98195
(206) 543-2350
Approximately 130 college-level courses
Many foreign-language courses

University of Wisconsin ♥ ★ ■
Independent Study, 432 N. Lake St.
Madison, WI 53706
(608) 263-2055
Approximately 195 college-level courses
Many foreign-language courses

University of Wisconsin, Plattville ✗
Extension Program
One Pioneer Plaza
Plattville, WI 53818
(608) 342-1468
Approximately 40 college-level courses
Mainly business and accounting

University of Wyoming ♥ ■
Correspondence Study Department
Box 3294, University Station
Laramie, WY 82071
(307) 766-5631
Approximately 100 college-level courses

Utah State University ♥ ■
Independent Study
Eccles Conference Center
Logan, UT 84322
(801) 750-2131
Approximately 100 college-level courses
Graduate courses in business/management, liberal arts/general studies, teacher education

Virginia Polytechnic Institute ■
3333 Norris Hall
Blacksburg, VA 24061-0202
(703) 231-5458
One graduate course, in engineering

Washington State University ♥ ■
Independent Study
208 Van Doren Hall
Pullman, WA 99164
(509) 335-3557
Approximately 100 college-level courses

Weber State College
Continuing Education
3750 Harrison Blvd.
Ogden, UT 84408
(801) 626-6600
Approximately 60 college-level courses

Western Illinois University ◆
Independent Study Program
318 Sherman Hall
West Adams Road
Macomb, IL 61455

(309) 298-2496
Approximately 70 college-level courses

Western Michigan University ♦ ■
Self-Instructional Programs, Ellworth Hall
Room B-102, West Michigan Ave.
Kalamazoo, MI 49008
(616) 383-0788
Approximately 75 college-level courses
Graduate course in business/management

Western Oregon State College ✗
Division of Continuing Education
Monmouth, OR 97361
(503) 838-8483
Approximately 40 college-level courses
14 fire-service administration courses, 5 graduate
level courses

Western Washington University ♦
Independent Study, Old Main 400
Bellingham, WA 98225
(206) 676-3320
Approximately 40 college-level courses

SOME FOREIGN SCHOOLS THAT OFFER CORRESPONDENCE COURSES

Australia
Adelaide College of TAFE
20 Light Squaare
Adelaide 5000 Australia
Over 300 external courses

Charles Sturt University
Albury Wodonga Campus
P.O. Box 789
Albury NSW 2640 Australia
Parks & rec, park management, and more

Curtin University
GPO Box U 1987
Perth WA 6001 Australia

Deakin University
Off-Campus Operations
Geelong 3217 Australia

Edith Cowan University
External Studies Dept., P.O. Box 830
Claremont, Western Australia 6010
Library studies, justice administration, youth work

Engineering Education Australia
Eagle House, 118 Alfred Street

Milsons Point NSW 2061 Australia
Continuing education for professional engineers

Flinders University
The Admissions Office
P.O. Box 2100
Adelaide SA 5001 Australia
Humanities, sciences, nursing

Hobart Technical College
School of External Studies, 26 Bathurst Street
Hobart, Tasmania 7000 Australia
Administration, business, applied science

Ipswich College of TAFE
The Centre for Mineral Industries Studies
P.O. Box 138
Booval QLD Australia
Mining studies

James Cook University
The Admissions Officer
Townsville, Queensland 4811 Australia

Macquarie University
New South Wales 2109 Australia

Monash Distance Education Centre
Churchill, Victoria Australia 3842
Applied science, visual arts, engineering, health

Northern Territory University
NT External Studies Centre
Darwin NT 0811 Australia
Professional courses

Open Training and Education Network
199 Regent Street, Redfern
NSW 2016 Australia

Queensland University of Technology
Kelvin Grove Campus
Locked Bag 2
Red Hill, Queensland 4059 Australia
Education, computers, health fields

St. Johns College, External Studies
P.O. Box 817
Newcastle 2130 Australia
Anglican theology

University of Central Queensland
Distance Education Centre
Rockhampton M.C.
Queensland 4702 Australia
Continuing professional education

University of New South Wales
P.O. Box 1, Kensington NSW 2033 Australia
Sports medicine, business, and more

University of South Australia
Underdale Campus, External Studies
Holbrooks Rd.
Underdale, South Australia 5032

University of Western Sydney
The Registrar
Hawkesbury, Richmond
NSW 2753 Australia
Agricultural education, applied science

Victoria University of Technology
G.P.O. Box 2476V
Melbourne, Victoria 3001 Australia
Technical continuing education

Canada

Acadia University
Division of Continuing Education
Wolfville, NS B0P 1X0 Canada
Includes a graduate course in teacher education

Athabasca University
Student Services, Box 10000
Athabasca, Alberta, Canada T0G 2R0
Approximately 120 college-level courses

British Columbia Institute of Technology
Health Part-Time Studies
3700 Wilingdon Avenue
British Columbia, V5G 3H2 Canada
All levels of health-studies courses

Dalhousie University
The Registrar
Halifax, NS B3H 4HT, Canada
Business, marketing, law, and more

Mount Saint Vincent University
EMF Room 121, 166 Bedford Hwy.
Halifax, NS B3M 2J6 Canada
Courses in allied health, business, tourism and hospitality

University of Calgary
Distance Education/Off Campus Credit
2500 University Drive NW
Calgary, Alberta T2N 1N4 Canada
About 20 courses

University of Manitoba
Room 166 Continuing Education Complex
Winnipeg, Manitoba R3T 2N2 Canada
74 courses

University of New Brunswick
Extension and Summer Session
P.O. Box 4400
Frederickton, NB E3B 5A3 Canada
Includes graduate courses in business/management, nursing, teacher education

University of Toronto
School of Continuing Studies
Distance Learning
158 St. George Street
Toronto, Ont M5S 2V8 Canada
Many courses

University of Waterloo
Teaching Resources and
Continuing Education
Waterloo, Ont N2L 3G1 Canada
Many fields, including interdisciplinary studies

Wilfrid Laurier University
75 University Avenue West
Waterloo, Ont N2L 3C5 Canada
Music, arts, science, business

Chile

Universidad Austal de Chile
Programa de Educacion Continua
Independencia 641
Valdivia, Chile

Costa Rica

Universidad Estatal a Distancia
Apartado 474-2050 de Montes de Oca
San Jose, Costa Rica

Hungary

Euro-Contact
P.O. Box 433
H-1371 Budapest, Hungary
Management and business administration

Indonesia

Universitas Terbuka
P.O. Box 6666
Jakarta 10001 Indonesia
Programs for teachers

Jamaica

Eagle Foundation for Enterprise
30 Grenada Crescent
Kingston 5, Jamaica, West Indies
Business

Kenya
University of Nairobi
Institute of Adult and Distance Education
P.O. Box 30197, Nairobi, Kenya
Kenyan history, religious studies, and Kiswahili

Korea
Korea Air & Correspondence University
169 Dongsung-Dong, Chongro-Ku
Seoul 110-791, Korea
Courses in languages, arts, law, agriculture

Norway
Jysk Aabent Universitet
Niels Juels Gade 84
DK-8200 Aarhus N, Denmark

NKI
P.O. Box 111
1341 Bekkestua, Norway
More than 250 courses

Norsk Fjernundervisning
P.O. Box 8197 Dep
0034 Oslo 1, Norway
Environmental education

Panama
Universidad Interamericana de Educacion a
Distancia
Urbanizacion Obarrio
Calle 57 y Abe Bravo
Edificio Tolima, Panama
Many lifelong learning courses

Portugal
Universidade Aberta
Palacio Ceia, Rua da Escola Politecnica 147
1200 Lisbon, Portugal
Teacher training, languages, and literature

Pakistan
Allama Iqbal Open University
Sector H-8, Islamabad, Pakistan
Mainly education

Sri Lanka
Open University of Sri Lanka
P.O. Box 21
Nawqala, Nugegoda Sri Lanka

Thailand
Sukhothai Thammathirat Open University
Bangpod, Pakkredl
Nonthaburi 11120 Thailand
Many fields

Vietnam
Vietnam National Institute of Open Learning
Vien Dao Tao Mo Rong
Nha B-101
Phuong Bach Koa
Quan Hai Ba Trung Hanoi, Vietnam
Mainly vocational and language courses

South Africa
Damelin Correspondence College
Damelin Center
Corner Plein & Hoekl Sts.
Johannesburg 2001 South Africa
*A wide range of high-school-level and professional
courses*

Promat Correspondence College
P.O. Box 95775, Waterkloof 0145
Weavind Park 0184
Pretoria, South Africa

University of Cape Town
School of Education
Rondesboch 7700, South Africa
Primary education for working teachers

Sweden
University of Umea
901-87 Umea, Sweden
More than 150 courses

Tanzania
University of Dar Es Salaam
Institute of Adult Education
P.O. Box 20679
Dar Es Salaam, Tanzania
African history, Kiswahili, national development

Zimbabwe
Zimbabwe Distance Education College
Moffat Street/Albion Road
P.O. Box 316
Harare, Zimbabwe
Management, administration, agriculture courses

*Recognized accrediting agencies can be a
powerful force in combating phony schools.*

♦12♦
Credit for Life Experience Learning

Experience is the name everyone gives to their mistakes.
OSCAR WILDE

The philosophy behind credit for life experience learning can be expressed very simply: Academic credit is given for what you know, without regard for how, when, or where the learning was acquired.

Consider a simple example: Quite a few colleges and universities offer credit for courses in typewriting. For instance, at Western Illinois University, Business Education 261 is a basic typing class. Anyone who takes and passes that class is given three units of credit.

An advocate of credit for life experience learning would say: "If you know how to type, regardless of how and where you learned, even if you taught yourself at the age of nine, you should still get those same three units of credit, once you demonstrate that you have the same skill level as a person who passes Business Education 261."

Of course not all learning can be converted into college credit. But many people are surprised to discover how much of what they already know is, in fact, creditworthy. With thousands of colleges offering hundreds of thousands of courses, it is a rare subject indeed that someone hasn't determined to be worthy of some credit. There is no guarantee that a given school will honor a given learning experience, or even accept another school's assessment for transfer purposes. Yale might not accept typing credit. But then again, the course title often sounds much more academic than the learning experience itself, as in "Business Education" for typing, "Cross-Cultural Communication" for a trip to China, or "Fundamentals of Physical Education" for golf lessons.

Here are eight major types of life experience that may be worth college credit, especially in nontraditional degree-granting programs:

1. Work. Many of the skills acquired in paid employment are also skills that are taught in colleges and universities. These include, for instance, typing, filing, shorthand, accounting, inventory control, financial management, map reading, military strategy, welding, computer programming or operating, editing, planning, sales, real estate appraisals, and literally thousands of other things.

2. Homemaking. Home maintenance, household planning and budgeting, child reaing, child psychology, education, interpersonal communication, meal planning and nutrition, gourmet cooking, and much more.

3. Volunteer work. Community activities, political campaigns, church activities, service organizations, volunteer work in social service agencies or hospitals, and so forth.

4. Noncredit learning in formal settings. Company training courses, in-service teacher training, workshops, clinics, conferences and conventions, lectures, courses on radio or television, noncredit correspondence courses, etc.

5. Travel. Study tours (organized or informal), significant vacation and business trips, living for periods in other countries or cultures, participating in activities related to other cultures or subcultures.

6. Recreational activities and hobbies. Musical skills, aviation training and skills, acting or other work in a community theater, sports, arts and crafts, fiction and nonfiction writing, public speaking, gardening, visiting museums, designing and making clothing, attending plays, concerts, and movies, and many other leisure-time activities.

7. Reading, viewing, listening. This may cover any field in which a person has done extensive or intensive reading and study, and for which college credit has not been granted. This category has, for instance, included viewing various series on public television.

8. Discussions with experts. A great deal of learning can come from talking to, listening to, and working with experts, whether in ancient history, carpentry, or theology. Significant, extensive, or intensive meetings with such people may also be worth credit.

THE MOST COMMON ERROR MOST PEOPLE MAKE

The most common error most people make when thinking about getting credit for life experience is confusing *time spent* with *learning*. Being a regular churchgoer for 30 years is not worth any college credit in and of itself. But the regular churchgoer who can document that he or she has prepared for and taught Sunday school classes, worked with youth groups, participated in leadership programs, organized fund-raising drives, studied Latin or Greek, taken tours to the Holy Land, or even engaged in lengthy philosophical discussions with a clergyman, is likely to get credit for those experiences. Selling insurance for 20 years is worth no credit—unless you describe and document the learning that took place in areas of marketing, banking, risk management, entrepreneurial studies, etc.

It is crucial that the experiences can be documented to a school's satisfaction. Two people could work side by side in the same laboratory for five years. One might do little more than follow instructions—running routine experiments, setting up and dismantling apparatus, and then heading home. The other, with the same job title, might do extensive reading in the background of the work being done, get into discussions with supervisors, make plans and recommendations for other ways of doing the work, propose or design new kinds of apparatus, or develop hypotheses on why the results were turning out the way they were.

It is not enough just to say what you did, or to submit a short resumé. The details and specifics must be documented. The two most common ways this is done are by preparing a life experience portfolio (essentially a long, well-documented, annotated resumé), or by taking an equivalency examination to demonstrate knowledge gained.

PRESENTING YOUR LEARNING

Most schools that give credit for life experience learning require that the student make a formal presentation, usually in the form of a life experience portfolio. Each school has its own standards for the form and content of such a portfolio, and many, in fact, offer either guidelines or courses (some for credit, some not) to help the nontraditional student prepare the portfolio.

Several books on this subject have been published by the Council for Adult and Experiential Learning. For a list of current publications, contact CAEL, 243 Wabash Ave., Chicago, IL 60606, (312) 922-5909.

CAEL also offers sample portfolios: $65 for introductory materials plus four large sample portfolios, or $80 for nine portfolios, representing seven schools. It may be worth trying to convince a local public or community college library to acquire these materials.

A man who had considerable success gaining upper division credit for his own experiential learning now publishes a guidebook and offers a personal consulting service in this area. Information is available from William Kemble, National College Studies, Student Assistance Division, Dept. BG1, 675 Blue Mountain Rd., Saugerties, NY 12477, phone (914) 246-0801.

The following list should help to get you thinking about the possibilities, by presenting a sampling of some 24 other means by which people have documented life experience learning, sometimes as part of a portfolio, sometimes not:

- official commendations
- audiotapes
- slides
- course outlines
- bills of sale
- exhibitions
- programs of recitals and performances
- videotapes
- awards and honors
- mementos
- copies of speeches made
- licenses (pilot, real estate, etc.).
- certificates
- testimonials and endorsements
- interviews with others
- newspaper articles
- official job descriptions
- copies of exams taken
- military records
- samples of arts or crafts made
- samples of writing
- designs and blueprints
- works of art
- films and photographs

HOW LIFE EXPERIENCE LEARNING IS TURNED INTO ACADEMIC CREDIT

It isn't easy. In a perfect world, there would be universally accepted standards, and it would be as easy to measure the credit value in a seminar on refrigeration engineering as it is to measure the temperature inside a refrigerator. Some schools and national organizations *are* striving to create extensive "menus" of nontraditional experiences, to insure that anyone doing the same thing would get the same credit.

There continues to be progress in this direction. Many schools have come to agree, for instance, on aviation experience: a private pilot's license is worth four semester units, an instrument rating is worth six additional units, and so forth.

The American Council on Education, a private organization, regularly publishes a massive multivolume set of books, in two series: *The National Guide to Educational Credit for Training Programs* and *Guide to the Evaluation of Educational Experiences in the Armed Forces* (see Bibliography for details), which many schools use to assign credit directly; others use them as guidelines in doing their own evaluations. A few examples will demonstrate the sort of thing that is done:

A nine-day Red Cross training course called The Art of Helping is evaluated as worth two semester hours of social work.

The John Hancock Mutual Life Insurance Company's internal course in technical skills for managers is worth three semester hours of business administration.

Portland Cement Company's five-day training program in kiln optimization, whatever that may be, is worth one semester hour.

The Professional Insurance Agents' three-week course in basic insurance is worth six semester units: three in principles of insurance and three in property and liability contract analysis.

The U.S. Army's 27-week course in ground surveillance radar repair is worth 15 semester hours: 10 in electronics and five more in electrical laboratory.

The Army's legal-clerk training course can be worth 24 semester hours, including three in English, three in business law, three in management, etc.

There are hundreds of additional business and military courses that have been evaluated already, and thousands more that will be worth credit for those who have taken them, whether or not they appear in these A.C.E. volumes.

THE CONTROVERSY OVER GRADUATE CREDIT FOR LIFE EXPERIENCE LEARNING

As Norman Somers writes, "Powerful forces in graduate education have declared the granting of credit for prematriculation experiences anathema. Many professors and graduate deans have spoken out against the assessment of learning experiences which have occurred prior to a student's formal enrollment."

The policy of the Council of Graduate Schools is that "no graduate credit should be granted for experiential learning that occurs prior to the student's matriculation." It should, they insist, be given "only when a graduate faculty and dean of an accredited institution have had the opportunity to plan the experience, to establish its goals, and to monitor the time, effort and the learning that has taken place."

In other words, if I enroll in a school and then study and master advanced statistical techniques, they should give me, say, nine units of credit. But if, say, I learned those techniques during 20 years on the job as chief stat-

istician for the Bureau of the Census, no credit should be given.

Fortunately, many schools and organizations, including the influential American Council on Education, disagree with this policy. Their guidelines, described earlier, regularly include recommendations for graduate credit, based on "independent study, original research, critical analysis, and the scholarly and professional application of the specialized knowledge or discipline."

SOME INSPIRATION

There are always some people who say, "Oh, I haven't ever done anything worthy of college credit." We have yet to meet anyone with an IQ higher than room temperature who has not done at least some creditworthy things. Often it's just a matter of presenting them properly, in a portfolio. Just to inspire you, then, here is a list of 100 things that *could* be worth credit for life experience learning. The list could easily be 10 or 100 times as long. Please note the "could." Some reviewers in the past have made fun of this list, suggesting that we were saying you can earn a degree for buying Persian rugs. Not so. We suggest, for instance, that a person who made a high-level study of Persian art and culture, preparatory to buying carpets, and who could document the reading, consultations, time spent, sources, etc., could probably earn some portfolio credit for this out-of-classroom endeavor. Here, then, the list:

Playing tennis
Preparing for natural childbirth
Leading a church group
Taking a body-building class
Speaking French
Selling real estate
Studying gourmet cooking
Reading War and Peace
Building model airplanes
Traveling through Belgium
Learning shorthand
Starting a small business
Navigating a small boat
Writing a book
Buying a Persian carpet
Watching public television
Decorating a home or office
Attending a convention
Being a summer-camp counselor
Studying Spanish
Bicycling across Greece
Interviewing senior citizens
Living in another culture
Writing advertisements
Throwing a pot
Repairing a car
Performing magic
Attending art films

83

Welding and soldering
Designing and weaving a rug
Negotiating a contract
Editing a manuscript
Planning a trip
Steering a ship
Appraising an antique
Writing a speech
Studying first aid or CPR
Organizing aCanadian union
Researching international laws
Listening to Shakespeare's plays on tape
Designing a playground
Planning a garden
Devising a marketing strategy
Reading the newspaper
Designing a home
Attending a seminar
Playing the piano
Studying a new religion
Reading about the Civil War
Taking ballet lessons
Helping a dyslexic child
Riding a horse
Pressing flowers
Keeping tropical fish
Writing press releases
Writing for the local newspaper
Running the PTA
Acting in little theater
Flying an airplane
Designing a quilt
Taking photographs
Building a table
Developing an inventory system
Programming a home computer

Helping in a political campaign
Playing a musical instrument
Painting a picture
Playing political board games
Serving on a jury
Volunteering at the hospital
Visiting a museum
Attending a great books group
Designing and sewing clothes
Playing golf
Having intensive talks with a doctor
Teaching the banjo
Reading the Bible
Leading a platoon
Learning Braille
Operating a printing press
Eating in an exotic restaurant
Running a store
Planning a balanced diet
Reading *All and Everything*
Learning sign language
Teaching Sunday school
Training an apprentice
Being an apprentice
Hooking a rug
Learning yoga
Laying bricks
Making a speech
Being Dungeonmaster
Negotiating a merger
Developing film
Learning calligraphy
Applying statistics to gambling
Doing circle dancing
Taking care of sick animals
Reading this book

HE STUDIED LAW AT HOME
AND WROTE HIS LESSONS ON
THE BACK OF A SHOVEL.
NOW HE'S ON THE $5 BILL.
A PUBLIC SERVICE MESSAGE FROM
THE ACME SHOVEL COMPANY

♦ 13 ♦
Credit by Learning Contract

An oral agreement isn't worth the paper it's written on.
SAMUEL GOLDWYN

A mainstay of many nontraditional degree programs is the learning contract, also known as a study plan, study contract, degree plan, etc. It is essentially a formal agreement between the student and the school, setting forth a plan of study the student intends to undertake, goals he or she wishes to reach, and the action to be taken by the school once the goals are reached—normally the granting either of a certain amount of credit or of a degree.

A well-written learning contract is good for both student and school, since it reduces greatly the chances of misunderstandings or problems after the student has done a great deal of work, and the inevitable distress that accompanies such an event.

Many counseling clients have been distressed, even devastated, to discover that some project on which they had been working for many months was really not what their faculty advisor or school had in mind, and so they would be getting little or no credit for it.

Indeed, one of the authors had a similar sort of experience. After John had worked for nearly two years on his Doctorate at Michigan State University, one key member of his faculty guidance committee suddenly died, and a second transferred to another school. No one else on the faculty seemed interested in working with him, and without a binding agreement of any sort, there was no way he could make things happen. He simply dropped out. (Three years later, a new department head invited him back to finish the degree, and he did so. But a lot of anguish could have been avoided if he had had a contract with the school.)

A learning contract is legally binding for both the student and the school. If the student does the work called for, then the school must award the predetermined number of credits. In case of disputes arising from such a contract, there are usually clauses calling for binding arbitration by an impartial third party.

Looking at examples of a simple, and then a somewhat more complex, learning contract should make clear how this concept works.

A SIMPLE LEARNING CONTRACT

The Background
In the course of discussing the work to be done for a Bachelor's degree, the student and her faculty advisor agree that it would be desirable for the student to learn to read in German. Rather than take formal courses, the student says that she prefers to study the language on her own, with the help of an uncle who speaks the language. If the student had taken four semesters of German at a traditional school, she would have earned 20 semester hours of credit. So the learning contract might consist of these eight simple clauses:

The Contract
1. Student intends to learn to read German at the level of a typical student who has completed four semesters of college-level German.

2. Student will demonstrate this knowledge by translating a 1000-word passage from one of the novels of Erich Maria Remarque.

3. The book and passage will be selected and the translation evaluated by a member of the German faculty of the college.

4. The student will have three hours to complete the translation, with the assistance of a standard German-English dictionary.

5. If the student achieves a score of 85% or higher in the evaluation, then the college will immediately award 20 semester hours of credit in German.

6. If the student scores below 85%, she may try again at 60-day intervals.

7. The fee for the first evaluation will be $100, and, if necessary, $50 for each additional evaluation.

8. If any dispute shall arise over the interpretation of this contract, an attempt will be made to resolve the dispute by mediation. If mediation fails, the dispute will be settled by binding arbitration. An arbitrator shall be chosen jointly by the student and the school. If they cannot agree in choosing an arbitrator, then each party will choose one. If the two arbitrators cannot agree, they shall jointly

appoint a third, and the majority decision of this panel of three shall be final and binding. The costs of arbitration shall be shared equally by the two parties.

This contract has the four basic elements common to any learning contract:
1. The student's objectives or goals.
2. The methods by which these goals are to be reached.
3. The method of evaluation of the performance.
4. What to do in case of problems or disagreement.

The more precisely each of these items can be defined, the less likelihood of problems later. For instance, instead of simply saying, "The student will become proficient in German," the foregoing agreement defines clearly what "proficient" means.

A MORE COMPLEX LEARNING CONTRACT

What follows is an abridgement of a longer learning contract, freely adapted from some of the case histories provided in a catalog from the late, lamented Beacon College.

Goals

At the end of my Master's program, I plan to have the skills, experience, and theoretical knowledge to work with an organization in the role of director or consultant, and to help the organization set and reach its goals; to work with individuals or small groups as a counselor, providing a supportive or therapeutic environment in which to grow and learn.

I want to acquire a good understanding of and grounding in group dynamics, how children learn, and why people come together to grow, learn, and work.

I am especially interested in alternative organizations. I want to have the skills to help organizations analyze their financial needs, and to locate and best utilize appropriate funding.

Methods

◆ Theory and Skill Development (40% of work)

I shall take the following three courses at Redwood Community College [courses listed and described] = 20% of program.

After reading the following four books [list of books], and others that may be suggested by my faculty advisor, I shall prepare statements of my personal philosophy of education and growth, as a demonstration of my understanding of the needs of a self-directed, responsible, caring human = 10% of program.

I shall attend a six-lesson workshop on power dynamics and assertiveness, given by [details of the workshop] = 10% of program.

◆ Leadership and Management Practicum (30% of work)

I shall work with the Cooperative Nursery School to attempt to put into practice the things I have learned in the first phase of my studies, in the following way: [much detail here]. Documentation shall be through a journal of my work, a log of all meetings, a self-assessment of my performance, and commentary supplied by an outside evaluator = 15% of program.

I shall donate eight hours a week for 20 weeks to the Women's Crisis Center, again endeavoring to put into practice the ideas which I have learned [much detail here on expectations and kinds of anticipated activities] = 15% of program.

◆ Organizational Development, Analysis, and Design (30% of work)

I shall study one of the above two groups (nursery school or crisis center) in great detail, and prepare an analysis and projection for the future of this organization, including recommendations for funding, management, and development = 20% of program.

Documentation will be in the form of a long paper detailing my findings and recommendations and relating them to my philosophy of growth and organization development. This paper will be read and evaluated by [name of persons or committee] = 10% of program.

Outcome

Upon completion of all of the above, the college will award the degree of Master of Arts in organization development. [Arbitration clause.]

Learning contracts are truly negotiable. There is no right or wrong, no black or white. Someone who is good at negotiating might well get more credit for the same amount of work, or the same degree for a lesser amount of work, than a less skillful negotiator.

Some schools will enter into a learning contract that covers the entire degree program, as in the second example. Others prefer to have separate contracts, each one covering a small portion of the program: one for the language requirement, one for science, one for humanities, one for the thesis, and so forth.

It is uncommon, but not unheard of, to seek legal advice when preparing or evaluating a learning contract, especially for a long or complex one covering an entire Master's or doctoral program. A lawyer will likely say, "It is better to invest a small amount of money in my time now, rather than get into an expensive and protracted battle later, because of an unclear agreement." Dozens of colleges and universities are sued every year by students who claim that credits or degrees were wrongfully withheld from them. Many of these suits could have been avoided by the use of well-drawn learning contracts.

◆14◆
Credit for Foreign Academic Experience

How much a dunce that has been sent to roam
Excels a dunce that has been kept at home.

WILLIAM COWPER

There are many thousands of universities, colleges, technical schools, institutes, and vocational schools all over the world offering courses that are at least the equivalent of work at American universities. In principle, most universities are willing to give credit for work done at schools in other countries.

But can you imagine the task of an admissions officer faced with the student who presents an Advanced Diploma from the Wysza Szkola Inzynierska in Poland, or the degree of Gakushi from the Matsuyama Shoka Daigaku in Japan? Are these equivalent to a high-school diploma, a Doctorate, or something in between?

Until 1974, the U.S. Office of Education helped by evaluating educational credentials earned outside the United States and translating them into approximately comparable levels of U.S. achievement. This service is no longer available, as the government has chosen, instead, to suggest some private nonprofit organizations that perform such evaluations.

It is important to note that these organizations are neither endorsed, licensed, nor recommended by the U.S. government, nor is there any regulation of them. The various organizations would appear to have very different ways of going about their work, often yielding quite different results. For instance, the external Master's degree of a large old Royal Chartered British university was evaluated as the exact equivalent of a U.S. regionally accredited Master's degree by three agencies and as not even at the level of an American Bachelor's degree by a fourth.

These organizations are used mostly by the schools themselves, to evaluate applicants from abroad or with foreign credentials, but individuals may deal with them directly, at relatively low cost. Many schools accept the recommendations of these services, but others will not. Some schools do their own foreign evaluations.

It may be wise, therefore, to determine whether a school or schools in which you have interest will accept the recommendations of such services before you invest in them. Depending on the complexity of the evaluation, the cost runs from $60 to $150. Some of the services are willing to deal with non-school-based experiential learning as well. The services operate quickly. Less than two weeks for an evaluation is not unusual.

Typical evaluation reports give the exact U.S. equivalents of non-U.S. work, both in terms of semester units earned, and of any degrees or certificates earned. For instance, they would report that the Japanese degree of Gakushi is almost exactly equivalent to the American Bachelor's degree.

Given the significant differences in the opinions of these services, if one report seems inappropriate or incorrect, it might be wise to seek a second (and even third) opinion.

Organizations performing these services include, in alphabetical order:

Educational Credential Evaluators, Inc.
P.O. Box 17499
Milwaukee, WI 53217   (414) 289-3400

Education Evaluators International, Inc.
P. O. Box 5397
Los Alamitos, CA 90721   (310) 431-2187

International Consultants of Delaware, Inc.
914 Pickett Lane
Newark, DE 19711   (302) 737-8715

International Credentialing Associates, Inc.
150 2nd Avenue N,
Suite 1600
St. Petersburg, FL 33707   (813) 821-8852

International Education Research Foundation
P. O. Box 66940
Los Angeles, CA 90066   (310) 390-6276

International Transcript Evaluation Division
C.E.I.E. Specs.
10 Legend Lane
Houston, TX 77024   (713) 464-6753

Joseph Silmy & Associates, Inc.
P.O. Box 248233
Coral Gables, FL 33124   (305) 666-0233

World Education Services
P. O. Box 745

Old Chelsea Station
New York, NY 10011   (212) 966-6311

For those interested in educational equivalents for one particular country, there is the world education series of books or monographs published by AACRAO, the American Association of Collegiate Registrars and Admissions Officers (One Dupont Circle NW, Suite 330, Washington, DC 20036). Each publication in this series describes the higher education system in a given country, and offers advice and recommendations on how to deal with their credits.

The problem with these AACRAO reports is that they are issued with such low frequency that many of them are way out of date, and of minimal usefulness.

In the early 1990s, the Australians (whose higher education system is similar to that of the US and Canada) attempted to deal with this problem by commissioning the researching and writing of comparative monographs on the educational equivalency of 83 countries, all at the same time. The monographs are published by the Australian Government Publishing Service, GPO Box 84, Canberra ACT 2601, Australia. (John did the initial research and writing for 15 of these monographs.)

*"Well, it's not too much fun, but they said I'd get my
diploma if I can keep this up for another two hours."*

◆ 15 ◆
The Credit Bank Service

We give no credit to a liar,
even when he speaks the truth.
CICERO

A lot of people have very complicated educational histories. They may have taken classes at several different universities and colleges, taken some evening or summer-school classes, perhaps some company-sponsored seminars, some military training classes, and possibly had a whole raft of other informal learning experiences. They may have credits or degrees from schools that have gone out of business, or whose records were destroyed by war or fire. When it comes time to present a cohesive educational past, it may mean assembling dozens of diverse transcripts, certificates, diplomas, job descriptions, and the like, often into a rather large and unwieldy package.

There is, happily, an ideal solution to this problem: the Regents Credit Bank, operated by the enlightened Department of Education of the State of New York, and available to people anywhere in the world.

The Regents Credit Bank is an evaluation and transcript service for people who wish to consolidate their academic records, perhaps adding credit for non-academic career and learning experiences (primarily through equivalency examinations). The Credit Bank issues a single widely accepted transcript on which all credit is listed in a simple, straightforward, and comprehensible form.

The Credit Bank works like a money bank, except that you deposit academic credits, as they are earned, whether through local courses, correspondence courses, equivalency exams, and so forth. There are seven basic categories of learning experience that can qualify to be "deposited" in a Credit Bank account, and of course various elements of these seven can be combined as well:

1. College courses taken either in residence or by correspondence from regionally accredited schools in the U.S., or their equivalent in other countries.

2. Scores earned on a wide range of equivalency tests, both civilian and military.

3. Military service schools and military occupational specialties that have been evaluated for credit by the American Council on Education.

4. Workplace-based learning experiences, such as company courses, seminars, or in-house training from many large and smaller corporations, evaluated by the American Council on Education or the New York National Program on Noncollegiate Sponsored Instruction.

5. Pilot training licenses and certificates issued by the Federal Aviation Administration.

6. Approved nursing performance examinations.

7. Special assessment of knowledge gained from experience or independent study.

The first six categories have predetermined amounts of credit. The CLEP basic science exam will always be worth six semester units. Fluency in Spanish will always be worth 24 semester units. Xerox Corporation's course in repairing the 9400 copier will always be worth two semester units. The army course in becoming a bandleader will always be worth 12 semester units. And so forth, for thousands of already evaluated nonschool learning experiences.

The seventh category can be extremely flexible and variable. Special assessment is a means of earning credit for things learned in the course of ordinary living or job experience. The Credit Bank assesses this learning by appointing a panel of two or more experts in the field. Except in rare cases, it is necessary to go to Albany, New York, to meet with this panel.

The panel may wish to conduct an oral, written, or, in the case of performers, performance examination. They may wish to inspect a portfolio of writing, art, or some other sort of documentation. Following the evaluation, whatever form it may take, the panel makes its recommendations for the amount of credit to be given. This has, in practice, ranged from zero to more than 80 semester units, although the typical range for each separate assessment is probably from 15 to 30 credits.

The Credit Bank has, for example, conducted special assessments in journalism, ceramics, Hebrew language, electronics engineering, aircraft repair and maintenance, and Japanese culture studies, among many others.

There is a $480 fee to set up a Credit Bank account, which includes evaluation of prior work (except special assessments), and one year of update service. After the first year, there is a $90 fee each time a new "deposit" is made.

Work that is, for whatever reason, deemed not creditworthy may still be listed on the transcript as "noncredit work." Further, the Credit Bank will only list those traditional courses from other schools that the depositor wishes included. Thus any previous academic failures, low grades, or other embarrassments may be omitted from the Credit Bank report.

Students who enroll in the Regents College of the University of the State of New York automatically get Credit Bank service, and do not need to enroll separately.

The address is Regents Credit Bank, Regents College, University of the State of New York, 7 Columbia Circle, Albany, NY 12203, (518) 474-3703.

♦16♦

Accredited Schools with Nonresident Programs

Education is hanging around until you've caught on.
ROBERT FROST

The schools that follow offer Bachelor's, Master's, and/or doctoral programs that are accredited by one of the recognized accrediting agencies and which require no residency whatsoever. Chapters 17 and 18 describe the short-residency schools, and those requiring that one live reasonably near the campus. Unaccredited schools, or those accredited by unrecognized agencies, are described in chapters 19-21. Programs on which we had insufficient information are listed in Chapter 29.

The basic format of each listing is as follows:

Name of School   **Bachelor's, Master's,**
Address   **Doctorate, Law, Dip**loma
City, State Zip Country
Contact name

Fields of study offered
Year established
Legal/ownership status (nonprofit or proprietary, independent, or state- or church-run), Tuition

Phone, toll-free phone (if any)
Fax

Key to tuition codes:
$ = free or very low cost
$$ = inexpensive
$$$ = average
$$$$ = expensive
$$$$$ = very expensive

(As costs change so quickly, it would be foolish to give dollar amounts. If no symbol is given, it's safe to assume that the school did not provide us with this information.)

American Military University   **M**
9104P Manawssas Drive
Manassas, VA 22110
John E. Jessup, Ph.D., Academic Dean
Military studies
1994
$$$
(703) 330-5398
(703) 330-5109 fax
New school offering a totally nonresident Master of Arts in Military Science. Shortly after they began offering degrees, AMU was awarded accreditation from the Distance Education and Training Council (formerly the National Home Study Council). At presstime they were still awaiting state authorized status from the state of Virginia. A maximum of 15 (of the 36 required) credit-hours can come from some combination of transfer credits, ACE-approved military training, and life experience learning.

Arizona State University   **M**
Distance Learning Technology
Tempe, AZ 85287
Elizabeth Craft, Director
Engineering
1885
Nonprofit, state $$$
(602) 965-6738
(602) 965-1371 fax
Arizona State's distance learning program offers an M.S. in engineering wholly through cable, public television, and ITFS televised courses that can be viewed at two public sites and 21 corporate locations in the Tempe area, as well as a large number of courses in other subjects available by cable, public television, and/or ITFS nationwide, via the National Technological University.

Arts and Sciences University   **B**
Department of University Correspondence Courses
Rangoon, Myanmar
Many fields

1920
Nonprofit, state
Auto 31144
More than 25,000 students are enrolled in this, the only nontraditional university in Myanmar (formerly Burma). Bachelor of Arts, Science, Economics, or Law can be earned entirely through correspondence study, plus passing necessary examinations. Some courses are also given through radio lectures.

Athabasca University   B, M
Box 10,000
Athabasca, AB T0G 2R0 Canada
Michael Neville
Many fields
1970
Nonprofit, independent $$
(403) 675-6168
An open distance-education institution serving more than 10,000 students across Canada and, as the result of a recent policy change, the United States and Mexico as well. Bachelor's degrees in administration, arts, general studies, English, history, sociology/anthropology, psychology, Canadian studies, information systems, and French. All distance-education courses are offered through sophisticated home-study packages. Students set up their own study schedules and work at their own pace. There are eight degree programs: Bachelor of Administration, Bachelor of Arts, Bachelor of Commerce, Bachelor of General Studies, Bachelor of Nursing, Bachelor of Science, an M.B.A. program, which costs nearly $20,000 (Canadian) and requires several short visits to the campus, and a new Master of Distance Education, in which much of the instruction and interaction occurs by modem. All students are assigned a telephone tutor to whom they have toll-free access. Some courses are supplemented by radio and television programs, audio- and videocassettes, seminars, laboratories, or teleconference sessions.

Auburn University   M
Graduate Outreach Program, 202 Ramsay Hall
Auburn, AL 36849
Tracy Dowdy, Outreach Program Coordinator
Business, engineering (8 areas)
1856
Nonprofit, state $$$$
(334) 844-5300
(334) 844-2519 fax
Auburn offers an almost totally nonresident M.B.A. and Master of Engineering in a range of fields, including aerospace, chemical, civil/environmental, electrical, computer science, materials, mechanical and industrial engineering. Graduate courses are taped in on-campus classrooms and mailed to distance students, who must keep the same pace as resident students. Limited credit available for life-experience learning. The M.B.A. requires 3 to 5 days on campus for an oral exam; the engineering degrees require one day for oral exams. Students must be within a 3-day delivery range, and currently live in 38 states.

Ball State University   M
Muncie, IN 47306
Thomas Bilger, Registrar
Education, business administration
1918
Nonprofit, state $$
(317) 289-1241
Master of Education program, including a special program in psychometrics, can be completed entirely through evening study. M.B.A. can be completed through satellite TV courses in cooperating workplaces. The phone number for the M.B.A. program is (317) 285-1931; the contact person is Tamara Estep.

Bemidji State University   B
Center for Extended Learning, Deputy Hall 110
Bemidji, MN 56601
Lorraine F. Cecil
English, history, vocational education, social studies, criminal justice
1913
Nonprofit, state $$
(218) 755-3924
(218) 755-4048 fax
Some credit for life experience and prior learning may be applied toward the degree requirements. New credit is earned through on-campus classes, extension classes in other cities, and independent guided home study. Learning packages (a syllabus, books, and sometimes audio- or videocassettes) are provided. Continued contact with B.S.U. is maintained in a variety of ways: by mail, telephone, exchange of cassettes, and conferences with academic advisors. As the Coordinator of External Studies put it, "Unique solutions exist for unique situations."

Berean College   B
1445 Boonville Ave.
Springfield, MO 65802
Zenas J. Bicket
Bible and theology studies
1985
Nonprofit, independent $$
(417) 862-2781
(417) 862-8558 fax
Accredited by the Distance Education and Training Council, a recognized agency. All courses can be completed by correspondence, and qualified students can also earn credit by examination and for certain types of life experience. Primarily for religious workers (clergy, missionaries). Many of Berean's correspondence courses are available in Spanish.

Board of Governors B.A. Degree Program   B
200 Hilton Plaza
700 E. Adams
Springfield, IL 62701
Many fields
Nonprofit, state $$$
(217) 782-6392
(217 524-7741 fax
Totally nonresident B.A. in a number of fields offered through the Illinois Board of Governors State Universities program, which includes Chicago State, Eastern Illinois, Governors State, Northeastern Illinois, and Western Illinois. Up to 105 credits may be awarded for transfer courses, military and other life-experience learning, and ACT, CLEP, DANTES and departmental exams. Home-study courses offered by correspondence, television, audio- and videocassette, newspaper, and e-mail, and independent study.

Boise State University   M
1910 University Drive
Boise, ID 83725
Joann Fenner
Instructional and performance technology
1932
Nonprofit, state $$
(208) 385-1312, (800) 824-7017, ext. 1312
In Idaho: (800) 632-6586, ext. 1312
(208) 385-1856 fax
Totally nonresident M.S. in instructional and performance technology (the study of human performance problems in various business and industry settings), offered via real-time computer conferencing courses. Applicants must have access to a compatible computer and modem for at least two hours a day, five days a week, and preferably a fax machine as well.

Brandon University   B, M
270 18th St.
Brandon, MB R7A 6A9 Canada
D. Bower, Dean of Students
Education, general studies, arts, science, music, nursing, mental health
1880
Nonprofit, independent $$$
(204) 728-9520
(204) 726-0210 fax
Brandon offers the Bachelor of Education and General Studies, B.A., B.S., Bachelor of Music, and Master of Music through evening, spring, and summer programs. Its Northern Teacher Education Programme is offered in seven residential centers, and also makes use of "traveling professors," who fly in regularly to remote communities in order to offer courses and advice. Many of Brandon's students are descended from the native peoples of the region.

British Columbia Open University
See: Open Learning Agency

California Institute of Asian Studies
See: California Institute of Integral Studies

California Institute of Integral Studies   B, M, D
765 Ashbury
San Francisco, CA 94117
John Axtell
Many fields
1968
Nonprofit, independent $$$
(415) 753-6100
(415) 753-1169 fax
Master's degrees are offered in business, drama therapy, East-West psychology, integral counseling psychology, integral health education , organizational development & transformation, philosophy and religion, social and cultural anthropology, somatics, and women's spirituality. The Ph.D. is available in integral studies, East-West psychology, and philosophy & religion, and social and cultural anthropology. Psy.D. is available in clinical psychology. Most programs involve a combination of intellectual study, personal experience of psycho-spiritual growth processes, and practical fieldwork in counseling, community service, teaching, or creative independent study. Also offers a B.A. completion program geared to working adults who need up to 45 credits to finish their degree. Formerly California Institute of Asian Studies.

California State University, Chico   B, M
Center for Regional and Continuing Education
Chico, CA 95929-0250
Leslie J. Wright, Associate Dean
Computer science, environmental planning, public administration, social science, and California studies
1887
Nonprofit, state $$$$
(916) 898-6105
(916) 898-4020 fax
Chico State offers short-residency and non-resident degrees. There is a B.A. in environmental planning, public administration, and social science; M.A. in California studies, environmental planning, and social science, and the Master of Public Administration, all with elements of independent study and credit for prior learning. In addition, both a B.S. and an M.S. in computer science are offered to corporate subscribers across the nation, entirely through interactive satellite TV. Individulas cannot participate in these latter programs without workplace sponsorship.

California State University, Dominguez Hills   M
SAC, Room 2126
1000 E. Victoria St.
Carson, CA 90747
Arthur L. Harshman
1960
Nonprofit, state $$
(310) 516-3743
(310) 516-3449 fax
Domingeuz Hills's External Degree Program in Humanities offers a nonresidential Master of Arts in history, literature, philosophy, music, theater arts/film, and art. The program is offered by "parallel instruction." Nonresidential students do all the work that residential students do, in the same general time frame, but do not attend classes. Total of 30 semester hours for the degree. Eighty percent must be earned after enrolling. Credit for independent study projects, correspondence courses, and a thesis or a creative project. Communication with faculty by mail and telephone. A full-time student can finish in one academic year. (This is a rare opportunity to earn an accredited Master's degree non-residentially. We are biased. Marina Bear completed her M.A. here in 1985, and is a testimonial to the program.) The M.S. in quality assurance requires 33 semester hours, with attendance at various business locations in southern California. The total cost is $4400. Contact person for quality assurance: Eugene Watson.

California State University, Los Angeles   B
Department of Technology
5151 State University Drive
Los Angeles, CA 90032
Chief Ray Shackelford, Advisor
Fire protection administration
1947
Nonprofit, state $$$
(213) 343-4550
Bachelor of Science in fire protection administration and technology through a variety of nontraditional means, including interactive televised courses broadcast to workplaces or various public sites, teleconferencing, and videocassette. Enrollment limited to the Los Angeles basin and surrounding counties.

California State University, Northridge   M
18111 Nordhoff St.
Northridge, CA 91330
Cora Connor, Coordinator, Instructional TV Network
Engineering
1958
Nonprofit, state $$
(818) 885-2355
(818) 885-2316 fax
Master of Science in engineering in a nontraditional mode, with element of independent study, and credit for prior experience, through televised courses. This program is primarily for employees of the Naval Air Warfare Weapons Division (formerly Naval Weapons Center) and Edwards Air Force Base, but local residents can also take advantage of it.

Central Michigan University   B, M
Extended Degree Program
Rowe Hall 126
Mt. Pleasant, MI 48859
Robert Trullinger, Director
Administration, management, supervision
1892
Nonprofit, state $$
(517) 774-3719, (800) 688-4268
(517) 774-3542 fax
The M.S. in administration program offers the graduate degree through intensive classes given at various locations nationwide (in Michigan, Washington, D.C., Hawaii, and locations throughout the Southeast and Midwest). One can earn a general administration and management degree, or specialize in public or health services administration. All programs are operated under the sponsorship of companies, military bases, or professional organizations. In most cases, anyone may enroll, whether or not they have an association with the sponsor. Twenty-one semester hours (of 36 required) must be completed through Central Michigan; up to 10 units can come from prior learning assessment. C.M.U. also offers programs in community college administration in Canada. For Michigan residents, there is also a program leading to a Bachelor of Individualized Studies, or a B.A. or B.S. in liberal studies. Thirty units towards each of these degrees must be earned from C.M.U.

Centre de Télé-Enseignement   B, M
Universitaire
6 Ave. H. Maringer
B.P. 33.97
Nancy, F-54015 France
Prof. Jean-Marie Bonnet
Many fields
Nonprofit, state
83-40-02-45
The Centre is a confederation of seven universities (including the Centre National de Télé-Ensignment) offering degree studies by correspondence, based primarily on taped lectures (in French, of course), with supplementary written materials. The tapes are available by mail, and are also broadcast on the radio and available at various regional centers. Students must first enroll in one of the participating universities (Besançon, Dijon, Metz, Mulhouse, Nancy, Reims, or Strasbourg), and then in the Centre. Even though all coursework is done through the Centre, the degree is awarded by the university. Bachelor's studies are offered in many fields; the Master's in only a few.

Chadron State College   M

Dept. of Education
1000 Main St.
Chadron, NE 69337
Roger Wess, Director of Interactive Distance Learning
Business administration
1911
Nonprofit, state $$
(308) 432-6364
(308) 432-6464 fax

Distance learning M.B.A. available to residents of 25 counties in western and central Nebraska, through a number of nontraditional modes of instruction, including CD-ROM, televised courses, computer conferencing and bulletin boards, e-mail, videocassette, and tele- and videoconferencing. Open policy means no requirements for admission.

Charter Oak State College   B

66 Cedar Street
Newington, CT 06111-2646
Helen Giliberto
Many fields
1973
Nonprofit, state $$
(203) 677-0076, (800) 842-2220 (CT only)
(203) 677-5147 fax

Charter Oak college is operated by the Connecticut Board for State Academic Awards, and offers the Bachelor of Arts and Bachelor of Science. Each student is responsible for amassing 120 semester units, which may come from courses taken elsewhere, equivalency examinations, military study, correspondence courses, or portfolio reviews. As soon as the 120 units are earned, with at least half in the arts and sciences, and 36 in a single subject or major area, the degree is awarded. Only students resident in the U.S. may enroll. Original name: Connecticut Board for State Academic Achievement Awards.

Chicago City-Wide College   Dip

Center for Open Learning
226 W. Jackson Blvd.
Chicago, IL 60606-6997
Patrick McPhilimy
Many fields
Nonprofit, state $
(312) 855-8213

Chicago's Center for Open Learning has been offering courses via television for over 30 years. Now, students who cannot view courses on TV can watch them on video at learning centers in their communities. Proctored exams are required, and students have the option of meeting with course coordinators. The school does not grant degrees, but courses can be transferred to a Bachelor's program elsewhere. This program is currently available to residents of Chicago and its outlying areas only.

City University   B, M

335 116th Avenue SE
Bellevue, WA 98004
Robert VanWoert
Many fields
1973
Nonprofit, independent $$$
(206) 643-2000 (800) 426-5596
(206) 637-9689 fax

Bachelor of Science in accounting, aviation management, business administration, fire command administration, and health care management, as well as an M.B.A., M.P.A., and M.Ed. are offered entirely by home computer (using e-mail), or by more traditional means. City University offers programs in 26 Washington cities, as well as Portland, Oregon; Santa Clara, California; several British Columbia locations; Zurich, Switzerland; and Frankfurt, Germany, leading to a Bachelor's in Business Administration or Health Care Administration, or an M.B.A. or M.P.A. (public administration). A B.S.N. (nursing) program is offered through evening study, and programs in computer science by evening or weekend study.

In 1995, City introduced its InRoads system, providing many aspects of its distance learning programs via the Internet: registering, paying tuition, communicating with faculty and other students, and so on. The home page address is http://www.cityu.edu/inroads/welcome/html

Clarkson College   B, M

101 South 42nd St.
Omaha, NE 68131-2739
Distance Education Coordinator
Business administration, management, health service, nursing
1888
Nonprofit, independent $$$$
(402) 552-2288, (800) 647-5500
(402) 552-3369 fax

Clarkson offers a B.S. in business administration and an M..S. in management (with a concentration in either health service management or business) entirely through distance-learning methods. The Bachelor's may be completed entirely through Clarkson, or by building on an Associate's in science, or courses taken for another B.S. Credit available for life-experience, through portfolio evaluation, military learning, and standardized tests. Clarkson also offers graduate health-related programs in nursing and health service management which can be completed through distance learning, with the exception of several weeks on campus for clinical experience.

Cogswell College

See: Open Learning Fire Service Program

College for Financial Planning   M

4695 S. Monaco St.
Denver, CO 80237

Glen Steelman, Registrar
Personal financial planning
1972
Nonprofit **$$$$$**
(303) 220-1200
(303) 220-5146 fax
The National Endowment for Financial Education offers, through its College for Financial Planning, an M.S. in personal financial planning, wholly through distance education, with emphasis in four fields: wealth management, or estate, tax, or retirement planning. The 12-course program is designed for applicants with some financial services background; students without such a background must successfully complete a special noncredit "Foundations in Financial Planning" course before they will be admitted. Accreditated by the North Central Association.

College of Great Falls   B
1301 20th St. S.
Great Falls, MT 59405
R. K. Bohne, Division Head
Accounting, business administration, counseling psychology, criminal justice, human services, microcomputer management, paralegal studies, sociology
1932
Nonprofit, church **$$$$**
(406) 761-8210
(406) 454-0113 fax
B.A. and B.S. in the above fields for residents of Montana and Alberta, Canada, through distance-learning techniques including teleconferencing, telephone instruction, and audio- and videocassette. Open-admissions policy applies to the fields of counseling psychology, criminal justice, human services, paralegal studies, and sociology.

Colorado State University   M
SURGE Program
Division of Continuing Education
Spruce Hall
Fort Collins, CO 80523
Debbie Sheaman, Registrar
Business, engineering, computer science, statistics, human resource development, industrial hygiene
1870
Nonprofit, state **$$$$**
(303) 491-5288 (800) 525-4950
(303) 491-7885 fax
The Colorado SURGE program is an innovative method of delivering graduate education to working professionals who cannot attend regular on-campus classes. Master's degrees are offered in business administration, management, computer science, human resource development, industrial hygiene, statistics, and engineering (agricultural, chemical, civil, electrical, and mechanical). Established in 1967, it was the first video-based graduate education program of its kind in America Regular Colorado State graduate courses are videotaped in specially equipped classrooms and sent via UPS with other coursework materials either directly to a student's home or to a participating site coordinator. Workload for SURGE students is the same as for the in-class students. This program is offered only to students residing in the continental United States or on U.S. military bases. (See also, National Universities Degree Consortium)

Columbia Union College   B
External Degree Programs
7600 Flower Ave.
Takoma Park, MD 20912
Charlotte Conway, Director of Records
Business administration, psychology, religion
1904
Nonprofit, church **$$$**
(301) 891-4080, (800) 835-4212
(301) 270-1618 fax
The Bachelor of Arts can be earned entirely through correspondence study. Credit available for standard equivalency examinations and/or work experience once the student has earned at least 24 semester hours in the program. At least 30 units (between eight and 12 courses) must be earned after enrolling. Students may select as an area of concentration business administration, psychology, or religion, but the psychology degree can not be completed entirely through home study. Every student must write a major paper, related to literature, religion, or arts, or pass a comprehensive examination, to qualify for graduation. The school is owned by the Seventh Day Adventist Church but non-church-members are welcome. Students may live anywhere in the world, but all work must be done in English.

Connecticut Board for State Academic Achievement Awards
See: Charter Oak State College

Darling Downs Institute of   B, M
Advanced Education
P.O. Box Darling Heights
Toowoomba, 4350
Australia
G. Edmondson, Senior Administration Officer
Applied science, arts, business, education, engineering
Nonprofit, state
(617) 631-2100
Degree programs make extensive use of audio- and videotapes, as well as written materials. Evening courses and external study programs are offered.

Deakin University   B, M
Off-Campus Studies
Victoria, 3217 Australia
Humanities, social studies, education

1975
Nonprofit
Deakin operates as an open university, for Australians only, with voluntary attendance at tutorials and weekend schools. The Bachelor of Arts is offered in humanities, social studies, and education; also, a Bachelor of Education, Master's in education, education administration, and business administration. Special entry offers the opportunity for adults who haven't completed high school to enroll in the B.A. program.

Dyke College   B
112 Prospect Ave.
Cleveland, OH 44115
Michael L. Blauner
Business areas
1848
Nonprofit, independent $$
(216) 696-9000
Adult students can complete a Bachelor of Science in management, marketing, accounting, health services management, and other business areas at their own pace, with guidance from professional mentors. All work may be done nonresidentially, but since occasional on-campus meetings with mentors are strongly recommended, the program is only available to residents of northeastern Ohio. Options for earning credit include home study (according to a learning contract), group study at various locations, life/work experience and/or proficiency exams (both at 1/3 tuition), and/or previous credit transfer. Tuition can be greatly reduced by life/work experience credit and proficiency exams. The first such program approved by the Ohio Board of Regents, this is the oldest and largest external degree program in Ohio.

Eastern Illinois University   B
Charleston, IL 61920
Kaye Woodward
Many fields
1895
Nonprofit, state $$
(217) 581-5618
(217) 581-2722 fax
Bachelor of Arts, with a minimum of 15 units to be earned on campus. Eastern Illinois is one of five members of the Board of Governors Bachelor of Arts program, a nontraditional program designed to allow working adults the chance to complete most of their requirements off-campus, through independent study, equivalency examinations, and credit for life experience. A major is not required. Skills and knowledge acquired by nonacademic means can be evaluated for academic credit. See also: Board of Governors B.A. Degree Program

Electronic University Network   B, M, D
1977 Colestin Road

Hornbrook, CA 96044
Steve Eskow
Business, liberal arts, psychology
1983
Proprietary $
(503) 482-5871, (800) 22LEARN
(503) 482-7544 fax
The Electronic University Network offers undergraduate courses for credit as well as Master's and Doctoral programs from accredited institutions, using the America OnLine computer bulletin board service to connect students with instructors, other students, and support services such as a library and student union. A personal computer (IBM or Macintosh) with a modem is required. Study is self-paced and in most programs may begin at any time. Affiliated schools change from time to time. They include the on-line doctorate of the California Institute for Integral Studies, the MBA of Heriot-Watt University, an M.S. in international relations from Salve Regina College, and several Associate's and Bachelor's programs. America OnLine subscribers type "Keyword EUN" to reach EUN online. Non-subscribers need to call or write the EUN office.

Embry-Riddle Aeronautical University   B, M
Department of Independent Studies
600 S. Clyde Morris Blvd.
Daytona Beach, FL 32114-3900
Thomas W. Pettit
Aeronautics
1926
Nonprofit, independent $$$
(904) 226-6397
(904) 239-6927 fax
Bachelor of Science in professional aeronautics and a Master of Aeronautical Science with no traditional classroom attendance. Applicants must have certified commercial or military training and professional experience in any of the following: air traffic control, airways facilities, aviation weather, electronic operations, flight operations administration, navigation systems, certified flight instructor, or pilot (airline command, air carrier, military, corporate, regional airline). Up to 36 semester hours may be awarded for professional training and experience. Bachelor of Science in aviation business administration is also offered, with no aviation experience required. Credit for CLEP and other exams, and work at accredited schools. Tuition includes study guides and audiotapes; there is an additional rental fee for videotapes. Textbook prices vary. The Master's degree work is available on a computer network; locally proctored exams are required.

Empire State College   B, M
Center for Distance Learning
2 Union Ave.

Saratoga Springs, NY 12866-4390
Daniel Granger, Director
Business, human services, interdisciplinary studies
1971
Nonprofit, state $$
(518) 587-2100, (800) 468-6372 (NY only)
(518) 587-5404 fax
A part of the State University of New York, Empire State College provides programs in 40 locations across New York State. The primary mode of study is independent study guided by faculty mentors. Together, students and mentors develop a degree program within the college's 11 broad areas of undergraduate study. Credit is given for college-level learning gained from work and other life experience. The Bachelor's degree can be completed entirely by independent, faculty-guided study; classroom attendance generally not required. The Master of Arts requires four days on campus at the beginning and end of each semester, and is offered in business and policy studies, labor and policy studies, and culture and policy studies. They combine independent study with three three-or-four day weekends on campus each year. In addition, the Center for Distance Learning offers structured courses and degree programs in business administration, human services, and interdisciplinary studies for students seeking more structured learning without classroom attendance or travel; faculty guidance is by mail and telephone. Empire State also offers the Open Learning Fire Service Program.

Faith Bible College   B
4501 Shed Road
Bossier City, LA 71111
Rev. Bill Walsworth
Bible studies/theology, religious education
1976
$$$$
(318) 746-8400
(318) 747-9634 fax
B.A. may be earned entirely by independent study. Joint degree offered with ICI University in Dallas, which is accredited by the Distance Education and Training Council. The joint degree is more expensive, but is accredited.

FernUniversität   M, D
Feithstrasse 152
D-5800 Hagen, Germany
Information Division
Many fields
1974
Nonprofit, state $
0-23-31-804-2408
0-23-31-804-2763 fax
West Germany's Distance Teaching University offers the Master's and Doctorate through completion of correspondence study units, plus examinations (which must be taken in Germany). Instruction is through a combination of written materials and audiocassettes. All courses are self-paced, and include mathematics, electrical engineering, computer science, economics, law, educational science, social science, and the arts. The university operates about 63 study centers in Germany, Austria, Switzerland, and Hungary for the assistance and guidance of students. All instruction in German, although a nice color brochure is available in English. More than 1,450 of FernUniversität's over 50,000 students live outside of Germany.

George Washington University   M
2201 G St.
Washington, DC 20052
William Lynch, Educational Technology Leadership
Educational technology, electrical engineering, computer science
1821
Nonprofit, independent $$$$
(202) 994-1700
(202) 994-5870 fax
Distance-learning M.A. in educational technology and M.S. in electrical engineering/computer science through a range of nontraditional teaching methods, including cable television (Mind Extension University), computer conferencing and bulletin boards, e-mail, and videocassettes. Also, interesting residential programs in the fields of education, humanities, the social sciences, criminal justice, urban learning, forensics, telecommunication operations, and administration.

Georgia Institute of Technology   M
Continuing Education
Atlanta, GA 30332-0240
Dr. W. Denney Freeston, Director
Engineering, computer science
1885
Nonprofit, state $$$$
(404) 894-3378, (800) 225-4656
(404) 894-5520 fax
This school's video-based instruction system allows working professionals to earn an M.S. entirely through videotaped classes and proctored exams from anywhere in the U.S. (and, in some cases, from other countries as well). The available majors are electrical engineering (with options in computer engineering, digital signal processing, and power and telecommunications), environmental engineering, health physics/radiological engineering, industrial engineering, and nuclear engineering. While the degree is expensive, many companies have tuition-reimbursement plans for their employees.

Governors State University   B
BOG Program
University Park, IL 60466
Otis O. Lawrence, Director of Assessment

Many fields
1969
Nonprofit, state $$
(708) 534-4092

B.A. may be earned through weekend, evening, and summer programs, as well as telecourses completed through the Board of Governors B.A. Degree Program. Fifteen credit hours must be completed through Governors State or one of the other Board of Governors institutions (Chicago State University, Eastern Illinois University, Northeastern Illinois University, or Western Illinois University). These units may be earned through independent study, telecourses, and on- or off-campus courses, so it is theoretically possible to earn this degree without ever setting foot on campus. There are also evening and weekend courses, and credit is awarded for nonacademic prior learning and equivalency exams.

Grand Valley State University   B

Grandlink Satellite Programs
301 West Fulton
Grand Valley, MI 49504
Terry Gorsky
Nursing
1960
Nonprofit, state $$$
(616) 771-6618
(616) 771-6520 fax

B.S. nursing degree completion program for holders of an R.N. or A.D.N., through courses beamed to six sites in Michigan (Alma, Benton Harbor, Harrison, Muskegon, Scottville, and Sidney).

Grantham College of Engineering   B

34641 Grantham College Road, P.O. Box 5700
Slidell, LA 70460-5700
Philip L. Grantham, Director of Student Services
Engineering technology, computer sciences
1951
Proprietary $$
(504) 649-4191, (800) 955-2527
(504) 649-4183 fax

Nonresident Bachelor's degrees in engineering technology, with an emphasis in either computers or electronics. Grantham's electronics-emphasis program is designed for people who already have practical experience in the field and laboratory; for the computer technology major, no prior experience is required. Students are given up to two years to complete each phase of the four-phase program; 402 lessons and 8 exams in all, but a highly motivated person could complete them much more quickly. All applicants must have already completed 21 unit-hours elsewhere (in English, history, etc.) and must have access to a personal computer. New B.S. in computer science program. Accreditation is from the Distance Education and Training Council.

Griggs University   B

12501 Old Columbia Pike
Silver Spring, MD 20904
Joseph E. Gurubatham, President
Religion, theological studies
Nonprofit, church $$
(301) 680-6570
(301) 680-6577 fax

The venerable Home Study International, which has offered correspondence courses for decades, now has a degree-granting university. Their B.A.'s in religion and theological studies are accredited by the Distance Education and Training Council.

Heriot-Watt University   M

US Distributor: 6921 Stockton Ave.
El Cerrito, CA 94530
John Bear
Business administration, construction management, acoustics, TESL
1821
$$$
(510) 528-3777, (800) THE WATT (843-9288)
(510) 528-3555 fax

Heriot-Watt offers the only accredited M.B.A. program that does not require a Bachelor's degree or entrance examinations and that can be done entirely by home study. With more than 10,000 students in over 120 countries (including more than 2,000 in the U.S. and Canada), it is, by far, the largest M.B.A. program in the world. The only requirement for earning the degree is passing nine rigorous three-hour exams, one for each of the required nine courses (marketing, economics, accounting, finance, strategic planning, etc.). The exams are given twice a year on hundreds of college campuses worldwide (some 100 in the U.S. and Canada). Students buy the courses one at a time, as they are ready for them. The courses consist of looseleaf textbooks (average: 500 pages) written by prominent professors specifically for this program. Courses are not interactive: there are no papers to write, quizzes, or other assignments, and no thesis. Each course averages about 150 hours of study time, so the entire M.B.A. can be completed in one year, but 18 to 24 months is more common. Hundreds of major corporations recognize and pay for the degree. *The Economist Intelligence Unit* includes Heriot-Watt in their report, "Which MBA: a critical guide to the world's best programmes." Heriot-Watt University has a 350-acre campus in Edinburgh, Scotland, with more than 10,000 on-campus students pursuing Bachelor's, Master's and Doctorates in many scientific, technical, and business fields. But only the M.B.A. and Master's degrees in acoustical science, vibration studies, construction management, and TESL are done by distance learning. John Bear is the sole distributor of Heriot-Watt courses in North America; there are also agents and distributors in thirty other countries. For information on the M.B.A., write to Dr. Bear in California. In Canada, write 204, 120 Robertson Road, Nepean, ON K2H 5V1 Canada; phone (800) 446-6288 or (613) 726-0205, fax (613) 726-9563. For information on the technical and TESL degrees, write to the main campus: Heriot-Watt University, Edinburgh EH14 4AS, Scotland.

Indiana University   B
Systemwide General Studies
Owen Hall 101
Bloomington, IN 47405
Louis Holtzclaw, Associate Director, Extended Studies
General studies
1975
Nonprofit, state $$
(812) 855-3693, (800) 342-5410, IN (800) 334-1011
fax: (812) 855-8680
Bachelor of General Studies available entirely through nonresidential study. The degree can be done without a major. One hundred and twenty semester units are required, of which at least 30 must be earned from Indiana University. All 30 can be via independent study by correspondence. One quarter of the units must be upper division (junior or senior) level. The university also has evening courses, a weekend college, and a course to assist in developing a life experience portfolio.

Indiana University Southeast   B
School for Continuing Studies
4201 Grant Line Road
New Albany, IN 47150
General studies
1941
Nonprofit, state $$
(812) 941-2315
Bachelor's in general studies may be earned through a combination of weekend, evening, television, and correspondence study. Intensive summer courses are also available. Credit for independent study, self-acquired competencies, military training, and by examination. All coursework may be completed through the university's correspondence division. Students from outside the U.S. are welcome, and should direct their inquiries to Indiana University, Owen Hall, Bloomington, IN 47405-5201. The telephone number is (812) 855-3693.

Instituto Politecnico Nacional   B
Avenida Instituto Politecnico Nacional
Mexico D.F., 14, Mexico
Carlos Leon Jinojosa, Secretary
Economics, international trade
1936
Nonprofit, state $
52-5-754-4706
Mexico's open university system (sistema abierto de

ensenanza) offers the Bachelor's degree in economics and international trade entirely through distance study, through study guides, slides, movies, records, and videocassettes, as well as group seminars held at various locations throughout Mexico. All work must be done in Spanish. The degree is awarded mainly on the basis of one's performance on final examinations.

International School of   M
Information Management
50 S. Steele St.
Suite 805
Denver, CO 80047
Mary Adams, Vice President
Information resources management,
business administration
1987
Proprietary $$$
(303) 752-3742, (800) 441-4746
(303) 752-4044 fax
An M.S. in information resources management and an M.B.A. with a focus in information resources management are offered via "electronic campus, where instructor-guided learning takes place using the school's own telecommunications network and computer bulletin-board service. A thesis or major independent study project is required of every student. Accreditation is from the Distance Education and Training Council.

Judson College   B
Marion, AL 36756
David E. Potts, President
Many fields
1838
Nonprofit, church $$$
(205) 683-5123, (800) 447-9472
(205) 683-5147 fax
Wholly nonresident Bachelor's degrees, for women over the age of 21 only, through an individualized study program based on a learning contract. Credit for prior life learning through portfolio assessment, standard equivalency exams, and proficiency tests prepared by Judson faculty. Students can major in art, biology, business, chemistry, CIS, criminal justice, English, fashion merchandising, home economics, history, interior design, mathematics, psychology, religious studies, or sociology.

Kansas Newman College   B
Off-Campus Nursing Division
3100 McCormick
Wichita, KS 67213
Sr. Glenda Reimer, Director
Nursing
1933
Nonprofit, church $$$$
(316) 942-4291

(316) 942-4483 fax
B.S. in nursing geared to allowing R.N.s in rural Kansas to obtain their degree by videocassette instruction.

Kansas State University   B
Non-Traditional Study Program, Umberger Hall
Division of Continuing Education
225 College Court
Manhattan, KS 66506
Cynthia Trent, NTS Coordinator
Interdisciplinary social science and agriculture, animal sciences, and industry
1863
Nonprofit, state $$$
(913) 532-5687, (800) 622-2KSU
(913) 532-5637 fax
Kansas State offers two Bachelor's-degree completion programs: the Bachelor of Science in interdisciplinary social science, and the Bachelor of Science in agriculture, animal sciences and industry, with an animal products option. Applicants to either program must already have earned at least 60 semester college credits toward either the B.S. in social science (a 120-credit -hour program) or the B.S. in agriculture (127 credit hours). Students may transfer up to 90 credits to KSU, and assessment of prior learning is available after acceptance into the program. NTS students must earn at least 30 credits from KSU, which can be accomplished through television courses, cablecast across the United States on ME/U, the Education Network. (See also: National Universities Degree Consortium.)

Lakehead University   B
Regional Centre, Room RC 0009
Thunder Bay, ON P7B 5E1 Canada
Environmental assessment, tourism, recreation resources management
Nonprofit, state
(807) 346-7730
(807) 343-8008 fax
The Bachelor of Arts, as well as certificates in environmental assessment, tourism, and recreation resources management can be earned through distance learning. Each course package includes a manual, audio and/or video cassettes, and possibly supplementary reading and self-test materials. Students mail in up to six assignments per course, and take examinations on specified dates at about 30 locations in northern Ontario (or other Canadian locations, by special arrangement). Students are encouraged to participate in group tutorials by teleconference.

Lehigh University   M
205 Johnson Hall
Bethlehem, PA 18015
Peg Kercsmar, Program Administrator

Chemistry, chemical engineering
1865
Nonprofit, independent $$$$$
(215) 758-5794
(215) 674-6427 fax
M.S. in chemistry or chemical engineering through a highly innovative program that is, at present, available only to corporate-sponsored groups. Classes are delivered nationwide via satellite television, and students can interact in real-time by calling an 800 number. Lehigh is also in the process of implementing an interactive computer-based system that allows distance-education students and professors to communicate by writing on an electronic "blackboard."

Loma Linda University   M
School of Public Health
Office of Extended Programs
Nichol Hall, #1706
Loma Linda, CA 92350
Glen Blix
Public health
1905
Nonprofit, church $$$
(909) 824-4595, (800) 854-5661
(909) 824-4577 fax
The Extended Program at Loma Linda University's School of Public Health offers a unique and practical way for midcareer health professionals to obtain a Master of Public Health (M.P.H.) degree in either health promotion or health administration while maintaining their present employment. The format includes a combination of independent study (pre- and post-lecture assignments) and extensive student/instructor contact. The student is not required to spend time on campus at LLU. Instead, instructors travel to various sites in the United States to meet with students in intensive three-day class sessions; one per quarter at each site. The program is geared to the needs of physicians, dentists, nurses, and other health professionals who wish to become qualified to organize health programs, engage in health promotion activities, and so on.

Madurai University   B, M
Palkalai Nagar
Madurai, 625 021,   India
T. B. Siddalingaiah, Director
Various fields
Nonprofit, state $
Bachelor's and Master's in both Arts and Commerce through a combination of correspondence study and examinations. (Indian universities generally award their degrees entirely by examination.) Madurai offers a wide range of correspondence courses designed to prepare students for its own examinations, which must generally be taken in India, but may be taken overseas by special permission.

101

It is necessary to take the courses, or you will not be allowed to take the examinations.

Mary Washington College B, M
1301 College Avenue
Fredericksburg, VA 22401
Stanley L. Groppel
Liberal studies, business administration, engineering
Nonprofit, state $$$$
(703) 899-4614
Bachelor of Liberal Studies is available through evening and summer programs. Thirty hours of residential credit is required. Credit for independent study, nonacademic prior learning by portfolio assessment, and by examination. Distance-learning M.B.A. and M.E. (engineering) through satellite television and telephone instruction. The M.B.A. is open to Virginia residents only, the M.E. to students worldwide.

Mind Extension University B, M
9697 E. Mineral Ave.
P.O. Box 3309
Englewood, CO 80155-3309
ME/U Education Center
Many fields
Independent $$$$
(800) 777-MIND
The cable education network called Mind Extension University, or ME/U, delivers live high school and college courses from more than 24 educational experts and regionally accredited colleges and universities. Through cable television, satellite, videotape, and other related transmission technologies, ME/U provides educational enrichment opportunities through basic viewing to people in over 19.5 million households, offices, schools and military bases. All students logistics, except for academic evaluation and transcript documentation, occur between the student and the ME/U Education Center, which can be reached through a toll-free number. The programs are prepared by each individual university and, just like on-campus education, range from lively and engaging to dry and tedious. The channel is on the air 24 hours a day.

Mount Saint Vincent University B
EMF Room 121
166 Bedford Hwy.
Halifax, NS B3M 2J6 Canada
Carolyn Nobes, Open Learning Coordinator
Tourism and hospitality
1925
Nonprofit, church $$$
(902) 457-6511, (800) 665-3838
(902) 457-2618 fax
Bachelor's in tourism and hospitality management (B.T.H.M.) offered nonresidentially throughout Canada by teleconferencing, telephone instruction, and videocassette.

National Technological University M
700 Centre Avenue
Fort Collins, CO 80526-1842
Lionel Baldwin
Technological fields
1984
Nonprofit, independent $$$$
(303) 484-6414
(303) 484-0668 fax
NTU offers a wide range of graduate courses and noncredit short courses in technological subjects. These are transmitted by satellite digital compressed video from 45 university campuses from Alaska to Florida to corporate, government, and university worksites. Working professionals and technical managers take the classes, often in "real time" (as they are being taught on the campuses), with telephone links to the classrooms. NTU offers the M.S. in computer engineering, computer science, electrical engineering, engineering management, hazardous waste management, health physics, management of technology, manufacturing systems engineering, materials science and engineering, software engineering, and special majors. In addition, about 400 short courses are broadcast on the NTU Network each year.

National Universities Degree Consortium B
Colorado State University/Continuing Education
Spruce Hall
Fort Collins, CO 80523
Joan Bowen
Varied fields
Nonprofit $
(303) 491-5288, (800) 525-4950
(303) 491-7885 fax
The National Universities Degree Consortium was established to offer flexible, nontraditional degree completion programs to adult and part-time students nationwide. Nine universities are participating already: Colorado State, Kansas State, Oklahoma State, University of Maryland, University of New Orleans, University of Oklahoma, University of South Carolina, Utah State, and Washington State. Courses are delivered over local cable TV, with the assistance of ME/U: The Education Network. If a student cannot receive the cablecast, videotapes can be provided. Coursework also includes interactive multimedia, computer networks, teleconferencing, live instruction, and correspondence courses. Currently, four full degree programs are offered: B.A. in Management, B.S. in Criminal Justice, Interdisciplinary Social Science, or Agriculture, Animal Science, and Industry.

New Jersey Institute of Technology B
Office of Distance Learning
University Heights, NJ 07102
Leon Jololian, Director of Curriculum

Information systems
1881
Nonprofit, state **$$$$**
(201) 596-3168
(201) 596-5777 fax
Bachelor of Arts in information systems offered entirely through distance learning, using videotaped courses, on-line conferencing, fax, and phone to stay in touch. Distance students study along with on-campus students, on the same schedule, and examinations can be administered in remote locations by an approved proctor.

New School for Social Research   M
Media Studies Admissions Office
Room 401, 66 W. 12th St.
New York, NY 10011
Elizabeth Ross
Media studies
1919
Nonprofit, independent **$$$**
(212) 229-5630
Master of Arts in media studies, which combines theoretical offerings with advanced production coursework. Offered through the communication department, it is designed for both media professionals and students considering further graduate study. Evening and independent study, or students can take some or all of their classes on-line through their personal computers.

New York Institute of Technology   B
Room 417, Theobald Hall
P.O. Box 8000
Old Westbury, NY 11568
Marshall Kremers, On-Line Director
Business administration, interdisciplinary studies, behavioral sciences
1955
Nonprofit, independent **$$$$**
(516) 686-7712, (800) 222-NYIT
(516) 484-6830 fax
Through the On-Line Campus, this school offers the B.S. in business administration (with a general management option), interdisciplinary studies, and behavioral sciences (with four concentrations: criminal justice, community mental health, psychology, and sociology). Credit available for prior learning experiences, by portfolio assessment, and for equivalency exams. All learning takes places over computer modem, by teleconferencing. The off-campus programs were formerly offered through American Open University.

North Central Bible College   B
Carlson Institute
910 Elliot Ave. S.
Minneapolis, MN 55404
Daniel Neary, Director of Admissions and Records

Church ministries, Christian education
1930
Nonprofit, church **$**
(612) 343-4430
(612) 343-4435 fax
Wholly nonresident Bachelor of Arts or Sciences in church ministries or Christian education. Credit available for life-experience learning through portfolio assessment, and for equivalency exams. Twenty-seven of the 130 credits required must be earned from North Central; this can be accomplished through their correspondence courses.

Ohio University   B
External Student Program
301 Tupper Hall
Athens, OH 45701
Rosalie Terrell
Specialized studies
1804
Nonprofit, state **$$**
(614) 593-2150, (800) 444-2420
(614) 593-0452 fax
The Bachelor of Specialized Studies (B.S.S.) degree can be earned entirely though nonresident study. The External Student Program provides a counseling and advising service, and also acts as a liaison in dealing with other university offices. Credit for the degree can come from assessment of prior learning experiences, correspondence courses, independent study projects, and courses on television. In many correspondence courses, one can take the examination only. If you pass, credit for the course is given. These exams can be administered anywhere in the world and must be supervised. Forty-eight quarter hours of credit must be completed after enrolling at Ohio. The university also has offered a college program for the incarcerated, at unusually low cost.

Oklahoma Baptist University   B
500 West University
Shawnee, OK 74801
Mr. Jody Johnson, Dean of Admissions
Christian studies
1910
Nonprofit, church **$**
(405) 275-2850
(405) 878-2069 fax
Bachelor of Arts in Christian studies through a (for now) wholly nonresident program (there is a plan to begin requiring a one-week summer session). The school's mission is to educate ministers, those who have responded to God's calling but not yet begun to serve as ministers, and laypeople who wish to become better-equipped servants of God in their own churches. Credit for military credit and by examination; coursework is through guided distance study and supervised fieldwork.

Oklahoma State University　　M
512 Engineering North
Stillwater, OK 74078
Bill Cooper, Extension Director
Engineering, business administration
1890
Nonprofit, state $$$
(405) 744-5146
(405) 744-5033 fax
M.S. in electrical, mechanical, or chemical engineering available nationwide and in Canada and Mexico, through the National Technical University's online courses. Also, a B.S. in electrical engineering and an M.B.A. offered by video to participating corporate sites. Contact for the M.B.A. is Karen Flock at (405) 744-5208. See also: National Universities Degree Consortium

Old Dominion University　　B, M
5215 Hampton Blvd.
Norfolk, VA 23529
Engineering, nursing, business, professional communications, criminal justice
1930
Nonprofit, state $$$$
(804) 683-3000, (800) YOUR-BSN nursing
(804) 683-4505 engineering
(804) 683-5253 nursing fax
B.S. in civil, mechanical, or electrical engineering technology and nursing, business, professional communications, and criminal justice; M.S. in nursing or a number of engineering fields (civil and environmental, electrical and computer, mechanical, and engineering management) through a variety of nontraditional means, including public and cable television, satellite and closed-circuit television courses delivered to remote sites, teleconferencing, videocassette and conferencing, and telephone instruction. Contact for engineering technology program is Dr. William D. Stanley, at (804) 683-3775. Nursing program can be done wholly nonresidentially, with clinical practicums arranged in your area.

Open Learning Agency　　B
P.O. Box 82080
Burnaby, BC V5C 6J8 Canada
Arien Heath
Many fields
Nonprofit, state $$
(604) 431-3110
(604) 431-3386 fax
Formerly the British Columbia Open University, which had been a degree-granting institution. Now they offer a wide range of nonresident courses—by audio- and videocassette, teleconferencing, and other methods—which can be applied to degree programs at other universities,
as well as a limited number of their own degrees.

Open Learning Fire Service Program　　B
FEMA National Fire Academy, Field Program
16825 South Seton Ave.
Emmitsburg, MD 21727-8998
Edward J. Kaplan
Fire administration, fire prevention technology
1977
Federal government sponsored
(301) 447-1127, (800) 238-3358
Accredited Bachelor's degree in fire services areas, through independent study courses taken from any of seven universities and colleges. The program is offered through seven regional colleges (all accredited): Cogswell College (California), University of Cincinnati, University of Memphis, Western Oregon State College, The University of Maryland University College, Western Illinois University, and Empire State College. All work is done by independent study. Students are sent a course guide, required textbooks, and their assignments. They communicate with instructors by mail and telephone. Supervised exams can be taken locally.

Open University　　B, M, D
Walton Hall
Milton Keynes, Buckinghamshire, MK7 6AA
England
C. R. Batten
Arts, education, mathematics, social science, science, technology, management studies
1969
Nonprofit, state
(0908) 274066
Established in 1969, Great Britain's Open University is now one of the largest distance education institutions in the world. Students study in their own homes and on their own schedules, using a combination of correspondence texts and audio- and videocassettes and the Internet computer network. Study can lead to a degree, a certificate, or a diploma. Some courses have week-long summer schools or weekend residential schools, and some require that the applicant be a resident of the U.K. or other European country. Associate students may study single courses for personal interest or professional updating. There are currently over 75,000 undergraduate and 20,000 associate students registered as well as some 7,000 higher degree students. Credit is earned through a combination of achieving a specified level of continuous assessment and passing the course examination. Open University offers some courses on the Internet, and plans many more. Online information is available from "General-Enquiries@open.ac.uk" or WWW: http://hcrl.open.ac.uk/

Open University of Israel B
U.S. office: American Friends of the Open University
330 West 58 Street, Suite 4A
New York, NY 10019
Many fields
1974
Nonprofit, independent **$$**
USA: (212) 713-1515 Israel: 972 (3) 646-0460

Israel's first open university offers the Bachelor's degree on completion of 18 home study courses. Each course consists of a home study kit, which may include written materials (in Hebrew only), laboratory equipment, simulation games, videotapes, etc. Each course requires 16 to 18 weeks to complete, with a 15- to 18-hour a week time commitment. Courses are available in natural sciences, life sciences, social sciences, mathematics, computer science, education, international relations, Jewish studies, management, and humanities. Noncredit courses are also offered in management enrichment, computers, video production, and cultural enrichment. Study group formation is encouraged, and tutorial sessions are held in study centers throughout Israel. Formerly Everyman's University.

Open University of the Netherlands B, D
P. O. Box 2960
6401 DL Heerlen, Netherlands
Marga Winnubust
Many fields
1984
State **$**
(045) 76-2222
(045) 71-1486 fax

The Netherlands's first nontraditional university offers a wide range of self-study courses in seven general fields: law, economics, management and administration, technology, natural science, social sciences, and cultural studies. In this program, modeled on Britain's Open University, credit is earned solely by passing examinations, and tutoring is available in study centers around Holland, or by telephone anywhere in the world. However, as their catalog puts it, "the language of the great majority of courses is, naturally, Dutch. As yet, only a few courses, or sections of courses, are available in English."

Queens University B
Division of Part-Time Studies
Kingston, ON K7L 2N6 Canada
German, political studies, psychology
1841
Nonprofit, state
(613) 545-2471

A Bachelor of Arts degree (15 courses in total) concentrating in German, political studies, or psychology can be completed entirely through correspondence. Study involves use of textbooks, tapes, and course notes written by instructors. Students submit assignments for grading and write final examinations under supervision at various centers worldwide. Telephone contact with instructors is possible. Other concentrations can be fulfilled by taking a combination of correspondence courses through Queens and by transferring Queen's-approved courses from other universities to complete degree requirements.

Regents College
See: University of the State of New York

Regis University B, M
3333 Regis Blvd.
Denver, CO 80221-1099
Many fields
1877
Nonprofit, church **$$$$**
(303) 458-4300, (800) 967-3237
(303) 458-4273 fax

Regis's University Without Walls program allows adults to complete a B.A. degree in almost any field and/or an M.A. degree in liberal studies through an individualized program of study in their home communities. Undergraduates can design a program of study which includes transfer credit from other regionally accredited colleges and universities, guided independent study, internships, workshops, seminars, credit by examination, and credit by assessment of prior learning acquired through experience. Master's degree students may concentrate their study in one of four areas: psychology, education, social sciences, or language and communication. Study for the Master's degree includes guided independent study and interactive seminars held once per semester. Also, B.A. in business administration, computer information systems, and accounting; M.S. in management and CIS through accelerated courses offered evenings and weekends at multiple locations in the Denver area. The undergraduate business major is also offered in western Colorado in Glenwood Springs and Steamboat Springs in cooperation with Colorado Mountain College. Undergraduate courses are offered in five- to eight-week formats; graduate courses are offered in seven-week formats.

Rensselaer Polytechnic Institute B, M
Satellite Video Program, CII 4011
Troy, NY 12180
Susan Bray, Director
Technical communication, engineering, computer science, business administration
1824
Nonprofit, independent **$$$$$**
(518) 276-6216

The M.B.A. is available through evening study. There are accelerated programs in which a Bachelor's and a medical, dental, or law degree can be earned in a total of six years. Several nonresident Master's programs are open to corporate subscribers; classes are by videocassette and at the industrial site. They are: the M.S. in technical communication, engineering (materials, manufacturing systems, mechanical, management, or microelectronics manufacturing), and computer science. Also, certificate programs in a number of technical fields.

Roger Williams University B
1 Old Ferry Road
Open Program
Bristol, RI 02809
William Dunfey
Many fields
1945
Nonprofit, independent $
(401) 254-3530
(401) 254-3480 fax
On-campus degrees in many fields; off-campus B.S. in industrial technology, business administration, public administration, administration, administration of justice, and historic preservation. Credit given for prior-learning assessment, military training, CLEP and other exams, and prior college attendance. While enrolled, one may earn credit from external courses, independent studies, internships, and day, evening, summer, and special classroom courses.

Salve Regina University M
Graduate Extension Study
100 Ochre Point Ave.
Newport, RI 02840-4192
Sr. Rosselina McKillop, Dean of Admissions
International relations, management and information systems, human resource management, liberal studies
1934
Nonprofit, church $$$$$
(401) 847-6650, (800) 637-0002
(401) 847-0372 fax
The Master of Arts in international relations, human resource management, and liberal studies and an M.S. in management and information systems are offered almost entirely through distance learning, with a two-week summer residency requirement. Instruction is by correspondence courses, with regular mail and telephone faculty contact, leading to guided independent study. Several degree programs can be earned entirely by using a personal computer over the America OnLine bulletin board system. See Electronic University Network for details

Southeastern College of the B
Assemblies of God
1000 Longfellow Blvd.
Lakeland, FL 33801
Religious fields
1935

Nonprofit, church $$$
(813) 665-4404, (800) 854-7477
(813) 666-8103 fax
Totally nonresident B.A. in Bible studies, Christian education, missions, and pastoral ministries, through credit for prior experience, equivalency exams, and correspondence courses, phone/mail instruction, supervised fieldwork, and independent study, guided by a learning contract.

Stanford University M
School of Engineering, SITN
401 Durand
Stanford, CA 94305-4036
Carolyn Schultz, Associate Director
Engineering, computer science
1885
Nonprofit, independent $$$$$
(415) 725-3000
(415) 725-3000 fax
Stanford offers a distance-learning M.S. in engineering or computer science to corporate and government subscribers, through closed-circuit television, teleconferencing, and other nontraditional methods. Students outside the live broadcast area must spend one quarter in residency.

Thomas Edison State College B, M
101 West State St.
Trenton, NJ 08608-1176
Jack Phillips, Registrar
Many fields
1972
Nonprofit, state $
(609) 984-1100
(609) 984-8447 fax
Bachelor's degrees in 119 areas of specialization. Unlimited credit can be earned through portfolio assessment (handbook available), Edison's own exams in dozens of subjects, guided study (correspondence courses using texts and videocassettes), courses by computer (many available through Edison's innovative CALL system: Computer Assisted Lifelong Learning), equivalency exams (over 400 available), military, business, and industry courses and training programs, PONSI, television-show-based courses (centered on, for example, PBS's The Story of English, Cosmos, etc.), licenses and certificates (C.P.A.: up to 33 credits, FAA Mechanic certificate/ Airframe and Power Plant rating: up to 55 credits; FAA Air Traffic Control Specialist: up to 60 credits, etc.), and transfer credit from accredited colleges. Unique academic advising available to enrolled students on an 800 number. Foreign students are welcome, with certain restrictions. A long-awaited Master's degree in business (although not an MBA) is due to be introduced right around the time this book goes to press.

Troy State University   B
P. O. Drawer 4419
Montgomery , AL 36103-4419
Dr. James R. Macey
Professional studies
1887
Nonprofit, state $$
(334) 241-9553
(334) 670-3774 fax
Bachelor of Arts or Science in professional studies can be earned through a combination of learning contracts with Troy State University in Montgomery (TSUM), TSUM television courses, transfer credit from and transient credit at other regionally accredited colleges/universities, and prior learning assessment (credit by examination; evaluation of previous training in the military, business and/or industry; and portfolio assessment). Majors are available in resource management (business), English, history, political science, social science, and psychology. Students must complete a minimum of 50 quarter hours under TSUM sponsorship.

Universidad Estatal a Distancia   B, M
Calle 23 B 25, Av. 108
San Jose,   Costa Rica
Celedolnio Ramirez
Education, business, agriculture, social service, health services, administration
1977
Nonprofit, state
25-8788
Costa Rica's state university for distance learning offers correspondence study consisting of written units, slides, and audio- and videocassettes, leading to the Bachelor's or Master's in the above fields. A Bachelor's can be earned in about two years of study. Evening and weekend instruction is also offered on campus.

Universidad Mexicana del Noreste   B
5a Zona No. 409, Apartado Postal No. 2191J
Col. Caracol
Monterrey, N.L. Mexico
Banking, finance, leisure time management
1974
40-12-05
This open-university program offers the Bachelor's degree in banking and finance, and in management of leisure time, based on study by learning guide and audiocassette. About four years are required to complete the degree.

Universidad Nacional Abierta   B
Avenida Gambria 18, San Bernadino
Caracas, 101,   Venezuela
Many fields
1975
Nonprofit, state

Venezuela's open university offers the Bachelor's degree in social sciences, management, land and sea sciences, engineering, mathematics, and physics. Students work at their own pace through teaching modules consisting of printed and audio-visual materials. Some courses are offered on radio or television. Laboratory work, where required, may be done at the university or at other institutions.

University of Alaska   B, M
706 C Gruening Building
Fairbanks, AK 99775
Education, rural development, social work
1917
Nonprofit, state $$$
(907) 474-7225
(907) 474-7225 fax
Programs for rural Alaska residents include a B.Ed. and an M.Ed., and B.A. in rural development or social work. Instruction is by a variety of nontraditional means, including audio- and videocassette, e-mail, and teleconferencing. Faculty and administrative support services are decentralized and located in various regional campuses and centers.

University of Dallas   M
Graduate School of Management
1845 East Northgate Drive
Irving, TX 75062-4799
Stan Croder
Health services management
1956
Nonprofit, church $$$$
(214) 385-7696 (800) 832-5622
(214) 721-5254 fax
M.B.A. in health services management available entirely by courses offered at health-care worksites (hospitals and other facilities). Only employees of facilities receiving either the HSTN Network or the Westcott network over their cable service may enroll. The program takes 2–3 years. Students who already have an M.B.A. earn the Master of Management instead.

University of Delhi   B, M
School of Correspondence Courses
and Continuing Education
5 Cavalry Lines
Delhi, 110007,   India
Ruddar Datt, Principal
Many fields
1962
Nonprofit, state $
725-7600
The correspondence programs and degrees are only for residents of India, and for Indian citizens resident in other countries.

University of East Asia — B, M

G. P. O. Box 3001
Macau
T. L. Tomaz
English language, Chinese law
1981
Private $$
The College for Lifelong Education offers wholly non-resident external programs in the English language using printed matter, audio, and videotapes. There is and English-language home study program in Chinese law. Programs have been designed with the cooperation of Britain's Open University and New Zealand's Massey University. This is Macau's only university; its local name is Universidade da Asia Oriental.

University of Houston — M

Off Campus Institutes
Houston, TX 77204-2162
Sandy Frieden, Director
Engineering
1927
Nonprofit, state $$
(713) 395-2629
M.A. in electrical or industrial engineering through courses beamed to remote sites (other schools, and some corporate sites) around the Houston area.

University of Hull — M

Asia Pacific Management Centre, International Plaza
10 Anson Road #09-17
Singapore 0207
Business administration
1927
$$$$
(65) 225-2825
(65) 225-3605 fax
The University of Hull offers a distance learning M.B.A. to businesspeople in Singapore, in conjunction with the independent Asia Pacific Management Centre. Students typically complete seven three-month "learning cycles" of evening and weekend classes, as well as a major second-year project. Faculty is apparently drawn entirely from Hull in England.

University of Idaho — M

Video Outreach Program
40 Janssen Engineering Building
Moscow, ID 83844
Thomas H. Miller, Director
Engineering, computer science, psychology
1889
Nonprofit, state $$
(208) 885-6373, (800) 824-2889
(208) 885-6165 fax
Master's degrees in electrical, mechanical, civil, geo-logical and computer engineering, computer science, and psychology (human factors) are offered non-residentially via the Video Outreach program. The school stresses that this is an intensive program that requires high levels of discipline and commitment from students.

University of Illinois at Urbana-Champaign — M

422 Engineering Hall, 1308 W. Green St.
Urbana, IL 61801
Linda Krute, Coordinator
Engineering, mechanics
1867
Nonprofit, state $$$
(217) 333-6634
(217) 333-0015 fax
M.S. in mechanics or a number of engineering fields (mechanical, general, electrical, or nuclear), through telephone instruction and videocassette. On-campus courses are taped, and shown at off-campus locations around the state. Admission to this program is highly competitive.

University of Iowa — B, M

116 International Center
Iowa City, IA 52242
Scott Wilcox, Educational Adviser
Liberal studies, computer science
1847
Nonprofit, state $$$$
(319) 335-2575 (800) 272-6430
(319) 335-2740 fax
Nonresident Bachelor of Liberal Studies, through public television, videocassette, and teleconferencing, for students who have completed 62 undergraduate credits elsewhere. M.S. in computer science geared mainly to corporate subscribers in the Iowa City area, although others are admitted on a space-available basis. Instruction is through closed-circuit television, and one graduate-level seminar on campus is required. Contact for M.S. program: Wayne Prophet, (319) 335-2050. See also: Quad Cities Graduate Center

University of London — B, M, D, L

Senate House, Malet St.
London, WC1E 7HU England
Many fields
1836
Nonprofit, state $$
(071) 636-8000 ext. 3139
(071) 636-5894 fax
London had the world's first external degree program and, after over a century and a half, it is still among the most popular. They do have an annoying policy that only holders of their own Bachelor's degree can enroll in M.Phil. or Ph.D. programs, but offer an increasing number of degrees specifically geared to correspondence

students. Five Master's degrees are recommended for distance-learning students: agricultural development, distance education, environmental management, and organizational behavior/occupational psychology. In classics, French, law, and most of the undergraduate programs, academic guidance is less extensive. Courses are non–time-limited and students work at their own pace to complete an individualized program. Assessment is by examination and (for some degrees) by thesis. Examinations in the U.S. are administered by the Educational Testing Center of Princeton, New Jersey.

University of Maryland University College
See: Open Learning Fire Service Program

University of Massachusetts at Amherst M
Video Instructional Program (VIP)
College of Engineering
Marcus Hall, Box 35115
Amherst, MA 01003-5115
Elisabeth D. Bowman
Mathematics and statistics, public health, management, and many engineering-related fields
1863
Nonprofit, state $$$$
(413) 545-0063
The Video Instructional Program (VIP) is an established distance-learning program providing graduate education to working engineers across the country. Using videotaped lectures and/or satellite broadcasts, professionals can enroll in the same classes offered to on-campus students, in both degree and nondegree formats. The Master of Science degrees are offered (engineering management and electrical and computer engineering), as well as noncredit/training courses in a variety of engineering-related disciplines.

University of Memphis
See: Open Learning Fire Service Program

University of Minnesota B
Program for Individualized Learning
201 Westbrook Hall
Minneapolis, MN 55455
Kent Warren, Admissions Coordinator
Many fields
1851
Nonprofit, state $$
(612) 624-4020
(612) 624-6369 fax
Nonresident B.A. and B.S. degrees for students in Minnesota and adjacent states and provinces who are willing to take responsibility for designing and implementing their degree programs. The program offers no courses or exams of its own; instead, it assists students in using resources at the university, at other institutions, and in the commu-

nity. These might include local or correspondence courses, independent study projects, and assessment of prior learning. At least a year of study is required after admission. Since there are no predesigned majors or prescribed curricula, each student develops an individualized degree plan. A set of standards, called graduation criteria, provide a framework for structuring and assessing degree programs. Requirements include an area of concentration, broad learning in the liberal arts, and a command of written English. Programs are not available in general business administration, accounting, public school teaching, engineering, or computer science.

University of Montana M
School of Business Administration
Missoula, MT 59812
Larry Gianchetla, Dean
Business administration
1893
Nonprofit, state $$$
(406) 243-6195
M.B.A. offered by televised courses at sites in Billings, plus computer conferencing and instruction by telephone and fax.

University of Nevada—Reno B
Division of Continuing Education
206 Midby Byron Bldg.
Reno, NV 89557
Neal A. Ferguson, Dean
General studies
1874
Nonprofit, state $$
(702) 784-4046, (800) 233-8928
(702) 784-4801 fax
Bachelor of General Studies program allows students who have already completed an Associate's degree elsewhere to earn a self-designed, wholly nonresident Bachelor's through a range of nontraditional methods, including correspondence courses and telecourses.

University of Northern Colorado M
College of Continuing Education
Greeley, CO 80639
Leon M. Zaborowski, Dean
Various fields
1889
Nonprofit, state $$$
(303) 351-1890
(303) 351-1880 fax
Wholly nonresidential Master's degrees for **adult students residing in Colorado only.** Applicants must also have at least three years' experience in their field (although no credit is given for life-experience learning, it is awarded for equivalency exams.) Degrees include: Master of Arts in education (eight areas of concentration), agency counseling, or communication, and

M.S. in statistics, operations research, or secondary science teaching. Instruction takes place through correspondence course, audio- and videotapes, televised courses, e-mail, telephone instruction, independent study, supervised fieldwork, and other innovative methods.

University of Northern Iowa   B
Center for Credit Programs
1222 West 27th Street
Cedar Falls, IA 50614
Liberal studies
1876
Nonprofit, state $$$
(319) 273-2311
(319) 273-3509 fax

The Bachelor of Arts in liberal studies can be earned entirely by correspondence from the University of Northern Iowa. There are no majors in the program, but students must earn 12 credits in three of these five areas: humanities, communication and arts, science and math, social sciences, and professional fields (business, education, etc.) Credit is also earned through guided correspondence study courses. Students mail in assignments and take proctored exams. Credit can also be earned through on-campus evening and weekend courses, televised courses, off-campus course sites throughout Iowa, courses from other regionally accredited four-year colleges (both on-campus and correspondence), and telebridge courses. "Telebridge" is a statewide system of two-way audio conferencing which permits classes to be held at remote locations. To qualify for admission, a student must live in the United States and have completed 62 transferable units or have an Associate's degree. At least forty-five semester hours must be earned at the Iowa Regents Universities (University of Iowa, Iowa State University, University of Northern Iowa). See also: Quad Cities Graduate Center

University of Phoenix   B, M
Online Program Administrative Offices
101 California Street, Ste. 505
San Francisco, CA 94111
Terri Hedegaard, V.P. Operations
Business, management
1976
Proprietary $$$$
(415) 956-2121, (800) 388-5463
(415) 541-0761

In 1976, the University of Phoenix, with campuses or offices in five western states, began offering three degrees entirely via computer, by using a modem: a B.S. in business administration, an M.B.A., and an M.S. in management, all designed for midcareer professionals, and all available completely nonresidentially. Students get their assignments, have group discussions, and ask questions of their professors online, without leaving their homes or offices. Each class meeting is spread out over an entire week, allowing busy students to complete their work at the most convenient time for them. Computer training and orientation is provided once a student enrolls. Phoenix also offers Bachelor's and Master's programs in business through evening and weekend study in many large West Coast cities. The university's main address is 4625 E. Elwood Street, P.O. Box 52076, Phoenix, AZ 85072; the Arizona phone numbers are: (602) 966-8577 and (800) 366-9699.

University of South Africa   B, M, D
P. O. Box 392, Muckleneuk Ridge
Pretoria, 0001 South Africa
Many fields
1909
Nonprofit, state $
(012) 429-3111
(012) 429-2565 fax

UNISA offers Bachelor's, Master's, and Doctorates entirely by correspondence. Examinations are taken at South African embassies and consulates worldwide. Degrees at all levels are offered in arts, science, law, theology, education, and economic and management sciences through a technique called "tele-tuition," using course materials, tapes, slides, etc. A minimum of 10 courses is required for the Bachelor's degree, which takes at least three years to complete. The government-subsidized program is relatively inexpensive. Before registering, undergraduate students must obtain a Certificate of Full or Conditional Exemption from the South African Matriculation Examination, obtained from the Matriculation Board, P.O. Box 3854, Pretoria, South Africa 0001 (this is not necessary for students who already hold "a recognized or accredited" Bachelor's degree). People worldwide are admitted. Syllabuses and course descriptions are available free of charge from the registrar. Note: A reader who has mastered the intricacies of dealing with UNISA has written a very helpful, detailed 110-page manual on how to do it. See the Bibliography for information on how to order this $15 report.

University of Surrey   M, D, L
Guildford
Surrey, GU2 5XH England
Elizabeth Oliver (education), P. Kangis (business)
Education, management, law
$$
(44-1483) 300800 (education), 259347 (business)
Fax (44-1483) 300803 (education), 259511 (business)

Distance-learning M.S. in education in the Department of Educational Studies "designed for educators and human resource personnel in all forms of post-compulsory education and training. The full course consists of eight "modules," plus a research dissertation. Each module takes about three months to complete, so it is possible to finish the M.S. in three years, although students are allowed six years. As only two of the 25 possible modules require face-to-face workshops, most students will have no trouble completing the degree through correspondence alone. No exams. The Surrey European Management School offers distance learning Master's and Doctorates in business, management, administration and law.

University of the State of New York B, M
Regents College
7 Columbia Circle
Albany, NY 12203-5159
C. Wayne Williams, Executive Director
Business, liberal arts, nursing, and technology
1784
Nonprofit, state $
(518) 464-8500
(518) 464-8777 fax
B.A., B.S., and M.A. by nonresidential study. The largest and, along with Thomas Edison State College, the most popular nonresident degree program in the U.S. Part of the oldest educational agency in America, The University of the State of New York, Regents College has no campus and offers no courses of its own. It evaluates work done elsewhere, and awards its own degrees to persons who have accumulated sufficient units, by a broad variety of means. Credit for nonduplicative college courses (both classroom and distance) and many noncollege learning experiences (company courses, military, etc., evaluated as college-level). Regents College recognizes many equivalency exams and offers its own as well, given nationwide and, by arrangement, at foreign locations. Each degree has its own faculty-established requirements with regards to areas of emphasis, but they are not restrictive. The program is described in brochures and catalogs, sent free to all who request them. If nonschool learning experiences cannot be assessed easily at a distance, or by exam, the student may go to Albany, New York, for an oral examination. Regents College makes available to enrolled students a service called DistanceLearn, which is a computer database of nearly 7,000 proficiency examinations and courses offered by other schools that can be completed through home study. In late 1996, Regents will initiate new standards in awarding credit based on exams, in which the score on the exam will determine the amount of credit awarded. It will still be possible to earn 30 units for one GRE exam, but only by scoring in the top 20% of those taking the exam. This is an incentive for students and prospective students to take some exams before fall of 1996.

A long-awaited graduate-level distance degree, the Master of Arts in Liberal Studies, is just starting up; interested students should contact the school for details.

University of Waterloo B
Correspondence Office
Waterloo, ON N2L 3G1 Canada
B. A. Lumsden, Associate Director
Many fields
1957
Nonprofit, state $
(519) 888-4050
Bachelor's degrees can be earned entirely through correspondence, including a non-major B.A. or B.S., a B.A. with a major in classical studies, economics, English, geography, history, philosophy, psychology, religious studies, or social development studies, and a Bachelor of Environmental Studies in geography. Credit is considered for prior academic experience, but none for experiential learning. The programs are available to people residing in Canada and the United States, but U.S. citizens pay three to four times as much tuition. All courses are offered on a rigid time schedule, in which papers and exams must be done by very specific times. As a result, there have been postal delivery problems with some U.S. students. (Suggestion: there is a maximum of six assignments per course; it might well be worth the expense of sending them in via Federal Express or fax.)

University of Wisconsin—Platteville B
Extended Degree Program
506 Pioneer Tower
1 University Plaza
Platteville, WI 53818-3099
John C. Adams, Director
Business administration
1866
Nonprofit, state $$
(608) 342-1468, (800) 362-5460 (WI only)
(608) 342-1466 fax
Limited to residents of Wisconsin, although wholly external. B.S. in business administration through correspondence courses, with some credit for experiential learning, military and other training, and proficiency exams.

University on the Air B
Taipei, Taiwan
Juang Huai-i, President
Many fields
1986
Nonprofit, state $
(02) 282-9355
Degree courses are offered entirely by radio and television. Full-time students must be over 20 and hold a high-school diploma; anyone can study part-time. Sixty of the total 128 required credits must be in one field of study. More than 30,000 students enrolled; all instruc-

tion is in Chinese.

Upper Iowa University   B
External Degree Program
P. O. Box 1861
Fayette, IA 52142
Dave Fritz
Accounting, management, marketing,
public administration
1857
Nonprofit, independent $$$$$
(319) 425-5251, (800) 553-4150
(319) 425-5271 fax
Upper Iowa's External Degree Program offers the opportunity to earn a B.S. in accounting, management, marketing, or public administration through directed independent study, with learning packets containing assignments and other course materials. Lessons may be faxed. Frequent interaction with the faculty by phone or mail is encouraged. An optional two-week summer session is offered on the Fayette campus, allowing students to complete six semester hours of credit. Home-study courses are available in a wide variety of fields, from accounting to chemistry, history to fine arts. Previous college work, job and military training, and other educational experience is evaluated for credit.

Uppsala University   B, M
External Study Programme
P. O. Box 256
Uppsala, S-751 05, Sweden
Birgitta Hyden
Many fields
1477
Nonprofit, state $
46-18-181877
Correspondence courses (in Swedish only) in law, business administration, development studies, international relations, political science, and English and French, for Swedes living in other countries. The courses come from the university and from Hermods, the Swedish National Correspondence Institute. Books, tapes, and assignments are mailed to Swedish nationals worldwide. Examinations may be taken at any Swedish embassy or consulate. Instruction in Swedish.

Washington State University   B
Extended Academic Programs
204 Van Doren Hall
Pullman, WA 99164
Ms. Terry M. Flynn, Director of Admissions
Social sciences
1890
Nonprofit, state $$$
(509) 335-3557, (800) 222-4978
(509) 335-0945 fax
The Bachelor of Social Sciences can be earned entirely

nonresidentially, with credit for prior learning, equivalency exams, and new instruction through correspondence and television courses, guided independent study, audio and videocassettes, and telephone instruction. See also: National Universities Degree Consortium

Western Illinois University   B
Non-Traditional Programs
5 Horrubin Hall
Macomb, IL 61455
Hans Moll, Director
Many fields
1899
Nonprofit, state $$
(309) 298-1929
(309) 298-2400 fax
The Board of Governors B.A. can be earned entirely by correspondence study. Fifteen of 120 semester hours must be earned through one or a combination of BGU Universities, and 40 must be upper division. The 15 units that must be earned through enrollment at a BGU University can be done by correspondence, on-campus in Macomb, or through extension courses at locations around the state. Students who did not graduate from an Illinois high school must pass an exam on the U.S. and Illinois state constitutions, or take an equivalent course in political science. All students must pass a university writing exam. Western Illinois provides a helpful guide to the preparation of a prior learning portfolio. Credit for learning experiences and many equivalency exams. The total cost of the program depends on the number and type of courses taken. The cost of assessing a life experience portfolio is only $30. Students from other countries are admitted, but they must have a U.S. address to which materials can be sent. See also: Board of Governors B.A. Degree Program, Governors State University, Open Learning Fire Service Program, Quad Cities Graduate Center.

Western Michigan University   B, M, D
Kalamazoo, MI 49008
Stanley E. Henderson
Many fields
1903
Nonprofit, state $$
(616) 387-1000
B.S. in general university studies available through the Campus III/Weekend College Program; concentrations include applied liberal studies, health studies, technical scientific studies, and applied professional studies. In addition, the following degrees are available entirely through off-campus regional centers: B.S. in general university studies and production technology, Master and Doctor of Public Administration, Master of Public Administration in health care administration, Master of Social Work, M.B.A., Master in Educational Leadership,

Master in Early Childhood Education, Master in Elementary Education, Master in Reading, M.S. in vocational education, engineering management, industrial engineering, and mechanical engineering, and Master in Industrial Psychology. Residency requirements can be satisfied through work completed at a WMU Regional Center.

Western Oregon State College
See: Open Learning Fire Service Program

Wilfrid Laurier University   B
Part-Time Studies
75 University Ave. West
Waterloo, Ont. N2L 5N3 Canada
Doug Witmer, Director
Sociology
(519) 884-1970
(519) 884-8829 fax

Wholly nonresident B.A. in sociology through teleconferencing and videocassette, offered to students worldwide. Applicants must be at least 21 years old and have two years' work experience.

World College   B
Lake Shores Plaza
5193 Shore Drive
Suite 113
Virginia Beach, VA 23455-2500
Electronic engineering technology
(804) 464-4600

World offers a Bachelor of Electronic Engineering Technology through independent study. All lab equipment, parts, and software are provided (student must have access to a computer), and the program's 300-plus experiments can be completed in the home. Accredited by the Distance Education and Training Council.

"Don' wanna work on my dissertation. Wanna play with my horsie."

"Do you really mean to sit there and say that you aren't going to approve my thesis because I refused to give you a hickey?"

Accredited Schools with Short Residency Programs

I forget what I was taught. I only remember what I learned.
PATRICK WHITE

The schools that follow offer Bachelor's, Master's, and/or doctoral programs that are accredited by one of the recognized accrediting agencies and can be completed with a short time on campus (or at another prescribed location). The intention of such programs, in virtually every case, is that they can be done by people who have regular jobs and wish to keep them. Accredited wholly nonresidential programs are described in chapter 16. Unaccredited schools, or those accredited by unrecognized agencies, are described in chapters 19-21. Programs on which we had insufficient information are listed in Chapter 29.

The basic format of each listing is as follows:

Name of School   **Bachelor's, Master's,**
Address   **Doctorate, Law, Dip**loma
City, State Zip Country
Contact name
Fields of study offered
Year established
Legal/ownership status (nonprofit or proprietary, independent, or state- or church-run), Tuition

Phone, toll-free phone (if any)
Fax

Key to tuition codes:
$ = free or very low cost
$$ = inexpensive
$$$ = average
$$$$ = expensive
$$$$$ = very expensive

(As costs change so quickly, it would be foolish to give dollar amounts. If no symbol is given, it's safe to assume that the school did not provide us with this information.)

American College   **M**
270 Bryn Mawr Ave.
Bryn Mawr, PA 19010
Shirley P. Steinman, CLU, ChFC
Professional
1927
Nonprofit, independent $$
(215) 526-1478
(215) 526-1310 fax
Offers an external Master of Science in financial services and a Master of Science in management, through a combination of distance courses and two one-week residency programs. Also offers the Chartered Life Underwriter (CLU) and Chartered Financial Consultant (CFC) designation programs.

American Technological University   **M**
P.O. Box 1416 Hwy. 190 West
Killeen, TX 76540
Laura Henderson, Admissions Advisor
Technological fields
1973
Nonprofit, independent
(817) 526–1150
Correspondents report substantial credit was given them toward a degree for prior learning and career experience. The school does not wish to appear in this book, but when we leave them out, people write and say, "why didn't you put them in?" so this brief notice is a compromise.

Andrews University   **D**
Berrien Springs, MI 49104
Cyril Connelly, Director of Enrollment
Education
1874
Nonprofit, church $
(616) 471-7771
The Ed.D. and Ph.D. can be earned entirely through summer residency over several summers.

Antioch University   **M**
Antioch International

Individualized Master of Arts Program
800 Livermore St.
Yellow Springs, OH 45387
Karen J. Haas
Many fields
1852
Nonprofit, independent $$$$
(513) 767-6325
(513) 767-6461 fax
Student-designed programs leading to the Master of Arts degree; requires two five-day seminars on Antioch's Yellow Springs, Ohio campus. Each student develops an individualized curriculum under the direction of two degree committee members who are recruited by the student and approved by Antioch University, then complete the coursework in their own community. Coursework may include independent study, research, practicums, workshops, conferences, tutorials, and traditional courses at other institutions. Thesis is required. Popular fields include conflict resolution, peace studies, counseling, applied psychology, creative writing, environmental studies, women's studies, and education. Antioch also offers educational programs through campuses in Los Angeles, Santa Barbara, Seattle, Keene, New Hampshire, and other locations worldwide.

Atlantic Union College   B
Adult Degree Program
South Lancaster, MA 01561
Ottilie Stafford
Many fields
1882
Nonprofit, church $$
(508) 368-2000, (800) 282-2030
(508) 368-2015 fax
Students take one "unit" each semester. A "unit" is a six-month study project, requiring two weeks on campus, and the balance of the time in independent study. A minimum of at least the two final units must be taken within the Adult Degree Program; hence four weeks of residency is required to earn the Bachelor's degree. Bachelor's degrees are offered in art, behavioral science, communications, computer science, education, English, history, interior design, modern languages, personal ministries, physical education, psychology, regional studies, religion, theology, and women's studies. Experiential learning credit through portfolio appraisal.

Atlantic University   M
67th and Atlantic Ave, Box 595
Virginia Beach, VA 23451
Keith Vonderohe
Transpersonal studies
1930
Nonprofit $$
(804) 428-1512

Originally established in 1930 by the Edgar Cayce Foundation, but dormant from 1932 to 1985. The program is interdisciplinary, exposing learners to the transpersonal aspects of psychology, science, and various spiritual traditions. The M.A. can be earned with eight correspondence courses and two courses taken in residence; these two can be taken in one intensive summer session. Accreditation is from the Distance Education and Training Council, and was awarded in 1994.

Bard College   B
Continuing Studies Program
Annandale-on-Hudson, NY 12504
Mary Backlund, Director of Admissions
Many fields
1860
Nonprofit, independent $$$$
(914) 758-6822
Bachelor of Arts, Bachelor of Science, and Bachelor of Professional Studies, designed "to meet the special needs of adults who have left college without completing their studies." Credit for prior learning experiences and for achievement measured by standard proficiency tests. Students attend evening seminars and classes which meet two hours each week; they may also meet with tutors for advanced study twice a month over the course of a 15-week term, or enroll in the regular daytime undergraduate classes. Minimum time to complete the degree is one academic year (10 months), and 30 of the required 124 units must be earned from Bard.

Bishop Clarkson College   B
333 S. 44th St.
Omaha, NE 68131
Nursing, health sciences, radiology
1888
Nonprofit, independent $$$$
(402) 552-3100
(402) 552-2899 fax
B.S. in nursing or radiology technology, M.S. in nursing or health sciences management through a combination of traditional courses, credit for exams, audio- and video-taped classes, independent study, instruction by phone, mail, or e-mail, supervised fieldwork, computer-assisted instruction, and externships. Students must attend one on-campus evaluation in Nebraska, and "geographically distant" RN undergrads meet with faculty three to four times each semester. Graduate courses meet three weekends out of every 12-week trimester.

Bluefield State College
See: West Virginia Board of Regents B.A. Program

Boricua College   B
3755 Broadway
New York, NY 10032

Francia Castro
Liberal arts, natural and social sciences, business, education
1974
Nonprofit, independent **$$**
(212) 694-1000
Bilingual (Spanish/English) college, offering a B.S. through individualized instruction, independent study, and field internships.

Brigham Young University B
305 Harman Building
Provo, UT 84602
Robert W. Spencer
Independent studies
1875
Nonprofit, private **$$**
(801) 378-4351
(801) 378-5278 fax
The Bachelor of Independent Studies Degree program involves independent study and a short period of on-campus study. The degree requires attendance at a maximum of five two-week seminars on campus, one for each of five areas of study. Students who have earned 32 or more semester hours of accepted college credit within the past 10 years may transfer those credits into the program. Only one study area may be waived by a CLEP exam, and only with a score of 610 or higher.

Burlington College B
95 North Ave.
Burlington, VT 05401
David Joy
Liberal arts and humanities
1972
Nonprofit, independent **$$$**
(802) 862-9616
(802) 658-0071 fax
Bachelor of Arts through the primarily nonresident "Independent Degree Program" (IDP). IDP students must have completed 60 college credits and have "strong writing skills and a track record in independent study," and must be able to spend four days on the Vermont campus at the beginning of each semester. IDP students must complete a minimum of 30 credits through the program, regardless of prior experience. Although programs are highly individualized, the school specifically encourages applicants whose interests fall in the fields of fine arts, feminist studies, humanities, psychology, transpersonal psychology, or "almost any liberal arts area(s) of study." Formerly Vermont Institute of Community Involvement.

Caldwell College B
External Degree Program
9 Ryerson Ave.
Caldwell, NJ 07006

Marilyn S. Goodson
Many fields
1979
Nonprofit, church **$$$$**
(201) 228-4424
Bachelor's degrees in business administration, English, foreign languages, history, psychology, religious studies, and sociology. This is primarily an off-campus, independent study program which utilizes tutorial relationships with professors. Students spend one weekend per semester on campus. Credit is given for life experience assessment and by examination.

California State University, Sacramento B, M
6000 J St.
Sacramento, CA 95819
Larry D. Galsmire
Many fields
1947
Nonprofit, state **$$**
(916) 278-6111
The following degree programs have at least some nontraditional elements, including independent study and internships: Bachelor of Arts, Bachelor of Science, Bachelor of Music, Master of Arts, Master of Science, and Master of Social Work. In addition, there is an M.B.A. available largely through teleconferencing (two to four semester-long sessions are required on-campus). The phone number for more information on that program is (916) 278-5974.

Calumet College B
2400 New York Ave.
Whiting, IN 46394
Cindy Hillman
Many fields
1951
Nonprofit, church **$$**
(219) 473-4215
Bachelor's degrees in general studies, social studies, humanities and arts, business administration, and other individualized programs. Up to 75 percent of the units required can come from an assessment of prior learning experience. A course is offered in the preparation of life experience portfolios. An off-campus degree-completion program was established in 1987. In this program, adult students who have already completed 60 credit hours can earn their B.S. in management in 54 weeks, attending class one evening per week.

Capital University B
Adult Degree Program
330 Renner Hall
Columbus, OH 43209
Gary Smith
Many fields

1976
Nonprofit, church **$$$**
(614) 236-6996
A university without walls program begun in 1976 by the Union for Experimenting Colleges and Universities and taken over in 1979 by the venerable Capital University. Beginning students must complete the equivalent of 124 semester credit hours, largely through guided independent study. A Bachelor of Arts, with various majors, or a Bachelor of General Studies, with no major, can be earned. All students must complete a senior project, showing Bachelor's-level abilities and serving as a learning experience. The university maintains Adult Degree Program offices in Cleveland and Dayton as well. Evening and weekend courses and credit for experiential learning available through portfolio assessment/competency statement development.

Charles Sturt University   B, M, D
Locked Bag 676
Wagga Wagga, NSW 2650 Australia
Many fields
1989
Nonprofit
(069) 22-2121
(069) 22-2922 fax
In 1989, Mitchell College of Advanced Education and Riverina-Murray Institute of Higher Education merged to form this school. According to their literature, about two-thirds of Charles Sturt's students study by distance education, and the school is active in developing correspondence courses for other universities. Degrees are offered in a range of fields, grouped into five basic departments: arts, commerce, education, health studies, and science and agriculture.

Chicago State University   B
University Without Walls
9501 S. King Dr.
Chicago, IL 60628
Michelle Howard-Vital
Many fields
1867
Nonprofit, state **$$**
(312) 995-2455
(312) 995-2457 fax
Most University Without Walls students enter with some prior college experience, and are expected to be actively engaged in their proposed field of study and to commit 20 hours a week to the program. Students "identify their own educational needs and propose means to satisfy them," with the help of a faculty advisor and learning coordinators. All students must satisfy general ed requirements in English composition, humanities, mathematics, and natural and social Sciences. Other work may include traditional classes, seminars, readings, research, reports and

surveys, and so on. In the last term, every student must complete a final project demonstrating mastery in his or her field. See also: Board of Governors B.A. Degree Program

College of Saint Scholastica   M
1200 Kenwood Avenue
Duluth, MN 55811-4199
Jennifer Reynolds Jenner, Ph.D.
Management
1912
Nonprofit, church **$$$$**
(218) 723-6150
An M.A. in management through four and a half years of independent study, with a 14-day residency required each year, usually in the summer, as well as completion of a final project.

Columbia University   D
Teachers College, 525 W. 121st St.
New York, NY 10027
Robert E. Furno, Acting Director of Admissions
Education
1887
Nonprofit, independent **$$$$$**
(212) 678-3000
The Doctor of Education is offered through an innovative program called AEGIS: Adult Education Guided Independent Study. The program requires two years to complete, largely through guided independent study, with advisement by correspondence, telephone, or optional campus visits. Participants must attend a seminar on campus one Saturday each month, plus a three-week intensive summer session for both summers of enrollment. The program is designed for experienced, self-directed professionals with at least five years of experience in program development or administration of adult education or training. Admission is highly competitive; about 20 students are admitted every other year.

Corpus Christi State University   B, M
Family Nurse Practitioner Program
Corpus Christi , TX
Christell Bray, Program Director
Nursing
Nonprofit, state **$**
(512) 994-2463
(512) 993-4204 fax
B.S. and M.S. in nursing through a regional interactive television system, providing training toward practice as a family nurse practitioner. Some on-campus residency.

Davis and Elkins College   B
Mentor-Assisted Program, 100 Campus Dr.
Elkins, WV 26241
Kevin D. Chenoweth, Director of Admissions

Various fields
1904
Nonprofit, church $$$$
(304) 636-1900
(304) 636-8624 fax
The Bachelor of Arts or Science in business, management, and other fields can be completed by correspondence courses and independent study, with assistance and guidance by telephone or with a total of two weeks on the campus, in a few short visits over the course of the program.

De Montfort University   B, M, D
Centre for Independent Study
The Gateway, Leicester LE1 9BH, England
Alison M. Cork, Head of Centre
Many fields
1897
Nonprofit, state $$$
(44-116) 257-7015
(44-116) 257-7625 fax
The former Leicester Polytechnic, which became a university in 1992, offers a variety of Bachelor's, Master's, and Doctorate programs largely through independent study, with minimal residence required on the campus in England. Most programs are based on a learning contract, or agreement negotiated between the student and the university. When one is accepted into the program, one is assigned a mentor/supervisor, usually a member of the university staff, who will guide them through their program, and assist in the formulation of a research or study proposal. Normally the mentor meets with the student once during each term. While this is often done in person, it is possible that it could be done by telephone, mail, or email. In lieu of formal examinations, the university conducts "continuous assessment" through a variety of coursework assignments, plus a major project or thesis which accounts for at least forty percent of the total. An oral examination is held at the end of each program. Master's and Doctorates are available in 39 departments of the university, including accounting, architecture, chemistry, computer science, education, electrical engineering, graphic design, human resource management, land management, law, mathematics, nursing and midwifery, physical education, performing arts, pharmacy, textile and fashion, and visual arts. A Bachelor's degree is not required for entry into graduate programs for those who have relevant prior learning gained through their work or personal development.

Eastern Michigan University   M
Division of Continuing Education
Ypsilanti, MI 48197
Paul T. McKelvey, Dean of Continuing Education
Educational administration

1849
Nonprofit, state $$
(313) 487-1081
Master of Arts in educational administration, with much of the work possible through independent or off-campus study, in combination with on-campus meetings and seminars. Several on-campus courses are available on weekends. The Master of Liberal Studies offers the opportunity to design an individualized interdisciplinary program; there is also a specialized M.L.S. in women's studies with an emphasis on feminist scholarship.

Eckerd College   B
Program for Experienced Learners, P.O. Box 12560
St. Petersburg, FL 33733
Dana E. Cozad
History, business management, human development, organizational studies
1959
Nonprofit, independent $$
(813) 864-8226, (800) 234-4735
(813) 864-8422 fax
External Bachelor's degrees available to U.S. residents only, through weekend, evening, and summer programs. Credit by examination, and for directed independent study and prior learning. No physical residency is required, but students must complete at least nine courses through Eckerd College. Two correspondents report that Eckerd encouraged them to enroll in the evening program instead, saying that "most external students end up there anyway."

Elizabethtown College   B
One Alpha Drive
Elizabethtown, PA 17022
Barbara R. Maroney
Professional and liberal studies
1899
Nonprofit, church $$$
(717) 361-1411, (800) 877-2694
Bachelor of Professional Studies and Bachelor of Liberal Studies in religious studies, offered through the EXCEL program. Majors offered in the B.P.S. degree program are: accounting, business administration, communications, criminal justice, early childhood education (non–teaching certification), human services, medical technology, and public administration. Applicants must have a minimum of seven years work experience related to the major field of study and at least 50 semester hours of college study, grade C or better, at regionally accredited institutions, and reside within 400 miles of the college. Credit awarded for CLEP/DANTE exams, certain structured noncredit learning, and (up to 32 semester hours) for experiential learning in the major field of study.

Ferris State University B

Gerholz Institute for Lifelong Learning
Big Rapids, MI 49307
Jeffrey Cross
Environmental health
1884
Nonprofit, state **$$**
(616) 592-2340, (800) 562-9130 (MI only)
(616) 592-2990 fax

Bachelor of Science in industrial and environmental health management offered through the College of Allied Health Science as an external degree program for qualified students anywhere in the United States. (Three years of work experience in the field of environmental health are required for admission to the program.) All of the requirements for the degree can be met through assessment of prior learning experience and a combination of equivalency examinations, independent study, faculty-directed study, home study courses, and special projects. All students must attend a three-week summer session on campus. Prior learning assessment can take as long as a year, and is done for a flat fee of around $250. Off-campus programs in health systems management, nursing, business administration, computer information systems, accountancy, maritime management, and vocational/occupational education (manufacturing, engineering technology, automotive management, construction management) are available at selected sites in Michigan.

Fielding Institute M, D

2112 Santa Barbara St.
Santa Barbara, CA 93105
Sylvia Williams
Psychology, human and organizational development
1974
Nonprofit, independent **$$$$$**
(805) 687-1099
(805) 687-4590 fax

Students must attend a five-day admissions workshop in Santa Barbara (held March, June, and September) before enrolling. This is the only required residency. Regional research sessions and academic seminars are offered at various locations throughout the year. The human and organizational development program offers an Ed.D., a Ph.D. in human and organizational systems or human development, a D.H.S. (Doctor of Human Services), and a Master's degree. The psychology program offers a Ph.D. in clinical psychology. The degrees are neither fast nor easy, but are designed to enable mid-career professionals to attain advanced degrees. It typically takes three to six years to complete the requirements for a doctoral degree. The psychology program has a residency requirement that can be completed through attendance at local student meetings. All students and faculty must have access to an electronic network which offers electronic mail, bulletin board service, and academic seminars.

Florida Atlantic University M

777 Glades Rd.
Boca Raton, FL 33431
W. Douglas Trabert, Director of Instructional Services
Engineering, nursing, education, sciences
1961
Nonprofit, state **$$**
(407) 367-3690
(407) 367-3668 fax

Degrees including M.S. and M.E. in engineering fields (civil, computer science, electrical, manufacturing systems, mechanical, and ocean engineering) through closed-circuit television and videocassette, offered statewide. Some on-campus residency required.

Framingham State College B

100 State St., P.O. Box 2000
Framingham, MA 01701
Walter Czarnec
Liberal studies
1839
Nonprofit, state **$$**
(617) 626-4550

Bachelor of Arts in liberal studies in which units may be earned through equivalency exams, independent study, correspondence study, prior learning experiences, and "non-credit educational experiences." The remaining units must be earned by taking courses on campus, through a series of weekend or summer seminars, or by making other arrangements satisfactory to the advisory committee.

Goddard College B, M

Plainfield, VT 05667
Peter Burns
Many fields
1938
Nonprofit, independent varies
(802) 454-8311, (800) 468-4888
(802) 454-8017 fax

Goddard has been a pioneer in nontraditional, progressive education for more than 50 years. They offer nontraditional options for studies in business and organizational leadership, education, psychology and counseling, natural and physical sciences, feminist studies, visual and performing arts, literature and writing, and social and cultural studies (history, philosophy, religious studies). The first eight days of each semester are spent in residency, where the work of the coming semester is planned. Students may choose to do the majority of their coursework off-campus while maintaining contact by mail every three weeks. Both Bachelor's and Master's programs require a minimum enrollment: two semesters for the Bachelor's, three for the Master's. Credit is available for prior learning, but life experience credit is given only at the Bachelor's level.

Graceland College B

Outreach Program, Division of Nursing
700 College Avenue
Lamoni, IA 50140
Lewis Smith, Jr., Student Information Director
Nursing, liberal studies, addiction studies
1895
Nonprofit, church $$$$
(515) 784-5000, (800) 537-6276
(515) 784-5480 fax

B.S. in nursing designed for working R.N.s, and B.A. in liberal studies. Courses include projects, home study-texts, learning guides (developed by Graceland faculty), videotapes, tests, and final proctored exam. Students are provided a toll-free number for contact with instructors. Up to 64 credit hours can come from evaluation of prior education and experience. B.S.N. program has clinical components; student can come to campus to fulfill these or find a college-approved preceptor to monitor their progress in their own community. There are mandatory two-week residency sessions twice a year.

Holborn College B, L

200 Greyhound Road
London, W14 9RY U.K.
J. R. Fairhurst
Law, business
1970
Independent $$$
(171) 385-3377
(171) 381-3377 fax

Offers the B.S. in economics and, through an affiliation with the University of Wolverhampton (formerly Wolverhampton Polytechnic), an LL.B. (Honours) which may qualify graduates to take the Bar in England. Both programs take a minimum of three years to complete, and were originally tutorials for the University of London's exams. Holborn's catalog notes that its degrees, legitimate in their own right, "can also be used by students as an access programme" to the prestigious London degrees. The LL.B. can be completed entirely by mail, with the exception of exams held yearly in London, Hong Kong, Kuala Lumpur, and elsewhere by special arrangement. Only first-year B.S. courses are offered by distance learning, after which students have the option of full-time, weekend, or intensive two-day pre-exam courses.

Humanistic Psychology Institute

See: Saybrook Institute

Huron University B, M

3-5 Palace Gate
London, W8 5lS England
Gordon Bennett, Provost
Many fields
1883

$$$$
071-584-9696
071-589-9406 fax

This London program of South Dakota–based Huron offers B.A., B.S., and M.B.A. Fields of study include art, art history, international relations, CIS, management, international business marketing, finance, applied economics, humanities and European studies, with independent study and international internship options. One year must be spent in residence.

International Management Centres B, M
(USA) Inc.

3050 Post Oak Blvd., Ste. 400
Houston, TX 77056
Robert L. Stein
Management, business administration,
training and development
1964
Nonprofit $$$$$
(713) 960-7171
(713) 784-9605 fax

This is the U.S. agency for a U.K.-based program (headquartered in Buckingham) offering the Bachelor's and Master's in management, business administration, and training and development. Credit for prior learning on Bachelor program except final credits. All programs are work-based action learning and must have a sponsorship of employers. Short residency requirements are at tutorial centers in one of 25 countries worldwide or in companies for groups of managers. Accredited by the Distance Education and Training Council. Formerly associated with Northland Open University.

Iowa State University B, M

204 Carver Hall
Ames, IA 50011-2010
Karsten Smedal, Director of Admissions
Many fields
1858
Nonprofit, state $$
(515) 294-5836, (800) 262-3810
(515) 294-0565 fax

The university offers an external degree called the Bachelor of Liberal Studies, primarily for residents of Iowa who are able to attend one of the off-campus centers around the state or occasional courses on the Ames campus. Previous Iowa State students with sufficient credit may also be eligible for the program. In addition, evening and weekend courses are offered toward degrees in agriculture, business, design, education, engineering, family and consumer sciences, and liberal arts and sciences. Upper-division B.S. in agriculture (for students who have completed their first two years of study elsewhere) and Master of Agriculture (M.Ag.) largely through locally available satellite and cable television programs, as well as videotaped programs. Many

121

courses require one Saturday on campus per credit, plus one week during the summer. See also: Quad Cities Graduate Center

John F. Kennedy University   B, M
12 Altarinda Rd.
Orinda, CA 94563
Ellnea Bloedorn, Registrar
Many fields
1964
Nonprofit, independent $$$
(510) 254-0200

Many innovative Bachelor's and Master's programs, in fields including liberal studies, museum studies, business administration, holistic health education, sport psychology, and more. While many courses are available on a part-time basis, all of JFK's degree programs require on-campus classroom attendance, with the exception of a Master's in career development, which has only a two-week summer residency. The university sees a major role for itself in helping adults to accomplish midcareer changes (their average student is 37 years old).

Kings College   B
Gateway Adult Program
Wilkes-Barre, PA 18711
Darlene A. Gavenonis
Many fields
1946
Nonprofit, independent $
(717) 826-5865

Darlene A. Gavenonis, Office Coordinator for the school's Center for Lifelong Learning, has written asking us not to describe Kings College's innovative degree program. For more details, you will need to contact the school directly.

Lesley College   B, M
29 Everett St.
Cambridge, MA 02138
Kimberly J. Kautz
Many fields
1909
Nonprofit, independent $$$$
(617) 349-8482, (800) 999-1959
(617) 349-8717 fax

Bachelor or Master of Science in cooperation with the National Audubon Society, involving a combination of coursework and expeditions. Audubon's Expedition Institute has a two-year program, or a field component: camping, hiking, canoeing, skiing, backpacking, and cycling all over America. Students gain practical knowledge of astronomy, anthropology, ecology, etc. The balance of the time is spent in classes at Lesley. The M.S. involves a year or a year and a half on Audubon expeditions and three or four courses at Lesley. Students may switch between Lesley and Audubon. Also offers short-residency Bachelor's and Master's programs in a variety of concentrations. Limited-residency B.S. and B.A. programs in behavioral science, human services, and education. Weekend and independent study are used. The M.A. and Master of Education are offered as independent-study degree programs, allowing individualized curricula developed by graduate students and faculty advisory teams.

Liberty University   B, M
School of LifeLong Learning
3765 Candlers Mountain Road
Lynchburg, VA 24506
Tom Clinton, Associate Provost
Religious and business fields
1971
Nonprofit, church $$
(804) 522-4700, (800) 228-7354

Liberty's "School of LifeLong Learning" offers accredited degrees largely through home study. Bachelor's degrees can be earned in church ministries, business administration, and psychology; Master's in counseling or religion. Six to 12 credit-hours (two to four classes) are normally required to be taken in residence; this can be accomplished during summer or other holiday seasons. Faculty are regularly available, and a toll-free number is provided for all communications. While residential students at Liberty must have accepted Jesus Christ as their personal savior, external students are not required to have done so. The founder of Liberty is the Rev. Jerry Falwell.

Lindenwood College   B, M
St. Charles, MO 63301
Arlene Taich
Many fields
1827
Nonprofit, independent $$$
(314) 949-2000

B.A., B.S., M.A., and M.S. through the College for Individualized Education, in administration, psychology, health administration, gerontology, valuation sciences, communications, and human and organizational development may be earned through evening and summer programs. The International Valuation Sciences degree program is primarily an off-campus degree program for experienced appraisers. There is a two-week on-campus session each year for at least two years. Credit for independent study, nonacademic prior learning, and by examination.

Linfield College   B
McMinnville, OR 97128
Vicki Lind, Director of Continuing Education
Management, systems analysis, liberal studies
1849
Nonprofit, church $$$$
(503) 472-4121, ext. 247

(503) 472-9528 fax
Residential degree programs offered at a number of Oregon locations. B.S. in management and B.A. in systems analysis or liberal studies, in which nearly 80% of the necessary units can come from a combination of assessment of prior learning and equivalency exams. A required course assists the student in preparing a life-experience portfolio.

Loyola College   B, M
4501 N. Charles
Baltimore, MD 21210
William J. Bossemeyer III, Director of Admissions
Business, accounting, education, nursing
1852
Nonprofit, church $$$
(800) 221-9107
B.A. in accounting and general business through evening study; Bachelor of Education can be earned evening and weekends; M.A. in psychology, evenings, weekends, and afternoons; M.B.A., evening; and Master of Education, afternoons, evenings, and weekends. B.S. in nursing for R.N.s can be completed largely by videocassette, although at least two days on campus are required (one for orientation, and the first day of the student's first nursing course).

Maine Maritime Academy   M
Castine, ME 04420
Wallace S. Reed
Maritime Management
1941
Nonprofit, state $$$$
(207) 326-4311
Master of Science in maritime management through a modular graduate degree program that can be completed "without career interruption." This is a business degree with emphasis on marine issues. Courses are scheduled in compact four-week modules that allow participants to remain fully employed while studying. A total of seven four-week modules are required for the Master's. The tuition fee includes books and materials.

Mankato State University   B, M
Alternative Degree Program
South Rd. and Ellis Ave.
Mankato, MN 56002
Many fields
1866
Nonprofit, state $$$
(507) 389-2463
(507) 389-1040 fax
B.S. in open studies and M.S. in continuing studies, for alternative students whose "personal, educational, or career goals require a program not confined to the demands of a specific discipline." Credit awarded for military experience, equivalency exams, television courses, independent

study, and supervised fieldwork. Attendance at an annual on-campus seminar is required.

Marshall University
See: West Virginia Board of Regents B.A. Program

Mary Baldwin College   B
Adult Degree Program
Staunton, VA 24401
James P. McPherson
Many fields
1842
Nonprofit, church $$$$
(703) 887-7003, (800) 822-2460
(703) 886-5561 fax
Bachelor of Arts program in which virtually all of the work can be done independently, or at a distance. The program is entirely nonresidential. Students need to come to the campus only once, for a day of orientation. Advanced standing is given for work done at other schools, equivalency examinations, and the assessment of prior learning. The degree program has regional offices in Richmond, Charlottesville, and Roanoke, Virginia, in addition to the main office in Staunton. The degree requires a minimum of nine months to complete.

Marywood College   B
Off-Campus Degree Program
2300 Adams Ave.
Scranton, PA 18509-1598
Patrick J. Manley, Director
Business administration, accounting
1915
Nonprofit, church $$$$
(717) 348-6235, (800) 836-6940
(717) 348-1817 fax
The Bachelor of Science degree in accounting or business administration is earned through a combination of distance-learning (114 credits) and two two-week residencies (12 credits) held on the campus: one midway through the program, and one near the end. A minimum of sixty (60) of the required 126 credits must be earned after enrolling at Marywood. Transfer credit is available through the evaluation of prior learning. A deferred tuition payment plan is available, as well as financial aid for those who qualify. Program technology includes audio-video as well as electronic mail.

Massey University   B, M
Centre for University Extramural Studies
Private Bag 11555
Palmerston North, New Zealand
T. K. Prebble
Many fields
1960
Nonprofit, state $

0-6-356-9099

Massey offers an external degree program, in which the majority of work can be completed by correspondence study, utilizing books, audio- and videocassettes, regional courses, and short on-campus courses. Degrees are offered in humanities, social sciences, science, business studies, agricultural science education, and technology. At present, enrollment in most courses is restricted to citizens of New Zealand.

Mercy College B, M
555 Broadway
Dobbs Ferry, NY 10522
Ralph W. Conant
Many fields
1950
Nonprofit, independent $$$
(914) 693-4560

Bachelor's degrees through a wide variety of methods designed to accommodate the adult student, including evening classes held twice a week for eight weeks; once-a-week Friday or Saturday classes for 16 weeks; and a home-study program for students who prefer to work independently (on-campus orientation session, midterm, and final exam required). Also, summer and January intersession programs. Parallel scheduling is designed to accommodate students who work rotating shifts, such as police and nurses, with the same class taught both day and evening, so that the student may attend either one. Credit is awarded for life achievement and by examination. In addition, the school offers a four-year bilingual program for Spanish-speaking students, and an extensive support program for the learning-disabled.

Metropolitan State University B
700 E. 7th St.
St. Paul, MN 55101
Janice Harring-Hendon, V.P., Marketing
Many fields
1971
Nonprofit, state $$
(612) 772-7777

Metropolitan State University is a pioneer in nontraditional programs, offering flexible Bachelor's and Master's programs, including an individualized Bachelor of Arts, Bachelor of Arts in accounting, business administration, human services, information and computer systems, nursing, professional communications, and a Master of Management and Administration. Daytime, evening, and weekend classes are offered in facilities throughout the Twin Cities area.

Murray State University B, M
Bachelor of Independent Studies
P.O Box 9
Murray, KY 42071-0009
Hughie G. Lawson, Director
Independent studies, nursing
1922
Nonprofit, state $
(502) 762-4159, (800) 669-7654
(502) 762-3593 fax

Bachelor of Independent Studies through correspondence study, television, and contract learning courses, as well as experiential credits. Many weekend and evening classes are available. Twenty-four of the 128 required semester hours must be taken with Murray State. Departmental challenge exams are available in some fields. If the exam is passed, credit is awarded. All students must attend a day-long seminar, held on Saturdays in April, August, and December. Admission to the program is based on satisfactory completion of the seminar. All students must earn credit in basic skills, humanities, science, social sciences, and electives, and complete a study project. Murray State charges a relatively low fee for portfolio assessment. Also, an M.S. for R.N.s who already have a B.S. in nursing, offered by remote television at three sites within a 100-mile radius of the campus. The contact for that program is Marcia Hobbs, at (502) 762-2193. Overseas applicants are not accepted.

New Hampshire College B, M
2500 North River Rd.
Manchester, NH 03106
Anne F. Lilly, Senior Program Asst.
Human services, social work
1932
Nonprofit, independent $$$
(603) 668-2211
(603) 644-3150 fax

Bachelor's and Master's can be earned entirely through weekend study (classes meet once a month, all day, for four months). The undergraduate program in human services (concentrations in counseling, administration, labor studies, and criminal justice) is designed to allow people with prior experience to enter as freshmen, sophomores, or juniors, depending on their prior work. The M.S. in human services has concentrations in administration, gerontology, and community service. There is also a Master of Social Work. A full-time student taking three classes would be at the college for one long weekend (Friday through Sunday) or two adjacent weekends (two Saturdays and a Sunday, or vice versa) each month. This program is also offered in London, through Lansdowne College.

Northeastern Illinois University B, M
5500 N. St. Louis Ave.
Chicago, IL 60625
Miriam Rivera
Liberal arts, education, business
1961

Nonprofit, state $$
(312) 583-4050
Bachelor of Arts with a minimum residency requirement of 15 semester hours, which can be completed in four months on campus. One of the five Illinois universities participating in the Board of Governors Bachelor of Arts program (see description under separate listing). Credit is given for life experience and all prior learning experiences. New credit may be earned through regular courses at any of the five schools in the program, or by correspondence study and independent study. (The five Board of Governors schools started out with almost identical programs, but now two, Western Illinois and Governors State, offer totally nonresident programs).

Northern Arizona University   B, M
P.O. Box 6235
Yuma, AZ 85366
Gus Cotera, Executive Director
Education, liberal studies
1899
Nonprofit, state $$$
(602) 344-7721
(602) 344-7743 fax
B.A. in liberal studies and Master of Education through courses beamed in real-time two-way video from the main campus at Flagstaff to remote sites statewide. Remote students can ask questions and otherwise participate as though they were present in the classroom. Some on-campus residency required.

Northwood University   B
External Plan of Study
3225 Cook Rd.
Midland, MI 48640
Donald L. Knight, Associate Dean
Management, accounting, computer science, marketing, economics
1959
Nonprofit, independent $$
(517) 631-1600, (800) 445-5873
(517) 832-9590 fax
Bachelor of Business Administration can be earned in either business or accounting with a total of six days on campus. Credit is given for prior learning and for equivalency exams. The external plan of study has many courses which can be passed by taking an open-book exam. All students must attend two three-day seminars on campus, write a thesis, and pass a final oral examination "which will last for several hours and be based on questions provided to the student in advance." Fees are quite variable depending on the approach a student takes. Northwood has offered this program at other locations around the U.S., including sites in California, Florida, Indiana, Louisiana, Michigan, and Texas.

Norwich University   B, M

Vermont College
College St.
Montpelier, VT 05602
Gregory Dunkling
Liberal studies, visual art, writing, art therapy
1834
Nonprofit, independent $$$
(802) 828-8500, (800) 336-6794 (outside VT)
(802) 828-8855 fax
Vermont College of Norwich University offers several of the longest-running external degree programs in North America for adult learners. The programs are structured to allow students great latitude in designing their studies in conjunction with faculty mentors. The Adult Degree Program (B.A.), begun in 1963, features short residencies in Vermont (9 days every six months or one weekend a month), alternating with study at home. Faculty guide and support student work in the liberal arts, including psychology and counseling, literature and writing, management, and education. The Graduate Program, started in 1969, offers self-designed studies in the humanities, arts, education, and social sciences including psychology and counseling. Regional meetings are held quarterly or monthly by program faculty. Students work with two advisors, a core faculty member who is responsible for a geographical region of the country and a field advisor, a local expert in the student's field of study. The M.A. in art therapy offers a 15-month program which includes summer residencies in Vermont. M.F.A. in writing or visual arts through off-campus programs with 9-day residencies twice a year in Vermont.

Nova Southeastern University   D
3301 College Ave.
Fort Lauderdale, FL 33314
Stephen Feldman, President
Education, administration, business, computer systems, social and systemic studies, liberal studies, psychology, speech and language, law
1964
Nonprofit, independent $$$$
(305) 475-7300, (800) 541-6682
(305) 475-7621 fax
Nova University has one of the more nontraditional doctoral programs ever to achieve regional accreditation. The typical student attends one group meeting a month (generally two or three days), plus two one-week residential sessions, and from three to six practicums which emphasize direct application of research to the workplace. Total time: about three-and-a-half years. The university also offers a Doctor of Arts in information science in which students use interactive computers. A major part of instruction in this program is through teleconferencing, TELNET, and TYMENET. Residential work has been offered in 23 states. Nova will consider offering the program in the continental United States wherever a cluster

of 20-25 students can be formed. Formerly Nova University; they recently merged with Southeastern Medical School, hence the name change.

Nova University
See: Nova Southeastern University

Oklahoma City University   B
Competency-Based Degree Program
N. W. 23rd at N. Blackwelder
Oklahoma City, OK 73106
Melissa Lamke
Many fields
1901
Nonprofit, state $$$
(405) 521-5265, (800) 633-7242, ext. 8
(405) 521-5264 fax
A Bachelor of Arts or Science degree can be earned by utilizing a combination of alternative methods: independent study, seminars, assessment of prior learning, and traditional courses. Each student must visit the campus to attend an orientation workshop, and additional campus visits may be necessary. The university has asked us to point out that the program may be suitable for some distance students; however, it may not meet the needs of others. An evaluation of each student's educational situation is necessary.

Oral Roberts University   B
Center for Lifelong Education (CLLE)
7777 South Lewis Ave.
Tulsa, OK 74171
Jeff L. Ogle
Church ministries, Christian care and counseling, business administration, elementary Christian school education
1965
Nonprofit, church $$
(918) 495-6238, (800) 678-8876
(918) 495-6033
The B.S. is offered largely through home study and independent study, with one week per year on campus. Credit is given for experiential learning, independent study, and equivalency exams. Applicants must sign a pledge not to use tobacco or alcohol, not to lie, cheat, curse or steal, and promise to participate in an aerobics program, attend church, avoid homosexual behavior, and to commit their lives to Jesus.

Ottawa University   B, M
1001 S. Cedar
Ottawa, KS 66067-3399
Harold D. Germer
Many fields
1865
Nonprofit, church $
(913) 242-5200, (800) 255-6380
(913) 242-7429 fax
Ottawa offers nontraditional Bachelor's programs in many

fields, and a Master's in human resources, through "adult centers" in Kansas City, KS, and Phoenix, AZ, as well as teacher certification programs at the Ottawa campus. Evening classes, and credit for life-experience learning through portfolio assessment, as well as equivalency exams and self-paced independent study. There are plans to open a third nontraditional center in Milwaukee in the very near future. The school suggests that interested students contact the closer campus directly; the addresses and phone numbers are:
Ottawa University Kansas City, 10865 Grandview, Bldg. 20, Overland Park, KS 66210; (913) 451-1431
Ottawa University Phoenix, 2340 W. Mission Lane, Phoenix, AZ 85021; (602) 371-1188
Directed studies (individually scheduled courses) are offered for individuals and small groups. They begin at any time and students progress at their own speed.

Pennsylvania State University   M
256 Applied Sciences Bldg.
University Park, PA 16802
Professor Alan Stuart
Acoustics
1855
Nonprofit, state $$$$
(814) 863-4128
Master of Science in acoustics through a special program for employees of the U.S. Navy and its contractors nationwide. Learning takes place through compressed-video television courses; one two-week summer session required.

Portland State University   M
P.O. Box 751
Portland, OR 97207-0751
Katherine Novy
Business administration
1946
Nonprofit, state $$$
(503) 725-3000, (800) 547-8887, ext. 4822
(503) 725-4882 fax
P.S.U.'s School of Extended Studies offers what they call a "statewide M.B.A." at 12 colleges, community colleges, local businesses, and corporate sites throughout Oregon, and one site in Washington. A new site can be established in a community where at least six students will enroll in the program. Classes meet two evenings a week, and students must also get involved in a study group with others at their site. One week after each lecture is delivered on campus, statewide M.B.A. students view that class on videotape. There is a toll-free phone number so students can communicate with faculty concerning coursework. The program takes three years to complete, and all students must go to the P.S.U. campus twice a year for special case study classes.

Prescott College   B

Adult Degree Program
220 Grove
Prescott, AZ 86301
Lydia Mitchell
Management, counseling, teacher education, human services, individually designed liberal arts programs
1966
Nonprofit, independent $$$
(602) 776-7116
(602) 776-5137 fax
Prescott's Adult Degree Program offers a student-centered independent-study format, using instructors from a student's home community. Students normally take two courses every three months, meeting weekly with local instructors wherever they live. (Prescott helps locate them.) Students must come to the college for a weekend orientation at the beginning of their program, and for an additional liberal arts seminar, also held on a weekend. Degree programs can be individually designed to meet students' goals. Entering students normally have a minimum of 30 semester hours of prior college work. One year enrollment with Prescott is required to earn the degree. Credit for prior college-level learning can be awarded through the writing of a life-experience portfolio.

Princeton Theological Seminary   D
CN 821
Princeton, NJ 08542-0803
Marija S. DiViaio, Program Assistant
Ministry
1812
Nonprofit, church $$
Doctor of Ministry (D.Min.) for working ministers through a program that consists largely of indepndent study. All participants are required to attend three on-campus workshops of two to three weeks; the entire program usually takes three to four years to cmplete.

Purdue University   B, M, D
West Lafayette, IN 47907
William J. Murray, Director of Admissions
Education, engineering, technology, management, pharmacy
1869
Nonprofit, state $$
(317) 494-1776
(317) 494-0544 fax
B.S. in technology or pharmacy; M.S. in engineering for fully employed engineers (primarily through televised or live classes at the worksite) and in education (generally through summer classes) for persons already working in the field. M.S. in management is available entirely by home-computer classes (Macintosh only), plus a total of 12 weeks on campus. Master's in pharmacy and Pharm.D. available in part through videocassette. A variety of evening and weekend programs for adult students are offered in

various Indiana cities.

Ramkhamhaeng University   B
Huamark
Bangkapi
Bangkok, 10240 Thailand
Business, humanities, education, science, political science, economics, law
1971
Nonprofit, state $
(02) 318-0860
(02) 318-0917 fax
With over 400,000 students, Ramkhamhaeng, which operates on the open-admissions system, is one of the world's largest universities. Bachelor's degrees are offered through a combination of on-campus lectures, lectures shown on videotape at centers around the country, and courses broadcast nationally on 44 radio stations. Cooperative arrangements with the University of Pittsburgh, City University of New York, Southern Illinois University, and the University of Surrey.

Regent University   M
Center for Extended Learning
Virginia Beach, VA 23464
Mike Gray, Enrollment Manager
Business, management
1977
Nonprofit $$$$
(804) 424-7051, (800) 477-3642
The M.B.A. and the M.A. in management can be earned through a combination of correspondence courses, guided independent study, audio- and videocassettes, and instruction by telephone and mail, plus a total of two one-week periods on campus. An accelerated program allows students who have completed three years of undergraduate work (90 semester hours) and have five years work experience to enroll in the Master's program without completing a Bachelor's. The university integrates traditional Judeo-Christian ethical principles in the teaching of each course.

Rice University   M
School of Engineering, P.O. Box 1892
Houston, TX 77251
Hardy M. Bourland, Associate Dean
Electrical engineering, computer science
1891
Nonprofit, independent $$$$$
(713) 527-4955
(713) 285-5300 fax
Master's in electrical engineering or computer science (M.E.E. or M.C.S.) offered to members of local industry, primarily through the Educational TV network. Some on-campus time is required for advising, seminars, and exams.

Rikkyo University   D

3-chome, Nishi-Ikebukuro, Toshima-ku
Tokyo, 171 Japan
S. Furuichi
Many fields
1874
Nonprofit, independent
(03) 985-2204
Doctoral degrees solely on the basis of a submitted dissertation (which can be in English), plus a series of written examinations taken in Japanese in Tokyo. Rikkyo was established by an American bishop in 1874, and was taken over by the Japanese in 1920. Applicants are asked to request a copy of the regulations governing the awarding of degrees at Rikkyo before submitting any materials. Once a preliminary application (a 2,000-word summary of the dissertation and a curriculum vita) is accepted, then the full work is presented. The applicant then goes to Japan to take written exams in the topic of the dissertation, and in two languages other than his or her native one. If the applicant's level of academic achievement is commensurate with others who have earned the Doctorate at Rikkyo, then the degree is awarded. Also known as Saint Paul's University.

Rochester Institute of Technology B, M
1 Lomb Memorial Dr.
Rochester, NY 14623
Richard Fuller
Technical fields, art, design, graphic arts, photography
1829
Nonprofit, independent $$$$
(716) 475-4089, (800) CALL-RIT
(716) 475-5089
B.S. in many technical fields, including engineering and computer science, as well as photography and graphic arts; M.S. in engineering technology or business technology, all through a combination of evening study, independent study, and some fieldwork. B.S. in electrical/mechanical technology has no on-campus requirement for applicants who live outside New York state and have an Associate's degree (in-state students must complete two courses on campus). M.S. in mathematical statistics requires two short on-campus seminars, plus independent study and a thesis. M.S. in software technology can be earned nonresidentially through a variety of nontraditional methods, including videocassettes, e-mail, cable television courses, and courses on disk.

Saint Francis Xavier University M
Department of Adult Education
Antigonish, NS B2G 1C0 Canada
Chair, Department of Adult Education
Education
1853
Nonprofit $$
(902) 867-3952

(902) 867-5153 fax
A Master's degree in adult education is offered through a short residency and guided independent study, often with an "area specialist" in the student's home town. Applicants must have at least two years experience in adult education.

Saint Joseph's College B, M
External Degree Program, Department 840
Windham, ME 04062-1198
Jamie Morin-Reynolds, Director
Health care administration, business administration, professional arts, long term care, radiologic technology
1912
Nonprofit, church $
(207) 892-6766, (800) 752-4723
(207) 892-7480 fax
Programs offered through faculty-directed independent study, with campus-based advising and instruction: Bachelor of Science in health care administration (with majors in general health care and long term care), business administration, professional arts (a degree-completion program for licensed health care professionals), and radiologic technology (a degree-completion program for rad techs); M.S. in health services administration. B.S. requires a three-week residency on-campus in Windham, Maine; M.S., two weeks.

Saint Mary's College (Minnesota) M
2510 Park Ave.
Minneapolis, MN 55404
Marilyn Frost, Dean
Human development and education
1912
Nonprofit, church $$$
(612) 874-9877
The Master of Arts in human development is for persons living within a 100-mile radius of Minneapolis, St. Paul, Winona, or Rochester, Minnesota. The Master of Arts in education program is for those living within the state of Wisconsin. All students must spend some time on the graduate campus in Minnesota or at a central location in Wisconsin. This residency may be as little as one weekend. Credit is given for completion of learning contracts negotiated between the student and the advisor. Most students complete the Master's in 24 to 30 months.

Saint Mary-of-the-Woods College B, M
External Degree Program
Saint Mary-of-the-Woods, IN 47876
Kathi Anderson
Many fields
1840
Nonprofit, church $$
(812) 535-5106, (800) 926-SMWC
(812) 535-4613 fax

Majors offered at the Bachelor's level include accounting, business administration, management, marketing, English, humanities, journalism, gerontology, paralegal studies, psychology, social science, theology, early childhood education, elementary education, kindergarten/primary education, and secondary education certification. Master's degrees available in pastoral theology. Life experience credit awarded to those with college-level knowledge acquired other than in a classroom environment. Students are guided by faculty via mail and phone in off-campus independent study, punctuated with brief on-campus residencies (an average of one day per semester). Only women are awarded the Bachelor's degrees, but both sexes can earn the Master's degree.

Saint Paul's University
See: Rikkyo University

Saybrook Institute   M, D
450 Pacific, 3rd Floor
San Francisco, CA 94133
Kathy Trimble, Director of Admissions
Psychology, human science
1970
Nonprofit, independent $$$$$
(415) 433-9200, (800) 825-4480
(415) 433-9271 fax
Courses are offered in an independent study format: a course guide is provided, specifying the required readings and including written lecture materials prepared by the faculty. Students may design their own courses as well. Student work focuses within four areas of concentration: clinical inquiry, systems inquiry, health studies, and consciousness studies. All students must attend a five-day planning seminar in San Francisco, and two one-week national meetings each year. Degrees can take from two to four years to complete. Many well-known psychologists have been associated with Saybrook (Rollo May, Stanley Krippner, Richard Farson, Nevitt Stanford, Clark Moustakas, etc.). Saybrook, until 1982, was called the Humanistic Psychology Institute.

Skidmore College   B, M
University Without Walls
Saratoga Springs, NY 12866
Robert H. Van Meter
More than 50 majors
1911
Non-profit, independent $
(518) 584-5000
(518) 584-7963 fax
Above address is the contact for the university without walls. For the external Master's degree program (also short residency), contact: Lawrence Ries, Director, Master of Arts in Liberal Studies, (518) 584-5000. Skidmore is one of the pioneers of the nontraditional movement, having offered a university without walls program since 1970. It is possible to earn their Bachelor of Arts or Bachelor of Science with a total of three days on campus: one for an admissions interview, a second for advising and planning, and

the third to present a degree plan to a faculty committee. Skidmore makes it clear that they hold their graduates to "standards of knowledge, competence and intellectual attainment which are no less comprehensive and rigorous than those established by traditional . . . programs." In addition to fulfilling all other requirements in the degree plan, each student completes a final project demonstrating competence in one's field. Students can major in any of the dozens of fields offered by Skidmore or, with the assistance of faculty advisors, devise a self-determined major. In 1992 Skidmore launched a Master's program in interdisciplinary studies, modeled on its highly successful undergraduate program.

Sonoma State University   B, M
1801 E. Cotati Ave.
Rohnert Park, CA 94928
Frank M. Tansey, Dean of Admissions
Psychology
1960
Nonprofit, state $
(707) 664-2778
The B.A. in psychology can be completed entirely through evening courses, and there is a one-year external Master's in psychology. Although there is no requirement to take any specific classes for the Master's, students must attend occasional meetings with a faculty advisor. The program is designed jointly by student and faculty, and can include coursework, fieldwork, research, and independent study. Applicants must have a Bachelor's degree, one year of graduate-level experience in humanistic psychology, and 9 unit of credit previously earned (in residence or by extension) from Sonoma State. A requirement of basic knowledge in psychology can be met through courses or by examination. About 40 new applicants are admitted each fall.

Southern Methodist University   B, M
Evening and Summer Studies
Dallas, TX 75275-0382
Robert Patterson
Many fields
1911
Nonprofit, church $$$$
(214) 768-5465
Bachelor of Social Science, Bachelor of Humanities, and Master of Liberal Arts, all through evening study in the School of Continuing Education. In the North Texas area, students can earn an M.S. in engineering management, operations research, computer engineering or science, mechanical, or electrical engineering largely through satellite television courses, visiting the campus only for exams.

Southern Oregon State College   B, M
1250 Siskiyou Blvd.
Ashland, OR 97520
Larry Nollenberger, Director of Program Advising
Many fields
1926
Nonprofit, state $$

(503) 482-3311

At the undergraduate level, "Special Academic Credit" (credit by examination, equivalency exam, prior learning experience, and correspondence courses) may be applied to degree programs. Fields include business, education, performing arts, nursing, social sciences, sciences, math, and humanities. Up to 90 credits may be earned in this manner. Assessments based on a portfolio prepared by the student after taking a required course on how to do so. Students must complete 45 credits at SOSC, exclusive of prior learning credit. An M.S. in education is available to working teachers, mainly through courses viewed at distant sites, videocassette, computer conferencing, and telephone instruction. One summer session, or several weekend courses required. Contact for Master's program is David Hoffman, at (503) 552-6283.

Southwest Baptist University   B
1600 University Avenue
Bolivar, MO 65613
Ben Sells, Enrollment and Admissions
Applied science, nursing
1878
Nonprofit, church $$$$
(417) 886-8883
(417) 886-8897 fax
Bachelor of Science in applied science or nursing, with a minimum of four weeks on campus, for a special summer term. Credit awarded for life-experience learning, through portfolio assessment. Additional learning takes place through audio- and videotaped classes, correspondence courses, cooperative education, independent study, and supervised fieldwork.

Southwestern Adventist College   B
Keene, TX 76059
Marie Redwine
Many fields
1893
Nonprofit, church $$$
(817) 645-3921, (800) 433-2240
(817) 556-4742 fax
B.A., B.S., and Bachelor of Business Administration through the Adult Degree Program (ADP). Virtually all work can be completed at a distance, following an eight-day admission seminar, held each March, June, and October. Credit is earned by transfer of credit, proficiency exams, credit for prior learning (portfolio), and independent study by mail, computer, and telephone. ADP students pay 80 percent of the tuition of on-campus students. Majors include business, communication, education, English, office administration, computer science, religion, social science, and history.

Southwestern Assemblies of God College   B
1200 Sycamore

Waxahachie, TX 75165
Jim Jessup, Director of Adult Education
Education
1927
Nonprofit, church $$$
(214) 937-4010
(214) 923-0488 fax
Bachelor's in adult and continuing education through a largely nonresidential program open to anyone who makes a statement of Christian faith. Instruction is through audio- and videocassette, teleconferencing, and computer conferencing; students must spend two days on-campus at the beginning of each semester, for registration.

Southwestern College   B, M
Winfield, KS 67156
Douglas M. Mason, Director of Admissions
Human resources, manufacturing technology, total quality management, education
1885
Nonprofit, church $
(316) 221-4150
(316) 221-3725 fax
Southwestern offers Bachelor's-completion programs in human resources, manufacturing technology, and total quality management through evening and weekend courses, with credit available for life-experience learning and CLEP exams, as well as an M.Ed. with some nontraditional aspects. Residents of Cowley County, Kansas (wherein Southwestern is located) who are over 65 years of age may take courses free of charge.

Sri Lanka Institute of Distance Education   B
P. O. Box 1537
Maligawatte, Colombo, Sri Lanka
Science, technology, management, mathematics
Higher National Diplomas in science, technology, management, and mathematics through correspondence studies, with occasional face-to-face meetings at one of 12 national centers. Some fields require attending laboratory sessions. Instruction is given in English, Sinhala, and Tamil.

State University College   B
Cooper Center
Brockport, NY 14420
Marsha R. Gottovi
Science, natural science, social science
1835
Nonprofit, state $$
(716) 395-2211
Bachelor of Liberal Studies, with a minimum of three weeks on campus for an annual seminar. The degree is offered in science, natural science, and social science. Students may design their own concentrations or majors. Credit is given for prior learning experiences, both formal and informal, as well as for equivalency exams, indepen-

dent study, and correspondence courses. The minimum time of enrollment is one academic year (nine months).

Stephens College   B
College Without Walls, Campus Box 2121
Columbia, MO 65215
LuAnna Andrews
Many fields
1833
Nonprofit, independent $$$
(314) 876-7125, (800) 388-7579
(314) 876-7248 fax
Bachelor of Arts in business, psychology (clinical counseling or general), philosophy and religion, health care and a second area, allied health and a second area, philosophy, law and rhetoric, and liberal arts, as well as student-initiated majors combining two or more disciplines. Bachelor of Science in health information management (processing program to advance to RRA) as well as early childhood and elementary education. Degree requirements can be met through independent study. Students may also earn credits through short-term, intensive courses, CLEP exams, prior learning portfolios, approved courses taken locally, etc. Students attend a three-semester-hour introductory liberal studies seminar at Stephens College prior to admission. The course is offered in seven-day or double-weekend formats several times throughout the year. A minimum of 30 semester hours must be completed with Stephens College faculty. Open to women and men 23 years of age and older.

Syracuse University   B, M
Independent Study Degree Programs
Syracuse , NY 13244-6020
Robert Colley, Director
Many fields
1870
Nonprofit, independent $$$$$
(315) 443-3284
(315) 443-1928 fax
B.A. in liberal studies; B.S. in business administration, criminal justice, or restaurant and food-service management; M.A. in advertising design or illustration; M.B.A., Master of Library Science, Master of Social Science, and M.S. in nursing, all with short residency on campus and independent study in between. All undergraduate degrees and the M.B.A. require three seven-day residencies per year. The average completion time for the M.B.A. is two and a half years; the Bachelor's degrees take a minimum of one year (30 credits) for people with substantial transfer credit, though in practice most students take quite a bit longer. The Master of Social Science requires two 14-day sessions on campus in July (but not necessarily two consecutive sessions); alternative sessions are offered in Washington D.C. and London. The M.A. degrees, which are taught by many of the country's best-known art direc-

tors, designers, and illustrators, require three two-week summer sessions on campus and several shorter sessions offered in New York, San Francisco, Chicago, and other metropolitan areas. The M.L.S. requires three two-week summer sessions, and four additional weeks over a two-year period. The M.S. in nursing requires four short summer sessions.

Trinity College   B
Individualized Degree Program
Hartford, CT 06106-3100
Denise T. Best, Assistant Director
Many fields
1823
Nonprofit, independent $$$$
(203) 297-2150
Bachelor of Arts and Bachelor of Science in a wide range of fields, including art history, American studies, biochemistry, classics, computer sciences, economics, history, mathematics, philosophy, public policy studies, theater arts, women's studies, and other fields. Degree programs are individually tailored, and amount of time on campus varies by program—some can be completed entirely through independent study, others require laboratory work or a limited number of on-campus classes. Tuition, as well, is tailored to a student's class standing, and their courseload.

Trinity University   M
715 Stadium Drive
San Antonio, TX 78212
Richard C. Elliott
Health care administration
1869
Nonprofit, independent $$$$
(512) 736-7011
(512) 736-7696 fax
Master's in health care administration available almost entirely through home study. Each course begins with an intensive three-day on-campus program, followed by independent home study. Support is offered in the form of regular teleconferencing sessions with the instructor.

Union Institute   B, M, D
440 E. McMillan St.
Cincinnati, OH 45206-1947
Jennifer King Cooper, Admissions Coordinator
Many fields
1964
Nonprofit, independent $$$$$
(513) 861-6400, (800) 543-0366
(513) 861-0779 fax
Union was established by the Union for Experimenting Colleges and Universities, a consortium including some large state universities, to be, in effect, their al-

ternative program. The undergraduate "University Without Walls" Bachelor's degree may involve independent study, directed reading, internships, on-the-job education, classroom instruction, tutorials, etc., as well as credit for prior learning experiences. The required residency involves a weekend colloquium (held in various locations) and occasional seminars. At least nine months are required to earn the degree. The Ph.D. begins with a 10-day "entry colloquium" held in various locations. The candidate develops a committee of at least five, including two peers and two experts of his or her own choosing, and works with them to establish a learning agreement, including an internship. All Ph.D. students must attend at least three five-day seminars at least six months apart, and another 10 days' worth of meetings with three or more other learners, or 35 days total. A typical Doctoral program takes two to four years, culminating in a Project Demonstrating Excellence: a standard or nonstandard dissertation project, showing that the student is able to perform creatively. A comparable, but shorter Master's degree program is available as well. Earlier name: Union Graduate School.

Universidad Autonoma Nacional de Mexico B
Circuito Exterior de la Ciudad Universitaria
Mexico, D.F. 04510 Mexico
Jorge Carpizo McGregor, Rector
Many fields
Nonprofit, state $
550-52-15
Mexico's national open university has prepared substantial course texts, each created by a team that includes academics, audio-visual specialists, and a graphic designer. Each text consists of a work guide, written materials, boxes of laboratory or field experiments, self-revaluation materials, and perhaps movies, tapes, and other audio-visual aids. Students must visit the university to take an examination after completing each course; there are courses offered in dental surgery, poultry breeding, English literature, Hispanic literature, history, economics, philosophy, sociology, education, law, business administration, psychology, nursing, international relations, mass media, and accounting.

Universidad de San Jose M, D
Regional Information office
7891 W. Flagler St.
Suite 123
Miami, FL 33144
Johnny Ortega
Administrative sciences, education and humanities, psychology and behavioral science, social science, biological science, science.
1976
Nonprofit, private $$$$

(305) 225-3500
The International Post-Graduate School offers nonresidential instruction in the English language, with a two-week on-campus residency requirement. Students are able to complete their studies for a post-graduate degree off-campus under the direct guidance of an academic advisor. The Master's program must be completed in less than three years, the Doctorate in less than five. Two study options are offered: a curriculum-based program for students who have the need to take traditional coursework in addition to the thesis/dissertation, and a research-based program for qualified students who already possess the necessary theoretical knowledge and experience in their area of expertise.

Universidad Nacional de B
Educacion a Distancia
Ciudad Universitaria
Madrid, 28040 Spain
Elisa Perez Vera, Rector
Many fields
1972
Nonprofit, state
(91) 449-3600
Spain's national open university offers degrees in a wide range of academic subjects. Each group of 150 students has a professor-tutor responsible for guidance and personal contact. More than 40 centers around the country (including 11 within large business, government, and military offices) are available for seminars, conferences, and lectures. Most work is done at a distance by use of written and audio-visual materials.

Universidad Nacional de Educacion B
"Enrique Guzman y Valle"
La Cantuta, Chosica, Peru
Literature, science, geography, mathematics, industrial technology
1905
Nonprofit, state $
91-00-52
Peru's national open university pilot project is for working teachers. It offers them correspondence courses and short-residency study; most work is done at a distance.

Universiti Sains Malaysia B
Minden
Penang, Malaysia
Many fields
Nonprofit, state
604-887812
B.A. and B.S. students work for a minimum of 5 and a maximum of 12 years toward the degree, mainly by correspondence and independent study using printed ma-

terials, tapes, and slides mailed to them. Tutorials are conducted by means of a two-way audiographic communication system linking the school with 10 regional centers. Students are required to come to campus once a year for a three-week residential program.

University of Alabama, New College   B, M
External Degree Program, P. O. Box 870182
Tuscaloosa, AL 35487-0182
Harriet Cabell
Many fields
1831
Nonprofit, state $$
(205) 348-6000
(205) 348-6544 fax

The Bachelor of Arts or Bachelor of Science may be earned entirely through nonresident independent study, with the exception of a two-day degree planning seminar on the campus at the start of the program. At least 32 semester hours of work must be completed after admission. This can be by out-of-class contract learning, correspondence courses, television courses, weekend college, prior learning evaluation, or on-campus courses at the university. Interdisciplinary degrees offered in human services, humanities, social sciences, natural sciences, applied sciences, administrative sciences, and communication. A 12-semester-hour senior project is required of all students. Academic advising and planning can be done by telephone. A Master's in criminal justice that requires just two weeks on campus is offered through the College of Continuing Studies, Box 870388, Tuscaloosa, AL 35487-0388. There often seems to be a waiting list to get into this program.

University of Calgary   B, M
Distance Education
Calgary, Alberta T2N 1N4 Canada
Irene Meek
Nursing, education
1980
Nonprofit, state $$$$
(403) 220-7346
(403) 284-4879 fax

Degree-completion program for R.N.s leads to a B.S. in nursing, through teleconferencing and videocassette. M.Ed. also available though nontraditional means.

University of Colorado—Boulder   M
Center for Advanced Training in Engineering
Campus Box 435
Boulder, CO 80309
Engineering
1876
Nonprofit, state $$$
(303) 492-6201

(303) 492-5105 fax

Master of Engineering offered to working adults through distance learning methods, in the following concentrations: aerospace, civil, electrical/computer, or software engineering, engineering management, telecommunication, and computer science. Students take one class per semester, finishing the degree in three and a half years. Distance-learning options include audio- and videocassettes, independent study, and television courses.

University of Colorado—Denver   M
Executive Program in Health Administration
P.O. Box 480006
Denver, CO 80248
Health administration
1912
Nonprofit, state $$$$$
(303) 623-1888, (800) 228-5778

Master of Science in health administration for working health-care professionals, primarily through computer conferencing and e-mail. Students must attend intensive on-campus sessions in Denver approximately four times throughout the two-year program. Instruction is by faculty from 11 accredited health-administration programs that make up the Western Network for Education in Health Administration (for information on the California-based Network, call 510-642-0790). Most if not all students are currently working in hospitals, community clinics, group practices, long-term care facilities, public-health agencies, and other health-related organizations.

University of Delaware   B, M
Clayton Hall
Newark, DE 19716
Richard B. Fischer, Director of Continuing Education
Many fields
1833
Nonprofit, state $$
(302) 831-2741

Bachelor of Arts or Bachelor of Science in accounting, chemistry, computer and information services, criminal justice, engineering technology, English, history, nursing, and psychology, as well as an M.B.A. and M.Ed., all through evening study. B.S. in nursing for R.N.s by videocassette, with only one weekend required on campus (will change to three weekends in the near future, according to the school). Contact for this program: Madeline Lambrecht, (302) 831-8368.

University of Durham   M
Business School
Mill Hill Lane
Durham City, DH1 3LB U.K.
John F. Ross
Business administration
1988

Nonprofit, state $$$$
(119) 374-2219
(191) 374-3389 fax
In mid 1988 Durham introduced a distance learning M.B.A. (they have offered a traditional M.B.A. since 1967). The program is administered by the University Business School to students in more than 40 countries. The three-to-four-year course of study combines specially written distance-learning materials, annotated texts, audiotapes, and one week per year of intensive residential seminars (first year excluded).

University of Evansville   B
Center for Continuing Education
1800 Lincoln Ave.
Evansville, IN 47722
Lynn R. Penland
Many fields
1854
Nonprofit, church varies
(812) 479-2981
(812) 479-2320 fax
The External Studies Program offers a B.A. or B.S. in virtually any field (although not generally in the technical or professional, such as mathematics, chemistry, engineering, computer science, nursing, and education) through a combination of classroom and correspondence courses, coursework from nontraditional sources, proficiency exams, independent study, and credit for life-experience learning. Students develop their own individualized plans in a two-day, on-campus educational planning workshop. Students can take up to 10 years to finish their self-paced degree program. Credit available for military and other life-experience learning, by portfolio assessment, and for a range of equivalency exams.

University of Kentucky   M, D
Lexington, KY 40506
Eugene R. Williams, Information Services
Business, public administration, engineering, family studies, education
1865
Nonprofit, state $$
(606) 258-9000
(606) 257-4000 fax
M.B.A. and Master of Public Administration may be earned through a combination of weekend and evening classes. Master of Engineering or Mineral Engineering, M.S. in family studies or special education, and Ed.D. in a number of concentrations all available through courses beamed to a large number of remote sites, with a brief residency requirement (usually one or two summer sessions).

University of La Verne   D
College of Graduate & Professional Studies

1950 Third Street
La Verne, CA 91750
Thomas R. Harvey, Program Chairperson
Educational management
1891
Nonprofit, independent $$$$
(714) 593-3511
(714) 593-0965 fax
This three-year doctoral program, designed primarily for the practicing school administrator, leads to an Ed.D. in educational management. It requires two nine-day seminars on campus, as well as several "regional cluster meetings" with faculty and other students. Students meet regularly in locations convenient to them, followed by periods of independent study.

University of Maryland   B
University College
College Park, MD 20742
Paul Hamlin
Technology & management, behavioral & social sciences, humanities, fire science, business, nuclear science, paralegal studies
1856
Nonprofit, state $$
(301) 985-7722, (800) 888-UMEC
(301) 454-0399 fax
University College, the continuing higher education campus of the University of Maryland System, offers B.A. and B.S. degrees in flexible formats through its Open Learning Program. Attendance is optional except for the introductory session and examinations. There are regional educational centers throughout the Washington-Baltimore area. A primary concentration in fire science is offered via independent study in a six-state region and the District of Columbia. Credit is available for relevant college-level prior learning. Paralegal training. See also: National Universities Degree Consortium

University of Massachusetts at Amherst   B
University Without Walls
University of Massachusetts
Amherst, MA 01003
Elizabeth Brinkerhoff
Humanities, sciences, social sciences, engineering, business, health sciences.
1863
Nonprofit, state $$$
(413) 545-1378
Amherst's University Without Walls helps nontraditional students attain a B.A. or B.S. degree through the University of Massachusetts, while working around the kinds of work and family responsibilities most college freshmen don't have. Each UWW student designs his or her own area of study, aided by a UWW advisor. UWW students satisfy the University's graduation requirements through

transfer credits, regular university coursework, and independent studies. UWW also awards credit for life experience based on an extensive portfolio review. The program cannot be done through correspondence; students must live within commuting distance of Amherst or Springfield, Mass.

University of Mindanao   M
College of Education, Bolton St.
Davao City
Mindanao Island, Philippines
Paquita Gavino
Education
1946
Nonprofit, independent
The university's on-the-air project offers a Master's degree in education entirely through radio broadcasts. Students submit terms papers, prepare workbooks, and take examinations at the university.

University of Minnesota   M
ISP Executive Study Program
School of Public Health
D-309 Mayo Bldg., Box 97
420 Delaware St. S.E.
Minneapolis, MN 55455-0381
1851
Public health, healthcare administration
(612) 624-1411
(612) 626-1186 fax
Two very competitive Master's programs, a Master of Healthcare Administration (M.H.A.) and Master of Public Health (M.P.H.), through three-year programs that require two weeks on campus each year. Students work on correspondence packets, and meet monthly with a preceptor in their area. The school stresses that these are *not* entry-level programs and that, in fact, the higher up the administrative level you are, the more likely you are to be admitted.

University of Missouri at Columbia   B
College of Agriculture Food and Natural Resources
Nontraditional Study Program
215 Gentry Hall
Columbia, MO 65211
Richard Linhardt
General agriculture
1839
Nonprofit, state $$
(314) 882-6287
(314) 882-6957 fax
Bachelor of Science in general agriculture is awarded for at least 128 semester hours including required courses and electives. Options for earning credit include college coursework, correspondence study, extension courses, CLEP, departmental examination, and evaluation of life

learning experience. Only students who have not enrolled in any school full-time for at least five years are accepted. Prior college-level work is required. Students with less than 60 hours of college work are discouraged. The program is not available to persons outside the United States.

University of Natal   M, D
King George V Avenue
Durban 4001,   South Africa
Many fields
1910
Nonprofit, state
031-816-9111
031-816-2214 fax
Natal's Master's and Doctoral degrees are research-based, which means that there is no coursework; the degree candidate does individual, independent research, culminating in a thesis that is submitted for in-person examinations. Requirements for specific degrees may vary; fields include business administration, agriculture, architecture, arts, commerce, economics, education, engineering, languages, medicine, science, and social sciences.

University of Nebraska—Lincoln   M, D
Division of Continuing Studies
157 Nebraska Center
Lincoln, NE 68583-0900
Nancy Aden
Engineering, business administration, computer science, education, journalism, home economics
1869
Nonprofit, state $$$
(402) 472-1924
(402) 472-1901 fax
M.S. in several engineering fields (industrial and management systems, manufacturing systems, mechanical) and computer science, and an M.B.A. through teleconferencing, e-mail, and courses beamed to distance-learning sites around the state. Ed.D. in curriculum and instruction requires only one summer session on campus. They want readers to be very clear that the one thing they do not offer is an external degree.

University of New Brunswick   B, M
Extension and Summer Session
P.O. Box 4400
Fredericton, NB E3B 5A3 Canada
John Morris, Director
Education, nursing
Nonprofit, state
(506) 453-4646
(506) 453-3572 fax
B.A. and M.A. in education available to residents of the New Brunswick province through tele- and videoconferencing, with one or two summer sessions required. B.S. in nursing for R.N.s available nationwide

and to residents of Bermuda, through audiocassette, public television, and teleconferencing.

University of New England　　　B, M
Distance Education and Open Learning Center
Armidale, NSW 2351 Australia
J. Chick, Director
Many fields
1938
Nonprofit, state $
(067) 73-2661
(067) 71-1644 fax

Bachelor's and Master's degrees are offered in accounting, arts, letters, Asian studies, science, computer science, economics, agriculture, administration, leadership, and urban and regional planning through the Department of External Studies. Instruction is by the same faculty that teach on-campus courses, and is via various media, including printed lecture notes, interactive TV and radio, video- and audiocassettes, and printed lecture notes. Students must attend a certain number of residential vacation sessions on campus; voluntary weekend sessions are also available, the majority of them in Sydney. Enrollment in most programs is restricted to full-time residents of Australia, or Australians with resident status who are temporarily overseas.

University of North Carolina at Chapel Hill　M
Regional Degree Programs & Off-Campus Programs
CB #7400
McGavran-Greenberg Hall
Chapel Hill, NC 27599
Barbara Chavious
Public health, health care administration
1793
Nonprofit, state $$
(919) 966-7364
(919) 966-6961 fax

The Executive Master's programs offer working health professionals the opportunity to earn a Master of Public Health in either management or dental health and a Master of Health-care Administration over three years, with six on-campus weeks per summer, and two each January. Applicants must have at least three years' experience in their field or a Doctoral-level professional degree in an appropriate field.

University of North Dakota　　　B, M
Grand Forks, ND 58202
Alice C. Poehls, Admissions
Nursing, medical technology, business and public administration, social work, engineering
1883
Nonprofit, state $$$$
(701) 777-2011
(701) 777-3650 fax

Degree programs through courses sent to distance sites around the state, by videocassette, interactive television, public and educational network TV, and fax. B.S. in nursing, medical technology, and engineering, Bachelor of Social Work, M.P.A., and M.B.A. On-campus time varies by program; can be as little as two weeks.

University of Oklahoma　　　B, M
College of Liberal Studies
660 Parrington Oval
Norman, OK 73019
Dan A. Davis, Associate Dean
Liberal studies
1890
Nonprofit, state $
(405) 325-1061
(405) 325-7605 fax

Bachelor and Master of of Liberal Studies with two or three weeks each year on campus, plus directed independent study. B.L.S. students work in three areas: humanities, natural sciences, and social sciences. Sessions on-campus are required each year, but three of the four years may be waived, based on prior study or passing of an equivalency exam. In the fourth year the student completes an in-depth study and attends a mandatory seminar. There is an upper-division option for applicants with two years of college, which allows them to begin with a five-day residential seminar and complete all three phases in about a year, with the final seminar required, as with the four-year B.L.S. There are no majors; students do elective study based on their interests. The M.L.S. is largely for people with specialized Bachelor's degrees who wish a broader education; it begins with a two-week on-campus seminar. See also: National Universities Degree Consortium.

University of Pittsburgh　　　B, M
External Studies Program
3808 Forbes Ave.
Pittsburgh, PA 15260
Sandra Haber
Psychology, economics, history, business administration
1787
Nonprofit, state $$$$
(412) 624-7210

Bachelor of Arts in psychology, economics and history, as well as core courses required for any degree offered in the College of General Studies (the University of Pittsburgh's evening college). Faculty-prepared self-instructional manuals and textbooks are used by students who complete the majority of their coursework at home. Attendance is expected at the three three-hour Saturday workshops held for each course at the Pittsburgh campus. Students may choose from among 14 testing sites located throughout Western Pennsylvania to take exams when they are ready to do so. Courses, faculty, tuition and transcript credits are the same as for Pitt's traditional classroom-based programs. Also, an M.B.A. through two different nontraditional formats: the executive M.B.A., for students who live within a 150-mile radius of Pittsburgh and can attend one weekend class every other week, and the "Flex-M.B.A.," offered to participants throughout the world, with a 14-week residency requirement that can be fulfilled two weeks at a time over two years. Contact for these Master's programs is A. C. "Skip" Gross, Jr., at (412) 648-1604.

University of Sarasota   M, D
5250 17th Street, Suite 3
Sarasota, FL 34235
Ned B. Wilson, Provost and CEO
Business, education
1969
Nonprofit, independent $$$$
(813) 379-0404, (800) 331-5995
(813) 379-9464 fax
Master of Business Administration, Master of Arts in Education (M.A.Ed.), and Doctor of Education, with a number of areas of concentration, and Doctor of Business Administration . Some intensive coursework in Florida is required. Courses are in the summer, with one-week seminars in winter and spring. Total residency may be as short as six weeks. The university's programs consist of seminars, supervised individual research, and writing, combined with the residential sessions. Master's candidates either write a thesis or complete a directed independent-study project. Doctoral students must write a dissertation. Many of the students are teachers and school administrators. (Originally known as Laurence University, the predecessor of the Laurence University that opened in California and is now the University of Santa Barbara.)

University of South Carolina   M
Columbia, SC 29208
T. Luther Gunter, Registrar
Library and information science, engineering, business administration
1801
Nonprofit, state $$$$
(803) 777-0411
The University of South Carolina beams courses to distance-learning sites by satellite; other learning takes place through e-mail, and audio- and videocassette. They offer a Master's in library and information science (M.L.I.S.) through centers in South Carolina, West Virginia, and Georgia; an M.S. or M.E. in a variety of engineering fields (chemical, civil, mechanical, electrical, and computer), though a program for working engineers, and an M.B.A. through a program that requires 15 Saturday sessions on-campus per year. See also: National Universities Degree Consortium

University of South Florida   B
4202 E. Fowler Ave.
Tampa , FL 33620
Kevin E. Kearney, Director, BIS
1956
Nonprofit, state $$$
(813) 974-4058, (800) 635-1484
(813) 974-5101 fax
The Bachelor of Independent Studies program requires from four to six weeks on campus, spread out over three summers. All students must have knowledge of other broad areas of study: social sciences, natural sciences, and humanities. Each area has an extensive program of guided independent study and a two-week on-campus seminar for research, writing, peer interaction, and, when relevant, laboratory experience. Two areas can be waived for students who have sufficient work background, provided they pass an equivalency exam. All students must write a thesis and defend it orally in a one-day examination on campus. The average student takes over five years to complete the degree, but there is a wide range. Applicants with an A.A. degree—or an A.S. in certain health-related fields—qualify for a two-area curriculum, with no thesis required.

University of Tennessee, Knoxville   M
Knoxville, TN 37996
Gordon Stanley, Director of Admissions
Engineering
1794
Nonprofit, state $$$
(615) 974-1000
(615) 974-3536 fax
M.S. in a wide number of engineering fields (including aerospace, chemical, electrical and computer, science and mechanics, industrial, mechanical, management, etc.) available nationally by videocassette. There is also a corporate M.S. program through courses at a distance center in Kingsport, or at local businessplaces, and a similar program geared to government employees and contractors (but open to locals as well) offered in Oak Ridge.

University of Virginia   M
Televised Graduate Engineering, Thornton Hall
Charlottesville, VA 22903
George L. Cahen, Jr., Assistant Dean
Engineering
1819
Nonprofit, state $$$$
(804) 982-4051
(804) 924-4086 fax
Master of Engineering in a number of fields, including chemical, civil, electrical, materials science, mechanical and aerospace, nuclear, and systems engineering, available nationwide by satellite television. Classes are televised live to numerous locations throughout the U.S. in the evening hours, four days a week.

University of Wales — M, D
University Registry, Cathays Park
Cardiff, CF1 3NS Wales
Many fields
Nonprofit, state $
(1222) 22656

External Ph.D.'s may be pursued at any of the campuses of the university. Each candidate works with a supervisor, who is a present or former full-time member of the academic staff. An applicant must have an approved Bachelor's degree, demonstrate that there are adequate facilities at the "home base" for pursuing research (library, laboratory, archives, etc.), and be able to pay regular visits to the university (typically three visits a year to meet with the director of studies, or one month a year in continuous work). Initial inquiries to the department head of the relevant department, or the registrar of the institution chosen. They are: University College of Wales, Aberystwyth, Dyfed SY23 2AX; University College of North Wales, Bangor, Gwynedd LL57 2DG; University of Wales College, Cathays Park, Cardiff CF1 3XA; University College of Swansea, Singleton Park, Swansea SA2 8PP; Saint David's University College, Lampeter, Dyfed SA48 7ED; University of Wales, College of Medicine, Heath Park, Cardiff CF4 4XN.

University of Warwick — M
66 Banbury Rd., Wolsey Hall
Oxford, OX2 6PR England
Business
Nonprofit, state $$$

Students anywhere in the world may register with Warwick and then pursue the M.B.A. from home, with the aid of a distance-learning course developed by Wolsey Hall, a private school that has, for many years, offered distance-learning courses for the University of London's external degrees. There is an eight-day residency each year on campus in England, or in Hong Kong, Singapore, or Malaysia. The period of study is usually four years, roughly 12 hours a week, but it can be three years if the dissertation is completed during the final year of study. There is direct contact with tutors. Wolsey Hall also offers a free six-lesson course in essential study skills for those who have been away from academic learning for a while. Optional weekend seminars are held three times a year in England, Hong Kong, Singapore, and Malaysia. Access to a personal computer is desirable but not essential.

University of Wisconsin—Green Bay — B
Individualized Learning Programs Office
Green Bay, WI 54301
Katherine Olski, Director
General studies
1978
Nonprofit, state $$
(414) 465-2423

Nontraditional program is available only to Wisconsin residents; B.A. in general studies requires at least two seminars held on-campus on Saturdays. Program includes independent study, research projects, internships, radio and television courses, and other learning methods.

University of Wisconsin—Madison — M
Engineering Outreach
1415 Johnson Dr., Rm. 2713
Madison, WI 53706-1691
Helene Demont, Program Assistant
Engineering
1849
Nonprofit, state $$$
(608) 262-5516
(608) 262-6400 fax

M.S. in nuclear engineering, power electronics, or engineering controls, primarily through satellite television and videocassette. Three weeks on campus required for a summer intersession laboratory course.

University of Wisconsin—River Falls — B
Extended Degree Program
College of Agriculture
River Falls, WI 54022
Gary Rohde, Dean
Agriculture
1874
Nonprofit, state $$
(715) 425-3239 (800) 228-5421
(715) 425-3304 fax

B.S. in agriculture for residents of Wisconsin and Minnesota only. Most of the coursework can be completed through home study, with occasional visits to the River Falls campus (actual number of visits will depend on the courses taken). Credit for agricultural life experience through portfolio assessment, and for departmental and CLEP exams. Financial aid is available.

University of Wisconsin—Superior — B
Extended Degree Program
Old Main 237
Superior, WI 54880
Carolyn A. Petroske
Many fields
1893
Nonprofit, state
(715) 394-8487

Bachelor of Science can be completed entirely through off-campus independent faculty-guided study. However, on-campus conferences with faculty are required. The student designs an individualized major based on personal or career goals. Competency-based, self-paced courses developed by the university faculty in a wide variety of fields are the primary mode of learning, in addition to learning contracts. The student has the option of requesting credit for prior learning through the development of a portfolio. The program is open to Wisconsin residents and Minnesota residents who qualify for reciprocity.

University of Wyoming   B, M
Off-Campus Degree Programs
Laramie, WY 82071
Richard A. Davis, Director of Admissions
Public administration, social science, administration of justice, adult education, speech pathology
1886
Nonprofit, state $$$
(307) 766-1121, (800) 448-7801, ext. 5
(307) 766-2271 fax
B.A. in social science or administration of justice, M.A. in adult education, M.S. in speech pathology, and Master of Public Administration through distance-learning courses, including videotaped lectures and an innovative audio teleconferencing technique. The social science program is upper division only; it is assumed that students will transfer in 60 credits of lower-division coursework from another institution. The M.S. requires at least two summers on campus.

Vermont Institute of Community Involvement
See: Burlington College

Virginia Polytechnic Institute and   M
State University
College of Engineering, 333 Norris Hall
Blacksburg, VA 24061
Benjamin S. Blanchard, Assistant Dean
Engineering
1872
Nonprofit, state $$$$
(703) 231-5458
(703) 231-7248 fax
M.S. or M.E. in various engineering fields (electrical, mechanical, system, civil, and industrial), though satellite courses available nationwide, and audioconferencing.

Walden University   M, D
155 Fifth Ave. South
Minneapolis, MN 55401
Glendon Drake
Administration/management, education, human services, health services
1970
Nonprofit, independent $$$$$
(612) 338-7224, (800) 444-6795
(612) 338-5092 fax
Walden has just inaugurated a Master's degree program in educational technology. More information can be found on-line by e-mailing help@waldenu.edu or calling their 800 number. Their doctoral program serves midcareer professionals with a Master's or equivalent. Doctoral programs (Ed.D. or Ph.D.) can be completed through a combination of independent study, intensive weekend sessions held regionally, personal interaction with the faculty, and a three-week summer residency at Indiana University. Admissions workshops are held in a dozen or more cities in the U.S. and Canada each year. Each student is guided by a faculty advisor, with a reader and external consultant/examiner added at the dissertation stage. Each student completes a series of "knowledge area modules," in areas ranging from research methodology to social systems. Ed.D. candidates must complete a 200-hour supervised internship. The school's academic policy board is chaired by Harold Hodgkinson, former director of the National Institutes of Education.

Weber State University   B
Office of College of Health Professions
Outreach Program
3750 Harrison Blvd.
Ogden, UT 84408-4011
William E. Smith
Allied health sciences
1889
State $$
(801) 626-6785, (800) 848-7770, ext.7164
(801) 626-7558 fax
B.S. in allied health sciences, with concentrations in health administrative services, advanced radiological sciences, respiratory therapy, and advanced dental hygiene. Up to 46 credit hours for CLEP exams, and up to 15 for two full years military service. At least 45 credit hours must be taken through WSU, through intensive workshops and independent study. Correspondence courses include textbooks, study guides, modules, video- and audiotapes, and other learning aides prepared by the instructor. Student is assigned an instructor for each course, and keeps contact by phone and mail. Student has up to six months to complete each course. Workshops are four three- to four-day sessions per year at various sites, including Billings, MT and Seattle, WA, or two six day "super sessions" at WSU. Exact number required depends on student's precise field of study.

Webster University   M
470 E. Lockwood Avenue
St. Louis , MO 63119
Charles E. Beech, Director of University Admissions
Business, computers, health
1915
Nonprofit, independent
(314) 968-6900
Now, here's the problem. Their innovative Master's programs, offered in dozens of locations around the U.S., used to be described in glowing terms in this book. We received more than 20 letters from people who enrolled as a result of our report and were happy. Then the coordinator of

Experiential and Individual Learning wrote and demanded that we stop providing information on their programs. So we left them out for one edition and, needless to say, got a bunch of letters from people saying, in effect, "How come you didn't put anything in about Webster?" And as we were working on this edition, Charles E. Beech, Director of University Admissions, wrote to ask that the school be deleted, although he didn't explain why. To find out, you'll have to write to him at the address above.

West Virginia Board of Regents B.A. Program   B

203 Student Services Bldg.
West Virginia University
Morgantown, WV 26506
Alan W. Jenks, Coordinator
Many fields
1867
Nonprofit, state $$
(304) 293-0111

This B.A. program requires a minimum of 15 semester hours in residence at any of the member schools in the state, and states that "as long as the student can provide evidence that he/she possesses college equivalent knowledge or skills, his/her achievements will be credited and recognized as applicable toward this degree program." The evaluation of life experience costs a modest $50, regardless of the amount of credit granted. The member schools are: Bluefield State College, West Virginia State College, Concord College, West Virginia Tech, Fairmont State College, West Virginia University, Shepherd College, West Liberty State College, Marshall University, and Glenville State College.

West Virginia Institute of Technology   B

Regents B.A. Degree Program
Montgomery, WV 25136
Many fields
1895
Nonprofit, state $$$
(304) 442-3071
(304) 442-3059 fax

B.A. largely through credit for life-experience and academic learning, equivalency exams, independent study, correspondence courses, supervised fieldwork, and televised classes. Fifteen credit hours must be earned on-campus.

Westminster College (Pennsylvania)   B

New Wilmington, PA 16172
Jesse Thomas Mann, Associate Dean
Many fields
1852
Nonprofit, church
(412) 946-7120

Jesse Thomas Mann, Associate Dean of the College, has written asking us not to describe their innovative Bachelor's degree program. For further information, then, you will need to contact the school directly, or see separate listing in this book under East Central College Consortium

Wolverhampton Polytechnic (London)

See: Holborn College

Accredited Schools with
Nontraditional Residential Programs

I find the three major administrative problems on a campus are
sex for the students, athletics for the alumni, and parking for the faculty.
CLARK KERR, WHEN PRESIDENT OF THE UNIVERSITY OF CALIFORNIA

The schools that follow offer Bachelor's, Master's, and/or doctoral programs that are accredited by one of the recognized accrediting agencies and are, in one way or another, nontraditional, although residency is required. Generally such programs are for people who already live in the vicinity of the school or are willing to relocate. Chapters 16 and 17 described the nonresident and short residency accredited schools. Unaccredited schools, or those accredited by unrecognized agencies, are described in chapters 19-21. Programs on which we had insufficient information are listed in Chapter 29.

The basic format of each listing is as follows:

Name of School   Bachelor's, Master's,
Address   **D**octorate, Law, **Dip**loma
City, State Zip Country
Contact name

Fields of study offered
Year established
Legal/ownership status (nonprofit or proprietary, independent, or state- or church-run), Tuition

Phone, toll-free phone (if any)
Fax

Key to tuition codes:
$ = free or very low cost
$$ = inexpensive
$$$ = average
$$$$ = expensive
$$$$$ = very expensive

(As costs change so quickly, it would be foolish to give dollar amounts. If no symbol is given, it's safe to assume that the school did not provide us with this information.)

Aalborg University Centre   B, M, D
Langagervej 2
P.O. Box 159
DK-9100, Aalborg, Denmark
P. Peter Lykke
Economics, engineering, business, social work, humanities
1974
Nonprofit, state $
(98) 1585-22
Students at this experimental Danish university spend one year in residential study, then work on independent-study projects in small groups. All degrees are based on passing examinations.

Abingdon University Institute
25 Sun St., Hitchen
Hertfordshire, SG5 1AH England
P. Graham
Has not responded to several requests for information about their nontraditional programs.

Acadia University   B
Wolfville, NS BOP 1X0 Canada
D.J. Green
Many fields
Nonprofit, state
(902) 542-2201
Although many courses are offered through correspondence and by teleconference, and a limited number of courses may be transferred from elsewhere, the school wants prospective students to be aware that it is not possible to complete all degree requirements nonresidentially. Many courses offered on audio- or videotape.

Adams State College   M
Department of Teacher Education
Alamosa, CO 81102
Philip Gore, Director of Field Services
Education
1921

Nonprofit, state $$$
(719) 589-7121
(719) 589-7522 fax
Field-based M.A. in elementary or secondary education for working, accredited teachers. Sixteen of the required thirty credit-hours must be taken in residency, the rest can be earned through assessment of prior learning, correspondence and television courses, audio- and videocassettes, and supervised fieldwork. Academic assistance, tutoring, job-placement, and financial aid available.

Adelphi University   B, M, D
University College ABLE Program
Garden City, NY 11530
Ellen Hartigan
Many fields
1896
Nonprofit, independent $$$
(516) 877-3400
(516) 977-3296 fax
B.A. and B.S. available through the ABLE (Adult Baccalaureate Learning Experience) Program, which offers evening and weekend classes during the fall, spring, and summer. The program, which is based on a four-credit system, provides flexible scheduling of classes, including regular courses that meet once weekly. Some courses meet seven times; others meet five times. Credit for prior learning and by examination is possible.

Alabama State University   B
Continuing Education
915 S. Jackson St.
Montgomery, AL 36195
Arthur D. Barnett
Many fields
1874
Nonprofit, state $$
(205) 293–4291
Bachelor's degree can be earned through weekend, evening, and summer programs. Credit for independent study, nonacademic prior learning, and by examination.

Alaska Pacific University   B, M
4101 University Dr.
Anchorage, AK 99508
Curt E. Luttrell
Many fields
1957
Nonprofit, church $$$
(907) 561-1266
Credit for independent study, nonacademic prior learning, and by examination. Thirty-six credits in residency required. Only private university in Alaska. Programs in liberal arts, elementary education, human resources, communications, natural resources, values and service, and management.

Albertus Magnus College   B
Accelerated Degree Program
700 Prospect Street
New Haven, CT 06511
Richard J. Lolatte, Dean of Admissions
Many fields
1925
Nonprofit, independent $$$$$
(203) 773-8550
(203) 773-3117 fax
Up to 21 credits toward a B.A. or B.F.A. may be awarded for prior learning, including a wide range of exams. Additional credit may be earned through independent study and/or supervised fieldwork.

Albright College   B
Evening Program
P.O. Box 15234
Reading, PA 19612
Jean Clavert, Evening Division Director
Business, computer science
1856
Nonprofit, church $$$$$
(215) 921-2381
(215) 921-7530 fax
B.S. in accounting, business administration, or computer science through evening courses. Up to half the required credits can come from transfer coursework, exams, and/or portfolio assessment.

Alvernia College   B
Reading, PA 19607
Abby L. Pfaffman
Many fields
1958
Nonprofit, independent $$$
(215) 777-5411
(215) 777-6632 fax
Abby L. Pfaffman, the Assistant Director of Admissions, has written asking us not to describe the school's weekend, evening, and summer programs. For more information, contact Ms. Pfaffman directly.

Alverno College   B
Weekend College, 3401 S. 39th St.
P.O. Box 343922
Milwaukee, WI 53234-3922
Mary Claire Jones
Nursing, professional communication, business, management
1887
Nonprofit, independent $$$
(414) 382-6100
(414) 382-6354 fax
Classes involve intensive study, close working relationships

with faculty, and maximum opportunity for self-directed study. The weekend program is a complete college experience with over 1,100 women attending. Previous college credit is not required. B.S.N. Nursing completion for R.N.'s.

Amber University   B, M
1700 Eastgate Drive
Garland, TX 75041
Judy George, Director of Admissions
Many fields
1971
Nonprofit, independent $$$$
(214) 279-6511
(214) 279-9773 fax
Amber is an upper-level and graduate university, offering the B.A., B.S., B.B.A., M.S., M.A., and M.B.A. to adult students (applicants must be over 21 years old; undergraduates must have completed 30 credits of coursework elsewhere). Credit awarded for CLEP exams, military experience, and by portfolio review. Courses meet once a week in the evening or on weekends, with four 10-week sessions each year.

American International College   B
1000 State St.
Springfield, MA 01109
Elizabeth Ayres
Business, human services
1885
Nonprofit, independent $$$
(413) 747-6325
The degree is available through evening and weekend study through the College of Continuing and Graduate Studies. A REACH program offers special support for older students who have never attended college.

American Schools of   M, D
Professional Psychology
220 S. State St.
Chicago, IL 60604
Kim Rauner
Clinical psychology
(800) 626-4123
The American Schools of Professional Psychology (ASPP), which includes the Illinois School of Professional Psychology (ISPP), the Minnesota School of Professional Psychology (MSPP), and the Georgia School of Professional Psychology (GSPP), was established to provide extensive practical training in the area of professional psychology. The M.A., offered at ISPP and GSPP, and the Psy.D. (Doctor of Psychology), offered at all three locations, emphasize the "practitioner" focus in the field of clinical psychology, and all of ASPP's curriculum and field training prepares students to obtain diverse careers in the mental health field. The Psy.D. degree at ISPP is accred-

ited by the American Psychological Association (APA).

American University   B, M, D
4400 Massachusetts Ave., N.W.
Washington, DC 20016
Marcelle Heershap, Director of Admissions
Many fields
1893
Nonprofit, church $$$$
(202) 885-6000
(202) 885-6014 fax
Degrees in a variety of fields can be earned through evening classes, credit for life and job experience, examinations, study abroad, and community-operated programs. The university hosts a "Washington Semester" program. In the innovative Bachelor of Liberal Studies program, a total of 75 credits (of the 120 required for a B.A. in liberal studies) can be transferred from other four-year institutions, and 30 more can come from portfolio evaluation. Forty-five units, however, must be earned in residency. The degree program is designed by the student and can focus on the humanities, social sciences, or natural sciences.

American University of Paris   B
31 Ave. Bosquet
Paris, 75007 France
Christine Broenins
Many fields
1962
Nonprofit, independent $$$$
(331) 45559173
Bachelor's degrees in international business administration, international affairs, art history, French studies, European cultural studies, computer science, international economics, and comparative literature are offered through year-round study in Paris. Summer sessions are also offered. All instruction is in English. The student body is about half American and half from 60 other countries. New York office is at 80 E. 11th St., Suite 434, New York, NY 10003, (212) 677-4870. Formerly American College in Paris.

Anna Maria College   M
Paxton, MA 01612
Donna Varney, Director of Admissions
Business
1946
Nonprofit, church $$$
(617) 757-4586
The M.B.A. can be earned in from 12 to 18 months of intensive weekend study at centers in either Paxton or Boston.

Aquinas College   B, M
Continuing Education Program
1607 Robinson Road, SE
Grand Rapids, MI 49506

Education, business, Christian ministry
1922
Nonprofit, church $$$$$
(616) 459-8281
(616) 732-4485 fax

Aquinas's mission is to provide a career-oriented liberal arts education, in a Catholic Christian context, to persons beyond conventional college age. Credit is given for life-experience learning, independent study, and some supervised fieldwork. Degrees awarded include the B.A. in general education, B.S. in business administration, M.A. in teaching and Master of Management.

Armstrong State College   B, M

11935 Abercorn St.
Savannah, GA 31406
Thomas P. Miller, Director of Admissions
Business, education
1935
Nonprofit, state $$
(912) 925-4200

Bachelor of Arts, Bachelor of Science, Bachelor of Business Administration, Master of Educational Administration, and M.B.A. are offered entirely through evening study.

Armstrong University   B, M

2222 Harold Way
Berkeley, CA 94704
Ronald Hook, President
Business
1918
Proprietary $$$
(510) 848-2500
(510) 848-9438 fax

Bachelor's and M.B.A. are offered through day or evening study; accreditation is from the Association of Independent Colleges and Schools.

Audrey Cohen College   B, M

345 Hudson St.
New York, NY 10014-4598
Steven Lenhart, Director of Admissions
Human service, business, administration
1964
Nonprofit, independent $$$$
(212) 989-2002
(212) 924-4396 fax

Bachelor of Professional Studies in human service or business; Master of Science in administration. Largely adult population; three full semesters a year give students the option of completing the four-year undergraduate preparation in under three years, and the graduate degree in one year. Each semester focuses on a broad area of activity critical to professional work in the global economy (such as "working effectively in groups," or "acting as an effective supervisor"). Students complete five classes each semester, culminating in a "constructive action" at their worksite or volunteer placement which demonstrates an understanding of the semester's theme. Cohen's Field Development and Job Placement Office helps students identify employment or internship sites, as needed.

Augustana College   B, M

29th and Summit
Sioux Falls, SD 57197
Dean Schueler, Director of Admissions
Many fields
1860
Nonprofit, church $$$
(605) 336-5516

The Twilight Degree Program offers a Bachelor of Arts through courses given in the evening, at the noon hour, or on weekends. Credit for independent study, nonacademic prior learning, and by examination. See also: Quad Cities Graduate Center

Aurora University   B, M

347 S. Gladstone
Aurora, IL 60506-4892
Ellen Goldberg, Registrar
Many fields
1893
Nonprofit, independent $$$
(708) 844-6517

Undergraduate degrees in almost all fields can be earned through evening study. Degree offerings include many career areas (accounting, business administration, management, marketing, economics, communication, criminal justice, recreation administration, social work, nursing), as well as liberal arts. Credit for life, vocational, and military experience, etc., assessed through Life Experience/Education Assessment Program. Self-designed degree programs in many areas. Master's degree programs in career/professional areas (education, nursing, social work, business, information science, recreation administration). All Master's coursework offered in evenings, on campus or at various off-campus sites.

Averett College   B, M

Adult and Continuing Education
420 West Main Street
Danville, VA 24541
Harold Henry, Dean
Business administration
1859
Nonprofit, church $$$$
(703) 893-0663, (800) 849-9223
(804) 791-5637 fax

Eighty-one of the 123 hours required for a Bachelor of Business Administration, or 30 of the 36 for an M.B.A., can come from life-experience learning, credit for exams, and correspondence courses. Averett stresses that this is a highly structured, rigidly paced program for adult students who want to get their degree as quickly as possible, without interruption.

Avila College   B
Weekend College
11901 Wornall Road
Kansas City, MO 64145
Many fields
1916
Nonprofit, church $$$$
(816) 942-8400
(816) 942-3362 fax
Ninety-eight of the required 128 credits for a Bachelor of General Studies from Avila can come from transfer credit, portfolio assessment, CLEP exams, and school-administered exams. The additional 30 credits are earned through weekend courses designed for students of all ages, but particularly those with family or career responsibilities.

Baker University   B, M
School for Professional & Graduate Studies
6800 College Blvd., Ste. 500
Overland Park, KS 66211
Donald Clardy, Dean
Business, management, liberal arts
1858
Nonprofit, church $$$$
(913) 594-6451
(913) 594-6721 fax
B.B.A., M.B.A., M.S. in management, and Master of Liberal Arts tailored to adult learners. Bachelor's applicants must have completed 60 credits and been employed in their field for at least three years (the school recommends that undergraduate applicants should be at least 23 years old, graduate students at least 25). At the undergraduate level, some credit can be awarded for military experience, exams, and by portfolio assessment. Forty-four (of 124) credits for the B.B.A. must be earned from Baker. Distance-learning options include correspondence and televised courses and independent study.

Baldwin-Wallace College   B, M
275 Eastland Rd.
Berea, OH 44017
Linda L. Young, Registrar
Many fields
1845
Nonprofit, church $$$
(216) 826-2900
Bachelor of Arts, Bachelor of Science, Bachelor of Science in education, Bachelor of Music, Bachelor of Music Education. Some programs available through evening study or the weekend college, which meets on alternate weekends. Credit accepted for prior learning and CLEP Examina-

tions. Credit also considered for military experience and programs in training per recommendations from the American Council on Education. Master of Business Administration available through evening and Saturday programs. Master of Business Administration Executive program meets on alternate weekends. Master of Arts in Education available evenings during the regular academic year and days during the summer.

Barat College   B
Lake Forest, IL 60045
Loretta Brickman, Director of Admissions
Many fields
1858
Nonprofit, independent $$$$
(708) 234-3000
Bachelor of Arts through a combination of coursework and credit for prior learning experiences. Evening students may complete majors in management and business, human resource emphasis, computing and information systems, and communication arts. Barat also offers a degree completion program for nurses, awarding up to 60 credit-hours for their professional training, plus additional credit for CLEP scores and work achievements.

Barry University   B, M, D
11300 NE 2nd Ave.
Miami , FL 33161
Mr. Robin R. Roberts, Dean of Admissions
Many fields
1940
Nonprofit, church $$$$
(305) 758-3392
Degrees are offered in accounting, management, marketing, computer science, economics, finance, philosophy, and psychology. Credit for prior professional and work experience. Classes held in various location throughout southern Florida.

Baruch College   B, M
17 Lexington Ave.
New York, NY 10010
John Fisher, Director of Admissions
Business and public administration
1919
Nonprofit, state
(212) 725-3000
The college of the City University of New York offers the Bachelor of Business Administration, M.B.A., and Master of Public Administration, entirely through evening study.

Bellarmine College   B, M
Newburg Rd.
Louisville, KY 40205
Maria Poschinger

Business, nursing
1950
Nonprofit, independent **$$**
(502) 452-8255 (800) 633-5114
Bachelor's and Master's degrees in business and nursing can be completed through the FLEX (Flexible Learning, Education eXcellence) plan. Classes generally meet once a week at any of the seven Louisville locations or six outreach locations around the state. Select courses are also offered in an accelerated seven-week format. Credit is given for prior learning and by examination.

Bellevue College   B, M
Galvin Road at Harvell Drive
Bellevue, NE 68005-3098
Many fields
1965
Nonprofit, independent **$$**
(402) 293-3766
(402) 293-2020 fax
Bellevue offers evening and weekend classes and summer sessions leading to B.A. and B.S. degrees in many fields. They also offer a Bachelor of Technical Studies (BTS) program in management, business administration, information management, or commercial art designed for graduates of community colleges, and a Bachelor of Professional Studies in business administration of technical services, criminal justice administration, health care management, management, management of human resources, or sales and marketing (this is an accelerated program designed for working adults to complete their degree in about a year. Applicants for the B.P.S. must have an Associates degree or 60 credits, be employed, and have "relevant work experience.") A Master of Arts in management is also offered, in a concentrated 16-month program.

Bentley College   B
175 Forest Street
Morrison Hall, Room 200
Waltham, MA 02154
Professional studies
1917
Nonprofit, independent **$$$$$**
(617) 891-2000
(617) 891-2569 fax
The B.S. in professional studies may be completed in one of the following concentrations: government, applied ethics, behavioral science, communication, or legal studies. Independent study and supervised fieldwork possible. Up to 75 of 120 required credits can come from transfer credit, portfolio assessment, and a number of exams. The average part-time student takes seven to eight years to complete this degree.

Bethany College

See: East Central College Consortium

Bethel College   B
McKenzie, TN 38201
Linda Dicus
Many fields
1842
Nonprofit, church **$$**
(901) 352-1000 (800) 441-4940
Credit is given for life experience learning and for internships, and some evening courses are available. Bethel offers 19 basic majors, and it is possible for students to initiate their own, as well.

Bethune-Cookman College   B
Continuing Education Program
640 2nd Ave.
Daytona Beach, FL 32114
Roberto Barragan, Director of Admissions
Many fields
1904
Nonprofit, church **$$$$$**
(904) 255-1401
(904) 257-7027 fax
B.A. and B.S. awarded in fields specifically directed toward "occupational and professional development, personal enrichment, community problems, and critical issues." Credit for ACT and CLEP exams, and for supervised fieldwork.

Birmingham Southern College   B, M
Adult Studies Program
Box A-52, Arkadelphia Rd.
Birmingham, AL 35254
Natalie Davis, Dean
Business, management, education, economics
1856
Nonprofit, church **$$$$$**
(205) 226-4600
(205) 226-4627 fax
Self-paced B.A. and B.S. in accounting, business administration, economics, education, and human resources management, as well as individualized interdisciplinary majors, and an M.A. in public and private management, through evening and weekend classes, independent study, and supervised fieldwork.Undergraduate applicants must have a full-time job, preferably in their field. Up to 72 semester hours awarded for transfer credit, CLEP and departmental exams, and portfolio assessment.

Bloomsburg University   B
School of Extended Programs and Graduate Study
Bloomsburg, PA 17815
Michael Varneck, Dean
Many fields
1839
Nonprofit, state **$$**

(717) 389-4004

A maximum of 60 credits toward the Bachelor's degree (of 128 required) can be earned through assessment of prior and experiential learning, alone or in combination with equivalency exams and departmental challenge exams prepared by the university. Bloomsburg offers evening classes and television courses; 32 of the last 64 credits must be earned in residency.

Boston Architectural Center   B
320 Newbury Street
Boston, MA 02115
Ellen Driscoll, Admissions Coordinator
Architecture, interior design
1889
Nonprofit, independent $$$$$
(617) 536-3170
(617) 536-5829 fax

This unique program offers a Bachelor of Architecture through a "concurrent work curriculum program," in which students earn credit for working in their field by day, and take classes at night. Limited credit available by transfer and portfolio assessment.

Boston College   B
Chestnut Hill, MA 02167
Louise M. Lonabocker
Many fields
1863
Nonprofit, church $$$$
(617) 552-8000

All the courses required for the Bachelor of Arts degree in American studies, business, economics, English, history, political science, psychology, and sociology can be earned entirely through evening study. Most courses are taught for two-and-a-half hours, one evening per week.

Boston University   B, M
Metropolitan College
755 Commonwealth Ave.
Boston, MA 02215
Arlene F. Becella
Many fields
1839
Nonprofit, independent $$$$$
(617) 353-3000

Bachelor of Liberal Studies, Bachelor of Science, Master of Criminal Justice, Master of Liberal Arts, Master of Science in computer information systems, Master of Urban Affairs, and Master of City Planning may be earned through evening or weekend study with the university's Metropolitan College. The Overseas Program, primarily for military and Department of Defense employees, offers Master of Science in business administration, Master of Science in management, Master of Science in computer information systems, Master of Education, Master

of Arts in international relations, and Master of Science in mechanical engineering. Locations include Belgium and Germany. Credit for prior learning, independent study, and by examination.

Bowling Green State University   B, M
Office of Continuing Education
300 McFall Center
Bowling Green, OH 43403
Joan Bissland
Many fields
1910
Nonprofit, state $$
(419) 372-8181

B.A. degrees in arts and science, business administration, health and human services, and technology, available through evening study. Master's degree program in organizational development, through a degree plan involving a combination of on-campus and independent study. Other evening Master's programs, including an M.B.A. Credit for prior learning, or by exam, and by portfolio assessment. The school wants us to emphasize that every degree has a nonnegotiable residency requirement.

Bradley University   B, M
1501 W. Bradley Avenue
Peoria, IL 61625
Gary R. Bergman
Many fields
1897
Nonprofit, independent $$$
(309) 677-1000

Bachelor's and Master's degrees may be earned through evening, weekend, and summer programs, as well as courses offered on-site at business and industrial locations. Special programs in nursing, engineering, education, computer science, business, manufacturing, international studies, radio and television, and international business. See also: Quad Cities Graduate Center

Brenau University   B, M
One Centennial Circle
Gainesville, GA 30501
Business and public administration, management, education, nursing, art
1878
Nonprofit, independent $$$$$
(404) 534-6299
(404) 534-6114 fax

B.A. and B.S. in business administration, human resource management, public administration, and education (middle grades and elementary); B.S. in nursing; B.F.A.; M.B.A.; and M.Ed. in middle grades and elementary education through some combination of weekend classes, online computer classes, audio- and videocassettes, independent study, newspaper courses, supervised fieldwork, and courses offered off-campus. Up to 151 of the 196 credits for a Bachelor's (or 10 of the 50-55 for the Master's) may come from transfer credit, military experience, portfolio assessment, and CLEP, DANTES, and departmental exams.

Briar Cliff College   B
3303 Rebecca St.
P.O. Box 2100
Sioux City, IA 51104-2100
Sean Warner, Ph.D.
Many fields
1930
Nonprofit, church $$$
(712) 279-5460
Briar Cliff offers evening and weekend courses in nursing, human resource management, business administration, accounting, mass communications, theology, and psychology, and an extensive internship program. There is also a weekend B.S.N.-completion program for registered nurses. "Project Assess" provides credit for life experience.

Bridgeport Engineering Institute   B
785 Unquowa Road
Fairfield, CT 06430
Engineering
1924
Nonprofit, independent $$$$$
(203) 259-5717
(203) 259-9372 fax
B.S. in the following engineering fields: electrical, mechanical, information systems, and manufacturing, through part-time evening study. Up to 103 of the 139 credits required may come from transfer credit, CLEP and departmental exams, and portfolio assessment.

Bryant College   B, M
Evening Division
Smithfield, RI 02917
Nancy G. Parchesky, Dean of Admissions
Business administration, criminal justice
1863
Nonprofit, independent
(401) 232-6000
Bachelor of Science in business administration or criminal justice and M.B.A., all offered entirely through evening and weekend study.

California School   M, D
of Professional Psychology
2749 Hyde St.
San Francisco, CA 94109
Patty Mullen
Psychology, organizational behavior
1969
Nonprofit, independent $$$$$
(415) 346-4500
Ph.D. and Psy.D. programs in clinical psychology, Ph.D. programs in industrial and organizational psychology, and a part-time M.S. program in organizational behavior, offered at campuses in Berkeley, Fresno, Los Angeles, and San Diego. Some evening and weekend courses are scheduled. Clinical Ph.D. programs at all campuses and Clinical Psy.D. program at Los Angeles are accredited by the American Psychological Association.

Cambridge College   M
Institute of Open Education
15 Mifflin Place
Cambridge, MA 02138
Bruce Grigsby
Management, education
1970
Nonprofit, independent $$$
(617) 492-5108, (800) 877-GRAD
(617) 349-3545 fax
Graduate programs in education and management through evening and weekend classes designed specifically for the working professional with a Bachelor's degree and five years' work experience in their field. Students who have not earned a Bachelor's but have ten years' experience may first be admitted to the school's two-to-three semester Graduate Studies Preparation Program, which prepares them for grad work. Most students can finish the Master of Education in one year, and the Master of Management in less than two.

Campbell University   B, M
P.O. Box 546
Buies Creek, NC 27506
Herbert V. Kerner
Many fields
1887
Nonprofit, church $$$
(919) 893-4111, ext. 2275
The Bachelor's and Master's can be earned entirely through evening and weekend study, and are open to active military personnel, veterans, and civilians.

Campbellsville College   B
Organizational Administration Major
200 W. College St.
Campbellsville, KY 42718
R. Trent Argo, Director of Admissions
Organizational administration
1906
Nonprofit, church $$$$$
(502) 465-8158
(502) 789-5020 fax
Bachelor of Science in organizational administration tailored for adult nontraditional students (applicants must

be at least 23 years old and have completed 60 credits elsewhere), to prepare them for a career in administrative leadership. A Southern Baptist school, Campbellsville presents all material "from a Christian perspective." Credit available for various exams, and life and military experience by portfolio review. Thirty of the required 128 credits must be earned after enrolling, but distance-learning options include correspondence courses, independent study, and supervised fieldwork.

Canisius College   B, M
2001 Main St.
Buffalo, NY 14208
Penelope H. Lips, Director of Admissions
Technical and liberal studies
1870
Nonprofit, independent $$$$
(716) 888-2200
Bachelor of Science in technical and liberal studies may be earned through evening and summer programs. Credit for independent study, nonacademic prior learning, and by examination. Up to 50 percent of the credit can come from work done at other approved institutions.

Cardinal Stritch College   B, M
Office of Adult Education
6801 N. Yates Rd.
Milwaukee , WI 53217
David Wegener
Many fields
1937
Nonprofit, church $$$
(414) 352-5400
Bachelor's degrees are offered in many fields. Credit for experiential learning. The business/economics degree can be earned entirely through evening study. Programs that meet one evening a week lead to Bachelor's and Master's degrees in business and management and a Master's in health services administration. In addition, a certificate in sales productivity and management and a certificate in international business are offered through Programs in Management for Adults.

Carroll College   B, M
Part-Time Studies Program
100 N. East Avenue
Waukesha, WI 53186
Jan Schoben, Director of Part-Time Studies
Business, accounting, communications, computer science, education, nursing, psychology
1846
Nonprofit, church $$$$$
(414) 547-1211
(414) 524-7139 fax
B.S., B.A. (majors in business, accounting, communications, computer science, education, nursing, and psychol-

ogy), and Master of Education available entirely through night classes. Credit for military experience, command of a foreign language, and applicable work experience, as well as CLEP (up to 48 credits), AP, and departmental exams. Very flexible schedule; correspondence courses, independent study, and supervised fieldwork available.

Carson-Newman College   B, M
Extension Division, Russell Ave.
Jefferson City, TN 37760
Jack W. Shannon, Director of Admissions
Many fields
1851
Nonprofit, church $$$
(615) 475-9061
Bachelor of Arts and Bachelor of Science in many fields, available entirely through evening study. Credit by examination, independent study, and for military experience. Self-designed majors are available. Master's degree offered in education.

Castleton State College   B, M
Castleton, VT 05735
Lyle Gray
Teacher and nursing education, business, liberal arts
1787
Nonprofit, state $$
(802) 468-5611
Bachelor's and Master's can be earned through weekend, summer, and evening classes. Special programs in nursing education. Credit for independent study, nonacademic prior learning, and by examination.

Cedar Crest College   B
Allentown, PA 18104
Curtis D. Bauman, Registrar
Many fields
1867
Nonprofit, church $$$$
(215) 437-4471
Bachelor's degree in any of 30 majors may be earned through weekend, evening, and summer classes (minimum of 30 credits must be earned after enrolling). Special programs include nursing, accounting, legal assistant, nuclear medical technology, and genetic engineering technology. Credit for life experience and by proficiency exam.

Centenary College (Louisiana)   B
P.O. Box 41188
Shreveport, LA 71134-1188
Caroline Kelsey, Director of Admissions
Many fields
1825
Nonprofit, church $$$
(318) 869-5131
Bachelor of Arts, Bachelor of Science, and Bachelor of

Music can be earned entirely through evening study.

Centenary College (New Jersey)   B
400 Jefferson St.
Hackettstown, NJ 07840
Michael McGraw
Many fields
1867
Nonprofit, independent $$$
(908) 852-1400, ext. 215
Bachelor's may be earned in fields including equine studies, fashion, interior design, art and design, communication, education, business, liberal arts, psychology, history, math, and English, through weekend, evening, and summer programs. Credit for independent study, nonacademic prior learning, and by examination.

Central Washington University   B, M
Ellensburg, WA 98926
Business fields, electronic engineering, law and justice, education
1890
Nonprofit, state $$$
(509) 963-1111
(509) 963-1241 fax
B.S. in accounting, business administration, or electronic engineering technology; B.A. in law and justice or education (majors in early childhood or special ed); Master of Education in reading or education administration, through off-campus courses "at convenient times and places" for working adults. Credit for military experience and some exams, independent study, and supervised fieldwork.

Central Wesleyan College   B, M
Leadership Education for Adult Professionals
Box 497, CWC
Central, SC 29630
James B. Bross, Adult and Graduate Studies
Management, Christian ministries
1906
Nonprofit, church $$$$
(803) 639-2453
(803) 639-0826 fax
B.S. in management of human resources, M.A.'s in organizational management and Christian ministries, all "guided by a Christian worldview." The Leadership Education for Adult Professionals (LEAP) program is designed to allow adult learners with previous college work to finish their degrees while still working. Applicants for the B.S. program must have already completed 60 credits in their field; for the M.A., two years' work experience. Maximum of 68 credits awarded for nontraditional prior learning, by portfolio review. Credit for various exams. Students must enroll full-time, which entails class one night per week and an additional study-group meeting each week. Many courses are held off-campus, and some may be taken through guided independent study.

Chaminade University   B
3140 Waialae Ave.
Honolulu, HI 96816-1578
Faye E. Conquest
Many fields
1955
Nonprofit, independent $$
(808) 735-4711
Bachelor of Arts, Science, Business Administration, and Fine Arts offered through accelerated evening programs on military bases, as well as the main Honolulu campus. Weekend and summer programs are also available. Credit for military training, independent study, and examinations.

Chapman College   B, M
333 N. Glassell St.
Orange, CA 92666
Michael Drumins, Director of Admissions
Many fields
1861
Nonprofit, independent $$$$$
(714) 997-6611
(714) 997-6713 fax
Regional education centers are located at over 50 military bases and civilian locations nationwide. Terms of 6, 8, 9, and 10 weeks are available. Some instruction uses T.A.P.E., a telecommunication-assisted program of education.

Cincinnati Bible College and Seminary   B, M
2700 Glenway Ave., P.O. Box 04320
Cincinnati, OH 45204-3200
Shawn Case
Religious fields
1824
Nonprofit, church $$
(513) 244-8100
The Bachelor of Arts, Science, or Music is offered in many fields, ranging from Christian education to Christian ministry to ministry to the deaf. There are also emphases offered in a number of areas such as journalism, psychology, and teacher education. A total of 13 fields of study are available. The Master of Arts can be earned by taking courses in module form. Master's degrees are offered in 11 areas of concentration. Accredited by the North Central Association and the American Association of Bible Colleges.

City University of New York   B, M
City College
138th St. at Convent Ave.
New York, NY 10031
Nancy Campbell, Director of Enrollment
Many fields
1847

Nonprofit, state **$**
(212) 650-6477
Fields include engineering, architecture, medicine, liberal arts, science, and performing arts. Up to 30 credits may be earned though the Center for Work Education's life experience thesis program, which is designed primarily for working adult members of labor unions. It offers flexible scheduling, weekend classes, and life experience credit. This program's phone number is (212) 650-5301. The Center for Vocational Teacher Education's program—(212) 650-8358—leads to state certification and a B.S. in vocational education.

City University of New York   B
Baccalaureate Program, Graduate Center North
25 W. 43rd Street, Suite 300
New York, NY 10036
Many fields
1961
Nonprofit, state **$$$**
(212) 642-1600
(212) 642-2642 fax
Bachelor of Arts and Bachelor of Science for self-motivated students who want to design their own individualized programs (with faculty guidance). Students are encouraged to take advantage of the wide range of resources available through CUNY's 17 undergraduate colleges, as well as its graduate school. Applicants must have completed at least 15 and no more than 90 credits towards the 120-credit degree. Limited credit awarded for nonclassroom learning, ACT, CLEP, DANTES, and departmental exams, and military experience. The school's material states that, "because students enter the program with from 15 to 90 earned credits, it is not uncommon for a full-time student to graduate within 1 1/2 years; a part-time student after two to three years."

Clark University   B, M
College of Professional and Continuing Education
950 Main St.
Worcester, MA 01610
Thomas Massey
Many fields
1953
Nonprofit, independent **$$**
(508) 793-7217
Bachelor of Arts in liberal arts, Master of Public Administration; and Master of Arts in liberal arts offered entirely by evening study or summer programs.

Cleveland State University   B, M
E. 24th and Euclid
Cleveland, OH 44115
Richard C. Dickerman
Many fields
1964

Nonprofit, state **$$**
(216) 687-2000
Bachelor of Arts, Science, Business Administration, Education, and Engineering; and the M.A., M.S., Master of Urban Affairs, and M.B.A. through evening study and/or Saturday classes.

Coker College   B
Evening and Summer School
Hartsville, SC 29550
Business administration, education, sociology
1908
Nonprofit, independent **$$$$$**
(803) 383-8010
(803) 383-8197 fax
The Bachelor of Science in business administration (concentrations in accounting, finance, operations management, or marketing) and Bachelor of Arts in sociology (concentrations in criminology or social work) can be completed entirely through night classes; the B.A. in education is earned through night classes plus an internship in a local school and a semester of student teaching. Credit for exams and military experience, by portfolio review.

College Misericordia   B
Lake St.
Dallas, PA 18612
David M. Payne, Dean of Admissions
Many fields
1924
Nonprofit, church **$$$**
(717) 675-2181
Bachelor of Arts in many fields through weekend study; Bachelor of Science in Nursing, B.A. in business, and Bachelor of Music through evening study. Master's degrees in nursing, occupational therapy, education, and human services administration. Evening and weekend courses. A Bachelor's degree can be earned in four years of evening study.

College of Mount Saint Joseph   B
Division of Continuing Education
Cincinnati, OH 45233
Mary Kay Meyer, Director of Continuing Education
Many fields
1920
Nonprofit, church **$$$$$**
(513) 244-4805
The PM College offers Bachelor's degree programs in accounting, business administration, computer information, graphic and interior design, paralegal studies, liberal arts, nursing, social work, management communication, and religious and pastoral ministry in classes that meet one evening a week. The Weekend College offers the Bachelor in business administration, communication arts, human services, gerontological studies, accounting, lib-

eral arts, or management of nursing services. Weekend classes meet five weekends out of each 13-week term. Each class is three-and-a-half hours long; three can be taken between Friday and Sunday evening. Credit is available for experiential learning.

College of Mount Saint Vincent   B
263rd and Riverdale Ave.
Riverdale, NY 10471
Lenore M. Mott, Director of Admissions
Many fields
1847
Nonprofit, independent $$$
(212) 549-8000
B.A. and B.S. programs in more than 30 fields through evening, summer, and weekend programs (every other weekend), both on- and off-campus. Also special B.S. for R.N.'s. Up to 30 credits may be granted for experiential learning; credit by examination also possible. More than 250 established internships are available for students. The is also a College Emeritus, with substantially reduced tuition, for students over the age of 55 who have not studied since high school, or have limited college experience.

College of New Rochelle   B
School of New Resources
New Rochelle, NY 10801
Patricia Furman
Liberal studies, liberal arts
1972
Nonprofit, independent $$
(914) 632-5300
The School of New Resources has six campus sites in the greater New York area—one in New Rochelle and one in each of the five boroughs. Degrees can be earned through evening and weekend study. Credit is given for life experience learning.

College of Notre Dame of Maryland   B
4701 N. Charles St.
Baltimore, MD 21210
Sharon A. Houst, Director of Admissions
Many fields
1873
Nonprofit, church $$$$
(410) 435-0100
(410) 435-5937 fax
Bachelor of Arts in 22 majors through weekend, summer, and January programs. Credit for nonacademic prior learning, independent study, and by examination. The literature reminds us, several times, that this Notre Dame is neither in Paris nor in South Bend, but in Baltimore.

College of Saint Catherine   B
2004 Randolph Ave.
St. Paul, MN 55105

Lisa Hubinger
Many fields
1905
Nonprofit, church $$$
(612) 690-6505, (800) 945-4599
College degree programs for adult women. Bachelor of Arts in business administration, philosophy, applied ethics, economics, communication, information management, nursing, occupational therapy, social work, and elementary education through weekend college. Some evening classes are available. Credit for CLEP exams, and through CARL, the Credit for Academic Relevant Learning program.

College of Saint Francis   B, M
500 Wilcox St.
Joliet, IL 60435
Charles Beutel
Health arts
1920
Nonprofit, church $$$
(815) 740-3360
Bachelor of Science program with a major in health arts for registered nurses and other health professionals. Students are required to complete at least eight courses and may do so at any of the 100 locations in 17 states, from New Mexico to Pennsylvania. New locations are added regularly. Classes meet one evening a week. Full-time students may complete the degree in less than a year, while those taking one course at a time will normally take two and a half years. One hundred and twenty-eight semester units are required for the degree, of which 32 must be earned after enrollment. Health professionals can receive up to three years of credit for previous education and experience through the Prior Learning Assessment Program. A Master's degree program in health services administration is also available off-campus at 40 locations in 14 states.

College of Saint Mary   B
1901 S. 72nd St.
Omaha, NE 68124
Many fields
1923
Nonprofit, church
(402) 399-2400
Saint Mary's weekend college offers a Bachelor of Science degree in business administration, computer information management, marketing, management, human resources management, and human services. Summer and evening study programs are also available; B.S.N. programs for nurses. Credit by examination and portfolio assessment.

College of Saint Rose   B
432 Western Ave.
Albany, NY 12203

Beryl Heidorn
Many fields
1920
Nonprofit, independent $$$
(518) 454-5143
Bachelor of Arts or Bachelor of Science of which up to 75 percent of the required credits may be earned through an assessment of prior learning experiences. The assessment can take three months or more. Only students matriculated at the College of Saint Rose are considered for assessment.

College of Saint Scholastica   B, M
1200 Kenwood Ave.
Duluth, MN 55811 USA
Christabel D. Grant
Nursing, physical therapy, medical technology
1912
Nonprofit, church $$$
(218) 723-6000
Bachelor's and some Master's degrees may be earned through summer and evening classes. Credit for independent study and nonacademic prior learning, and by examination.

College of Santa Fe   B, M
Graduate and External Programs
1600 St. Michael's Drive
Santa Fe, NM 87501-5634
Dolores E. Roybal
Business administration, education, psychology, humanities
1947
$$$$
(505) 473-6177
Bachelor's degrees in business administration, education, humanities, organizational psychology, psychology, and public administration, M.A. in education, and M.B.A. offered on an accelerated (five terms per year) evening and weekend schedule. Credit toward a degree may be accepted from CLEP exams, nonacademic learning, course challenges, and life experience, by portfolio review. An "assessment course" provides the opportunity for any student to assemble a prior learning portfolio of up to 48 units, under close academic supervision. Classes are offered in Santa Fe, Albuquerque, Los Alamos, and at other selected sites throughout the state all year.

College of Staten Island   B
130 Stuyvesant Place
Staten Island, NY 10301
Elaine Bowden, Registrar
Many fields
1955
Nonprofit, state $
(718) 390-7733

The college is part of the City University of New York and offers Bachelor's degrees in many fields. Qualified students may enter the CUNY Baccalaureate Program, a university-wide program offering individualized courses of study. Credit is earned for classes held on-campus; limited credit may be earned for classes held off-campus and at work sites, independent study projects, work experience, and prior learning experience. Credit by examination, departmental challenge exams, and internships. Noncredit courses available to prepare adult students returning to college.

Colorado Christian University   B
School of Graduate and Professional Studies
180 S. Garrison St.
Lakewood, CO 80226
Gene R. Marlatt, Dean
Several fields
1914
Nonprofit, church $$$
(303) 234-1478
The B.S. in management of human resources, computer information systems management, Christian leadership, or elementary education can be earned in 12 months (18 months for CISM) through evening or weekend programs, if the participant has an A.A. or 56 hours of transferable credit, is at least 25 years old, and prepares a life experience portfolio (which can be worth up to 34 units). Centers in Lakewood, Denver, Colorado Springs and Grand Junction, Colorado. Formerly Rockmont College. No connection whatever with a defunct diploma mill called Colorado Christian University.

Columbia College   B
1001 Rogers St. (10th and Rogers)
Columbia, MO 65216-0001
Virginia J. Ponder, Evening & Community Ed.
1851
Nonprofit, church
(314) 875-8700
Offers evening degree programs. Has not responded to two requests for more information.

Columbia College of Nursing   B
2121 E. Newport
Milwaukee, WI 53271
Nursing
1901
Nonprofit, independent $$$$
(414) 961-3530
(414) 961-4121 fax
Bachelor of Science in nursing through a joint program with Carroll College. Credit for CLEP and departmental exams; nontraditional course options include correspondence classes, independent study, and supervised fieldwork. At least 32 of the required 128 credit-hours must be completed after enrollment.

Concordia University   B, M
12800 North Lake Shore Dr.
Mequon, WI 53092
David Zersen
Management and communication, liberal arts, health care, nursing, and criminal justice
1881
Nonprofit, church $$$
(414) 243-4399

Concordia offers Bachelor's degrees in an accelerated modular format, for full-time working adults. Additional credits can be earned through portfolio assessment, telecourses, correspondence courses, challenge exams, and independent study. School accepts PONSI and ACE recommendations as well as CLEP and DANTE scores. Centers are in Mequon, Appleton, Green Bay, Madison, and Kenosha, Wisconsin; Fort Wayne and Indianapolis, Indiana; St. Louis, Missouri; and New Orleans, Louisiana. Video-assisted guided independent study can be taken anywhere in the U.S. Has recently added a Master's degrees in 20 subject areas, in which much of the coursework and other interaction takes place over the Internet, with only one week required on campus.

Converse College   B
Converse II Program
580 E. Main Street
Spartanburg, SC 29302
Many fields
1889
Nonprofit, independent $$$$$
(803) 596-9000
(803) 596-9158 fax

The Converse II program is designed to encourage adult women (24 years old and up) to return to school for a B.A., B.F.A., or Bachelor of Music. Some credit for CLEP exams and by portfolio review; students with theater or music performance experience may exempt some classes; independent study and supervised fieldwork options. CII features simplified application procedure, reduced fees, special financial aid, flexible scheduling, and individualized counseling to women who meet the stated criteria.

Covenant College   B
Quest Program
Lookout Mountain, TN 30750
Dennis Miller
Organizational management
1955
Nonprofit, church $$$
(706) 820-1560

The Bachelor of Arts in organizational management through an innovative program in which groups of 12 to 20 students meet one evening a week for 52 weeks. Nine courses are offered during this period, for one to five weeks each.

All students complete a major research project, applying management and organizational behavior studies to a problem or need in their fields or workplaces. All work is done in "a biblical framework"; Covenant is affiliated with the Presbyterian Church of America. A degree program can begin whenever and wherever 12 to 20 students are ready. Applicants must have 60 semester units of credit and five years of work experience to qualify. CLEP and military credit are accepted. Students earn up to 31 units toward graduation (not admission) from life experience. The program is offered in Chattanooga, Tennessee, and four satellite locations within a 30-mile radius.

Creighton University   B, M
California St. at 24th
Omaha, NE 68178
Shirley L. Dooling
Nursing
1878
Nonprofit, independent $$$
(800) 544-5071, ext. 2043

The Accelerated Nursing Curriculum program offers persons with a B.A. or B.S. in another field the opportunity to earn a professional degree (B.S.N.) in nursing in one year. There is also a three-year Bachelor's/Master's option. Financial aid is available.

Dallas Baptist University   B
3000 Mountain Creek Parkway
Dallas, TX 75211
Luther McCollister
Many fields
1898
Nonprofit, church $$
(214) 331-8311

Most courses are offered evenings and weekends. The Bachelor of Applied Studies program awards up to 30 hours of credits for prior learning experiences in marketing, management, business administration, management information systems, criminal justice, accounting, psychology, public administration, pastoral ministries, social services, and other areas. Credit is generously but realistically awarded for government, military, and other career training. The program has been in existence since 1974 and collaborates with many companies to bring education to the off-campus student.

Dallas Theological Seminary   M
Extension Programs
3909 Swiss Avenue
Dallas, TX 75204
Eugene W. Pond, Director of Admissions
Biblical studies
1924
Nonprofit, independent $$$$
(214) 824-3094

(214) 841-3642 fax
M.A. in biblical studies offered through evening and weekend courses at six locations around the country (San Antonio, Houston, Tampa, FL, Philadelphia, Chattanooga, TN, and Birmingham, AL). Courses are taught by local pastors and scholars, as well as regular full-time faculty from the Dallas campus, who fly in to the remote locations. Applicants must provide a letter of recommendation from their church.

Dartmouth College   M
M.A.L.S. Admissions
6092 Wentworth Hall
Hanover, NH 03775-3526
Rogers Elliott
Liberal studies
1769
Nonprofit, independent $$$$$
(603) 646-3592
Dartmouth College's Master of Arts program in liberal studies is designed to let adults continue a liberal-arts education (each student plans his or her own course of study; there are no core courses and no majors). Students typically attend for three summers, or five consecutive terms. (About 40 percent of the 200 currently active students are from out of the area). The program combines classes, a weekly colloquium, student-led seminars, independent study, and a thesis. Meals and housing are available on the Dartmouth campus, if desired. Seventy-five percent of M.A.L.S. students receive some form of financial assistance.

De La Salle University   B
College of Saint Benilde
2544 Taft Avenue
Manila, Philippines
Divina Edralin, Dean
Business, accounting, management, industrial design
1911
Nonprofit, church $$
57-28-15
57-27-73 fax
This Philippine university offers a B.A. in management interdisciplinary studies and a B.S. in business administration, industrial design, business management, or accountancy; all programs designed for working students employed in public services, education, commerce and industry, or other private agencies.

De Paul University   B, M
25 E. Jackson Blvd.
Chicago, IL 60604
Susan Thornton
Many fields
1898
Nonprofit, state $$$
(312) 362-6709

De Paul University's School for New Learning offers alternative B.A. and M.A. programs at three campus locations through weekend and evening programs. Each degree is individually designed, with credit given for learning from life and work experience. The Master of Arts in liberal studies offers adult students the opportunity to design a multidisciplinary liberal arts curriculum, emphasizing team-taught courses and colloquia. All classes meet one evening per week. Students take four core courses, two colloquia, and six elective courses, and finish by completing an "integrating project."

Defiance College   B
701 N. Clinton St.
Defiance, OH 43512
Penny D. Bell
Many fields
1850
Nonprofit, church $$$
(419) 784-4010
Bachelor of Art and Bachelor of Science in a wide variety of fields, through weekend, evening, and summer programs. Credit for prior learning, independent study, and by examination. A two-semester interdisciplinary core course is required of all students. In addition to many traditional majors, unusual majors include municipal and industrial recreation, natural systems, therapeutic recreation, environmental science, and restoration ecology.

Delaware Valley College   B
Doylestown, PA 18901
Stephen W. Zenko, Director of Admission
Business, biology, computer systems, management
1896
Nonprofit, independent $$$
(215) 345-1500
The Bachelor of Science in business, biology, computer systems, and management is available entirely through evening study.

Dominican College of Blauvelt   B
Weekend and Accelerated Evening Programs
10 Western Highway
Orangeburg, NY 10962
Many fields
1952
Nonprofit, independent $$$$$
(914) 359-7800
(914) 359-2313 fax
B.S. in nursing (for R.N.'s only), occupational therapy, business, accounting, management, computer information systems, or business administration, and B.A. in humanities entirely through weekend and accelerated evening classes. Credit for military and other life experience learning through portfolio assessment, and for a range of exams. Optional independent study and supervised fieldwork for credit.

Drake University
B, M, L

2507 University Ave.
Des Moines, IA 50311
Thomas F. Willoughby, Director of Admission
Many fields
1881
Nonprofit, independent $$$$$
(515) 271-3181
(515) 271-2831 fax

B.A. and B.S. available entirely through evening and weekend classes in the following majors: accounting, computer information systems, economics, finance, general business, insurance, international business, management, marketing, nursing completion, psychology, and sociology. Study may also design individualized majors. Master's degrees through evening and weekend study in adult education/ training and development, education, business administration, counselor education, general studies, mass communications, nursing, and public administration.

Drexel University
B, M

32nd and Chestnut
Philadelphia, PA 19104
Keith Brooks, Associate Dean of Admissions
Many fields
1891
Nonprofit, independent $$$$
(215) 895-2000

Bachelor of Science in architecture, business administration, engineering, or general studies; Master's in business administration, home economics, or library science, all available through evening study. The M.L.S. (library science) can be earned through evening and weekend classes in two years or less.

Drury Evening College
B

900 N. Benton Ave.
Springfield, MO 65802
Sue Rollins
Many fields
1873
Nonprofit, independent $$$
(417) 865-8731, ext. 207

Bachelor of Science may be earned in many fields entirely through evening and weekend study. Advanced placement possible by CLEP or credit by proficiency examination.

East Central College Consortium
B

Hiram College
Hiram, OH 44234
Gary G. Craig, Director of Admissions
General studies, sciences, humanities and arts, business administration, health
1850
Nonprofit, independent $$$$

(216) 569-5278

A consortium of seven liberal arts colleges that cooperate to offer the B.A. in general studies, sciences, humanities and arts, business administration, and allied health. Registration at one of the colleges and fulfillment of some residency requirements are mandatory. The schools are Heidelberg College, Hiram College, Marietta College, Mount Union College and Muskingum College (all in Ohio), Bethany College (West Virginia), and Westminster College (Pennsylvania).

East Tennessee State University
B, M, D

P.O. Box 70731
Johnson City, TN 37614-0731
Nancy Dishner
Many fields
1911
Nonprofit, state $$
(615) 929-4213

The Bachelor of General Studies (B.G.S.) degree program provides a learner-centered alternative to traditional programs in which adult students develop individualized interdisciplinary academic programs specifically tailored to their learning needs.

Eastern Connecticut State University
B, M

83 Windham St.
Willimantic, CT 06226
Arthur C. Forst
Liberal arts and sciences, business, education
1889
Nonprofit, state $$$
(203) 456-5286

Bachelor's may be earned through weekend, evening, and summer programs. Credit by examination and for prior nonacademic and military learning. Up to 60 credits can be earned through CLEP exams. Higher tuition for out-of-state students.

Eastern Oregon State College
B, M

Division of Continuing Education
La Grande, OR 97850
Lee Insko
Many fields
1929
Nonprofit, state $$
(503) 962-3378

Bachelor's degree may be earned through weekend, evening, and summer programs. Credit for independent study, cooperative work experience, assessment of prior learning, weekend college, and by examination. Master's in teacher education (M.T.E.) available largely through distance learning methods (locally televised courses, tele- and computer conferencing, satellite television), with one summer session on-campus. The contact for the M.T.E. is Jens Robinson, at (503) 962-3772.

Eastern Washington University   B

Cheney, WA 99004
Roger Pugh, Admissions Officer
General studies
1882
Nonprofit, state $$–$$$$$
(509) 359-2397

Bachelor of Arts in general studies, specifically for persons with professional or paraprofessional experience, such as mechanics, computer programmers, police officers, nurses, secretaries, firefighters, draftspeople, and others. Twenty-five percent of degree work must be done after enrollment, which usually translates into about one academic year (nine months). A main advantage here is the school's willingness to give life-experience credit to people in fields that other schools might not agree were creditworthy. We have heard from a few people who enrolled in Eastern Washington long enough to get credit for, say, their secretarial experience, and then transferred this credit to another, faster school.

Edinboro University of Pennsylvania   B

Edinboro, PA 16444
Terrence Carlin
Many fields
1857
Nonprofit, state $$
(814) 732-2000

Bachelor of General Business, Bachelor of Arts in English, speech communication, geography, or psychology, and Bachelor of Science in education or industrial and trade leadership, through evening, weekend, and summer programs. Credit for nonacademic prior learning, independent study, and by examination. Prior learning assessment is done in Edinboro's Life Experience Center and can take a month or less. For a small fee, they will conduct a brief inspection of one's resume or credentials and advise whether or not they think it is worthwhile to go ahead with the more expensive complete assessment. Edinboro's Opportunity College is designed to help adult students earn credit while continuing employment and family responsibilities.

Elmhurst College   B

Office of Adult and Transfer Admission
Elmhurst, IL 60126
Elizabeth D. Kuebler
Many fields
1871
Nonprofit, independent $$$
(708) 617-3069

Bachelor's degree through weekend, evening, and summer study. Elmhurst offers a degree completion program for working registered nurses, with courses offered in Chicago-area hospitals, and a special accelerated program in business administration. Credit for independent study, prior learning experience, and by examination.

Elmira College   B

Park Place
Elmira, NY 14901
William S. Neal
Many fields
1855
Nonprofit, independent $$$$
(607) 735-1724

Bachelor of Science and Master of Science, both in education, available entirely through evening study. Fields of concentration include accounting, business, chemistry, computer information systems, education, general studies, human services, mathematics, nursing, psychology, and social studies.

Elon College   B, M

Elon College, NC 27244
Mark R. Albertson
Business, education
Nonprofit, church
(919) 584-9711

All Bachelor's degrees, an M.B.A., and a Master of Education are available through evening study.

Emmanuel College   B, M

Adult Learner Degree Program
400 The Fenway
Boston, MA 02115
Jacqueline Armitage, Assistant Dean
Liberal arts, health and business administration, nursing, management, education, ministry, public policy
1919
Nonprofit, church $$$$$
(617) 277-9340
(617) 735-9877 fax

Bachelor of Liberal Arts, B.S. in health administration, business administration, and nursing; M.A. in human resource management, education, educational pastoral ministry, clinical pastoral counseling, public policy making; Master in School Administration, and Master in School Special Education Technology, all for adult students (age 23 and older). Courses offered late afternoons, evenings, weekends, and summers; accelerated courses are offered at various off-campus sites. Credit for a variety of exams, and up to 16 credits for appropriate life-work experience, through portfolio assessment.

European University Institute   D

Via dei Roccettini, 5
San Domenico di Fiesole, 50016 Italy
Emile Noel, Principal
Many fields
1976
Nonprofit, state

(055) 50921

The institute was established in 1976 by the then nine members of the European Economic Community, although about 20 percent of students today come from outside of the Common Market countries. Students plan independent-study projects under the guidance of faculty tutors and research supervisors, and the degree of Ph.D. is awarded on completion and publication of a dissertation. Fields of study include economics, history and civilization, law, political science, and social sciences.

Evergreen State College   B, M
Olympia, WA 98505
Doug Scrima
Many fields
1967
Nonprofit, state $$
(206) 866-6000

Students have the option of creating independent contracts for individual study or research, which is supervised under a faculty mentor. Groups of two or more students may work under a group contract. Credit is given for prior experiential learning and internship programs involving, for instance, work in local hospitals, clinics, or businesses. Full-time and half-time interdisciplinary programs are available on campus as well. The half-time program is geared to working adults, and offers the same courses taken by the majority of Evergreen students, through evening and weekend instruction. Students involved in independent study are still expected to visit the campus and meet with their faculty mentors at least once a month. All transfer students must earn at least 45 of the last 90 quarter hour credits while enrolled at Evergreen to be eligible for a degree.

Fairfield University   B
General Studies Program
Fairfield, CT 06430
General studies
1942
Nonprofit, independent $$$$$
(203) 254-4000
(203) 254-4060 fax

B.A. or B.S. in general studies for working adult students whose educational needs cannot be met by traditional programs. Applicants must be at least 25 years old, and have at least a three-year "interruption in formal education." Up to 75 credits of the 120 required may be awarded for life-experience learning; credit also available for various equivalency exams. Some courses taught through audio- and videocassette and television courses, as well as independent study.

Fairhaven College   B
Western Washington University
Bellingham, WA 98225

Ronald D. Riggins, Acting Dean
Many fields
1893
Nonprofit, state $$$
(206) 676-3000
(206) 676-3037 fax

Fairhaven offers students a fair amount of latitude in designing their own programs for the B.A., B.S., B.F.A. (fine arts), and Bachelor of Music, including a combined B.A./ Bachelor of Education program; all programs can combine regular courses, credit from equivalency exams, independent study, supervised fieldwork, and other practical experiences related to the student's academic goals.

Fairleigh Dickinson University   B, M, D
285 Madison St.
Madison, NJ 07940
Rita Bennett, Director of Admissions
Many fields
1958
Nonprofit, independent $$$
(201) 593-8900

B.A., B.S., M.A., M.S., and Doctor of Education programs, offered through centers at Madison, Rutherford, and Teaneck, primarily through evening study. The Doctorate, in educational leadership, consists of formal courses, seminars, and internships, as well as independent study and research. The school also offers a "success program" for persons over the age of 25 who have never attended (or never finished) college. A number of accelerated programs offer the opportunity to complete two degrees together in less time than they would normally take separately, including five-year B.A./M.P.A. (public administration), B.A./M.B.A., B.A./M.A. in psychology, and B.A./M.A. in teacher education, as well a rare six-year B.S./M.D. or B.S./D.M.D. in medicine or dentistry. Also, degree-completion programs for professional athletes over the age of 22.

Fayetteville State University   B, M
Murchinson Rd.
Fayetteville, NC 28301
Denise F. Mahone, Administrative Services
Many fields
1867
Nonprofit, state $
(919) 486-1111

B.A. and B.S. for military personnel, their dependents, and local residents. All work can be completed through weekend and evening study. Some credit given for prior learning experiences and for equivalency exams. There are 24 majors available at the Bachelor's level, and four Master's programs: business administration, administration and supervision, special education, and elementary education.

Florida Institute of Technology   M
Graduate Admissions Office
150 W. University Blvd.
Melbourne, FL 32901
Director of Admissions
Many business and technical fields
1958
Nonprofit, independent $$$
(407) 768-8000
(407) 984-8461 fax
M.B.A. in 10 fields and M.S. in computer science, electrical engineering, management, space technology, and many other fields, offered to military and civilians at 15 locations in Florida, New Jersey, Alabama, New Mexico, Virginia, Louisiana, and Maryland. Has incorporated the programs of the former International Graduate School of Behavioral Psychology. FIT has threatened to sue us for mentioning, in earlier editions, the circumstances under which the chairman of their board of trustees resigned— an event described in detail in at least a half a dozen Florida newspapers but no longer in this publication.

Florida State University   M
4750 Collegiate Drive
Panama City, FL 32405
William Jerome Barnes, Associate Dean
Engineering
1851
Nonprofit, state $$$
(904) 872-4750
(904) 872-4199 fax
Master of Science in electrical or mechanical engineering, with a number of specialties in each field, through compressed-video television courses offered electronically from the Tallahassee campus to sites in Panama City.

Fontbonne College   B, M
Options Program
6800 Wydown Blvd.
St. Louis, MO 63105
Bob Ratcliffe, Dean
Business administration
1917
Nonprofit, church $$$$
(314) 862-3456
(314) 889-1451 fax
Bachelor of Business Administration and M.B.A. through the "Options Program," a flexible course of study geared to students over the age of 25 with at least two years' relevant work experience (three for the Master's) who have completed at least 60 credits elsewhere. Credit available for life-experience learning and equivalency exams. All coursework is based in the real-life workplace, and courses meet one night a week for four hours. Every M.B.A. student is issued a laptop computer for coursework, which they may then keep after graduation.

Fordham University   B
School of General Studies
Bronx, NY 10458
Kathleen Caltagirone
Liberal arts, business, premedical
1841
Nonprofit, independent $$$$
(212) 579-2486
Bachelor of Arts, Bachelor of Science, and Bachelor of Business Administration available entirely through evening study or Saturday classes. Credit is given for life experience learning. There is an Esperanza Center for adult Hispanic students, and a separate adult admissions office.

Fort Wright College
See: Heritage College

Francis Marion University   B
Bachelor of General Studies Program
P.O. Box 100547
Florence, SC 29501
General studies
1970
Nonprofit, state $$$
(803) 661-1362
(803) 661-1165 fax
The Bachelor of General Studies program is offered for adult students (generally over the age of 25) who have earned a variety of college credits, often at a number of institutions, but have not met specific requirements for any one major. Some credit for equivalency exams; up to 90 of the 120 required hours may be transfer credits. Nontraditional study options include independent study and courses by correspondence, newspaper, and television.

Franklin Pierce College   B
Rindge, NH 03461
Louis D. D'Allesandro
Management, marketing, CIS, accounting, general studies
1962
Nonprofit, independent $$$$
(603) 889-6146
Bachelor of Science in accounting, computer information systems, financial management, management, marketing, and general studies through weekend, evening, and summer programs offered at satellite campus location. Credit for nonacademic learning available.

Franklin University   B
201 S. Grant Ave.
Columbus, OH 43215
Kitty Miller
Many fields
Nonprofit, independent

(614) 341-6231
Bachelor's degrees offered through evening courses, with credit for experiential learning through proficiency testing and portfolio assessment.

Fresno Pacific College   B
Management of Human Relations Program
1717 S. Chestnut Ave.
Fresno, CA 93702
Management of human relations
1944
Nonprofit, church $$$$
(209) 453-2000
(209) 453-2007 fax
B.A. in management of human relations through a "compressed-time program" for working adults who have at least seven years' experience in their field. Up to 30 units may be awarded for portfolio assessment, and 70 from transfer credit. The final 30 credits must be earned from Fresno Pacific. Correspondence courses and independent study available.

Friends World Program of   B
Long Island University
Southampton, NY 11968
Carol Gilbert
Many fields
1965
Nonprofit, independent $$$
(516) 283-4000
Bachelor of Arts degree is earned by combining academic study with independent field research and internships around the world. Faculty at campuses and program centers in the U.S., Costa Rica, England, Israel, Kenya, India, China, and Japan offer four- to 12-week residential programs for cultural orientation, language immersion, and learning plans designed prior to the independent field study, which may be carried out in these and other countries. (Since 1965, F.W.C. students have studied in over 70 different countries.) Students may choose from traditional liberal arts majors, as well as such fields as third world development, peace and conflict resolution, UN studies, holistic and traditional healing, appropriate technology, animal behavior, women's studies, and many interdisciplinary majors.

Gannon University   B
University Square
Erie, PA 16541
Laura Lewis-Clemons
Management, administrative studies
1925
Nonprofit, church $$$$
(814) 871-7000
(814) 871-7338 fax
B.S. in management or administrative studies through evening, weekend, and summer courses, especially for students interested in church, career, and social leadership. Although the school is run by the Roman Catholic church, they stress that "the university's environment is one of inclusiveness and cultural diversity."

Gardner-Webb College   B
GOAL Program
Boiling Springs, NC 28017
Many fields
1905
Nonprofit, church $$$
(704) 434-2361
(704) 434-6246 fax
The GOAL (Greater Opportunity for Adult Learners) program allows students who have already completed 64 units elsewhere to finish a B.A. or B.S. entirely through evening classes. Fields offered are: B.S. in business administration, business management, health management, accounting, MIS, nursing, human services, or social science (with a concentration in criminal justice); B.A. in religion. Classes are offered at 11 North Carolina locations; credit also available for military experience, proficiency exams, independent study, and supervised fieldwork.

George Fox College   B
Department of Continuing Studies
Newberg, OR 97137
Human resources management
1891
Nonprofit, church $$$$
(503) 538-8383   (503) 537-3830 fax
B.A. in human resources management for students with at least two years of previous coursework. Credit available for life-experience learning through portfolio assessment and proficiency exams; cooperative education and independent study are possible.

George Mason University   B, M
Office of Individualized Studies
4400 University Dr.
Fairfax, VA 22030
Patricia M. Riordan
Individualized studies
1957
Nonprofit, state $$
(703) 993-2084
In the Bachelor of Individualized Studies degree (B.I.S.), units may be earned by alternative means, such as equivalency exams or credit for life-experience learning. Applicants must have at least eight years of post–high-school experience in their field. Students work with an academic advisor to design and complete a program of study. A total of 30 units must be completed at George Mason or certain other northern Virginia schools. A Master of Arts in Individual Studies (M.A.I.S.) is available to adult students with at least two years' work ex-

perience in the proposed area of study. At least six hours of graduate-level work must be completed before enrolling. Each M.A.I.S. student works out an individual course of study with a faculty member who will supervise the performance of that work. A special project is required, and evening study is available for residential programs.

Georgetown University
Liberal Studies Office
306 ICC Building
Washington, DC 20057
Phyllis O'Callaghan
We've heard that they offer some nontraditional programs, but thus far Dr. O'Callaghan has not responded to our requests for more information.

Georgia School of Professional Psychology
See: American Schools of Professional Psychology

Georgia Southern University   B
Landrum Box 8092
Statesboro, GA 30460
General studies
1906
Nonprofit, state $$$
(912) 681-5611
(912) 681-0196 fax
Bachelor of General Studies allows nontraditional students to combine up to 145 hours of prior liberal-arts education and/or credit from military experience and proficiency exams with 45 units in residence in the specialization of their choice.

Georgia Southwestern College   B
800 Wheatley St.
Americus, GA 31709
Diane Burns
Social science, business administration
1906
Nonprofit, state $$
(912) 928-1279
Bachelor of Arts and Bachelor of Science in social science and business administration, entirely through evening study.

Georgian Court College   B
Evening Division
900 Lakewood Ave.
Lakewood, NJ 08701-2697
Sister Dorothy Lacework, Director
Many fields
1908
Nonprofit, church $$$$
(908) 364-2200
(908) 367-3920 fax

B.A. in art, art history, chemistry, humanities, mathematics, physics, psychology, sociology, or special education; B.S. in accounting, biology, or business administration, entirely though evening study. Some credit for military experience and a wide range of proficiency exams, as well as cooperative education, independent study, and supervised fieldwork.

Golden Gate University   B, M, D, L
536 Mission St.
San Francisco, CA 94105
Archibald Porter, Dean of Admissions
Many fields
1901
Nonprofit, independent $$$
(415) 442-7272
B.A. in many management-related fields; B.S. in accounting, insurance management, and transportation; M.B.A.; M.P.A.; M.S. in accounting and taxation; combined M.B.A. and law degree; and a D.P.A. or D.B.A. all entirely through evening and/or weekend study. An "executive M.B.A." program for experienced managers meets every other weekend for 20 months. Off-campus courses are offered in locations around California (including L.A., Sacramento, and San Diego) and at military bases across the country (Arizona, Florida, Idaho, Nevada, New Hampshire, New Mexico, North and South Carolina, Virginia, and Washington, as well as Guantanamo Bay, Cuba). Two Bear family members happily attended Golden Gate before moving on to schools with broader course offerings.

Guilford College   B
Center for Continuing Education
5800 West Friendly Ave.
Greensboro, NC 27410
Mary T. Vick, Director
Many fields
1837
Nonprofit, church $$$$
(910) 316-2000
(910) 316-2951 fax
B.A., B.S., and B.F.A. in a number of fields, entirely through evening courses. Credit for up to 64 units of prior academic education; an additional 16 can come from proficiency exams. Independent study and supervised fieldwork also available.

Hamline University   M
Snelling and Hewitt Ave.
St. Paul, MN 55104
Jack K. Johnson
Public administration
1854
Nonprofit, church $$$$

(612) 641-2800

Master's in public administration through an evening program for public administrators, corporate managers, and lawyers.

Hampshire College   B

Amherst, MA 01002
Audrey Y. Smith
Many fields
1970
Nonprofit, independent $$$$$
(413) 549-4600

The B.A. is earned by completing three levels of study. In Division I (basic studies), students spend three or four semesters in residence taking courses and pursuing research. In Division II (concentration), they gain mastery of their chosen fields through independent study, foreign study, internships, and/or more courses. In Division III (advanced studies), they complete a major project. Each student designs a course of study in close collaboration with faculty. Interdisciplinary study is available in all major liberal arts disciplines.

Harvard University   B, M

Extension School, 51 Brattle St.
Cambridge, MA 02138
Michael Shinagel, Dean
Many fields
1636
Nonprofit, independent $$
(617) 495-4024

Nearly 600 courses in over 65 fields of study on an open-enrollment basis. Bachelor of Liberal Arts in extension studies, Master of Liberal Arts (A.L.M.) in extension studies, certificate of special studies in administration and management, certificate of advanced study in applied sciences, certificate in public health. English as a Second Language program. Half the units for the Bachelor's degree must be earned at Harvard (in the Extension School, the Summer School, or the regular university). All work for the Master's degree must be completed at Harvard. There is a foreign language requirement, and a thesis must be submitted.

Hawaii Pacific University   B, M

1166 Fort Street Mall, #203
Honolulu, HI 96818
Director of Admissions
Many fields
Nonprofit, independent $$$
(808) 544-0249

The Honolulu campus offers various Bachelor's degrees and an M.B.A. through Adult Continuing Education, for adults who wish to remain fully employed. Credit is given for work experience, military training, and equivalency exams. The M.B.A. offers concentrations in various specialties, as well as an internship option. The Hawaii Loa

campus in Kaneohe offers a Bachelor in Organizational Management through an accelerated program for working adults. Up to 30 of 124 credits required can come from life-experience learning, through portfolio assessment, and another 30 from equivalency exams. Applicants must have already earned 60 credits (through the just-mentioned methods, or prior traditional learning); the program meets one night a week and every other Saturday, for 18 months. The Kaneohe campus is at 45-045 Kamehameha Highway, Kaneohe 96744, phone (808) 233-3100.

Heidelberg College   B

310 E. Market St.
Tiffin, OH 44883
Raymond A. Wise
Many fields
1850
Nonprofit, church
(419) 448-2000

Bachelor of Arts and Bachelor of Science in accounting, allied health, business administration, health services management, psychology, and public relations. Up to 75 percent of the necessary credits may be earned through an assessment of prior learning experiences, which is done on the basis of a portfolio prepared by the student. The assessment fee is $575. Nontraditional courses are available, based on a learning contract model. There is also a weekend college, which meets from Friday evening through Sunday morning during the fall, spring, and summer terms. See also: East Central College Consortium.

Heritage College   B, M

3240 Fork Road
Toppenish, WA 98948
Barbara Gfeller
Many fields
1907
Nonprofit, independent $$$
(509) 865-2244

Master of Education through intensive weekend courses on both Toppenish and Omak campuses. Bachelor's degrees available entirely through evening study, with credit for prior learning experiences and equivalency examinations. Credit for work experience available through on-campus LINK program. Formerly known as Fort Wright College.

Hiram College   B

Hiram, OH 44234
Nancy Moeller
Various fields
1850
Nonprofit, independent $$
(216) 569-5161

Bachelor of Arts offered entirely through weekend study.

The weekend college meets from Friday evening through Sunday noon, every other weekend. Programs available in fine arts, humanities, social sciences, communications, business management, and allied health. The degree can be completed in a minimum of two academic years; 90 credit hours must be completed at Hiram College. See also: East Central College Consortium.

Hofstra University B
New College, 1000 Fulton Ave.
Hempstead, NY 11550
Kathe Sweeney
Many fields
1935
Nonprofit, independent $$$
(516) 463-5823
(516) 565-4104 fax
Hofstra's New College is a small interdisciplinary liberal arts college offering the B.A. in humanities, natural sciences, social sciences, creative studies, or interdisciplinary studies, based on a combination of individual study on campus, internship projects off campus, and classroom work. Within New College, there is a university without walls program for "able adults who can spend only limited time on campus, but whose life situations provide opportunity for full- or part-time learning." This individualized program awards degrees based on development of abilities and competencies, rather than accumulation of credit-hours. New College students can earn up to 32 credits by examination. Many of Hofstra's traditional courses are offered in the evening as well.

Holy Names College B
3500 Mountain Blvd.
Oakland, CA 94619
Carol Sellman
Various fields
1868
Nonprofit, independent $$$
(415) 436-1120
Holy Names's weekend college offers a Bachelor of Arts in business administration/economics, human services, humanistic studies, and nursing; an M.B.A., and an M.A. in English. Classes meet every other weekend for three trimesters. Academic programs and support services are designed for the adult who works full-time.

Hood College B, M
Rosemont Ave.
Frederick, MD 21701
Katherine Joseph
Many fields
1893
Nonprofit, independent $$$$
(301) 663-3131
Bachelor's degrees in many fields, in which units may be

earned through an assessment of prior learning experiences, conducted by Hood's Learning Assessment and Resource Center. Master of Arts in human sciences for in-service teachers and others, through late afternoon, evening, and summer study.

Howard Payne University B
HPU Station
Brownwood, TX 76801
General Studies Program
General studies
1889
Nonprofit, church $$$$
(915) 646-2502
(915) 643-7835 fax
Degree-completion program for students who have already accumulated 60 credits, and have employment experience in their field. Credit for life-experience learning through portfolio assessment, as well as for a range of equivalency exams. The school does offer correspondence courses.

Hunter College B, M
695 Park Ave.
New York, NY 10021
William Zlaty
Many fields
1870
Nonprofit, state $$
(212) 772-4490
Bachelor of Arts, Bachelor of Science, and Master's degrees in many fields, available entirely through evening study. There are combined Bachelor's/Master's programs in anthropology, economics, English, history, mathematics, music, physics, and sociology.

Illinois Benedictine College B, M
5700 College Rd.
Lisle, IL 60532
Jane L. Smith, Director of Admissions
Many fields
1887
Nonprofit, church $$$$$
(708) 960-1500
(708) 960-1126 fax
Bachelor's degrees in over 30 fields, including accounting, elementary education, health sciences, philosophy, Spanish, and computer science; M.B.A.; Master of Public Health, and M.S. in management of information systems, counseling psychology, fitness management, and management and organizational behavior, all entirely through evening study. Credit is given for prior work and life-experience learning. Formerly Saint Procopius College.

Illinois School of Professional Psychology

163

See: American Schools of Professional Psychology

Indiana Central College
See: University of Indianapolis

Indiana Institute of Technology B
1600 E. Washington Blvd.
Fort Wayne, IN 46803-1297
Donald E. St. Clair
Business administration
1930
Nonprofit, independent $$$
(219) 422-5561, ext. 251
Bachelor of Science in business administration. Credit is given for independent study and nonacademic prior learning, and correspondence courses are available.

Indiana State University M
Terre Haute, IN 47809
Lowell Anderson
Human resources, occupational safety
1865
Nonprofit, state $$$
(812) 237-2642
M.S. in occupational safety management or human resource development for higher education and industry (yes, that's the full name of the degree!) through interactive television, offered at sites statewide. Students may also obtain videocassettes of courses when needed. The contact for occupational safety is Portia Plummer at (812) 237-3071.

Indiana University Northwest B
3400 Broadway
Gary, IN 6408
William D. Lee, Director of Admissions
General studies
1921
Nonprofit, state $$$
(219) 980-6500
(219) 980-6670 fax
Bachelor of General Studies program designed for students who cannot attend school on a traditional schedule, or those who have prior credit and/or experience in a wide range of fields. Up to 30 credits (of 120 total required) can come from prior experience, through portfolio review; additional credit for CLEP, DANTES, and other exams. After enrollment, students have access to correspondence courses, supervised fieldwork, and other nontraditional options.

Indiana University of Pennsylvania D
Indiana, PA 15705
George E. McKinley, Director of Admissions
English and American literature
1875
Nonprofit, state $$
(412) 357-2100
(412) 357-6213 fax
Indiana University (city of Indiana, state of Pennsylvania) offers a Ph.D. in English and American literature and in English (rhetoric and linguistics) in which the course work can only be done in two summers of study, with independent study in between. Programs are arranged to accommodate teaching schedules of secondary, community, and four-year college teachers. With this flexibility of scheduling, graduate students can pursue their studies without interrupting their careers. Comprehensive exams and a dissertation beyond course work are required. The language requirement can be met by coursework, exams, linguistics courses, or knowledge of a computer language. This is a rigorous program for serious students who wish to be challenged intellectually.

Indiana Wesleyan University B, M
LEAP Program
4406 S. Harmon St.
Marion, IN 46953
David J. Spittal, Vice President of Adult Studies
Business administration, management
1920
Nonprofit, church $$$$$
(317) 674-6901
(317) 677-2499 fax
The LEAP (Leadership Education for Adult Professionals) program is designed for working adult students, and offers a B.S. and an M.S., both in management or business administration. (Undergraduate applicants must have at least two years of employment experience and 60 credits completed elsewhere; graduate applicants, three years employment). Up to 40 credits can come from portfolio assessment and equivalency exams. Students are required to meet one night a week in class for four hours, and an additional night out of class, also for four hours. The school stresses that these are very intense "lockstep" programs.

Inter-American University B
405 Ponce De Leon
Hato Rey, PR 00919
Judith Mendez, Director of Admissions
Many fields
1960
Nonprofit, independent $
(809) 758-8000
Bachelor's degree in many fields can be earned through evening and weekend study, summer school, and through a university without walls program. This last, which requires one visit a week to campus, was originally designed for working law enforcement officers but other types of applicants are accepted.

International College B

8695 College Pkwy.
Fort Myers, FL 33919
Elias Ursitti
Business administration, accounting, CIS, management
(813) 482-0019
Bachelor of Science in the above fields offered through independent study and/or "parallel enrollment," a nontraditional program that combines on-campus courses with off-campus job experience. Up to 25 percent of credit toward a degree can come from assessment of prior life-experience learning.

International Graduate School of Behavioral Science
See: Florida Institute of Technology

International University (Europe)   B, M
The Avenue
Bushey, Watford, WD2 2LN UK
Gordon Bennett, Director
Business, engineering, human behavior, international relations
Nonprofit, independent $$
(1923) 49067
Bachelor's and Master's degrees are offered in residence on the campus near London, in association with the accredited United States International University, San Diego.

Iona College   B
715 North Ave.
New Rochelle, NY 10801-1890
Isabel Cavanagh
Various fields
1940
Nonprofit, independent $$$
(914) 633-2000
Bachelor of Arts and Bachelor of Science can be earned entirely through evening, weekend, and summer programs.

Iowa Wesleyan College   B
Office of Continuing Education
601 N. Main Street
Mount Pleasant, IA 52641
David C. File, Director
Many fields
1842
Nonprofit, church $$$$$
(319) 385-8021
(319) 385-6296 fax
B.A. in accounting, business administration, elementary education, psychology, sociology, and criminal justice; B.S. in nursing, and Bachelor of General Studies, through some combination of evening, weekend, and summer courses, independent study, supervised fieldwork, and televised courses. Credit for prior military and other experience through portfolio assessment, and

equivalency exams.

Jacksonville State University   B
227 Stone Center
Jacksonville, AL 36265
Jerry D. Smith, Dean of Admissions
General studies
1883
Nonprofit, state $$$
(205) 782-5781
(205) 782-5291 fax
Bachelor of General Studies through a program that allows students greater freedom to select an individualized course of study, and gives some credit for military experience and possibly other, by portfolio assessment, equivalency exams, and televised courses.

Jacksonville University   B, M
College of Weekend Studies
2800 University Blvd. N.
Jacksonville, FL 32211
James A. Anderson, Director
Many fields
1934
Nonprofit, independent $$$$
(904) 744-3950
(904) 744-0101 fax
Bachelor of General Studies, Bachelor of Science, including a specialization in nursing (B.S.N.), Executive M.B.A., and M.A. in teaching, all entirely through weekend and independent study. Undergraduate applicants must have already completed 30 units elsewhere, and both undergrad and graduate applicants must have five years employment or other related experience. Credit for military and other life-experience learning through portfolio assessment, and for equivalency exams.

James Madison University   B
Harrisburg, VA 22807
General studies
1908
Nonprofit, state $$$$
(703) 568-6211
An individualized Bachelor of General Studies that can be tailored to adult returning students' needs. Applicants must have completed 30 units, and have been out of high school for at least four years. Credit for life-experience and military learning, through portfolio assessment, as well as a range of equivalency exams.

Johns Hopkins University   B, M, D
School of Continuing Studies
102 Shaffer Hall
3400 N. Charles Street
Baltimore, MD 21218
Stanley C. Gabor

Business, education, liberal arts
1876
Nonprofit, independent $$
(410) 516-8490
(410) 516-7704 fax
Bachelor of Liberal Arts; Bachelor of Science; Master of Arts in teaching; Master of Drama Studies; Master of Liberal Arts; Master of Science in business, counseling, education, information and telecommunication systems for business, interdisciplinary science studies, marketing, organization and human resource development, real estate, and special education, and Doctor of Education all offered through evening and weekend courses. The School of Continuing Studies operates off-campus centers in downtown Baltimore, Columbia, Montgomery County, Maryland, and Washington, D.C.

Johnson State College   B

External Degree Program
Johnson, VT 05656
Eileen Boland
Many fields
1828
Nonprofit, state $$
(802) 635-2356 ext. 290
This individually tailored Bachelor's degree is set up to allow native Vermonters to earn a self-designed degree, working with a mentor/advisor. Experiential learning credit is accepted as part of the 60 unit-hours needed for entry, and/or the 122 minimum for graduation. Students must earn 30 credits while enrolled in the program, through independent or correspondence study and on- or off-campus coursework.

Kansas Wesleyan University   B

100 E. Claflin
Salina, KS 67401
Richard Keist
Many fields
1886
Nonprofit, church $$$
(913) 827-5541
B.A. and B.S. available in accounting and finance, arts and communication, business administration and economics, computer science, pre-engineering, pre-law, pre-ministerial, teaching, social services, and many health sciences areas. KWU has recently initiated a Bachelor of Applied Science in business that they feel is particularly well suited to the nontraditional student.

Kean College   B

Morris Ave.
Union, NJ 07083
Brian Lewis
Many fields
1855

Nonprofit, state $$
(201) 527-2000
Some degree requirements can be earned through an assessment of prior learning experiences, based on assessment of a student-prepared portfolio.

Keller Graduate School of Management   M

10 S. Riverside Plaza
Chicago, IL 60606
Business administration
1973
Proprietary $$$$
(312) 454-0880
Keller offers a practitioner-oriented M.B.A. program for working adults entirely through evening or weekend study at five Chicago locations, as well as in Phoenix, Arizona; Kansas City, Missouri, Milwaukee, Wisconsin, and two locations in California: Pomona and Long Beach. They purchased the DeVry Computer Schools in 1987.

Kingston University   M

Kingston Hill, Kingston upon Thames
Surrey, KT2 7LB England
Julie Brown
Business administration
1984
Nonprofit, public $$$
(081) 547-2000
(081) 547-7178 fax
Two-year M.B.A. through a distance-learning program, with one weekend on-campus required per month for intensive group study and individual counseling. Geared to midcareer executives who wish to develop their skills.

Lake Erie College   B

391 W. Washington St.
Painesville, OH 44077
Barbara Emch
Many fields
1856
Nonprofit, independent $$$
(216) 352-3361
Bachelor of Arts, Bachelor of Science, and Bachelor of Fine Arts may be earned through weekend and evening study. Special programs: business administration, equestrian studies. Credit for nonacademic prior learning and by examination.

Lamar University   B, M, D

4400 Pt. Arthur Rd.
Beaumont, TX 77710
Elmer G. Rode, Registrar
Many fields
1923
Nonprofit, state $

(409) 880-8969

B.A. and B.S. can be earned entirely through evening and summer programs; some Saturday classes in graduate-level education.

Landsdowne College
B, L

43 Harrington Gardens
London, SW7 4JU England
Gordon Bennett, Ph.D., President and Dean
Business, fine arts, interior design
(11) 373-7282

Landsdowne follows the curriculum of the accredited New Hampshire College, of Manchester, New Hampshire, and, upon completion of the coursework in London, the student earns their B.S. from New Hampshire. A comparable program is also offered with Drury College in Missouri. Landsdowne also prepares for London University's degree-examinations for the Bachelor of Laws. Its academic council is composed of five present or former administrators of excellent American nontraditional degree programs or schools. B.A. and B.F.A. programs also available.

Lebanon Valley College
B

Annville, PA, 17003
Karen D. Best
Many fields
1866,
Nonprofit, church $$
(717) 867-6100

Bachelor of Arts and Bachelor of Science available through weekend, evening, or summer programs. Evening classes meet once a week during the academic year and twice during the summer. Weekend classes meet Friday nights or Saturdays. There is a special two-week intensive term in mid May, during which students can complete one entire course. Degrees are offered in a wide variety of fields, including accounting, administration for health care professionals, computer information systems, management, and social service. Credit for experiential learning, and by examination.

Lewis-Clark State College
B

500 8th Ave.
Lewiston, ID 83501
Steven J. Bussolini, Director of Admissions
Business, social work, nursing, general studies
1893
Nonprofit, state $$
(208) 799-5272

Although the American Council on Education's book, the Electronic University, reports that Lewis-Clark offers nonresident Bachelor's degrees which can be earned through a combination of audio- and videocassettes, televised and correspondence courses, and guided independent study, the college tells us that the ACE is in error.

Lincoln University
M

Jefferson City, MO 65101
Gary Scott
Various fields
1866
Nonprofit, state $$
(314) 681-500

Master of Education, Master of Arts, and Master of Business Administration may be earned through evening or summer programs. Credit for independent study and by examination.

Long Island University
B, M

C. W. Post Campus
Brookville, NY 11548
Nishan Najarian, Dean
Many fields
1954
Nonprofit, independent $$$
(516) 299-0200

This school's weekend college offers a Master of Professional Studies in criminal justice, Master of Public Administration in health care administration and public administration, and a Master of Science in medical biology, as well as evening classes that can be applied to 174 degree programs at the C. W. Post Campus. The PLUS Program gives special attention to the educational needs of adult students who are preparing for a career change or a move up the ladder. Credit for life experience and by examination awarded toward degree fulfillment. The Office of Adult Services serves as the initial point of contact for many adults by providing free educational and career counseling.

Louisiana State University
B, M, D

Evening School
388 Pleasant Hall
Baton Rouge, LA 70803
Rita Culross
General studies coursework
1855
Nonprofit, state $$$
(504) 388-6297

Bachelor of Arts in history, English, sociology, and business administration; Bachelor of Science in mathematics, psychology, and computer science; Master of Library Science at New Orleans and Shreveport; Master of Science in petroleum engineering at New Orleans; Master of Arts in education at Eunice and Alexandria; Ph.D. in education at Shreveport, all through evening study.

Lourdes College
B

6832 Convent Blvd.
Sylvania, OH 43560
Mary Ellen Briggs

Individualized studies, religious studies, other fields
1958
Nonprofit, church $$
(419) 885-5291, Ohio only (800) 878-3210
Bachelor of Individualized Studies through evening, weekend, and summer programs. Credit for prior learning, independent study, and by examination. Evening and weekend courses in many fields of study, including business, gerontology, music, occupational therapy, recreational therapy, psychology, nursing, social work, sociology, and art.

Loyola University (Louisiana)   B
6363 St. Charles Ave.
New Orleans, LA 70118
Marjorie Dachowski, Director of Admissions
Many fields
1912
Nonprofit, church $$$
(504) 865-2011
They have what sounds like an interesting and innovative Bachelor of Liberal Studies degree, and an interesting and innovative Master's program as well, but they don't want to be in this book, so you'll have to find out from Marjorie Dachowski, Director of Admissions. Tell her John Bear sent you.

Loyola University of Chicago   B
Mundelein College of Loyola
6525 N. Sheridan Road, SKY 204
Chicago, IL 60626-5385
Paula V. DeVoto
Many fields
1870
Nonprofit, church $$$
(312) 670-3000
(312) 508-8008 fax
Loyola has recently expanded its part-time undergraduate program through affiliation with the formerly independent Mundelein Weekend College. The new program awards B.A. and B.S. degrees in a wide range of fields, including physical and life sciences, humanities, social work, business administration, and education. Students have a choice of day, evening, weekend, or summer courses and, according to a 1992 note in Loyola's newsletter for part-time students, the school "continues to alter its identity as it adapts to the rhythm of the times while clinging resolutely to its essential mission: offering adult students access to higher education."

Madonna University   B, M
36600 Schoolcraft Rd.
Livonia, MI 48150
Ursula Murray, Academic Advising
Many fields

1947
Nonprofit, church $$
(313) 591-5174
B.A. and B.S. programs are offered in many fields, often through evening classes. Life-experience credits awarded in many areas, including allied health management, business, computer science, criminal justice, gerontology, home economics, and nursing. Such prior learning needs to be described in detail and documented, and is evaluated by means of portfolio assessment, challenge exam, or national standardized tests (CLEP). Cooperative education for credit can be arranged. Thirty semester units in residency required for the degree.

Malone College   B
515 25th St.NW
Canton, OH 44709
Management
1892
Nonprofit, church $$$$
(216) 471-8100
(216) 454-6977 fax
B.A. in management through an accelerated, intensive degree-completion program (applicants must have completed at least 60 credits, and be 25 or older). Credit for prior learning through portfolio assessment, and for equivalency exams, cooperative education, and independent study.

Manchester College   M
North Manchester, IN 46962
Gregory K. Miller, Dean
Accounting
1889
Nonprofit, church $$$$
(219) 982-5000
Master's in accounting can be earned entirely through evening study.

Manhattan College   B
School of General Studies
Bronx, NY 10471
John J. Brennan, Dean of Admissions
General studies
1853
Nonprofit, independent $$$
(718) 920-0100
Bachelor of Science in general studies may be earned through evening and summer programs. Cooperative nursing program with E. McConnell Clarke School of Nursing.

Marian College   B, M
45 South National Ave.
Fond du Lac, WI 54935
Carol Reichenberger, Enrollment Services
Education, business administration, nursing, radiology

1936
Nonprofit, church $$$$
(414) 923-7650, (800) 262-7426
(414) 923-7154 fax
Degree-completion programs leading to Bachelor of Business Administration or B.S. in nursing, operations management, or radiologic technology, as well as an M.A. in education and an M.S. in quality, values, and leadership. Credit for challenge exams and prior nonacademic learning by portfolio assessment. Courses scheduled to meet the needs of working adults.

Marietta College   B, M
215 Fifth Street
Marietta, OH 45750-4005
Dennis R. Deperro
Economics, management, accounting, psychology, and liberal arts and learning
1835
Nonprofit, independent $$$$
(800) 331-7896
Bachelor of Arts in economics, management, accounting, psychology, and liberal arts; Master of Arts in liberal learning through day, evening, and weekend study. Credit available for life experience. See also: East Central College Consortium.

Marquette University   B
1212 W. Wisconsin Avenue
Milwaukee, WI 53233
David Buckholdt, Director of Enrollment
Many fields
1881
Nonprofit, church $$$
(414) 288-7302
Marquette's part-time studies division offers day, evening, and Saturday courses leading to the Bachelor's degree in engineering, criminology and law, political science, advertising, journalism, public relations, organization and leadership, and interpersonal communications.

Mars Hill College   B
Center for Continuing Education
Mars Hill, NC 28754
Raymond C. Rapp
1856
Nonprofit, church $$$
(704) 689-1166
Bachelor of Science, Bachelor of Arts, and Bachelor of Social Work available through summer and evening classes. Special programs include allied health, social work, and elementary education. Credit for nonacademic prior learning, independent study, and by examination must be completed as part of a regular program at Mars Hill or one of the two off-campus centers in Asheville or Burnsville.

Martin University   B, M
2171 Avondale Place
Indianapolis, IN 46218
Jane Schilling, Academic Dean
Many fields
1977
Nonprofit, independent $$$
(317) 543-3235
(317) 543-3257 fax
Martin University's stated mission is "to the poor, the minority, and the adult learner." The average student is 40 years old. They offer the Bachelor's degree in many fields, including accounting, pre-law, chemistry, biology, business, human services, African-American studies, genetic counseling, substance abuse, social services, and music. Many courses through evening and Saturday study. Master's in community psychology and urban and ministry studies. Assessment of prior learning for life-learning credit.

Marygrove College   B, M
8425 W. McNichols Rd.
Detroit, MI 48221
Karin Jahn, Director of Admissions
Many fields
1910
Nonprofit, church $$$$
(313) 862-8000
(313) 864-6670 fax
B.A., B.S., B.F.A., Bachelor of Music, Bachelor of Social Work, Bachelor of Business Administration, Master of Arts, and Master of Education, all or largely through evening classes. Credit for life-experience learning through portfolio assessment, for equivalency exams, and for cooperative education, independent study, and television courses.

Marylhurst College for Lifelong Learning   B, M
Marylhurst, OR 97036
Keith W. Protonentis
Many fields
1893
Nonprofit, independent $$$
(503) 636-8141
Bachelor of Arts in communication, humanities, human services, social science, science/math, arts, crafts, and interdisciplinary studies; Bachelor of Fine Arts; Bachelor of Science in management; Bachelor of Music; Master of Science in management; M.B.A.; and M.A. in art therapy. Baccalaureate graduation requirements include a minimum of 40 quarter hours of credit through Marylhurst (22 percent of the degree). Credit is earned by taking Marylhurst courses, courses at other schools, or by correspondence, and through independent studies.

Fifty percent of the graduates utilize the credit for Prior Learning Experience Program to complete their degrees. The average student is 38 years old and enters with about two years of college.

Marymount College   B
Tarrytown, NY 10591
Gina Campbell
Many fields
1907
Nonprofit, independent $$$
(800) 724-4312
Bachelor of Arts and Bachelor of Science degrees in such fields as psychology, English, history, economics, business, information systems, and elementary education may be earned by spending every second or third weekend on campus to complete as many as twelve credits per term. Weekend courses run from Friday evening through Sunday afternoon. Credit for prior experiential learning.

Maryville University of St. Louis   B
13550 Conway Rd.
St. Louis, MO 63141
Robert L. Adams
Many fields
1872
Nonprofit, independent $$$
(314) 576-9300
Bachelor's degree programs in management, information systems, psychology, sociology, nursing, and communications are offered through evening and weekend courses. Credit for experiential learning.

Metropolitan State College of Denver   B
P.O. Box 173362
Denver, CO 80217-3362
Kenneth C. Curtis, Dean of Admissions
Many fields
1963
Nonprofit, state $$
(303) 556-8514
Up to half the units required for the Bachelor's degree can come from assessment of prior learning experiences. The assessment is based on a student-prepared portfolio, and the cost is based on the number of units awarded.

Miami Institute of Psychology   D
8180 N. W. 36th St., Second Floor
Miami, FL 33166
Jorge A. Herrera, Assistant V.P.
Psychology
1966
Nonprofit, independent $$$
(305) 541-8970
The accreditation is for the main campus, the Caribbean Center for Advanced Studies, in Puerto Rico.

Ph.D. and Psy.D. degrees are offered in general clinical psychology, clinical psychology and criminal justice, clinical gerontological psychology, and clinical neuropsychology. Some courses available through evening or weekend study.

Michigan State University   M
Office of Admissions and Scholarships
250 Administration Building
East Lansing, MI 48824
William H. Turner
Many fields
1855
Nonprofit, state $$$
(517) 355-8332
John's alma mater offers the M.B.A. through evening study at Troy; M.A. in advertising, journalism, and counseling in Birmingham; M.A. in teacher education in Saginaw, Flint, Grand Rapids, and Kalamazoo; Master of Science in nursing in Benton Harbor; Master of Social Work in Sault Ste. Marie and Traverse City. Also, Michigan State offers the M.A. in education through part-time and independent study centers in Japan, England, Thailand, and the Philippines.

Midway College   B
512 E. Stephens St.
Midway, KY 40347
Robert Parrent, Dean of Enrollment
Business administration
1847
Nonprofit, church $$$$
(606) 846-4421   (606) 846-5349 fax
B.A. in business administration entirely through evening classes. Credit for prior learning experiences, equivalency exams, independent study, and supervised fieldwork.

Millersville University of Pennsylvania   B
Millersville, PA 17551
Darrell C. Davis
Many fields
1855
Nonprofit, state $$
(717) 872-3024
Bachelor of Arts in English, business administration, economics, history, mathematics, computer science, political science, psychology, social work, and physics may be earned through evening classes or summer sessions. Special program for registered nurses leads to B.A. in nursing. Millersville offers no degree program that can be earned exclusively through evening or summer classes.

Millsaps College   B
Adult Degree Program
Jackson, MS 39210
Harrylyn G. Sallis, Dean for Adult Studies
Liberal studies

1890
Nonprofit, church $$$$$
(601) 974-1000
(601) 354-2624 fax
The Adult Degree Program is scheduled so as to allow adult students to pursue a Bachelor of Liberal Studies while continuing full-time work. Credit awarded for prior learning experiences through portfolio assessment and for equivalency exams, independent study, and supervised fieldwork.

Milwaukee School of Engineering   B, M

1025 N. Broadway
P. O. Box 644
Milwaukee, WI 53201
Sandra Everts
Engineering, engineering technology, business, and management
1903
Nonprofit, independent $$$
(414) 277-7300
Bachelor of Science in engineering technology, business, and management; Master of Science in engineering and engineering management, entirely through evening study. Courses are also offered at corporate facilities, other off-campus locations, and via videotape.

Minnesota School of Professional Psychology

See: American Schools of Professional Psychology

Mississippi State University   B, M

Office of Continuing Education
P.O. Drawer 5247
Mississippi State, MS 39762
Political science, public policy administration, business administration, general studies
1878
Nonprofit, state $$$
(601) 325-2131
(601) 325-7455 fax
Bachelor of General Studies, M.A. in political science or public policy administration, and M.B.A. through nontraditional programs, including short, intensive semesters and weekend classes. Credit for equivalency exams.

Moorhead State University   B

External Studies Program
Moorhead, MN 56563
Lois Fisher
Many fields
1885
Nonprofit, state $$
(218) 236-2181
Bachelor's degrees in many fields available to students within a 100- to 150-mile radius of the university. Assessment of prior learning is part of the program and is based on evaluation of student-prepared portfolios and interviews with faculty from appropriate departments. Testing, either through oral interviews or in written form, is required in most areas. The assessment fees, which are quite low, are based on the number of units awarded. This program is not open to students outside of the region. Many classes are offered on weekends.

Moravian College

Division of Continuing Studies
Bethlehem, PA 18018
Bernard J. Story
They do have relevant programs. But according to Mr. Bernard J. Story, they do not wish to appear in this book. For details, you'll have to contact Mr. Story.

Mount Saint Mary College   B, M

Powell Ave.
Newburgh, NY 12550
J. Randall Ognibene, Director of Admissions
Many fields
1954
Nonprofit, independent $$$
(914) 561-0800
Bachelor's degree programs in business management and administration, sociology, social sciences, and interdisciplinary studies; Master's in computer science, nursing, and public relations, through evening and weekend study.

Mount Saint Mary's College (California)   B

12001 Chalon Road
Los Angeles, CA 90049
Sister Merrill Rodin
Business, psychology
1925
Nonprofit, church $$$$
(310) 476-2237
Bachelor of Science in business and Bachelor of Arts in psychology, through evening and weekend classes. Credit for prior experience by portfolio assessment, and for equivalency exams, independent study, and supervised fieldwork.

Mount Saint Mary's College (Maryland)   B

Bachelor of General Studies Program
Emmitsburg, MD 21727
General studies
1808
Nonprofit, church $$$$
(301) 447-6122
(301) 447-5755 fax
Bachelor of General Studies in a degree-completion program (applicants must have completed 85 of the 120 total credits for the degree elsewhere). Credit awarded for prior life and military experience by portfolio assessment, and also for equivalency exams, independent study, and su-

pervised fieldwork.

Mount Union College   B

1972 Clark Ave.
Alliance, OH 44601
Amy Tomko, Director of Admissions
Many fields
1954
Nonprofit, church $$$$
(216) 821-5320 ext. 2590
(216) 821-0424 fax

Bachelor's degrees in many fields, in which up to 75 percent of the required units can come from an assessment of prior learning experiences in a program called CARE (Credit for Academically Relevant Experience). The assessment is based on a portfolio, examinations, and/or faculty interviews. The assessment fee is based on the number of units, and is generally about a third the usual cost of that number of units. Courses are also offered through a weekend college program. See also: East Central College Consortium

Muskingum College

See: East Central College Consortium

Naropa Institute   B, M

2130 Arapahoe Ave.
Boulder, CO 80302
Michelle Graves
Many fields
1974
Nonprofit, independent $$$$
(303) 444-0202

Naropa offers an M.A. and upper-division B.A. degrees, nondegree study, and a summer program. Education at Naropa combines the disciplines of the classroom with those of personal awareness through contemplative practices such as sitting meditation, aikido, t'ai chi, and others. The combination is intended to cultivate both academic strength and the desire to contribute to the world with understanding and compassion. B.A. programs in "InterArts Studies" (dance/movement, music, and theater), early childhood education, environmental studies, interdisciplinary studies, psychology, religious studies, and writing and literature. M.A. programs in art therapy, gerontology, counseling, and psychotherapy; M.F.A. in writing and poetics. Study-abroad programs in Bali and Nepal.

National Institute for Higher Education

See: University of Limerick

National University   B, M, D, L

University Park
San Diego, CA 92108
Louise Clark
Many fields
1971
Nonprofit, independent $$$
(619) 563-7100

Each course is offered in intensive one-month modules, meeting in the evenings and selected Saturdays. Some daytime classes are offered. More than 600 courses begin each month, 12 times a year. Courses are offered in San Diego, Fresno, Irvine, Los Angeles, Sacramento, San Jose, Stockton, and Vista, California, and in San Jose, Costa Rica. Students may freely transfer from one center to another. Degrees include a Bachelor of Business Administration, B.A. in behavioral science, B.A. in interdisciplinary studies, Bachelor of Technical Education, B.S. in computer science, M.B.A., M.B.A. in health care administration, M.A. in business with emphasis in human services management or real estate management, and Master of Public Administration.

National-Louis University   B, M

2840 Sheridan Rd.
Evanston, IL 60201
Scott Heck, Director of Admissions
Many fields
1886
Nonprofit, independent $$$
(312) 256-5150

Bachelor of Arts in applied sciences, in which up to 75 percent of the required units can come from an assessment of prior learning and college transfer credit. The college utilizes what it calls the "field-experience model," in which the student follows an intense program of classes (one four-hour session per week) and individual study, while remaining fully employed. The M.S. in management requires 59 four-hour meetings (once a week for 15 months); M.S. in adult and continuing education, 52 weekly meetings (13 months). National-Louis also has a Bachelor's completion program in management and education, designed for registered, licensed, certified allied health professionals. This program lasts 13 months and requires 49 one-night-a-week class meetings. Programs are offered around Illinois and in St. Louis, Missouri; McLean, Virginia; Beloit, Wisconsin; Tampa, Florida; Atlanta, Georgia, and Heidelberg, Germany. Formerly called National College of Education.

Nazareth College   B, M

Continuing Education Program
Rochester, NY 14610
Paul W. Kenyon
Liberal arts, education
1924
Nonprofit, independent $$$
(716) 586-2525

Bachelor of Arts in liberal arts and Master's in education, for persons over 21, offered entirely through evening study.

Nebraska Wesleyan University   B

Institute for Lifelong Learning
5000 St. Paul Ave.
Lincoln, NE 68504
Many fields
1887
Nonprofit, church $$$$
(402) 466-2371
(402) 465-2179 fax

Bachelor of Arts and Bachelor of Science in many fields, including nursing, through evening classes, with an open admissions policy. Credit for equivalency exams, independent study, and supervised fieldwork.

Neumann College   B

Liberal Studies Program
Aston, PA 19014
Mark Osborn, Director of Admissions
Many fields
1965
Nonprofit, church $$$$
(215) 459-0905
(215) 459-1370 fax

Bachelor of Arts or Science in liberal studies, through programs designed to accommodate the schedules and commitments of adult students. Concentrations in accounting, computer and information management, elementary and early childhood education, humanities, marketing, business administration, health care administration, human resource development, and psychology. Credit awarded for life experience learning, by portfolio assessment, equivalency exams, cooperative education, independent study, and supervised fieldwork.

New College of California   B, M, D, L

50 Fell St.
San Francisco, CA 94102
Katrina Fullman
Humanities (many fields), psychology, poetics, law
1971
Nonprofit, independent $$$
(415) 863-4111

New College has offered its Bachelor of Arts, Master of Arts, and J.D. degrees using a variety of different approaches, including evening courses, weekend courses, and the weekend college for working adults (a series of long weekend seminars with independent study sessions in between, on-the-job practica, tutorials, and credit for prior learning experience.) In 1989, New College took over the nontraditional programs of Antioch University West. The B.A. is offered in humanities (including art, writing, psychology, politics, Latin American studies, anthropology, and much more). There is an M.A. in psychology and in poetics (a unique program combining the critical study and creative writing of poetry). The Science Institute offers science courses designed for people planning to at-

tend professional schools in the health care field. New College was started by Father Jack Leary, former president of Gonzaga University. Traditional courses are offered, generally in three-hour sessions. (The name "New College" comes from Oxford University where their New College was established in the 13th century.)

New York University   B, M

Gallatin Division
715 Broadway, 6th Floor
New York, NY 10003
Richard Avitabile *or* Frances R. Levin
Many fields
1831
Nonprofit, independent $$$$
(212) 998-7370

Created in 1972, the Gallatin Division offers mature, self-directed students the opportunity to plan an individualized program of study in more than 150 majors. The Bachelor of Arts degree allows students to combine coursework taken in most of the schools of NYU with internships, private lessons in the arts, and independent study. Students are expected to be thoroughly conversant with a list of great books as a graduation requirement. (Courses in great books and classic texts are offered as part of the curriculum.) Credit for life experience is also available. An extensive internship program offers the opportunity for internships in education, arts and arts administration, media, business, and public/social service. The Master of Arts in Individualized Study involves coursework, internships, and independent study under the supervision of a faculty advisor. A scholarly, creative, or performance thesis is required. Credit is given for career experience learning.

Niagara University   B, M

Niagara, NY 14109
George C. Pachter, Dean of Admissions & Records
Many fields
1856
Nonprofit, independent $$$$$
(716) 286-8700, (800) 462-2111

Credit for life experience learning, challenge exams, and equivalency exams, such as CLEP. Bachelor's in business, nursing, education, arts, and sciences may be earned through day, evening, and summer programs. Niagara has six divisions: College of Arts and Sciences, College of Business Administration, College of Nursing, College of Education, Travel, Hotel, and Restaurant Administration, and the Division of General Academic Studies.

Nordenfjord World University   B, M, D

Skyum Bjerge, Snedsted
Thy, DK-7752 Denmark
Many fields
1962

$$$
45-7-936-234
This is actually six separate schools, to which students come from all over the world for anything from a semester to an entire degree program. New Experimental College, one of the six, was established with the goal of developing a self-perpetuating community of scholars that would have a worldwide effect on technology, economics, and social planning. Although it's not officially recognized by the Danish government, many students arrange with schools in their home countries (including America, where accredited schools have agreed to recognize Nordenfjord) to award degrees based on work done there. Instruction is largely through teacher-directed independent study, with some classes and seminars. Rule and plans are made in the "ting," a New Age–sounding group meeting. Students nearing the end of their work may call for a "high ting," a combination exam and celebration in which work is presented and discussed. Other units of Nordenfjord specialize in communications, arts and crafts, language, and philosophy.

North Adams State College   B
Office of Continuing Education
North Adams, MA 01247
Gerald F. Desmarais, Director of Admissions
Business administration, computer science, sociology
1894
Nonprofit, state **$$**
(413) 664-4511
B.S. in business administration or computer science and B.A. in sociology offered through evening degree programs.

North Carolina State University   B, M, D
P. O. Box 7103
Raleigh, NC 27695
George R. Dixon
Many fields
1887
Nonprofit, state **$$$**
(919) 515-2434
Bachelor's degrees in many fields, including design, forest resources, and textiles. Evening study available. No credit for work or life experience, but credit by exam available. Master of Public Affairs and Master of Industrial Engineering programs may be offered through evening study at various centers around the state (Charlotte, Fayetteville, Greensboro, and Raleigh). Some courses are also offered by cable television in the Raleigh area, or by videocassette.

North Carolina Wesleyan College   B
Rocky Mount, NC 27804
Josie Williams
Accounting, business administration, computer informa-
tion systems, justice and public policy
1956
Nonprofit, church **$$$**
(919) 985-5197
Bachelor's degree in accounting, business administration, computer information systems, and justice and public policy may be earned through evening and summer programs. For North Carolina residents only.

North Central College   B, M
30 N. Brainard St.
Naperville, IL 60566
Susan J. Moore
Many fields
1861
Nonprofit, church **$$$**
(312) 420-3000
Bachelor of Arts in accounting, communications, computer science, management, marketing, and management information systems may be earned through weekend or evening programs offered in Naperville and Schaumburg/Rolling Meadows. Bachelor of Science in Computer Science through evening studies. North Central also has a weekend college that meets Friday evening and Saturday, normally every other weekend; six meetings per term.

North Dakota State University   B, M
College of University Studies
Morrill Hall 112
Fargo, ND 58105
Roger D. Kerns, Dean
Many fields
1890
Nonprofit, state **$$**
(701) 237-7014
(701) 237-8482 fax
Bachelor of University Studies degrees through individually tailored programs in many fields, some available at remote sites, by two-way video. There is a residency requirement of one year or 30 semester credits. Students may earn credit for prior work, and educational and military experiences. The assessment must be done after enrollment and is part of a degree proposal prepared by the student in consultation with an advisor. There is no fee for the assessment. Students usually have a major emphasis or thrust to their proposed course of study but they do not have a major. They may combine previous academic credit, credit for life experience and nontraditional education, and courses offered by any department on campus. Also, M.Ed. or M.S. in counseling, with a number of specializations, largely through two-way video, beamed to designated sites around the state. Some on-campus residency required. Contact for Master's programs: Robert Nielsen (701) 237-7676.

Northeastern University B, M, D, L

360 Huntington Ave.
Boston, MA 02115
Philip R. McCabe
Many fields
1898
Nonprofit, independent $$
(617) 437-2000

Northeastern offers what UNESCO calls "the world's leading program in cooperative education." They have asked us to delete their listing from this book, but we have chosen not to do so, since the program is of interest to so many people. Most of Northeastern's more than 50,000 students are employed half-time at companies all over the U.S.—while one-half of the students are attending classes, the other half are working full-time. Every three to six months, they switch. In many cases, two students work together to hold a full-time job in business or industry. Some evening classes are offered. Degrees at all levels are offered in this manner in a wide variety of subjects, from social science to engineering to pharmacology, nursing, and criminal justice.

Northern Illinois University

See: Quad Cities Graduate Center

Northwest Christian College B

Degree Completion Program
828 E. 11th Ave.
Eugene, OR 97401
Managerial leadership
1895
Nonprofit, church $$$
(503) 343-1641
(503) 343-3727 fax

Bachelor of Science in managerial leadership, designed for the adult student (applicants must have five years of experience in their field, and have completed 75 credits elsewhere). Maximum of 46 credits awarded through portfolio assessment; credit also available for equivalency exams. All students must complete a 60-credit managerial leadership curriculum, which includes 18 credit-hours of bible study.

Northwestern College B

3003 Snelling Avenue N.
St. Paul, MN 55113
Organizational administration
1902
Nonprofit, independent $$
(612) 631-5100
(612) 631-5269 fax

Degree-completion program awards the B.S. in organizational administration to adult students (25 or older) who have completed at least 86 credits (of 188 required) elsewhere. Credit awarded for equivalency exams, life and

military-experience learning by portfolio assessment, and for licenses such as real estate and financial counselor. Particular emphasis is placed upon integrating Christian values, ethics, and faith into the curriculum.

Northwestern University B, M

University College
339 E. Chicago Ave.
Chicago, IL 60611
Louise Love, Associate Dean
Many fields
1851
Nonprofit, independent $$$$
(312) 503-6950
(312) 503-4942 fax

Bachelor's and Master's may be earned through evening and summer programs. Bachelor's degrees offered in anthropology, art history, communications, computer studies, economics, English, environmental studies, fine and performing arts, history, mathematics, organization behavior, philosophy, political science, psychology, radio/tv/film, and sociology. The Master's degrees are in liberal arts and English.

Nyack College B

Adult Degree Completion Program
Nyack, NY 10960
Judith S. Krom, Dean
Organizational management
1882
Nonprofit, church $$$$$
(914) 358-1710
(914) 358-1751 fax

Bachelor of Science in organizational management through a degree-completion program for students who have already earned 60 credits (of 120 total) elsewhere. Credit for life-experience learning, by portfolio assessment, equivalency exams, cooperative education, correspondence courses, independent study, phone/mail instruction, and supervised fieldwork. Classes meet once a week for four hours and, according to the school, are more like business seminars than traditional courses. They involve research, discussion, and group problem-solving exercises with peers.

Ohio State University B, M

Division of Continuing Education
2400 Oletangy River Rd.
Columbus, OH 43210
James J. Mager, Director of Admissions
Many fields
1870
Nonprofit, state $$
(614) 292-3980

Evening and weekend courses are offered, leading to the following degrees: B.A. in English or history, B.S. in many fields, Bachelor of Business Administration, and M.A. in education, English, history, or journalism. Credit for life-experience learning. Telephone-assisted language program in eastern European languages. Counseling, trouble-shooting, and workshops are available from Ohio's Department of Continuing Education.

Oregon State University   B, M
Office of Continuing Education
327 Snell Hall
Corvallis, OR 97331
Don Olcott, Assistant Director
Liberal studies, education
1868
Nonprofit, state $$$
(503) 737-0123   (503) 737-2400 fax
The Bachelor of Arts and Bachelor of Science are offered in liberal studies, for adult students who have already earned at least 90 units elsewhere. Credit for equivalency exams and through independent study, supervised fieldwork, and television courses. The Master of Education in training and development is a practical, work-based degree.

Our Lady of the Lake University   B
411 S. W. 24th St.
San Antonio, TX 78285
Loretta Schlegel
Computer science, management, health care management, human resources, liberal studies
1911
Nonprofit, church $$$$
(210) 434-6711
Bachelor's and Master's in computer information systems, management, human resources and organization, health care management, and liberal studies, through weekend study. All classes are scheduled for four hours every other Saturday or Sunday. Credit may be earned through several testing programs and a portfolio process for evaluation of life/work experience at a cost of one-third the usual tuition for credit awarded. A 36-semester-hour M.B.A. can be earned in two years. This program utilizes the Decision Theater, a teaching laboratory using computer simulations and models to present real life business situations, enabling students to apply managerial theories to everyday situations.

Pace University   B
1 Pace Plaza
New York, NY 10038
Liberal studies, general studies
1906
Nonprofit, independent $$$$
(212) 346-1200   (212) 346-1933 fax
Bachelor of Arts in liberal studies and Bachelor of Science in general studies through programs designed to accommodate the adult working professional. Credit

awarded for military training and life-experience learning, through portfolio assessment, as well as for a range of departmental and equivalency exams.

Pacific Oaks College   B, M
5 Westmoreland Place
Pasadena, CA 91103
Marsha Franker
Human development
1945
Nonprofit, independent $$$$
(818) 397-1351
The College Outreach Extension provides in-service training for ECE educators. They offer B.A., M.A., and certificate programs designed for part-time students who are working professionals. Evening and weekend courses are offered in Southern California as well as in the San Francisco area, Portland, San Diego, Phoenix, and Seattle.

Palm Beach Atlantic College   B
901 S. Flager
West Palm Beach, FL 33401
Rich Grimm, Dean of Admissions
Human resource management
1968
Nonprofit, church
(407) 650-7700
(407) 835-4342 fax
Bachelor of Human Resource Management through a program tailored to the needs of fully employed adults who have earned at least 40 credits already (up to 30 can come through assessment of life experience portfolio and military training). Program is designed to be full-time, one night a week, for 54 weeks. A student entering with 60 credits can expect to finish in one year.

Park College   B, M
Parkville, MO 64152
Randy Condit
Many fields
1875
Nonprofit, church $$$
(816) 741-2000
Park's portfolio plan is an individualized degree completion program for adults, based on a learning contract which specifies credit for prior experience and new work to be done in classrooms and through independent study. Evening classes are offered in the Kansas City area, and degree completion centers are operated on or near military bases in a dozen states. There is a Master of Public Affairs and graduate study in religion for clergy and lay leaders of the Reorganized Church of Jesus Christ of Latter Day Saints.

Pepperdine University   B, M, D

24255 Pacific Coast Hwy.
Malibu, CA 90265
Robert L. Fraley, Dean of Admissions
Many fields
1937
Nonprofit, independent **$$$$$**
(213) 456-4000
Bachelor of Science in many fields, Master of Arts in education or general psychology, M.S. in educational computing, educational therapy, school management, or administration, Doctor of Education in institutional management or community college administration, all available through a combination of weekend and evening classes in the Los Angeles area. Also, an M.B.A. program for business leaders.

Philadelphia College of Textiles and Science   B, M

Evening Division, School House Lane and Henry Ave.
Philadelphia, PA 19144
John T. Pierantozzi, Director of Admissions
Business, computers, design, science, textiles, nursing
1884
Nonprofit, independent **$$$**
(215) 951-2700
Most of their Bachelor of Science degrees can be earned entirely through evening study. There is a special B.S. for registered nurses (their R.N. training counts for half the needed credits), and another for other health-care professionals. M.B.A. classes meet one evening a week in Bucks and Montgomery counties. Credit given for prior learning, through examination.

Pittsburg State University   M

Pittsburg, KS 66762
Ange Peterson
Many fields
1903
Nonprofit, state **$$**
(316) 231-7000
Master's degrees in many fields can be earned on a part-time basis while remaining fully employed. The university serves students from the states of Kansas, Missouri, and Oklahoma.

Plymouth State College   M

Plymouth, NH 03264
Clarence W. Bailey, Director of Admissions
Education
1871
Nonprofit, state **$$**
(603) 536-5000
Master of Arts for classroom teachers, based on two eight-week summer sessions, with independent study during the nine months in between.

Polytechnic University   M

6 Metrotech Center
Brooklyn, NY 11201
Ellen H. Hartigan, Dean of Admissions
Engineering, science, mathematics, management
1854
Nonprofit, independent **$$$$$**
(718) 643-5000, (800) POLYTEC
(718) 260-3136 fax
Master of Science in mathematics, management, science, and engineering (aerospace/mechanical, electrical, and civil), through evening study at several New York locations.

Pratt Institute   B

200 Willoughby Ave.
Brooklyn, NY 11205
Judy Aaron
Many fields
1887
Nonprofit, independent **$$$$**
(718) 636-3669, (800) 331-0834
Credit awarded for portfolio/work experience/special examinations evaluation. Applicants intending to seek credits by this route should notify the school, but the evaluation process will begin only after the student is registered. Work experience must be substantiated by resumé, letters of certification from the applicant's employer(s), and a portfolio. There is a fee for all such evaluations, and for all credits awarded.

Providence College   B, M

Providence, RI 02918
Michael G. Backes, Director of Admissions
Many fields
1917
Nonprofit, church **$$$$**
(401) 865-1000
Bachelor of Arts, Bachelor of Science in business administration or law enforcement, and M.B.A., all available entirely through evening study.

Quad Cities Graduate Center   M

639 38th Ave.
Rock Island, IL 61201
Jenet Lessner, Ph.D.
Many fields
1969
Nonprofit, independent **$$$**
(309) 794-7376
The center is sponsored by the University of Illinois, Northern Illinois University, the University of Iowa, Teikyo Marycrest University, Augustana College, Iowa State University, University of Northern Iowa, Western Illinois University, St. Ambrose University, and Bradley University. The degree is issued by one of these ten, depending on the program selected. Degrees of-

177

fered include Master of Arts, Master of Science, M.S. in education, M.S. in engineering, and Master of Business Administration, all available entirely through evening study.

Queens College B

Adult Collegiate Education
65-30 Kissena Blvd.
Flushing, NY 11367
Betty W. Mason, Director of Admissions
Many fields
1937
Nonprofit, state $$
(212) 520-7000

Bachelor of Arts program for persons over 30 years old through this division of the City University of New York. Learning consists of weekend seminars, tutorials, exemption exams, work credit, and supervised independent study. Classes are scheduled to fit the needs of the student. One year of residency is usually required.

Radford University B

Continuing Education
P.O. Box 6917
Radford, VA 24142
Vernon L. Beitzel, Director of Admissions
General studies
1910
Nonprofit, state
(703) 831-5000   (703) 831-5970 fax

Bachelor of General Studies consists of a coursework core of arts and sciences courses (English, math, history, etc.), plus an individualized concentration or major. Liberal credit awarded for prior academic and nonacademic work, by portfolio assessment, as well as equivalency exams, and independent directed study. Applicants must be at least 25 years old and have completed 30 or more units of college-level work.

Ramapo College of New Jersey B

505 Ramapo Rd.
Mahwah, NJ 07430
N. E. Jaeger
Many fields
1969
Nonprofit, state $$
(201) 529-7500

Through a combination of evening and/or Saturday classes, degree-seeking students may complete all degree requirements in biology, business administration (several concentrations), chemistry, computer science, economics, environmental studies, and psychology. Degree-seeking students who are restricted to Saturday study, and who have met the college's general education requirements, may complete a degree in business administration, with a

concentration in accounting, management or marketing. Up to 75 credits can be earned by equivalency tests, and through PLEX, the Prior Learning Experience Program.

Research College of Nursing B

Accelerated B.S. Option
2316 East Meyer Blvd.
Kansas City, MO 64132
Nursing
1980
Nonprofit, independent $$$$
(816) 276-4700

Bachelor of Science in nursing through an accelerated program that allows students to earn the degree in as little as two years full-time, or four years part-time. Credit awarded for equivalency exams, particularly R.N. work, and by portfolio assessment.

Rhode Island College B

600 Mount Pleasant Avenue
Providence, RI 02908
William H. Hurry, Dean of Admissions
General studies
1854
Nonprofit, state $$$
(401) 456-8000
(401) 456-8379 fax

Bachelor of General Studies in either human studies or business institutions, through a program designed for adults who have been out of school for at least five years. Both majors are broadly interdisciplinary. Credit for departmental and other equivalency exams, television courses, independent study, and supervised fieldwork.

Richmond College B, M

Queens Rd.
Richmond, Surrey, TW10 6PJ England
William Petrek
Many fields
(181) 940-9762
(181) 332-1596 fax

Richmond is an accredited American college operating in London, with an international student body. The school offers B.A. degrees in 13 fields and an international M.B.A. Their degree-granting authority comes from the Educational Institution Licenture Commission of the District of Columbia.

Rider College B

2083 Lawrenceville Rd.
Lawrenceville, NJ 08648
Susan C. Christian, Director of Admissions
Business administration, chemistry, office administration, liberal studies
1865

Nonprofit, independent $$$$
(609) 896-5042
B.A. in liberal studies, B.S. in business administration, chemistry, and office administration, all available entirely through evening study.

Robert Morris College   B
Narrows Run Rd.
Coraopolis, PA 15108
Don L. Fox
Science
1921
Nonprofit, independent $$$$
(412) 262-8200
Bachelor of Science, in which all coursework can be done in the evening.

Rockford College   B, M
5050 E. State St.
Rockford, IL 61108
Miriam King, V.P. for Enrollment Management
Many fields
1847
Nonprofit, independent $$$$
(815) 226-4050, (800) 892-2984
(815) 226-4119 fax
B.A. in many fields, B.S. in general education, B.F.A., M.A. in teaching, and M.B.A., all available through evening courses.

Rockhurst College   B, M
1100 Rockhurst Road
Kansas City, MO 64110
Jack Reichmeier
Economics, industrial relations, psychology, sociology, business administration
1910
Nonprofit, church $$
(816) 926-4000
Bachelor of Science and Bachelor of Arts available through evening study; M.B.A. through evening and weekend classes. Cooperative Education Program allows students to alternate semesters of college with full-time salaried work. Internships and practica in communication, psychology, and politics.

Rockmount College
See: Colorado Christian University

Rocky Mountain College   B
Billings, MT 59102
Richard Widmayer, Academic Vice President
Liberal arts, general studies
1878
Nonprofit, church $$$$$
(406) 657-1020

(406) 259-9751 fax
Bachelor of Arts in liberal arts/general studies through computer conferencing, videocassette, and telephone instruction. One semester generally required on-campus. Essentially a degree-completion program, it offers upper-division general education courses, and courses in education, business, and Native American culture (through the Tribal College Telecommunications Exchange).

Rollins College   B, M
Hamilton Holt School, Evening Degree Programs
1000 Holt Avenue, #2725
Winter Park, FL 32789-4499
Charles Edmondson
Many fields
1885
Nonprofit, independent
(407) 646-2232
Offers Bachelor of Arts degree through evening and weekend study in anthropology/sociology, economics, English, environmental studies, humanities, international affairs, organizational behavior, organizational communication, psychology, and urban and public affairs. Also offers Master of Liberal Studies degree, an interdisciplinary program for adults, in the evenings on a part-time basis. Classes meet one evening per week during the 14-week term.

Roosevelt University   B
430 S. Michigan Ave.
Chicago, IL 60605
Albert Bennett, University College
General studies
1945
Nonprofit, independent $$$
(312) 341-3500
(312) 341-3655 fax
Bachelor of General Studies in a variety of programs ranging from hospitality management to computer science (32 concentrations available); prior-learning credit available. The degree is offered through the University College, for persons over 25 years of age. Classes are held evenings and weekends in Chicago and the suburbs, as well as off-campus. Roosevelt offers the "discovery program," through which individuals with no Bachelor's degree can, through a year or less of testing, enter a Master's degree program directly. A Master's degree in General Studies is offered on-campus. No relation to the large diploma mill also called Roosevelt University.

Roskilde University Center   B, M
Postbox 260
Roskilde, DK-4000 Denmark
Henrik Toft Jensen
Many fields
1972

179

Nonprofit, state
(46) 75 77 11

An experimental university, specializing in interdisciplinary studies. Clusters of approximately 60 students, five teachers, and a secretary work together in a house for two years, during which time subgroups work together on interdisciplinary research and creative projects in humanities, social science, and natural science. Nearly 4,000 students are involved. The two years of basic studies are followed by one-and-one-half to three-and-one-half years of specialized studies, leading to the degree. Subjects include foreign language, international development, sociotechnological planning, public relations, and sciences. The school wants to be sure we make it clear that all instruction is in Danish, and that it is difficult, although not impossible, for foreigners to gain access.

Rowan College of New Jersey   B
Office of Admissions
Glassboro, NJ 08028
Marvin G. Sills, Director of Admissions
Many fields
1923
Nonprofit, state $$
(609) 863-5346   (609) 863-6553 fax

Bachelor's degrees in many fields, in which some credit can come through an assessment of prior learning experiences, equivalency exams, and transfer credit. There is no fee for the assessment once one has enrolled. Rowan regards itself as "very traditional," and does not want to hear from applicants looking for a nontraditional program, please.

Rutgers University   B
University College
P. O. Box 93740
Camden, NJ 08102-3740
Deborah E. Bowles, Director of Admissions
Various fields
1927
Nonprofit, state $$
(609) 757-6104

Bachelor of Arts and Bachelor of Science in accounting, computer science, management, physics, microelectronics, English, and psychology available through summer and evening classes in Camden.

Sacred Heart University   B, M
5151 Park Avenue
Fairfield, CT 06432
Douglas J. Bohn, University Registrar
Many fields
1963
Nonprofit, independent $$$$$
(203) 374-7999

B.A., B.S., M.A., M.S., and M.B.A. available through

evening study. Cooperative education and credit for life/work experience and equivalency exams are available at the Bachelor's level.

Sage Evening College   B
140 New Scotland Ave.
Albany, NY 12208
Robert E. Pennock
Many fields
1949
Nonprofit, independent $$$
(518) 445-1717

All degree programs are available entirely through evening study. Fields of study include psychology, health education, business, nursing, computer science, sociology, art, and more. Up to 30 of the required 120 units in the Bachelor's program can come from credit for experiential learning.

Saint Ambrose College   B
518 W. Locust St.
Davenport, IA 52803
Patrick O'Connor
Many fields
1882
Nonprofit, church $$$
(319) 383-8765

Bachelor of Arts, Bachelor of Science, and Bachelor of Elected Studies may be earned through weekend, evening, and summer programs. Special degree-completion program for nurses, and credit for nonacademic prior learning and by examination.

Saint Edwards University   B, M
3001 S. Congress
Austin, TX 78704
Joseph O'Neal
Many fields
1885
Nonprofit, independent $$$
(512) 448-8700

Bachelor's degree program through New College in business, humanities, and social sciences, in which some of the degree requirements can be met by assessment of prior learning. The assessment is based on analysis of a portfolio prepared by the student in a special research course offered for that purpose. The cost is based on a fee for each credit awarded. Saint Edwards also offers a Bachelor of Arts in behavioral sciences and criminal justice. Bachelor of Business Administration, and Master of Business Administration, and M.A. in human resources, through evening study.

Saint Francis College   M
Loretto, PA 15940
Edwin M. Wagner

Industrial relations
1847
Nonprofit, church **$$$$**
(814) 472-3026
M.A. in industrial relations can be earned entirely through evening study at the college's branches in Harrisburg and Pittsburgh, or at the home campus in Loretto.

Saint John's College   M
Graduate Institute
Santa Fe, NM 87501
Director
Liberal studies
1864
Nonprofit, independent **$$**
(505) 982-3691
Saint John's has long been known for its full-time undergraduate programs based entirely on a study of great books of Western civilization. They also offer an innovative Master of Arts in liberal studies, also based on great books, over a period of four eight-week summer sessions in four consecutive years, and/or a fall and spring term program of two evenings a week. The program is offered on both the New Mexico campus and the school's Maryland campus, and students are encouraged to move from one to the other. (Maryland address: Saint John's College, Graduate Institute, Annapolis, MD, 21404 (301) 263-2371).

Saint Joseph's University College   B, M
5600 City Ave.
Philadelphia, PA 19131
Randy H. Miller, Director of Admissions
Many fields
1851
Nonprofit, church **$$$**
(215) 879-7300
B.A. and B.S. offered in more than 30 majors and Master's in business administration, chemistry, computer science, education, health administration, health education, public safety, criminal justice, gerontological services, and American studies, all through evening study. Nontraditional students may also obtain Bachelor's degrees full- or part-time through the Continuing Education program. Up to 65 credits may be transferred from four-year colleges, and 64 from two-year schools. An R.N. may count for up to 60 credits.

Saint Leo College   B
State Rd. 52
St. Leo, FL 33574
Office of the Associate VP of CDL
Psychology, business, public administration, criminology
1889
Nonprofit, church **$$$$**
(904) 588-8236

Bachelor's in psychology, business, public administration, or criminology available through weekend, evening, or summer programs. Weekend students attend classes every other weekend.

Saint Mary College   B
4100 S. 4th St., Traffic Way
Leavenworth, KS 66048
Domenic Teti
Many fields
1923
Nonprofit, church **$$**
(913) 682-5151, (800) 752-7043
Evening programs in Leavenworth in the following majors: accounting, business administration, computer science, human services (client services or criminal justice), and liberal studies. Saint Mary also offers an evening degree-completion program in Kansas City, Kansas, known as the 2 Plus Two program. There is a facility in Johnson County. Saint Mary also offers classes and weekend workshops for teachers, which apply toward certificate renewal, including computer classes through the state-approved Teacher Education Program in computer studies.

Saint Mary's College (California)   B, M
Extended Education
P. O. Box 5219
Moraga, CA 94575
Robert Roxby, Dean
Management, health services administration, procurement and contract management
1863
Nonprofit, church **$$$**
(510) 631-4900
The programs offered are: Bachelor of Arts in management or health services administration, Master of Science in health services administration or procurement and contract management, and a paralegal certificate program. The Bachelor's program is based on a learning contract. All students complete a core curriculum, a field-work project, and various other courses comprising an area requirement. To enter the program, applicants must have 60 units of previous academic credit and work experience in the degree area.

Saint Peter's College   B, M
2614 Kennedy Blvd.
Jersey City, NJ 07306
Robert J. Nilan, Dean of Admissions
Many fields
1872
Nonprofit, church **$$$**
(201) 333-4400
The degree programs are available through evening, weekend, and summer courses. Credit awarded for life experience learning and equivalency exams. Courses also offered

at a branch campus in Englewood Cliffs.

Saint Procopius College
See: Illinois Benedictine College

Sam Houston State University   B, M, D
Huntsville, TX 77431-2087
R. A. Reiner, Associate V.P.
Many fields
1879
Nonprofit, state $
(409) 294-1002
Many subjects are offered through evening and weekend courses. Two-thirds of the coursework for any degree must be completed on-campus. Correspondence courses are offered at the undergraduate level only and a maximum of six correspondence courses (18 semester credit hours) may be applied to an undergraduate degree. The only Doctorate offered is in criminal justice.

San Francisco State University   B, M
Extended Education
1600 Holloway Ave.
San Francisco, CA 94132
Peter Dewees
Many fields
1899
Nonprofit, state $
(415) 338-1377
Associate Dean Jo Volkert wrote asking us to remove SF State's listing, as disappointed readers have apparently misunderstood the school's offerings in the past. However, that would mean omitting a program that many will still find useful. The problem is that although SFSU offers "degree credit courses," the extension program does not issue any degrees. No matter how many courses an extension student completes, he or she must still apply to SF State University (the traditional branch) or another school, to complete a degree.

San Jose State University   B
Washington Square
San Jose, CA 95192
Edgar Chambers
Health care administration, community health/occupational health education
1857
Nonprofit, state $
(408) 924-1000
Bachelor of Science in health care administration and in community health/occupational health education. Credit is earned through coursework, examinations, directed independent study, and field internships.

Sangamon State University   B, M
Springfield, IL 62708
Dennis Frueh, Acting Director of Admissions

Many fields
1969
Nonprofit, state $$
(217) 786-6626, (800) 722-2534
Sangamon's INO, or individual option program, is based partially on a university without walls model. A learning proposal is developed, a learning contract negotiated, and the student pursues the Bachelor's degree through selected off-campus study, internships, foreign study, independent study, or exchange with other institutions. Evening and weekend classes are offered. Credit for prior learning.

Sarah Lawrence College   B, M
Bronxville, NY 10708
Alice K. Olson
Liberal arts, fine arts
1926
Nonprofit, independent $$$$$
(914) 395-2205
The Center for Continuing Education offers adults the opportunity to earn the Bachelor of Arts through part-time daytime coursework and independent study. Weekly seminars are combined with regular individual conferences with faculty. An individually designed M.A. is also available through the Office of Graduate Programs.

Schiller International University   B, M
U.S. Admissions Office
453 Edgewater Dr.
Dunedin, FL 34698-4964
Walter Leibrecht
Many other fields
1964
(813) 736-5082, (800) 336-4133 outside FL
Schiller International University is an accredited independent coeducational American university with an international focus offering undergraduate and graduate degree programs and semester, summer, and full-year study-abroad programs at 10 campuses in six countries: Dunedin, Florida; Central and Greater London, England; Paris and Strasbourg, France; Heidelberg and Berlin, Germany; Engelberg and Leysin, Switzerland; and Madrid, Spain. Fields of study include international business administration, international relations/diplomacy, international hotel/tourism management, and many more. English is the language of instruction at all campuses, and SIU students can transfer among SIU's campuses without losing any credits.

School for International Training   B, M
Kipling Rd., P.O. Box 676
Brattleboro, VT 05302-0676
Neal Mangham
International studies, language education
1964
Nonprofit, independent $$$$

(802) 257-7751, (800) 451-4465 outside VT
(802) 258-3248 fax
Bachelor of International Studies, through the World Issues Program, a junior/senior year program that combines intensive on-campus study with an overseas internship of at least 27 weeks. M.A. in teaching foreign languages (or English as a second language) and M.A. in intercultural management, which concentrates on developing skills useful in international and intercultural professions. Both M.A.s include an internship, and may be completed in 12 to 16 months.

Seattle Pacific University

3307 Third Avenue West
Seattle, WA 98119
1891
Nonprofit, church $$$$
(206) 281-2050
We've heard that they offer some nontraditional programs, but thus far they have not responded to our requests for more information.

Seattle University   B, M, D

Broadway and Madison
Seattle, WA 98122-4460
Lee Gerig, Dean of Admissions
Many fields
1891
Nonprofit, church $$$
(206) 296-5800
Master of Arts in education, Master of Education, Master of Business Administration, Master of Public Administration, Master of Software Engineering, Master of Religious Education, Master of Ministry, Master of Pastoral Ministry, Master of Psychology, and Doctor of Education in educational leadership, all through evening study, summer school, and with some weekend classes. Bachelor's degrees through evening classes in the following fields: accounting, criminal justice, finance, international business, management, nursing, business economics, general business, liberal studies, marketing, and public administration.

Shaw University   B

CAPE
118 E. South St.
Raleigh, NC 27611
Many fields
1865
Nonprofit, church $$$$
(919) 546-8200   (919) 546-8301 fax
Bachelor of Arts and Bachelor of Science for persons who could not otherwise pursue a degree (due to jobs, family obligations, military status, incarceration, distance from campuses, or other special considerations) through the Centers for Alternative Programs of Education (CAPE), located throughout North Carolina. Credit for life-experience and military learning, by portfolio assessment, as well as a wide range of equivalency exams.

Shimer College   B

438 N. Sheridan Rd.
P.O. Box A500
Waukegan, IL 60079
David Buchanan
General studies, humanities, natural sciences, social sciences
1853
Nonprofit, independent $$$
(708) 623-8400
Shimer was once affiliated with the University of Chicago and still bases its curriculum on original source material and the Socratic, or shared inquiry, method in classes no larger that twelve. The small community combined with the college's organization encourages intense student involvement in all aspects of the college. Degrees may also be earned through a weekend program meeting once every three weekends.

Siena Heights College   B

1247 Siena Heights Dr.
Adrian, MI 49221
Norman A. Bukwaz, Dean of External Programs
Health, business, general studies, trade and industrial areas
1919
Nonprofit, church $$$
(517) 263-0731
The degree completion program offers the opportunity to earn the Bachelor's degree in many fields. Substantial credit is given for prior life experience. Up to 80 percent of the required 120 semester hours can be earned through the assessment (including courses taken elsewhere). New work is done through a combination of evening and weekend classes. The program is designed for students who have already completed at least two years of college.

Silver Lake College   B, M

Career Directed Programs Office
2406 South Alverno Road
Manitowoc, WI 54220
Sandra Schwartz, Director of Admissions
Management, manufacturing systems engineering, technology, accounting, organizational behavior
1935
Nonprofit, church $$$$
(414) 684-5955, (800) 236-4752
B.S. in management, manufacturing systems engineering, technology, and accounting, and M.S. in management and organizational behavior offered through classes that meet one or two evenings a week, in centers located in Appleton,

Green Bay, Fond du Lac, Neenah, Wausau, and the Lakeshore area. Credit awarded for prior academic and nonacademic learning, internships, equivalency exams, and coursework at other schools.

Simmons College   B
Continuing Education
300 The Fenway
Boston, MA 02115
Carol H. Pooler, Director
Many fields
1899
Nonprofit, independent $$$$$
(617) 738-2000   (617) 738-2099 fax
B.A. and B.S. programs for women aged 23 and older, offered on a flexible schedule, including a weekend and evening program for registered nurses. A fair amount of credit toward the degree can be earned through portfolio assessment and equivalency exams (up to 80 of the total 128 credits for all transfer assessment, and 82 from exams, although 48 credits must be earned after enrollment).

Simpson College   B
Adult and Continuing Education
701 N. C St.
Indianola, IA 50125
Ronald De Jong, Director of Admissions
Accounting, computer science, communication studies, English, management
1860
Nonprofit, church $$$$
(515) 961-6251
(515) 961-1498 fax
Bachelor of Arts in accounting, computer science, communication studies, English, or management offered through day, evening, Saturday, or accelerated programs. Classes are held in Indianola and in West Des Moines. Credit for professional licenses, military, and other life experience, through portfolio review, as well as for a wide range of equivalency exams, cooperative education, independent study, and supervised fieldwork.

Sioux Falls College   B
1501 S. Prairie Ave.
Sioux Falls, SD 57105
Susan J. Reese, Director of Admissions
Organization and management
1883
Nonprofit, church $$$$
(605) 331-5000
(605) 331-6615 fax
Working adults who have already earned two to three years' worth of college credit can earn the B.A. in organizational management in 17 months, attending class one evening

per week. Credit for prior life-experience and military learning, through portfolio assessment, as well as equivalency exams. Some courses offered at a distance, through audio- and videocassette.

South Dakota State University   B
College of Arts and Sciences, Adm. 122
Brookings, SD 57007
Herbert E. Cheever, Dean
Many fields
1881
Nonprofit, state $$$
(605) 688-4151
(605) 688-5822 fax
South Dakota State offers a number of nontraditional ways to earn credits toward a Bachelor of General Studies, B.A., or B.S., including equivalency exams, cooperative education, correspondence courses, newspaper and television courses, independent study, and supervised fieldwork.

Southeastern Massachusetts University
See: University of Massachusetts—Dartmouth

Southeastern University   M
501 Eye St. SW
Washington, DC 20024
William H. Sherrill, Dean of Admissions
Business, public administration, accounting, taxation
1879
Nonprofit, independent $$$
(202) 488-8162
(202) 488-8093 fax
On Saturdays and Sundays, Southeastern offers an M.B.A., M.S. in accounting or taxation, and Master of Business and Public Administration. Classes last all day, once a week, and the degree requires 36 credit hours for completion.

Southeastern University of the Health Sciences   D
College of Pharmacy
1750 NE 168th Street
North Miami Beach, FL 33162
William D. Hardigan, Dean
Pharmacology
1979
Nonprofit, independent $$$$
(305) 949-4000
(305) 957-1606 fax
Rigorous but flexible program allows working pharmacists who possess either a B.S. or an M.S. to earn the Pharm.D. while remaining fully employed. Courses are offered in the evenings, and students can vary their pace according to work schedule. Some credit for life experience and departmental exams, as well as supervised fieldwork.

Southern Arkansas University   B
SAU Box 1240
Magnolia, AR 71753
James Whittington, Director of Admissions
Business administration, industrial technology
1967
Nonprofit, state $$
(501) 574-4500
(501) 574-4520 fax
Degree-completion programs for holders of an Associate's degree, through weekend classes. Two degrees available: B.S. in industrial technology, and Bachelor of Business Administration. Limited credit for work and military experiences, and for equivalency exam and PBS telecourses. Credit for independent study and supervised fieldwork.

Southern Illinois University   M
Carbondale, IL 62901
Roland Keim
Many fields
1869
Nonprofit, state $$
(618) 453-2121
Master of Science in administration of justice, through coursework, independent study, and work projects. Master of Science in engineering biophysics through coursework plus a field internship. Master of Arts in rehabilitation administration, with five weeks of independent study for each week spent on campus. Weekend program in industrial technology. Programs offered at selected military bases.

Southern Vermont College   B
Monument Road
Bennington, VT 05201
Kathryn True
Many fields
1926
Nonprofit, independent $$$
(802) 442-5427
Bachelor's degree program for licensed practical nurses offered through the evening extension program, and many courses through evening, weekend, and summer classes. Bachelor's degrees in accounting, business, English, environmental studies, communications, criminal justice, health services, human services, resort management, private security, and social work. Telecourses can fulfill some degree requirements. Independent study and internships are an important element of degree programs, and students with special interests are encouraged to formulate their own degree programs, with the help of a faculty or staff advisor.

Southwest State University   B
Marshall, MN 56258
Charles R. Richardson, Director of Admissions
Humanities, social science, education, business, science, technology
1963
Nonprofit, state $$
(507) 537-6286
Bachelor's degrees may be earned in the above fields through evening classes.

Southwest Texas State University   B
San Marcos, TX 78666
Many fields
1899
Nonprofit, state $$$
(512) 245-2111
(512) 245-2033 fax
Bachelor of Applied Arts and Sciences offered through schedules that accommodate the nontraditional learner. Credit for life and work experience learning, through portfolio assessment, equivalency exams, cooperative education, correspondence courses, and supervised fieldwork.

Spalding University   B
Weekend College
851 S. Fourth St.
Louisville, KY 40203
Shirley L. McBrayer, Director
Business administration, communication, liberal studies, nursing
1814
Nonprofit, independent $$$$
(502) 585-9911
(502) 585-7158 fax
Weekend college offers the Bachelor of Arts and Bachelor of Science in business administration, communication, liberal studies, and nursing, through courses that meet about five times per 11- to 12-week session. Credit available for life-experience learning, through portfolio assessment, as well as a number of equivalency and departmental exams, cooperative education, independent study, and supervised fieldwork.

Spring Arbor College   B
Alternative Education
106 Main St.
Spring Arbor, MI 49283
Darlene T. Mefford
Management, human resources, health fields, family life education
1873
Nonprofit, church $$$
(517) 750-1200, ext. 363
Bachelor of Arts degree can possibly be earned in 12 to 18 months through weekend, evening, and/or summer programs if participant has junior status, is employed full time, is 25 years old or older, and prepares a portfolio of life

experience for evaluation. Four majors available: management of human resources, management of health sciences and gerontology, management of health promotion, and family life education.

St. Ambrose University
See: Quad Cities Graduate Center

St. Francis College   B
180 Remsen St.
Brooklyn, NY 11201
Thomas Brennan
Special studies
1884
Nonprofit, independent $$$$
(718) 522-2300
Bachelor of Science in special studies designed for non-traditional students seeking a flexible program of study tailored to individual needs and interests. Up to 98 credits accepted from other schools and equivalency exams toward a degree. Credit also given for experiential learning. Up to 10 credits may be awarded to armed forces veterans.

State University of New York (Buffalo)   B, M
Millard Fillmore College
3435 Main St.
Buffalo, NY 14214
Kevin Durkin, Director of Admissions
Many fields
1946
Nonprofit, state $$
(716) 829-2202
More than 350 evening classes each semester, in fields including arts and sciences, management, nursing, engineering, and architecture, with credits applicable to various degree programs.

State University of New York College   M
at Plattsburgh
Center for Lifelong Learning
Kehoe 413
Plattsburgh, NY 12901
Liberal studies
1889
Nonprofit, state $$$
(518) 564-7000
(518) 564-7827 fax
Master of Arts in liberal studies offered in five broad fields: administration and leadership, educational studies, English language and literature, historical studies, and natural sciences. Student may enroll at any time. Credit for military experience and independent study. Courses are offered in the evening on the Plattsburgh campus, at the Plattsburgh military base, and at several additional sites in northern New York state.

State University of New York   B
at Old Westbury
College at Old Westbury, P. O. Box 210
Old Westbury, NY 11568
Michael Sheehy, Director of Admissions
Many fields
1967
Nonprofit, state $$$$
(516) 876-3073
B.A., B.S., and Bachelor of Professional Studies, in which some units can be earned through a combination of assessment of prior experience, and taking equivalency exams.

Stetson University   B
421 Woodland Boulevard
Deland, FL 32720
Linda F. Glaver
Many fields
1883
Nonprofit, church $$$
(904) 822-7100
Bachelor of Arts and Bachelor of Science in many fields through evening study. Bachelor of Science in medical technology in conjunction with area hospitals. Credit for equivalency exams.

Suffolk University   B, M
Beacon Hill
Boston, MA 02108
William F. Coughlin
Many fields
1906
Nonprofit, independent $$$
(617) 573-8000
Bachelor of Arts, Bachelor of Science, Master of Business Administration, and Master of Public Administration, all available entirely through evening study. Cooperative program, where students work in jobs related to their majors and graduate in four and a half years (with summer sessions).

Swinburne University of Technology   B
P. O. Box 218, John St.
Hawthorn, Victoria, 3122 Australia
Ian McCormick
Applied science, engineering, business, graphic design
1908
Nonprofit, independent $$$
(613) 819 8647
Swinburne runs cooperative education programs in applied science, engineering, business and graphic design. Under this program, students are placed in 12-month, full-time paid industrial work. During this period each student's progress is monitored by a staff member. Students learn in both academic and work settings. Assistance is given to place overseas students in work-experi-

ence settings in their home countries.

Tarkio College   B
Tarkio, MO 64491
Richard Phillips, Director of Admissions
Business, management
1883
Nonprofit, church $$$
(816) 736-4131
Bachelor of Science in business administration, management, and related fields, requiring evening classes that meet once a week for eight weeks. Evening and weekend classes held in Missouri, at centers in St. Louis, Jefferson City, and Kansas City. Life experience credit is possible.

Technion Institute   M
Faculty of Industrial Engineering and Management
The Technion
Kiryat Hatechnion, Haifa, 3200 Israel
Industrial management
Nonprofit, state
Master of Science in industrial management requiring one day a week on the campus in Haifa.

Teikyo Loretto Heights College   B
3001 S. Federal Blvd.
Denver, CO 80236
Doraleen Hollar, Dean of Admissions
Many fields
1918
Nonprofit, independent $$$$
(303) 936-8441, ext. 221
Loretto offers a university without walls program that allows enrollees to earn the Bachelor of Arts with little or no time spent on campus. The SAAD (Students at a Distance) program is available to students of all ages in the Rocky Mountain area. The degree requires 128 semester units, of which at least the final 30 hours must be earned consecutively after enrolling. But these can be earned through a variety of nontraditional means as well as regular courses: independent reading and research, seminars in the field, independent field practica, and assessment of prior learning experiences, CLEP and challenge exams, etc. Students are expected to meet periodically with faculty advisors, but those advisors are sometimes able to travel to a student's home location.

Teikyo Marycrest University   B
1607 West 12th St.
Davenport, IA 52804
Catherine Linnenkamp, CHM
Many fields
1939
Nonprofit $$$
(319) 326-9226

Degrees in accounting, business administration, professional communication, computer science, pre-law, social work and special studies. Credit for experiential learning and by examination. See also: Quad Cities Graduate Center

Tennessee Wesleyan College   B
College St.
Athens, TN 37303
James G. Harrison
Business management, accounting
1857
Nonprofit, church $$
(615) 745-7504
The Bachelor of Applied Science in business management or accounting is designed to meet the needs of adult learners who have two years of business-related college studies. Evening classes are held in Knoxville, Chattanooga, Athens, and Oak Ridge, Tennessee.

Texas Christian University   B
Office of Extended Education, P. O. Box 32927
Fort Worth, TX 76129
Derek S. Skaggs
General studies
1873
Nonprofit, church $$$
(817) 921-7130
Bachelor of General Studies program, available entirely through evening study. At least 30 of the required 124 semester hours must be earned at T.C.U. Credit is given for prior academic work, and for equivalency exams, including a series of exams developed at the university.

Texas Tech University   D
Lubbock, TX 79409
Albert B. Smith, Coordinator of the Higher Education Program
Education
1923
Nonprofit, state $
(806) 742-3654
Although Professor Albert B. Smith, Coordinator of the Higher Education Program, has asked us to remove this listing, we found Texas Tech's programs described in other directories, and so have decided to leave them in here, particularly since they offer the Ed.D. in higher education with the possibility of a much shorter residency than most traditional Doctoral programs. Professor Smith may be willing to tell you about their programs.

Thomas Jefferson University   B
1020 Locust St.
Philadelphia, PA 19107
Thomas Coyne
Nursing
1824
Nonprofit, independent $$$$

(215) 955-8890

The College of Allied Health Sciences offers a B.S. in nursing through evening classes. Applicants must have two years of prior college experience.

scheduled to meet the needs of working adults (applicants must be over 25 years old and have already taken two college-level courses). Limited credit available for equivalency exams.

Towson State University   B

College of Continuing Studies
Towson, MD 21204
Norma R. Long, Dean
Many fields
1866
Nonprofit, state $$
(800) CALL-TSU

Bachelor of Arts and Bachelor of Science in many fields, including business administration, psychology, chemistry, mass communications, accounting, education, liberal arts and sciences, and computer science, can be completed through evening study. Also weekend and summer courses. Credit for independent study, nonacademic prior learning, and by examination.

Trinity College   B, M

PACE
208 Colchester Ave.
Burlington, VT 05401
Kathleen H. Berard, Director of Nontraditional Admissions
1925
Nonprofit, church $$$
(802) 658-0337   (802) 658-5446 fax

Trinity College offers four programs for adult students to begin or resume their education. The PACE program, with a Monday through Friday schedule, offers 28 majors for a B.S./B.A. degree. The Weekend College has classes every other Saturday and/or Sunday for eight weekends a semester, with five majors. The Evening Degree program, offering only a Bachelor of Business Administration, meets two evenings a week for six eight-week terms. Finally, the Graduate Education program offers an M.Ed. to applicants who have taught for at least one year, and have access to a classroom. A minimum of 30 credits in the B.A./B.S. must be earned at Trinity. Applicants are eligible for advanced placement through transfer credit and credit for approved life/work and military experience.

Tufts University   B

REAL Program, Office of Undergraduate Education
Medford, MA 02155
David D. Cuttino, Dean of Admissions
Many fields
1852
Nonprofit, independent $$$$
(617) 628-5000
(617) 381-3703 fax

B.A. and B.S. in many fields through part-time programs

Tulane University   B, M

University College
125 Gibson Hall
New Orleans, LA 70118
Louis Barrilleaux, Dean
Paralegal studies, social studies, computer information systems, general studies, applied development/health
1834
Nonprofit, independent $$$$
(504) 865-5000

B.A. in paralegal studies or social studies, B.S. in CIS, or Bachelor of General Studies, through classes scheduled to meet the needs of working adults. Credit for CLEP exams, independent study, and supervised fieldwork. M.A. in applied development/health through evening and weekend classes, with the option to complete the program through distance learning. All full-time graduate students get use of a computer, and free Internet access.

Tusculum College   B, M

P. O. Box 5049
Greeneville, TN 37743
Diane Keasling
Many fields
1794
Nonprofit, church $$$
(615) 636-7312

Some degree programs are offered through evening classes, and at off-site locations in Knoxville and Chattanooga.

United Nations University   Dip

Toho Seimi Bldg., 15-1 Shibuya 2-Chome
Shibuya-ku, Tokyo, 150 Japan
Professor Heitor Gurgulino de Souza
International affairs
1975
Nonprofit, independent $
(03) 3499-2811
(03) 3499-2828 fax

Based on U Thant's idea for a worldwide network of advanced research and training institutions devoted to "pressing problems of human survival, development and welfare." UNU is affiliated with academic establishments worldwide but does not, as yet, grant degrees of its own. UNU is currently conducting research in five broad fields: universal human values and global responsibilities, the world economy and development, global life-support systems, advances in science and technology, and population dynamics and human welfare. To date, Japan and several other countries have contributed over $100 million to UNU; the US has yet to contribute a cent.

United States International University   B, M
The Avenue
Bushey, Herts, WD2 2LN England
Richard Gregson
Business, engineering, hotel management, international relations, human behavior
Nonprofit, independent $$
(1923) 249067
Bachelor's and Master's degrees are offered in residence on the campus near London, in association with the accredited United States International University in San Diego.

United States Sports Academy   M
1 Academy Dr.
Daphne, AL 36526
Glenn Snyder
Sports-related fields
1972
Nonprofit, independent
(205) 626-3303, (800) 223-2668
(205) 626-1149 fax
The Master's degree is offered in sports management, sports medicine, sports coaching, sports fitness management, and sport research. This program involves two summers on the Academy's Daphne, Alabama campus and a "mentorship" in your home community.

Universidad Iberoamericano   B
Prolongacion Paseo de la Reforma 880
Av. Lounas de Santa Fe
Mexico, D.F. 01210 Mexico
Carlos Vigil Avalez
Sociology, theology
1943
570-6198
The Bachelor's degree in sociology or theology is based largely on individual study, with study guides, required weekly group sessions on the university's campus, and individualized tutorials with the faculty, as requested by the student. The time involved is at least five years.

Universidade da Asia Oriental
See: University of East Asia

Université de Paris VII-Vincennes   B, M, D
Route de la Tourelle
Paris, CEDEX 12, 75571, France
Many fields
Nonprofit, state
The Vincennes campus of the University of Paris is known as the "university of second chance." The more than 30,000 students come from more than 100 countries. Degrees in languages, linguistics, social sciences, fine arts, theater, and cinematography through evening, small-group, and student-directed study.

University Center at Harrisburg   B, M
2986 N. 2nd St.
Harrisburg, PA 17110
A. Jane Collier
Many fields
Nonprofit, independent
Cost varies
(717) 787-0866
An educational consortium involving the 14 institutions of the state system of higher education and Elizabethtown College. This consortium offers various degree programs, primarily through evening and weekend study.

University of Alabama at Birmingham   M
Executive Health Administration Program
Webb Bldg., Room 560
Birmingham, AL 35294-3361
Health administration
1966
Nonprofit, state $$$$
(205) 934-4011
Intensive 24-month "Executive Program" for experienced health-services providers who want to earn an M.S. in health administration while remaining fully employed. Learning occurs on-campus, weekends and evenings, and by correspondence courses, e-mail, and independent study. Applicants must have at least three years' worth of midlevel experience in their field.

University of Arizona   B, M, D
Tucson, AZ 85721
Jerome Lucido
Many fields
1885
Nonprofit, state $$
(602) 626-3958
Evening programs leading to the B.A. in general studies, M.B.A., M.Ed. in reading or bilingual/bicultural education, Ph.D. in higher education or educational foundations, and Pharm.D. There is a public administration program primarily for police officers. Several programs are offered in Sierra Vista/Ft. Huachuca including an M.S. in electrical engineering via microwave link and a B.S. in nursing. Correspondence and independent study programs can be part of some degree programs (the M.S. in engineering, for example, requires only one semester on campus).

University of Arkansas   M
Fayetteville, AR 72701
Collis Geren
Operations management, education, engineering
1871
Nonprofit, state $$
(501) 575-4401

(501) 575-7575 fax

Residence requirements for some graduate degrees may be completed off-campus at Graduate Resident Centers located in Camden, Fort Smith, Little Rock, Monticello, Pine Bluff, and Russellville (in Arkansas); at military bases at Blytheville and Little Rock (in Arkansas), at Millington, Tennessee, and in Bolivia. Not all degrees may be completed at all centers. Degrees offered include an M.B.A., M.Ed., and M.S. in engineering, among others.

University of Baltimore   B, M, D
Charles at Mount Royal
Baltimore, MD 21201
Clare MacDonald, Director of Admissions
Many fields
1925
Nonprofit, state $$
(301) 625-3348

Bachelor's, Master's, M.B.A., and J.D. may be earned through evening and summer programs. Fields of study include computer science, criminal justice, corporate communication, law, political science, and others. There is an accelerated Bachelor's/Master's program in which some courses can be applied to the requirements for both degrees simultaneously.

University of Bridgeport   B, M
Bridgeport, CT 06601
Walter Wager
Various fields
1927
Nonprofit, independent $$$$
(203) 576-4000

Bachelor of Arts, Bachelor of Science, Bachelor of Elective Studies, Master of Business Administration, Master of Science in liberal arts, bio-nutrition, counseling, education, business, and engineering, all through evening or weekend study.

University of California, Berkeley   M
Haas School of Business
M. B. A. Evening Program
1170 Market St.
San Francisco, CA 94102
David H. Downes
Business administration
1868
Nonprofit, state $$$
(415) 621-3591

Traditional M.B.A. available entirely through evening classes from the Graduate School of Business.

University of California, Davis   B, M
Davis, CA 95616
Gary Tudor, Director of Admissions
Various fields
1905
Nonprofit, state $$
(916) 752-2971

The Academic Re-entry Program provides readmission advising for older students who are re-entering an academic program after work and life experience. Admission "in exception" may be possible for persons who do not meet the formal admissions requirements if they present evidence of academic potential (test scores, recent coursework, "late bloomers", etc.) Part-time status may be elected by persons who are employed, retired, have family responsibilities, or health problems. No evening classes are offered.

University of California, Irvine   B, M
Campus Dr.
Irvine, CA 92717
James E. Dunning, Director of Admissions
Various fields
1965
Nonprofit, state $$
(714) 856-5011

M.S. in educational administration and M.A. in social ecology or in teaching of Spanish, all through evening study. There is a five-year combined Bachelor's/Master's in business administration.

University of California, Los Angeles   M
John E. Anderson Graduate School of Management
405 Hilgard Avenue
Los Angeles, CA 90024-4151
Thomas E. Lifka
Business administration
1919
Nonprofit, state $$
(301) 825-2032   (301) 206-4151 fax

Master of Business Administration offered through two programs: the Executive MBA, a two-year series of Friday and Saturday courses open to successful executives with at least eight years' experience in business and the Fully Employed MBA, a three-year evening program.

University of California, Santa Barbara   B, M
Santa Barbara, CA 93106
William Villa
1944
Nonprofit, state $$
(805) 893-3641

Bachelor of Arts in law and society, through evening study in the College of Letters and Science; Master of Science in electrical engineering or computer science through e-mail and videocassette, among other instruction methods. B.A. in liberal arts through a distance center in Ventura that is equipped with academic advisers, a computer lab, and library research programs.

University of Central Florida

P.O. Box 25000
Orlando, FL 32816
1963
Nonprofit, state $
(407) 823-2000

We've heard that they offer some nontraditional programs, but thus far they have not responded to our requests for more information.

University of Chicago   M

5801 Ellis Ave.
Chicago, IL 60637
Maxine Sullivan
Business administration
1891
Nonprofit, independent $$$$$
(312) 753-1234

The Master of Business Administration is offered in two nontraditional modes: entirely through evening study at a downtown Chicago location, and in an Executive Program requiring one day at the downtown location every week for two years, plus a five-day residency seminar.

University of Cincinnati   B

Cincinnati, OH 45221
Director of Admissions
Many fields
1819
Nonprofit, state $$
(513) 556-1100

Bachelor's degree in natural science, social science, engineering, humanities, arts, and business administration, which may be earned entirely through evening study. There is an extensive cooperative education program, a weekend university, and an innovative "learning at large" program. See also: Open Learning Fire Service Program

University of Connecticut   B

Stamford, CT 06903
Ann G. Quinley, Director of Admissions
Many fields
1881
Nonprofit, state $$
(203) 322-3466

Bachelor of Arts and Bachelor of General Studies through evening classes. Credit for independent study and by examination.

University of Denver   B, M

New College
2300 S. York St.
Denver, CO 80208
Roger Campbell
Many fields
1864
Nonprofit, independent $$$$
(303) 871-1200

Bachelor of General Studies in data processing, communications, or liberal arts, as well as a Master of Special Studies and Master of Liberal Arts, all through weekend and evening classes. There is also a special Bachelor's in business, for women, through the weekend college, which meets every other weekend.

University of Detroit   B, M

4001 McNichols Rd.
Detroit, MI 48221
Robert A. Mitchell, S. J.
Many fields
1877
Nonprofit, independent $$$
(313) 927-1000

Evening classes leading to a wide variety of Bachelor's and Master's degrees, including a Bachelor of Business Administration in accounting, economics, finance, management, marketing, and personnel, B.A. in criminal justice, B.S. in engineering, nursing, and human resource development, M.B.A., Master of Computer Science, Master of Engineering, Master of Engineering Management, and Master's in criminal justice, education, health services administration, and health care education, among others. Also offers certification programs in elementary and secondary education.

University of Dubuque   M

2000 University Ave.
Dubuque, IA 52001-5050
John Wiemers, MBA Director
Business administration
1852
Nonprofit, private $$$$
(319) 589-3301   (319) 556-8633 fax

M.B.A. for fully employed students, through evening classes on-campus in Dubuque or at distance-learning centers in Singapore, Hong Kong, and Malaysia. A basic level of business knowledge is required; most students are employed in their fields while working on the degree, which can be completed in less than two years.

University of Findlay   B, M

1000 N. Main St.
Findlay, OH 45840
Doris Salis, Dean of Adult and
Continuing Education
Many fields
1882
Nonprofit, church $$$$$
(419) 424-4600

Bachelor of Arts or Bachelor of Science can be earned in 58 majors, including business administration, accounting, computer science, systems analysis, and social work, through summer, weekend, and/or evening study. Unusual majors include equestrian studies, nuclear medicine technology, and hazardous waste studies.

University of Georgia   B, M, D
Athens, GA 30602
Claire Swann, Director of Admissions
Business administration, early childhood education, public administration
1785
Nonprofit, state $$
(404) 542-2112
Bachelor's and Doctoral programs offered through evening and independent study, the latter limited to the equivalent of one academic year. Master's in early childhood education and public administration available through evening study.

University of Guam   B, M
U. O. G. Station
Mangilao, 96923 Guam
Kathleen R. Owings, Director of Admissions
Many fields
1952
Nonprofit, state $$
(671) 734-9450
Bachelor's degree may be earned through evening and summer programs. Many majors in the colleges of arts and science, education, agriculture and life sciences, and business and public administration.

University of Hawaii—Manoa   B, M, D
2444 Dole St.
Honolulu, HI 96822
David Robb, Interim Director of Admissions and Records
Many fields
1907
Nonprofit, state $$
(808) 956-8975
B.A., B.S., M.A., M.S., M.B.A., Ed.D. and Ph.D. in many, many fields, including history, anthropology, mathematics, sociology, educational administration, biology, botany, dance ethnology, Hawaiian, engineering, health sciences, physics, all through evening study. Some classes are given at Hickham Air Force Base.

University of Hawaii—West Oahu   B
96-043 Ala Ike
Pearl City, HI 96782
Stella L. T. Asahara, Student Services Coordinator
Humanities, social science, professional studies
1976
Nonprofit, state $
(808) 456-5921
Bachelor's degree programs in humanities (English, history, or philosophy), social services (anthropology, psychol-

ogy, sociology, political science, or economics), or professional studies (business or public administration) are available through daytime and/or evening classes. All degrees can be earned entirely through evening study. Instead of a major in one of these areas, students may pursue study related to a major theme, such as American studies, Asian studies, justice administration, etc. Courses are also offered on weekends, and at three off-campus locations.

University of Illinois
See: Quad Cities Graduate Center

University of Indianapolis   B, M
1400 E. Hanna Ave.
Indianapolis, IN 46227
C. R. Stockton
Many fields
1902
Nonprofit, private $$$
(317) 788-3368
A variety of Bachelor's and Master's degrees can be earned entirely through evening study. The Executive M.B.A. program meets one Friday and three Saturdays each month. In this program, it is possible to earn the degree in two years (comprising 19 Fridays and 50 Saturdays). Formerly called Indiana Central College.

University of Kansas   M
102 Bailey Hall
School of Education, Graduate Division
Lawrence, KS 66045
Robert Sanders
Public administration, education
1864
Nonprofit, state $$
(913) 864-2700
Master of Public Administration through evening study, and Master of Science in Education through evening study and at the Kansas City campus (K.U. Regents Center).

University of Laverne   B, M
S. C. E., 1950 3rd St.
La Verne, CA 91750
Adeline Cardenas-Clagu
Many fields
1891
Nonprofit, independent $$$$
(714) 593-3511, ext. 501
Bachelor's or Masters may be earned through evening, weekend, and summer programs. Fields include liberal arts, graduate and professional studies, business, communications, behavioral sciences, education, child development, pre-medicine, and pre-law. Residence centers in California, Alaska, Greece, and Italy.

University of Limerick   B, M, D
National Technological Park
Limerick, Ireland
P. A. Cashell
Many fields
Nonprofit
353-61-333644

The University of Limerick was established by the Irish Government to meet the special needs brought on by the rapid expansion of the Irish economy and its membership in the European Community, which it accomplishes through its programs as well as through wide interaction with the business, industrial, government and community sectors in the Irish and international spheres. Formerly known as National Institute for Higher Education.

University of Louisville   B, M, D
S. 3rd St.
Louisville, KY 40292
Mary Ann Penner
Many fields
1798
Nonprofit, state $$
(502) 588-7070

Eighty degree programs at the Bachelor's, Master's, and Ph.D. level are available through part-time and/or evening studies. Evening and weekend courses are offered on the main campus and at two other sites. University of Louisville offers counseling for adults thinking of entering or returning to college, and evening workshops on topics of relevance. The Adult Commuter Center and Evening Student Services (ACCESS) provides a place for adults to call their own for typing, studying, and conversation, as well as university functions (admissions, bookstore, financial aid, etc.)

University of Maine   B, M
Continuing Education
122 Chadbourne Hall
Orono, ME 04469
Robert C. White, Director
Many fields
1865
Nonprofit, state $$$
(207) 581-6192

Bachelor of University Studies, Bachelor of Science in elementary education, Master of Arts in English or speech, M.B.A., M.S. in education or medical technology, Master of Liberal Studies, and Master of Public Administration, all of which may be earned through evening classes given at Orono, as well as many off-campus extension centers.

University of Mary   B, M
7500 University Dr.

Bismark, ND 58501
Steph Storey
Various fields
1957
Nonprofit, church $$$
(701) 255-7500, (800) 288-6279

Business and accounting programs available through evening study. Some weekend classes. Credit for prior learning, equivalency exams, and independent study.

University of Massachusetts—Boston   B
College of Public and Community Service
Boston, MA 02125
Ronald E. Ancrum, Director of Admissions
Public, community, legal, and human service, housing and community development
1964
Nonprofit, state $$
(617) 929-7000

Bachelor's degree program in the above fields; many of the required units can come from an assessment of prior learning experiences, but there is still a one-year required residency at the university.

University of Massachusetts—Dartmouth   B
Old Westport Rd.
North Dartmouth, MA 02747-2300
Raymond M. Barrows
Many fields
1895
Nonprofit, state $$
(508) 999-8000

Bachelor's degree in criminal justice, sociology, psychology, English, electrical engineering technology, humanities/social science, management, accounting, junior and senior years of nursing program, and others. Up to 25 percent of the required units can be earned through a for-fee assessment of prior learning experience. The assessment is based on evaluation of a portfolio, which is prepared in a class given for that purpose, through the Division of Continuing Education. Formerly Southeastern Massachusetts University.

University of Memphis   B
University College
Memphis, TN 38152
John Y. Eubank, Dean of Admissions
Many fields
1912
Nonprofit, state $$
(901) 454-2000

Bachelor of Professional Studies in alcohol and drug abuse services, aviation administration, biomedical administration, commercial aviation, fire administration, and fire prevention technology, health care fields, human services, organizational leadership, orthotics/prosthetics, paralegal services, printing management, services for the aging, and women's studies. All students are required to have on-the-job experience which will be evaluated through internships and/or portfolio assessment. The University College also offers the Bachelor of Liberal Studies in African-American studies and women's studies. Other individualized programs may be designed where credit for experiential learning and nontraditional instruction can be evaluated. Formerly Memphis State University.

University of Miami   B, M, D
P. O. Box 248025
Coral Gables, FL 33124
Deborah Triol-Perry, Dean of Enrollment
Many fields
1925
Nonprofit, independent $$
(305) 284-2211
M.B.A. with classes held every weekend, for fully-employed persons sponsored by their employers. Miami offers an intriguing Honors Program in medicine, biomedical engineering, law, and marine and atmospheric science. Well-qualified applicants (including high school seniors) are admitted simultaneously to the Bachelor's and the Doctoral programs.

University of Michigan   M
200 Hill St.
Ann Arbor, MI 48109
Glenda K. Radine
Social work, education, nursing
1817
Nonprofit, state $$
(313) 764-5300
The University of Michigan offers graduate courses in social work, and occasionally nursing, through the off-campus program, sponsored by the respective departments and by the Extension Service. Independent study courses at the graduate level as well as the undergraduate level are available through the Extension Service. It is not, however, possible to earn an entire degree through either the off-campus program or the independent study program. Students anywhere in the world can take independent study courses. The School of Business Administration has an evening M.B.A. program.

University of Missouri at St. Louis   B
8001 Natural Bridge Rd.
St. Louis, MO 63121
Mimi La Marca
General studies
1963
Nonprofit, state $$
(314) 553-5451
The Continuing Education division offers extension courses during the day and evening at various locations. There is a Bachelor of General Studies program. Some credit is given for life experience learning.

University of Nebraska—Omaha   B
College of Continuing Studies
Omaha, NE 68182
John Flemming, Director of Admissions
General studies
1908
Nonprofit, state $$
(402) 554-2393
(402) 554-3472 fax
Courses from many sources, with credits leading to the student-planned Bachelor of General Studies degree, offered "to established adults only." Credit for life-experience and amnesty for past college failures; 24 credit hours must be earned in residence after enrollment.

University of New Hampshire   B, M
Division of Continuing Education
6 Garrison Ave.
Durham, NH 03824
Stanwood C. Fish
Various fields
1866
Nonprofit, state $$$
(603) 862-2015
A variety of part-time and/or evening classes leading to a Bachelor's for registered nurses, B.S. in engineering technology for experienced engineers, Master of Public Administration, and Master of Library and Information Studies.

University of New Haven   B
300 Orange Ave.
West Haven, CT 06516
Dany Washington
Many fields
1920
Nonprofit, independent $$$$
(203) 932-7000
Bachelor's degrees in all fields except applied mathematics, natural sciences, English, and world music can be earned on a part-time basis through the Division of Continuing Education, which has day and evening divisions. More than 50 majors are available. Among the unusual ones are air transportation management, arson investigation, forensic science, dietetics, fire science, music and sound recording, and tourism and travel administration.

University of New Mexico
Division of Continuing Education
1634 University Blvd. N.E.
Albuquerque, NM 87131 1889
Nonprofit, state $
(505) 277-0111
(505) 277-6019 fax

We've heard that they offer some nontraditional programs, but thus far they have not responded to our requests for more information.

University of New Orleans
See: National Universities Degree Consortium

University of Pennsylvania   B, M
Credit Programs, College of General Studies
3440 Market St.
Suite 100
Philadelphia , PA 19104-3335
Richard Hendrix, Director
Liberal arts & sciences
1740
Nonprofit, independent $$$$
(215) 898-7326
Bachelor of Arts through College of General Studies, a division of Penn's School of Arts and Sciences in which part-time evening students earn the same degree as full-time day students at about one-third the regular tuition. Master of Liberal Arts and Master of Social Gerontology also offered in the evening. Only one Saturday class (biology) is offered, and no credit for life-experience learning.

University of Puerto Rico   B
P. O. Box 5000
Mayaguez, PR 00709
Antonio Santes, Director of Admissions
Education
1911
Nonprofit, state $
(809) 834-4040
Bachelor's in education for employed teachers, through evening, weekend, and summer classes. Offered through the Division of Academic Extension and Community Services, which was created to provide educational opportunity to the adult working population, disadvantaged groups, and minorities.

University of Quebec Télé-Université   B
2635, Boulevard Hochelaga, 7th Étage
Case Postale 10700,
Sainte-Foy, Quebec G1N 4M6 Canada
Jean-Guy Beliveau
Many fields
1972
Nonprofit, state $
(418) 657-2262
(418) 657-2094 fax
Télé-université is one of the 11 units of the huge University of Quebec. A university without walls program, it offers courses in human and social science, communication, business administration, environmental sciences, computer-assisted education, science and technology, language, distance education, and more. Students use textbooks, special student guides, video- and audiotapes, television, teleconferencing, and computer networks under the guidance of an assigned tutor/mentor.

University of Redlands   B, M
1200 E. Colton Ave.
Redlands, CA 92374
Stephen Hankins, Dean of Admissions
Liberal arts, business, information systems
1907
Nonprofit, independent $$$$
(909) 793-2121
Degree programs for working adults throughout Southern California through Redlands's Whitehead Center: B.S. in business and management or information systems, and an M.B.A. Forty units may be earned through portfolio assessment of prior learning. Applicants must have already earned at least 40 units from another institution. The school's Johnson Center offers residential undergraduate programs in which students have almost total academic freedom to create their own majors, or to take advantage of interdisciplinary or custom-designed traditional majors. Johnson students are "graded" by narrative evaluation, mostly live in the same dormitory, and are expected to address issues of community and cross-cultural awareness.

University of Rhode Island   B, M
College of Continuing Education
199 Promenade St.
Providence, RI 02908
Walter A. Crocker
General studies, business administration, others
1892
Nonprofit, state $$
(401) 277-3807
Bachelor of Arts, Bachelor of Science, and Bachelor of General Studies degrees. Master of Arts, Master of Business Administration, Master of Public Administration, and Master of Science in Labor and Industrial Relations. Most liberal arts majors offered, plus counseling/human services and manufacturing engineering. Classes meet once a week on Saturday mornings or in evenings. Three major sites for courses, plus at local businesses around the state.

University of Richmond   B
Richmond, VA 23173
Thomas N. Pollard, Jr., Dean of Admissions
Applied studies
1830
Nonprofit, state $$$$
(804) 289-8133
Bachelor's of Applied Studies available only through evening study.

University of San Francisco   B, M

College of Professional Studies, Ignatian Heights
2130 Fulton Street
San Francisco, CA 94117
Judith Donaldson
Many fields
1855
Nonprofit, church $$$$
(415) 666-2062
(415) 666-2793 fax

The College of Professional Studies administers a variety of undergraduate and graduate programs for working adults, and undergraduates may received credit for experiential learning through USF's Experiential Learning Center. Classes meet one evening a week and/or on Saturdays at a number of California locations. Degrees offered include a Bachelor of Public Administration, B.S. programs in organizational behavior, information systems management, and applied economics; Master's programs in environmental management, public administration, human resources and organization development, and nonprofit administration.

University of Saskatchewan   B

Division of Extension, 326 Kirk Hall
Saskatoon, SK S7N 0W0 Canada
Many fields
1907
Nonprofit, state $$$$
(306) 966-5563
(306) 966-5590 fax

Wide variety of studies offered through evening, distance-education, and off-campus courses in agriculture, arts and sciences, commerce, education, health care administration, horticulture, and nursing.

University of Scranton   B

Dexter Hanley College
Gallery Building
Scranton, PA 18510-4582
Shirley M. Adams, Director
Many fields
1888
Nonprofit, church $$$$
(717) 941-7400
(717) 941-6369 fax

Nineteen evening degree programs leading to Bachelor of Arts or Bachelor of Science, including two designed for R.N.s. Credit for a variety of life experience learning, through portfolio assessment, and for equivalency exams. In addition to evening classes, learning can take place through audio- and videocassettes, independent study, supervised fieldwork, and televised courses.

University of South Alabama   B

Department of Adult Personalized Study
Alpha East 214

Mobile, AL 36688
Many fields
1963
Nonprofit, state $$$$
(205) 460-6101
(205) 460-7205 fax

Bachelor of Arts and Bachelor of Science in many fields, through weekend college and other programs tailored to the needs of adult learners. Credit for life and military experience and for a range of equivalency exams; nontraditional options include audio- and videotaped courses for home study, cooperative education, and independent study.

University of Southern California   B, M, D

University Park
Los Angeles, CA 90089
Duncan Murdoch, Director of Admissions
Many fields
1880
Nonprofit, independent
(213) 740-8775
(213) 740-6364 fax

In the past, USC has offered a wide range of evening and weekend classes, international programs, and other interesting nontraditional options, both on campus and at distant locations. However, when we wrote to ask about any changes for this edition, Mr. Murdoch wrote back to say that because we had made an error in reporting some USC program in the past, he wasn't going to tell us anything now. So you'll have to ask him directly, at the number and address above, what programs still exist.

University of Southern Mississippi   B, M

Box 5006
Hattiesburg, MS 39406
Danny W. Montgomery
Education
1910
Nonprofit, state $$
(601) 266-5006

The work for several Bachelor's and Master's degrees in education can be completed by evening and weekend study, or over two summer sessions.

University of Tampa   B

School of Continuing Studies
401 W. Kennedy Blvd.
Tampa, FL 33606
H. Griffin Walling, Dean
Liberal studies, computer information systems, management and marketing
1931
Nonprofit, independent $$$$
(813) 253-3333
(813) 251-0016 fax

Bachelor of Liberal Studies, B.S. in computer information systems, and Bachelor of Marketing and Management through evening and summer classes, as well as other nontraditional programs. Credit awarded for life experience learning and for taking equivalency exams, as well as correspondence courses, independent study, and supervised fieldwork.

University of Tennessee at Chattanooga   B, M
615 McCallie Ave.
Chattanooga, TN 37402
Ray P. Fox, Dean of Admissions
Many fields
1886
Nonprofit, state $$
(615) 755-4141
Bachelor of Arts, Bachelor of Science, Master of Business Administration, Master of Science, and Master of Education, available almost entirely through evening study. Some credit may be given for prior work and volunteer experience through the Individualized Education Program.

University of Tennessee Space Institute   M
B. H. Goethert Parkway
Tullahoma, TN 37388
Max Hailey
Industrial engineering, engineering management, aviation systems
Nonprofit, state $$$$
(615) 393-7201
(615) 393-7201 fax
M.S. in industrial engineering or engineering management through distance-leaning centers. Also, through a separate distance-learning program (contact: Ralph Kimberlin, phone (615) 393-7411, fax (615) 455-5912), an M.S. in aviation systems, including flight testing, aircraft design, aviation meteorology, air traffic control, and airport management. Students in this program are required to spend one day on the UTSI campus, defending their thesis.

University of Texas   B, M, D
Arlington, TX 76019
R. Z. Prince, Director of Admissions
1895
Nonprofit, state $$
(817) 273-2011
Bachelor of Arts, Master of Arts in many fields, almost entirely through evening study.

University of Toledo   B, M
Adult Liberal Studies, University College
Toledo, OH 43606
Thaddeus McHugh, Associate Dean
Many fields
1872
Nonprofit, state $$
(419) 537-2051
(419) 537-4940 fax
The Adult Liberal Studies program offers people over the age of 25 the opportunity to earn a bachelor's degree through a combination of independent study, evening classes, regular coursework, and a thesis. All students begin with an introductory planning seminar. Credit is given for CLEP exams. Nine seminars are given in various fields of study, usually one evening a week, for a total of 54 of the required 186 quarter hours. Thirty-five hours of traditional courses must be taken, before writing a thesis in an area of special interest. Toledo also offers 2 + 2 programs that allows Associate's degree holders to complete an accelerated Bachelor's in any of a number of fields.

University of Tulsa   B, M, D
600 S. College Ave.
Tulsa, OK 74104-3189
John C. Corso, Dean of Admission
Business, arts and sciences, engineering, law
1894
Nonprofit, independent $$$$$
(918) 631-2510
(918) 631-3187 fax
All business majors, the M.B.A., and the J.D. are offered through evening study. Student-designed majors are available through the College of Arts and Sciences. Some degree programs can incorporate summer terms, with six- and 12-week sessions.

University of Utah   M
Salt Lake City, UT 84112
John S. Landward, Director of Admissions
Business administration, administration, engineering
1850
Nonprofit, state $$
(801) 581-7200
Master of Business Administration, Master of Engineering, and Master of Administration may be earned entirely through evening study.

University of Washington   B
UW Extension, GH-21
Seattle, WA 98195
Richard Lorenzen, Director
General studies
1861
Nonprofit, state $$$
(206) 543-2100
(206) 543-9285 fax
The B.A. in general studies is an upper-division degree-completion program that allows students who have completed 75 credits elsewhere to complete a degree part-time (usually over three to four years). Some instruction can take place by correspondence courses, but this is essentially a part-time residential program.

University of West Florida   B, M
11000 University Pkwy.
Pensacola, FL 32514
Peter Metarko, Enrollment Services
Many fields
1963
Nonprofit, state $$
(904) 474-2000   (904) 474-3131 fax
B.S. in business administration, M.B.A., Master of Education, and M.A. and M.S. in many fields. Credit available for life-experience learning and equivalency exams, as well as independent study, supervised fieldwork, and, at the Bachelor's level only, cooperative education.

University of West Los Angeles   B
1155 W. Arbor Vitae St.
Inglewood, CA 90301-2902
Teri Canon, Dean of Paralegal Studies
Paralegal
1966
Nonprofit, independent $$
(310) 215-3339
Bachelor of Science in paralegal studies for transfer students can be earned through two to three years of evening classes.

University of Wisconsin—Oshkosh   B
800 Algoma Blvd.
Oshkosh, WI 54901
Marvin Mengeling
Liberal studies
1871
Nonprofit, state $$
(414) 424-0234
One hundred twenty-eight credits are required for a Bachelor of Liberal Studies, and it is possible to earn 101 of them through weekend classes. Credits earned through any combination of transfer credits from accredited institutions, evening classes, independent study, accredited television courses, CLEP examinations, and challenge examinations may be applied to this degree. A minimum of 30 credits in residency is required. A prerequisite course that is offered four times a year must be completed to enter the program. Students take one course at a time, meeting three weekends per course. Inexpensive on-campus housing is available for weekend students.

University of Wisconsin—Platteville   B
Extended Degree Program
Pioneer Tower 513
Platteville, WI 53818
John C. Adams, Director
Business administration
1866
Nonprofit, state $$
(608) 342-1468, (800) 362-5460 WI only
The Extended Degree Program offering the Bachelor's degree in business administration (with optional minor in accounting) is open to Wisconsin residents only. Areas of concentration are finance, marketing, management, and human resource management. Credit can be earned through individualized study and evaluation of prior learning achieved through work and life experience.

University System of New Hampshire   B
School for Lifelong Learning
Dunlap Center
Durham, NH 03824
Victor B. Montana
General studies, professional studies (management, behavioral sciences)
1972
Nonprofit, state $$
(603) 862-1692
Bachelor of General Studies and Bachelor of Professional Studies by independent study, for adults who have already earned at least 60 credit hours elsewhere. Courses are available evenings, weekends, and by videocassette. Learning contracts, credit for life experience learning, and self-designed degree programs are offered.

Upsala College   B, M
Center for Adult Degrees
East Orange, NJ 07019
Selma Brookman, Director of Continuing Education
Many fields
1893
Nonprofit, church $$$
(201) 266-7102
Bachelor of Arts and Bachelor of Science can be earned entirely through evening study in the Division of General Studies. Special R.N. programs. Other courses through weekend study. Credit by examination, and for life-experience learning.

Urbana University   B
College Way
Urbana, OH 43078
Thomas A. Gallagher
Business, social sciences, education, natural science, preprofessional
1850
Nonprofit, independent $$$
(513) 652-1301
B.S. and B.A. through weekend, evening, and summer programs held at the main campus in Urbana or at branch campuses in Bellefontaine, Dayton, and Columbus. Self-designed majors and credit for independent study are available, but 30 hours of coursework must be completed at Urbana.

Utah State University   B, M
Electronic Distance Education
Logan, UT 84322-3702
Business administration, psychology, social sciences, rehabilitation counseling, education
1888
Nonprofit, state $$$
(801) 750-2028
(801) 750-3880 fax
Degree programs offered by telephone and video conferencing at 37 sites in Utah and two in Colorado. Degrees offered: B.S. in business administration or psychology, M.S. in rehabilitation counseling or home economics education, and Master of Social Science in human resource management. See also: National Universities Degree Consortium.

Valley City State University   B
Alternate Learning Program
Valley City, ND 58072
LaMonte H. Johnson, Director of Admissions
Many fields
1889
Nonprofit, state $$$
(701) 845-7102
(701) 845-7245 fax
Bachelor of University Studies, B.A., and B.S., including a special B.S. in education, through programs tailored to the needs of adult students. Credit available for life-experience learning and for equivalency exams, as well as cooperative education, independent study, and supervised fieldwork.

Valparaiso University   B, M
Valparaiso, IN 46383
Many fields
1859
Nonprofit, church $$$$
(219) 464-5000
(219) 464-5381 fax
Bachelor of Arts in many fields, Master of Music, Master of Education, M.S. in nursing, and M.A. in liberal studies or applied behavioral science, through a variety of nontraditional residential programs, as well as cooperative education, independent study, and supervised fieldwork. Credit awarded for a wide range of equivalency exams.

Vanderbilt University   M
Owen Graduate School of Management
Nashville, TN 37203
Thomas B. Hambury
Business administration
1873
Nonprofit, independent $$$$$
(615) 322-2513
Designed for midcareer executives and professionals who want to complete the M.B.A. degree in 22 months of full-time study without giving up their jobs. Classes meet all day Friday and Saturday of alternate weekends.

Villanova University   B
University College
Villanova, PA 19085
J. R. Johnson
Many fields
1842
Nonprofit, church $$$$
(215) 645-4500
Bachelor's may be earned through weekend, evening, and summer programs. Fields of study include many majors in liberal arts and sciences, accountancy, business administration, engineering, and nursing.

Virginia Commonwealth University   B, M
821 W. Franklin St., Box 2526
Richmond, VA 23284
Horace Woolridge
General studies, interdisciplinary studies
1837
Nonprofit, state $$
(804) 367-1222
Bachelor of General Studies for working adults. Individually developed degree requirements in the form of an individualized curriculum plan. Encouragement to utilize CLEP, military, and noncollege health-related education. Some use of courses taught at other institutions of the Capital Consortium for Continuing Higher Education. Program requires a minimum of 30 credits to be completed at VCU in regular day, evening, or weekend classes. Master of Interdisciplinary Studies Program, serving evening and part-time graduate students, enables students to combine studies in three graduate programs into a coherent, individualized, multidisciplinary program. Program is a joint venture with Virginia State University in Petersburg and requires some study at VSU. Thesis or final project is required.

Virginia State University   B
P.O. Box FF
Petersburg, VA 23803
Individualized studies
1882
Nonprofit, state $$$
(804) 524-5000
(804) 524-6506 fax
The Bachelor of Individualized Studies program allows "mature students" to create a personalized program that meets their educational goals, in conjunction with an academic advisor. Credit awarded for life/work and military experience and equivalency exams.

Washington University   B, M
University College, One Brookings Drive
St. Louis, MO 63130
Jane Smith
Arts and sciences
1853
Nonprofit, independent $$$$
(314) 935-6700
Bachelor of Science, Master of Arts, Master of Liberal Arts, Master of Health Science, and Advanced Certificates in international affairs and nonprofit management available through evening study in the University College, a division of Arts and Sciences.

Wayland Baptist University   B, M
1900 W. 7th
Plainview, TX 79072
Lorraine Nance, Director of Academic Services
Occupational education, occupational technology, business, religion
1908
Nonprofit, church $$
(806) 296-5521
Bachelor of Science in occupational education, in which over 75% of the necessary units can be earned through an assessment of prior learning experiences. Wayland learning centers are located in Amarillo, Lubbock, Wichita Falls, San Antonio, and Honolulu, as well as on the main campus in Plainview. A degree plan is prepared upon request either prior to or after enrollment, based on documentation submitted by the student. The assessment generally takes less than one month, and there is no cost to the student.

Wayne State University   B
College of Lifelong Learning
Interdisciplinary Studies Program
6001 Cass
Detroit, MI 48202
Howard Finley
General studies
1868
Nonprofit, state $$
(313) 577-0832
The Bachelor of Interdisciplinary Studies and the Bachelor of Technical and Interdisciplinary Studies degrees are offered through a combination of television courses, four-hour day or evening workshops, and weekend conferences. Students must complete credit hours in the social sciences, humanities, science and technologies, electives, and interdisciplinary advanced studies. A minimum of 40 semester hours must be completed within the Interdisciplinary Studies Program. Students are welcome to take courses in the other colleges at Wayne State University. Courses are offered at a variety of locations within the Detroit metro area.

Wellesley College   B
Elizabeth Kaiser Davis Degree Program
Office of Continuing Education
Wellesley, MA 02181
Many fields
1875
Nonprofit, independent $$$$
(617) 283-2237
(617) 283-3639 fax
Special program for women over the age of 24 whose education has been interrupted by at least two years. Credit for some equivalency exams.

Wentworth Institute of Technology   B
550 Huntington Ave.
Boston, MA 02115
Robert A. Schuiteman, Dean of Admissions
Technical, design fields
1904
Nonprofit, independent $$$
(617) 442-9010, ext. 264
Wentworth's weekend college offers Bachelor's degrees in architectural building construction, computer science, construction management, electronics, interior design, and mechanical technical management.

West Coast University   B, M
440 S. Shatto Place
Los Angeles, CA 90020-1765
Roger A. Miller, Director of Admissions
Engineering, computers, business, other fields
1909
Nonprofit, independent $$$
(213) 487-4433
Certificate program in pre-health sciences, Bachelor of Science in engineering (mechanical, electrical, electromechanical, industrial), computer science, industrial technology, and business administration; Master of Science in engineering (aerospace, electrical, mechanical, systems), computer science, management information systems, acquisition and contract management, engineering and technical management, business administration, and international business administration. All courses available through evening and weekend study at locations in Los Angeles, Orange, San Diego, Ventura, and Santa Barbara counties. Credit for nondegree courses (business, military); and for life experience, by challenge examination.

West Virginia Graduate College   M, D
P. O. Box 1003
Institute, WV 25112
K.A. O'Neal, Director of Admissions
Many fields
1972
$$

(304) 766-2000

Uses classrooms of other institutions to offer Master's degrees in education, counseling, humanities, psychology, business, engineering, environmental studies, and information systems. Educational Specialists degrees are offered in school psychology and education. Doctor of Education is offered in cooperation with West Virginia University. Classes are offered in late afternoon and evening in many locations in West Virginia. Intensive short courses and workshops are available throughout the year. Formerly West Virginia College of Graduate Studies.

West Virginia University B, M
P.O. Box 6009
Morgantown, WV 26506-6009
Glenn Carter, Director of Admissions
Education, business administration, nursing
1867
Nonprofit, state $$
(304) 293-2121

B.S. and M.S. in nursing through satellite courses, which can be viewed at 16 public sites statewide, and teleconferencing. Some on-campus clinical courses may be required, on a case-by-case basis. Master of Arts in education and M.B.A. available through evening study. "Academic forgiveness" of any less-than-wonderful grades more than five years old. See also: West Virginia Board of Regents B.A. Program.

Western International University B, M
10202 N. 19th Ave.
Phoenix, AZ 85021
Elena Pattison, Director of Admissions
Business, accounting, computers, management, general studies
1978
Nonprofit, independent $$
(602) 943-2311

B.S. in accounting, management, or computer information science, B.A. in general studies, M.B.A., M. S. in accounting or computer information science, offered by evening study on campuses in Arizona and overseas in London. Courses are given in an "accelerated semester" format, in which each course takes one month, meeting two evenings a week. The undergraduate degrees can be completed in 29 months; the Master's in 12. Advanced standing may be awarded to students who prove competent in and can demonstrate knowledge of course content as, for example, through portfolio assessment or challenge examination.

Western Maryland College M
Westminster, MD 21157
Joseph S. Rigell, Director of Admissions
Sensory impairment, education of the deaf
1867

Nonprofit, independent $$$$
(301) 848-7000

M.Ed. and M.S. in sensory impairment, two programs designed to prepare professionals to teach the hearing-impaired and to work with the hearing and visually impaired. Courses are conducted during late afternoon and evening hours, except in the summer. Programs can also be completed in three consecutive nine-week summer sessions, with provision for independent study at home in between.

Western Network for Education in Health Administration
See: University of Colorado

Western New England College B, M
School of Continuing Higher Education
Springfield, MA 01119
Judy Cadden
1919
Nonprofit, independent $$$
(413) 782-1259, (800) 325-1122

Bachelor's and Master's degrees in many fields offered through part-time evening study.

Western Washington University B, M
Extended Programs, 516 High St.
Bellingham, WA 98225
Ken Symes, Director
Human services, electronics engineering, fashion marketing, education
1893
Nonprofit, state $$$
(206) 676-3000
(206) 676-3037 fax

B.A. in human services or fashion marketing, B.S. in electronics engineering technology, and Master of Education through evening, weekend, and correspondence classes, and independent study.

Westfield State College B, M
Western Ave.
Westfield, MA 01086
John Marcus
Many fields
1838
Nonprofit, state $
(413) 568-3311

Weekend, evening, and summer classes leading to a Bachelor of Arts, Bachelor of Science, Master of Arts, Master of Science, Master of Education, and Certificate of Advanced Graduate Study.

Westminster College (Utah) B
Office of Adult and Extended Education
1840 S. 13th East
Salt Lake City, UT 84105
Betsy Campbell

Many fields
1875
Nonprofit, independent **$$$**
(801) 488-4200
Bachelor's degrees in 27 fields. Up to one third of the necessary units may be earned by an assessment of prior learning experiences. Some degrees in business and the social sciences may be earned through evening programs. Assessment is limited to students admitted to a degree program and is done after enrollment, at a cost of $252 for the class and a $350 assessment fee.

Whitworth College   B, M
Spokane, WA 99251
Dale E. Soden Ph.D.
Accounting, business, education, teaching, liberal studies
1890
Nonprofit, church **$$$**
(509) 466-3222
Bachelor of Arts in accounting, business management, and education, Master of Education, Master in Teaching (MIT), and Bachelor of Liberal Studies through evening and summer programs and independent study. The tuition for degrees earned in the evening and summer is approximately one quarter of that for daytime programs.

Widener University   B
Weekend College
Rm. 137, Kapelski
Chester, PA 19013
Nursing, business administration, psychology
1821
Nonprofit, independent **$$$$**
(215) 499-4000
(215) 876-9751 fax
B.S. in nursing or business administration and B.A. in psychology entirely through weekend classes, augmented by extensive out-of-class independent study and supervised fieldwork. Credit for life-experience learning and equivalency exams.

Wilmington College   B, M, D
320 Dupont Highway
New Castle, DE 19720
Michael E. Lee, Dean of Admissions
Many fields
1967
Nonprofit, independent **$$$$**
(302) 328-9401
(302) 328-9442 fax
Wilmington offers a number of nontraditional approaches to degree-earning, including accelerated B.S. programs for

working R.N.s, and a number programs that allow credit for life-experience learning and challenge examinations, including Bachelor's degrees in education, behavioral science, criminal justice, accounting, aviation management, banking and finance, communication arts, human resources management, and nursing, M.B.A., M.S. in human resources management, M.Ed., and an Ed.D. (for employed teachers or schools administrators only).

Winona State University   B, M
Adult Continuing Education & Extension
Winona, MN 55987
Pauline Christensen, Chair
Many fields
1858
Nonprofit, state **$$**
(507) 457-5000
Bachelor's degrees in arts, sciences, business, education, nursing, and paralegal; M. S.in education, counseling, and educational administration, and an M.B.A. Adult students in undergraduate degrees, except teaching or nursing, may qualify for life-experience credit. Many courses available evenings. Minimum of 48 credits required from WSU.

Wittenberg University   B
School of Continuing Education
P. O. Box 720
Springfield, OH 45501
Kenneth G. Benne
Many fields
1845
Nonprofit, church **$$$$**
(513) 327-6231
(513) 327-6340 fax
The degrees of B.A. in Liberal Studies and a B.A. degree completion program for registered nurses can be done entirely through evening study. Adults can also enroll in more than 30 daytime degree programs. Credit is given for standard equivalency exams, and special exams will by devised in areas not covered by standard tests.

Xavier University   B, M
Center for Adult and Part-time Students
Cincinnati, OH 45207
Susan Wideman
Various fields
1831
Nonprofit, church **$$$**
(513) 745-3355
Xavier offers a Bachelor of Liberal Arts, a Bachelor of Science in business administration, and other Bachelor's degrees in modern foreign languages, computer science, and communication arts, through weekend and evening study. Extremely low tuition is available for people over 60.

◆19◆

Unaccredited Schools with Nonresident Programs

One could get a first class education from a shelf of books five feet long.
CHARLES ELIOT, WHEN PRESIDENT OF HARVARD

This chapter includes schools that claim to be accredited, but whose accreditation comes from an agency that is not recognized by the U.S. Department of Education. This does not necessarily mean that the school is bad, or its claims illegal, but it *does* mean that said accreditation is not likely to be helpful in those situations in which an accredited degree is required.

The basic format of each listing is as follows:

Name of School   **Bachelor's, Master's**
Address   **Doctorate, Law, Diploma**
City, State Zip Country
Contact name

Fields of study offered
Year established
Legal/ownership status (nonprofit or proprietary, independent, or state- or church-run), Tuition

Phone, toll-free phone (if any)
Fax

Key to tuition codes:
$ = free or very low cost
$$ = inexpensive
$$$ = average
$$$$ = expensive
$$$$$ = very expensive

(As costs change so quickly, it would be foolish to give dollar amounts. If no symbol is given, it's safe to assume that the school did not provide us with this information.)

Adam Smith University   **B, M**
2200 Main St.
Suite 500
Wailuku, HI 96793
Donald Grunewald
Many fields
1991
$$
(808) 242-1819, (800) 732-3796
fax: (500) 446-8771
Degrees based on assessment of work done at accredited schools elsewhere, and on life experience and independent study. The literature indicates President Grunewald has his Doctorate from Harvard, is former president of Mercy College, and lives in New York. The university formerly operated from a mail receiving service in Louisiana, which did not meet Louisiana's 1994 standards. Now it operates from a Hawaii, which does not regulate schools. Accreditation is claimed from the unrecognized World Association for Universities and Colleges.

American Coastline University   **B, M, D**
5000 W. Esplanade, Suite 197
Metairie, LA 70006
Raymond Chasse
Many fields
1986
$$
(818) 766-3810
Established in California by Raymond Chasse, formerly with Pacific Western University, now with Summit University. Offers programs in Louisiana, California, and Hawaii; degree programs include science, technology, engineering, commerce and economic studies, community services and human services, counseling, and religious studies. Offers on-line interactive and indepedent-studies programs on GENIE and DELPHI, with student conferences available on CompuServe and America OnLine.

American Commonwealth University
See Foundation for Economic Education

American Graduate School of Business

Place des Anciens-Fosses
1814 La Tour-de-Peilz
Switzerland
Spero C. Peppas, Director
(21-944) 95-01
(21-944) 95-04 fax
Offers traditional reisdential courses in business. Accreditation is claimed from the unrecognized agency, World Association of Universities and Colleges.

American Graduate University   M

733 N. Dodsworth Ave.
Covina, CA 91724
Paul R. McDonald, Sr., President
Government contracting, acquisition management
1975
Proprietary $$$
(818) 966–4576
(818) 915-1709 fax
M.B.A. with a specific focus on federal government contracting, and a Master of Acquisition Management. Courses may be taken entirely by correspondence, or by attending seminars given at various locations around the U.S. The university is accredited by the National Association of Private Nontraditional Schools and Colleges, a legitimate but unrecognized accreditor. A Bachelor's degree is required for admission. The 24-person faculty is composed of accountants, lawyers, and business and government executives. Had been authorized to grant degrees by the state of California and is now a candidate for approval under the new laws.

American Institute for   B, M
Computer Sciences

2101 Magnolia Ave., Suite. 200
Birmingham, AL 35205
Lloyd Clayton, Jr.
Computer science
1989
$
(800) 767-2427
B.S. and M.S. in computer science, entirely through correspondence. Some credit is offered for life experience, in the form of tuition reduction. No faculty are listed in the catalog, although the school did provide us with background on three instructors (two had Master's degrees, the third expected to receive a Bachelor's shortly.) Clayton also established Chadwick University and two health-related universities. All four schools are located in Birmingham, but students from the state of Alabama are not accepted. We were given one explanation of this policy by the state of Alabama, and another by Dr. Clayton. Claims accreditation from the World Association of Universities and Colleges, an unrecognized agency.

American International Open University

See: Clayton University

American International University   D

Box 225
Canoga Park, CA 91305
Peter Levenson
Metaphysics, parapsychology, pastoral hypnotherapy
$
(818) 883-0840
(818) 710-8671 fax
Unaccredited Doctorates in Metaphysics, Parapsychology, and Pastoral Hypnotherapy. School operates from the same address as the American Association for Parapsychology. The typed, photocopied brochure offers handy advice, such as a list of things your Doctoral degree can do for you, including "Psychologically, the title 'Doctor' gives greater stature to pastoral counselors," and "Increased salary or chance for promotions," among others. There is or was some connection with Hawaii International University, and there was formerly an address in California. There is no connection with a diploma mill of this name which operated from California in the 1970s and early 1980s.

American University in London   B, M, D

Archway Central Hall, Archway Close
London N19 3TD England
Khurshid A. Khan
Liberal arts, business, engineering, sciences
1984
Nonprofit, independent
$$–$$$$
0044-71-263-2986
0044-71-281-2815 fax
The University operates under the laws of the State of Iowa (which registers, but does not investigate schools). Originally established as the London College of Science and Technology in 1984. Name changed to "American University of London" in 1986 and to "American University in London" in 1994. Their literature claims that AUL undergraduate credits are accepted for transfer at many accredited U.S. schools. Resident B.B.A., B.S., M.B.A., M.S., and Ph.D. courses are also offered through eight AUL-affiliated colleges in London, Abu Dhabi, Canada, Saudi Arabia, and Pakistan. Nonresident (external) degree programs at all levels are offered through the Distance Learning Center. Credit is earned through independent study, prior work, examination, and military courses. Each student works under one or more adjunct faculty through guided independent study and research. A thesis and examination is required of Master's (one year) and Ph.D. (two years). Candidates with prior credit may apply for "transfer student" status.

American World University   B, M, D

312 E. College St., #205
Iowa City, IA 52240
Maxine Asher, President
Many fields
Nonprofit $$
(319) 356-6620
(319) 354-6335 fax

Dr. Maxine Asher responded to our detailed letter of inquiry about American World's program and students, saying she considered some of the questions, including the school's intended new location in Iowa (the original address was in Louisiana), and the faculty's credentials, among other claims made in the school's literature, to be an invasion of "the right-to-privacy law," and demanding not to be listed in this guide. Subsequently, according to the *New Orleans Times-Picayune*, American World University failed to meet licensing standards set by the Louisiana Board of Regents (Dr. Asher asked the newspaper for a retraction; they declined.), and was ordered to cease operating in the state. whereupon the office was moved to Iowa, a state which automatically registers schools. They are accredited by the World Association of Universities and Colleges, an unrecognized agency started by the two founders of American World University, Dr. Asher and Dr. Franklin T. Burroughs, former president of Armstrong University.

Australian College of   Dip
Applied Psychology

245 Broadway
P.O. Box 43
Broadway, N.S.W. 2007 Australia
Lionel Davis
Counseling, psychotherapy
1983
$$
(02) 660 8100

This school offers diplomas, not degrees, in counseling and psychotherapy, child psychology, and managing for success. Courses can be done either in class or by home study. Counseling workshops are held twice a year. They are recommended but not mandatory for correspondence students.

Barrington University   B, M, D

381 Park Avenue South, Suite 617
New York, NY 10016
Steven M. Bettinger, President
Business administration
1993
$$$
(212) 889-3773, (800) 680-5870
(212) 447-0804 fax

Offers business degrees at all levels. Although its literature has listed an address in Vermont, the state department of education writes that the school is not operating legally in that state. Indeed, the school's own literature states "keep in mind that Barrington was chartered in 1993 in the state of Vermont but does not get it's [sic] degree granting status from the state." It is not clear to us where the degree-granting authority *does* come from. President Bettinger writes that "Our school was originally chartered in Vermont, but markets its programs from New York, Virginia and Florida." In a subsequent communication, he said the school was registered in Iowa, and planned to register in Zurich, Switzerland. Accreditation claimed from the World Association of Universities, an unrecognized agency. Original name: Barrington College, later Barrington American University.

Bernadean University   D, L

13615 Victory Blvd., Ste. 114
Van Nuys, CA 91401
Joseph Kadans, Ph.D.
Many fields
Nonprofit, church
(818) 225-9650, (800) LIBER-WAY

A division of the Church of Universology, they have offered correspondence degrees in everything from theology to astronutrition to law. The two-room headquarters is in a Los Angeles suburb. Bernadean used to be in Nevada but lost permission to operate in that state. Founder and president Joseph Kadans, Ps.D., N.D., Th.D., Ph.D., J.D., is licensed to practice law. At times, Bernadean has been recognized by the Committee of Bar Examiners in California. At one point, the school offered a certificate good for absolution of all sins to its graduates. In late 1994, even though Bernadean was neither accredited nor state approved, it seemed to continue operating without problems.

Brighton University   B, M, D

1164 Bishop St., Ste 124
Honolulu, HI 96813 USA
Rev. Clif Soares
Many fields
1991
Nonprofit, church $
(808) 524-5411, ext. 75

A "Christian University of the United Congregational Church," offering degrees in a wide variety of fields, including business, psychology, social work, and Biblical studies. All students are required to take one course in Christian religion, regardless of their own religion. All programs are completed through independent study projects, with credit given for all "acceptable" courses already completed in one's field. Branch seminaries in China, Korea, and Abu Dhabi. Brighton formerly used an address in Louisiana, and at presstime was applying for license to operate in Idaho, where a building had been rented. Accreditation is claimed from the unrecognized Association of Christian Schools and Colleges.

California Coast University   B, M, D
700 N. Main St.
Santa Ana, CA 92701
Thomas M. Neal, Jr., President
Engineering, education, behavioral science, business
1974
Proprietary $$
(714) 547-9625, (800) 854-8768
California Coast was one of California's first nonresident universities. Degrees are offered at all levels in engineering, education, behavioral science, and business, with credit given for prior academic learning and certain equivalency exams. All department heads and adjunct faculty hold degrees from traditional schools. The university operates from its own building in a Los Angeles suburb, and maintains a lending library to ensure availability of textbooks for all students, worldwide. Combined programs allow one to earn the Bachelor's and Master's or Master's and Doctorate simultaneously. Accreditation is from the National Association of Private Nontraditional Schools and Colleges, an unrecognized but legitimate agency. Former name: California Western University. Approved to grant degrees by the state of California.

California National University   B, M
16909 Parthenia St., Ste. 303
North Hills, CA 91343
Joseph Benjoya, President
Business administration, engineering, health care management
$$$$
(818) 830-2411, (800) 782-2422
(818) 830-2418 fax
B.S. in health care management, engineering (computer, electrical, environmental, mechanical, quality control), and a number of business administration concentrations (accounting, business law, international business, MIS, marketing, etc.); M.B.A., M.S. in engineering, and professional Master's programs in health care management, MIS, and human resource management. All degrees can be attained wholly through distance learning, and students from around the world are welcomed. Up to 75 percent of credit toward a degree can come from transfer credit, challenge exams such as CLEP, and life experience learning, through portfolio assessment. California National has won approval to grant degrees from the state of California.

California Pacific University   B, M, D
10650 Treena St. #203
San Diego, CA 92131
N. C. Dalton, Ph.D.
Business, management, human behavior
1976
Nonprofit, independent $$
(619) 695-3292

Bachelor's, Master's, and Doctorate in business administration, and M.A. in management or human behavior, entirely by correspondence study using the school's "highly structured programs." Limited experiential credit is given at undergraduate level only. Students are supplied with study guides written by university faculty, to accompany recognized textbooks in the field. The school is "committed to the training and education of business managers and leaders in the technical, quantitative, and theoretical areas of business management, without neglecting the all important human side of business enterprise."

California Western University
See: California Coast University

Canadian School of Management   B, M
335 Bay St., Suite 1120
Toronto, ON M5H 2R3 Canada
Christine van Duelmen, M.A., F.CAM
Business, management
1976
Nonprofit, independent $$
(416) 360-3805
(416) 360-6863
The Canadian School of Management offers nonresident degrees in business administration, health services administration, nursing administration, management, diplomatic and consular studies, and facilities management. Credit is given for prior learning experience as documented in a portfolio. C.S.M. is a member of the International University Without Walls Council, which operates from its premises. Until 1991, accredited by the Distance Education and Training Council. According to DETC, the accreditation was revoked at least in part because of CSM's connection with the unaccredited Hawthorne University in Utah. Until late 1994, CSM was affiliated with the University of King's College, Toronto. UKC was founded in 1827 and received a royal charter to grant degrees. The charter was abandoned in 1850. Claiming that a royal charter never expires, David Anderson, formerly of the University of Toronto, opened a new UKC in 1992 and claims that degrees can legally be granted. The matter is under dispute by various parties. Students who completed work at CSM received UKC degrees. UKC retroactively conferred a degree on all CSM alumni. CSM had been affiliated with Northland Open University, which had an address but not a presence in Yellowknife, Northwest Territories. CSM was registered with the Louisiana Board of Regents, using a convenience address in Metairie, Louisiana. There are five affiliated schools outside Canada: CSM Institute of Graduate Studies (Pakistan), CSM College of Advanced Management (Hong Kong), Korey International University and CSM Institute of Graduate Studies (UK), and CSM Institute of Graduate Studies, South Asia.

Capital City Religious Institute

3858 North St.
Baton Rouge, LA 70802
Rev. J. R. Williams
Has not responded to several requests for information about their nontraditional programs.

Century University   B, M, D

6400 Uptown Blvd NE
Suite 398-W
Albuquerque, NM 87110
Donald Breslow
Many fields
1978
Proprietary $$$
(505) 889-2711
(505) 889-2750 fax

Organized primarily for professional administrators with extensive experience in their fields. Programs are by "guided independent study," which involves one-on-one faculty counseling, and credit for demonstrated work experience, but no classes. Students must devote at least nine months (one academic year) to the program. Many of the adjunct faculty, who often make up part of a student's dissertation committee, hold Century University Doctorates. In 1990, Century moved from Los Angeles to Albuquerque. Century claims accreditation from an unrecognized accrediting agency. Like many other schools, they have misrepresented the findings of a study on the acceptance of nontraditional degrees. A late 1994 change in New Mexico's school licensing law may have an eventual effect on Century's status.

Chadwick University   B, M

2112 11th Ave. South
Suite 504
Birmingham, AL 35205
Tavia Sorrell
Business
1989
Proprietary $$
(205) 252-4483, (800) 767-2423
(205) 252-4480 fax

Completion of Bachelor's requires nine home-study courses (45 credit hours); eight (42 credit hours) for the M.B.A. One of four schools established and operated by Lloyd Clayton, Jr. (The others are the American Holistic University, American Institute of Computer Science, and Dr. Clayton's School of Natural Healing). Chadwick claims accreditation from the World Association of Universities and Colleges, an unrecognized agency . Students from the state of Alabama are not accepted. In August, 1995, we were given one explanation of this policy by Dr. Joe Miller with the state of Alabama, and another by Chadwick.

City Business College

See: International University (Missouri)

City University Los Angeles   B, M, D

3960 Wilshire Blvd.
Los Angeles, CA 90010-3306
Henry L. N. Anderson
Business, education, humanities, nursing
1974
Nonprofit, independent $$
(213) 382-3801
(800) 262-8388 (outside CA)
(213) 382-8481 fax

CityUnivLA (that is how they refer to themselves throughout their literature) regards itself as a "finishing school" for students whose studies were interrupted earlier in life. Applicants should have at least two years of college credit toward a Bachelor of Business Administration, B.S. in engineering or nursing, M.B.A., M.S. in engineering, M.S. or M.A. in Education, or Ph.D. in humanities. Law degrees qualify students for the California bar exam. Degree completion may include home study, internships, classes or lecture series, projects, and other activities in the area of concentration. A Bachelor's Challenge Examination allows anyone who has completed 75 percent of the work toward their degree elsewhere to earn a Bachelor's by examination in one weekend. CityUnivLA has claimed accreditation from several unrecognized agencies, and lists Muhammad Ali, Ethel Kennedy and Coretta King as recipients of honorary degrees. "Campuses" are claimed in many other countries. A few we checked out were the homes or offices of alumni.

College of Southeastern Europe   M

22 Academias Avenue
Athens, Greece 10671
Achilles C. Kanellopoulos, President
Business
(30-1) 361-7681
(30-1) 360-2055

A member university of the World Association of Universities and Colleges (an unrecognized accrediting agency), they offer residential programs at the graduate level in business administration and related areas.

Columbia Pacific University   B, M, D, L

1415 3rd St.
San Rafael, CA 94901
Richard L. Crews
Many fields
1978
Proprietary $$$
(415) 459-1650
(800) 227-0119 in CA
(800) 552-5522 outside CA
(415) 459-5856 fax

Nonresident degrees in many fields through schools of arts and sciences, administration and management, and health and human services. The faculty all have graduate degrees; most have accredited Doctorates and hold, or have held, faculty positions at other major colleges and universities. Degrees are based on credit for prior learning, completion of a core curriculum normally requiring 12 to 18 months (covering research methods, creative thinking, learning techniques, etc.), and a major project, thesis, or dissertation. Columbia Pacific claims more than 5,000 students worldwide, and 500 adjunct faculty. President Crews (his M.D. is from Harvard) and Dean of Faculty Lester Carr (formerly president of the accredited Lewis University in Illinois) have been the owners and chief officers of CPU since its establishment.

Columbia Southern University   B, M, D
650 S. McKenzie St.
Foley, AL 36535
Thomas Colley, Registrar
Occupational safety & health, environmental engineering, business administration
1993
$$
(800) 977-8449
Degrees at all levels and certificates of compliance in the area of environmental compliance management. While the programs look impressively comprehensive, we are concerned that the school has claimed accreditation from the unrecognized and controversial Accrediting Commissions International, and that Richard Hoyer, Ph.D., Dean of the University and Professor of Environmental Science, has his own doctorate from an unaccredited religious school, Meridian University, and serves as a mentor for Chadwick University. We are concerned that the university uses the Sosidian and Sharp study to imply that its degrees will be widely accepted, when that study dealt only with accredited Bachelor's and Associate's degrees. Finally, the literature quotes census data on the increased earning a doctorate will produce, when that data, too, is based only on legitimately accredited degrees. Former name: University of Environmental Sciences.

Columbia State University
See chapter 25, Diploma Mills.

Cook's Institute of Electronics Engineering   B
Hwy. 18, P.O. Box 20345
Jackson, MS 39029
Wallace L. Cook
Electronics engineering
1945
Proprietary $$$$
(601) 371-1351
Bachelor of Science in Electronics Engineering, entirely

through correspondence study, involving completion of 36 courses. Advanced placement (and reduced tuition) available for experienced electronic technicians with satisfactory prior schooling. At least 15 of the 36 courses must be completed after enrolling. The school literature explains in great detail why they are not accredited (they say no home study engineering program is; this was so at one time), and makes clear the distinction between their B.S.E.E. and the correspondence B.S. in Engineering Technology as offered by some other home study programs. Wallace Cook, the owner, established this school more than 45 years ago. Accreditation is from the unrecognized but legitimate National Association for Private Nontraditional Schools and Colleges.

Eastern Nebraska Christian College
See: Saint John's University

Eastern University   B, M, D
Note: the president of Eastern University was unhappy with some things John wrote on the Internet. As a peace offering, John offered to print a listing for said school exactly as President Welker wrote it, as long as he (John) did not disagree with it. John had not expected such a lengthy statement, but John does keep his promises, so here it is, precisely as written. The fact that President Welker subsequently called John "sleazy" and wrote that he was contacting the Attorney General and the Federal Trade Commission, urging them to take action against this book because of comments with which he disagreed (on another school) was a disappointment.

"John, I expect that you will honor your commtiment [sic] to place the information on Eastern University exactly as it is worded in this document. I look forwar [sic] to hearing from you soon. I remain.[sic] Most Cordially, Dr. Will Welker
STATEMENT OF PURPOSE
Eastern University is dedicated to the belief that all people should have a chance to develop and extend their skills and knowledge and to increase awareness of their roles and responsibilities as citizens. The university is devoted to serving the educational needs of individuals seeking alternatives to traditional methods and recognition for knowledge and skills already attained. The university assumes a responsibility for helping meet the requirements for trained manpower in a global economic environment through cooperative effort with business, industry, professions, trades, and government. Adults may enroll in associate through doctorate degree programs. Administrators and faculty act as mentors and counselors to assist students with decisions concerning their educational and occupational goals.
PROGRAMS
Eastern University offers an external degree (distance education) program with a faculty mentor working with each student to design and complete an individualized Plan of Study. Students have control over program content and particular course content. Programs offered include business administration, management, transportation management, health care management, accounting, computer science, religious studies, law enforcement or police science, child care and development, counseling and therapy, hospitality management, transportation management, computer science, para-legal, nursing (for nurses with a two or three year nursing degree) and education. Students may also design and

submit a personally designed degree program (in most disciplines), for review and approval.

The university is an open admissions university and offers the opportunity for adult students to earn a degree through distance learning including communication by Internet. Eastern University offers credit for work and life experiences, previous college work, business education, workshops/seminars attended, military service and others.

Eastern University began operation on October 22, 1993 and is licensed as a degree-granting university by the New Mexico Commission on Higher Education. The university is affiliated with the New Mexico Association of Private Schools, the American Association for Collegiate Independent Study and the New Mexico Commission on Higher Education. Eastern University offers Associate, Bachelor's, Master's and Doctorate degree programs, moderately priced, and with flexible programs and schedules to accommodate the student. The university currently has fifty-six faculty mentors each with a master's and/or doctorate degree in the teaching field.

NO INTEREST payment plans available.

Call 1-(800) 801-5980/505-294-2772 for Catalog, e-mail, or write
Eastern University
2535 Wyoming NE, Suite B
Albuquerque, NM 87112
You may enroll by e-mail: eastuniv@usa.net"

Eula Wesley University   B, M, D
900 E. Cornell
Ruston, LA 71270
Samuel Wesley, President
Business, sociology, religious studies
$$
(318) 255-4396

Established in Phoenix, in founder Samuel Wesley's home. Wesley told an *Arizona Republic* reporter that his own Doctorate has been earned from Eula Wesley, "after his thesis . . . was reviewed by member of the . . . board of directors," whom he identified as two local educators. Both denied ever being on the board, or conferring the degree. "They're lying," Wesley told the reporter. Then, according to the article, "Wesley later admitted . . . his degree was an honorary one, and had been awarded by . . . James Jenkins, an unemployed janitor, and Eula Wesley, Wesley's mother." In Arizona, the school was accredited by the unrecognized International Accrediting Commission for Schools, Colleges, and Theological Seminaries, whose founder, George Reuter, according to the *Republic*, came to Phoenix, but never visited the "campus."

Eurotechnical Research University   B, M, D
P.O. Box 516
Hilo, HI 96721
Science, engineering, karate
1983
Proprietary $$$
(713) 785-5040

(810) 629-5908 fax

Established in California in 1983 and moved permanently to Hawaii in 1989, where it operated from the bedroom of university president James Holbrook's rented home. At one time, we respected the quality and integrity of Eurotech's activities, primarily the awarding of doctorates based on research performed in nonacademic settings, usually an industrial or government laboratory. 1n 1990, however, Eurotechnical became affiliated with the Rockwell College of Applied Arts and Science, an Ohio karate school with no listed phone, run by Harold Mayle, a man whose only degrees were purchased from the Universal Life Church. Eurotechnical awarded Mayle a Ph.D. *and* a D.Sc. based on his karate skills, and has awarded other doctorates to Rockwell personnel for their karate experience. Rockwell has claimed that Eurotechnical was fully accredited, a claim later withdrawn. John had counted Professor Holbrook as a friend, but Holbrook refused to communicate with John after John expressed amazement at the above-mentioned developments. A diploma mill called Leiland College of Arts and Science, which sells degrees for under $100, operated from a Hawaiian post-office box. Holbrook told a Hawaiian reporter he knew nothing about Leiland, but the reporter determined that Holbrook had in fact rented the box. Holbrook would not comment on this matter. Holbrook, the sole proprietor and staff member at the time, died in early 1994. Robert Simpson (Ph.D., Eurotech) assumed control. At presstime, President Simpson, who lives in Texas, told us that he chose not to reveal the physical location of the university, but assured us there were exciting building plans in the future, as well as important development of a health-related patent (we asked, but he chose not to reveal the patent number). We await further developments with interest.

Fairfax University   B, M, D
2900 West Fork Dr. #200
Baton Rouge, LA 70827
Alan Jones, Administrator
Many fields
1986
Nonprofit, independent $$
(504) 292-3496

"Programme Participants" (students) work at their own pace, assisted by a "Program Supervisor" (faculty members), to complete work required by a learning contract. On completion of this work plus a paper, thesis, or dissertation, and the approval of an external assessor, the degree is awarded. John and his wife Marina were two of the four founders of Fairfax; they resigned two months after the first enrollment, in 1986. They thought they had parted company with Alan Jones and his partner amicably, but soon after Jones attempted (unsuccessfully) to persuade California authorities to prevent John from selling this book, because he didn't like some of the things said in it, and later sued John and Marina in an unsuccessful attempt to involve them in a lawsuit between Fairfax and Columbia Pacific (for whom he used to work). When John visited the above address he found no Fairfax office, only a secretarial service that apparently forwards mail and messages to Jones and his colleague Malcolm Large in England.

Feather River University .... B
P.O. Box 1900
Paradise, CA 95969
W. Jay Murphy
Martial arts
1984
Nonprofit
(916) 872-4404

Feather River's program allows recognized martial arts practitioners (Judo, Tang Soo Do, Tae Kwan Do, etc.) to combine their verifiable Eastern martial arts training and rank with previously earned college or university credit, toward a conventional university degree. Several of the school's board members are nationally ranked martial arts champions.

Foundation for Economic Education .... M, D
30 South Broadway
Irvington-on-Hudson, NY 10533
Hans F. Sennholz
Economic theory, business
$$$$
(914) 591-7230
(914) 591-8910 fax

The Foundation does not issue its own degrees, but students who complete the coursework for the M.A. or Ph.D. in economic theory or history or for an M.B.A. receive the degree from American Commonwealth University. According to the Foundation's literature, Professor Sennholz has served as an academic advisor and "learning resource specialist" for American Commonwealth for over ten years, and this is his way of working more closely with students in his field of interest. Details of each degree program "depend primarily upon the previous preparation of the candidate," and instruction may be conducted in face-to-face classes, seminars, workshops, individual meetings, or teleconferences.

Freie und Privat Universität .... D
Degersheimerstrasse 29
Herisau AR, 91000, Switzerland
L. Mattei, President
Industrial sciences
(41-71) 52 35 25
(41-92) 26-11-64 fax

The university is not recognized by the Swiss Central Office for Higher Education, and the degrees are not recognized in Germany. Degrees offered in industrial sciences (political economy, marketing, insurance, banking, organization, and data processing). They also use the French

(Université Libre et Privé) and Italian (Universita Libera e Privata) versions of their name. Students are "offered the opportunity to turn their prior academic experience, expertise, and skills into a doctoral dissertation." Accreditation is claimed from the unrecognized World Association of Universities and Colleges.

Frederick Taylor University .... B, M, D
346 Rheem Blvd., Suite 203
Moraga, CA 94556
Mansour Saki, President
Management, business administration
(510) 284-1880, (800) 988-4MBA
fax: (510) 378-0908

Work in a number of fields is done by guided independent study, leading to a B.S. in management, B.B.A., or M.B.A. Areas of concentration in taxation, health care administration, information systems, and international business. Credit given for life experience (up to 30 units) and challenge exams. Foreign students welcome.

Gestalt Institute of New Orleans .... Dip
3500 St. Charles Ave., Ste 208
New Orleans, LA 70115
Ann Teachworth
Gestalt therapy
1976
Proprietary $$
(504) 891-1212

Evening and weekend courses leading to two levels of diploma (not degree), and a correspondence program providing written assignments and audio- and videotapes for students unable to attend in person at any of their three locations (New Orleans, New York, Santa Cruz). Registered with the Louisiana Board of Regents, an automatic, nonevaluative process.

Golden State University
See: Honolulu University of Arts, Sciences, and Humanities. No connection to the diploma mill of the same name.

Greenwich University .... B, M, D, L
103 Kapiolani
Hilo, HI 96720
Douglas Capogrossi, President
Many fields
1972 (International Institute), 1990 (Greenwich)
$$
(808) 935-9934, (800) FOR-HILO
(808) 969-7469 fax

Greenwich evolved from the International Institute for Advanced Studies, one of the oldest nontraditional graduate schools in the U.S, which still exists as a part of Greenwich. Each student's learning (however it occurred) is matched against standards for what a degree-holder should know. Greenwich then helps the student fill in any gaps in that learning, through guided independent study using a learning contract developed by student and faculty mentors. A major paper, thesis, or dissertation is required. Bachelor's programs are open only to students who have already earned 60 credits, or the equivalent. Law programs are non-Bar-qualifying. Headquartered in Hawaii's second-largest city, Greenwich maintains offices in Australia and has affiliations with schools in Malaysia, Warnborough College in the U.K., and New Zealand. The Greenwich School of Theology is based in England. John was the first president of Greenwich, serving full-time for 18 months (from early 1990 through mid 1991). See chapter 7 for a discussion of the school-licensing situation in Hawaii. Greenwich has been pursuing accreditation with the Pacific Association of Schools and Colleges, a legitimate but unrecognized accreditor.

Harmony College of Applied Science B, M, D
1434 Fremont Ave.
Los Altos, CA 94022
Rev. Roy B. Oliver, Ph.D. D.D.
Spiritual science, spiritual healing (which includes spiritual healing, magnetic healing, mind healing, and divine healing), philosophy, psychology, natural healing
$
(415) 967-1232
Students work through self-paced programs on a one-to-one basis with professors, keeping in touch by mail and phone. Credit available for professional and life experience, nontraditional studies, and through their special test program. Thesis of 2,500 words required for all degrees.

Hawthorne University (Utah)
They have threatened with such vigor to sue us into oblivion if we said anything whatsoever about their school that we won't at this time, other than to point out that the regional accreditation they have claimed relates to a high school they operate, and not to university-level programs, and that founder Alfred W. Munzert claims his own Ph.D. from the "Brantwood Forest School" in England, a school we can't locate. (The name is reminiscent of the Brant*ridge* Forest School, described in chapter 25, Diploma Mills.)

Heed University B, M, D, L
Alumni and Information Center, P.O. Box 311
Hollywood, FL 33022
Marvin Hirsch
Psychology, philosophy, education, business administration, law
1970
Nonprofit, independent $$$
(305) 925-1600
B.A., B.S., M.A., M.S., M.B.A., Ph.D., Ed.D., D.B.A., Doctor of Arts, Doctor of Psychology, and Doctor of Juridical Science (S.J.D.) all entirely through correspondence.

The Ph.D. and S.J.D. require dissertations, the other Doctorates do not. In 1986, Heed moved from Florida, where they had been for 16 years, to the U.S. Virgin Islands, although they still operate an information center at the address above. Heed once operated Thomas Jefferson College of Law in California, which was recognized by the Committee of Bar Examiners, and awards law degrees through correspondence study, including a four-year J.D., graduates of which may take the California bar, an S.J.D., and a non–bar-qualifying J.D. that may be completed in as little as six months.

Honolulu University of Arts, B, M, D
Sciences, and Humanities
500 Ala Moana Blvd., #7-400
Honolulu, HI 96813-4920
Warren Walker, President
Many fields
1978
Independent $$
(808) 955-7333
Degrees at all levels can be earned through correspondence courses in dozens of fields of study. Formerly Golden State University, which operated from four cities in California.

Institute of Professional M
Financial Managers
16/22 Great Russell St.
London WC1B 3TD, UK
Felix Orogun, Course Director
Business adminstration
1992
071-580-9407
071-323-1766 fax
A new and probably legitimate, self-paced MBA, which we are still looking into.

International Institute for Advanced Studies
see: Greenwich University

International Open University
11814 Coursey Blvd., #341
Baton Rouge, LA 70816
Satish Shetty
Has not responded to several requests for information about their nontraditional programs.

International University (Missouri) B, M, D
1301 S. Noland Road
Independence, MO 64055
John W. Johnston, Chancellor
Many fields
1973
Nonprofit, independent $$
(816) 461-3633
Degrees at all levels are offered through correspondence

study. Claims to be accredited, but not by any recognized agency. The catalog claims "107 affiliated colleges in 28 countries," but names none of them, nor does it give the sources of faculty members' degrees. There is, or has been, some affiliation with the Sussex College of Technology, which has been identified as a degree mill by every major British newspaper and educational authority. This affiliation has been, however, vigorously defended by International's vice president and dean of faculty as being "legal" and "valid," since Sussex degrees "are definitely accepted in many countries." (We are not aware of any.) City Business College operates from the same address (178 Goswell Road) as this school's London office.

Kennedy-Western University   B, M, D
1459 Tyrell Lane
Boise, ID 83706
Paul Saltman, President
Many fields
1984
Proprietary $$$
(208) 375-4542, (800) 933-2228
(208) 375-5402 fax

Degrees in business administration and management, criminal justice, education, engineering, MIS, psychology, environmental safety, and computer science, with credit given for prior academic and nonacademic learning, and challenge exams. Every student works with an academic support team consisting of a resident faculty advisor, adjunct faculty member in the student's area, and a senior employee at the student's place of work who agrees to evaluate their progress. Admission requires portfolio assessment, and five years of degree-related field experience. Course of study involves challenge exams and independent study, culminating in the writing and defense of a thesis or dissertation. International students welcome, but they pay higher fees. Kennedy-Western moved from California to Idaho in 1990, and also has an office in Honolulu. Accreditation is being pursued through the unrecognized but legitimate Pacific Association of Schools and Colleges.

Kensington University   B, M, D, L
124 S. Isabel St.
Glendale, CA 91209
Alfred A. Calabro, J.D.
Business, engineering, social sciences, education, law
1976
Proprietary $$
(818) 240-9166, (800) 423-2495
fax: (818) 240-1707

The programs are specifically designed for the mature adult student who is capable of and committed to self-directed study. All required coursework is accomplished by individual study, with guidance and instruction provided by faculty mentors. Most coursework consists of assigned texts, exams, and projects. An individually tailored study plan is developed for each student. Nonrequired seminars and programs are offered periodically nationally and worldwide through Kensington University affiliates. The Kensington University College of Law is registered with the Committee of Bar Examiners, and its students qualify to take the California Bar exam, where they have had reasonably good success. Kensington was denied approval by the state of California in August, 1994. They successfully obtained a writ in court which permits them to continue operating unless the state decides to pursue the matter further, which had not happened at press time.

Kent College
See: La Salle University

Knightsbridge University   B, M, D
U.K. Administration Office, 1 Palk Street
Torquay, Devon TQ2 5EL England
Michael Bishop, Administrator
Many fields
$$
(44-1803) 201-830
(44-1803) 201-831 fax

The university's authorization to award degrees comes from their registration in the Caribbean nation of Antigua & Barbuda. Students have the choice of working on modular taught courses or earning degrees based on thesis evaluation. Degrees are offered in business administration, theology, sociology, English literature, psychology, astronomy, and many others. The university, under new management since 1994, has advertised extensively using an address in Denmark, and is now administrated from the west of England.

Koh-I-Noor University
See: University of Santa Monica

LA International University   D
3317 Sugar Mill Road
New Orleans, LA 70065
Bill Lemoine
Many fields
$$$
(504) 469-7000, (800) LAIU-PHD

Doctoral students must have a Bachelor's upon application, but apparently not a Master's. The student can spend three weeks (in the summer or winter) in New Orleans completing their proposal; spend one weekend a month in New Orleans, and finish in three months, plus an additional week to actually write the proposal; overseas students can exercise the second option at local centers (LA's literature does not list where). Literature says that students are provided computers and software by the school.

LaSalle University   B, M, D, L
P.O. Box 4000
Mandeville, LA 70470
Terri Turow, Executive Director
Many fields
1986
Nonprofit, church $$
(504) 624-8932, (800) 283-0017

Degrees are offered in many fields of study entirely by correspondence study. The university's literature states that "the purpose and mission of LaSalle University is to provide education . . . in Biblical studies, theology, and in theocentric (God-centered) studies in applied fields" such as holistic health care, theocentric psychology, management degrees in business and public administration, criminal justice management, health services management, hotel and restaurant management, computer science, and engineering. It goes on, "the Biblical Christian perspective serves as the framework and intertwining basis for the conduct of all educational programs at LaSalle." All programs are offered through the education ministry of the World Christian Church and are denominational, theocentric, and nonsecular. Acceptance as a student is acceptance into the church's educational ministry. LaSalle is accredited by the Council on Postsecondary Christian Education, a part of the World Christian Church, and has not requested listing by the U.S. Department of Education. Same management as Kent College of Louisiana.

Lael University
7851 Lindbergh Blvd.
Hazelwood, MO 63042
La Verne Anderson
Has not responded to several requests for information about their nontraditional programs.

Lafayette University
See: Notre Dame de Lafayette University

Leland Stanford University
P.O. Box 80234
Baton Rouge, LA 70898
Thomas W. Cook
Has not responded to several requests for information about their nontraditional programs. Certainly wins the chutzpah-in-naming award.

Los Angeles University   M, D
6862 Vanscoy Ave.
North Hollywood, CA 91605
D. E. Brimm, Director
1964
Nonprofit, independent
(213) 87-0792

In the last edition, we noted that the University had not responded to three requests for information on their pro-grams. For this edition, Director Brimm has responded, by demanding that we say nothing about his university. Since we know nothing about it, other than that the address is an unmarked home in a residential neighborhood, there is nothing we *can* say.

Louisiana Capital University
1923 Roosevelt Ave.
Kenner, LA 70062
Charles Parks
Has not responded to several requests for information about their nontraditional programs.

Louisiana Christian University
The Charleston Towers
900 Ryan St., Suite 402
Lake Charles, LA 70601
Edward Adams
Has not responded to several requests for information about their nontraditional programs.

Mellen University   B, M, D
Box 450
Lewiston, NY 14092
Herbert Richardson, President
1993
Proprietary
(800) 635-5368

The university is an outgrowth of the Edwin Mellen Press, a large academic publishing house specializing in short-run editions of specialized academic texts. In a long cover story, the respected academic magazine *Lingua Franca* called the press "a quasi–vanity press cunningly disguised as an academic publishing house . . . the brainchild of Herbert Richardson, a former University of Toronto professor of religion and one-time Moonie apologist with a Ph.D. in the sociology of religion from Harvard . . ." Richardson is suing the magazine over this article, published in the September 1993 issue (available for $6 from Lingua Franca, 22 W. 38th St., New York, NY 10018 (212) 302-0336). Advertising in the *Toronto Globe and Mail*, Mellen University has offered "a fully accredited British MPhil or PhD by writing a thesis for external examination." Mellen claims to be accredited because they are chartered on the commonwealth island of Turks and Caicos, and follow the British system of "quality control (accreditation)." The catalog says "Mellen University has earned a license from the government of the Turks and Caicos Islands and, virtually, the British government." The "virtually" is presumably because Turks is a commonwealth country. *Lingua Franca* claims Mellen's first graduating class consisted of 11 ministers from North Carolina who "were interviewed for half an hour each by Frederic Will (whose field is comparative literature), after which Will deemed all 11 candidates qualified for Ph.D.'s." A long front-page article in the *Toronto Globe and Mail* suggests that the University of Toronto, where Professor Richardson had tenure, was considering dismissing him, and that Richardson planned to contest this, should it happen (a few months later he was, indeed, dismissed). Mellen advertises a Bachelor's degree based on life experience. A friend—who has two earned Doctorates—left a message on their answering machine asking for a catalog. He instead received a letter saying, "Based on our conversation, achieving the degree you so richly deserve is well within your grasp. It is amazing how many are like yourself, with all the knowledge and experience, and without the recognition and credentials." Dr. Richardson has also announced his intent to acquire the campus of a defunct college in Dodge City, Kansas, and open the University of Western Kansas on the site, but the *Washington Post,* in an unflattering story on Mellen, says this plan has fallen through.

Midwestern University
See: Saint John's University (Louisiana)

Mole Ltd. University
10117 Florence Ct.
River Ridge, LA 70123
C. Denver Mullican
Has not responded to several requests for information about their nontraditional programs.

More University
P.O. Box 652
Lafayette, CA 94549
Registrar
1978
$$$$$
(510) 930-6972
Has not responded to several requests for information about their nontraditional programs.

New World College   B, M, D
3154B College Dr. #546
Baton Rouge, LA 70808
Robert F. Kephart
Many fields
1986
Proprietary $$$
No listed telephone
Self-paced programs in many fields, including unique self-designed programs (subject to college approval), based on learning contract designed by "the mature, self-directed, self-motivated student" and a college-assigned faculty preceptor. The New World Center for Advanced Studies, a division of New World College, provides non-residential degree programs for fire, life safety and related professional fields. Nonrequired seminars and workshops are available in the U.S.A., Belize, Costa Rica, Monaco, Mexico, Japan, Korea, Singapore, and Thailand.

Newport University   B, M, D, L
2220 University Dr.
Newport Beach, CA 92660
Ted Dalton
Business, education, psychology, human behavior, law, engineering, religion
1976
Proprietary $$$$
(714) 631-1155
(714) 631-0555 fax
Students earn credit toward their degrees through directed independent study, practica, seminars, and workshops, as well as experiential credit. Study centers are maintained in 19 countries across Europe and Asia. Newport programs in business, education, psychology, human behavior, law, engineering, and religion are approved by the state of California. Originally known as Newport International University.

North American University   B, M, D
13402 N. Scottsdale Rd.
Suite B-150
Scottsdale, AZ 85254-4056
Melissa Braudaway, Registrar
Religious and health-related fields
1992
$$$
(602) 948-3353, (800) 321-6917
(602) 948-8150 fax
N.A.U. offers degrees at all levels in health and religious fields, including pastoral psychology, pastoral wellness, psychotherapy, Christian spirituality, and comparative religion, entirely through distance learning. Credit for life experience and equivalency exams. It is worrisome that the school's photocopied catalog misquotes and misinterprets the Sosidian and Sharp study's findings on the acceptance of nontraditional degrees (the government-funded study covered only accredited Bachelor's and Associate's degrees). Apparently no connection with a diploma mill of the same name which operated from Arizona and Florida in the 1980s, or another diploma mill of this name which operated from Utah and Hawaii in the 1990s.

Northland Open University   B, M
204 Lambert St., Financial Plaza
Suite 200
Whitehorse, Yukon Y1A 3T2 Canada
Joyce Edwards, Registrar
Commerce, technology, health administration, business administration
1976
$
(800) 263-1619
Northland was established in 1976 for the purpose of providing mid-career professionals with access to higher learning. The address was in Yellowknife, Northwest Territo-

ries, although the university apparently never actually operated there. Northland offers undergraduate programs in commerce, technology, and health administration, as well as an M.B.A., with only one or two full weeks of residence required. Each student communicates with faculty members and works closely with faculty advisors in their area. The schools does not offer any courses itself, with the exception of the M.B.A.'s research component, but evaluates and awards credit for exams, life experience, and coursework taken elsewhere. Northland has had an affiliation with the Canadian School of Management, and is a member of the International University Without Walls Council and the International Council on Distance Education (housed at the Canadian School of Management).

Notre Dame de Lafayette University   B, M, D
10730 Bethany Dr., Ste. 102
Aurora, CO 80012
Msgr. John Thompson, Vice President
Many fields
Nonprofit, church
(303) 368-5541

Initially called just Lafayette University. Degrees in divinity studies, religious education, pastoral wellness, psychotherapy, theology, counseling, and pastoral psychotherapy. A 1989 catalog states that Lafayette is "the only accredited institution in the U.S." offering degree courses in nutromedical arts and sciences. But, apparently, no nutrimedicine courses are offered, and Lafayette's accreditation comes from its own church, the Mercian Rite (Orthodox) Catholic Church. No names appear in the catalogs. Father Thompson writes, "Please know that Lafayette University is state accredited," but the Colorado Commission on Higher Education does not accredit schools, and wrote to us in 1992 that Lafayette only "marginally qualifies" for state authorization. In late 1994, the state of Colorado closed the school, which thereupon moved to Minnesota. Shortly after, according to the Denver newspapers, thousands of dollars worth of computer equipment that had been reported as stolen in Colorado was found in the Minnesota office.

Nova College   B, M, D
P. O. Box 67004
Northland Village
Calgary, AB T2L 2L2 Canada
Reg. P. Farley
Any field
1977
Nonprofit, independent $
No listed phone

In 1987 Nova College stopped public operations in Canada, but continues from a convenience address on the Isle of Man. Degrees are based almost entirely "on the process of a survey and the formulation of a portfolio for each student." Credit is given for formal and informal

education, tests taken anywhere in the world, life experience, military background, etc. A thesis is generally required for graduate degrees. Paintings, the writing of a book, or other material may be accepted in lieu of a thesis. Nova's fees may be greatly reduced for those in special circumstances (unemployed, incarcerated, etc.) Not to be confused with the accredited Nova University (which actually has a component called Nova College).

Occidental University of Saint Louis
See: International Institute for Advanced Studies

Open University of America   B, M, D
3916 Commander Dr.
Hyattsville, MD 20782
Mary Rodgers, Chancellor
Many fields
1968
Nonprofit, independent $$
(301) 779-0220

Established in 1968 by Dr.s Daniel and Mary Rodgers, this school grants degrees entirely on the basis of prior achievements. The catalog is large and, at first glance, impressive. But in response to a routine request for information, Chancellor Rodgers, who apparently runs the university from the basement of her home, wrote back saying, "Your attempt to extort data from me by blackmail method (sic) is reprehensible . . . Be advised that you are not at liberty to criticize, extol, describe, interpret or represent knowledge about the Open University of America in any way." We can't determine whether they are still operating, but in late 1994, the university number was still listed with the phone company, although the phone was answered merely, "Hello." Not approved by the Maryland Board for Higher Education. We shall say no more.

Pacific Western University   B, M, D
2875 S. King Street
Honolulu, HI 96826
R. Frank Sutter
Many fields
1977
Proprietary $$
(808) 951-0911, (800) 423-3244
(310) 471-6456 fax

Degrees can be completed entirely through correspondence study, typically following a short writing assignment plus credit for prior experience (job, military, company training, industrial courses, seminars, etc.) Professional and career-oriented off-campus independent study programs lead to degrees in business, management science, engineering, physical and natural sciences, social science, education, and the helping professions. Pacific Western lost their permission to operate in California and Louisiana in 1994. All programs were to be offered through their Hawaii office, although university administration remains in California. In late 1994, however, the University secured a writ permitting them to continue operating in California unless the state decides to pursue the matter further.

Paideia B, M, D
Koningin Wilhelmina Plein 29 (P. O. Box 69667)
1060 CS Amsterdam, Netherlands
Policy studies
(31-20) 618-2804

Paideia is a university on the World Wide Web of the Internet. It focuses its attention on how liberal and policy studies illumine public dialogue and political, cultural and economic responsibility. Its WWW server provides studies guides and agendas that serve as a framework for conferencing, email, home pages, and portfolios. An M.A. represents two years of half time participation. Provision exists for B.A. completion and the Ph.D. WWW server: http://www.nl.net/~paideia/ Email: paideia@inter.nl.net

Saint John's University B, M, D
31916 University Circle
Springfield, LA 70462
Arthur E. Winkler, President
Many fields
Nonprofit, church, $$
(504) 294-2129

St. John's University of Practical Theology offers degrees in religion and theology, metaphysics, psychology, addictionology, hypnotherapy, parapsychology, business, police science, social justice, security and private investigation, social services, education, and journalism. There is also a high school equivalency program that has been accepted by some traditional colleges. Hundreds of home-study classes, ranging from foot reflexology to "the confidence man" to "creating a succe$$ful hypnotherapy center." There is free tuition for prisoners. Accreditation is claimed from two unrecognized theological agencies. The American Counselors Society and the National Society of Clinical Hypnotherapists operate from the same address; neither has a listed telephone number. Former names: Eastern Nebraska Christian College, Midwestern University. Former locations: Nebraska, Missouri, and Ponchatoula, Louisiana. No relation to an unaccredited St. John's University that operated from New Orleans in the 1980s. The name of the road leading to St. John's has been changed from Pat's Lane to University Circle.

Saint Martin's College and Seminary M, D
P. O. Box 12455
Milwaukee, WI 53212
Evelyn Pumphrey, Registrar
Business, divinity, ministry
Nonprofit, church $$$
(414) 264-2455

Master's in business, Master of Divinity, and Doctor of Ministry offered residentially, but students unable to pursue regular classes may work through the Department of Extension Studies. Certificate programs are available in Black theology, thanatology, Christian education, and pastoral education. State approved programs in alcohol and substance abuse.

Senior University B, M, D
200-7577 Elmbridge Way
Richmond, BC V6X 3X5 Canada
Abdul Hassam, Dean of Faculty
Arts and sciences, administration and management, health and human servies, religious studies and sacred traditions
1993
(604) 244-7754
(604) 244-9952 fax
Proprietary, $$$

The university's primary focus is on serving people "who seek continuing education to facilitate their evolution through the life transitions they face after their 50th birthday." A minimum of twelve months of guided independent study, under the one-on-one guidance of a faculty member, by mail, telephone, fax, or computer E-mail. All students engage in an independent guided study of the impact of lifestyle on health, including a self-evaluation of lifestyle habits. Although only the Canadian address appears in the literature, the degree-granting authority comes from the state of Wyoming, and the literature states that the university "is centered on the campus of the Lifelong Learning Center in Evanston, Wyoming." Senior University is appropriately registered with the Post-Secondary Education Commission of British Columbia. The president, based in Ontario, is Dr. Stephen Griew, former president of Athabasca University, Canada's first distance learning university. The university was co-founded and is owned by Dr. Hassam and Dr. Les Carr, co-founder and Dean of Faculty of Columbia Pacific University, whose programs and literature Senior University closely reflects, but for the focus on students over the age of fifty. Forty senior core faculty are listed. Three of the six doctorate-holding senior administrators have unaccredited doctorates.

Sierra University B, M, D
Suite D-207
2900 Bristol St.
Costa Mesa, CA 92626
1975
Nonprofit, independent $$$$$
(714) 545-1133

Students study with an instructor on an individual basis. They meet weekly with their instructor and utilize local learning resources. Life-experience credit may be granted at the undergraduate level. B.A., M.A., Ph.D. degrees offered in business, religion, psychology, health administration, public administration, communications, education, and human behavior.

Somerset University — B, M, D

The Admissions Office
Illminster, Somerset, UK TA19 0YA
Arts, science, business, law, music, theology
1982
Proprietary **$$**
(504) 889-3385

Degrees at all levels are earned through correspondence study. In the past, correspondence has been to a convenience address in Metairie, Louisiana, but now it appears to be going directly to England, even though the university cannot legally operate in England. The school's catalog lists a number of officers and faculty with traditional British credentials. Graduate degrees are based on faculty-guided research leading to writing and presenting a thesis. The Doctorates in law, science, and divinity are awarded entirely based on prior work. Founder Raymond Young previously operated Harley University from his hair salon in London. There has been an affiliation with Villarreal University of Peru.

Southern California University for Professional Studies — B, M

1840 S. 17th St., #240
Santa Ana, CA 92701
Donald Hecht
Business, management, marketing, health care administration, internal relations
1978
Private **$$**
(714) 480-0800, (800) 477-2254

The degrees offered by home study are: the Bachelor of Business Administration with a concentration in marketing, management, or accounting; and the M.B.A. Courses are offered by mail, phone, and audiotape. Each course may be completed in four to 16 weeks. A minimum of 10 courses (40 units) must be completed through the University. Undergraduate credit given for other college work, vocational and business school courses, training, seminars and military service. We were annoyed when SCUPS distributed what they said was a reprint from this book, but they had changed it to make it more favorable. They agreed not to do this any more. Approved by the state of California. Accreditation claimed from the World Association of Universities andColleges, an unrecognized accreditor.

Southern International University — B, M, D

818 Howard Ave., Ste. 500
New Orleans, LA 70113
Denis K. Muhilly, President
Psychology, human behavior, fine arts, business
(504) 522-2652
(504) 522-2594 fax

Degrees at all levels in psychology, human behavior, fine arts, and business through wholly nonresident programs. Although a fax from Dr. Muhilly mentioned the school's "privileged one-on-one methodology of instruction" and "distinguished international faculty," a request for further information went unanswered.

Southwest University — B, M

2200 Veterans Blvd.
Kenner, LA 70062
Grayce Lee, President
Various fields
1982
Proprietary
(504) 468-2900, (800) 433-5923
(504) 468-3213 fax

Southwest University was established in 1982, in Phoenix, Arizona, by its president, Dr. Grayce Lee, and administrator Dr. Reg Sheldrick. (Sheldrick also established the school now called Newport University). Southwest maintains a curriculum development office in Omaha, Nebraska. Bachelor's and Master's degrees in business administration, computer science, education, counseling/hypnotherapy, criminal justice, environmental studies, and other fields. In late 1994, the Board of Regents of Louisiana attempted to close Southwest University. The University went to court, where the closing order was quashed, and the university was subsequently licensed by the Board of Regents, with Southwest agreeing to stop offering doctorates.

Summit University — B, M, D

7508 Hayne Blvd.
New Orleans, LA 70126
Mel Maier Suhd, President
Many fields
1988
Nonprofit, religious **$$**
(504) 241-0227
(504) 243-1243 fax

Summit University is an "assessment university," with the stated mission of "critically assessing a person's lifelong learning." They award degrees at all levels and in virtually any field. Students are evaluated by a provost, who determines how many credits are needed to earn the desired degree and, with the student (Summit prefers the term "learner"), explores community resources that will be used to earn those credits. Such resources may include lectures, workshops, seminars, on-the-job training or learning, volunteer work, courses at other schools, etc., as well as credit for prior learning. Summit is registered with the state of Louisiana. Several of the administrators have been involved with accredited nontraditional programs in the past.

U.S. College of Music — Dip

18 Haviland St., Suite 22
Boston, MA 02115
John Amaral, Director
Music
1977

$$

$$
(617) 266-2886
In the past, the U.S. College of Music has offered degrees in conjunction with Greenwich University and, although that affiliation has ended, they are likely to offer degrees again. Currently, they are offering a wide selection of diplomas in music-related fields grouped into three specialization areas: artistic (arranging, performing, multimedia scoring, etc.), science (computer science, electrical engineering), and business (music business manger, financial management, etc.)

Universitas Sancti Martin — D

902 Arlington Center, Suite 137
Ada, OK 74820
A. Mason James, Admissions Chairman
(800) 359-1186
A questionable-sounding school, apparently based in Reynosa, Mexico, although all correspondence goes through Oklahoma, and directory assistance in Reynosa has no listing for such a university. A correspondent was told that he could receive a doctorate under St. Martin's "challenge" program, wherein "all independent course study requirements will be waived in lieu of a scholarly paper." Claims accreditation from the possibly nonexistent InterAmerican Association of Postsecondary Colleges and Schools, and recognition from the similarly suspect National Diet and Nutrition Association. At presstime, Dr. James had not responded to a detailed letter requesting clarification of these and other issues.

Université Libre et Privé

See: Freie und Privat Universität

University de la Romande — B, M, D

c/o Neil Gibson & Co.
P.O. Box 3
Sudbury, Suffolk CO10 6DW England
Many fields
Proprietary $$
(1787) 278-478
Pay attention, this is complex. UDLR was established in Sudbury, England, by Neil Gibson & Company. The spokesman for Neil Gibson was John Courage. Then a book was published on nontraditional degrees, by a William Ebbs, calling UDLR the best nontraditional school in the world. John Courage and William Ebbs do not, in fact, exist. They were both pseudonyms for one man, Raymond Seldis, of Neil Gibson & Company. Early advertising identified UDLR as a private and fully accredited Swiss university. The claimed accrediting agency turned out not to exist. The university later advertised from a post office box on the Isle of Man, clearly stating that it is not accredited—but the mail goes to Sudbury, as it always has. This is all legal under British law. Degrees are earned by writing a thesis, which can be quite short. Seldis has apparently now left, and UDLR is in new hands. Neil Gibson & Company also used to sell degrees that even they admitted were fake, from the University del Puerto Monico, Panama. See also: Knightsbridge University.

University of America — B, M, D

365 Canal St., Ste. 2300
New Orleans, LA 70130
James W. Benton
Many fields
1987
Proprietary $$
(504) 561-6561, (800) 347-8659
Degrees in a wide range of fields can be earned through independent study. Same management as the Theological University of America. Apparently quite actively offering degrees in Thailand.

University of Berkley — B, M, D

19785 Twelve Mile Road West, Suite 324
Southfield, MI 48076
Rev. Dr. Victor J. Pancerev, Director, Public Affairs
1993
Nonprofit $$
(814) 825-6604
Although the address is in Michigan, the telephone is in Erie, Pennsylvania, as is the postmark on the catalog envelope. Degrees are offered in virtually any subject, from parapsychology to dance, computer engineering to hypnosis. No faculty or staff are listed in the catalog. The university is part of the Society of God and Pantheistic Philosophy. Pancerev did not respond to several letters asking about the faculty, the Pennsylvania connection, the location of the campus, etc. No connection, needless to say, with the University of California at Berkeley.

University of Kings College

See: Canadian School of Management

University of Leicester — M

University Road
Leicester, UK LE1 7RH
(0533) 522-522
fax: (0533) 522-200
Business administration, criminal justice, security management
Leicester offers distance-learning courses leading, in two and a half years, to an MBA. The program incorporates instruction, examination, and a dissertation. The school's Singapore campus offers an M.S. in criminal justice or security management entirely through home study. Each program consists of five courses, each culminating in a 10–20 page term paper, then a sixth course followed by a comprehensive exam. At that point, one gets a certificate of achievement; for the Master's, an additional 50-page

218

thesis is required. The Singapore address is: IAHE Consultants PTE LTD., 1 Selegie Road, #05-03, Paradiz Centre 0718, Singapore.

University of Metaphysics   B, M, D
11684 Ventura Blvd.
Studio City, CA 91604
This school is operated by the International Metaphysical Ministry, offering Bachelor's, Masters, and Doctorates, including a one-year program in which students can earn all three through self-paced correspondence courses (48 lessons for the Bachelor's, an additional 18 plus a 6,000-word thesis for the Master's, and an additional 10,000-word dissertation for the Doctorate.)

University of Sciences in America
412 North Fourth St. #200
Baton Rouge, LA 70802
Edward Song
Has not responded to several requests for information about their nontraditional programs.

University of the Rockies   B, M, D
3525 S. Tamarac Dr., #270
Denver, CO 80237
Lyman Snyder, Ed.D.
Education, ministry
1981
(800) 292-0555
Founded in 1981 as the Christian Learning Institute of Denver. The present name was adopted in 1987. All coursework is completed through supervised independent study. Most faculty are part-time working practitioners with professional degrees in their area of teaching. A toll-free phone allows students throughout the U.S. and Canada to be connected with their instructors as necessary. Final exams are mailed to approved proctors in the student's geographic area. Credit is granted for documented experiential learning and by examination.

University of Twente   M
Faculty of Educational Science and Technology
P.O. Box 217
7500 AE Enschede, Netherlands
Mr. Jan Nelissen
Educational and training systems design
Nonprofit, state $$$
31-53-893-588
31-53-356-531 fax
The Master of Science in educational and training systems design can be completed through a resident year in Holland, or through distance learning to groups of students, usually a group of co-workers at a sponsoring workplace, through workshops and electronic course delivery.

Warnborough College   B, M, D
Boars Hill
Oxford, OX1 5ED U.K.
B. D. Tempest-Mogg, President
Many fields
1973
$$$$
(44) 865-730901
(44) 865-327796 fax
Offers residential and nonresidential degrees in liberal arts, scientific studies, and professional studies. A 7-minute CD put out by Warnborough spends its first three minutes describing Oxford University, with which there is no connection. Much attention is devoted to the fact that people like Albert Einstein, Bertrand Russell, Madame Curie, and Mahatma Gandhi "have all walked the halls and found a place of inspiration among Warnborough's 13-acre campus." They may have set foot on the grounds, but if so, it was long before Warnborough College was established. The announcer on the CD intones, "No other college can offer such a combination of historical depth and academic excellence." We beg to disagree. There is an affiliation with Greenwich University.

Washington School of Law   M, D
Washington Institute for Graduate Studies
2268 E. Newcastle Dr.
Salt Lake City, UT 84093
Gary James Joslin
Taxation
1986
Nonprofit, independent $$$
(801) 943-2440
Lawyers and CPAs may earn a Master's in taxation (LL.M. Tax for lawyers, M.S. Tax for CPAs) after 360 hours of study, in residence or by videocassette. Most students take two years to complete the program. The college uses what it identifies as the most advanced integrated system of textbooks on taxation of any graduate tax program. The doctorate (J.S.D. for lawyers, Ph.D. for CPAs) requires the Master's in taxation, and a book-length dissertation of publishable quality, which must be defended before a panel of specialists. The school is accepted for CPE credit by the Treasury, Internal Revenue Service for Enrolled Agents, the National Association of State Boards of Accountancy, and by the state boards of accountancy of virtually all states requiring such approval, and is registered with the Utah Board of Regents. Accreditation is claimed from the Accrediting Commission for Higher Education of the National Association of Private Nontraditional Schools and Colleges, a legitimate but unrecognized agency.

Weimar College   B
20601 W. Paoli Ln.
Weimar, CA 95736
Herbert E. Douglass, President
1978

Nonprofit, independent **$$**
(916) 637-4111
Has been authorized to grant degrees by the state of California. Did not respond to three requests for information on their programs.

Westbrook University   B, M, D

404 North Mesa Verde
Aztec, NM 87410
Sandi Pasker
Many fields
1988
$$$$
(505) 334-1115, (800) 447-6496
(505) 334-7583 fax
Programs in, among other subjects, business administration, psychology, naturopathy, holistic science, religious counseling, herbology, iridology, blood and urine analysis, chromotherapy, mythology, and metaphysics, and an individualized program in anything else the student wants. In the latter case, a student finds a mentor in the desired field who will help them work out a plan of study/learning contract, evaluate the work, and recommend awarding of the degree when the contract has been completed. Thesis required for Master's and Doctorate. Accreditation claimed from three unrecognized agencies. A change in New Mexico's school licensing law in late 1994 may have an effect on Westbrook.

Western Graduate College   B, M

Merium Complex, 3rd Floor
Bahadur Shah Zafar Road
Karachi-74300, Pakistan
Rafat H. Wasty, Executive Director
Business administration, computer information systems
1994
$
21-494-0586
21-476-115 fax
Bachelor's and Master's in business administration (B.B.A. and M.B.A.), and B.S. or M.S. in computer science through external degree programs. This school has an affiliation with American University in London, an unaccredited, Iowa-registered school located in England.

Western States University   B, M, D

P. O. Box 430
Doniphan, MO 63935
Olga Bowman
Many fields
(314) 996-7388
This school's attorneys have demanded that we not say anything about the school. Fair enough. But about the school's founder, Glenn Hudson, we will mention that his Doctorate is from the University of England at Oxford, a diploma mill whose proprietors were sentenced to federal prison in 1987 for selling degrees for $200 each. Hudson's Bachelor's and Master's are from Metropolitan College Institute, a nonexistent school that sells degrees for $100.

William Howard Taft University   B, M, L

10061 Talbert Ave.
Fountain Valley, CA 92708
David L. Boyd, J.D., CPA
Business
1976
Proprietary
(714) 850-4800   (800) 882-4555
Programs for tax professionals who are interested in small-business management and entrepreneurship, including an MBA, M.S. in taxation, B.S. in laws and a Juris Doctor program that qualifies graduates to take the California Bar Exam.

World University Colleges

548 Beatty St.
Vancouver, BC V6B 2L3 Canada
R. S. Rodgers, President
Many fields
(604) 685-7095
(604) 685-7095 fax
Has not responded to several requests for information about their nontraditional programs.

ATTENTION CORRESPONDENCE SCHOOL STUDENTS:
BUY THE NEW QUILL-O-MATIC HAT
and never again will you run out of
ink while writing your final exam!
CALL 1-800-"INKWELL" TODAY!

"I'm sorry I've missed the last 19 Saturday classes, Professor Kleindienst, but we homeschooling mothers have so little spare time. I appreciate your offer for private tutoring in your office, but I think I'll give it a miss."

◆20◆

Unaccredited Schools with Short Residency Programs

A log in the woods, with Mark Hopkins at one end and me at the other—
that is a good enough university for me.
PRESIDENT JAMES GARFIELD

The schools that follow offer Bachelor's, Master's, and/or doctoral programs that are not accredited by one of the recognized accrediting agencies, and which require a short period of residency to earn the degree. Such programs are typically intended for people who will remain fully employed while pursuing the degree. Accredited schools are described in chapters 16-18. Programs on which we had insufficient information are listed in Chapter 29.

The basic format of each listing is as follows:

Name of School   **Bachelor's, Master's**
Address   **Doctorate, Law, Diploma**
City, State Zip Country
Contact name

Fields of study offered
Year established
Legal/ownership status (nonprofit or proprietary, independent, or state- or church-run), Tuition

Phone, toll-free phone (if any)
Fax

Key to tuition codes:
$ = free or very low cost
$$ = inexpensive
$$$ = average
$$$$ = expensive
$$$$$ = very expensive

(As costs change so quickly, it would be foolish to give dollar amounts. If no symbol is given, it's safe to assume that the school did not provide us with this information.)

American Commonwealth University B, M, D
2801 Camino del Rio South
San Diego, CA 92108-2630
Henry W. Gaylor, Jr., Ph.D.
Business, psychology, humanities
1986
$$$$
(619) 298-9040, (800) 962-7097
After completing a short initial seminar (40 hours over five days) and formulating a learning contract, "learners" complete their education through "decentralized, direct delivery of instruction in the learner's community." No correspondence instruction or independent study; all learning activities are accomplished through face-to-face meetings with University-assigned adjunct professors in the learner's area. All ACU learners must complete Foundational Learning Modules, which may consist of traditional courses, seminars, workshops, or individualized one-to-one sessions, as set out in the contract. The University's Learning Resource and Research Center is a member of the Online Computer Library Center (OCLC). Credit is allowed for verifiable structured prior learning experience at the undergraduate level only. Originally known as William Lyon University.

Asia Pacific International University B, M, D
155 Cyril Magnin Street
San Francisco, CA 94102-2129
Business fields
(415) 834-2748
(415) 834-2758 fax
Asia Pacific offers the following degrees: Bachelor of Business Administration in financial management, information technology, or marketing management; Bachelor of Science in manufacturing management; M.B.A. in international management; Master of Information Systems, and Doctor of Business Administration in international management. All programs are offered through courses that meet about once a month, on a weekend. Bachelor's students also have the option of studying at the school's New Zealand and Vancouver campuses.

223

Berne University D
Administrative Office
P.O. Box 1080
Wolfeboro Falls, NH 03896
Dale L. Berne, Rector
Many fields
1993
$$$$
(603) 569-UNIV
(603) 569-5003 fax

Berne offers the Doctor of Business Administration, Ed.D., Doctor of Public Administration, Doctor of Theology, and Ph.D.'s in education, governmental studies, health services, international relations, psychology, and social work. Students spend one month in an "intensive academic residency semester," at the school's Nevis campus (in the West Indies), followed by two semesters of nonresidential work under the guidance of a faculty advisor. Applicants must have a Master's degree or the equivalent, and at least one year's work in their field. Also offers a "Certificate of Advanced Graduate Studies," for one semester in Nevis and one under an advisor. The catalog refers to "the finest international faculty possible," but none is listed. Financial aid is offered "in the form of low-interest Nevisian government loans when available." Advertising for Berne says that the university is accredited in the U.S. and Britain. The US accreditation is from Accrediting Commission International, an unrecognized agency. British accreditation is from World-Wide Ministries of the United Kingdom, not a recognized accreditor.

Bob Jones University B
Office of Extended Education
1700 Wade Hampton Blvd.
Greenville, SC 29614
General studies, arts and sciences, religious fields, education
Church **$$$**
(800) BJ-AND-ME
(800) 2-FAX-BJU fax

Degree-completion program leading to a Bachelor of General Studies, and other Bachelor's degrees in which up to 30 credits can come by correspondence, from a religious school whose brochure says "Religiously, our testimony is, 'Whatever the Bible says is true.'"

(The) Graduate School of America M, D
121 South 8th St. Suite 730
Minneapolis, MN 55416
Don Smithmier, Academic Office
Education, human services, organization and management, interdisciplinary studies
1993
Proprietary **$$$$**
(612) 924-2374, (800) 987-1133
(612) 339-8022 fax

The Graduate School of America is a major, well-funded, and ambitious new effort to create a nontraditional institution along the lines of Walden University and the Union Institute: long periods of guided independent study and research, with an intensive summer residency. The Ph.D. can be earned in as little as two years. President Harold Abel has been president of three accredited universities, including Walden and Central Michigan. Board chairman Stephen Shank is an attorney and former president and CEO of Tonka Corporation. TGSA, as the school calls itself, has received permanent institutional approval from the Minnesota Higher Education Coordinating Board. The approval was unanimous, despite vigorous opposition from traditionalists, including the chancellor of the state university system, who went on record as "strenuously opposing" TGSA as a "mail order school." TGSA is actively pursuing accreditation with the North Central Association and, since NCA is the agency that accredited Walden and Union, the prospects are good that candidacy will be achieved. The school's catalog and other materials are comprehensive and well-designed.

Institute for Professional Studies B, M, D
7611 Natural Bridge Road
St. Louis, MO 63121
Dorothy Lupascu
Business administration
1989
Nonprofit, independent **$$$**
(314) 383-0550 (800) 510-0550

Ph.D. in administration from a program designed, according to the Institute's catalog, to "meet the educational and professional development needs of mid-career professionals and to promote the concept of 'servant leadership.'" A minimum of 36 credits (of 48 required) must be taken from the Institute, including 24 in residency, which can be accomplished in two six-week summer sessions. Students take one comprehensive final exam, and write a dissertation focusing on "servant leadership," a field that encompasses such areas of concentration as counseling, human resource management, marketing, and education and training. Also has a Native American studies program, dedicated to helping American Indians receive culturally sensitive external undergraduate and graduate degrees. The student is required to obtain tribal approval of his or her program, making the tribe a part of the educational process.

Institute for the Advanced Study M, D
of Human Sexuality
1523 Franklin St.
San Francisco, CA 94109
Robert T. McIlvenna
Human sexuality
1976
Proprietary **$$$**

(415) 928-1133

Degrees offered are Master of Human Sexuality, Ph.D., Ed.D., and Doctor of Human Sexuality. Minimum of nine weeks' residency for the Masters (three weeks in each of three trimesters); 15 for the Doctorate (five trimesters), although additional residency is encouraged. The school's founders, including such prominent sexologists as Kinsey's coauthor, Wardell Pomersoy, designed these programs to rectify what they believe is "a woeful lack of professionals who are academically prepared in the study of human sexuality." Many courses available on videocassette; comprehensive exams and a basic research project are expected of all students. Each Doctorate addresses a different emphasis—scientific inquiry, academic skills, or therapy and counseling. The Institute is approved by the state of California.

Institute of Imaginal Studies   M, D
47 Sixth St.
Petaluma, CA 94952
Psychology
(707) 765-1836

Offers weekend Master's and doctoral programs in psychology that qualify graduates to sit for the MFCC and Psychology License exams. Classes meet one weekend a month for nine months, and for one week during the summer. Students take three courses each quarter; the Doctorate takes three years of coursework post-M.A., four years post-B.A.

Institute of Transpersonal Psychology   M
250 Oak Grove Ave.
Menlo Park, CA 94025
Psychology, counseling
1975
$$$$
(415) 326-1960

The Institute offers two external degree programs: a 21-month M.A. in transpersonal studies and a 27-month Master of Transpersonal Psychology. Both programs typically begin with a brief (usually about nine days each year), intensive on-campus seminar, after which students complete their coursework through home study, with telephone support from assigned mentors. Graduates do not qualify to take state licensing exams for counselors.

La Jolla University   B, M, D
5005 Texas St., 4th floor
San Diego, CA 92108-3725
William Pickslay
Business administration, psychology, behavioral studies
1977
Proprietary $$
(619) 293-3760
(619) 293-3737 fax

Permits independent study by petition, in a student-directed "learner program." Pickslay writes that the school has been moving towards a "more traditional stance," but the self-guided option is still available: "Essentially the student must justify it because of special circumstances."

Nomad University
P. O. Box 2128
Seattle, WA 98111
No degrees
Nonprofit, independent $
(206) 746-1886
(206) 746-6871 fax

Nomad presents public classes for groups of 500 or more in cities worldwide. The say that they do not seek accreditation or grant degrees because "education should be for discovery, not for approval." The lovely little catalog goes on, "Not all that we call education is to be found within the ivy-covered walls of Academia. Nomad University pitches its all-encompassing tent under the open sky wherever the conditions for learning are good. . . . There are great teachers all around us. Nomad University has assembled in our movable camp the best guides, storytellers, wizards, bards, enchantresses, seers, adventurers, old ones, healers, clowns, warriors, and adepts. . . . Because we learn from our colleagues, we are a true college. Because the walls move with the wind, we remember where the true university is." The first three courses are $25 each, and you are not told what they will be; you simply pay and then go. It is all rather charming.

Open University (Florida)   M
24 South Orange Ave., P. O. Box 1511
Orlando, FL 32802
Business, entrepreneurial studies
Donald M. Mikula, Vice President for Academic Affairs
1987
Proprietary, $$$$
(407) 649-8488, (800) 874-0388
(407) 843-4866

The sole focus of the university is educating adults in skills associated with entrepreneurship and small business ownership. The Executive MBA begins with a one-week residency in Orlando, followed by nine months of distance learning, working through modules provided by the university. Then the sequence is repeated: a second week on campus, and additional modules over the next nine months. Students are in regular communication with faculty and advisors using fax, computer E-mail, and teleconferencing. Programs can be customized to match specific student interests. Founder and president Laurence J. Pino is an attorney, author of books on entrepreneurship, and publisher of *Wealth Builder Monthly*.

Oxford Graduate School   M, D
American Centre for Religion/Society Studies

505 Oxford Drive
Dayton, TN 37321
Hollis L. Green
1982
Nonprofit, church $$$$
(615) 775-6597

We'd better let the catalog speak for itself: "Flexible residency through the concept of reading for a degree. Qualifying examinations make Oxford available to worthy students and exit examinations validate the quality of the education. . . . [The] program accepts only experienced Christian scholars who are qualified by academic standing and practical experience. The program requires an evident balance between orthodoxy and orthopraxis [and is] primarily an andragogic educational model with synergogic learning designs." The D.Phil. program is structured "to develop distinct patterns of expectations regarding the understandings, knowledge, skills and competencies expected of D.Phil candidates . . . [and] develop and implement a basic strategy for translating programmatically projected expectations into actual patterns of student progress."

Oxford Open MBA Office   M

66 Banbury Road
Oxford, OX2 6PR UK
0865 31010
Had not responded to requests for information about their programs at presstime.

Pacific States University   M, D

1516 S. Western Ave.
Los Angeles, CA 90006
Steven Kase, President
Many fields
1928
Nonprofit, independent $$
(213) 731-2383
Master of Arts, Doctor of Education, Doctor of Product Development, and Ph.D. programs, primarily through nonresidential independent study. A six-week summer session, either in Los Angeles or London, England, is required. The university was founded in 1928 as an engineering school, and still offers residential programs in various fields. The graduate degrees are offered with a specialty in administration, general education, or psychology, and can be completed in less than a year.

Pacifica Graduate Institute   M

249 Lambert Road
Carpinteria, CA 93013
Kathy Snow
Psychology
1974
Nonprofit, independent $$$
(805) 969-3626
(805) 565-1932 fax

M.A. in counseling psychology through weekend courses held once a month. The Institute is approved by the state of California, so graduates are eligible to take the M.F.C.C. license exam and clinical psychologist exam. Also offers an overseas program in which classes at the Santa Barbara campus are supplemented with summer sessions in Hawaii and selected international locations for the purpose of "recognizing the importance of cultural diversity, native rituals, mythological traditions, and the physical landscape as primary architects of the human experience of psyche." Formerly the Human Relations Institute.

The Graduate School of America

See: Graduate School of America. The "The" is part of the name, but that wreaks havoc with alphabetizing.

The Open University (Florida)

See: Open University (Florida). The "The" is part of the name.

University of Santa Barbara   M, D

4050 Calle Real #200
Santa Barbara, CA 93110
Julia Reinhart Coburn, President
Education, business
1973
Nonprofit, independent $$
(805) 967-0020
(805) 967-6289 fax

M.A. and Ph.D. in education, MBA, M.S. in business administration, international business, and a number of business-related fields. All courses of study contain an international studies component and an ethics emphasis. The programs all require a minimum residency of three weeks in Santa Barbara, for intensive seminars preparatory to self-guided research. The resident faculty and non-resident advisors all have traditional Doctorates. Degree candidates must complete courses and independent study work, and pass an examination in each study area. Originally established in Florida as Laurence University. Candidate for accreditation by the Pacific Association of Schools and Colleges, an unrecognized but legitimate accrediting agency.

Western Institute for Social Research   B, M, D

3220 Sacramento St.
Berkeley, CA 94702
John Bilorusky
Psychology, education, social sciences, human services/community development
1975
Nonprofit, independent $$
(415) 655-2830
Degrees at all levels, primarily for people concerned

with educational innovation and/or community and social change, through a combination of residential and independent study. The typical student is enrolled for two to three years, which must include two months per year residency or several days every couple of months. The approach involves intensive study with a faculty advisor and in small seminars, and projects combining practical and intellectual approaches to community and educational problems. The school has been approved by the state of California. Formerly Western Regional Learning Center.

Western Regional Learning Center

See: Western Institute for Social Research

William Carey International University   B, M, D

1539 E. Howard Street
Pasadena, CA 91104
International development
Nonprofit, independent $$
(818) 398-2142
(818) 398-2111 fax

Approved by the state of California to grant degrees. A recent request for a catalog was met with a form letter apology that no catalogs were available, as they were being revised. The fact sheet did say that they offer degrees at all levels in the field of international development, focusing on "the work of voluntary organizations involved in cross-cultural service."

William Lyon University

See: American Commonwealth University

LESSON 2
HOME STUDY
COURSE IN
WINEMAKING
INTERNATIONAL SCHOOL
OF MAIL ORDER
OENOLOGY
AND HIGH COLONICS

◆21◆
Unaccredited Schools with Nontraditional Residential Programs

"Whom are you?" he asked, for he had been to night school.
GEORGE ADE

The schools that follow offer Bachelor's, Master's, and/or doctoral programs that are not accredited by one of the recognized accrediting agencies, and which require a moderate amount of residency to earn the degree. Such programs are typically intended for people who live near the school, or can spend long periods of time nearby.. Accredited schools are described in chapters 16-18. Programs on which we had insufficient information are listed in Chapter 29.

The basic format of each listing is as follows:

Name of School   Bachelor's, Master's,
Address   Doctorates, Law, Diplomas
City, State Zip Country
Contact name

Fields of study offered
Year established
Legal/ownership status (nonprofit or proprietary, independent, or state- or church-run), Tuition

Phone, toll-free phone (if any)
Fax

Key to tuition codes:
$ = free or very low cost
$$ = inexpensive
$$$ = average
$$$$ = expensive
$$$$$ = very expensive

(As costs change so quickly, it would be foolish to give dollar amounts. If no symbol is given, it's safe to assume that the school did not provide us with this information.)

California Graduate Institute   M, D
1100 Glendon Ave.
11th Floor
Los Angeles, CA 90024
Marvin Koven
Psychology and psychotherapy
1968
Nonprofit, independent $$
(213) 879-1533
Established to expand the scope of traditional graduate study in psychology and psychotherapy. Faculty are practicing professionals in the field of mental health. Curriculum includes clinical psychology, behavioral medicine, psychoanalysis, and marriage, family, and child counseling. Graduates are eligible to take California licensing exams.

California Graduate School of Marital and Family Therapy
See: California Graduate School of Psychology

California Graduate School   M, D
of Psychology
1859 Scott Street
San Francisco, CA 94115
Neil Kobrin
Counseling, clinical psychology
1976
Nonprofit, independent
(415) 771-8995
Master's degree and Psy.D. in Marriage, Family, and Child counseling, Psy.D. in clinical psychology, and D.M.F.C. (Doctor of Marital, Family, and Child Therapy) all through evening and weekend courses. Counseling programs are approved by the state of California, so graduates can take state licensing exams. Formerly called the California Graduate School of Marital and Family Therapy.

California International University B, M
2706 Wilshire Blvd.
Los Angeles, CA 90057
Moonkyu Park, Acting President
Business fields
1973
Nonprofit, independent $$
(213) 381-3719
Degrees in business management and international business, specially tailored for international students who use English as a second language. Evening classes. Authorized to grant degrees by the state of California.

Cambridge Graduate School M, D
of Psychology
3456 W. Olympic Blvd.
Los Angeles, CA 90019
Michael Callahan
Psychology
1982
Proprietary $$
(800) 472-1932
Weekend and evening classes for professionals already working in psychological service areas. The programs are approved by the state of California, enabling graduates to sit for state licensing exams in clinical psychology and in marriage, family, and child counseling.

Center for Psychological Studies D
1398 Solano Ave.
Albany, CA 94706
Margaret S. Alafi, Ph.D.
Clinical and developmental psychology
1979
Nonprofit, independent $$$
(510) 524-0291
Mature professionals who have completed a Master's degree or its equivalent can earn a Ph.D. in clinical or developmental psychology from the Center; concentration in organizational psychology is possible. Both Doctorates are approved by the California State Department of Education and meet educational requirements for the psychology license. Students receive ample faculty support, and are encouraged to pursue their own research interests for dissertations. Part-time study is available, and the academic calendar is geared to the needs of working students. Classes meet in the evenings and on weekends. Approved for veterans' benefits. Formerly the Graduate School of Human Behavior.

Center Graduate School M
19225 Vineyard Lane
Saratoga, CA 95070
Robert Baratta-Lorton
Mathematics education
1980

Nonprofit, independent $
(408) 867-3167 (800) 395-6088
This school's sole offering is a Master of Arts in education, with a specialization in elementary mathematics. The coursework is designed for current or prospective mathematics resource teachers at the elementary-school level.

Central Texas College
P.O. Box 3461, Bldg. 7801
Fort Polk, LA 71459
James Anderson
Has not responded to several requests for information about their nontraditional programs.

College for Financial Planning
See: National Endowment for Financial Planning

Eubanks Conservatory of Music and Arts B, M
4928 S. Crenshaw Blvd.
Los Angeles, CA 90043
Raymond Cho
Music
1951
Nonprofit, independent $$
(213) 291-7821
The Bachelor's and Master's degrees are offered in performance (classical or jazz) theory and composition, accompaniment, church music, and music history. Courses are offered evenings and weekends. There are a few correspondence courses, and limited credit is given for life experience learning. The conservatory is approved to grant degrees by the state of California.

European University B
Rue de Livourne 116-120
1050 Brussels, Belgium
Ludo Lambrechts
Many fields
(02) 648-67-81
(02) 648-59-68 fax
The full-color literature is impressive looking, but we remain confused, and correspondence with President Lambrechts has not cleared everything up. To their credit, they reproduce "affiliation agreements" from Troy State and Central State universities (both accredited), in which those schools agree to accept E.U.'s students into their M.B.A. programs. Membership is claimed in the American Association of Collegiate Schools of Business, an organization we cannot locate. There is an American *Assembly* of Collegiate Schools of Business, but E.U. is not a member. The school's literature states that more than 1,500 students are enrolled in the residential Bachelor's program in language, business, information systems, hotel administration, or public relations, and that the university operates its own radio station. Courses also given in Antwerp and in Montreux, Switzerland.

Graduate School of Human Behavior
See: Center for Psychological Studies

Hawthorne University (California)   B, M, D
Cotati, CA 94952
General studies
1982
(707) 795-7168
Hawthorne opened in the fall of 1982, offering degrees at all levels in general studies, with an emphasis at the Master's level in humanistic computer studies. (The Bachelor's was offered as a convenience for those going on to higher degrees.) In 1988, the university was still in operation, although apparently no longer authorized by the state of California. Hawthorne evolved from a formerly state-approved school named Paideia, now apparently alive but dormant in Berkeley. Indeed, seven of Hawthorne's 10 faculty members have their highest degree from Paideia. The school utilizes the "Paideian process," in which interdisciplinary groups of 12 or so meet each week, and the entire school meets one Saturday a month.

Hispanic University   B, M, D
262 Grand Ave.
Oakland, CA 94610
B. Roberto Cruz
Education, business, health care, computer science
1981
Nonprofit, independent
(510) 451-0511
A multilingual, multicultural approach to higher education. Also at: 135 E. Gish Road, San Jose CA 95112, (408) 441-2000.

Human Relations Institute   M
5200 Hollister Ave.
Santa Barbara, CA 93111
Counseling psychology
Nonprofit, independent $$$
(805) 967-4557
The degree is available through weekend courses held once a month. The institute is approved by the state of California, so graduates are eligible to take the M.F.C.C. licensing exam.

Inner City Institute for Performing and Visual Art
1308 S. New Hampshire Ave.
Los Angeles, CA 90006
C. Bernard Jackson
1966
$$$$
(213) 387-1161
The Institute is apparently temporarily closed, but they do expect to reopen. Interested parties should contact them directly for more information.

Institut P-2000   B, M
P.O. Box 5211
Zurich 8022 Switzerland
Ivana Andretta, President
(41-1) 241-4183
(41-1) 241-3033
According to a publication of the World Association of Universities and Colleges (an unrecognized accrediting agency), this member university "is a scholastic entity for therapy, psychological therapy, and psychosomatic therapy at the levels of Practitioner, Bachelor's, and Master's proficiency." Programs are residential.

International University of America   M, D
220 Montgomery St., Suite 1900
San Francisco, CA 94104
Matthew Bernstein
Business administration (with emphasis in international business management)
1980
State approved $$$$
(415) 397-2000
(415) 397-2052 fax
M.B.A. and a Ph.D. /Doctor of Business Administration program is "designed for managers and executives who seek exposure to state-of-the-art international business theories and practice." Seven courses must be completed during a one-year residency, followed by a minimum of two years' work on a dissertation, which can be done anywhere. The 20 students accepted each year must have completed at least two years of successful professional experience; M.B.A.-holders are preferred. Students who have completed two full quarters at IUA in San Francisco may apply for admission to the Asian Center in Hong Kong for a quarter; special two week seminars in Hong Kong or four weeks in Paris are also options. IUA is a member of, but not accredited by, the unrecognized agency World Association of Universities and Colleges.

Koh-I-Noor University
See: University of Santa Monica

Los Angeles Institute and Society   M, D
for Psychoanalytical Studies
1100 Glendon Ave., Suite 933
Los Angeles, CA 90024
Ernest S. Lawrence
Psychoanalytic training
1970
Nonprofit, independent $
(310) 208-3090
Systematic training for mental-health professionals. A four-year program of coursework, personal analysis, supervised analyses, and a case presentation. Students must already have a license to practice in the state of California.

Northwestern Polytechnic University   B
4378 Enterprise St.
Fremont, CA 94539
Barbara Brown
Electrical engineering, computer systems engineering
1984
Nonprofit, independent **$$$**
(510) 657-5911
Their program offers the last two years of a four-year course of studies. All accepted students must have completed 50 to 60 semester hours of general studies before enrolling. Credit for documented life, work, and military experience and equivalency exams. Students may request a challenge exam in any course, given during the first two weeks. If they pass, they get credit for the course. A degree can be earned in 15 to 19 months of evening study.

Nyingma Institute   Dip
1815 Highland Place
Berkeley, CA 94709
Tarthang Tulku Rinpoche
Human development based on Tibetan Buddhism
1973
Nonprofit, independent Cost varies
(510) 843-6812
Curriculum includes philosophy, psychology, language study, meditation practice, history, culture, and comparative studies.

One Institute of Homophile Studies   M, D
3340 Country Club Dr.
Los Angeles, CA 90019
David G. Cameron
Homophile studies
1956
Nonprofit, independent **$$$**
(213) 735-5252
Interdisciplinary curricula in anthropology, biology, sociology, history, literature, psychology, etc., of male and female homosexuality. Some credit for life experience learning. Some courses by evening and weekend study. Authorized to grant degrees by the state of California. Graduate degrees in homophile studies only. No other degrees; highly specialized technical training.

Palo Alto School of Professional Psychology
See: Western Graduate School of Psychology

Reid College of Detection of Deception   M
250 S. Wacker
Chicago, IL 60606
Brian C. Jayne, Dean
Polygraph techniques
1971
Proprietary **$$**

(312) 876-1600, (800) 255-5747
The college began as a school held in the laboratories of John Reid, a polygraph specialist. Now, an M.S. in detection of deception is offered through a six-month course in Chicago, plus the writing of a thesis, which can be done at a distance. Applicants must have an accredited Bachelor's degree. The program consists of lectures, laboratory work, and an internship. There is a final written exam, and each student must conduct two polygraph examinations under the scrutiny of the Degree Granting Board. Six-month programs begin each January and July. The college is authorized to grant its M.S. by the superintendent of public instruction.

Rosebridge Graduate School   M, D
of Integrative Psychology
1040 Oak Grove Road, Ste. 103
Concord, CA 94518
R. K. Janmeja Singh, Dean
Psychology
1978
$$$$
(510) 689-0560
Rosebridge offers evening and weekend courses leading to an M.A. in counseling psychology or a Psy.D. in a number of specializations, including addiction treatment, women's psychology, parapsychology and paranormal research, and strategic hypnotherapy. The Master's program meets California state educational requirements for licensure as a Marriage, Family, and Child Counselor, meaning that graduates are qualified to sit for the state licensing exam.

Rudolph Steiner College   B
9200 Fair Oaks Blvd.
Fair Oaks, CA 95628
Judith Blatchford
Education and arts
1976
Nonprofit, independent **$$**
(916) 961-8727
Program includes a "foundation year," an arts program, and Waldorf training based on the insights of Rudolf Steiner and others. If general education requirements have been met elsewhere, the B.A. may be earned through this study. The school is approved by the state of California to grant degrees.

Ryokan College   B, M, D
11965 Venice Blvd.
Los Angeles, CA 90066
Alvin P. Ross
Human behavior, counseling psychology, clinical psychology
1979
Nonprofit, independent **$$**

(213) 390-7560

The programs are for mature, career-oriented people with at least two years of undergraduate college work. Classes are held in supportive small group settings. The college is approved by the state of California to grant degrees.

Southeast Asia Interdisciplinary Development Institute   M, D

Taktak Dr., Atipolo Rizal
AC - P.O. Box 267
Quezon City, Philippines
Msgr. Patricio R. Getigan, HP, Ph.D.
Organizational development and planning, instruction development and technology
Nonprofit $$
(632) 665-4791

The M.A., M.A./Ph.D., and Ph.D. are offered by S.A.I.D.I. in organizational development and planning. Students work with a faculty committee to plan an independent study program, including Socratic and practicum conferences. The programs are offered using a modular system, allowing an integrative and experiential approach to learning. Since the courses are self-paced, the student may take from 15 to 32 months to complete the modules.

Southeastern Institute of Technology   B, M, D

200 Sparkman Dr.
Huntsville, AL 35807
Raymond C. Watson, Jr., President
Applied science, engineering, management, business administration
1976
Nonprofit, independent $$
(205) 837-9726

Residential courses for the M.S. in engineering or management, M.B.A., and Doctor of Engineering, Management, or Science. Bachelor's degree are not offered separately, but may be combined with a Master's program. All faculty are professional practitioners. Doctoral students may complete their degrees away from Huntsville if they begin the program there. All programs licensed and approved by the state of Alabama.

University for Humanistic Studies   B, M, D

2002 Jimmy Durante Blvd.
Del Mar, CA 92014
Greg Sanders
Psychology
1977
Nonprofit $$
(619) 259-9733

Degrees in psychology, including marriage, family, and child counseling and transpersonal studies; clinical health education; body therapy; body psychology; and specialized (individualized) studies. Coursework is primarily classroom based, evening and weekend. Dissertation re-

quired of all Doctoral students. Written comprehensive examination and thesis required of all Master's students. Some programs require an oral exam as well. Master's degrees take at least 18 to 24 months to complete; Doctoral degrees take at least two and a half to three years. Bachelor's degrees take 9 to 12 months for every 45 quarter units of study needed (180 units needed to graduate). Inka dinka doo.

University of Santa Monica   M

Center for the Study & Practice of Spiritual Psychology
2107 Wilshire Blvd.
Santa Monica, CA 90403
Norm Frye
Applied psychology, counseling psychology
1976
State approved $$
(310) 829-7402

Competency-based M.A. programs in which students earn the degree by demonstrating knowledge, skills, and qualities of efficiently relating with themselves and others. According to the school's materials, they are "guaranteed to positively transform your life while you earn a Master's degree! . . . dynamic graduate programs on the cutting edge where psychology interfaces with spirituality." Both programs (applied psychology and counseling psychology) have an emphasis in spiritual psychology. A Certificate of Completion option is available for those not seeking a degree. The M.A. in counseling psychology provides the appropriate professional training meeting the educational qualifications for licensing as a Marriage, Family, and Child Counselor in California. Formerly called Koh-I-Noor University.

Western Graduate School of Psychology   M, D

575 Middlefield Rd., Suite B
Palo Alto, CA 94301
John Emanuele, President
Clinical psychology
1978
Nonprofit, independent $$$
(415) 325-0804

The Ph.D. in clinical psychology is offered to working professionals, through classes offered in the late afternoon and evening. Normally, two years of classes plus a lengthy period of supervised fieldwork are required. Students who have knowledge in a specific subject area may take challenge examinations, rather than the entire course. The program is approved by the state of California, and thus graduates can take the state licensing exams without further qualification. Formerly Palo Alto School of Professional Psychology.

World University of America   B, M, D

107 N. Ventura St.
Ojai, CA 93023
Benito F. Reyes, President
Many fields

1974
Nonprofit, independent $$
(805) 646-1444
Degrees and vocational certificates offered in many fields of study, including counseling psychology (graduates are qualified to test for the Marriage, Family, and Child Counseling license), global studies, yoga, spiritual ministry, and hypnotherapy. The school's stated goal is "to promote spiritual growth within the framework of an academic curriculum." Not affiliated with the formerly accredited World University of Puerto Rico.

Yuin University   B, M, D
2007 East Compton Blvd.
Compton, CA 90221
Acupuncture, Oriental medicine, Christian theology, business
Proprietary
(310) 609-2704
(714) 861-1910 fax
Offers degrees in the above fields through evening, weekend, and off-campus study. Authorized to grant degrees by the state of California.

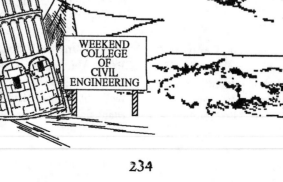

WEEKEND
COLLEGE
OF
CIVIL
ENGINEERING

♦ 22 ♦
High School Diplomas and Associate Degrees

Education is what remains when you have
forgotten everything you learned in school.
ALBERT EINSTEIN
(ALSO ATTRIBUTED TO B. F. SKINNER)

HIGH SCHOOL DIPLOMAS BY CORRESPONDENCE STUDY

The first thing to say is that, even if you have not completed high school, you probably will not need to do so in order to enroll in a nontraditional college degree program.

The high school diploma is the usual "ticket of admission" to a traditional university. However, many universities, both traditional and nontraditional, believe that anywhere from two to seven years of life or job experience is at least the equivalent of a high school diploma. So if you are over the age of 25, you should have no trouble finding schools that do not require a high school diploma. If you are between 18 and 25, you may have to shop around a little, or may find it necessary to complete high school (or its equivalent) first.

Here are the five ways to complete high school (or its equivalent) by nontraditional means:

The High School Division of a University

While many of the universities with correspondence programs listed in chapter 12 offer high-school-level correspondence study as well as college-level, only two major universities actually award high school diplomas entirely through correspondence study. These diplomas are the exact equivalent of a traditional high school diploma, and are accepted everywhere.

Texas Tech University High School

Guided Studies Program, Division of Continuing Education, P.O. Box 42191, Lubbock, TX 79409   Phone (806) 742-2352 or (800) MY COURSE

University of Nebraska at Lincoln

Independent Study High School, 269 Nebraska Center for Continuing Education, 33rd and Holdredge Streets, Lincoln, NE 68583   Phone (402) 472-1926

State Department of Education

The state of North Dakota offers people throughout the United States and worldwide the opportunity to earn a high school diploma by studying correspondence courses. North Dakota Department of Public Instruction, Division of Independent Study, P. O. Box 5036, State University Station, Fargo, ND 58105   Phone (701) 239-7282

State Equivalency Examinations

Each of the 50 states offers a high school equivalency examination, sometimes called the G.E.D., which is the equivalent of a high school diploma for virtually all purposes, including admission to college. Although each state's procedures differ, in general the examination takes from three to five hours, and covers the full range of high school subjects: mathematics, science, language, history, social studies, etc. It must be taken in person, not by mail. For the details in any given state, contact that state's Department of Education in the state capital.

(Two members of our family have taken the equivalency exam when they were 15, partway through the 10th grade. As soon as they learned they had passed, they left high school forever. One immediately enrolled in college; the other worked for three years, and then entered a university. Neither had any problem with college admission as a result of their equivalency diploma. And both ended up as straight-A students, despite the lack of whatever they might have learned in three years of high school.)

Private Correspondence Schools

There are quite a few private, usually proprietary (profit-making) schools or institutes that award high school diplomas or equivalency certificates through correspondence study. They tend to be more expensive and not quite as widely accepted as the university programs or the state equivalency exams. On the other hand, they may be faster and more generous in the credit given for prior experience.

Here are four accredited schools offering such programs:

American School
850 E. 58th St., Chicago, IL 60637
(312) 947-3300

Home Study International
P. O. Box 4437, Silver Spring, MD 20914
(800) 394-GROW

International Correspondence Schools
Pacific High School
925 Oak St., Scranton, PA 18515
(717) 342-7701 or (800) 233-4191

Robert M. Millburn High School
14416 Jefferson Davis Highway, Suite 12
Woodbridge, VA 22191
(703) 494-0147

Home Education

There is a large and growing movement toward educating children at home. It isn't easy, but it can be richly rewardin and much help and support is available, largely through the auspices of John Holt's organization. Holt is the author of *How Children Fail* and other books on educational reform, and founder of a magazine called *Growing Without Schooling*. Information is available from Holt Associates Book and Music Store, 2269 Massachusetts Ave., Cambridge, MA 02140.

ASSOCIATE'S DEGREES

The Associate's degree, a relatively recent innovation, is awarded by community and junior colleges at the conclusion of two full-time years of successful study, as well as being given halfway through the Bachelor's degree program by some (but not too many) Bachelor's-granting colleges.

The standard degrees are the A.A. (Associate of Arts) and A.S. (Associate of Science), but many other titles are used.

Thousands of different Associate's programs exist, and many of them are available by part-time, evening, or correspondence study. Many take into account life experience, previous courses, and/or credit by examination.

To describe or even list them all would have doubled the size of this book, and a reader survey a few years ago convinced us that only a tiny percentage of readers have interest in this degree. Fortunately, for those who are interested, there does exist a directory of such programs. It is called *A Directory of U.S. College and University Degrees for Part-Time Students,* and it is sold at bookstores and by the National University Extension Association, One Dupont Circle NW, Suite 360, Washington, DC 20036.

It is arranged alphabetically by states and cities, and lists more than 2,000 Associate's degree programs in all 50 states.

One interesting development is a new nationwide program planned by PBS that will allow students to earn Associate's degrees from local community colleges entirely through televised courses.

Get on the mailing list for the 13th edition of Bears' Guide. Leave a message at (800) 835-8535

♦23♦
Law Schools

The law is the true embodiment of everything that's excellent;
It has no kind of fault or flaw, and I, m'lords, embody the law.
W. S. GILBERT

The law is a curiosity of the academic world. On one hand, it is possible to graduate from a world-famous law school and not be able to practice law. And on the other hand, it is possible to practice law without ever having seen the inside of a law school.

What makes this unusual set of circumstances possible is, of course, the Bar exam. In all 50 states of this union, the way most people are "admitted to the Bar" is by taking and passing this exam. Each state administers its own exam, and there is the Multi-State Bar exam, which is accepted by most states for some or all Bar exam credit.

Until the 20th century, most lawyers learned the law the way Abraham Lincoln did—by apprenticing themselves to a lawyer or a judge or studying on their own and, when they had learned enough, taking the Bar. Although a few states theoretically still permit this practice, for all intents and purposes it survives only in California, where the study of law is, in many aspects, different from the rest of the U.S., which is why California is considered separately in this chapter.

In a few states, if one graduates from a law school in that state, it is not necessary to take that state's Bar exam in order to practice law. In a few states, graduates of unaccredited law schools may be permitted to take the Bar exam. There are two problems we have in reporting this: one is that the situation keeps changing—states seem regularly to revise or reinterpret their regulations—and the other is that rules and regulations seem often to be rather flexible or at least inconsistent in the way they are interpreted (see chapter 27, Bending the Rules).

THE BAR EXAM

The Bar exam has come under increasing criticism in recent years, on a number of grounds.

• There often seems to be little correlation between performance on the Bar and performance as a lawyer. Most Bar exams, for instance, do not test ability to do legal research, conduct interviews, or argue in court.

• A test score that will pass in one state will fail in another. Consider the score required to pass, in several states, in one recent year:

California:	145	Pennsylvania:	129
New York:	135	Texas:	128
Florida:	130	Wisconsin:	125

One critic has pointed out that if California test takers had gone en masse to New York, their pass rate would have been 74% instead of California's rather dismal 42% that year.

In recent years, the Bar exam has undergone frequent and major changes. Gordon Schaber, former chairman of the ABA's section on legal education, points out that the California exam underwent "10 serious structural changes" between 1974 and 1983, during which time the pass rate dropped 12%. Following significant changes in 1983, the pass rate dropped another 9%. The failure rate might have been higher, but nearly half the minority graduates at UCLA (which has the largest minority law student population in the state) chose not to take the California Bar exam. The pass rate for African and Hispanic Americans has been significantly lower than for other groups, although the majority of those who failed in California would have passed the New York or Pennsylvania exam with the same scores.

Although the quality of law education is generally felt to continue to improve, the percentage of people passing the Bar has steadily declined in recent years. As one example, Schaber cites the entering Stanford class of 1981, which had the highest LSAT (Law School Admissions Test) scores ever, and a grade point average of 3.79 on a scale of 4. Yet when this class graduated and took the Bar exam, only 75% passed—down 17% from a few years earlier.

Can it be, people are asking more and more, that there may be too many lawyers in the world, and the already-established ones are trying to limit the new competition? In recent years, the number of lawyers has increased at more than double the rate of the population as a whole. There are more lawyers in Chicago than in all of Japan; more in New York than in all of England.

THE LAW DEGREE

Until the early 1960s, the law degree earned in America was the LL.B., or Bachelor of Laws. An LL.D., or Doctor of Laws, was available at some schools as an advanced law degree, earned after several years of study beyond the LL.B. Many lawyers didn't like the idea that lots of other professionals (optometrists, podiatrists, civil engineers, etc.) put in three years of study after college and got a Doctorate, while lawyers put in the same time and got just another Bachelor's. Law schools took heed, and almost universally converted the title of the law degree to a J.D., which can stand for Doctor of Jurisprudence or Juris Doctor. Most schools offered their alumni the opportunity to convert their old LL.B.'s into nice shiny J.D.'s. One survey reported that a large percentage accepted, but another report suggests that very few of these actually *use* the J.D. professionally, still listing the LL.B. in legal directories.

THE SITUATION IN CALIFORNIA

California is the only state that permits study of law by correspondence, or with private tutors (normally lawyers or judges), and it is one of three states (Georgia and Alabama are the others) that regularly allows graduates of unaccredited law schools to take the Bar exam. (We say "regularly" because, as indicated earlier, there are apparently special case exceptions in other states, from time to time.)

There are two kinds of unaccredited law schools: approximately 20 that offer regular residential courses in California, often through evening and/or weekend study; and a handful that offer study entirely by correspondence. There used to be no requirement that the correspondence schools be located in California, but as of 1990, only graduates of California schools are permitted to take the Bar.

The California procedure works like this: after completing one year of law study, which must include a documented 864 hours of study (about 17 hours a week), the student must take the First Year Law Students' Qualifying Exam, known as the "Baby Bar." This is a consumer protection measure, to help students studying law nontraditionally determine whether or not they are making progress.

Once the Baby Bar is passed, the student then continues for three additional years of study, 864 hours a year. When at least four years have passed and at least 3,456 hours have been logged, the regular Bar exam may be taken.

Copies of past years' versions of the Baby Bar, with answers, may be purchased from the State Bar of California, P.O. Box 7908, San Francisco, CA 94129.

The Baby Bar is required of all students studying either with correspondence law schools or with unaccredited residential law schools. In the last three years, students from 15 correspondence schools and 26 residential unaccredited schools have taken the regular Bar exam.

CALIFORNIA EXAM PERFORMANCE

One could spend days studying and analyzing the huge amounts of data made available by the State Bar of California, giving pass rates by school, by date, by kind of school, by ethnic background, by number of previous exam attempts, and so forth. In an early edition of this book, we erred by basing calculations on the number of exam passes rather than the number of *people* who passed. If, for instance, one person failed the Bar 10 times, this should be counted as one person failing, and not 10, in calculating a school's pass-fail percentages.

Rather than fill this chapter with endless charts and tables, we have elected to present only the following data:

- Complete summary of statistics for a recent Bar exam.
- For unaccredited residential schools, first time exam takers' pass rates, cumulative for six consecutive Bar exams (three years).
- For correspondence law schools, just the last results.

Unfortunately, the California Bar does not make available results of the Baby Bar by individual schools, or even by the subcategories of "residential" and "correspondence." It would be most helpful if they did.

Please bear in mind that these statistics will vary considerably from year to year and school to school.

"In retrospect, that Ito chap did a fairly good job, but if I had been in charge, utilizing the principles I learned at the Feijoada Correspondence Law Institute, the trial would have been over in a week."

ALL CALIFORNIA BAR EXAM TAKERS

	TOOK	PASSED	PERCENT
All students	7,057	4,164	59.0%
First timers	5,254	3,875	73.8
Second timers	475	125	26.3
California accredited schools that are ABA-approved			
First timers	3,232	2,712	83.9
Repeaters	329	90	27.4
California accredited schools not ABA-approved			
First timers	676	296	43.8
Repeaters	535	69	12.9
California schools neither accredited nor approved			
First timers	98	24	24.5
Repeaters	149	4	2.7
Out of State law schools			
First timers	873	656	75.1
Repeaters	145	36	24.8
Correspondence law schools			
First timers	18	6	33.3
Repeaters	34	3	8.8
Private study with lawyer or judge			
First timers	3	1	33.3
Repeaters	5	0	0.0
Lawyers from other states			
First timers	282	149	52.8
Repeaters	247	40	16.2
Stanford University			
First timers	83	77	92.8
All applicants	86	79	91.9
Harvard University			
First timers	81	74	91.4
All applicants	82	75	91.5

UNACCREDITED RESIDENTIAL LAW SCHOOLS
FIRST TIME TAKERS ONLY, 6 CONSECUTIVE BAR EXAMS

	TOOK	PASSED	PERCENT
American College of Law	68	8	11.8%
California Northern U.	8	2	25.0
California Pacific School of Law	24	14	58.3
California Southern Law School	45	13	28.8
Central California U.	11	0	0.0
Citrus Belt Law School	15	5	33.3
Lincoln U. San Jose	35	22	62.8
Northwestern Calif. U.	2	0	0.0
Oakland College of Law	1	0	0.0
Pacific Coast U.	37	8	21.6
Peninsula U.	32	8	25.0
People's College	7	1	14.3
Simon Greenleaf School of Law	5	2	40.0
Southern Cal. Inst. of Law	5	3	60.0
Southern Cal. Inst. of Law Ventura	8	2	25.0
U. of Northern California	52	11	21.2
Western Sierra Law School	10	3	30.0

CORRESPONDENCE LAW SCHOOLS,
RECENT RESULTS

	Took	Passed	%
Bernadean University	2	0	0%
City U. Los Angeles	3	1	33
*Kensington U.	11	3	27
LaSalle U.	6	0	0
La Salle Extension	0	0	0
*Newport U.	5	2	40
*North American College	1	0	0
*Northwestern Cal. U.	8	6	75
Ocean U.	1	0	0
Southland U.	2	0	0
Thomas Jefferson College	2	0	0
U. of Central Calif.	1	0	0
U. of San Gabriel Valley	1	0	0
U. of Honolulu	3	1	33
*William H. Taft U.	14	5	36

*These are the only schools whose students may take the California bar. The others used to be qualified, and their graduates were given up to seven years to pass the bar.

To summarize three key numbers: the percent of first-time passers for
Traditional accredited law schools: 59%
Unaccredited residential law schools: 24%
Unaccredited correspondence law schools: 6%

Since these numbers are very small, it is probably wise to look both at results over a longer period of time (e.g., Thomas Jefferson has had no passes in more than 80 attempts since 1985), and trends (Kensington had a poor record in 1986-87, but an excellent one later on).

Bear in mind, also, that the unaccredited school results reflect only those students who passed the Baby Bar and went on to take the regular Bar. Since the Baby Bar pass rate was around 13%, at the last sitting, it is not unreasonable to suggest that the percent of people who start an unaccredited program and eventually pass the Bar is considerably less than those figures of 24% and 6%.

Opponents of the nontraditional approach argue that the lower pass rates "prove" that the approach cannot work. Supporters point out that truly dedicated and highly motivated students *do* pass, and that many of these people would never have been able to pursue the degree by traditional means. They also suggest that many people take the Bar exams as a matter of curiosity, with little expectation of passing.

It is clearly the case that for the would-be lawyer who cannot afford either the time or the money for traditional law study, or who cannot gain admission to an accredited law school, California approaches offer the best hope.

In addition to qualifying students for the California Bar, completion of unaccredited law programs may also qualify graduates to take the exams required for practice before U.S. tax and patent courts, workers compensation boards, the Interstate Commerce Commission, and various other federal courts and agencies. As with any degree program, potential students should satisfy themselves in advance that the degree will meet their personal needs.

THE CORRESPONDENCE LAW SCHOOLS

Many of these schools are described in more detail in chapters 16 through 21.

Bernadean University
13615 Victory Blvd., Ste. 114, Van Nuys, CA 91440
(818) 255-9650 or (800) LIBER-WAY
The school is not authorized to operate by the State of California even though it has been recognized by the Committee of Bar Examiners, an unusual situation. A part of the Church of Universology, which in the past has offered absolution from all sins to its graduates.

City University Los Angeles
3960 Wilshire Blvd., 5th Floor, Los Angeles, CA 90010
(213) 382-3801 or (800) 262-8388
Offers both a three-year non-Bar-qualifying and a four-year qualifying degree. At a recent sitting, 1 of 3 candidates (33.3%) passed the Bar.

Columbia Pacific University
1415 Third St., San Rafael, CA 94901
(415) 459-1650 or (800) 227-0119
Offers only a three-year non-Bar-qualifying degree in international law.

Greenwich University
103 Kapiolani, Hilo, HI 96720
(800) FOR-HILO
A non-bar-qualifying degree is offered to physicians and other health practitioners. Other specialized degrees (for accountants, engineers, clergy, etc.) will be offered at a later time.

Kensington University
124 S. Isabel St., Glendale, CA 91209
(818) 240-9166 or (800) 423-2495
At a recent sitting, 3 of 11 candidates (27.3%) passed the Bar.

LaSalle University
Mandeville, Louisiana
See Southland, this chapter. Graduates no longer qualify to take the California Bar. The law degree is a religious degree through the church that operates LaSalle. Potential students may wish to check first with the Consumer Protection Office of the Louisiana Attorney General's

office for an update on their current status.

Newport University School of Law
2220 University Dr., Newport Beach, CA 92660
(714) 631-1155
Formerly Newport International University. 2 of 5 candidates (40%) passed the Bar at a recent sitting.

North American College of Law
Apparently no longer operating in La Mirada, California

Northwestern California University
1750 Howe Ave., Suite 535, Sacramento, CA 95825
(916) 922-9303
The university divides its law studies into four parts. Students who complete the first two parts earn a Bachelor of Science in law. Those who complete three parts earn the J.D. degree but do not qualify to take the bar exam. Completion of four parts qualifies students to take the California bar. The university made headlines in the legal press in 1994 when six of its eight first-time bar exam takers passed, a rate that put them in the top five in the state. Tuition is a modest $1,200 for each of the four parts, plus the cost of study materials.

Southland University
Closed in California in the mid 1980s. La Salle University, Missouri, subsequently opened a school of the same name, under the same management, and using many of the same materials. LaSalle later moved to Louisiana.

Thomas Jefferson School of Law
A part of Heed University, with its main office in the Virgin Islands. See listing in Chapter 19.

William H. Taft University
10061 Talbert Ave., Suite 200, Fountain Valley, CA 92708
(714) 850-4800 or (800) 882-4555
5 of 14 candidates (35.7%) passed the Bar at a recent sitting.

Washington School of Law
2268 E. Newcastle Dr., Salt Lake City, UT 84093
(801) 943-2440
Offers non-Bar-qualifying programs: an L.L.M. and J.S.D. in taxation for lawyers

UNACCREDITED RESIDENTIAL LAW SCHOOLS
These schools all offer the standard law curriculum. Most have evening and/or weekend courses. While not accredited, they are approved by the California Bar. Only listed are those schools who have had at least one graduate take the Bar in the last three years.

American College of Law

401 S. Brea Blvd., Brea, CA 92621
(714) 671-0153 or (800) 843-5291
Offers evening and weekend courses.

Cal Northern School of Law
H St., Sacramento, CA 95814 (916) 447-7223
2 of 29 candidates (6.9%) passed the Bar at a recent sitting.

California College of Law
P. O. Box 449, Beverly Hills, CA 90213

California Southern Law School
3775 Elizabeth St., Riverside, CA 92506

Central California College of Law
2135 Fresno St., Room 317, Fresno, CA 93721

Lincoln University Law School
281 Masonic Ave., San Francisco, CA 94118

Northern School of Law
301 Salem St., Suite 1, Chico, CA 95926

Pacific Coast University School of Law
440 Redondo Ave., Room 203, Long Beach, CA 90814
(213) 439-7346
Between 1986 and 1991, 93 of 130 students who took the bar passed, an impressive 65% success rate.

Peninsula University College of Law
436 Dell Ave., Mountain View, CA 94043
(415) 964-5044

People's College of Law
660 S. Bonnie Brae St., Los Angeles, CA 90057
(213) 483-0083
The only student-governed collectively run law school, their program focuses on socially and politically conscious practice. One of nine candidates passed the bar at a recent sitting.

Simon Greenleaf School of Law
3855 E. La Palma Ave., Anaheim, CA 92807
(714) 632-3434, fax: (714) 630-6109
Recently announced a forthcoming merger with Trinity International University of Illinois.

University of Northern California
727 1/2 J St., Sacramento, CA 95814
(916) 447-7223
Two of 29 candidates (7%) passed the bar at a recent sitting.

Western Sierra Law School
6035 University Ave., Suite 2, San Diego, CA 92115
3 of 8 candidates (37.5%) passed the Bar at a recent sitting.

INTERSTATE LEGAL STRATEGIES

Since the rules for becoming a lawyer vary so much from state to state, the question often arises: what about qualifying to practice law in one state (an "easier" one), and then moving to another state to practice?

It is possible, but quite impractical. Twenty-seven of the 50 states permit lawyers from another state to take the Bar in their state, but, in all but a few cases, only after they have practiced in their "home" state for a minimum number of years, and only if their degree is from an ABA-approved, accredited school. The minimum waiting time ranges from 3 years in Maine and Wisconsin to 20 years in Connecticut, but is 4 or 5 years in most states. Indiana and Iowa will, under certain conditions, permit lawyers admitted in other states to take their Bar with no waiting period.

STUDYING LAW NIGHTS OR WEEKENDS

In previous editions, we included a list of law schools that offered the law degree entirely through evening and/or weekend study. This practice, once relatively rare, has grown so rapidly that there are now a great many schools doing it. Simply check any standard school directory or the yellow pages of your telephone book for this information.

PARALEGAL DEGREES

Many people who are intrigued by the law, and wish to be involved with the law, are unwilling or unable to pursue a law degree or to be admitted to the Bar. A fairly satisfactory solution for some of these people is to pursue an alternative degree, entirely by correspondence, or with short residency, in a law-related subject.

For instance, many people have earned nonresident Master's or Doctorate degrees in business law, law and society, import-export law, consumer law, and so forth. The titles of such degrees are things like M.A. in legal studies or Ph.D. in corporate law. Of course such degrees do not permit one to practice law. Many schools offering nonresident nontraditional degrees will consider such degree programs.

There are also many people with law degrees (both traditional and nontraditional, residential and correspondence) who have never passed the Bar, but who are still working in the law. They have jobs with law firms, primarily doing research, preparing briefs, etc. They cannot meet with clients or appear in court, but they are most definitely lawyers working in the law.

Some of the schools offering paralegal studies (but not degrees) by correspondence are:

Blackstone School

P. O. Box 871449, Dallas, TX 75287
(214) 418-5141 or (800) 826-9228
For many years, they did offer law degrees which quali-

fied for bar exams. Now the nephew of the founder is operating it as a paralegal school only.

School of Paralegal Studies

6065 Roswell Road N.E., #3118, Atlanta, GA 30328
(800) 223-4542
In addition to the professional paralegal program, offers advanced specialty programs for paralegals, in civil litigation, real estate law, will, trusts, estate administration, and corporate law. Graduates of the basic program may take their first advanced class for free.

University of Maryland

University College, College Park, MD 20742
(301) 985-7036, (800) 888-UMEC
Offers paralegal training through independent study, with a short residency requirement.

University of West Los Angeles

1155 W. Arbor Vitae St., Inglewood, CA 90301
(310) 215-3339
B.S. in paralegal studies for transfer students can be earned through two to three years of evening classes.

ANOTHER APPROACH TO LAW STUDY AND DEGREES

The Law Apprentice Program offers an interesting approach to becoming a lawyer, for people who live in one of thirteen states or the District of Columbia. Two approaches are available:

1. Training (by videotape plus telephone consulting) to improve the chances of passing the Bar in California or the five states plus D.C. where a person with a non-A.B.A.-approved law degree can take the bar. Students must also enroll in one of the California correspondence law schools.

2. Apprentice training (videotape, telephone, plus local internship with a lawyer) for those nine states where one can take the Bar without having a law degree, after an appropriate apprenticeship (which can be as long as four years).

The states where someone with a non-A.B.A. degree can take the bar are California, Connecticut, Georgia, Maine, North Carolina, and South Carolina, plus the District of Columbia;

The states where it is possible to take the bar based on apprenticeship study, without ever attending law school are Alaska, California, Maine, New York, Vermont, Virginia, Washington, West Virginia, and Wyoming.

L.A.P. provides the same law books used in most major law schools, plus hundreds of audio- and video-taped lectures, weekend workshops each month at several locations around the U.S., casebooks, hornbooks, and on-line access to law faculty. Regular classes are also offered every Saturday in the Denver, Colorado area.

Further information is available by telephoning L.A.P. at (303) 245-6750 or (800) 529-9383 or writing 2561 I Road, Grand Junction, CO 81505.

◆24◆
Medical and Other
Health-Related Schools

*Géronte: It seems to me you are locating them wrongly. The heart is
on the left and the liver is on the right.
Sganarelle: Yes, in the old days that was so, but we have changed
all that, and teach medicine by an entirely new method.*
MOLIÈRE

*Note: In previous editions, this chapter was restricted to schools
offering only the M.D. degree. Now, in response to many letters, it seems appropriate to expand it to include other schools
which offer only degrees related to the health sciences, nutrition, holistic healing, and so forth. The emphasis is on the "only,"
for there are many schools that offer programs in health sciences, nursing, etc., as just a small part of a much broader curriculum. Such schools are listed in chapters 16 through 21.
(There will probably still be many letters. The biggest wave of
angry complaint letters we've ever received was after one edition in which osteopathy was referred to as an "alternative"
medical therapy.)*

MEDICAL SCHOOLS

There are, of course, no legitimate correspondence medical schools, but there are some nontraditional approaches
to earning a traditional medical degree.

The traditional approach in the U.S. consists of attending a regular college or university for four or more
years to earn a Bachelor's degree (in any field; it need not
be scientific), and then going on to medical school for
another four years, after which the Doctor of Medicine
(M.D.) is awarded. Then one spends anywhere from two
to eight years of internships, residency, and training in
clinical specialities (surgery, psychiatry, etc.)

The problems caused by this huge expenditure of time
and money (tuition of $20,000 a year is not uncommon)
are compounded by the even greater problem of admission to a traditional medical school. The simple fact is
that the great majority of applicants are not admitted.
Many schools have anywhere from 10 to 100 applicants
for each opening. Although schools are not allowed, by law,
to have quotas by race or by sex, as they once did, they definitely have quotas based on age. Applicants over the age of
30 have a much harder time getting in, and those over 40
have almost no chance at all. The schools argue that their
precious facilities should not be taken up by persons who
will have fewer years to practice and to serve humanity.

Is There a Shortage of Doctors?

The reason it is so hard to get into medical school is that
there are not enough openings available. And the reason
there are not enough openings available is the subject of
bitter debate between and among medical and political
people.

The American Medical Association and the Association of American Medical Colleges both said throughout the 1980s that we would have too many doctors by
the 1990s. But in 1988, a major study conducted by the
RAND Corporation and the Tufts University School of
Medicine suggested that there may be some significant
shortages by the year 2000, especially in major areas of
specialty such as heart, chest, blood, kidney, gastrointes-
tinal, blood disease, cancer, and infectious disease.

The A.M.A. suggests that too many doctors, whether
from medical schools or from other countries, may mean
that U.S. doctors' skills could deteriorate because the physician "may not perform certain procedures frequently
enough to maintain a high level of skill." But RAND/
Tufts suggest that by 2000, cities with populations of
200,000 may not have anywhere near the specialists they
need.

Andy Rooney writes that "the A.M.A. sounds like a
bricklayers' union. The bricklayers want to limit membership in the union so that there will always be more
bricks that need to be laid than there are bricklayers to lay
them. Doctors don't want a lot of young doctors offering
their services for less so they can pay back the money they
borrowed to get through medical school."

ACCELERATED
MEDICAL PROGRAMS

One slightly nontraditional approach to the M.D. is that
of compressing the total elapsed time between high school
and receiving the M.D. by two or three years. Many schools
now offer a "3-4" program in which you enter medical

school after the third year of college, and receive the Bachelor's degree after the first year of medical school. While most accelerated programs take seven years, some take six (Boston University, Lehigh University, Wilkes College, for instance), and one (Wofford College in South Carolina) takes five. The U.S. is, apparently, moving very slowly toward the British system, in which one enters medical school right after high school, and earns the Bachelor of Medicine in four or five years. (In England, the Doctor of Medicine is a less common advanced degree.)

Ph.D. into M.D.

The first two years of medical school are usually spent learning the relevant academic subjects (anatomy, physiology, biology, etc.) On the assumption that a person who has already earned a Ph.D. in certain fields will have this knowledge, two schools—one in the U.S. and one in Mexico—offer a two-year M.D. to such people. Applicants must have a Ph.D. in the biological, physical, or engineering sciences, or in mathematics.

University of Miami
P.O. Box 520875, Miami, FL 33152
There is theoretically no age limit to this program, but applicants under 40 have preference. The program consists of eight and a half months of preclinical study, twelve and a half months of intensive medical study, and 10 weeks of elective clinical work. The total cost exceeds $25,000. Only 36 students are admitted each year, and competition is fierce. A few non–U.S. citizens are permitted in each class.

Universidad Autonoma de Ciudad Juarez
Apartado Postal 231, Ciudad Juarez, Chihuahua, Mexico
Juarez offers a special program for non-Mexicans. Since Juarez is right on the border with the U.S., some Americans choose to live in El Paso, Texas and cross the border to their classes each day.

FOREIGN MEDICAL SCHOOLS

In previous editions of this book, several pages were devoted to a discussion of the history, philosophy, and present practice of dealing with foreign medical schools: those in Mexico that cater to English-speaking students from the U.S. and elsewhere, and those throughout the Caribbean established to provide a medical education for Americans unable to get into an American medical school.

The situation is immensely complex, and almost impossible to evaluate for a nonmedical layman. Luckily, 1995 saw the return to print of what we have always considered to be the best reference in the field, a witty, information-packed, delightfully written, and heavily opinionated book called *Foreign Medical Schools for U.S. Citizens* by Carlos Pestana, M.D., Ph.D., a professor at the University of Texas medical school. Dr. Pestana self-publishes the book, and for people considering looking

outside the U.S. for a medical school, it is worth far, far more than the $20 he charges for it by mail (for ordering information, see the Bibliography of this book). In brief, his advice is not to even consider foreign school unless your MCAT exams scores are in the upper 20s or 30s. According to Dr. Pestana, most U.S. students who study abroad come back unable to pass the necessary examinations (currently the USMLE) to qualify for residency training and eventual licensure in the U.S. If this doesn't worry you, get his book, and/or try the schools listed below, under the heading "The Medical Schools."

Using Exam Pass Rates to Judge Schools
People who attend a medical school outside the U.S. and wish to be licensed in the U.S. must pass a qualifying exam, administered by the Educational Commission for Foreign Medical Graduates (3624 Market St., Philadelphia, PA 19104). One valuable measure used to evaluate foreign schools is the percentage of its graduates who take and pass the exam. In past years, the range is literally from 0 to 100%. Unfortunately, however, ECFMG no longer publishes data on exam pass rates, claiming that too many schools were misusing them in their marketing.

Here is an old set of numbers, from when ECFMG was releasing them, for all schools with 25 or more Americans taking the exam.

School, Country	Americans who took exam	passed exam	%
Sackler School of Medicine, Israel	33	33	100
St. George's U., Grenada	218	173	79
U. of the East, Philippines	27	12	44
Far Eastern U., Philippines	44	19	43
Universidad de Monterrey, Mexico	47	20	43
Universidad de Montemorelos, Mex.	26	11	42
U. of Santa Tomas, Philippines	45	19	42
Universita degli Studi di Roma, Italy	107	45	42
American U. of the Carib., Montserrat	363	146	40
Institut de Medicin, Romania	35	14	40
Ross U., Dominica	118	46	39
U. Autónoma Nuevo Leon, Mexico	37	14	38
U. Autónoma Guadalajara, Mexico	861	294	34
U. Autónoma Ciudad Juarez, Mex.	255	66	26
U. de Guadalajara, Mexico	35	9	26
National University of Athens, Greece	32	8	25
Universita degli Studi di Bologna, Italy	62	14	23
U. Nacional Autónoma, Mexico	34	7	21
Universidad de Sevilla, Spain	25	5	20
Católica Madre y Maestra, Dom. Rep.	68	11	16
U. Nordestana, Dom. Republic	63	10	16
Universidad de Zaragoza, Spain	49	7	18
U. Autónoma Santo Domingo, DR	90	12	13
U. Central del Este, Dom. Rep.	1139	167	13
U. Autónoma de Guerrero, Mexico	32	4	12
Aristotelian U. Thessalonika, Greece	32	3	9
Universidad de Santiago, Spain	37	2	5

ILLEGAL MEDICAL DEGREES

Very few fake school operators take the higher risk of offering fake medical degrees, although there are a handful of them sprinkled throughout chapter 25, "Degree Mills." Two of the largest operations were closed down in 1984 as a result of the F.B.I. Dip Scam operation: the Johann Keppler School of Medicine (which had operated from various addresses in Canada, Switzerland, the U.S., and Mexico), and the United American Medical College (operating from Louisiana and Florida). In both cases, the perpetrators went to prison. But the fake doctor who had been involved with both returned to the scene ten years later, apparently affiliated with a British school that purported to offer surgical training by correspondence study.

In the mid 1980s, it was discovered that two medical schools in the Dominican Republic, known as CETEC and CIFAS, were involved in selling M.D. credentials at a cost of $5,000 to $50,000. It has never been fully determined how many of the more than 5,000 M.D. degrees awarded by these two schools were genuinely earned and how many were sold to people who never attended the school.

More alarmingly, a major California university acknowledged that someone had tampered with their computer records, and had rigged the system to show that at least one unqualified person had a medical degree. Because the school did not retain any paper records whatsoever, they had no simple way to determine how many other fake medical alumni their computer claimed they had.

One man arrested and jailed as a medical-degree broker earned $1,500,000 in fees from his 165 clients, 44 of whom actually passed the foreign medical students' exam and were practicing medicine in the U.S.

Some of the fake schools listed in the chapter on diploma mills have sold medical degrees, most frighteningly sometimes under the name of legitimate schools. As recently as 1994, an Arkansas organization that advertised in *USA Today* was selling the M.D. of Stanford University, no questions asked, for under $400.

MEDICAL SCHOOL REFERRAL SERVICES

There are several services that claim they can smooth the way for Americans and others to deal with medical schools in other countries. Some also deal with dental and veterinary schools. Some apparently have a working arrangement with one particular school while others deal with a variety of schools. Here are some that have advertised regularly in the Sunday *New York Times* and elsewhere. The fees seem to range from $50 to $500 or more:

Foreign Medical Education Consultants
P. O. Box 9932, Berkeley, CA 94709 (no listed phone)

Medical Education Corporation
1655 Palm Beach Lakes Blvd., West Palm Beach, FL 33401, (305) 683-6222; 76 Orange Dr., Jericho, NY 11753, (516) 933-7448

Proven Student Service
P. O. Box 130094, Sunrise, FL 33313, (305) 748-5172

Worldwide Medical Education Institute
318 4th St., Union City, NJ 07087, (201) 867-2864

THE MEDICAL SCHOOLS

Some 60 or so foreign schools welcome students from the U.S. and other countries. Here are the ones most highly recommended by Dr. Pestana:

Faculté Libre de Médicine
Catholic University of Lille, Lille, France. Once welcomed American students through a representative in Pennsylvania. While they are no longer actively seeking American students, they assumedly know how to deal with them better than schools that never recruited.

Grenada School of Medicine
Grenada, West Indies
U.S. Office: One East Main St., Bay Shore, NY 11706-9990. Phone: (516) 665-8500 or (800) 899-6337. Fax: (516) 665-5590.

Ross University
Dominica, West Indies. U.S. office: International Educational Admissions, 460 West 34th Street, 12th Floor, New York, NY 10001. Phone: (212) 279-550; fax: (212) 629-3147.

Royal College of Surgeons
123 St. Stephen's Green, Dublin 2, Ireland. Phone: 011-353-1-478-0200. Fax: 011-353-1-478-2100. No U.S. office.

Sackler School of Medicine
University of Tel Aviv, Tel Aviv, Israel. U.S. office at 17 E. 62nd St., New York, NY 10021, (212) 688-8811. Fax is (212) 223-0368.
In Dr. Pestana's opinion, "this is without question the best foreign medical school that a U.S. citizen may attend."

Saint George's School of Medicine
Grenada, West Indies. U.S. office at One E. Main St., Bay Shore, NY 11706, (516) 665-8500.

Tuoro College/Technion University
Israel. U.S. office: Admissions Office/Biomedical Sciences, Tuoro College, Buildiong #10, 135 Carman Road, Dix Hills, NY 11746, (516) 673-3200. Fax: (516) 673-3432.

Universidad Autonoma de Guadalajara
Americans already resident in Mexico should contact the Foreign Students Office, Avenida Patria 1201, Lomas del Valle, 3A Seccion (Apartado Postal 1-440), Guadalajara, Jalisco, Mexico. Phone: 011-523-641-5051, ext. 32345.

U.S. office: 10999 IH-10 West, Suite 355, San Antonio, TX 782301356, (210) 561-9559 or (800) 531-5494. Fax: (210) 561-9562.

OTHER HEALTH-RELATED SCHOOLS

Note that most of the schools in this section are unaccredited. (Schools accredited by an unrecognized accrediting agency are listed as "unaccredited.")

American Academy of Tropical Medicine   Dip
16126 E. Warren
Detroit, MI 48224 USA
Ben Allie, M.D.
Tropical medicine
No residency, unaccredited
Nonprofit, independent $
(313) 882–0641
Offers diplomas and certificates, not degrees. The Academy is incorporated in Ohio, but since their literature indicates the work is not transferable as college credit, they are not regulated by the Ohio Board of Regents. Awards the designations of FAATH (Fellow of American Academy of Tropical Medicine) or FICTN (Fellow of International College of Tropical Medicine).

American College of Health Science
See: American Health Sciences Institute

American College of Nutripathy   B, M, D
P.O. Box 14430
Scottsdale, AZ 85251
Steven Calrow, Dean
Nutripathy, nutritional philosophy
No residency, 1976, unaccredited
$
(602) 946–5515
Offers a practical (as contrasted with theoretical) approach to the healing of body, mind, and spirit. The catalogue states that "nutripathy is the condensation of most all natural healing and counseling techniques available today [having] discarded the 'foo-foo' and kept the basic 'what works.'" Also offered: Doctor of Nutripathic Theology. The catalogue is sold for $13. Accreditation from the International Accrediting Commission for Schools, Colleges and Theological Seminaries, an unrecognized accreditor. Students "must have, or desire, an active relationship with God."

American College of Prehospital Medicine   B
365 Canal Street, Suite 2300
New Orleans, LA 70130
Richard Clinchy, Ph.D.
Emergency medical services
No residency, 1988, accredited
Proprietary $

(504) 561-6543
fax: (504) 561-6585
Bachelor of Science in emergency medical services, open to any licensed EMT professional at or above the level of EMT—Ambulance. Credit given for prior training, experience, and level of licensure. Accredited by the Distance Education and Training Council.

American Health Sciences Institute   Dip
1108 Regal Row
Austin, TX 78744
T. C. Fry
Nutritional and health sciences
No residency, 1982, unaccredited
Nonprofit, independent $
(512) 280-5566
This college awards a diploma in nutritional science on completion of 105 lessons, which takes a minimum of 48 weeks. The lessons are detailed and comprehensive presentations of the views of administrator T. C. Fry, who sees conventional medicine as "untrue in philosophy, absurd in science, in opposition to natural principles, contrary to common sense, disastrous in results, and a curse to humanity." The lessons cover diet and nutrition, mental and emotional well-being, physiology, and more. Former names: American College of Health Science, College of Life Science, and Life Science Institute.

American Holistic College of Nutrition   B, M, D
1704 11th Avenue South
Birmingham, AL 35205
Lloyd Clayton Jr., President
Nutrition
No residency, 1980s, unaccredited
Proprietary $
(205) 933–2215
The Bachelor's degree requires seven correspondence courses. The Master's requires six additional courses; the Ph.D. five more and a 30–40 page dissertation. It is possible to earn all three degrees at the same time by taking all the courses and writing the dissertation. The college no longer claims to be fully accredited. No faculty are listed. The seven-man advisory board includes two M.D.s. The president, Clayton, also purveys Dr. Clayton's herbs and homeopathics, and operates the Clayton School of Natural Healing (offering a Doctor of Naturopathy degree by correspondence) as well as Chadwick University and a computer school, although they say that the ventures are completely separate. Accreditation claimed from an unrecognized agency.

American Institute of Hypnotherapy   B, D
1805 E. Garry, #100
Santa Ana, CA 92705
Caroline Miller, Dean of Academic Studies

Hypnotherapy
No residency 1982, unaccredited
Proprietary **$$**
(714) 953–6857
Offers Bachelor's and Doctorates in hypnotherapy, entirely through correspondence study. Doctoral work involves either completion of courses and a practicum, or courses plus a final evaluation project. Tuition includes hypnotherapy certification course, and an extensive two-and-a-half-day hands-on training, presented year round at locations nationwide. Students are encouraged to finish their Ph.D. in about a year. Students and faculty are involved in hypnotherapy applications ranging from the clinical to the esoteric. The school will provide prospective students with a list of students and graduates who may be contacted. The faculty includes doctors of medicine, dentistry, and osteopathy. Authorized to grant degrees by the state of California.

Anglo-American Institute of Drugless Therapy Dip
30 Kinloch Rd.
Renfrew, Scotland
Naturopathy, osteopathy
No residency, 1911, unaccredited
Nonprofit, independent
(141) 886–3137
Until recently, this school offered a Doctorate in Naturopathy and a diploma in osteopathy entirely through correspondence study. However, due to new laws in the U.K., they are no longer allowed to grant Doctorates, and both programs now culminate in the diploma. The naturopathy program involves completing about 50 lessons by correspondence, in subjects ranging from anatomy and physiology to chiropractic and spondylotherapy (which appears to involve emptying the stomach and appendix by means of concussion, with positive effect, according to the catalog, on heart trouble, bust development, syphilis, and impotence). The Institute was established in 1911 in Indiana by a medical doctor, moved to Scotland in 1939, to England in 1948, and back to Scotland in 1977, and claims more than 7,000 graduates.

Arnould-Taylor Education, Ltd. B, M
James House, Oakelbrook Mill
Newent, Gloucestershire,
GL18 1HD England
Mrs. K. Aldridge, Managing Director
Physiatrics
No residency, 1947, unaccredited
(1531) 821875
Bachelor of Physiatrics and Master of Physiatrics, entirely through correspondence study. The course consists of seven lessons for each degree, with a paper to be written at the end of each lesson. Physiatrics is the study of body weight and its effects on psychological well-being. The senior tutor

is W. E. Arnould-Taylor. Since they are not officially empowered to grant degrees, they have apparently given themselves that right through their corporate charter. (This is legal in England.) They emphasize that the degrees are professional, not academic degrees, offered to persons already qualified in the field of physical therapy.

Bastyr College Dip
144 NE 54th Street,
Seattle, WA 98105
Russ Romans, Director of Continuing Ed.
Natural health and nutrition
Certificate, accredited
No residency
Nonprofit, independent
(206) 523-9585
1978
$$$
Bastyr awards a certificate in natural health and nutrition entirely through audio- and videotaped courses and telephone instruction; it is the only accredited school to offer such a program from a holistic perspective. The course of study is geared to healthcare professionals, employees of the natural-products industry, and interested laypeople.

California Acupuncture College D
711 S. Vermont Ave., #212
Los Angeles, CA 90025 USA
Steven Rosenblatt, President
Chinese medicine, herbal study, homeopathy
Residency, 1978, unaccredited
Nonprofit, independent **$$$**
(213) 470–9009
Campuses in Santa Barbara and San Diego. A three-year program preparing students to become practitioners of acupuncture and Oriental medicine. Courses are also offered in western sciences, herbology, and homeopathy. Authorized to grant degrees by the state of California.

California College for Health Sciences B, M
222 West 24th St.
National City, CA 91950
Judith Eberhart
Health services
1979, accredited
$$$
(619) 477-4800, (800) 221-7374
(619) 477-4360 fax
Bachelor of Science in health services management and Master of Science in community health administration and wellness promotion, entirely through home-study courses. Any course may be challenged by taking the final exam without taking the course. The program prepares health professionals to become health promotion specialists working in private industry or education. Nondegree programs are offered in wellness management, wellness program

development, and wellness counseling. The school is accredited by the Distance Education and Training Council.

Clayton School of Natural Healing
See: American Holistic College of Nutrition

College of Life Science
See: American Health Sciences Institute

Dr. Jay Scherer's Academy of Natural Healing   Dip
1443 S. St. Francis Dr.
Santa Fe, NM 87501
Steven Rosenblatt, President
Massage therapy
Residency, 1979, unaccredited
Nonprofit, independent $$
(505) 982-8398

Diploma program trains students for a career as a certified massage therapist, including qualifying them to sit for the New Mexico State Board of Massage's licensing exam. Two six-month full-time programs are offered per year. Classes meet Monday through Thursday, 9 to 5. A maximum of 26 students take the course together. An integral part of the program is a practicum and internship requiring a minimum of 80 supervised massages, all of which take place outside of class.

Dominion Herbal College   Dip
7527 Kingsway
Burnaby, British Columbia
V3N 3C1 Canada
Judy Nelson, D.C., President
Traditional herbalism
No residency, unaccredited
Proprietary $
(604) 521–5822
fax (604) 526-1561

The title of "Chartered Herbalist" is awarded to students who complete a 58-lesson correspondence course in herbalism. A Master Herbalist program, and one in clinical herbal therapy, are also offered. Summer seminars are not required but are recommended. The school seems to be well-regarded in the profession.

Donsbach University
See: International University for Nutrition Education

Emerson College of Herbology   M
582 Cummer Ave.
Willowdale, Ontario M2K 2M4 Canada
Herbology
No residency, unaccredited
(416) 733–2512
$$$

Master of Herbology title is awarded on successful completion of 33 correspondence lessons (a total of 550 pages),

covering botanic medicine, phytotherapy, pharmabotanics, and herbalism. Lessons are mailed in three at a time, graded, and returned with the next set of lessons.

Galien College of Natural Healing   Dip
B.C.M. Forest
London WC1N England
Munawar A. Kanday, Principal
Alternative healing, biochemics, education
No residency, unaccredited
$$$$

Twenty correspondence courses, each of which takes about six months to complete, in generally health-related fields (accupressure, aromatherapy, homeopathy, etc.), although Galien's offerings also include haircutting techniques, religious studies, and marketing. These credentials may offer some opportunity for misinterpretation. For instance, anyone who completes the "diploma in naturopathic medicine" course may use the initials "N.D." after their name.

Heartwood Institute   Dip
220 Harmony Lane
Garberville, CA 95442
Robert Fasic, president
Massage therapy, hypnotherapy, polarity therapy, clinical nutrition
Residency, 1977, unaccredited
Proprietary $$
(707) 923–2021
fax (707) 923-4906

Three-and nine-month residential programs for comprehensive career training in fields including addictions therapy, Swedish/Esalen massage, and alternative psychotherapy, among others. Students do their coursework "with a sensitive, talented faculty in the warmth and support of a nurturing community." Formerly known as California College of the Natural Healing Arts, an institution that awarded Bachelor's and Master's in health-related fields.

International College of Natural Health Sciences   B, M, D
100 Wigmore Street
London, W1H 0AE England
Melvyn S. Davis, Director of Education
Nutrition, homeopathy, reflexology
No residency, unaccredited
$
(171) 486–0431

Students are supplied with texts, and must pass proctored examinations. A thesis (unspecified length) is required for graduate degrees which many students will complete in less than a year. The combined B.S.-M.S.-Ph.D. program might take longer. The literature refers to the College "having the authority to confer degrees." The only possible "authority" could come from their own corporate charter, in which they give themselves the right to grant degrees. (They are "part of The Wigmore Organisation Ltd.") This sort of thing is apparently legal in England.

International University for Nutrition Education   B, M, D
1161 Bay Blvd.
Chula Vista, CA 92011
Jacob Swilling, President
Holistic nutrition
No residency, 1978, unaccredited
Nonprofit, independent $$
(619) 424-7590

The school's staff believes that the trend in medicine is away from dangerous drugs and indiscriminate surgery; instead, they teach the concepts of self-care through holistic principles, with an emphasis on nutrition. The university has its own large building, offering residential classes and conducting nutritional research. The founder, Kurt Donsbach, has his own line of vitamins and nutritional aids. Authorized to grant degrees by the state of California. Formerly Donsbach University, of Huntington Beach and Concord, California.

Life Science Institute
See: American Health Sciences Institute

Northern Institute of Massage   Dip
100 Waterloo Road
Blackpool, Lancashire, England FY4 1AW
K. Woodward
Massage
Short residency, 1924, unaccredited
$$$
(1253) 403-548

Two diploma programs are offered: a remedial massage course for students who aspire to a career in remedial massage and manipulative therapy, and a massage therapy course, which is a more general, fitness-oriented program for people who want, for example, to work in health clubs. Learning takes place through correspondence courses, with test papers due at the end of each lesson. Students must attend the school proper for practical class instruction at relevant stages in the course program, although overseas students may, in some cases, do all of their residency at once. Higher-level diploma in advanced remedial massage and manipulative therapy available to students who satisfactorily complete postgraduate training in advanced massage, with appropriate clinical experience.

Pacific School of Nutrition   Dip
1257-12 Siskiyou Blvd.
Ashland, OR 97520
Michael Megarit, Dean
Nutrition, business, herbology
No residency, unaccredited
$
(503) 770-4373

Correspondence programs leading to certification as a nutritionist or nutritionist and herbologist, through written tutorials. Those who have completed the certified nutritionist program may take a course in business and financial programs for the health professional.

Samra University of Oriental Medicine   M
2828 Beverly Blvd.
Los Angeles, CA 90057
Norman Bleicher, President
Oriental medicine, acupuncture, herbology
Residency, 1975, unaccredited
Nonprofit, independent $$$$$
(213) 487-2672;
fax (213) 487-0607

Clinical facilities to serve the needs of the community. Classes are taught day, evening, and weekends in English, Chinese, and Korean. Minimum time required to earn a degree is 36 months; all students must complete 60 semester credits of general/technical education (some of this requirement can be met with military training). Approved to grant degrees by the state of California.

School of Natural Healing   M
P.O. Box 412
Springville, UT 84663
John Christopher, President
Herbology
Short residency, unaccredited
$
(801) 489-4254

A program offering the Master of Herbology degree, largely through home-study courses, with seven-to-nine-day seminars by the school's founder, John R. Christopher.

SMAE Institute   Dip
The New Hall, Bath Road.
Maidenhead, Berks, England SL6 4LA
Michael J. Batt, FSSCh.
Physiotherapy, surgical chiropody
Short residency, 1919, unaccredited
(1628) 21100
$$$

While part of each program can be done through correspondence courses, some lectures and on-campus practical training are required. Physiotherapy program includes massage, joint manipulation, and medical electricity. It can be completed in three years, with several two-to-three-day residential sessions each year in England. The chiropody program takes about two years; the final exam must be taken in England, followed by 100 hours of practical training in the school clinic.

South Baylo University   B, M, D
12012 S. Magnolia St.

Garden Grove, CA 92641
David Park, President
Acupuncture, Oriental medicine
Residency. 1978, unaccredited
Nonprofit, independent **$$**
(714) 534–5411
Authorized to grant degrees by the state of California. Did not respond to three requests for information on their programs.

Southwest Acupuncture College   M
712 W. San Mateo
Santa Fe, NM 87501
Oriental medicine, acupuncture

Residency, unaccredited
(505) 988–3538
Three-year program leading to the M.S.O.M. degree.

Wild Rose College of Natural Healing   Dip
1220 Kensington Rd. N.W., Suite 302
Calgary, Alberta T2N 3P5 Canada
Terry L. Willard, Director
Wholistic healing, herbalism
No residency, unaccredited
(403) 270–0936
Correspondence programs leading to a Wholistic Healing Degree (WHD), or Master Herbalist certificate. Both programs require a thesis of publishable quality.

"Trust me. I'm a doctor."

Degree Mills

When you deal with a degree mill,
it is like putting a time bomb in your resumé.
It could go off at any time, with dire consequences.
JOHN BEAR

In most earlier editions of this book, the degree mill section began with the following sentence: "Degree mills have been around for hundreds of years, and they are still flourishing all over the world."

Then, for ten or more years, we were able to report that the number of currently operating phony schools significantly diminished as a result of the "DipScam" diploma-mill task force of the FBI, whose work helped secure indictments and, in most cases, convictions of a great many people who were responsible for the operation of scores of phony colleges and universities.

Unfortunately, the trend has reversed and things are getting worse again. With the winding down of DipScam in the early 1990s, and the advent of inexpensive laser printers, color copiers, overnight delivery services, 800, 888, and 500 telephone numbers, faxes, computer bulletin boards, and other accessible technology, diploma mills have made a real comeback, both in the U.S. and Europe.

There are dozens of places where one can buy Bachelor's, Master's, Doctorates, even law and medical degrees, with no questions asked, on payment of fees of anywhere from one dollar to several thousand. To demonstrate this, in September, 1994, John purchased (for $53) an extremely authentic-looking law degree (Doctor of Jurisprudence) of Harvard University, from an outfit in Florida that has been advertising nationally, complete with an 800 phone number. Transcripts were available as well. And no, we will not provide the address, or those of any other illegal schools. We have no wish to give them business. And our lawyer has advised us that we could be considered "accessories before the fact" should someone buy a fake degree and use it to defraud others. (We will, of course, cooperate with law enforcement officers and bona fide investigative reporters.)

One of the main reasons that fake schools continue to exist is that it is so very difficult to define legally exactly what is meant by the term "diploma mill" or "degree mill."

Surely any school that will send you a Ph.D. by return mail on payment of $100, no questions asked, is a fraud. But what about a school that requires a five-page dissertation before awarding the Doctorate? How about 20 pages? 50? 100? 200? Who is to say? One man's degree mill is another man's alternative university. And nobody seems to want the government stepping in to evaluate doctoral dissertations before permitting schools to grant degrees. Would you want [insert the name of your least-favorite politician] grading your thesis?

Another large gray area is the one dealing with religious schools. Because of constitutional safeguards in the U.S. guaranteeing separation of church and state, most states have been reluctant to pass any laws restricting the activities of churches—including their right to grant degrees to all who make an appropriately large donation. In many states, religious schools are not regulated, but are restricted to granting religious degrees. But in some, like Hawaii, if you established your own one-person church yesterday, you could start your university today, and award a Ph.D. in nuclear physics tomorrow.

WHY ARE DEGREE MILLS ALLOWED TO OPERATE?

The answer is that, as just indicated, it is almost impossible to write a law that will discriminate clearly between legitimate schools and mills. Any law that tries to define something that is subjective—obscenity, pornography, threatening behavior, or the quality of a school—is bound to be controversial. There can never be a quantitative means for, in effect, holding a meter up to a school and saying, "This one scores 83; it's legitimate. That one scores 62; it's a degree mill."

Also, degree mills that do not muddy their own local waters, but sell their products only in other states or other countries, are more likely to get away with it longer. A goodly number of degree mills have operated from England, selling their product only to people in other countries (primarily the U.S., Africa, and Asia). Many British authorities seem not to care as long as the only victims are foreigners, and authorities in the U.S. find it virtually impossible to take action against foreign businesses.

After decades of debating these matters (even Prince

Charles made a speech about the diploma mill problem), Britain has taken two tiny steps. Step one is to forbid unrecognized schools to call themselves a "University." However, this law had been in effect for about three minutes when England's leading diploma mill, the Sussex College of Technology, found the loophole. The law declares that it pertains to everyone enrolling after April 1, 1989. Sussex immediately began offering to backdate applications to March 31, 1989, which appears not to be illegal. It remains to be seen how long they can get away with this. Step two is to require that unrecognized schools must say in their literature that they do not operate under a Royal Charter or an Act of Parliament (the two ways schools become legitimately recognized in Britain). This, however, is unlikely even to be noticed by degree-buyers in other lands.

Other states and jurisdictions have tried to craft laws that would permit legitimate nontraditional schools to operate while eliminating degree mills. For instance, for many years California had a law that stated that the main requirement for being authorized by the state to grant degrees was ownership of $50,000 worth of real property. That law was apparently passed to eliminate low-budget fly-by-night degree mills. But $50,000 ain't what it used to be, and from the 1960s through the early 1980s, dozens of shady operators declared that their home or their book collection was worth $50,000 and proceeded to sell degrees with wild abandon.

In 1978, John had the pleasure of advising the 60 Minutes people from CBS on which California "universities" they might wish to send Mike Wallace in to expose. The proprietor of California Pacifica University was actually arrested while Wallace was interviewing him, and soon after pleaded guilty to multiple counts of mail fraud, and went off to federal prison. Two years later, California Pacifica was still listed in the state's official publication, the *Directory of California Educational Institutions*.

California, thankfully, has tightened things up considerably in the last few years, by eliminating the "authorized" category, and adding requirements that there must be elements of instruction provided by state-*approved* schools. Once again, of course, we have a law trying to define subjective matters.

In 1990, John had the further pleasure of appearing on the nationally syndicated program Inside Edition to help expose yet another major degree mill, North American University. Its proprietor, Edward Reddeck, who had previously been to prison for running another fake school, was convicted on multiple counts of mail and wire (telephone) fraud, and sent to federal prison for a few years.

Another reason for the proliferation of degree mills in the past is that the wheels of justice ground very slowly, when they ground at all. Dallas State College was shut down by authorities in Texas in 1975. The same perpetrators almost immediately opened up as Jackson State University in California. When the post office shut off their

mail there, they resurfaced with John Quincy Adams University in Oregon. It took 12 more years and a major effort by the FBI before the Dallas State perpetrators were finally brought to justice in a federal courtroom in North Carolina in late 1987, nearly two decades and millions of dollars in revenues after they sold their first Doctorate. Details shortly.

It was the entry of the FBI into the diploma mill arena that changed the rules of the game.

DIPSCAM

In the late 1970s, the Federal Bureau of Investigation launched an operation called DipScam (for Diploma Scam), which methodically investigated degree-granting institutions from coast to coast and, abroad, with some cooperation from Scotland Yard and other foreign authorities as well.

John consulted with the FBI on matters of degree mills from 1979 until 1992, when arch diploma mill exposer, Special Agent Allen Ezell, retired, and DipScam wound down.

The FBI looked into hundreds of unaccredited schools. Some were found to be harmless, innocuous, even good, and no actions were taken. When there was evidence of chicanery, a search warrant was issued, and FBI vans hauled off tons of papers and records. In many cases, but not all, a federal grand jury handed down indictments. And when they did, in many, but not all, cases the indictees pleaded guilty to mail or wire (telephone) fraud, and received fines and sentences in federal prison. When this has happened, it is described in the listing for those schools later in this chapter.

The wording of the federal grand jury indictments is quite wonderful. Here is a sample, from one indictment. (This is just a small excerpt from a thick document.)

SCHEME AND ARTIFICE: Count One: That from some unknown time prior to on or about [date] and continuing through some unknown time after [date] within the Western District of North Carolina and elsewhere in the United States, [defendants] did knowingly, intentionally, and unlawfully combine, conspire, confederate and agree with each other and with others to the Grand Jurors both known and unknown, to commit offenses against the United States, that is, having devised and intending to devise a scheme and artifice to defraud and for obtaining money by false and fraudulent pretenses, representations and promises, for the purpose of executing said scheme and artifice to defraud and attempting do so knowingly and intentionally placing and causing to be placed in a post office and an authorized depository for mail matter, and causing to be delivered by United States mail according to the direction thereon, matters and things to be sent and delivered by the

United States Postal Service, in violation of Title 18, United States Code, Sections 1341 and 2, and knowingly and intentionally transmitting and causing to be transmitted by means of wire communication in interstate commerce, certain signs, signals and sounds, to wit, interstate telephone conversations, in violation of Title 18, United States Code, Section 1343.

In other words, they sent fake degrees by mail, and made interstate phone calls to their customers.

In its earlier days, DipScam went after the fake medical schools—the most dangerous degree-sellers of all. They were quickly able to shut down the two worst perpetrators, Johann Keppler School of Medicine and the United American Medical College, and send their respective founders to prison.

DipScam's largest case came to its grand finale in a federal courthouse in Charlotte, North Carolina, in October 1987, with John present as an expert witness and observer. On trial were the seven perpetrators of a long string of degree mills, most recently including Roosevelt University, Loyola University, Cromwell University, University of England at Oxford, Lafayette University, DePaul University, and Southern California University, as well as several fake accrediting agencies.

More than 100 witnesses were called over a two-and-a-half-week period, including many who established the substantial size and scope of bank deposits and investments made by the defendants. Witnesses from Europe testified to the mail forwarding services the defendants used in England, France, Belgium, Germany, Holland, and elsewhere.

The circuslike atmosphere was not helped by the fact that Jim and Tammy Faye Bakker, Jessica Hahn, and company, were appearing in the courtroom right next door, and so the grounds of the courthouse were covered by photographers and reporters, none of whom took much interest in the DipScam trial.

Two of the minor players were dismissed by the judge for lack of definitive evidence, but the five main defendants were found guilty by the jury on all 27 counts of mail fraud, aiding and abetting, and conspiracy. They were sentenced to prison terms ranging from two to seven years.

Even though the DipScam project is no longer active, the FBI, the postal inspectors, and some crusading state agencies are still actively working to keep fake schools from operating and phony degrees from being sold.

WHY DEGREE MILLS PROSPER

The main reason—really the only reason—for the success of degree mills (and drug dealers, and pornographers) is, of course, that people keep on buying their product. They crave the degrees and somehow, despite much evidence to the contrary, they really believe that they are going to get away with it.

Unfortunately, many newspapers and magazines continue to permit the perpetrators to advertise. For years, the otherwise reputable *Psychology Today* and *New York Times* regularly ran ads for phony schools, and turned a deaf ear to the pleas of many, John included, to stop disseminating these frauds. In 1989, when the totally fraudulent University of North America began advertising in *USA Today,* he telephoned and wrote their advertising department, suggesting that they were doing their readers a disservice by running those ads. The reply, in effect, was that no one had complained (except him), so they would keep on running the ads. Several of the major diploma mills continue to use *USA Today,* as well as *The Economist* and other otherwise legitimate publications.

We must warn you, as emphatically as we can, that it is taking a very big risk to buy a fake degree, or to claim to have a degree that you have not earned. It is like putting a time bomb in your resumé. It could go off at any time, with dire consequences. The people who sell fake degrees will probably never suffer at all, but the people who buy them often suffer mightily.

In part as a result of all the publicity the FBI activities have gotten, credentials are being checked out now as never before. *Time* magazine, in an article on fake degrees (February 5, 1979), said that "with the rate at which job candidates are now fibbing on resumes and faking sheepskins, graduate schools and companies face detective work almost every time they see an application. . . . Checking up on about 12,000 inquiries a year, U.C.L.A. finds two or three frauds a week. For its part, Yale has accumulated a file of 7,000 or so bogus Old Blues."

Often people get caught when something unexpectedly good happens in their lives, and they become the focus of the news media, which love stories involving fake degrees.

DEGREE MILLS IN THE NEWS

Here is just a small sampling of the stories from our overflowing file on people who have gotten in trouble over degrees and credentials in recent years.

♦ The Chairman of the Board of a major Florida university resigned, after it became known that he had bought his degrees from an Oklahoma diploma mill. And when we put the name of the school in an earlier edition, the school's lawyers threatened to sue for 'revealing' what had been page one news in the papers. Talk about killing the messenger if you don't like the message!

♦ Two recent presidential candidates had problems over credentials claims. Joseph Biden's campaign literature "misstated" the nature of his graduate degrees, and Pat Robertson's official biography had to be changed from saying that he did "graduate study, University of London" to "studied briefly at the University of London" after the revelation he had taken only a short undergraduate seminar on art for Americans.

♦ The Superintendent of Schools for California's second largest school district lost his job and faced serious legal consequences when the Stanford Ph.D. he had claimed for years turned out to be a phony one.

♦ A popular columnist for *Forbes* magazine, Srully Blotnick, was dropped from the magazine when his Ph.D. credentials (as well as his research methodology) came under close scrutiny.

♦ Arizona's Teacher of the Year (a major honor in that state) was found to be using a Doctorate he had never earned. A $10,000 prize had to be returned.

♦ The biggest business scandal in Sweden in half a century, the Fermenta affair, was triggered when a former employee of a major industrialist, believed to be the richest man in Sweden, charged (correctly) that the industrialist had lied about possessing two Doctorates. According to *The Economist* magazine, "Fermenta's share price halved as this charge about bogus qualifications spread." A billion-dollar deal with Volvo was canceled in the wake of the scandal.

♦ During the New York City parking meter scandals, one of the government's star witnesses, according to the *Daily News,* "admitted he has a bogus Doctorate from Philathea College. . . ."

♦ In 1985, Congressman Claude Pepper convened a congressional panel, which asserted that more than 500,000 Americans have obtained false credentials or diplomas. (Pepper's staff got him a Ph.D. from Union University. All "Dr. Pepper" allegedly had to do was submit four book reports, which his staff wrote for him.)

♦ As a result of accumulating over 7,000 "client" names from its diploma mill raids, the FBI identified more than 200 federal employees, including 75 in the Defense Department, with bogus degrees.

♦ Congressman Ron Wyden of Oregon said that as many as 40,000 physicians who failed their qualifying exams may nonetheless be practicing medicine.

♦ According to *Sports Illustrated,* the owner of the Indianapolis Colts, Robert Irsay, made the "frequent boast that he played Big Ten football at the University of Illinois, while getting a degree in electrical engineering." The magazine says he neither played football nor earned a degree.

♦ A fake degree scandal rocked Indonesia, with the revelation that a war hero turned businessman was bilked of huge sums of money by an executive of his shipping line, who had been hired because of his Doctorate in economics from a U.S. degree mill, Thomas Edison College of Florida and Arkansas (not the legitimate one in New Jersey).

♦ And even in Russia . . . one Alexander Shavlokhov was arrested for selling at least 56 fake degrees of the Gorky Agricultural Institute, at 1,000 rubles each, to industrialists around the country. (Note: Russia refuses to allow us to advertise this book in that country; they say there is no need for it.)

TWO OTHER INSIDIOUS ACADEMIC FRAUDS

In addition to those who sell fake degrees, there are two other "services" that undermine the academic establishment.

One is the so-called "lost diploma replacement service." If you tell them you had a legitimate degree but lost it, they will replace it for a modest fee. That's why John has a Harvard "Doctor of Neurosurgery" diploma hanging on his wall (next to his real Michigan State one). The Harvard phony sold for $49.95. When the FBI raided one such service, in Oregon (they had been advertising in national publications), they found thousands of blank diplomas from hundreds of schools—and records showing an alarmingly large number of clients.

The other is term paper and dissertation writing services. Several of them put out catalogues listing over a thousand already written term papers they will sell, and if they don't have what you want, they will write anything from a short paper to a major dissertation for you, for a $7 to $10 a page.

HOW THIS CHAPTER HAS CHANGED

Earlier editions used to include all those schools that John regarded as diploma mills, religious and otherwise. The problem with this approach was that many of the schools were, in fact, operating legally, either because they were church-run, or because they were in locations with few or no laws regulating schools. Until 1985, for instance, Arizona had no laws whatsoever regulating universities and degrees, and so a good many degree mills operated from that state. Now, every state but Hawaii has some form of law regulating or registering or approving or accrediting colleges and universities. Some states are very thorough in their licensing process; others have little or no evaluative process, but simply register any school that applies for registration.

Long ago, this chapter also used to give the addresses of the degree mills. We've become convinced that this served no legitimate or useful purpose, so the detailed addresses have been deleted, and we will not supply them if you write to us.

Finally, there are a handful of schools that we firmly believe are diploma mills, but we do not have sufficient proof to say so in print, and we do not enjoy being sued. These schools have been listed among the regular schools, generally with descriptions that are less than wonderful, but factual.

Some of these borderline institutions were written about in a major series of articles that appeared in the Arizona *Republic* a few years ago. The *Republic* received many threats from lawyers and aggrieved school operators, but was never sued over their series. The articles have been reprinted in a booklet called *Diploma Mills: The Paper Merchants.* The booklet is out of print. If you can't find it in a library, we can make you a photocopy for $10 (includes first class postage). Write to John Bear, P. O. Box 7070, Berkeley, CA 94707. But don't buy this expecting to get the addresses of the mills; they aren't there either.

THE DIPLOMA MILLS

"E&T" stands for *Education & Training*, a British magazine that used to report regularly on European and other degree mills. "COE" stands for the Council of Europe, an intergovernmental agency based in Strasbourg, France, which keeps track of what they believe are degree mills in Europe and elsewhere. At press time, we read in the London *Times Higher Education Supplement* that the University Grants Commission of India had just released a list of 125 "fake universities" that have arisen in India in recent years. We hope to obtain that list in order to list these places in subsequent printings.

Academy College of Holy Studies Sheffield, England. Identified as a degree mill by E&T.

Academy of the Science of Man See: University of the Science of Man

Accademia di Studi Superiori Minerva Milan, Italy. Identified as a degree mill by COE. However, the courts decided otherwise. In District Court of Fiorenzuola d'Arda in 1958, one Amorosa d'Aragona Francesco was brought to trial for using a degree from this school. The court apparently ruled that the school may not be great but it is legal. It moved from Bari to Milan a few years later, and then went out of business.

Accademia di Studi Superiori Phoenix Bari, Italy. Identified as a degree mill by COE. Very likely the same as the school listed above.

Accademia Universale de Governo Cosmo-Astrosofica-Libero de Psico-Biofisica Trieste, Yugoslavia. Identified as a degree mill by COE. Can you imagine what their school cheers sound like?

Accademia Universitaria Internazionale Rome, Italy. Identified as a degree mill by E&T.

Adams Institute of Technology See: National Certificate Company

Addison State University Ottawa, Canada. Bachelor's, Master's, and Doctorates in almost any field but medical or dental are sold for about $30.

Alabama Christian College See: R/G Enterprises. No connection with a legitimate school of this name in Montgomery, Alabama.

Albany Educational Services Northampton, England. Offers to act as an agent to obtain American Bachelor's, Master's, and Doctorates for a fee of $150 to $250. Letters to the director, L. W. Carroll, asking which schools he represents, have not been answered.

Albert Einstein Institut Zurich, Switzerland. Sells the phony degrees of Oxford Collegiate Institute (of the International University). One of the many fake degree operations of Karl Xavier Bleisch.

American College in Switzerland Berne, Switzerland. Totally phony Doctorates are offered by yet another of "Professor Doctor" Karl Xavier Bleisch's degree mills. Affiliations with Georgetown University and with the University of Florida are falsely claimed in this school's literature.

American Extension School of Law Chicago, Illinois. Identified as a degree mill by COE.

American Institute of Science Indianapolis, Indiana. Identified as a degree mill by COE.

American Institute of Technology See: Bureau for Degree Promotions.

American International Academy New York and Washington. Identified as a degree mill by COE.

American International University Established in California in the 1970s by Edward Reddeck (who was convicted of mail fraud for a previous diploma mill operation, and later went to prison for his University of North America using Missouri, Utah and Hawaii addresses). His employee, Clarence Franklin, left to establish American National University, and was later indicted by a federal grand jury. Degrees of all kinds were sold for $1,600 to $2,500, whether or not the required eight-page dissertation was written. No longer in operation. American International resurfaced briefly in 1987, using a Kansas City, Missouri, address which was a mail forwarding service.

American Legion University U.S. location unknown. Identified as a degree mill by E&T.

American Management Institute See: International Universities Consortium.

American Medical College (Burma) Rangoon, Burma. Identified as a degree mill by COE.

American Medical College (Idaho) Nampa, Idaho. Doctor of Medicine degrees have been awarded by this apparently nonexistent school. A student there (with a diploma mill undergraduate degree) provided what appears to be a letter from the Idaho superintendent of public instruction confirming that the school is appropriately registered with his office. There is no listed telephone for them in Nampa.

American National University Phoenix, Arizona. The university was established by Clarence Franklin, a California chiropractor formerly associated with American International University who was subsequently indicted by a federal grand jury for operating this school. Degrees were offered on payment of fees in the vicinity of $2,000. Accreditation was claimed from the National Accreditation Association, which had been established by Franklin and a colleague in Maryland. Apparently stopped operations in 1983 or 1984. Franklin was convicted of violation of federal law a few years later. A new and unrelated American National University was authorized in California in 1987.

American School of Metaphysics Location unknown. Identified as a degree mill by COE.

American University San Diego, California. Degrees of all kinds were offered on payment of a fee of $1,500 to $2,500. The claim was made that all degrees were "registered with the government" in Mexico, where the school was allegedly located. No longer in business.

American West University See: California Pacifica University. One of the many fake schools of Ernest Sinclair.

American Western University Operated from a mail drop in Tulsa, Oklahoma, in the early 1980s by Anthony Geruntino of Columbus, Ohio, who later went to federal prison for this school and his next venture, Southwestern University. American Western's mail delivery was stopped in late 1981 by the U.S. Postal Service, at which time a new address was utilized. Affiliated schools included the National College of Arts and Sciences, Northwestern College of Allied Science, Regency College, and Saint Paul's Seminary.

Amritsar University Amritsar, India. Identified as a degree mill by COE.

Anglo-American College of Medicine See: National College

Anglo-American Institute of Drugless Medicine See: National College

Aquinas University of Scholastic Philosophy New York. Identified as a degree mill by E&T.

Argus University Fairplay, Colorado. A fictitious university formed apparently just for fun in 1977. Its stated purpose is selling Doctorates to dogs and their humans. The founder writes that Argus "will confer a degree to any dog whose owner sends a check for $5 to Argus University." Same fee for humans, apparently.

Arya University Srinigar, India. Identified as a degree mill by COE.

Atlanta Southern University Atlanta, Georgia. See: California Pacifica University. Another of Ernest Sinclair's degree mills. The president of a large respectable university used to tell people his degree was from Atlanta Southern; he doesn't any more.

Atlantic Northeastern University Their address in New York was a mail forwarding service. They offered all degrees, using well-designed and printed promotional materials, almost identical to those used by Pacific Northwestern and Atlantic Southern universities. Fake (but realistic-looking) transcripts were available for an additional fee. Apparently no longer in business.

Atlantic Southern University Operated briefly from addresses in Atlanta, Georgia, and Seattle, Washington. The materials look identical to those of Pacific Northwestern University. Newspaper publicity in 1980 apparently caused them to cease operations.

Atlantic University New York. As a promotional gimmick once, Atlantic Monthly magazine offered an honorary Doctorate from Atlantic University to new subscribers. A harmless gag, perhaps, but we have now seen two instances in which Atlantic University appeared on a job-application resumé.

Australian Institute See: Bureau for Degree Promotions

Avatar Episcopal University London, England. Identified as a degree mill by E&T.

Avatar International University London, England. Identified as a degree mill by COE.

Ben Franklin Academy and Institute For Advanced Studies Washington, D. C. They offered Bachelor's, Master's, and Doctorates through correspondence study. "Deserving Americans" could request honorary Doctorates, which required a donation. They claimed to be "not just another degree mill, but a fully accredited degree-granting institution." The accreditation was from the American Association of Accredited Colleges and Universities which we could never locate. The former address (P.O. Box 1776) and former phone number (USA-1776) were the best part; at least it shows they had influence somewhere in Washington.

Benchley State University See: LTD Documents

Benson University Same management as Laurence University of Hawaii.

Bettis Christian University Arkansas. In the mid 1980s, Ph.D.'s were sold for $800 by two inmates of the Arkansas State Prison. Another instance of a "University Behind Walls."

Beulah College Nigeria and Texas. In 1990, offered to award an honorary Doctor of Humanities to anyone sending them $500.

Bible University Ambuhr, North Arcot, India. Identified as a degree mill by COE.

Bonavista University Douglas, Wyoming. All degrees were sold for fees of $500 to $700. Other Bonavista literature had been mailed from Sandy, Utah, and Wilmington, Delaware. No longer in business, at least at those locations.

Bosdon Academy of Music See: ORB

Boston City College See: Regency Enterprises

Bradford University Same management as Laurence University of Hawaii.

Brantridge Forest School See: Sussex College of Technology

Bretton Woods University New Hampshire. Diplomas of this alleged institution have been sold for $15 by a "collector of elite unit militaria" who says they were "obtained through various unknown third parties . . . Some are original unawarded certificates, while others could be reproductions."

British College of Soma-Therapy England. Identified as a degree mill by E&T.

British Collegiate Institute London, England. They used to sell degrees of all kinds for a fee of $100 to $300, through the London address, and an agent in Inman, Kansas. The provost was listed as Sir Bernard Waley, O.B.E., M.A., D.Litt. See also: College of Applied Science, London.

Broadhurst University See: West London College of Technology

Brownell University Degrees of this "University that does not now exist" were sold for $10, both by Associated Enterprises of Jacksonville, Florida, and Universal Data Systems of Tustin, California. An extra $5 bought a "professional lettering kit" so you could add any name and date you wish. School rings, decals, and stationery were sold as well. Since the sellers in Tustin (apparently two schoolteachers) slammed the door on a 60 Minutes crew some years ago, the degrees have apparently not been sold.

Brundage Forms Georgia. Brundage sells blank forms for all purposes. His college-degree form, which you can fill in yourself, costs less than a dollar. His motto is "No advice, just forms." Our motto is: "You can get in just as much trouble with a phony 50¢ Doctorate as with a phony $3,000 Doctorate."

Buckner University Texas. All degrees, including some in medicine, were sold for $45 each. They claim there is a real Buckner in Texas. There isn't. The literature says, "We believe this modestly-priced yet extremely impressive document will give you great enjoyment, prestige, and potential profitability." It is also likely to give you the opportunity to meet some nice people from your district attorney's office. The degrees were sold by University Press of Houston, and by Universal Data Systems of Tustin, California (which also sold Brownell and other fake diplomas).

Bureau for Degree Promotions Holland. Sells the fake degrees of Addison State University, Atlantic Southeastern University, the Australian Institute, American Institute of Technology, and International University of India for $50 to $100, and knighthoods at $500.

Calgary College of Technology Calgary, Canada. One of Canada's most ambitious degree mills offered the Bachelor's, Master's, and Doctorate for fees up to $275. The literature included a lengthy profile of the dean, Colonel R. Alan Munro, "Canada's premier Aeronaut." A recent book of heraldry lists "Colonel the Chevalier Raymond Allen Zebulon Leigh Munro, C.M., G.C.L.J., C.L., K.M.L.J., S.M.L.J., A.D.C., C.O.I., C.O.F., M.O.P., B.S.W., M.H.F., LL.B., M.A., LL.D., D.Sc.A., C.D.A.S., F.R.S.A., F.S.A. Scot, A.F.C.A.S.I., C.R.Ae.S., A.F.A.I.A.A., M.A.H.S., M.C.I.M., M.C.I.M.E." Could this be the same person? The Calgary catalog even included a telephone number. That phone was answered, "Spiro's Pizza Parlor." Truly. Could "Ph.D." stand for "Pizza, Home Delivery"?

California Christian College See: R/G Enterprises

California Institute of Behavior Sciences California. Humorous but well-designed Doctorates were awarded, at least in the 1960s, with the title of Doctor of Image Dynamics, citing "mastery of Machiavellian Manipulations . . . discovery of the failsafe Success Mechanism, and the fail un-safe Failure Mechanism . . . ."

California Institute of Higher Learning See: London Institute for Applied Research

California Pacifica University Hollywood, California. Widely advertised degree mill operated by Ernest Sinclair. Degrees from California Pacifica or almost any other school one wanted were sold for $3,500. The slick catalog showed photos of faculty and staff, all fictitious. Sinclair was the main subject of a CBS 60 Minutes exposé in April 1978. He pleaded guilty to three of the 36 counts on which he was arrested. While his trial was on, he opened yet another fake school, Hollywood Southern University. Sinclair's advertising was regularly accepted by the New York *Times* and other major publications. Two years after he was arrested, California Pacifica was still listed in the official California directory of authorized schools! Sinclair once sued John for $4 million for calling his degree mill a degree mill, but he went to prison before we went to trial. One report had it that he continued to sell degrees while in federal prison—if true, the first known instance of a "University Behind Walls" program.

Canadian Temple College of Life of the International Academy Burnaby, British Columbia, Canada. Identified as a degree mill by COE.

Capital College See: National Certificate Company

Cardinal Publishing Company Florida. They publish a variety of fake diploma forms and blanks.

Carlton University Same management as Laurence University (Hawaii).

Carnegie Institute of Engineering See: Regency Enterprises

Carolina Institute of Human Relations Sumter, South Carolina. Identified as a degree mill by COE.

Carroll Studios Illinois. Since 1988, they have been selling "College Diploma" forms for $2 each, in which the buyer must letter not only his or her own name but the name of the school and degree earned. Two dollars also buys you a marriage certificate, a birth certificate, a divorce certificate, and, if devastated by all of the above, a last will and testament.

Central Board of Higher Education India. Identified as a degree mill by COE.

Central School of Religion England, the U.S., Australia. Identified as a degree mill by E&T.

Central States Research Center Ontario, Canada. They sold well-printed fake diplomas "in memory of famous names." The samples they sent out included Christian College, the Ohio Psychological Association, and Sussex College of Technology. Another address in Columbus, Ohio.

Central University See: National Certificate Company

Charitable University of Delaware Identified as a degree mill by E&T.

Chartered University of Huron Identified as a degree mill by COE.

Chicago Medical College Fort Pierce, Florida. Their literature says that "Your beautiful 11 x 15 graudate [sic]

diploma is printed on the finest sturdy parchtone . . . . It will add prestige and beauty to your office." Or cell. The price of their medical degree is a mere $450.

Chillicothe Business College Ohio. Identified as a degree mill by E&T.

Chirological College of California Identified as a degree mill by COE.

Christian College See: Central State Research Center

Christian Fellowship Foundation See: Lawford State University

City Medical Correspondence College London, England. Identified as a degree mill by E&T.

Clayton Theological Institute California (the address appears to be a private home). Their Doctorate was awarded on completion of a dissertation of at least 25 words and a fee of $3. When this was done (John's dissertation was 27 words; he worked extra hard), he got a nice letter saying that he had indeed been awarded their Doctorate, but if he wanted the actual diploma, it would cost $50 more. Recent letters to the institute have been returned as undeliverable.

Clemson College See: R/G Enterprises

Clinton University Livonia, Michigan. For years, they sold fake degrees of all kinds for $25 and up, offering "a masterpiece so perfect, it absolutely defies detection." Mail to their address is now returned as undeliverable.

Coast University Another name for Gold Coast University; see them later in this chapter.

Colgate College See: R/G Enterprises

College of Applied Science London London, England. The college exists on paper only, but, like Brigadoon, it was real (well, almost real) for one day. As reported by a German magazine, a wealthy German industrialist bought a fake Doctorate from this place, and insisted that it be presented in person. The president, "Commander Sir" Sidney Lawrence enlisted the aid of his friend, "Archbishop" Charles Brearly, who runs several fake universities in Sheffield. They rented a fancy girls' school for the day, installed carpets and candelabra, and rented costumes for their friends, who dressed up as "counts hung around with medals, an abbess in a trailing robe . . . and the knights of the Holy Grail." The German arrived in a Rolls Royce, and received his degree in an impressive ceremony, which only cost him $15,000. Sir Sidney, incidentally, appends a rubber stamp to his letters saying, "Hon. Attorney General U.S.A."

College of Divine Metaphysics England. Identified as a diploma mill by E&T.

College of Franklin and Marshall See: Regency Enterprises

College of Hilton Head See: University of East Georgia

College of Hard Knocks See: USSI

College of Homeopathy Missouri. Identified as a diploma mill by E&T.

College of Journalism West Virginia. Identified as a diploma mill by E&T.

College of Life Florida. Honorary Doctorates were sold for $2, but the school has since gone away.

College of Natural Therapeutics See: International University

College of Naturatrics Missouri. Identified as a diploma mill by E&T.

College of Nonsense Nevada. "You can fool your friends and tell them you have a Doctorate degree. If they don't believe you, you can show your friends your Doctor degree." John bought a Doctor of Politics for $2. A Doctor of Martyrism, Cheerleading, or Nose Blowing would have been 50¢ extra. Silly stuff, but a better-printed diploma than many legitimate schools provide.

College of Spiritual Sciences England. Identified as a diploma mill by E&T.

College of Universal Truth Chicago, Illinois. Identified as a diploma mill by E&T.

Collegii Romanii See: International Honorary Awards Committee

Collegium Technologicum Sussexensis Britannia See: Sussex College of Technology

Colorado Christian University Subject of a landmark court case in which the state of New York successfully sued to prevent them from selling their degrees to New Yorkers, or to advertise in publications distributed from New York. No connection whatever with the accredited Rockmont College, which changed its name in 1989 to Colorado Christian University.

Columbia School Unknown U.S. location. Identified as a diploma mill by COE.

Columbia State University A currently-active diploma mill, using a mail forwarding and telephone answering service in Louisiana, but run by a man named Ronald Pellar (using the alias of "Douglas Ford") from southern California. Columbia State claims to be fully accredited (from a non-existent agency). They used to claim that Jonas Salk was an alumnus, until Salk protested; now they list other famous scientists, who clearly have never heard of this "school." Pellar, using the name "Herald Crenshaw," has published a book that looks very much like an earlier edition of this one, and indeed is largely copied from ours, but which identifies Columbia State as the best university in the United States (and, for good measure, identifies the quite legitimate Greenwich University, with which John was once associated, as the worst university in the United States). In 1994, Pellar managed, by a clever ruse, to steal the mailing list of recent buyers of this book. Those people were sent a newsletter from "U.S. Official Publications," in which Pellar, now using the alias "Edward Connelly," spent eight pages attacking this book (which he called a "brochure") and John Bear. Needless to say there is no such organization as "U.S. Official Publications." In 1995, we learned that Pellar used to be known as Doctor Dante, who was a well-known television hypnotist in the '50s, briefly married Lana Turner, served a prison term for attempted murder, and has, according to the Federal Trade Commission, operated a wide variety of scams under at least 40 aliases. John is often asked why he does not sue Pellar. Even though two lawyers advised that this was the clearest case of libel they'd ever seen, the cost of mounting a proper suit could easily reach six figures, and the probability of collecting a dime from this probably-75-year-old scoundrel following a courtroom victory is small.

Commercial University Delhi, India. Listed as a degree mill by COE. The Ministry of Education writes that it is a "coaching institution" whose degrees are "not recognised for any purpose." However a reader in Malaysia maintains that their B.Com. degree exam is comparable to those of University of London, and that at least one graduate has had his degree accepted by the Malaysian government.

Commonwealth School of Law Washington. Identified as a diploma mill by COE.

Commonwealth University California. Degrees of this nonexistent school were sold by mail for $40. Also sold by the same firm: Eastern State University.

Constantinia University In 1989, a mailing went out to Italian businessmen, offering them the opportunity to earn a doctorate from this apparently nonexistent school, in association with the accredited Johnson & Wales University (which denied any knowledge of the scheme). For $3,000, they would spend a week in New York, see Niagara Falls, and go home with a Doctorate. According to one source in Italy, more than 100 people signed up.

Continental University In 1990, a reader in Japan sent us a copy of a diploma (dated 1989) from the nonexistent school, allegedly in Los Angeles.

Cranmer Hall Theological College Identified as a diploma mill by E&T.

Creative University of Southeast London London, England. Identified as a diploma mill by E&T.

Cromwell University London, England. This diploma mill was one of many run for years by the Fowler family of Chicago, five of whom were sentenced to prison in late 1987 for these activities. Cromwell sold degrees of all kinds for $730, through a mail forwarding service. Accreditation was claimed from the nonexistent Western European Accrediting Society of Liederbach, West Germany.

Dallas State College Dallas, Texas. One of the first heavily advertised diploma mills, Dallas State flourished in the early 1970s under the guidance of at least one of the Fowler family of Chicago. In 1975, the attorney general of Texas permanently enjoined Dallas State from operating in that state.

Darthmouth College See: Regency Enterprises

De Paul University Paris, France. A diploma mill operated for years by the Fowler family, from a mail forwarding service in Paris. Operations ceased following five Fowlers' sentencing to prison in 1987. Degrees of all kinds were sold for $550, and accreditation was claimed from

the Worldwide Accrediting Commission, allegedly of Cannes, France. Other addresses used in Clemson, South Carolina, and Santa Monica, California.

Delaware Law School Identified as a diploma mill by E&T and we're sorry the people at the genuine Delaware Law School of Widener University are upset that we mention this, but don't blame us when diploma mill operators choose to use the same name as a legitimate school.

Diplomatic State University See: R/G Enterprises

Diplomatic University See: National Certificate Company

Earl James National University College Toronto, Canada. Identified as a diploma mill by COE.

Eastern Missouri Business College The nonexistent school established by the Attorney General of Missouri, in a sting operation. During its one day of existence, the head of the International Accrediting Commission for Schools, Colleges and Theological Seminaries visited the one-room office in St. Louis, overlooked the fact that the school had officers named Peelsburi Doobuoy and Wonarrmed Mann, overlooked the fact that the marine biology text was The Little Golden Book of Fishes, did not overlook the accreditation "fee" he was handed, and duly accredited the school, which disappeared forever the next day.

Eastern Orthodox University India. Identified as a diploma mill by COE.

Eastern State University See: Commonwealth University

Eastern University See: National Certificate Company

Ecclesiastical University of Sheffield See: University of Sheffield

Elysion College They used to offer degrees from various addresses in California, although the proprietor was in Mexico. Several book reports or essays and $500 were required to earn the degree. When the proprietor died, his daughter continued the operation from her home in San Francisco. She told authorities she was not operating the school, but an FBI analysis of her garbage revealed that she was, and after her indictment by a federal grand jury, and her guilty plea, Elysion College faded away.

Emerson University California. Identified as a diploma mill by COE.

Empire College of Ophthalmology Canada. Identified as a diploma mill by COE.

Episcopal University of London London, England. Identified as a diploma mill by E&T.

Episcopal University of Saint Peter Port Frankfurt, Germany. Identified as a diploma mill by E&T.

Études Universitaires Internationales Leichtenstein, Luxembourg. Identified as a diploma mill by COE.

Eugenia Institute of Metaphysics See: ORB

European College of Science and Man Sheffield, England. Identified as a diploma mill by E&T.

Evaluation and Management International Inglewood,

California. These folks have sent out a three-page, unsigned letter saying that on receipt of $2,100 they will arrange for the degree of your choice to be issued to you. They require 50 percent down before they reveal the name of the school that is to be your alma mater. Can anyone ever have fallen for this?

Evergreen University In 1989, large ads appeared in civil service and other newspapers, offering the degrees of this school, allegedly in Los Angeles. By the time we learned of it, just a month after the ads ran, the three phone numbers had all been disconnected, and mail was returned as undeliverable.

Faraday College England. Identified as a diploma mill by E&T.

Felix Adler Memorial University Charlotte, North Carolina. Identified as a diploma mill by E&T.

Florida State Christian College Fort Lauderdale, Florida. They used to advertise nationally the availability of Bachelor's, Master's, Doctorates, and honorary Doctorates, until both the postal service and the state of Florida acted to shut them down. They also operated Alpha Psi Omega, a professional society for psychological counselors.

Forest Park University Chicago, Illinois. Identified as a diploma mill by COE.

Four States Cooperative University Texas. Identified as a diploma mill by COE.

Franklin University Same management as Laurence University (Hawaii).

Geo-Metaphysical Institute New York. "Here's a great way to get instant status," said their national advertising, offering an ornate personalized and totally phony honorary Doctorate in geo-metaphysics for $5.

George Washington University California. They arose in 1995, selling honorary doctorates and professorships in the non-extent university, for "donations" between $3,000 and $7,000. All literature is in German, where the "university" is advertised, and such things are popular.

Georgia Christian University Georgia. The first pyramid scheme diploma mill. When you "graduate" (buy a degree), you become a professor and can sell degrees to others. When your students buy degrees and become professors, you become a dean and share in their profits, and so on, up the academic ladder.

German-American Dental College Chicago, Illinois. Identified as a diploma mill by COE.

Gold Coast University Hawaii. Opened by Edward Reddeck, previously imprisoned for operating other diploma mills. Later changed to Coast University. Although Hawaii authorities showed no interest, federal authorities closed the "school" in 1992 after Reddeck was indicted on many counts of mail fraud and conspiracy. He was convicted on all 22 counts in early 1993, and returned to prison.

Golden State University Operated from California and Colorado in the 1950s and 1960s. Exposed as a degree mill on Paul Coates's television program in 1958. No connection with the legitimate school of the same name that opened in 1979.

Gordon Arlen College England. Identified as a diploma mill by E&T.

Gottbourg University of Switzerland See: ORB

Graduate University See: National Certificate Company

Great Lakes University Higgins Lake, Michigan. One of several degree mills operated by W. (for Wiley!) Gordon Bennett. Degrees were sold for $200. Also used addresses in Dearborn and Berkley, Michigan, and Chicago.

Gulf Southern University Louisiana. The literature is identical to that used by several other mills, such as Pacific Northwestern and Atlantic Northeastern. Degrees were sold for $45 to anyone but Louisiana residents.

Hamburger University This is the training school for McDonalds, and they award the Doctor of Hamburgerology to graduates. Of course it's not a diploma mill; in fact, it has even been licensed to grant real Associate's degrees. But we are mentioning it here because we are convinced that anything that can be misused will be misused (see Atlantic University, above, for instance).

Hamilton State University Arizona. Sold degrees for $50 or less. The fake diploma says they are in Clinton, New York, home of the old and respectable Hamilton College. See also: Regency Enterprises and R/G Enterprises.

Hancock University, Tennessee. Arose briefly in 1995, with ads in USA Today, selling honorary degrees of all kinds, but after a month or so, they were no longer there.

Harley University London, England. John found the university in a tiny corner of the London College of Beauty Therapy. The salon receptionist was the university registrar. Ph.D. degrees were awarded on completion of a dissertation of less than 20 pages. The co-proprietor of Harley U. (who refused to tell us the source of his own Ph.D.) wrote that "the details in your booklet are totally untrue in every respect." The detailed questions then put to him in our reply to that letter were never answered. Harley University apparently is no more. Its proprietor later established Saint Giles University College and Somerset University.

Hartford Technical Institute See: Regency Enterprises

Hirshfeld College See: USSI

His Majesty's University of Polytechnics Sacramento, California. Used to sell honorary Doctorates in all subjects (but "no profanities or obscenities") for all of $5. But the "university" closed down many years ago, so please stop trying to write to them, so the former proprietor won't have to write us any more annoyed letters.

Hollywood College California. Identified as a diploma mill by E&T.

Hollywood Southern University See: California Pacifica University

Holy Toledo University American Educational Publishers has invented the delightful and humorous Doctorates of Holy Toledo U., offering the Doctor of Philosophy in Adorableness, Defrosting, Worrying, and other fields. They are nicely designed (the gold seal says, in small type, "My goodness how impressive!") and sold for $12 a dozen.

Honoré College See: ORB

Humberman University College Identified as a diploma mill by E&T.

Idaho College of Commerce See: International Universities Consortium.

Illinois State University See: Regency Enterprises

Imperial Philo-Byzantine University Madrid, Spain. Identified as a diploma mill by COE.

Independence University Missouri. Flourished in the late 1970s, offering degrees by correspondence, until exposés in the *Chronicle of Higher Education* and a Chicago newspaper helped close them down. The *Chicago Tribune* reported that the headmaster of a prestigious Chicago private school resigned "after disclosures that he was using the office there as a center of activity for the diploma mill." A community college president in Chicago subsequently lost his job for using an Independence Doctorate. There apparently is also a humorous and unrelated Independence University, offering realistic-looking diplomas from its School of Hard Knocks, and signed by "A. Harry World."

Independent Study Programs, Inc. Missouri. Degrees of all kinds sold in the late 1970s. No longer there.

Independent Universal Academy See: Independent University of Australia

Independent University of Australia Morwell, Victoria, Australia. Identified as a diploma mill by E&T. However, we are persuaded by material sent by persons familiar with the school that it was a legitimate and sincere attempt to establish an alternative university over the constant objections of the educational establishment. It survived from its founding in 1972 until the death of founder Ivan Maddern. Name changed to Independent Universal Academy after the government forbade use of the word "university."

Indiana State University See: Regency Enterprises

Institut Patriarcal Saint Irenée Beziers, France. Granted honorary Doctorates to the founder's American colleagues and perhaps others. See: Inter-State College.

Institute of Excellence Florida. All degrees, including medical and dental, at $10 each. The fake diplomas are very poorly printed, and say, in small type, "for novelty purposes only."

Inter-American University (Italy) Rome, Italy. Identified as a diploma mill by COE.

Inter-State College England, France. Established by Karl Josef Werres, granting honorary Doctorates from England. One of the recipients claims that the college is "legally chartered" to do this, but all that means is that in their corporate charter, they give themselves the right. See also: Institut Patriarcal Saint Irenée.

Intercollegiate University Incorporated in Kansas before World War II. As American Mercury reported, "Intercollegiate specialized in hanging its M.A. on some of England's minor men of God—for $50; and for a few dollars more, it was willing to bestow a dazzling D.C.L. Before the war this had grown into a roaring and profitable trade, but when wartime law prohibited sending money out of England, the Intercollegiate professors were obliged to suspend their work of international enlightenment."

Internation University U.S. Identified as a diploma mill by E&T.

International Academy for Planetary Planning See: International Honorary Awards Committee

International American University Rome, Italy. Identified as a diploma mill by COE.

International College of Associates in Medicine Texas. Used to offer a Ph.D. and a Doctor of Medical Letters on payment of modest fees.

International Honorary Awards Committee California. They sold a wide range of Doctorates and other awards, mostly for $100 or less. The well-designed doctoral diplomas come from Collegii Romanii, the International Academy for Planetary Planning, Two Dragon University, and the Siberian Institute. One can also buy diplomatic regalia including the Grand Cross of the Imperial Order of Constantine and the Sovereign Order of Leichtenstein, complete with rosettes, medals, and sashes. The late Francis X. Gordon, founder of all these establishments, had a delightful sense of humor about his work. His widow apparently carried it on.

International Protestant Birkbest College England. Identified as a diploma mill by E&T.

International Universities Consortium Missouri. In 1989, help-wanted ads appeared in the academic press, soliciting faculty for a consortium of nontraditional schools. Being the suspicious sort, John fabricated a resume of the most outrageous sort, under an assumed name, and submitted it. Shortly thereafter, his nom de plume was appointed to the faculty of what was alleged to be a group of eight "universities"—one a long-established diploma mill (London School for Social Research), one a school we have been suspicious about for years (Northern Utah University), and six new ones, characterized by the common theme that they do not appear to exist (no listed phones). They are: Southwestern University (allegedly in New Mexico), St. Andrews University (allegedly in Baha [sic] California, Mexico), Northwestern Graduate Institute (allegedly Montana), University of the West (allegedly Wyoming), Idaho College of Commerce (allegedly Idaho), and American Management Institute (no location given). Northern Utah actually issued a catalog, complete with the "faculty" names of all those boobs who answered the ad and signed up to be on the staff, no questions asked. But the address and phone numbers in the catalog are not working. Consortium president Warren H. Green writes that the whole scheme, which he defends as completely legitimate, has been canceled.

International University (Greece) Athens, Greece. The literature claims that the Doctorates are nonacademic, but nonetheless fully recognized as educational and professional degrees by the republic of Greece. The embassy of Greece has written to us that this is not a correct statement. The president is listed as a "Right Reverend Bishop Doctor," who later established a 'university' in Louisiana. There apparently was, at least at one time, an affiliation with International University of Missouri.

International University (India) Degrees of this institution are sold for $50 to $100 each by the Bureau for Degree Promotion in Holland.

International University (Louisiana) Louisiana. Opened in the early 1980s, offering degrees of all kinds. Accreditation was claimed from the North American Regional Accrediting Commission, which we have never been able to locate. Following a stern letter from the Louisiana Proprietary School Commission, International University apparently faded away. It was incorporated by relatives of a man who still runs a large nonresident university in Louisiana.

International University (Switzerland) Zurich, Switzerland. One of the many diploma mill operations of Karl Xavier Bleisch, this one selling Bachelor's, Master's, and Doctorates for $500 to $1,000. The literature has a photocopy of a San Jose State College diploma awarded to Celia Ann Bleisch in 1967. What can this mean?

Jackson State University Los Angeles, Nashville, Reno, Chicago. Sold degrees of all kinds for $200. The postal service issued "false representation orders" and stopped their mail years ago, and the perpetrators finally were sentenced to federal prison in 1987. No connection whatsoever with the legitimate school of this name in Mississippi.

Janta Engineering College Karnal, India. Identified as a diploma mill by COE.

Japan Christian College Tokyo, Japan. Identified as a diploma mill by COE.

Jerusalem University Tel Aviv, Israel. Degrees of all kinds are sold for $10 to $40 from this nonexistent university. Buyers must sign a statement that they will not use the degrees for any phony purpose.

Johann Keppler School of Medicine There are very few people daring or stupid enough to start a fake medical school. This was one of the most ambitious, complete with catalog, and an alleged faculty in Switzerland, Canada, and Mexico. The claim was made that the degrees were recognized in many countries. When John asked their representative (who telephoned to make sure he would put them in this book) which countries, he thought a while and then said, "Well, Mauritius for one." All addresses used were mail forwarding services. Accreditation was claimed from the American Coordinated Medical Society, a fake organization started by L. Mitchell Weinberg, who has been to prison several times for fake medical school operations, and who was involved with Keppler as well. Operations ceased in the wake of the FBI DipScam operation in 1983. Weinberg was indicted and sentenced to prison again.

John Hancock University See: Hancock University

John Quincy Adams College Portland, Oregon. A totally phony school, selling any degree for $250. Later used addresses in Illinois and Nevada. Operated by the Fowler family, five of whom were sentenced to prison in 1987.

Kentucky Christian University Ashland, Kentucky. They offered degrees in everything from chemical engineering to law at all levels for a $300 fee. Same auspices as Ohio Christian and Florida State Christian, all now defunct.

Kentucky Military Institute See: Bretton Woods University

Kenwood Associates Long Green, Maryland. For $15 each or three for $30, they will sell Bachelor's, Master's, or Doctorates in the name of any school, with any degree and any date. Then you can buy, for $12, a Jiu Jitsu Master Instructor certificate to flash when the authorities come to take you away.

Kingsley University See: Bradford University

Lafayette University Amsterdam, Netherlands, through a mail forwarding service. One of many fake schools operated by the Fowler family, five of whom were sentenced to prison for operating diploma mills, in late 1987. Degrees of any sort, with any date, were sold for $725. Accreditation was claimed from an equally fake accrediting agency, the West European Accrediting Society of Liederbach, West Germany.

Lamp Beacon University See: California Pacifica University

Laurence University Hawaii. All degrees in all fields except medicine and law, for a fee of $45. The literature says, "We are confident you will find the benefits you can obtain with a degree from Laurence University are very valuable indeed." The main benefit we can think of is a period of room and board at government expense. The same seller, Associated Enterprises, also issues the fake degrees of Benson University, Carlton University, Kingsley University, Buckner University, Franklin University, and Bradford University. There is, of course, no connection with the legitimate school formerly called Laurence University (now University of Santa Barbara) in California.

Lawford State University Maryland. They used to sell degrees of all kinds for $6.99 from a post office box in Baltimore, now closed. The other school names were Université de Commerce de (sic) Canada and the Christian Fellowship Foundation. The hard-to-decipher signatures on the quite-realistic-looking certificates were "Thoroughly Fake, Ph.D." and "Too Much Fun, Jr."

Leiland College of Arts and Sciences (Hawaii). Arose in 1992, offering degrees to martial artists for under $100. Diploma identical to that of Eurotechnical Research University whose president originally opened the post-office box used but later turned it over to a colleague, and denied any knowledge of Leiland.

Libera Universita di Psico-Biofisica Trieste, Yugoslavia (that's what their literature says, even though Trieste is now in Italy). Identified as a diploma mill by E&T.

Life Science College California and Oklahoma. The proprietors were arrested in 1981 for an array of charges, including selling Doctor of Divinity degrees, and income tax evasion through the operation of the college and the associated Life Science Church.

Lincoln-Jefferson University See: California Pacifica University

London College of Physiology England. Identified as a diploma mill by E&T.

London College of Theology England. Identified as a diploma mill by E&T.

London Educational College England. Identified as a diploma mill by E&T.

London Institute for Applied Research England. All right, he did it (as he's been saying in this book for 20 years now). In 1972, while living in England, John was involved in fund-raising for a legitimate school. He figured that since major universities were "selling" their honorary degrees for millions, why not use the same approach on a small scale? He and his associates created L.I.A.R. and ran ads in the U.S. reading "Phony honorary doctorates for sale, $25." Several hundred were sold, but the whole thing seemed to have upset half the world's educational establishment (the other half thought it was a good gag.) So L.I.A.R. was retired. Then an offer came from a Dutchman who lived in Ethiopia (you must believe us on this—who would make up such a story?) who wanted to trade 100 pounds of Ethiopian ear-pickers and Coptic crosses for the remaining L.I.A.R. certificates. Now he's selling them from Holland without the humorous disclaimer, and has added a bunch more fake school names. And if anyone would like some Ethiopian trinkets, have we got a deal for you! (Honestly!)

London School for Social Research London, England. The well-prepared literature offer degrees of all kinds for fees of up to $2,000. The address is in a dingy little building off Leicester Square, where John climbed five flights of stairs so narrow that he had to go up sideways, and at the top found the little one-room office of Archangel Services, a mail-forwarding service that told him they forward the London School mail to Miami. Some literature has also been mailed from Phoenix. See also: International Universities Consortium.

London Tottenham International Christian University England. Identified as a diploma mill by E&T.

Loyola University Paris, France. Through a mail-forwarding service, degrees of all kinds were sold for a pay-

ment of up to $650. The brochure claimed that "Many of our successful graduates have used their transcripts to transfer to other colleges and universities in the U.S.A." If this really did happen, it would have been only because of name confusion with the four legitimate Loyolas in the U.S. The perpetrators of this Loyola were sentenced to federal prison in 1987.

LTD Documents New York. Extremely well-done, and thus especially dangerous, fake diplomas with the name of any school and any degree printed on them for $69.50. Also, preprinted degrees from the nonexistent San Miguel College and Benchley State University for $49.50. They even explain how to "age" a certificate to make it look older.

Lyne College England. Identified as a diploma mill by E&T.

Madison State University See: R/G Enterprises.

Marcus Tullius Cicero University San Francisco, California. A Swiss company advertised in the International Herald Tribune that they could provide the "registered legal degree" of the so-called university for a mere $3,000. The diploma indicates that the university is "officially registered" with the secretary of state which, if true, simply means it is a California corporation. Checks are made payable to The Knights of Humanity. There is, of course, no such university in California or, presumably, anywhere else.

Marlowe University New Jersey and Florida. Active during the 1960s and 1970s, selling all kinds of degrees for $150 or less.

Marmaduke University California. Degrees of all kinds were sold for $1,000 and up. The literature reports that "usually the student qualifies for more advanced study than he initialy [sic] expected." Mention was made of a 30-day resident course in the use of lie detectors, but the voice on the phone (answered simply, "Hello") said it had been canceled "because of the building program." Marmaduke was actually once authorized by the state of California, back in the days (late 1970s) when such things were vastly easier.

Martin College Florida. They used to sell degrees of all kinds for $200. Graduates were required to pass some tough exams, as evidenced by this example given in the school's literature: "True or false—the Declaration of Independence was signed on the 4th of July by British Royalty."

Meta Collegiate Extension Nevada. Chartered in Nevada before World War II, they sold Ph.D.'s for $50, with a 20 percent discount for cash.

Metropolitan Collegiate They sell all degrees, including medical and dental, for $100 or less. The address is a mail-forwarding service which told us that they forward the mail to Yorkshire, England. It is hard to imagine that such things can be tolerated, but this place has been going for years. (We have this little fantasy in which the prime minister becomes gravely ill on a trip abroad, and the doctor who is summoned to treat him "earned" his Ph.D. from Metropolitan Collegiate.)

Millard Fillmore Institute In 1966, the year John earned his real Doctorate (from Michigan State University), Bob Hope received one of his first honorary Doctorates after making a large gift to Southern Methodist University. Aware that Millard Fillmore, our great 13th president, was the only president who routinely turned down offers of honorary Doctorates (including one from Oxford), John was inspired to create the fictitious Institute, to poke fun at the way universities trade honorary degrees for money. The ornate diploma read, "By virtue of powers which we have invented . . . the honorary and meretricious" title was awarded, "magna cum grano salis" (with a big grain of salt). Many were given away, and some were sold, complete with a cheap plastic frame, for five bucks. Most people thought it was amusing, but a few saw it as a threat to civilization as we know it, and so, after a few years, the fictitious gates of the institute were closed, perhaps forever.

Miller University Philadelphia, Pennsylvania. Identified as a diploma mill by E&T.

Milton University Maryland and New York. Identified as a diploma mill by E&T.

Ministerial Training College Sheffield, England. Identified as a diploma mill by COE.

Montserrat University California. Degrees of all kinds were sold for $10 or $20 from a post office box in San Francisco in this name and those of the equally fake Stanton University and Rochfort College. Apparently now defunct.

Morston-Colwyn University England and Canada. Identified as a diploma mill by E&T.

Mount Sinai University USA Identified as a diploma mill by E&T.

Nassau State Teachers College See: Regency Enterprises

National Certificate Company New York. These people sold the degrees of eight nonexistent universities at $20 to $30 each, and also sold a "make your own" kit consisting of a blank diploma and press-on letters. The eight fake schools are Diplomatic University, Central University, Capital College, Adams Institute of Technology, Eastern University, Western College, Graduate University, and the Southern Institute of Technology. Buyers must sign a statement saying they will not use them for any educational purpose. Suuuuure.

National College Kansas and Oklahoma. Doctorates of all kinds, including medical, were sold by "Dr." Charles E. Downs. Accreditation claimed from a bogus accrediting association established by "Dr." Weinberg, founder of several fake medical schools himself. See also: East Coast University.

National College of Arts and Sciences Once a very active mill, finally closed down by authorities in Oklahoma in 1982. Same ownership as American Western, Northwestern College of Allied Science, and other fake schools. A quite wonderful event in the annals of degree mills occurred when a state official in New York innocently wrote to National College to verify a Master's degree claimed by a job applicant. National College misinterpreted the letter, and sent a Master's degree to the state official, in his own name, complete with a transcript listing all the courses taken and grades received!

National Ecclesiastical University Sheffield, England. Identified as a diploma mill by E&T.

National Stevens University California. Identified as a diploma mill by E&T.

National University (Canada) Toronto, Canada. Identified as a diploma mill by COE.

National University (India) Nagpur, India. Identified as a diploma mill by COE.

National University of Colorado Denver, Colorado. Identified as a diploma mill by COE.

National University of Dakota South Dakota. Identified as a diploma mill by E&T.

National University of Sheffield Sheffield, England. Identified as a diploma mill by COE and E&T. No connection, of course, with the legitimate University of Sheffield.

Nebraska College of Physical Medicine England. Degrees in chiropractic and osteopathy are sold to people who, according to newspaper articles, are said to use them to practice medicine.

New Christian Institute of New England See: ORB

New York State College See: R/G Enterprises

Newcastle University England. Not to be confused with the legitimate University of Newcastle. Identified as a diploma mill by E&T.

North American College of the Artsy With the purchase of the Complete Conductor Kit, the Portable Maestro of St. Paul, Minnesota, awards a Master's degree from the North American College of the Artsy and Somewhat Musically Inclined.

North American University Utah, Hawaii, Missouri. Formerly University of North America. Degree mill, run by Edward Reddeck, who has twice gone to prison for educational frauds. A great many people were defrauded by this "school" largely because national publications like *USA Today* kept accepting his advertising. Enjoined from operating by Utah in 1989, but the order was ignored. Reddeck was indicted by a federal grand jury in 1992 for mail fraud and conspiracy, convicted in 1993, and imprisoned.

Northern Utah University/Northern Utah Management Institute They have been around for years, but now are apparently a part of the International Universities Consortium, described earlier in this chapter. The phone listed in Salt Lake City is not in service, and mail was returned as undeliverable in 1990.

Northwest London College of Applied Science London, England. Same location as the College of Applied Science, London. Also known as Northwest London

University. Links with several medical degree mills, including Keppler and the Chicago Medical School. The signature of Karl Josef Werres, founder of Inter-State College and Institut Patriarcal Saint Irenée, and past officer of two large American nontraditional schools, appears on their diploma. Professor Werres wishes people to know that he has nothing to do with this school, and that his name has been forged. Done.

Northwest London University See: Northwest London College of Applied Science

Northwestern College of Allied Sciences Oklahoma City, Oklahoma. Authorities in Oklahoma closed this mill down in 1982. It had been under the same management as American Western, National College, and several other fake schools operated under the cloak of the Disciples of Truth by James Caffey of Springfield, Missouri. Caffey was indicted by a federal grand jury in 1985, pleaded guilty, and was sentenced to prison.

Northwestern Graduate School Allegedly in Montana. See: International Universities Consortium.

Obura University London, England. Identified as a diploma mill by E&T.

Ohio Central College See: Regency Enterprises

Ohio Christian College One of the more active degree mills in the 1960s and 1970s, they sold degrees of all kinds for fees of $200 and up. Literature identical to that of Florida State Christian University, which was closed by authorities in that state. They claimed to be a part of Calvary Grace Christian Churches of Faith, Inc.

Ohio Saint Mathew University Columbus, Ohio. Identified as a diploma mill by E&T.

Open University (Switzerland) Zurich, Switzerland. One of the many diploma mills operated by Karl Xavier Bleisch.

ORB Virginia. A supermarket of phony degrees that offered diplomas from eight nonexistent institutions at fees of $5 to $65 each. The more authentic-sounding ones were more expensive. The schools were: Bosdon Academy of Music, Eugenia Institute of Metaphysics, Gottbourg University of Switzerland, Honoré College of France, New Christian Institute of New England, Royal Academy of Science and Art, Taylor College of England, and Weinberg University of Germany. ORB (other literature reveals that it stands for Occult Research Bureau) has been operated by Raymond Buckland, author and former curator of the Buckland Museum of Magick.

Oriental University Washington, D.C. Identified as a diploma mill by COE.

Oxford College of Applied Science Oxford, England. A diploma mill selling degrees of all kinds. Apparently operated from Switzerland by Karl Xavier Bleisch, who has been involved with many other degree mills.

Oxford College of Arts and Sciences Canada. Identified as a diploma mill by E&T.

Oxford Institute for Applied Research London, England. Fake honorary Doctorates sold for $250.

Pacific College Sold everything from high school diplomas to Doctorates for $75 because they believed that "everyone has the right to live and experience life according to his or her own convictions." This presumably includes convictions for fraud.

Pacific Southern University New Jersey and California. No connection whatsoever with a school of the same name that had state authorization, in Los Angles. *This* Pacific Southern operates from various post-office boxes and offers "degrees you can be pround [sic] of" at $250 each.

Pacific States College Degrees from this nonexistent school have recently been sold for $5 if blank; $15 if professionally lettered. The literature describes them as "some of the finest, most authentic looking college degrees on the market. It is almost impossible to distinguish them from the real thing."

Palm Beach Psychotherapy Training Center See: Thomas A. Edison College of Florida

Pensacola Trade School See: Regency Enterprises

People's National University USA. Identified as a diploma mill by E&T.

Philo-Byzantine University Madrid, Spain. Identified as a diploma mill by E&T.

Phoenix University (Italy) See: Accademia di Studi Superiori Phoenix.

R/G Enterprises Florida. They sold degrees from 10 schools with almost-real names at prices up to $37.50. The schools were: Alabama Christian College, California Christian College, Clemson College, Colgate College, Diplomatic State University, Hamilton Institute of Technology, Hamilton State University, Madison State University, New York State College, and Tulsa College. The literature says, "This offer not valid in states where prohibited by law," which doubtless encompasses all 50 of them.

Raighlings University See: USSI

Regency College See: American Western University

Regency Enterprises Missouri. They used to sell degrees with the names of real schools, often slightly changed, such as Stamford (not Stanford) University, or Texas University (not the University of Texas). Others included Cormell University, Indiana State University, Boston City College, the University of Pittsburgh, Illinois State University, Rockford Community College, Hartford Technical Institute, Carnegie Institute of Engineering, Stetson College, Nassau State Teachers College, Darthmouth College, Ohio Central College, College of Franklin & Marshall, and Pensacola Trade School. A blank diploma with a lettering kit was sold for $20. Buyers were asked to sign a statement that they would not use these phony diplomas for any fraudulent purposes, although it's hard to imagine any other use to which they could be put. Don L. Piccolo of Anaheim, California was indicted by a federal grand jury in 1985 for running Regency, and entered a guilty plea.

Rhode Island School of Law Identified as a diploma mill by E&T, which believed it to be in Wyoming.

Rochfort College See: Monserrat University

Rockford Community College: See Regency Enterprises

Roosevelt University Belgium. Degrees of any kind were sold for a "tuition" of $400 to $600. Also used an address in Zurich, Switzerland. Five of the proprietors were sentenced to federal prison in late 1987.

Royal Academy of Science and Art see: ORB

Royal College of Science Identified as a diploma mill by E&T. Apparently affiliated with, or the same as, Empire College of Opthalmology.

Saint Andrews Correspondence College Identified as a diploma mill by E&T.

Saint Andrews Ecumenical Foundation University Intercollegiate Identified as a diploma mill by E&T.

Saint Andrews University Allegedly in Mexico. See: International Universities Consortium

Saint John Chrysostom College London, England. Identified as a diploma mill by E&T.

Saint John's University India. Identified as a diploma mill by COE.

Saint Joseph University New York. They offered Bachelor's, Master's, Doctorates, and law degrees. Some of the literature was well-done, some of it was ludicrous—the name "Saint Joseph," for instance, was often inserted in gaps where clearly some other school's name had once appeared. The location was variously given as New York, Louisiana, and Colorado, even in the same catalog. Degrees cost from $2,000 to $3,000.

Saint Stephens Educational Bible College Los Angeles, California. The president of this institution, a Baptist minister, pleaded guilty to forgery and grand theft for issuing illegal credentials. He was fined $5,000 and placed on probation for five years, and Saint Stephens is no more.

San Francisco College of Music and Theater Arts In 1987, a San Francisco man began advertising this apparently nonexistent school in Chinese and African papers. Somehow, it was certified as legitimate by the Immigration and Naturalization Service. The *San Francisco Chronicle* reports that three Chinese dancers came to San Francisco to train at the school and ended up being forced to work as servants for its founder.

San Miguel College See: LTD Documents

Sands University Yuma, Arizona. Sold degrees of all kinds in the mid 1980s. Proprietor, Wiley Gordon Bennett, who operated from Tennessee, was convicted and sent to prison thanks to the FBI's DipScam operation.

School of Applied Sciences London and New York. Identified as a diploma mill by E&T.

School of Psychology and Psychotherapy England. Identified as a diploma mill by E&T.

Self-Culture University India. Identified as a diploma mill by COE.

Shield College (UK) See: USSI

Siberian Institute See: International Honorary Awards Committee

Sir Edward Heyzer's Free Technical College Hong Kong. Associated with the National University of Canada, identified as a diploma mill by COE.

South China University Hong Kong and Macau. Identified as a diploma mill by E&T.

South Eastern Extension College Essex, England. All degrees but medicine or law, at £20 for one or £45 for three. "Our degrees are indistinguishable from degrees issued by other colleges in the traditional way," the sales letter says. Same ownership as Whitby Hall College.

Southern California University California. One of the many fake school names used by the Fowler family, five of whom were sentenced to prison in 1987 for their part in running diploma mills worldwide. Degrees of all kinds were sold for $200 and up.

Southern Eastern University London, England. A diploma mill operated by a "Professor Swann-Grimaldi," which claimed the late Princess Grace of Monaco as a patron. The address used was that of the prestigious Royal Commonwealth Society, whose members can collect their mail there. Degrees were sold for fees of about $1,000 and up. Applications were to be sent to the professor's parents' home in Essex.

Southern Institute of Technology See: National Certificate Company

Southwestern University Tucson, Arizona and St. George, Utah. The university had its own impressive building in Tucson, with many of the trappings of a real school. But after they sold degrees to an FBI agent during the DipScam operation, several administrators were indicted by a federal grand jury. President Geruntino pleaded guilty, and served a term in federal prison. The names of more than a thousand Southwestern "alumni" were made public, and many jobs were lost as a result, including some in NASA and the Pentagon. Many students had enrolled following a glowing recommendation for the school from an educational guidance service in Columbus, Ohio that was also run by Geruntino.

Southwestern University Allegedly in Albuquerque, New Mexico. See: International Universities Consortium

Specialty Document Company California. In 1988, they were selling fake diplomas for a Doctor of Medicine, Doctor of Veterinary Medicine, Bachelor's, and Ph.D. certificates (no school specified) for $1 each, or 100 for $15. Imagine that! A medical degree for 15¢!

Spicer Memorial College India. Identified as a diploma mill by COE.

Stanton University: See Montserrat University

Staton University In the early 1980s, music teachers in North America received an invitation to join the American Guild of Teachers of Singing, upon which they would be awarded an honorary Doctorate from this nonexistent school, which was supposed to be in Ohio.

Stetson College See: Regency Enterprises

Sussex College of Technology Sussex, England. Perhaps the oldest of Britain's degree mills, Sussex is run by "Dr." Bruce Copen from his home, south of London. At the same address, but with different catalogs, are the Brantridge Forest School and the University of the Science of Man. Each offer "earned" degrees for which a few correspondence courses are required, and "extension awards" which are the same degrees and diplomas for no work at all. Honorary Doctorates are offered free, but there is a $100 engraving charge. "Professor Emeritas" [sic] status costs another $100. One flyer admits Sussex is not "accrediated" [sic] but goes on to say that "No student who has taken our courses and awards have to date had problems." This statement would not be accepted by, among many others, a former high-level state official in Colorado who lost his job when the source of his Doctorate was discovered. Sussex continues to advertise extensively in newspapers and magazines in the U.S. and worldwide. In 1988, a new British law came into effect, forbidding such "schools" to accept students who enrolled after May 1st. Sussex's solution to this minor annoyance was to offer to back-date all applications to April 30th, 1988—a creative response that British law apparently hasn't caught up with yet.

Taurus International University California. The claim is that the Taurus International Society was established in 1764 by James Boswell. The Ph.D. is sold for all of $2, and the Doctor of Whimsey for $1.

Taylor College of England See: ORB

Taylor University of Bio-Psycho-Dynamic Sciences was established in Chattanooga, Tennessee, in the early 1920s by some of that city's "most respected citizens, including a philanthropic capitalist, merchant prince, a dentist ... and a woman of high intelligence." The Doctorate sold for $115, or $103.50 cash in advance.

Temple Bar College Identified as a diploma mill by E&T.

Tennessee Christian University Tennessee. Affiliated with Ohio and Florida State Christian in the sale of fake degrees.

Texas Theological University Texas. Identified as a diploma mill by E&T.

Texas University See: Regency Enterprises

Thomas A. Edison College Florida and Arkansas. Totally fake school run by the Rt. Rev. Dr. George C. Lyon, M.D., Ph.D., LL.D., D.D. After twice being fined heavily and sentenced to prison for running fake schools in Florida, he moved to Arkansas, arriving with an entourage in a red Mercedes and a green Rolls Royce, and bought a vacant church for cash. But the FBI's DipScam operation caught up with him again, and Lyon, now in his 80s, went off to federal prison once again. Thomas A. Edison College managed to fool an awful lot of people over the years, and not just because it sounds like the legitimate nontraditional Edison in New Jersey. This Edison was listed in many otherwise reputable college guides (like *Lovejoy's*) as a real school

for years. Lyon's other nefarious enterprises have included the Palm Beach Psychotherapy Training Center, the Florida Analytic Institute, and an involvement with two phony medical schools, United American Medical College and the Keppler School of Medicine.

Thomas Jefferson University Missouri. In the early 1980s, catalogs were mailed from this school, allegedly in St. Louis (the address was a private home), but there was never a listed phone, and the postmark was Denver. Degrees at all levels were offered for $1,500 on up. The catalog was almost identical to that used by a legitimate California school. Letters were never answered. With the catalog came a Servicemen's Allotment Account form, for military people to have the "university" paid directly each month from their paycheck, into a bank account in New York.

Thomas University Pennsylvania. They used to sell fake degrees for up to $1,000. They claimed accreditation from the fake Middle States Accrediting Board.

Tremonte University See: USSI

Trinity Collegiate Institute England and Switzerland. The London mail service forwards the mail to Karl Bleisch, an operator of many diploma mills in Switzerland. According to an expose in the Times of London, Bleisch told the forwarding service that Trinity was a language school only, with "no question of awarding degrees." Within two months, he was handing out degrees in subjects from beer marketing to scientific massage. (One alumnus went on to start Inter-State College and Institut Patriarcal Saint Irenée.)

Tuit University Georgia. The Doctorates, sold for $10, are amusing when you read the small print, which says, for instance, that the recipient "has not had the time to do the necessary work leading to the degree of Doctor of Philosophy ... ."

Tulsa College See: R/G Enterprises

Two Dragon University See: International Honorary Awards Committee

United American Medical College A medical degree mill, operated from the apartment of its founder in Louisiana, and from a mail-forwarding service in Canada. The approach was almost identical to that of the Johann Keppler School of Medicine, described earlier. When owner L. Mitchell Weinberg was first arrested (1977) for violating Louisiana school laws, he maintained the school was fully accredited by the American Coordinated Medical Society in California. Indeed, said society wrote that "we of the accreditation committee feel that U.A.M.C. has the highest admission requirements of any medical college in the world ... due to the great leadership of it's [sic] President, L. Mitchell Weinberg." The founder and proprietor of the American Coordinated Medical Society is L. Mitchell Weinberg. In 1982, Weinberg pleaded guilty to charges of selling medical degrees and was sentenced to three years in federal prison.

United Free University of England Identified as a

diploma mill by E&T.

United States University of America Washington, Florida. The 11-page typewritten catalogue actually listed names of some legitimate faculty who had been duped into doing some work for "Dr." Frank Pany and the school he ran from his Florida home, using a Washington, DC mail-forwarding service. One of the faculty, the "Chairman of the Marriage Counseling Department," whose Doctorate was from U.S.U.A. was more candid. "You're in California," he said on the phone. "Why not deal with a degree service closer to home?" In the wake of an FBI visit, and a grand jury indictment in February 1986, "Dr." Pany departed suddenly for Italy.

Universal Bible Institute Birmingham, Alabama. The state declared it was a diploma mill, and ordered it closed, because doctoral degrees could be acquired in less than two months on payment of appropriate fees, and the school was not affiliated with any religious organization. According to Alabama authorities, the institute's president moved to Florida, taking all the records with him, as the Alabama investigation began.

Universal Ecclesiastical University Their Doctorates were offered in any field but law or medicine for a 10-page dissertation, and honorary Doctorates to anyone with "good moral character" plus $200 to spend. Our last letter to Professor Gilbert at the university's address in Manchester, England, was returned with the word "Demolished" written in big blue crayon letters across the front. Let us hope they were referring to the building, not the professor.

Universidad Brasileira Rio de Janeiro, Brazil. Identified as a diploma mill by COE.

Universidad Indigenista Moctezuma Andorra's only diploma mill—identified as such by COE.

Universidad Latino-Americana de La Habana Havana, Cuba. Identified as a diploma mill by COE.

Universidad Sintetica Latina y Americana El Salvador. Identified as a diploma mill by COE.

Universidad Tecnológica Nacional Havana, Cuba. Identified as a diploma mill by COE.

Universitaires Internationales Liechtenstein, India, Sudan, Morocco, Japan, etc., etc. Identified as a diploma mill by E&T.

Universitas Iltiensis England, Switzerland. Identified as a diploma mill by E&T.

Universitas Internationalis Studiorum Superiorium Pro Deo In 1989, they began offering "honoris causa" Doctorates from an address in New York, under the imprimatur of the Titular Archbishop of Ephesus.

Universitates Sheffieldensis See: University of Sheffield

Université de Commerce de Canada See: Lawford State University

Université des Science de l'Homme France. Same as University of the Science of Man. See: Sussex College of Technology.

Université International de Paris Paris, France. Identified as a diploma mill by COE.

Université Nouvelle de Paris Paris, France. Identified as a diploma mill by COE.

Université Philotechnique Brussels, Belgium, and Paris, France. Identified as a diploma mill by COE.

Université Voltaire de France Marseilles, France. Identified as a diploma mill by COE.

University College of Nottingham See: Whitby Hall College

University del Puerto Monico Panama. Degrees of this nonexistent institution were sold by Neil Gibson & Company in England, who also represented University de la Romande. They say that "the degree certificates are excellently presented and make a superb and unusual wall decoration. They are for self-esteem only but remain very popular indeed." The same management later opened Knightsbridge University.

University in London Same as Obura University. Identified as a diploma mill by E&T.

University of Cape Cod A school of this name was promoted in eastern Massachusetts in the early 1980s.

University of Corpus Christi Reno, Nevada. Affiliated with the Society of Academic Recognition. Identified as a diploma mill by E&T. No connection with the legitimate school formerly known as University of Corpus Christi but now a part of Texas A & I University.

University of Coventry England. Identified as a diploma mill by E&T. There is a legitimate university with the same name.

University of East Carolina See: University of East Georgia

University of East Georgia Georgia. Degrees in all fields, including medicine, psychiatry, surgery, and neurology sold for $500 and completion of a thesis on "a subject and length of your own choosing." Embarrassingly enough, John was duped by the first literature he received from proprietor John Blazer in 1975, but the game soon became clear. Blazer also operated the University of the Bahama Islands, the College of Hilton Head, the University of East Carolina, and the University of Middle Tennessee. In 1984, he was indicted by a federal grand jury as a result of the FBI's DipScam operation. He pleaded guilty to the charge of mail fraud and was sentenced to prison.

University of Eastern Florida Chicago, Illinois. Degrees of all kinds except medicine and law were sold for $40 each. The school claimed to be a "state chartered university" in Florida (not true).

University of England, University of England at Oxford London, England. Degrees of and kind were sold for about $200 by a school using both of these names. In 1987, the American proprietors were indicted by a federal grand jury. Five of them were found guilty and sentenced to prison. The founder of Western States University claims a degree from this institution (the school, not the prison)

University of Independence A realistic-looking diploma was given or sold as a promotional piece to independent businesspeople. The Ph.D. came from the School of Hard Knocks. A reader sent us a photo of a well-known author and lecturer, from a national magazine, showing the diploma prominently displayed on his wall. Only the school name, the man's name, and "Doctor of Philosophy" are readable. This is one way that even "gag" fake diplomas can be misused.

University of Man's Best Friend A lovely $2 Ph.D. in Love and Loyalty, with paw prints as signatures.

University of Middle Tennessee: See: University of East Georgia

University of North America Diploma mill operated by Edward Reddeck from a mail-forwarding service in Missouri in the late 1980s. After he was fined $2,500,000 for this operation, he fled to Utah, changing the name of the school slightly, to North American University (see separate listing). He was indicted for mail fraud and conspiracy in the spring of 1992, found guilty on all 22 counts in 1993, and sent back to prison.

University of Pittsburg See: Regency Enterprises

University of Rarotonga Fictitious school whose paraphernalia is sold on this South Seas island.

University of Saint Bartholomew After John gave a talk on diploma mills on Australian radio, a number of people called or wrote to mention a school by this name in Oodnadatta, Australia that merrily sold its fake product to Europeans.

University of Sealand Identified as a diploma mill by E&T.

University of Sheffield Sheffield, England. Also called Universitates Sheffieldensis, Ecclesiastical University of Sheffield. There is a legitimate, traditional University of Sheffield, and then there is this fake one, run (according to an article in the *Times* of London) by Charles Brearly, an auto mechanic who styles himself Ignatius Carelus, successor to Cardinal Barberini of Rheims. He is a sometime associate of "Sir" Sidney Lawrence, proprietor of the College of Applied Science, London. We have received a stern letter from the academic registrar of the real University of Sheffield, suggesting that "in order that our academic standing not be endangered, I would ask that your publication make it quite clear in the future that the college mentioned has no connection whatsoever with this institution." Done, and thanks for thinking that our little book could endanger your large, old, well-established university.

University of Sulgrave England. Identified as a diploma mill by E&T.

University of the Bahama Islands See: University of East Georgia

University of the Eastern United States Identified as a diploma mill by E&T.

University of the New World Arizona and Europe. Identified as a diploma mill by E&T.

University of the Old Catholic Church Sheffield, England. Identified as a diploma mill by E&T. Presumably the same management as the fake University of Sheffield.

University of the President Utah. They have sold honorary Doctorates in iridology, psionics, macrobiotics, endogenous endocrinotherapy, and dozens more, in exchange for a $25 "donation."

University of the Republic A fictitious school started by *Arizona Republic* newspaper reporters Jerry Seper and Rich Robertson as part of a series on degree mills, to show how easy it was to do such things in Arizona at the time. Public outrage led to a tough new school-regulating law being passed.

University of the Science of Man See: Sussex College of Technology

University of the West See: International Universities Consortium

University of Walla Walla California. Advertising in a national women's magazine offered a Doctor of anything ending in "ologist" for $18.90.

University of Winchester London, England. Same address as the London School of Social Research. The $15 diplomas have been widely advertised as "completely spurious, nonetheless as impressive as genuine."

University of Wyoming Of course there is a real one in Laramie, but there is also a fake one. A man named Cunning, using an address in London, England and literature printed in German, has been selling Ph.D.'s, law degrees, and alarmingly, M.D.'s of the University of Wyoming for about $500. We wrote to the general counsel of the real University of Wyoming, thinking they might be interested, but there's been no reply. (Since there's a purveyor of fake degrees named Wiley Bennett, one can't help wondering if they might some day get together, to form a Wiley and Cunning partnership.)

USSI Florida. In late 1994, they began selling a range of documents ranging from the obviously silly (such as Super Mom or Total Airhead) to the highly deceptive. "Diplomas" are offered from Hirshfeld University, Shield College (UK), Tremonte University, Wellingsburg University, Raighlings University, or the College of Hard Knocks. Degrees include Bachelor's, Master's, Doctorates, and law degrees, in a wide range of fields, for prices ranging form $59.50 to $101.50. A warning on the order form states "These novelty items (Certificates) are very realistic in appearance. In view, they may be mistaken as authentic certificates. USSI, it's [sic] staff and any hired agency or service are not liable for any representation by the purchaser of our products." More alarmingly, USSI also offers to produce diplomas from any university and for any degree. To test this, John ordered a medical degree from Harvard. Someone from USSI telephoned him and suggested that they would be willing to make a Harvard law degree instead, and that is what they did.

Vocational University India. Identified as a diploma mill by COE.

Washington International Academy New York.

Identified as a diploma mill by E&T.

Webster University (GA) Georgia. Identified as a diploma mill by E&T. (There is an accredited school of the same name in Missouri. No connection, of course.)

Weinberg University of West Germany See: ORB

Wellingsburg University See: USSI

Wellington University New Jersey. Offered some correspondents the apportunity to earn a Sri Lankan M.D. upon payment of $1,000. Because of that, this "university" has been moved from the chapter on medical schools to this one.

West London College of Technology London, England. Advertisements appearing in African magazines offered a 12-month correspondence program leading to various qualifications, including the M.B.A., "in association with Broadhurst University." The address given is a mail receiving and forwarding service in London, and there is no telephone. We can find no evidence of the existence of either the West London College or of Broadhurst University.

Western Cascade University California. Degrees of all sorts at $45 each. The address is a mail forwarding service. In an apparent effort to avoid prosecution, they will not sell their product to California residents.

Western College See: National Certificate Company

Western Orthodox University Glastonbury, England. Identified as a diploma mill by E&T.

Western Reserve Educational Services For years, they sold diplomas that they claimed to have "salvaged" from "genuine schools that have gone out of business" from an Ohio post office box. The proprietor, Robert Kim Walton, claimed to have been commended by the Sacred Congregation in Rome—not, one dares hope, for selling fake degrees.

Western University California One of the early American degree mills, operating from southern California (San Diego and Jacumba) in the 1940s and 1950s. A Western University with addresses in Georgia, Montana, Colorado, and Delaware has been identified as a diploma mill by E&T; one in India has been identified as a diploma mill by COE.

Whitby Hall College Essex, England. M. Palmer offers degrees of almost any kind for about $100, earned for your resumé and a poem, a story, or a two-page book review. His other school names are the University College of Nottingham, and South Eastern University.

Williams College Idaho. When the late Lane Williams left New Mexico to move his "college" to Mexico, he changed its name from Williams to Elysion. But Williams was apparently left in other hands, and continued to operate, selling Bachelor's and law degrees for about $300 each. See also: Elysion College.

Wordsworth Memorial University England and India. Identified as a diploma mill by E&T and by COE.

"We find you acceptable, sir. You will be issued a halo, a set of wings, and an honorary doctorate in the subject of your choice."

Honorary Doctorates

Why anybody can have a brain. That's a very mediocre commodity.
Back where I come from we have universities—seats of great learning—where men go to become great thinkers. And when they come out they think deep thoughts, and with no more brains than you have. But they have one thing you haven't got: a diploma!
Therefore by virtue of the authority vested in me by the Universitatis Committitatum E Pluribus Unum, I hereby confer upon you the Honorary Degree of Th.D.
That's, uh, er, ah, Doctor of Thinkology.
L. FRANK BAUM, THE WIZARD OF OZ

The probable origin of the honorary Doctorate was discussed in chapter 3. The persistence of this "degree"—indeed, its usage has grown tremendously, with more than 50,000 being awarded by major universities in the last decade—is one of the mysteries of the academic world, for there is nothing whatever educational about the honorary Doctorate. It is, purely and simply, a title that some institutions have chosen for a variety of reasons to bestow upon certain people (and a few animals).

That the title given is "Doctor"—the same word used for academic degrees—is what has caused all the confusion, not to mention most of the desirability of the honorary Doctorate. It is exactly as if the government were to honor people by giving them the title of "Senator" or "Judge." Whatever the reason, honorary Doctorates have become highly valuable, even negotiable, commodities.

Not everyone takes them seriously, however. When a German university handed its Doctor of Music diploma to the composer Handel, he rolled it into a dunce cap, placed it on the head of his servant, and said, "There! Now you're a Doctor, too."

Poet Robert Frost expressed particular delight at the announcement of his 40th honorary Doctorate (from Oxford), because he confessed that he had been having the decorative hoods given with each award made into a patchwork quilt, and now it would all come out even. He revealed this en route to England "to collect some more yardage."

When artist Thomas Hart Benton accepted an honorary degree from Rockhurst College, he gestured to the graduating class and said, "I know how those boys behind me feel. They're thinking 'I worked four years for this, and that bum gets it free.'"

One of the curiosities of the honorary Doctorate is that the title given rarely has much relevance to the recipient's qualifications. Hence we have actor Fess Parker getting a Doctor of Letters (from Tennessee, after portraying Davey Crockett), Robert Redford a Doctor of Humane Letters (from Colorado; he said it is "as important to me as my Oscar"), Times Square restaurant owner Dario Toffenetti a Doctor of Laws (from Idaho, for promoting the baked potato), and the late industrialist Clarence Mackay a Doctor of Music (but there was a logical reason for this: his daughter had married Irving Berlin).

Perhaps Mark Twain said it best:

It pleased me beyond measure when Yale made me a Master of Arts, because I didn't know anything about art. I had another convulsion of pleasure when Harvard made me a Doctor of Literature, because I was not competent to doctor anybody's literature but my own.... I rejoiced again when Missouri University made me a Doctor of Laws because it was all clear profit, I not knowing anything about laws except how to evade them and not get caught. And now at Oxford I am to be made a Doctor of Letters—all clear profit, because what I don't know about letters would make me a millionaire if I could turn it into cash.

Not all titles have been inappropriate, of course. In 1987, Mr. Rogers received a Doctor of Humanities (Bowling Green), and led the audience in singing "Won't you be my neighbor." Admiral Byrd received a Doctor of Faith and Fortitude. Charlie McCarthy, the impertinent ventriloquist's dummy, received a Master of Innuendo from Northwestern. Antioch University gave a Master of Communication to a campus switchboard operator, and Brooklyn College, which averages only one honorary degree every four years, gave a Doctor of Delectables to a longtime campus hot dog vendor. A heroic seeing-eye dog named Bonzo received a Doctor of Canine Fidelity from Newark University. A mule named Elwood Blues got a doctorate from Yale. And so it goes.

WHY HONORARY DOCTORATES ARE GIVEN

1. To Attract Celebrities to Campus

These humorous (or, some say, ludicrous) examples illuminate one of the four major reasons that honorary Doctorates are given: to bring publicity to the graduation ceremonies of the school. If a small college can lure a baseball star, a movie or television personality, or even the wife of a famous politician to the campus, the commencement is more likely to make the evening news and the next morning's papers, which may help student or faculty recruiting, fundraising, or membership in the alumni association. It may even increase the chances that a top high school quarterback will come to the school next year. Indeed, when John Carroll University awarded an honorary Doctorate to Miami Dolphins coach Don Shula, it almost certainly was not for his academic achievements. And that is why we have Dr. Marlon Brando, Dr. Henry Fonda, Dr. Dave Winfield (of the New York Yankees), Dr. Bob Hope (more than 40 times over), Dr. Captain Kangaroo,

---

Is There a Doctor in the House?

Here are some of the people who have been 'doctored' by major universities in recent years:

Doctor Ella Fitzgerald	Doctor J. Edgar Hoover
Doctor Bonnie Raitt	Doctor Dan Rather
Doctor Roger Maris	Doctor Charles Addams
Doctor Mr. Rogers	Doctor Captain Kangaroo
Doctor B. B. King	Doctor Robert Redford
Doctor Stevie Wonder	Doctor Margot Fonteyn
Doctor Dolores Hope	Doctor Marvin Hamlisch
Doctor Doctor Seuss	Doctor Dave Winfield
Doctor Bing Crosby	Doctor Norman Mailer
Doctor Max Factor	Doctor Leontyne Price
Doctor Gavin McLeod	Doctor Duke Ellington
Doctor Ted Williams	Doctor James Earl Jones
Doctor John Wayne	Doctor Kirk Douglas
Doctor Ozzie Nelson	Doctor Marcel Marceau
Doctor Arthur Ashe	Doctor Mrs. Anwar Sadat
Doctor Idi Amin	Doctor Sammy Davis Jr.
Doctor Jane Pauley	Doctor Walter Cronkite
Doctor Celia Cruz	Doctor Terry Bradshaw
Doctor Helen Hayes	Doctor Aretha Franklin
Doctor Billy Joel	Doctor Pinchas Zuckerman
Doctor Isaac Stern	Doctor Candace Bergen
Doctor Don King (how did he wear his hat?)	
and at least 50,000 more	

Dr. Michael Jackson, and thousands of others.

Sometimes the publicity is not the kind the school had in mind. St. Joseph's College, a Catholic school, offered its honorary Doctorate to columnist Ann Landers, then created a big flap by withdrawing it after Landers wrote a pro-abortion column. And as Louisiana Tech was presenting its honorary Doctorate to former football quarterback Terry Bradshaw, outraged alumni flew over the ceremony and dropped a cascade of leaflets protesting the award.

There is nothing new going on here. During the Revolutionary War, Harvard gave an honorary degree to Lafayette. When he heard this, Baron von Steuben urged his troops, then approaching Cambridge, to ride through town "like the devil, for if they catch you, they make a doctor of you."

2. To Honor Distinguished Faculty and Administrators

Honorary degrees are often given to honor distinguished faculty at the donating school, or other schools. This is perhaps the most academically defensible reason. In American society, there is nothing equivalent to the national honors given in many European countries (e.g., the Queen's Honours List in Britain, at which hundreds of people each year become knights, ladies, Members of the British Empire, etc.) The honorary Doctorate remains one of the few honors we have to bestow. And so, each June, from 40% to 60% of all honorary degrees go to unknown academics, often, it is said, in the hope that *their* school will honor someone from *our* school next year.

This practice has resulted in a new world record. In 1982, then-president of Notre Dame Father Theodore Hesburgh collected his 90th honorary title, eclipsing Herbert Hoover's record of 89. The good Father now has well over 100.

3. For Political Reasons

American presidents, British prime ministers and other statesmen are regularly so honored, and often take the opportunity to make major speeches. Winston Churchill used the occasion of receiving an honorary degree in Missouri to deliver his famous "iron curtain" speech, and General George Marshall announced the Marshall Plan while receiving an honorary Doctorate.

Although every American president has collected some honorary Doctorates (George Washington had seven), none caused quite the furor of Harvard's award of an honorary Doctor of Laws to President Andrew Jackson. The Sons of Harvard erupted in anger. John Quincy Adams wrote about how his alma mater had degraded herself, "conferring her highest literary honors on a barbarian who could not write a sentence of grammar and could hardly spell his own name." Harvard president Josiah Quincy responded, "As the people have twice decided that this man knows enough law to be their ruler, it is not for

Harvard College to maintain they are mistaken."

The ceremony itself must have been quite extraordinary. After Jackson had been given the sheepskin and expressed his thanks in a few short remarks, an aide reminded him that he was expected to make a speech in Latin. Thereupon, according to biographer Robert Rayback, he bellowed out, in tones of thunder, all the Latin he knew: "E pluribus unum, sine qua non, multum in parvo, quid pro quo, ne plus ultra." So much for Dr. Jackson.

Haverford College made a rather dramatic political statement when they awarded honorary Doctor of Laws degrees to the 3,000 inhabitants of a French village that helped save the lives of 2,500 Jews during World War II.

Withholding of honorary Doctorates has also been used to make political statements. In 1987, the governing body of Oxford University voted 738 to 319 to withhold an honorary Doctorate from Prime Minister Thatcher because of her role in cutting university research funds. And the proposed awarding of degrees to Richard Nixon has caused controversies in more than a few places—including his alma mater, Duke University, which ultimately turned him down. Indeed, one report had it that during the final days of Watergate, someone in the Nixon administration had the idea that an honorary Doctorate would give Nixon some favorable publicity for a change. The only school they could find that would agree to do it was General Beadle State College, and that is why Air Force One descended into South Dakota one day in the spring of 1974. (General Beadle subsequently changed its name to Dakota State, but denies there was any connection with the Nixon visitation.)

In 1988, it was revealed that the faculty of Dan Quayle's alma mater voted overwhelmingly to deny him an honorary Doctorate, largely because of his poor academic record, but they were overruled by the administration. The same thing happened when predominantly black South Carolina State College offered an honorary degree to Strom Thurmond. "No South Carolinan has done more over the past 40 years to impede the advancement of black people," said a petition signed by most faculty and students. They were overruled by president Albert Smith, hence we have Dr. Senator Thurmond.

The decision of a Jesuit school, Fairfield University in Connecticut, to award an honorary degree to Billy Joel produced some major objections from people who contended that Joel's song *Only the Good Die Young* was insulting to Catholics. He got his degree.

But former Secretary of Transportation Drew Lewis stunned a commencement audience at his alma mater, Haverford College, when he removed his purple doctoral hood after the honorary degree had been bestowed on him. He said that Quakers are supposed to act by consensus, but he had learned that a third of the faculty opposed his award because of his role in breaking the air traffic controllers' strike. The audience gave him a standing ovation.

4. For Money

Although schools sanctimoniously deny there is any connection whatsoever, they have regularly awarded Doctorates to academically undistinguished folks who just happened to donate a bundle of money. How long has this been going on? Well, in *A Distant Mirror*, Barbara Tuchman writes that in the 14th century, the University of Paris "had taken to selling degrees in theology to candidates unwilling to undertake its long and difficult studies."

A few centuries later, George Baker gave Harvard millions for a new business school. Harvard gave George Baker a Doctor of Laws along with their hearty thanks. John Archbold contributed a new football field to Syracuse University. Soon after, he was doctored by Syracuse University. William Randolph Hearst "traded" $100,000 and 400 acres of land to Oglethorpe University for an honorary Doctorate.

A few years ago, a British dry-goods merchant named Isaac Wolfson gave about $10 million to Cambridge University, and they not only gave him an honorary Doctorate, they named a college of the university for him. Then he made the same gift to Oxford, and they too both doctored him and named a college for him. Thus, as one London paper wrote in a caustic editorial, only two men in all history have had a college named for them at both Oxford and Cambridge: Jesus Christ and Isaac Wolfson. (The price seems to be going up. The Kellogg people invested more than $12 million before Oxford renamed another college in favor of the inventor of corn flakes.)

The Shah of Iran made a $1 million gift to the University of Southern California, whose president then hand-carried an honorary Doctorate to Iran. Around the same time, the University of Wisconsin exchanged an honorary Doctorate for a $2.5 million gift from oil millionaire C. George Weeks.

John Hope Franklin of the National Humanities Center worries, as do many others, about "the delicate matter of honorary degrees. One cannot help wondering in how many ways some institutions sell their souls in conferring them. . . . Better that a university cease to exist altogether than sell its soul."

One solution to this matter is to award the honorary degree first, in the hopes that the recipient will give the school his thanks in the form of a check or other favors. This approach made headlines a while back when the *Washington Post* uncovered the "Koreagate" scandal, in which 11 U.S. congressmen had accepted, among other favors, honorary Doctorates from South Korean universities, complete with all-expense luxury trips to Korea to collect them, in an apparent effort to win congressional approval of the Korean regime.

To their credit, three congressmen rejected the honorary Doctorates. But it is rare indeed for an honorary Doctorate to be turned down. Oxford University used to have a policy, before Richard Nixon came along, of offering an honorary Doctorate to every outgoing U.S. president. Of all those to whom it was offered, only good old Millard Fillmore turned it down, saying that he felt he had done nothing to merit it, and besides, the diploma was in Latin and he never accepted anything he couldn't read.

HOW TO GET AN HONORARY DOCTORATE

How, then, does the ordinary person, who is not a movie star, an athlete, or a millionaire, acquire an honorary Doctorate? There is no simple way, other than buying one from a less-than-respectable institution, or having one printed to order at the neighborhood print shop. Nonetheless, here are five possibilities:

1. Donate money. The question naturally arises, how little money does it take to buy an honorary Doctorate from a major accredited university? If the school is in financial trouble, as little as $10,000 has been said to turn the trick. The cheapest case we personally know about is $50,000 from an Arab businessman to an accredited California university whose building fund was in trouble.

A Los Angeles businessman once ran a small ad in *The New Republic* magazine, offering to donate $10,000 to any accredited school that would give him an honorary degree. When we contacted him, he told John he had gotten the degree, but refused to name the school.

2. Perform a valuable service. Honorary Doctorates have gone to heads of fundraising committees, who never gave a dime themselves, to real estate brokers who put together a big deal to acquire more land or refinance a mortgage for the school, to friends of friends of celebrities who managed to get the Senator or the Star or the Second Baseman to speak at the commencement, to a nurseryman who wangled the donation of hundreds of trees and supervised their planting on campus; to a golf pro who donated his time to the college team; and so on.

Lawyers are sometimes rewarded too. When Cecil Rhodes died in 1902 he left money for scholarships for "white American boys from all 13 states." The lawyer who got this legal mess untangled, and persuaded Parliament to come up with funds for "white American boys" from all the other states, got a Doctor of Civil Law from Oxford for his efforts.

Perhaps the most valuable service one can perform is finding a cash donor. Remember that $50,000 honorary Doctorate for an Arab businessman, just described? Well, the man who found that donor for the university in question also got an honorary Doctorate, as a finder's fee.

3. Capitalize on trends. Honorary Doctorates seem to be rather trendy things, and those trends seem to run for three to five years. For instance, in the late 1950s, space science was in vogue, and people ranging from Wernher von Braun to the founder of a local rocketry society were being honored. In the 1960s, it was the Peace Corps. Sargent Shriver, its first director, set a record that still stands by accepting seven Doctorates in one month (June, 1964), and a lot of other Peace Corps people and other youth workers were in demand on commencement platforms.

The 1980s seemed heavy on jazz and classical musicians, medical researchers, people who work with the handicapped, the very elderly (several people over 100 got them for no apparent reason other than survival), Vietnam veterans, economists, and public interest lawyers.

In the 1990s, more than a few kudos have gone to authors of children's books, radio talk show hosts, AIDS researchers or counselors, investigative reporters, coaches of non-major sports (lacrosse, rugby, field hockey, volleyball), and schoolteachers.

Some people have reported success by directly or, more often, indirectly contacting a school that has given a certain honorary degree this year, suggesting they may wish to consider a similar one next year.

4. Buy one. If all you really want is a fancy but meaningless document to hang on the wall (actually, all honorary Doctorates fit that description, but some may be perceived as more meaningless than others), some of the schools described in chapter 19 are likely to oblige, according to a recent article in *Spy* magazine (Feb. 1995). Of course any of the diploma mills would be more than pleased to dispense an honorary Doctorate on payment of a fee that can range from 50¢ to over $1,000, but you're on your own for locating those; we don't give out addresses. Another common source of honoraries are the Bible schools, some of which reward donors with honorary degrees. See Appendix E for more information on these.

But you'll do just as well at the local print shop, where you can have the type set for the diploma of your choice. Just don't get carried away and have a whole batch printed for sale to the public.

5. Wait. A few years ago, John wrote that "I think it is inevitable that one or more well-known, respectable, fully-accredited colleges, faced by the cash crunch that is upon so many worthy institutions, will face reality and openly put their honorary Doctorates up for sale." A few years later, it happened. A small, accredited college took out a national ad, suggesting a donation of $25,000. The accrediting agency got quite upset at this, and the offer was withdrawn. But later, the well-respected Embry-Riddle Aeronautical University bought a *Wall Street Journal* ad offering a Trusteeship of the University in exchange for a $1 million donation (from an otherwise qualified donor). That, too, caused a furor.

So maybe we are still a bit premature in saying, "Wait." It may be that the deals will continue to go on just below the surface for a while longer.

THE ETIQUETTE OF SOLICITING DEGREES

Here's one that Emily Post never had to deal with. How

straightforward should one be in letting it be known that one would like an honorary Doctorate? There is no way to know. Our feeling is that in the majority of situations, the direct approach is inappropriate. One must work through intermediaries—friends of school officials or trustees, who drop hints. But there are some schools and awards committees who seem to find the blunt approach refreshingly candid. These are people who realize and admit that what they are really doing is selling honorary degrees, so why not be up front? The president of a small eastern college told John that he was once approached by a second-rate actor who really wanted an honorary Doctorate, "just like Marlon Brando and Henry Fonda." They negotiated terms, and the degree was awarded the following June—presumably after the check cleared the bank.

On the other hand, a high U.S. Air Force official in Europe got a lot of unfavorable publicity when *Stars and Stripes* revealed that he had solicited honorary Doctorates for himself and some associates from universities that were doing contractual work for the air force. Two of the universities (Southern California and Maryland) turned him down. "It wasn't appropriate to ask for it, and it wasn't appropriate to give it," one school official said. But the third university gave it to him.

The army's counterpart in Europe, when asked if *he* would solicit honorary Doctorates, replied, "You've got to be out of your tree."

One of the more awkward solicitations came from actor George Wendt, better known as the beer-guzzling Norm on the popular sit-com *Cheers*. Here is how the Miami *Herald* reported the event:

Notre Dame Coach Lou Holtz looked toward a big Fighting Irish fan—a really big Fighting Irish fan—to motivate his team Friday night. George Wendt...burst into a frenzied pep rally unannounced as the 10,000-plus students chanted 'Norm!'
Wendt proclaimed that the Fighting Irish had some unfinished business to attend to Saturday. As far as motivation speeches go, though, this wasn't much of one. Other than the unfinished-business line, Wendt did little more than yell unintelligibly at the top of his lungs until he was dragged away. Wendt, who failed out of Notre Dame after three years, asked for an honorary degree, but Holtz gave him an autographed football instead....

THE WONDERFUL WACKY WORLD OF HONORARY DEGREES

Here are just a few of the recipients we learned about since the last edition of our book.

Recipient	School	What, why, etc.
Dr. Robin Williams	Juilliard	After lampooning Jesse Helms and Dan Quayle ("President Quayle, raise your right hand. No, your other right hand."), he said "I would like to do something from Hamlet. I just need a moment to prepare." As the crowd roared, he continued, "To be or...wait! I know this!"
Dr. Patrick Ewing	Shaw University	For his athletic abilities and his work with youth.
Dr. Sonny Bono	National Disaster Conference	The degree in disaster medicine was awarded after he helped carry stretchers following a bus accident in Palm Springs.
Dr. Bill Cosby	University of Maryland	"There are no courses in valet parking, waitressing and grinding coffee. You people are not prepared. You are well-educated and you look cute, but that's not going to do it."
Dr. Mother Teresa	University of Scranton	The degree is in social sciences; as soon as it was awarded, she had a police escort back to the Wilkes-Barre airport.
Dr. Sun Myung Moon	Shaw Divinity School	Dr. Moon was in prison for tax evasion at the time.
Dr. Oprah Winfrey	Morehouse College	Doctor of Humane Letters. She gave $1 million for a scholarship fund at the all-male school.
Dr. Goober	U. of North Alabama	George Lindsey, Goober on the Andy Griffith Show, was a sterling fund raiser for his alma mater.
Dr. Frank Sinatra	Stevens Institute	A third of the graduating class signed a petition objecting, not to Sinatra but to the fact the degree was in engineering. Sinatra was born in Hoboken, site of the school.
Dr. Bryant Gumbel	Bates College	"I was not the hardworking 4.0 student.... Life doesn't end when you graduate with less than a 3.0"
Dr. Elwood Blues	Yale University	This mule received a Doctor of Portage Equus for carrying rocks for the Yale geology team. "We don't consider this a joke," said a National Park Service spokesman. "It's not likely an honorary doctorate has ever been given to a mule before from an Ivy League school."
Dr. Mike Tyson	Central State University	After the ceremony, he told a reporter, "I'm successful, I'm young, I'm single, I'm rich, I have God in my life...and may I be permitted to say, you are such an incredible-looking woman."
Dr. Victor Borge	University of Denver	"Now that I'm a doctor," he said, "I think I have to get some malpractice insurance."
Dr. Jim Evans	Central Missouri State	He invented Cheerios.
Dr. Cinderella	Miami-Dade College	For her efforts at literacy, as part of a book fair.
Dr. Chevy Chase	Bard College	Speaking to his alma mater, he said, "Never tell the truth. Embellish, patronize, pander, use hyperbole, braggadocio, mollify, but never actually tell the truth. Your job is to act. Keep the dream alive. Also, never call me."
Dr. Alexander Solzhenitsyn	Dartmouth College	Doctor of Letters. He speaks almost no English, refused to be interviewed, and did not speak to the graduating class.
Dr. Dolly Parton	Carson-Newman College	Doctor of Letters for "her personal commitment to the educational and economic vitality of East Tennessee..."
Dr. Prince Charles	Harvard University	Ronald Reagan was to deliver the keynote address, but declined when Harvard refused him an honorary degree because of the controversy over his academic deficiencies. The Prince of Wales accepted. His eagerly-awaited first words on arrival at Logan Airport: "Hello, how are you?"

Recipient	School	What, why, etc.
Dr. Soupy Sales	Marshall University	The newspaper story was headlined "Degree better than pie in face," when his alma mater presented the award.
Dr. Paul McCartney	University of Sussex	"Just call me Dr. Rock." he said. Since he didn't do too well at school, "it was great to get this degree without having to revise [study] for it."
Dr. Oliver North	Liberty University	Chancellor Jerry Falwell called him an American hero and compared his legal predicament to the suffering of Jesus.
Dr. Magic Johnson	Rust College	He said, "This is the greatest and biggest day of my life. This tops any championship, any MVP I've won...."
Dr. Bob Hope	University of San Diego	On receiving his 44th honorary doctorate, he said, "I love commencement. I love the happy, ecstatic, joyous faces. But enough about the teachers."
Dr. Joe DiMaggio	Columbia University	When he was spotted in the procession, "applause grew and several people chanted 'Joe D., Joe D, Joe D.' He waved.
Dr. Steve Wozniak	University of Colorado	The Apple founder was expelled for tampering with the school's computer system. 25 years later, they gave him a doctorate.
Dr. Scott Hamilton	Bowling Green State Univ.	The gold medalist never attended the school, but he did learn to skate on the university's ice arena.
Dr. Jerry Lewis	South Central Tech College	He stuck a glass all the way into his mouth, hid behind a giant flower arrangement, then said, "I never know what's going to happen until I get to the podium. I'm guided by instinct."
Dr. Joseph Haydn	Oxford University	He wrote Symhony #92 to thank Oxford for awarding him the degree, but it wasn't done in time, so #91 was played at the ceremony.
Dr. Doctor J	University of Massachusetts	Julius Erving received the honorary doctorate at the same time as his earned Bachelor's in leadership and management.
Dr. Prince Philip	Asian Institute of Technology	For his work in saving the environment and wildlife.
Dr. Milt Hinton	Skidmore College	The Judge, patriarch of jazz bass players, played two songs on his stand-up bass in lieu of making a speech.
Dr. Tony Bennett	Art Institute of Boston	He said, "When I get into the art zone, I forget about any pains that I have." He said he paints and sings every day.
Dr. Ed McMahon	Catholic University	Watch for a diploma in your mailbox.
Dr. Michael Jackson	Fisk University	For his support of the United Negro College Fund.
Dr. Alex Haley	Coast Guard Academy	The author of *Roots* received the academy's first honorary degree. While at sea during World War II, he wrote letters to their girlfriends for shipmates at one dollar each.
Dr. Dustin Hoffman	Santa Monica College	He enrolled there to study music, but took an acting class and never looked back (and never graduated).
Dr. Stan Musial	Washington University	Stan the Man never went to college, but as the newspaper account said, "most college graduates can't hit a curve ball."
Dr. George Bush	University of Kuwait	For his "distinguished leadership, lofty stance, and honorable endeavors in...the triumphant restoration of Kuwait's independence and sovereignty."
Dr. George Wallace	Tuskeegee Institute	He said, "Very few people have one. You wouldn't have thought I'd have had that, would you? If I was a bad man, I wouldn't have gotten that. No way."
Dr. Nelson Mandela	Carabobo State University	He was offered hundreds; this one was from Venezuela.

Noted rule bender.

♦27♦
Bending the Rules

Any fool can make a rule, and every fool will mind it.
HENRY DAVID THOREAU

One of the most common complaints or admonishments we get from readers goes something like, "You said thus-and-so, but when I inquired of the school, they told me such-and-such." Often, a school claims that a program we have written about does not exist. Sometimes a student achieves something (such as completing a certain degree entirely by correspondence) that we had been told by a high official of the school was impossible.

One of the open secrets in the world of higher education is that the rules are constantly being bent. But, as with the Emperor's new clothes, no one dares point and say what is really going on, especially in print.

The purpose of this brief essay is to acknowledge that this sort of thing happens all the time. If you know that it happens regularly, then at least you are in the same boat with people who are already benefiting from those bent rules.

Unfortunately, we cannot provide many specific examples of bent rules, naming names and all. This is for two good reasons:

1. Many situations where students profit from bent rules would disappear in an instant if anyone dared mention the situation publicly. There is, for instance, a major state university that is forbidden by its charter to grant degrees by correspondence study. But they regularly work out special arrangements whereby students are carried on the books as residential, even though all their work is done by mail. Indeed, some graduates of this school have never set foot on its campus. If this ever got out, the Board of Trustees, the accrediting agency, and all the other universities in that state would probably have conniptions, and the practice would be suspended at once.

2. These kinds of things can change so rapidly, with new personnel or new policies, that a listing of anomalies and curious practices would probably be obsolete before the ink dried.

Consider a few examples of the sort of thing that is going on in higher education every day, whether or not anyone will admit it, except perhaps behind closed doors or after several drinks:

♦ A friend of John's, at a major university, was unable to complete one required course for her Doctorate before she had to leave for another state. This university does not offer correspondence courses, but she was able to convince a professor to enroll her in a regular course, which she would just happen never to visit in person.

♦ A man in graduate school needed to be enrolled in nine units of coursework each semester to keep his employer's tuition assistance plan going. But his job was too demanding one year, and he was unable to do so. The school enrolled him in nine units of "independent study" for which no work was asked or required, and for which a "pass" grade was given.

♦ A woman at a large school needed to complete a certain number of units before an inflexible deadline. When it became clear that she wasn't going to make it, a kindly professor turned in grades for her, and told her she could do the actual coursework later on.

♦ A major state university offers nonresident degrees for people living in that state only. When a reader wrote to say that he, living a thousand miles from that state, was able to complete his degree entirely by correspondence, John asked a contact at that school what was going on. "We will take students from anywhere in our correspondence degree program," she told him, "But for God's sake, don't print that in your book, or we'll be deluged with applicants."

♦ If we are to believe a book by a member of Dr. Bill Cosby's dissertation committee at the University of Massachusetts (*Education's Smoking Gun*, by Reginald Damerell), the only class attendance on Cosby's transcript was one weekend seminar, and the only dissertation committee meeting was a dinner party, with spouses, at Cosby's house.

♦ Partway through John's supposedly definitive final doctoral oral exam, a key member of his committee had to leave for an emergency. He scrawled a note, and passed it to the Dean who read it, then crumpled it up and threw it away. The grueling exam continued for several hours more. After it was over and the committee had congratulated John and departed, he retrieved the note from the

279

wastebasket. It read, "Please give John my apologies for having to leave, and my congratulations for having passed."

◆ A man applied to a well-known school that has a rigid requirement that all graduate work (thesis or dissertation) must be begun after enrollment. He started to tell an admissions officer about a major piece of independent research he had completed for his employer. "Stop," he was told, "don't tell me about that. Then you'll be able to use it for your Master's thesis."

◆ Mariah was initially denied admission to the University of California at Berkeley because of some "irregularities" on her high school transcript. (It was a nontraditional high school.) The high school's records had been destroyed in a fire. The former principal checked with the University, discovered that the admissions people would be glad to admit her, once the computer said it was OK. He typed up a new transcript saying what the computer wanted said. The computer said OK, and three years later, she graduated Phi Beta Kappa. But how many other applicants accepted the initial "No," not knowing that rules can often be bent?

◆ The Heriot-Watt University MBA by distance learning, with which John is involved, had a written policy stating that if a student failed an exam in a compulsory course twice, they could not continue in the program. Some students who had passed several courses, but then failed a course twice, were quietly offered another opportunity. Now, to its credit, the university has made this an official policy, and that particular rule no longer needs to be bent.

Please use this information prudently. It will probably do no good to pound on a table and say, "What do you mean I can't do this? John Bear says that rules don't mean anything, anyway."

But when faced with a problem, it surely can do no harm to remember that in many, many situations the rules have turned out to be far less rigid than a school's official literature would lead one to believe.

"Woweee! This home study course from the Mallowan Detective Institute is much more fun than I had expected."

◆28◆
Advice for People in Prison

*In the midst of winter I discovered
there was in me an invincible summer.*
ALBERT CAMUS

NOTE: More than a few readers and users of this book are institutionalized. We have invited a man who has completed his accredited Bachelor's, Master's, and Doctorate while in prison, and who consults often with inmates and others around the country, to offer his thoughts and recommendations. There is some very useful advice for noninstitutionalized persons as well. (The above quotation has been on Dr. Dean's bulletin board since he began his baccalaureate.)

Arranging Academic Resources for the Institutionalized
by Douglas G. Dean, Ph.D.

One obstacle for any institutionalized person interested in pursuing a degree is limited resources: availability of community faculty, library facilities, phone access, and financial aid. To overcome these, it helps to streamline the matriculation process. Time spent in preparation prior to admission can help avoid wasted effort and time when in a program, thereby reducing operating expenses and cutting down the number of tuition periods.

A second obstacle is finding ways to ensure that a quality education can be documented. Because courses are generally not prepackaged, it is the student's responsibility to identify varied learning settings, use a range of learning methods, find and recruit community-based faculty, provide objective means to appraise what has been learned, and indeed design the study plan itself.

Finding a Flexible Degree Program
Most well-established degree programs grant credit for a variety of learning experiences. In terms of cost and arrangements required, equivalency examinations and independent study projects are the most expedient. Credit for life-experience learning is another option sometimes offered. If a degree program does not offer at least two of these options, it is unlikely that the program as a whole will be able to accommodate the needs of the institutionalized student.

Writing a Competency-based Study Plan
The traditional method of acquiring credits is to take narrowly focused courses of two to four credits each. Since the nontraditional student must enlist his or her own instructors, find varied learning methods, and quantify the whole experience, the single-course approach creates much needless duplication of effort.

A better approach is to envision a subject area which is to be studied for 9 to 12 credits (e.g., statistics). As an independent-study project, the student identifies what topics are germane to the area (e.g., probability theory, descriptive statistics, inferential statistics); at what level of comprehension (e.g., introductory through intermediate or advanced); how the topic is to be studied (e.g., directed reading, programmed textbooks), and how the competencies acquired are to be demonstrated (e.g., oral examination, proctored examination including problem solving). This way, a single independent-study project can take the place of a series of successive courses in a given area (e.g., statistics 101, 201, 301).

Designing the Curriculum
Every accredited degree program has graduation requirements. These requirements broadly define the breadth of subject areas that comprise a liberal arts education and the depth to which they are to be studied. It is the responsibility of the external student not only to identify a curriculum fulfilling these requirements but, in most cases, to design the course content that will comprise each study module.

But how does a student know what an area of study consists of before he or she has studied it? The answer lies in meticulous preparation.

Well in advance of formally applying for an off-campus degree program, the prospective student should obtain course catalogs from several colleges and universities. Look at what these schools consider the core curriculum and what is necessary to fulfill the graduation requirements. With this broad outline in mind, the student can begin to form clusters of courses fulfilling each criterion. This approach helps shape the study plan academically rather than touch it up later as an afterthought.

Next, decide which subjects are of interest within each criterion area. Compare topical areas within each subject as described in the course listings and commonalities will emerge. From there, it is simply a matter of writing to the various instructors for a copy of their course syllabi. These course outlines will provide more detailed information about the subject matter and identify the textbooks currently used at that level of study.

Means of Study

Having decided what is to be studied, the student must then propose various ways to study it.

Equivalency exams (such as CLEP) enable the student to acquire credits instantly, often in core or required areas of study. This helps reduce overall program costs by eliminating the need for textbooks and tuition fees. More importantly, it helps reduce the number of special learning arrangements that must otherwise be made.

"Testing out" of correspondence courses (taking only the examinations, without doing the homework assignments) is another excellent way to acquire credits quickly. This can, however, be an expensive method since full course fees are still assessed. Nonetheless, if a student studies on his or her own in advance according to the course syllabus, and if the instructor can then be convinced to waive prerequisite assignments, it can be an efficient and cost-effective method to use.

Independent-study projects should form the balance of any study plan. With the topical areas, learning objectives, and learning materials identified, an independent study project allows the student to remain with the same instructor(s) from an introductory through an intermediate or advanced level of study. This eliminates the need for new arrangements to be made every two to four credits. An independent study project can take the form of simple directed reading, tutorial instruction, practicum work, or a combination of these methods, culminating in the final product.

Direct tutorial arrangements, similar to the European don system, commit a student to learn under a single instructor until he or she is convinced that the student has mastered a given subject at a predetermined level of competency. The tutoring itself may take the form of directed reading from both primary and secondary sources, writing and orally defending assigned topical papers, monitored practica, and supervised research projects. The caveat is that the tutor determines when a student has satisfied all study requirements, so the study plan should meticulously spell out the breadth and depth of what is to be studied.

One may also be able to use existing classroom courses as a setting in which to evaluate a student's mastery of a given subject. Some institutions periodically offer an on-site college or vocational course (e.g., communications skills). Instead of taking such a course for the standard 2 to 3 credits, the student could arrange for specific communication skills (composition, rhetoric) to be evaluated at a given level of mastery (beginning to advanced). In this single step, a student may be able to earn advanced credit and fulfill all the communication skills core requirements for graduation.

Various professions require practitioners to earn continuing education credits, usually through seminars and/or home study courses. These courses represent the latest knowledge in a given field, come prepackaged with an evaluation test, and are an excellent source of study material. The breadth and depth of specialization offered in such courses is especially useful to students with graduate or postgraduate aspirations.

Independent-study projects require the aid of qualified persons to act as community faculty, and to oversee personally the progress of the work. Therefore, it is highly advantageous to line up faculty in advance of entering the degree program. It is equally important to have alternates available in the event an instructor is unable, for any reason, to fulfill his or her commitment. It is better to anticipate these needs at the preparatory stage than to be scrambling for a replacement while the tuition clock is running.

Multiple Treatments of Subject Matter

The external student is often without benefit of lecture halls, interactions with other students, or readily available academic counseling services. For the institutionalized student, picking up the phone or stopping in to see a faculty member for help with a study problem are not options. This is why alternate methods of study are so valuable.

One approach is to use several textbooks covering the same subject matter. If something does not make sense, there is a different treatment of the subject to turn to.

Programmed textbooks make especially good substitute tutors. A programmed text breaks the subject matter into small segments requiring a response from the reader with periodic tests to check progress. Such texts are now available in many subject areas, but are particularly useful for the sciences. Titles can be obtained from the *Books in Print* subject guide, or by writing directly to textbook publishers.

Audio-visual (A-V) materials can, to some extent, make up for college life without the typical lectures and classes. Writing to A-V departments at large universities often yields a catalog of materials available for rental. These materials frequently take the form of a comprehensive tape series, and may address even the most advanced subject matter. When using such materials, it is best to work through the school or social service department of the student's institution of residence.

Some large campuses have lecture note services, which employ advanced students to attend class lectures and take copious lecture notes, which are then sold to students. Aside from gaining insights into good note-taking, these published notes are an additional treatment of course content, and can indicate what topical areas are given special emphasis. Such notes are especially recommended for new students.

Documenting Study

The administrators of a degree program must be convinced that there are acceptable ways to document what has been learned, and what levels of subject mastery have been achieved, without taking the student's word for it. Community faculty members may be asked to provide written or oral examinations, but it does not hurt to make their jobs easier.

It is highly recommended that each study project be evaluated using a number of means (objectives tests, essay exams, oral exams) and documented using a variety of methods (student narrative, faculty narrative, test results, final product, grade equivalent, etc.).

Self-evaluation, not unlike personal logs or journals, provides an excellent primary source from which to glean what a student truly knows, how they came to know it, and what new questions arise from the acquired knowledge. Any future employer or admissions counselor unfamiliar with non-traditional or off-campus degree programs can gain a fuller appreciation of the process through such narratives.

Likewise, a narrative evaluation written by the instructor provides a description of student competencies that ordinary assessment methods are unable to detect or reflect. Nuances of learning style, ability to converse in the field of study, and scholarly integrity are examples of such insights.

Depending on the subject at hand, the final product may take the form of a research monograph, video presentation, musical manuscript, senior thesis, etc.—whatever will best provide proof and record that the student has achieved the target level of competency in that field.

Most professions (accounting, psychology, law, medicine, etc.) have licensing and/or board certification examinations that must be taken. An industry has built up around this need, providing parallel or actual past examinations to help prepare students. By agreeing to take a relevant sample examination under proctored conditions, and negotiating cutoff scores in advance, the community faculty member is relieved of having to design his or her own objective examination for just one student. This approach adds validity to the assessment process, and provides a standardized score that has some universal meaning. This is an optional approach but may be worth the effort.

Recruiting Community Faculty

Just as it is easier for a student to organize a study plan into blocks of subject areas, a competency-based study plan

of this sort makes it easier for a prospective instructor to visualize what is being asked of him or her.

A typical independent study project would define for the instructor what specific topics are to be studied, what levels of mastery will be expected of the student, what textbooks or other materials will be used, and what is expected of the instructor.

Many traditional academics are unfamiliar with external degree programs. Consequently, they tend to assume that their role as instructor will require greater effort and time on their part than for the average student, who may expect their services in many roles, from academic advisor to tutor. The more an institutionalized student can do up front to define clearly the role and expected duties of the community faculty member, the more successful a student will be in enlisting instructors for independent study projects.

Instructors may sometimes be found on the staff of the institution where the student resides. They may also be found through a canvasing letter sent to the appropriate department heads at area colleges, universities, and technical schools. The same approach may be used to canvas departments within area businesses, museums, art centers, hospitals, libraries, theaters, zoos, banks, and orchestras, to name but a few. People are often flattered to be asked, providing it is clear to them exactly what they are getting into.

The more a student can operate independently, and rely on community faculty for little more than assessment purposes, the more likely a student will be successful in recruiting help, and thereby broadening the range of study options.

Revealing Your Institutionalized Status

It is generally proper and appropriate to inform potential schools and potential faculty of one's institutionalized status. (Many institutions now have mailing addresses that do not indicate they are, in fact, institutions.) Some schools or individuals may be put off by this, but then you would not want to deal with them anyway. Others may be especially motivated to help.

A recommended approach is to first make a general inquiry about the prospective school or program. With this information in hand, information intended for the general student, one may better tailor inquiries to specific departments or faculty, addressing your specific needs.

Financing the Educational Process

Unfortunately, there are virtually no generalizations to be made here, whatsoever. Each institution seems to have its own policy with regard to the way finances are handled. Some institutionalized persons earn decent wages, and have access to the funds. Others have little or no ability to pay their own way. Some institutions permit financial gifts from relatives or friends, others do not. Some schools make special concessions or have some scholarship funds available for institutionalized persons; many do not. One should contact the financial aid office of the prospective school with any such questions.

Again, start with a general inquiry, as would any student, then ask about the applicability of specific programs to your situation. Often a key element is to find someone on campus, perhaps in the financial aid office or your degree program, who is willing to do the actual legwork, walking your financial aid paperwork to various administrative offices. A financial aid package is of no use to anyone if it cannot be processed.

The denial of Pell grants to incarcerated people, starting in 1994, and the demise of Davis-Putter—the only foundation specializing in paying inmates' tuition—have made an already difficult process even harder.

In conclusion

Institutionalized students must be highly self-directed, and honest enough with themselves to recognize if they are not. Because the student lives where he or she works, it takes extra effort to set aside daily study time, not only to put the student in the right frame of mind, but also to accommodate institution schedules. It can mean working with a minimum number of books or tapes to comply with property rules. It can mean study periods that begin at 11 P.M., when the cellhall begins to quiet down. It means long periods of delayed gratification, in an environment where pursuing education is often suspect. And it is the greatest feeling in the world when it all comes together.

"When they told me I'd only have to read six books to earn my Master's through distance learning, it never occurred to me . . . "

◆29◆
Other Schools

*"There are more things in heaven and earth, Horatio,
than are dreamt of in your philosophy."*
WILLIAM SHAKESPEARE

This chapter replaces the old "Help Wanted" and "Good-bye" indexes; it lists all of the schools that, for whatever reason, are not listed in the other, previous chapters (16 through 24).

There are three main reasons why a school would be listed here rather than there:

1. They have been in earlier editions of this book, and are no longer in business (or findable by us, despite our best efforts);

2. They have been in earlier editions of this book, and, while they are still in business, they no longer offer the nontraditional program(s) earlier described;

3. They are schools which may offer (or have offered) certain degree programs nontraditionally, but about which we have not been able to learn enough information to give them a proper listing.

This represents the most complete compilation of "good-byes" ever—every school that has ever been listed in this book, going back to the first edition in 1974 and what, to the best of our knowledge, has happened to them.

The "best of our knowledge," however, isn't always that complete, and that is the reason for the third group of schools listed in this chapter: those on whom we have fragmentary information, but not enough for a full listing.

We Welcome Help of Two Kinds:

1. Help in checking out schools: Situations regularly arise in which we'd like to learn more about a certain school. Sometimes we are hindered by distance. One can often learn more from a brief in-person inspection than by hours of research or communication (such as, in an extreme but not uncommon case, when it turns out to be a mail-forwarding service.) Sometimes we are hindered by John's notoriety—some schools simply won't communicate with John Bear (or anyone named Bear) at all, or won't answer questions about their programs.

We do have an informal array of pen pals in cities around the world who have been very helpful in checking out schools, either in person or by correspondence—but more are always needed. If you would be willing to do this from time to time, please drop us a card or note to let us know. If you frequently travel to a certain city and could check out schools there, let us know that too. Thank you (John & Mariah Bear, P.O. Box 7070, Berkeley, CA 94707).

2. Help in learning about specific schools: We are regularly asked for information on certain schools, by law-enforcement officials, personnel officers, reporters, alumni, or other interested members of the public. Often we can help, but many times we cannot. If you know anything about the schools listed below, even if it is only a scrap of information or a bit of hearsay, please let us know. Thank you again. We won't use your name in any way—but if you'd prefer, anonymous letters are acceptable. (If you sent us a letter about any of these schools and see that your information was not incorporated, please don't be dismayed. In the past, updating was a much more haphazard affair. With this edition, we have also created a complete computerized database of every school in the book. Thus all comments can be easily added, for the next edition.)

Abilene Christian University Texas. At one time offered an accredited external M.S. in human relations or management.

Academic Credit University Started in Culver City, California by the former president of Southland University and some Ethiopian colleagues; mail now returned as undeliverable.

Academy of Open Learning They used to offer a Bachelor of Arts in valuation sciences for appraisers, but now mail to their former address in Geneva, Illinois is not answered and there is no listed phone.

Academy of Oriental Heritage A reader writes that this school offers courses in Chinese herbalism and a variety of other Oriental fields. Inquiries to their address in Blaine, Washington have not been answered.

Academy of Technical Sciences See: Bedford University

Advanced School of Herbology They were in Sacramento, California, but we cannot locate them now.

Airola College See: North American Colleges of Natural Health Science.

Ambassador College The school is still in existence in Big Sandy, Texas (formerly Pasadena, California), but no longer offers any nontraditional programs.

American College in Paris At one time offered Bachelor's degrees through summer or year-round study in Paris.

American College of Finance Formerly a California authorized school, but mail has been returned as undeliverable and there is no listed telephone in Sunnyvale, California.

American Floating University In the 1930s they offered Bachelor and Master of World Affairs degrees to students who studied while traveling on ocean liners. Now they have sunk from view. Constantine Raises of San Francisco was in charge.

American Institute of Traditional Chinese Medicine They had been a state-authorized school in San Francisco, but letters to them were returned as undeliverable, and there is no listed telephone number.

American International Open University See: Clayton University

American M & N University We believe that they are at 5000 Esplanade, #263, Metairie, LA 70006, and that Nancy Chien is in charge, but there has been no response to our requests for information

American National University They had been a state-authorized school, but mail to their La Palma, California address was returned as undeliverable and there is no listed telephone. Apparently there was no connection with a diploma mill of this name which operated from California and Arizona in the 1970s and early 1980s.

American Open University This was the name used for the nontraditional programs of the New York Institute of Technology, but it is apparently no longer in use.

American Open University This was a well-funded effort by a consortium of traditional universities to establish a nontraditional university in Lincoln, Nebraska, also using the name "University of Mid-America." But the project ended before any students were enrolled.

American Pacific University They were formerly a state-authorized school, but mail to the Costa Mesa, California address has been returned as undeliverable, and there is no listed telephone number there.

American Schools The address we have is 292 S. La Cienega Blvd, #10, Beverly Hills, CA 90211, but they have not responded to our inquiries. Len Nelson is the name we have.

American University of Oriental Studies Formerly a state-authorized school. Mail to their Los Angeles address returned as undeliverable, and there is no listed telephone number.

Americanos College We know that they are located at P.O. Box 12614, Latsia, Nicosia, Cyprus, but James Lehigh, Dean of Academic Development, has not responded to several requests for information about their nontraditional programs.

Amwealth University In the early 1990s, they were registered with the Louisiana Board of Regents (then an automatic process), but mail to the New Orleans address was returned as undeliverable, and there is no listed telephone number.

Ana G. Mendez University System We know that they are located at P.O. Box 21345, San Juan, Puerto Rico 00928, but no one has responded to several requests for information about their nontraditional programs.

Andrew Jackson College Originally established as American Community College, then Andrew Jackson University and Andrew Jackson University College, in Louisiana by Jean-Maximillien De La Croix de Lafayette. Subsequently used an address that was apparently Dr. De La Croix de Lafayette's home in Maryland, but now apparently no longer in business.

Andrew Jackson University College See: Andrew Jackson University

Anthony University Philadelphia. This unaccredited school offered degrees at all levels, but the phone has been disconnected.

Appalachian State University North Carolina. This accredited school used to offer a B.A. in which over 75% of the credits could come from life-experience learning.

Appraisal College Formerly registered with the Louisiana Board of Regents, then an automatic process. Mail to their Baton Rouge address is returned as undeliverable, and there is no listed telephone number.

Arnould-Taylor Education Ltd. No longer grants degrees because of changes in British higher education laws. Had offered both a Bachelor's and Master's in Physiatrics entirely through correspondence. Their material emphasized that these were professional—not academic—degrees offered to persons already qualified in the field of physical therapy.

Arthur D. Little Management Education Institute Cambridge, Massachusetts. Offered an accredited M.S. in international management education; asked to be deleted many years ago and we haven't heard from them since.

Asian American University Formerly authorized to grant degrees by the State of California. Letters to their San Diego address have not been answered, and there is no listed telephone number.

Atlanta Law School Georgia. Unaccredited, and now defunct, law school.

Atlantic Institute of Education An accredited Canadian program offering Master's degrees and Doctorates through distance learning. Closed after they lost their funding.

August Vollmer University Formerly authorized by the State of California. Mail to their address in Orange, California returned as undeliverable, and no listed telephone number.

Avon University Several bible school administrators have listed degrees from this school, which one said was founded in Boston in 1897, but we have been unable to locate it.

Azusa Pacific College California. At one time offered Master's degrees through evening study.

Babson College Wellesley, Massachusetts. Accredited evening M.B.A. discontinued.

Bay Area Open College California. At one time offered undergraduate degrees through a range of nontraditional methods. Affiliated with the traditional Wright Institute.

Beacon College Established in Boston and later moved to Washington, D.C., Beacon had probably the most flexible, most nontraditional Master's degree ever to achieve traditional accreditation, which was granted in 1981. Accreditation was subsequently lost due to licensing difficulties, and the school went out of business. Former name: Campus-Free College.

Bedford University Operated briefly in Arizona, offering degrees at a time when that state had no laws regulating schools. Closed in 1983. Had offered degrees in conjunction with the Academy of Technical Sciences of Beirut, Lebanon. According to the *Arizona Republic* newspaper, clients of the Educom Counseling Service in California were referred to Bedford as "the school most suited" to their needs. Educom was run by Thomas Lavin, formerly vice president of Kensington University, later Bedford's founder, later still an officer of Clayton University, and his daughter.

Bell Isles College See: College of the Palm Beaches

Ben Franklin Academy and Institute for Advanced Studies Washington, D.C. Offered unaccredited degrees at all levels entirely through correspondence, and for very little coursework.

Bentley Institute At one time, registered with the Louisiana Board of Regents, but apparently never accepted students, and no longer exists.

Berea School of Theology Letters to their address in Linton, Indiana were returned as undeliverable.

Berean Christian College A correspondent writes that he sent money to Berean at an address in Long Beach, California, but soon after his mail was returned and the phone was disconnected.

Berkeley International University In 1993, advertisements in The Economist magazine described a distance-learning M.B.A., but a visit to this school's San Francisco office yielded only the information that their catalog was not yet ready, and some biographical information on members of "The Berkeley Group," many with degrees listed from various Russian universities. Less than a year later, the phones had been disconnected and they were gone.

Beta International University Apparently now out of business (letters to their Chicago address have been returned to sender), Beta was an evangelical Christian school that offered nonreligious degrees of all kinds, including law, by correspondence. Claimed accreditation from "Af Sep," an organization with which we are not familiar. No names were given in their newsprint catalog other than a "Dr. Ellis."

Beverly Law School California. Alternative law school, no longer around.

Biscayne College See: Saint Thomas University

Blake College A reader asked for information on this school, which he said operated in both Mexico and Eugene, Oregon, but we have not been able to learn anything.

Body Mind College Barry Green at 149 Highway 1077, Madisonville, LA 70447 has not responded to our requests for information.

Borinquen University Medical School Mail to their last known address in Puerto Rico returned as undeliverable; cannot locate.

Boulder Graduate School This unaccredited school in Boulder, Colorado offered Master's degrees in psychology and counseling and in health and wellness, emphasizing a balance between academic training and experiential learning. Formerly the Colorado Institute of Transpersonal Psychology. Now out of business.

British Institute of Homeopathy A reader writes that they offer diploma and postgraduate courses in homeopathy. We asked for but never received information from their address in southern California.

California Acupuncture College Letters to their address in Los Angeles were returned as undeliverable. They had campuses in Santa Barbara and San Diego offering a three-year program preparing students to become practitioners of acupuncture and Oriental medicine. Courses were offered in Western sciences, herbology, and homeopathy. They were approved to grant degrees by the state of California.

California American University Formerly authorized by the State of California, but mail sent to their address in Escondido is returned as undeliverable and there is no listed telephone number. Had offered an M.S. in management involving a five-week summer session and tutorials directed by senior professors, all of whom had earned traditional Doctorates.

California Christian College of Los Angeles See: California Christian University

California Christian University Established in Los Angeles (then moved to Adelanto, California) by the Reverend Bishop Doctor Walter G. Rummersfield, B.S., Ms.D., Ps.D., GS-9, D.D., Ph.D.M., Ph.D., Ph.D., D.B.A., S.T.D., J.C.D., J.S.D. Formerly called California Christian College of Los Angeles; once authorized by the state of California to grant degrees. Honorary Doctorates were awarded on payment of a donation of "$1,000 or less." Dr. Dr. Dr. Dr. Dr. Dr. Dr. Dr. Rummersfield apparently transferred control to new management in the 1980s, but no one answers our letters, and there is no longer a listed phone in Adelanto.

California College of Commerce A letter to their Long Beach address was returned marked "forwarding order expired," and we cannot locate them.

California Institute of Electronics and Materials Science We have had no response to our inquiries to Lev I. Berger at 2115 Flame Tree Way, Hemet, CA 92343.

California College of Law Formerly authorized by the State of California, but letters to their Beverly Hills, California address were returned as undeliverable and there is no listed telephone number.

California Institute of the Arts Valencia, California. Accredited school no longer offers its B.F.A. with up to 75% life-experience learning credit.

California University for Advanced Studies In 1989 they lost their state authorization and closed their offices in Petaluma, California. The school maintained they were harassed out of existence. The state will not comment, other than to say that the school no longer met the requirements for authorization. Many enrolled students were allowed to complete degrees, but many others neither finished nor received refunds, and have been attempting unsuccessfully to locate University owner George Ryan. The "Roberta Bear" who was listed briefly as president is not known to either of us.

Campus-Free College See: Beacon College

Carthage College Kenosha, Wisconsin. Accredited school no longer offers its Bachelor's with over 75% life-experience learning credit.

Centro de Estudios Universitarios Xochicalco Cuernavaca, Mexico. There were actually two medical schools by this name: the original, which had recognized programs offered in conjunction with a school in Philadelphia, and the second, apparently an identical program started by a disgruntled faculty member of the first. Neither school is now in business.

Charles Dederich School of Law This unaccredited law school was operated by the Synanon Foundation. During the short time of their existence in Badger, California, they achieved an impressive success rate in bar exam passes, including 8 out of 9 one year.

Chase University Elmer P. Chase III sincerely attempted to start a university in various locations, most recently Kenner, Louisiana, but none of them got off the ground, and the effort has apparently been abandoned.

Chicago Conservatory College Offered accredited Bachelor's and Master's of music through evening study.

Christian Congregation, Inc. They used to issue honorary Doctorates in divinity, in return for a donation. Donors were encouraged to be as generous as circumstances and conscience permitted. Mail to the last address we had, in Monroe, North Carolina, has been returned as undeliverable.

CIFAS School of Medicine Santo Domingo, Dominican Republic. This large Caribbean medical school, which primarily served Americans, was found to be offering a legitimate education through the front door and selling M.D. degrees for up to $27,000 out the back door. Several administrators went to prison for so doing.

Clarksville School of Theology This Clarksville, Tennessee school offered Bachelor's, Master's, and Doctorates in theology under the guidance of W. Roy Stewart, a popular evangelist. As of 1988, there is no listed telephone number for the school.

Clayton University The phone is now answered "Clayton University Transcript Service," and the message says that the school is no longer accepting students. However, some readers have reported that Clayton is still operating in Europe and elsewhere. For many years, they operated as a nonresident institution based in Clayton, Missouri. Original name: Open University, and later American International Open University.

Clinical Hypnosis Center Florida. Apparently once offered an alternative degree in hypnotherapy. Probably the same as the Gracie Institute of Hypnosis.

Clinical Psychotherapy Institute At one time, authorized by the state of California. Letters to their address in San Rafael, California are returned as undeliverable and there is no listed telephone number.

Colby-Sawyer College New London, New Hampshire. No longer offers its accredited evening-study B.S. for women.

Colegio Jacinto Trevino Mercedes, Texas. Offered a bilingual B.A. in interdisciplinary studies to Chicano students through evening programs and community service. Letters returned as undeliverable.

College for Human Services New York. A one-time unaccredited human services Master's program, primarily for minority students.

College of Adaptive Education Sciences Inc. At one time registered with the Louisiana Board of Regents. Letters to their address in Baton Rouge have been returned as undeliverable, and there is no listed telephone number.

College of Clinical Hypnosis This Honolulu school used to offer a degree in clinical hypnosis through a $350 correspondence course. The founder and president "earned" his degree from Thomas A. Edison College, a notorious degree mill. In 1988, the phone was disconnected, and there has been no new listing.

College of Oriental Studies This Los Angeles school used to offer Bachelor's, Master's, and Doctorates in philosophy and religion, but they appear to have moved on.

College of Professional Studies Took on the international business programs that European University of America had run, but is apparently no longer operating. At least, mail has been returned and there is no listed number in San Francisco.

College of Racine Wisconsin. At one time offered a university without walls program.

College of the Palm Beaches West Palm Beach, Florida. Offered B.A. and M.B.A. through residential study, with a great deal of credit possible for prior experience. Unaccredited but licensed by the state. Declined to provide recent information. Formerly Bell Isles College, then University of Palm Beach.

Colorado Institute of Transpersonal Psychology See: Boulder Graduate School

Colorado Technical College Colorado Springs, Colorado. Used to offer a program through The Source, a computer correspondence system, but it was discontinued.

Commenius International University A 1981 article in *Monato,* an Esperanto-language magazine, featured an interview with the founder of this school, apparently located in San Diego. Mail addressed to the address given was neither answered nor returned as undeliverable, and there is no listed phone. The claim in the article that the university is "officially approved" by the state of California is not correct.

Concoria Institute La Verne, California. They offered a B.A. in business administration, and claimed an affiliation with Nova College in Canada. The director's Doctorate is from Elysion College, a now-closed California diploma mill.

Cooperating University of America Wilson, North Carolina. In the 1970s, a retired professor announced plans to establish a university by this name. The idea was to offer European students the opportunity to study in the U.S., in order "to prevent them from studying in Communist countries." We heard nothing about it until 1994, when a Swiss news magazine reported that Swiss professionals were using questionable credentials that came from a Swiss institute affiliated with the Cooperating University of America in North Carolina.

Creative Development Institute Manila, Philippines. An American reader reports that he was awarded a Ph.D. by this Filipino school, based entirely on his career experience and writings, without having to go to the Philippines. He says many other such degrees have been awarded but we have not been able to locate the school.

Crestmont College At one time registered with the Louisiana Board of Regents, but letters to their address in Baton Rouge have been returned as undeliverable, and there is no listed telephone.

Cyberam University Also known as Universidad Medico Naturalista Hispano-America. Had offered degrees of all kinds, from psychology to music to astrology, for fees of $150 to $300. Apparently no longer in business.

Darwin University A correspondent reported a degree mill of this name, but gave no further information.

DeHostos School of Medicine Puerto Rico. Questionable medical school. Letters returned as undeliverable.

Duarte Costa University Missouri. Questionable school operated by the Servants of the Good Shepherd. Would not give school's address or phone number when

their Altoona, PA headquarters was queried.

Earls Croft University A reader asks about this school, located at Redgrove House, 393 Lordship Lane, Dulwie, London, England. According to the school's administrative officer, R. D. Pendleton, the "university" is registered in Ireland and the school is accredited by the Life Experience Accreditation Foundation, which we've never heard of. We don't know anything more, except that it's not recognized, and it's illegal for unrecognized schools to call themselves "university" in England.

East Carolina University This legitimate school in Greenville, North Carolina no longer offers the M.A. in elementary education with a large independent-study element.

East Coast University They offered Master's and Doctorates in many subjects, with literature identical to that of the National Graduate School, National College (see Diploma Mill chapter), Roger Williams College, and National University. Their address was a residential hotel in St. Louis. When John asked for them there, the man at the desk acknowledged they got their mail there, but would say no more. They have used addresses in Mobile, Alabama; Tampa, Brooksville, and Dade City, Florida (also called Roger Williams College there), and Sweet Springs, Missouri. Recent mail to their various addresses has been returned as undeliverable. They claimed accreditation from the International Accredited Commission for Schools, Colleges, and Theological Seminaries, an unrecognized agency that was enjoined from operating by the state of Missouri.

Emmanuel College Oxford Oxford, England. The claim is made that degrees will be awarded solely on completion of a Master's thesis (about 100 pages) or doctoral dissertation (about 400 pages) and payment of about $1,800. They have not responded to our inquiries, and we are concerned about the lack of telephone, the absence of names on any of the literature we have seen, and the spelling, several times, of "Ph.D." as P.hD." Somewhat reassuring is their policy of not asking for any money until a proposal has been approved and a faculty advisor assigned, as well as the note, typed onto their flyer, that they are not part of the University of Oxford, and have no Royal Charter.

Escuela de Medicina Benito Juarez–Abraham Lincoln See: Escuela de Medicina Dr. Evaristo Cruz Escobedo

Escuela de Medicina de Saltillo Apparently defunct Mexican medical school.

Escuela de Medicina Dr. Evaristo Cruz Escobedo Also known as Universidad Interamericana and Escuela de Medicina Benito Juarez–Abraham Lincoln, they were one of the more controversial Mexican medical schools, and, as such, received a lot of bad press.

Essenes Research Foundation San Diego, California. They have awarded Ph.D.s through the Graduate School Consortium for the Religious Arts and Sciences. We have never been able to find an address or phone number for them.

Eureka Foundation A correspondent reported that "an open university known as the Eureka Foundation has commenced advertising in Australia." We have not been able to learn more about them.

European University of America They had offered a 10- to 14-month Master's program in San Francisco based around a major independent study project centering on international business, but that program is no longer offered, and none of their other offerings are nontraditional.

Evangel Christian University of America At one time, registered with the New Orleans Board of Regents, but letters to the address in Monroe, Louisiana have been returned, and there is no listed phone.

Extended Learning Program Ohio. A pilot program for external degrees that existed in the 1980s.

Flaming Rainbow University Flaming Rainbow University, an accredited Oklahoma university, officially closed its doors on February 18, 1992, thereby removing one of the more delightful university names from the arena.

Florida Institute of Remote Sensing Offered correspondence programs and, apparently, a degree in this field, involving interpretation of aerial photos, and other technology. No longer in existence in Marianna, Florida as best we can determine.

Franconia College New Hampshire. At one time offered many experimental and innovative programs.

Frank Ross Stewart University System This Centre, Alabama university has offered some courses from time to time, all taught by Mrs. Stewart. Honorary Doctorates have been offered to people who inquired about courses. Mrs. Stewart writes that "we do not find it attractive nor necessary" to be in this book. Well lade-da.

Franklin and Marshall College Lancaster, Pennsylvania. This accredited school at one time offered an M.S. in physics entirely through evening study.

Free University John once saw a diploma—a huge, spectacular diploma—on a wall. It awarded the "Academic degree of Bachelor of Dentistry" of the Free University for the recipient's exploits on a geographical expedition. We have never been able to locate the university, which was part of the International Federation of Scientific Research Societies. Possibly the same Free U. identified as a diploma mill by E&T magazine.

Freedom College Colorado Springs, Colorado and Santa Ana, California. Established in 1957 by Robert LeFevre, a well-known libertarian author. Later renamed Rampart College. Destroyed by heavy rains (was this a message?) in 1965, reopened in 1968, and closed for good in 1975. Later, LeFevre became president of Southwestern University, an Arizona degree mill that was closed following an FBI investigation.

Freedom University A correspondent asks about this school, which she says is in Albuquerque, New Mexico, but there is no listed phone there, nor can we find any information. Not clear if it is connected with the Freedoms in Florida and Colorado.

Freeman University Las Vegas, Nevada. We found them in a Las Vegas phone book, but can't find them in any school directory, nor have our letters to 4440 S. Maryland Parkway been answered.

Fremont College Officers of another university list Doctorates from this school, which they say was or is in Los Angeles, but we can find no evidence of it.

Galatia University A correspondent saw an advertisement for this school, which he thinks was in Salem, Oregon, and wrote for a catalog. He received a postcard saying they were temporarily out, and would send one soon. Nothing more was heard, and he has lost the address.

Grace University This West Indian medical school is apparently no longer actively recruiting American students.

Gracie Institute of Hypnosis See: Clinical Hypnosis Center

Graduate School for Community Development At one time, authorized by the state of California. Letters to the address in San Diego have been returned as undeliverable, and there is no listed phone.

Graduate School of Patent Resources Washington, D.C. This unaccredited but legit school offered advanced study in patent-related matters for lawyers, engineers, and businesspeople, but has no active programs at this time.

Graduate School of the Suggestive Sciences El Cajon, California. They offered Master's degrees and Doctorates in what they called "Hypnoalysis," but letters have been returned as undeliverable.

Granton Institute of Technology We have an address— 263 Adelaide St. West, Toronto, ON M5H 1Y3 Canada, and a name, Dayl Marks, but no one has ever answered our letters.

Great Lakes Bible College No longer offers correspondence courses leading to a degree.

Griffith University Queensland, Australia. A reader writes that they have introduced a "new kind of B.A. degree," but details have not been forthcoming.

Gulf States University Established in 1977 in South Carolina as Southeastern University. Moved to Louisiana a few years later. Offered doctoral programs requiring several weeks of summer residency in New Orleans. Following financial problems, the university closed in 1987. Many students who had not finished their degrees at the time transferred to the now-accredited University of Sarasota.

Hallmark University All we know about this is that an advertisement once ran in the Los Angeles Times offering a "University for sale" of this name.

Hawaii International University Apparently originated in California as American International University, then operated briefly from Hawaii, and administrator Diana Barrymore told us they would be moving to Iuka, Mississippi. No listed telephone number there.

Hawaii University Maui, Hawaii. Unaccredited school established by William Onapolis of Ohio in 1995 to award degrees to clients of his credit evaluation service. At presstime, we had not received the catalogue.

Headlands University Mendocino, California. Had offered innovative residential and nonresidential programs which are now dormant.

Highland University Athens, Tennessee. Once offered a 25-month Ed.D. program involving three four-week summer sessions with independent study in between. Now mail has been returned and there is no listed phone number in Athens. Originally chartered in North Carolina, moved to Sweetwater, Tennessee, then Athens.

Holistic Life University Flourished in San Francisco in the late 1970s and early '80s, but is no longer findable there. They offered coursework that they claimed could be applied to degree programs at Antioch, Redlands, and Sonoma State.

Holy Cross Junior College Merrill, Wisconsin. When the original school of this name went bankrupt, others began offering a Ph.D. program in psychology or education, from the Institute of Learning of Holy Cross Junior College. After a newspaper exposé, holders of the degree (most of them school administrators and psychologists) maintained that they had done substantial work and truly earned their degrees. Critics disagreed, and the school faded away.

Horizon University Established in Shelburne, Ontario, Canada, to offer off-campus degrees based on independent study, with credit for prior learning. Apparently a victim of a 1984 provincial law strictly regulating universities. At least, we cannot locate them now.

Houston International University They sent a letter saying "Sorry, we are no longer a university." Had specialized in social work and public administration education for Hispanics and other international students for whom English was a second language. Original name was Hispanic International University.

Howard University This accredited university no longer offers a university without walls program.

Independence University Missouri. In the mid 1950s, the National Association for Applied Arts and Sciences (an organization we'd never heard of) apparently established a credit bank similar to that of Regents. From this evolved Independence, a degree-granting entity. But it is no more.

Indiana Northern Graduate School of Professional Management Run from a small dairy farm in Gas City, Indiana, they once offered a Master of Professional Management degree, primarily through independent study, with some class meetings in various northern Indiana cities. Ceased operations in 1985. Originally called Indiana Northern University, but the "university" and the doctoral programs were dropped by agreement with the state of Indiana, which accredited the school. Run by the Most Reverend Bishop Dr. Gordon Da Costa, Ph.D., Ed.D., D.Sc., D.C., whose only earned degrees were from Indiana Northern, and who established several accrediting agencies which, in turn, accredited Indiana Northern.

Indiana Northern University See: Indiana Northern Graduate School of Professional Management

Institute for Information Management At one time, authorized to grant degrees by the state of California. Did not respond to three requests for information, and there is no listed telephone number in Sunnyvale, California.

Institute for Management Competency San Francisco, California. An unaccredited but state authorized Master's program has been discontinued.

Institute of Human-Potential Psychology Palo Alto, California. Offered an external Ph.D. program for a while. Name then changed to Psychological Studies Institute but that, too, seems to have faded away.

Institute of Open Education Massachusetts. Once offered working teachers a fully accredited M.Ed. through two summer sessions and independent study.

Institute of Paranormal Science Fremont, California. Announced the intention of offering a degree program in the early 1980s, but there is no evidence of them now.

Institute of Science and Mathematics The address is 1125 Red Cut Loop Road, West Monroe, LA 71292, but we don't know what goes on there, since Milton Peacock has never answered our letters.

Instituto de Estudios Iberamericanos Saltillo, Mexico. Offered Bachelor's, Master's, and Doctorates, mostly to Americans, with a five-week summer session in Mexico plus independent study. No longer in operation.

International Academy of Management and Economics A letter addressed to them at their last known address, in Manila (the Philippines), was returned stamped "gone away."

International Academy of Philosophy We know that they are located at Obergass 75, FL 9494 Schaan, Lichtenstein, but no one has responded to several requests for information about their nontraditional programs.

International College Los Angeles, California. Alas, this splendid idea did not survive. They offered Bachelor's, Master's, and Doctorates through private study with tutors worldwide. Apparently many of the well-known tutors (Lawrence Durrell, Yehudi Menuhin, Ravi Shankar, Judy Chicago, etc.) had very few (or no) students. Many of the students transferred to William Lyon University.

International College of Arts and Sciences We know that they are located at 2 Othonos Str., Maroussi 151 22,

Athens, Greece, and that there is some affiliation with the University of Indianapolis, but no one has responded to several requests for information about their nontraditional programs.

International Free Protestant Episcopal University See: Saint Andrew's Collegiate Seminary

International Graduate School Established in St. Louis in 1980 as the doctoral-level affiliate of the accredited World University (Puerto Rico), offering the Doctorate in business or education. They received candidacy for accreditation with the North Central Association in the remarkably short time of one year. However, the candidacy was withdrawn in late 1987, and in 1988 the school told the state of Missouri that it would be closing down.

International Graduate University They offered Ph.D. degrees in clinical psychology and behavioral science, through an affiliation first with American College of Switzerland and later with Florida Institute of Technology, but no longer.

International Institutes of Science and Technology At one time registered with the Louisiana Board of Regents as an unaccredited school, but letters to them are returned as undeliverable and there is no listed telephone number in Monroe, Louisiana, where they had been located.

International Japan University At one time, authorized by the state of California, but letters are undeliverable, and there is no listed telephone number in Orange, California.

International School of Business and Legal Studies Mail to their London, England address returned as unforwardable. This unaccredited school had awarded degrees entirely on the basis of an applicant's credentials, under somewhat unusual circumstances. They'd solicited agents in other countries, and offered to award degrees on the basis of agents' recommendations. They required that these agents have Doctorates, which they offered to provide for £450, £175 more for wig and gown.

International Studies in Humanistic Psychology In the 1970s they offered a nonresident Ph.D. in their field, from Cotati, California.

International University (California) Pasadena, California. A now-dormant unaccredited school that may or may not have had some ties to Southland University and/or its founder, James Kirk.

International University (Greece) Athens. This apparently unaccredited school (they claimed to be "fully recognized" by the government of Greece, but the Greek embassy disagreed) has ceased operations.

International University (New York) Letters are returned as undeliverable, and there is no listed telephone number in New York City. This unaccredited school, formerly incorporated on the West Indies island of St. Kitts, had offered Doctorates in psychoanalysis and

psychotherapy. It was apparently a legitimate and useful program, and the faculty had impressive credentials, but the New York connection and the difficulty of getting a catalog (they did not respond to five requests) were a bit odd.

International University of Applied Arts & Sciences At one time registered with the Board of Regents of Louisiana, but letters are returned as undeliverable, and there is no listed telephone in New Orleans.

Iowa Commonwealth College The Iowa State Coordinating Committee for Continuing Education at one time hoped to develop an external degree program by this name.

Irvine College of Business They have not responded to several requests for information. The address we have is 16591 Noyes Ave., Irvine, CA 92714.

James Tyler Kent College of Homeopathic Medicine Offered a five-year program in homeopathic medicine, from Phoenix, Arizona, but mail was returned and there is no listed phone in Phoenix.

Jamilian University Full-page advertisements in Omni magazine (and that ain't cheap) in 1987 and 1988 heralded the arrival of Jamilian University of Reno, Nevada, in which a "much-talked-about but little known group of mystics is offering to share" the "age old secrets for prolonging life and expanding intelligence." We chose not to invest $25 in the admissions package and they chose not to send us a catalog, so you will have to learn the secrets for yourself.

Jean Ray University A reader inquired about this school, allegedly in Namus, Belgium, from which a prominent person in his community had claimed a Doctorate, but we can find out nothing about it.

Jefferson College of Legal Studies At one time registered with the Board of Regents of Louisiana, but letters to their address are returned as undeliverable, and there is no listed telephone in Gretna, Louisiana.

John Marshall Law School Georgia. This unaccredited law school is, we are informed by a correspondent, currently seeking ABA accreditation.

John Rennie University At one time, authorized by the state of California, but letters are returned as undeliverable, and there is no listed telephone in Irvine, California.

Juarez-Lincoln Bilingual University Austin, Texas. Letters returned as undeliverable.

Keichu Technological Institute Registered with the Louisiana Board of Regents in 1988, but mail to the registered address is returned as undeliverable, and there is no listed phone. President Karl Marx was affiliated with Andrew Jackson University, formerly of Baton Rouge.

Keltic University A reader in England inquires about Keltic University, but letters to 3 Vicarage Close, Kirby Muxloe, Leicestershire have not been answered. There is certainly no recognized school by this name in England.

Kripalu Institute Summitt Station, Pennsylvania. They offered a Master's in humanistic studies. There was a connection with an International University in Kayavorahan, India, but the phone is disconnected and mail is returned as undeliverable.

Krisspy University We have been sent a transcript showing a Master's degree from Krisspy University of Bayamon, Puerto Rico, but cannot locate such a school. (Is it possible they merged with Rice University?)

La Salle Extension University This huge correspondence university discontinued operations in 1982, not long after losing their accreditation from the National Home Study Council (now the Distance Education and Training Council). They had been owned for many years by the Macmillan Publishing Company of New York.

Lawyer's University In late 1987, a law officer was trying to locate a school of this name, possibly in Florida or Los Altos, California. We could find no trace.

Lincoln University New Guinea. The degrees were based on writing up to 10 papers in a given field. Established in Arizona when that state had no school laws, it later moved to London England in 1987, where the address was a mail-forwarding service, and then to New Guinea. The university's founder seems to be a sincere scholar and, indeed, Lincoln may have achieved some level of acceptance. Claimed alumni included the head of government for the kingdom of Lesotho, and the former minister for education and culture in Ghana.

London International College Had offered degrees in cooperation with the unaccredited Andrew Jackson University College of Louisiana and, later, Maryland. Apparently out of business.

Lone Mountain College California. At one time offered an external Master's in psychology. The college was absorbed into the University of San Francisco, but the external degree did not survive.

Los Angeles College of Law See: Van Norman University

Los Angeles Psychoanalytic Society and Institute No longer offers degrees.

Los Angeles Psychosocial Center A letter requesting information was returned to sender, but Los Angeles information did have a new listing for them, which yielded a recorded message asking callers to leave a name and phone number for information about psychological services. No one has responded to our messages inquiring about the school's fate.

Louisiana Central University At one time they were registered with the Louisiana Board of Regents, but letters have been returned as undeliverable, and there is no listed telephone in Metairie, Louisiana.

Louisiana International University Inc. At one time they were registered with the Louisiana Board of Regents, but letters have been returned as undeliverable, and there is no listed telephone in New Orleans, Louisiana.

Louisiana Pacific University At one time they were registered with the Louisiana Board of Regents, but letters have been returned as undeliverable, and there is no listed telephone in Metairie, Louisiana.

Louisiana University of Medical Sciences Randolph Howes has not responded to information requests sent to 1158 Park Blvd., Baton Rouge, LA 70806.

Loyola Southwestern University A caller insisted that there is a school by this name in Baton Rouge, Louisiana, but neither we nor the authorities in Louisiana have heard of it or can find it.

Lyle University Operated for a while in the mid 1980s from New Orleans and Metairie, Louisiana, offering Bachelor's, Master's, and Doctorates at $750 for a complete program. Started by a Columbia Pacific University graduate, and quite similar in approach to C.P.U. No longer registered with the Louisiana board of regents, and therefore presumably no longer in business.

Magellan University Tucson, Arizona. According to *The Chronicle of Higher Education,* after 25 years as an administrator at the University of Arizona, a man named Bill Noyes plans to open an on-line university by this name. He plans to be up and running by 1996, and hopes to win accreditation for Magellan, which will offer instruction by videotape, CD-ROM, and modem. It sounds great, but at this early stage it's hard to know whether everything will work out as planned.

Magna Carta University California. Alternative law school, no longer around.

Manx University In 1987, there was an announcement that a university by this name was to open on the Isle of Man in 1992. A multimillion-pound fundraising appeal was said to have begun, and anyone making a donation, however small, was to become a trustee of the university, at least for a while. The people behind the endeavor chose to remain anonymous, and we can find no evidence that the school ever opened.

Marquis Guiseppe Scicluna International University Foundation In an earlier edition, John wrote that in 1987 the Universal Intelligence Data Bank (of Independence, Missouri) had written to businessmen in Asia offering them an honorary doctorate from this institution, on receipt of a $500 payment. Baron Marcel Dingli-Attard, of the Foundation, has assured us that the offer was only made to a limited number of people, not necessarily in Asia and, in any event, is no loner being made. Our apologies for the incorrect statements made earlier.

McDonough 35 Prep/Bernadean University At one time registered with the Louisiana Board of Regents, but letters have been returned as undeliverable and there is no listed telephone number in New Orleans. We don't know what the name means either, but Bernadean University *is* described in Chapter 23.

Mellen Research University Apparently a predecessor of Mellen University, it operated from San Francisco, but never granted degrees. Mail to their address is returned as undeliverable, and there is no listed telephone. Mellen is described in Chapter 19.

Mensa University A correspondent reports that Mensa, the international organization for people with high I.Q.s, was at one time associated very briefly with a Maryland university.

Meridian University This unaccredited Louisiana school, affiliated with the Buddhist Theosophical Society, had awarded degrees at all levels on the basis of prior coursework. Closed in 1995.

Metropolitan University Operated in Glendale, California in the 1950s, apparently quite legitimately, offering degrees with substantial life-experience credit. Long gone.

Mid-Valley College of Law Van Nuys, California. Unaccredited, and now defunct, law school.

Millikin University This accredited school no longer offers degrees through its Evening Division.

Missouri Central College Letters are returned and there is no listed telephone number in Clayton, Missouri. This unaccredited school's 10-page catalog had dedicated two pages to a misrepresentation of the Sosdian-Sharp study. No listed faculty or phone.

Morgan State College At one time offered a nontraditional degree program for urban African Americans, focusing on "black perspective and minority group problems," but no longer does so.

Mount St. Joseph's College Offered accredited Bachelor's degrees in which over 50% of credit could come from prior learning.

Mundelein College This independent, traditional school, in operation since 1929, had offered a Bachelor's in which up to 75% of credits could be earned through assessment. However, in late 1994, their phone was disconnected, and they were no longer listed in a major directory of accredited schools.

National Christian University At one time, there was one located in Richardson, Texas and another in Dallas. Then some ads appeared for the National Christian University of Missouri, but one was to write to the dean of theology in Oklahoma City. A National Christian also appears on the Council of Europe's list of degree mills. So far, we remain confused and they remain elusive.

National College for the Natural Healing Arts Birchdale, Minnesota. Offered programs leading to Bachelor's, Master's, and Doctorates in naprapathy, reflexology, iridology, homeopathy, acupuncture, cancer research, and so forth, possibly through nonresidential study. Mail has been returned and there is no listed phone number in Birchdale.

National College of Education Offered accredited Bachelor's degrees in which up to 75% of credit could come from prior learning.

National Graduate School See: East Coast University

National University (Missouri) See: East Coast University.

New York Institute of Photography We know that they are located at 211 East 43rd. Street, New York, NY 10017, but Don Scheff, the contact name we have on file, has not responded to several requests for information about their nontraditional programs.

Norfolk State University Virginia. Apparently once offered an external Master's degree in communication.

North American College of Acupuncture Vancouver, British Columbia, Canada. Offered correspondence studies in Chinese medical philosophy and principles of diagnosis. Mail has been returned.

North American Colleges of Natural Health Science San Rafael, California. Offered professional career education in holistic natural health sciences. Mail has been returned; no listed telephone. Formerly called Airola College.

North Continental University They have used a P.O. box in Santa Rosa, California, and at one time they put on demonstrations of sacred dance, but they were not state-authorized and our inquiries have never been answered.

Northern Virginia School of Law Letter are returned, stamped "box closed, no forwarding order," and there is no listed telephone in Alexandria.

Northwest University of Metaphysics Listed as the source of a degree for a faculty member at a traditional school. We have not been able to locate it.

Occidental Institute of Chinese Studies A reader asks about their degrees; he believes they are located somewhere in Florida, but we haven't found them.

Occidental Institute Research Foundation A reader said they offered nontraditional programs from P. O. Box 5507, Bellingham, WA 98227, but there has never been a response to our inquiries.

Ocean University At one time they were authorized to grant law and other degrees in California, but no longer. Operated from addresses in Lancaster and Santa Monica.

Open University See: Clayton University

Orange University of Medical Sciences A major article in the *Los Angeles Times* in 1982 announced the highly controversial impending opening of this investor-owned for-profit medical school. We've often wondered what happened, but haven't been able to find out.

Oregon Institute of Technology This accredited school no longer offers any sort of nontraditional program.

Our Lady of the Lake College of Nursing and Allied Health The name and address from which nothing has ever been sent, in response to our inquiries, is Ms. Maureen Daniels, 7500 Hennessy Blvd., Baton Rouge, LA 70808.

Pacific Coast University Registered with the Louisiana Board of Regents at one point, but mail to them is returned as undeliverable, and there is no listed telephone in Baton Rouge. Mark Zeltser was the man behind it.

Pacific College of Oriental Medicine At one time they were authorized by the state of California, but letters have been returned as undeliverable and there is no listed telephone in San Diego.

Pacific Institute for Advanced Studies At one time they were authorized by the state of California, but letters have been returned as undeliverable and there is no listed telephone in Studio City.

Pacific International University At one time, they were authorized to grant degrees by the state of California. They did not respond to three requests for information about their programs. Almost certainly unrelated to the Pacific International University that operated from Hollywood, California, at least through 1964, offering correspondence and residential degrees in science and engineering.

Pacific National University At one time they were authorized by the state of California, but letters have been returned as undeliverable and there is no listed telephone in Los Angeles.

Pacific School of Nutrition They offered correspondence programs leading to certification as a nutritionist and/or herbologist, through written tutorial. Mail to their last-known address is returned as undeliverable, and there is no listed telephone in Ashland, Oregon.

Pacific Southern University They had been authorized to grant degrees by the state of California, but when their authorization ended, they had apparently not qualified for state approval; at presstime they say that it is in process. They offered degrees by correspondence study in a wide range of subjects through schools of business and management, education, engineering, and human behavior.

Pennsylvania Military College Offered B.A. and M.B.A. through evening study.

People's University of the Americas A correspondent has reported that such a university exists, with an address at a post-office box in Solna, Sweden, from which no response has been heard.

Phoenix Medical School Phoenix, Arizona. Incorporated and began recruiting students even though the university existed, as an article in the *Arizona Republic* noted, only "on a few pieces of paper stacked on a rented credenza under a rented scenic picture in a small office [in] Mesa." President Gloria Coates announced an opening date for the university, but apparently it never came to pass.

Phoenix University The president of a bible school lists among his credentials a Ph.D. from the Bari Research Center of Phoenix University for archeological research, bestowed by its president, His Serene Highness Prince Francisco D'Aragona. We are unfamiliar with this institution but see (we suspect) Accademia di Study Superiori Phoenix in Chapter 22, Degree Mills. Certainly unrelated to the accredited University of Phoenix in Arizona.

Pitzer College California. Once offered an external B.A.

Point Park College Pittsburgh, Pennsylvania. Offered accredited Bachelor's degrees through weekend classes.

Prachathipok University Thailand's open university was announced as a totally nonresidential correspondence university, with courses by mail, radio, and television. It is unclear to us if Sukhothai Thammathirat Open University of Bangkok, which opened in 1980 and now has more than 150,000 students, is the same school.

Professional School for Humanistic Studies Listed as the source of the degree held by a faculty member at a traditional school. We have not been able to locate it.

Professional School of Psychological Studies At one time, authorized by the state of California. No response to three letters asking for information, and the person who answers the listed telephone says the school no longer exists, and good-bye.

Professional Studies Institute Phoenix, Arizona. Offered unaccredited Bachelor's, Master's, and Doctorates in physical and mental health fields, but can no longer be located.

Prometheus College Tacoma, Washington. Arose in the mid 1970s and rather quickly became a candidate for accreditation. Then suddenly they were gone—perhaps back to Olympus.

Protea Valley University Bernard Leeman established this school in Toowoomba, Australia in 1991, and registered it in Louisiana, with the intention of providing education for black South African exiles. He gained Archbishop Desmond Tutu's backing for the idea, but abandoned it in the planning stages when it became clear that majority rule was going to become a reality in South Africa.

Psychological Studies Institute See: Institute of Human-Potential Psychology

Quimby College Alamogordo, New Mexico. Offered a B.A. in life arts and an M.A. in spiritual studies and counseling. Locally controversial, perhaps in part because of the focus on aura balancing, and the assertion that the college had its start when the thoughts of Phineas P. Quimby, a New England watchmaker who died in 1866, were transmitted to an Alamagordo woman. No longer findable.

Radvis University A correspondent asks about this school, possibly located in Canada, and we can find no information.

Rampart College See: Freedom College

Rand Graduate Institute Santa Monica, California. At the time they asked to be left out of this book (in the mid '80s) they were offering an accredited apprenticeship-based Ph.D. in policy analysis.

Rem University A reader has inquired about nontraditional Doctorates in psychology issued by this establishment, possibly in South Euclid, Ohio, but we could find no evidence of it.

Ripon College Wisconsin. Offered accredited Bachelor's degrees in which up to 75% of credit could come from prior learning.

Roanoke College Virginia. Offered a variety of accredited Master's degrees through evening courses.

Rochdale College This legitimate, if unorthodox, institution in Toronto, Canada used to "award" honorary degrees for the college to anyone who made a modest donation, as a fundraising tool. The honorary Ph.D. had a watermark; when you held the diploma up to the light, you saw "Caveat Emptor."

Rockwell University Scottsdale, Arizona. They offered degrees of all kinds by correspondence study. The only requirement was the writing of a thesis. A former president of Loyola University in Louisiana was claimed to be one of the five founders. "An education for the 1980s" was their slogan, but they didn't make it through the '80s themselves.

Roger Williams College See: East Coast University. Not to be confused with the fully accredited school by the same name in Rhode Island.

Royal Orleans University At one time, they were registered with the Board of Regents of Louisiana, but mail is returned as undeliverable and there is no listed telephone number in Lake Charles, Louisiana.

Russell Sage College New York. Offered accredited Bachelor's and Master's degrees in education through evening courses.

Sacred Heart College A program offering a very short residency Bachelor's in management and criminal justice has been canceled, at least for the time being.

Saint Andrew's Collegiate Seminary In the late 1950s, Saint Andrew's was a small and apparently sincere and legitimate seminary in London, England offering Master's and doctoral work in theology and counseling. Later, to raise funds, the seminary offered honorary Doctorates to clergy and others who made donations. This evolved into awarding nonresidential degrees for life experience in the name of the Saint Andrew's Ecumenical Church Foundation Intercollegiate. This further evolved into a worldwide enterprise, again offering degrees entirely based on resumes, called the International Free Protestant Episcopal University. None of these entities survives today.

Saint Andrew's Ecumenical Church Foundation Intercollegiate See: Saint Andrew's Collegiate Seminary

Saint Bonaventure University Degrees through evening study no longer available.

Saint Cloud State University Minnesota. Offered accredited Bachelor's degrees in which virtually all credit could come from prior learning experiences.

Saint George Center for Training At one time, they were authorized to grant degrees by the state of California. There was no response to three requests for information on their programs, and there is no listed telephone number in Berkeley.

Saint Giles University College This England-based school offered nonresident Bachelor's, Master's, Doctorates, and certificates in psychology, physiatrics, teacher training, and science. The Doctor of Science program consisted of three lessons: (1) factors influencing children's sweet eating, (2) psychiatry and psychology, and (3) radiation and human health. Raymond Young was the moving force behind Saint Giles, Harley University, and Somerset University.

Saint John's College This London-based school, a division of City Commercial College, did not offer their own degrees, but conducted the coursework leading to a Bachelor's or an M.B.A. from an unspecified-in-their-literature nontraditional school in California. They apparently closed down in the wake of student protests.

Saint John's University A very small school established in Edgard, Louisiana by District Court Judge Thomas Malik, they used to offer nonresident degrees, but that program was discontinued. No connection with the other Saint John's University in Louisiana or the one in New York.

Saint Paul College and Seminary A reader asks about an honorary Doctorate that a co-worker claims from this institution, apparently in Rome, but we have not found it.

Saint Thomas University Had offered B.A., B.S., and Master's degrees through evening, weekend, and summer programs in the School of Continuing and Adult Education. Formerly called Biscayne College.

Samuel Benjamin Thomas University A grand plan by King Theophilus I of the Ashanti Kingdom to establish a distance learning university in Sierra Leone apparently has not yet come to pass.

San Diego State University California. Once offered external Bachelor's and Master's degrees.

San Francisco College of Acupuncture At one time, authorized to grant degrees by the state of California, but letters are returned as undeliverable and there is no listed telephone in San Francisco.

San Francisco Theological Seminary San Anselmo, California. They have discontinued their Doctor of Science of theology once offered through summer sessions, and do not wish us to describe their nonresidential Master of Arts in values program because "we are in the process of curriculum changes and it would be difficult to express the substance and location of the programs at this time."

Santa Barbara University Goleta, California. They appeared in the 1986 directory of schools put out by the state of California, offering Master's and Doctorates in business but by 1988 there was no telephone listing. Presumably not the same as University of Santa

Barbara (formerly Laurence University.)

Santa Fe College of Natural Medicine Santa Fe, New Mexico. Offered nonresidential Bachelor's, Master's, and Ph.D. programs as well as residential studies. Now there is no response to letters, and the phone has been disconnected.

School of Botany A reader has inquired about an honorary degree a colleague of his was using. Possibly in Spain, but we could not locate it.

Seattle International University Letters to the school have been returned as undeliverable, and there is no listed telephone number in Seattle or Federal Way, Washington. This unaccredited school had offered the B.B.A. and M.B.A. entirely through evening and weekend study.

Sedona College/Sedona University Sedona, Arizona. According to an article in the *Arizona Republic,* an application to operate this school was made in Arizona by two men, one a former employee of Southwestern University (whose owner was imprisoned for selling degrees), the other the police chief of Sedona, whose Doctorate was from De Paul University, a degree mill whose owners were sentenced to prison in 1987. According to a spirited defense of Sedona College in the *Sedona Times* newspaper (September 19, 1984), James H. Smith of California "purchased Sedona College from its founder, Ted Dalton" (president of Newport University). We are uncertain as to whether Sedona ever accepted students, but there is no listed phone for them in Sedona now. We have been told that there were actually two schools—Sedona College and Sedona University—perhaps quite independent of each other.

Sequoia University In 1984 a Los Angeles judge issued a permanent injunction against Sequoia University, which had operated from California and Oklahoma, and its president to cease operation until the school could comply with state education laws. The university had offered degrees in osteopathic medicine, religious studies, hydrotherapy, and physical sciences.

Shelton College This college, founded in Cape May, New Jersey, by fundamentalist radio preacher Carl McIntire, challenged New Jersey's school licensing law, claiming that it should be exempt from licensing under freedom of religion and speech precedents. New Jersey maintained that any exceptions to its right to license would diminish the value and integrity of degrees awarded in the state. We are researching the case.

Sonoma Institute Bodega, California. Offered training for an M.A. in humanistic and transpersonal psychology through a cooperative relationship with the University of Redlands. Apparently no longer in business.

Southeastern Graduate School South Carolina. At one time advertised that Doctorates were available in 100 fields, with a one-month residency. Literature made troublesome statements about accreditation eligibility.

Southeastern University See: Gulf States University

Southern Bible College A correspondent reports they offer a Bachelor's program in Christ-centered education for Christian missionaries entirely through evening study. Have not responded to many inquiries over the years.

Southern California Christian University No longer in business, at least not at the address we had for them in Los Angeles.

Southland University Southland University operated from Pasadena, California and later from Arizona in the 1980s. Following a visit from the FBI's "DipScam" diploma mill team, which carried off four truckloads of records, Southland closed. No indictments were handed down. La Salle University in St. Louis (later to move to Louisiana) subsequently opened under the same management with similar programs, including some law materials bearing the name Southland.

Southwestern University Law School California. Alternative law school, no longer around.

St. Louis University Missouri. Offered a number of degrees through evening study.

State University of Nebraska Used to offer a largely correspondence degree.

Stewart University System See: Frank Ross Stewart University System

Stratton College Navan, Ireland. An external degree program was announced by the college. Then the college was taken over by the Institute of Maintenance Engineering and the degree program was canceled.

Sukhothai Thammathirat Open University See: Prachathipok University

Sunshine University Probably (but we've never been sure) a gag or promotional diploma. The Ph.D. they sent John is quite attractive and appears to be signed by the mayors of three Florida cities and the chairman of the Pinellas County Commission.

Susan B. Anthony University Established in the 1970s by Dr. Albert Schatz, discoverer of the antibiotic streptomycin, this unaccredited school at one time offered degrees in education, environmental studies, and other fields, but no longer exists, according to Dr. Schatz, who ought to know.

Synthesis Graduate School for the Study of Man San Francisco, California. An ambitious-seeming endeavor that offered the M.A. and Ph.D. in psychology and medical synthesis. Buckminster Fuller and a Nobel laureate in medicine were on the board of advisors. Most faculty were disciples of Roberto Assagioli. But now the school is gone, as best we can determine.

Teachers University A reader asks about this school, which she believes used to exist in Miami, but we can find no evidence of them.

Temple University Philadelphia. Offered accredited degrees at all levels through evening study.

Tennessee Southern University and School of Religion Established in late 1981 for the purpose, according to founder O. Charles Nix, of "developing students with a special sense of social responsibility, who can organize and apply knowledge for human betterment." Mail to several Tennessee addresses was returned as undeliverable.

Thomas Jefferson College of Law Apparently no longer offering any nontraditional programs.

Tri-State College and University Several readers have asked about this institution, but letters to J. Roy Stewart at the Oxon Hill, Maryland address provided were never answered, and there was no listed telephone.

Tyler Kent School of Medicine Arizona. Health-related school, now apparently defunct.

Unification Theological Seminary Reverend Moon's Unification Church was denied the right to grant the Master of Religious Education degree at its Barrytown, New York seminary. By a four-to-three margin, New York's highest court determined that the board of regents acted on bona fide deficiencies (in the program) and not discrimination when they denied the degree-granting license.

Union College South Africa. Listed in another directory of alternative education as having a correspondence degree program, but inquiries were not answered.

Union University Los Angeles. Unaccredited and somewhat questionable school offered Master's degrees and Doctorates though nonresidential study.

United States Open University At one time, registered with the Board of Regents of Louisiana, but mail has been returned as undeliverable and there is no listed telephone number in Baton Rouge.

Universidad Boricua District of Columbia. A university without walls program primarily for Puerto Ricans.

Universidad Interamericana See: Escuela de Medicina Dr. Evaristo Cruz Escobedo

Universidad Medico-Naturalista Hispano-America See: Cyberam University.

Universidad Nordestana Dominican Republic. This foreign medical school is apparently no longer accepting American students.

University Associates Graduate School At one time authorized in California, the school closed in 1987.

University College Academy Christians International In 1987, John was sent a document submitted by a clergyman in Puerto Rico in support of a degree claimed from this entity. The document, purporting to be a certification by the state of New York that "University College" is legitimate and accredited, is clearly a fake. It has a number of misspellings, and is simply not true.

University College of Northern Cyprus We have seen help-wanted ads in which they sought a campus director for their "accredited American Degree programmes in business administration." But we were never able to learn the particulars.

University of Azania The name was registered in England by Bernard Leeman (see Lincoln University and Protea Valley University, this chapter), in the hope and expectation of establishing a school that would ultimately be located in a "free South Africa." (Azania is a name that some black South Africans have used for their country.)

University of Beverly Hills The University thrived as an unaccredited school in the 1970s and two of its presidents went on to start comparable schools, Century and Kennedy-Western. While UBH ostensibly closed in the mid 1980s, advertising (mostly in Asia) in its name went on for an additional four or five years, using an address in Council Bluffs, Iowa. A visitor to the Council Bluffs address found no University of Beverly Hills, but did find an educational service company whose manager became hostile when asked about the University.

University of California, Riverside Their off-campus Master of Administration program has been discontinued.

University of California, San Diego Their nonresidential Bachelor of Arts program has been discontinued.

University of California, San Francisco The M.S. in nursing through evening study has apparently been discontinued.

University of California, Santa Cruz Their B.A. in community studies through evening study has apparently been discontinued.

University of Canterbury Established by two prominent psychologists in Los Angeles, California in the late 1970s. They offered graduate degrees in psychology and other fields with a four-week residency requirement in either California or England, but within a few years they were gone.

University of Central Arizona Tempe, Arizona. Operated in the late 1970s, offering Doctor of Arts in education and Doctor of Business Management, based on readings, examinations, and a dissertation. The two founders agreed to a consent judgment and stopped awarding Doctorates.

University of Central California Sacramento, California. Once offered degrees of all kinds by correspondence, typically after a student responded to 100 to 200 multiple-choice, true-or-false, and essay questions to demonstrate competency, followed by independent study, a thesis, and an examination. They were authorized by the state of California, but both the "authorized" status and the university are no more.

University of Hartford They have some innovative programs that we would love to list in this book, but they apparently have all the students they need because Ms. Carole Olland, director of admissions, wants them left out, so we are leaving the out.

University of Healing Basically a religious school, they offered degrees at all levels. The University of Philosophy operated from the same California address. They claimed accreditation from God Unlimited, not a recognized agency.

University of Honolulu For a short while, they offered training for the California Bar, then sank from sight.

University of Mid-America A consortium of 11 midwestern universities, which was to establish the American Open University, spent $14 million from the National Institute of Education in organizing, and then went out of business in 1982 when the NIE shut its purse.

University of Mississippi Offered accredited external Master's degrees and Doctorates.

University of Nairobi A plan was announced in the early 1980s for an External Degree Programme in Kenya, but some years later it had not started, due to "unforeseen problems."

University of Naturopathy A reader inquires about a school of this name that he believed might be operating in East Orange, New Jersey, but there is no listed phone number there.

University of Palm Beach. See: College of the Palm Beaches

University of Philosophy See: University of Healing

University of Psychic Sciences Someone sent John a business card for this school, located in National City, California, but we have not been sent any information on what they do. Perhaps they haven't picked up the message we've been beaming them.

University of Puget Sound Offered accredited Bachelor's and Master's degrees through evening study.

University of Rochester Rochester, New York. No longer offers evening study degrees.

University of Saint Lucia School of Medicine This medical school was started on the Caribbean island of Saint Lucia by self-styled "Crazy Eddie" Antar, New York electronics magnate, but closed abruptly a year later, in early 1984, stranding students and faculty alike. Saint George's University in Grenada agreed to take qualified students, but only 37 of Saint Lucia's 127 were accepted there. No connection with Saint Lucia Health Sciences University.

University of South Dakota Offered accredited external M.B.A.

University of South Wales No longer offers nontraditional degrees.

University of the America's Professional Institute At one time, registered with the Board of Regents of Louisiana, but according to Thomas Lavin, who had also been affiliated with Kensington and Bedford Universities, the UOTA never opened for business, and no longer exists.

University of the Pacific Offered accredited Bachelor's degree in which over 80% of credit could come from prior learning.

University of the World A reader says that in 1988 it existed in La Jolla, California, but we can't find any evidence.

University of Toledo Offered accredited Master's and law degrees through evening study.

University of Utopia Letter asking for information was returned, and the phone number we'd been given was someone's personal answering machine.

University Without Walls/New Orleans Offered Bachelor's degrees. Now mail is returned, and there is no listed phone.

University Without Walls/Project Success North Hollywood, California. In the mid 1980s their literature described Bachelor's, Master's, and Doctorates in evolutionary systems design, but they are no longer there.

Valley Christian University Fresno, then Clovis, California. Degrees in many fields at all levels by correspondence. Letters neither answered nor returned; no listed telephone.

Van Norman University Los Angeles, California. Unaccredited, and now defunct, law school (degrees were offered through its Los Angeles College of Law).

Vermont State College System Many years ago, when we were more accommodating about such requests, they asked that their innovative external degree program (mainly for Vermont residents) not be listed.

Video University Jackson, Mississippi. In the early 1980s a major marketing effort was launched for Video U., which intended to offer many training courses. Now the phone has been disconnected.

Villarreal National University In 1988, this large Peruvian university (30,000 residential students) began offering completely nonresident Master's and Doctoral programs in English, at a cost of nearly $10,000, to people living in the U.S. From 1988 to 1991, there may have been certain irregularities, both in the U.S. and in Peru, that could affect the validity of degrees earned during that period. We have been informed that the American Council on Education in Washington, the U.S. Information Agency in Lima, the Council of Europe, in France, and the FBI may all have looked into these matters. In February of 1991, Villarreal entered into an affiliation with Somerset University, an unaccredited British school then using an address in Louisiana, whereby Somerset handled Villarreal matters in the U.S. This agreement apparently ended, and Somerset may no longer be involved. Despite frequent inquiries as of late 1994, no new information had been learned regarding this mysterious situation. Before learning of the pre–February 1991 problems, this book had listed the Villarreal program. The ongoing investigations and letters from aggrieved pre-1991 Villarreal students have persuaded us to withdraw that listing.

Washburn University Offered accredited Bachelor's degrees through evening study.

Washington International College Washington, D.C. They offered a B.A. with two weeks' residency, achieved accreditation candidacy status, and then went out of business in 1982.

Wellsgrey College Greeley, Colorado. Advertisements appeared in business publications offering the M.B.A. by computer, but mail was not answered and now there is no phone listing.

West London University A letter sent to them was returned with the notation "gone away."

Western Australia Institute of Technology No longer offers external degrees.

Western Colorado University Grand Junction, Colorado. Offered nonresident degrees in many fields at all levels. Accredited by the unrecognized National Association for Private Nontraditional Schools and Colleges, with whom they shared staff and office space. Financial problems set in, and the doors were closed in the mid 1980s.

Western Scientific University Opened in southern California in the early 1980s as a "Christian internal, external alternate degree program," offering M.D. (homeopathic) and various Bachelor's, Master's, and Doctorates. Original name: Western University. No longer there.

Western University See: Western Scientific University

Westminster College (Missouri) This old established school for men started a nontraditional campus in Berkeley, California, then closed same in 1977 when it became apparent that the California branch was not upholding the parent school's high academic standards.

Whitman University Years ago, John received a "prototype" 1985–1986 bulletin, offering Bachelor's, Master's, and Doctorates through guided independent study. Accreditation was claimed from the International Association of Non-Traditional Schools, England, an association we have not been able to locate. Students were asked to pay tuition in cash ($200 for the Ph.D., $600 for the B.A.), and to send it wrapped in carbon paper, in a thick envelope. Our letters asking for more information went unanswered, and recently have been returned by the post office.

Wichita State University At one time offered an accredited Bachelor's degree in which over 80% of credits could come from prior learning.

William Darren University A correspondent asked for information on this school, apparently in or formerly in Phoenix, but we could find no record of them.

Windsor University One of California's first nontraditional schools, Windsor opened in Los Angeles in 1972, soon became a candidate for accreditation, and had an affiliation with Antioch. But things fell apart in the wake of claims of misleading statements and falsified credentials, and Windsor is no more.

Woodrow Wilson College of Law Georgia. Unaccredited, and now defunct, law school.

World College West This innovative school in Petaluma, California offered a variety of weekend programs leading to degrees, but ran out of money and closed in 1993.

World Open University This now-defunct unaccredited South Dakota school offered graduate degrees through an association with the Li Institute of Science and Technology (LIST).

World University (Arizona) In the early 1980s we received quite a few inquiries about World University. Here's what we know: The "world headquarters of the secretariat" was in Tucson Arizona. There was a joint degree-offering venture with Columbia Pacific University. One transcript we saw identified it as "affiliated with University Danzig, USA." But now there is no listed telephone, and letters to President H. John Zitko have not been answered.

World University (Dominican Republic) Santo Domingo, Dominican Republic. It was a medical school incorporated in Puerto Rico, affiliated with the then-accredited International Institute of the Americas, and recognized by the World Health Organization. But the phone has been disconnected and mail has been returned.

World University (Puerto Rico) There used to be a fully accredited World University with headquarters in Hato Rey, Puerto Rico, and various branches or alliances in places around the U.S., including the International Graduate School in St. Louis and World University of Florida. But the school is no longer accredited if, indeed, they are there at all.

Yaacov College International We heard that this school offered innovative programs, but when we wrote for information to the address provided (at Y.C.I. World Trade Center in Rotterdam), the letters were returned.

The experiments at Shari Lewis University in cross-breeding a ram with the Encyclopaedia Britannica look promising.

Appendix A
Glossary of Important Terms

When ideas fail, words come in very handy.
J. W. GOETHE

academic year: The period of formal academic instruction, usually from September or October to May or June. Divided into semesters, quarters, or trimesters.

accreditation: Recognition of a school by an independent private organization. Not a governmental function in the U.S. There are more than 100 accrediting agencies, some recognized by the Department of Education and/or CORPA, and some unrecognized, some phony or fraudulent

ACT: American College Testing program, administrators of aptitude and achievement tests.

adjunct faculty: Part-time faculty member, often at a nontraditional school, often with a full-time teaching job elsewhere. More and more traditional schools are hiring adjunct faculty, because they don't have to pay them as much or provide health care and other benefits.

advanced placement: Admission to a school at a higher level than one would normally enter, because of getting credit for prior learning experience or passing advanced-placement exams.

alma mater: The school from which one has graduated, as in "My alma mater is Michigan State University."

alternative: Offering an alternate, or different means of pursuing learning or degrees or both. Often used interchangeably with *external* or *nontraditional.*

alumni: Graduates of a school, as in "This school has some distinguished alumni." Technically for males only; females are *alumnae.* The singular is *alumnus* (male) or *alumna* (female), although none of these terms are in common use.

alumni association: A confederation of alumni and alumnae who have joined together to support their alma mater in various ways, generally by donating money.

approved: In California, a level of state recognition of a school generally regarded as one step below *accredited.*

arbitration: A means of settling disputes, as between a student and a school, in which one or more independent arbitrators or judges listen to both sides, and make a decision. A means of avoiding a courtroom trial. Many learning contracts have an arbitration clause. See *binding arbitration; mediation.*

assistantship: A means of assisting students (usually graduate students) financially by offering them part-time academic employment, usually in the form of a teaching assistantship or a research assistantship.

Associate's degree: A degree traditionally awarded by community or junior colleges after two years of residential study, or completion of 60 to 64 semester hours.

auditing: Sitting in on a class without earning credit for that class.

authorized: Until recently, a form of state recognition of schools in California. This category was phased out beginning in 1990, and now all schools must be approved or accredited to operate. Many formerly authorized schools are now billing themselves as candidates for approval.

Bachelor's degree: Awarded in the U.S. after four years of full-time residential study (two to five years in other countries), or the earning of 120 to 124 semester units by any means.

binding arbitration: Arbitration in which both parties have agreed in advance that they will abide by the result and take no further legal action.

branch campus: A satellite facility, run by officers of the main campus of a college or university, at another location. Can range from a small office to a full-fledged university center.

campus: The main facility of a college or university, usually comprising buildings, grounds, dormitories, cafeterias and dining halls, sports stadia, etc. The campus of a nontraditional school may consist solely of offices.

Chancellor: Often the highest official of a university. Also a new degree title, proposed by some schools to be a higher degree than the Doctorate, requiring three to five years of additional study.

CLEP: The College-Level Examination Program, a series of equivalency examinations given nationally each month.

coeducational: Education of men and women on the same campus or in the same program. This is why female students are called coeds.

college: In the U.S., an institution offering programs leading to the Associate's and/or Bachelor's, and sometimes higher degrees. Often used interchangeably with *university,* although traditionally a university is a collection of colleges. In England and elsewhere, *college* may denote part of a university (Kings College, Cambridge) or a private high school (Eton College).

colloquium: A gathering of scholars to discuss a given topic over a period of a few hours to a few days. ("The university is sponsoring a colloquium on marine biology.")

community college: A two-year traditional school, offering programs leading to the Associate's degree and, typically, many noncredit courses in arts, crafts, and vocational fields for community members not interested in a degree. Also called *junior college.*

competency: The philosophy and practice of awarding credit or degrees based on learning skills, rather than time spent in courses.

COPA: The Council on Postsecondary Accreditation, a now defunct private nongovernmental organization that recognized accrediting agencies.

CORPA: The Commission on Recognition of Postsecondary Accreditation, a nationwide nonprofit corporation, formed in 1994, that has essentially taken over the role of *COPA* (see above) in evaluating accrediting agencies and awarding recognition to those found worthy.

correspondence course: A course offered by mail and completed entirely by home study, often with one or two proctored, or supervised, examinations.

course: A specific unit of instruction, such as a course in microeconomics, or a course in abnormal psychology. Residential courses last for one or more semesters or quarters; correspondence courses often have no rigid time requirements.

cramming: Intensive preparation for an examination. Most testing agencies now admit that cramming can improve scores on exams.

credit: A unit used to record courses taken. Each credit typically represents the number of hours spent in class each week. Hence a 3-credit or 3-unit course would commonly be a class that met three hours each week for one semester or quarter.

curriculum: A program of courses to be taken in pursuit of a degree or other objective.

degree: A title conferred by a school to show that a certain course of study has been completed.

Department of Education: The federal agency concerned with all educational matters in the U.S. that are not handled by the departments of education in the 50 states. In other countries, similar functions are commonly the province of a ministry of education.

diploma: The certificate that shows that a certain course of study has been completed. Diplomas are awarded for completing a degree or other, shorter course of study.

dissertation: The major research project normally required as part of the work for a Doctorate. Dissertations are

expected to make a new and creative contribution to the field of study, or to demonstrate one's excellence in the field. See also *thesis.*

Doctorate: The highest degree one can earn (but see *Chancellor*). Includes Doctor of Philosophy (Ph.D.), Education (Ed.D.), and many other titles.

dormitory: Student living quarters on residential campuses. May include dining halls and classrooms.

early decision: Making a decision on whether to admit a student sooner than decisions are usually made. Offered by some schools primarily as a service either to students applying to several schools, or those who are especially anxious to know the outcome of their application.

ECFMG: The Education Commission for Foreign Medical Graduates, which administers an examination to physicians who have gone to medical school outside the U.S. and wish to practice in the U.S.

electives: Courses one does not have to take, but may elect to take as part of a degree program.

essay test: An examination in which the student writes narrative sentences as answers to questions, instead of the short answers required by a multiple-choice test. Also called a *subjective test.*

equivalency examination: An examination designed to demonstrate knowledge in a subject where the learning was acquired outside a traditional classroom. A person who learned nursing skills while working in a hospital, for instance, could take an equivalency exam to earn credit in, say, obstetrical nursing.

external: Away from the main campus or offices. An external degree may be earned by home study or at locations other than on the school's campus.

fees: Money paid to a school for purposes other than academic tuition. Fees might pay for parking, library services, use of the gymnasium, binding of dissertations, etc.

fellowship: A study grant, usually awarded to a graduate student, and usually requiring no work other than usual academic assignments (as contrasted with an *assistantship*).

financial aid: A catch-all term, including scholarships, loans, fellowships, assistantships, tuition reductions, etc. Many schools have a financial aid officer, whose job it is to deal with all funding questions and problems.

fraternities: Men's fraternal and social organizations, often identified by Greek letters, such as Zeta Beta Tau. There are also professional and scholastic fraternities open to men and women, such as Beta Alpha Psi, the national fraternity for students of accounting.

freshman: The name for the class in its first of four years of traditional study for a Bachelor's degree, and its individual members. ("She is a freshman, and thus is a member of the freshman class.")

grade-point average: The average score a student has made in all his or her classes, weighted by the number of credits or units for each class. Also called G.P.A.

grades: Evaluative scores provided for each course, and often for individual examinations or papers written for that course. There are letter grades (usually A, B, C, D, F) and number grades (usually percentages from 0% to 100%), or on a scale of 0 to 3, 0 to 4, or 0 to 5. Some schools use a pass/fail system with no grades.

graduate: One who has earned a degree from a school. Also, the programs offered beyond the Bachelor's level. ("He is a graduate of Yale University, and is now doing graduate work at Princeton.")

graduate school: A school or a division of a university offering work at the Master's or doctoral degree level.

graduate student: One attending graduate school.

GRE: The Graduate Record Examination, which many traditional schools and a few nontraditional ones require for admission to graduate programs.

honor societies: Organizations for persons with a high grade point average or other evidence of outstanding performance. There are local societies on some campuses, and several national organizations, the most prestigious of which is called Phi Beta Kappa.

honor system: A system in which students are trusted not to cheat on examinations, and to obey other rules, without proctors or others monitoring their behavior.

honorary doctorate: A nonacademic award, given regularly by more than 1,000 colleges and universities to honor distinguished scholars, celebrities, and donors of large sums of money. Holders of this award may, and often do, call themselves "Doctor."

junior: The name for the class in its third year of a traditional four-year U.S. Bachelor's degree program, or any member of that class. ("She is a junior this year.")

junior college: See *community college.*

language laboratory: A special room in which students can listen to foreign-language tapes over headphones, allowing many students to be learning different languages at different skill levels at the same time.

learning contract: A formal agreement between a student and a school, specifying independent work to be done by the student, and the amount of credit the school will award on successful completion of the work.

lecture class: A course in which a faculty member lectures to anywhere from a few dozen to many hundreds of students. Often lecture classes are followed by small group discussion sessions led by student assistants or junior faculty.

liberal arts: A term with many complex meanings, but generally referring to the nonscientific curriculum of a university: humanities, arts, social sciences, history, and so forth.

liberal education: Commonly taken to be the opposite of a specialized education; one in which students are required to take courses in a wide range of fields, as well as courses in their major.

licensed: Holding a permit to operate. This can range from a difficult-to-obtain state school license to a simple local business license.

life-experience portfolio: A comprehensive presentation listing and describing all learning experiences in a person's life, with appropriate documentation. The basic document used in assigning academic credit for life-experience learning.

LSAT: The Law School Admission Test, required by most U.S. law schools of all applicants.

maintenance costs: The expenses incurred while attending school, other than tuition and fees. Includes room and board (food), clothing, laundry, postage, travel, etc.

major: The subject or academic department in which a student takes concentrated coursework, leading to a specialty. ("His major is in English literature; she is majoring in chemistry.")

mentor: Faculty member assigned to supervise independent study work at a nontraditional school; comparable to *adjunct faculty.*

minor: The secondary subject or academic department in which a student takes concentrated coursework. ("She has a major in art and a minor in biology.") Optional at most schools.

MCAT: The Medical College Admission Test, required by most U.S. medical schools of all applicants.

multiple-choice test: An examination in which the student chooses the best of several alternative answers provided for each question; also called an *objective test.* ("The capital city of England is (a) London, (b) Ostrogotz-Plakatz, (c) Tokyo, (d) none of the above.")

multiversity: A university system with two or more separate campuses, each a major university in its own right, such as the University of California or the University of Wisconsin.

narrative transcript: A transcript issued by a nontraditional school in which, instead of simply listing the courses completed and grades received, there is a narrative description of the work done and the school's rationale for awarding credit for that work.

nontraditional: Something done in other than the usual or traditional way. In education, refers to learning and degrees completed by methods other than spending many hours in classrooms and lecture halls.

nonresident: (1) A means of instruction in which the student does not need to visit the school; all work is done by correspondence, telephone, or exchange of audiotapes or videotapes; (2) A person who does not meet residency requirements of a given school and, as a result, often has to pay a higher tuition or fees.

objective test: An examination in which questions requiring a very short answer are posed. It can be multiple choice, true-false, fill-in-the-blank, etc. The questions are related to facts (thus objective) rather than to opinions (or subjective).

BEARS' GUIDE

on the job: In the U.S., experience or training gained through employment, which may be converted to academic credit. In England, slang for having sex, which either confuses or amuses English people who read about "credit for on-the-job experience."

open admissions: An admissions policy in which everyone who applies is admitted, on the theory that the ones who are unable to do university work will drop out before long.

out-of-state student: One from a state other than that in which the school is located. Because most state colleges and universities have much higher tuition rates for out-of-state students, many people attempt to establish legal residence in the same state as their school.

parallel instruction: A method in which nonresident students do exactly the same work as residential students, during the same general time period, except they do it at home.

pass/fail option: Instead of getting a letter or number grade in a course, the student may elect, at the start of the course, a pass/fail option in which the only grades are either "pass" or "fail." Some schools permit students to elect this option on one or two of their courses each semester.

PEP: Proficiency Examination Program, a series of equivalency exams given nationally every few months.

Phi Beta Kappa: A national honors society that recognizes students with outstanding grades.

plan of study: A detailed description of the program an applicant to a school plans to pursue. Many traditional schools ask for this as part of the admissions procedure. The plan of study should be designed to meet the objectives of the *statement of purpose.*

portfolio: See *life-experience portfolio.*

prerequisites: Courses that must be taken before certain other courses may be taken. For instance, a course in algebra is often a prerequisite for a course in geometry.

private school: A school that is privately owned, rather than operated by a governmental department.

proctor: A person who supervises the taking of an examination to be certain there is no cheating, and that other rules are followed. Many nontraditional schools permit unproctored examinations.

professional school: School in which one studies for the various professions, including medicine, dentistry, law, nursing, veterinary, optometry, ministry, etc.

PSAT: Preliminary Scholastic Aptitude Test, given annually to high school juniors.

public school: In the U.S., a school operated by the government of a city, county, district, state, or the federal government. In England, a privately owned or run school.

quarter: An academic term at a school on the "quarter system," in which the calendar year is divided into four equal quarters. New courses begin each quarter.

quarter hour: An amount of credit earned for each classroom hour spent in a given course during a given quarter. A course that meets four hours each week for a quarter would probably be worth four quarter hours, or quarter units.

recognized: A term used by some schools to indicate approval from some other organization or governmental body. The term usually does not have a precise meaning, so it may mean different things in different places.

registrar: The official at most colleges and universities who is responsible for maintaining student records and, in many cases, for verifying and validating applications for admission.

rolling admissions: A year-round admissions procedure. Many schools only admit students once or twice a year. A school with rolling admissions considers each application at the time it is received. Many nontraditional schools, especially ones with nonresident programs, have rolling admissions.

SAT: Scholastic Aptitude Test, one of the standard tests given to qualify for admission to colleges and universities.

scholarship: A study grant, either in cash or in the form of tuition or fee reduction.

score: Numerical rating of performance on a test. ("His score on the Graduate Record Exam was not so good.")

semester: A school term, generally four to five months. Schools on the semester system usually have two semesters a year, with a shorter summer session.

semester hour: An amount of credit earned in a course representing one classroom hour per week for a semester. A class that meets three days a week for one hour, or one day a week for three hours, would be worth three semester hours, or semester units.

seminar: A form of instruction combining independent research with meetings of small groups of students and a faculty member, generally to report on reading or research the students have done.

senior: The fourth year of study of a four-year U.S. Bachelor's degree program, or a member of that class. ("Linnea is a senior this year, and is president of the senior class.")

sophomore: The second year of study in a four-year U.S. Bachelor's degree program, or a member of that class.

sorority: A women's social organization, often with its own living quarters on or near a campus, and usually identified with two or three Greek letters, such as Sigma Chi.

special education: Education of the physically or mentally handicapped, or, often, of the gifted.

special student: A student who is not studying for a degree either because he or she is ineligible or does not wish the degree.

statement of purpose: A detailed description of the career the applicant intends to pursue after graduation. A statement of purpose is often requested as part of the admissions procedure at a university.

subject: An area of study or learning covering a single topic, such as the subject of chemistry, or economics, or French literature.

subjective test: An examination in which the answers are in the form of narrative sentences or long or short essays, often expressing opinions rather than reporting facts.

syllabus: A detailed description of a course of study, often including the books to be read, papers to be written, and examinations to be given.

thesis: The major piece of research that is completed by many Master's degree candidates. A thesis is expected to show a detailed knowledge of one's field and ability to do research and integrate knowledge of the field.

TOEFL: Test of English as a Foreign Language, required by many schools of persons for whom English is not the native language.

traditional education: Education at a residential school in which the Bachelor's degree is completed through four years of classroom study, the Master's in one or two years, and the Doctorate in three to five years.

transcript: A certified copy of the student's academic record, showing courses taken, examinations passed, credits awarded, and grades or scores received.

transfer student: A student who has earned credit in one school, and then transfers to another school.

trimester: A term consisting of one third of an academic year. A school on the trimester system has three equal trimesters each year.

tuition: In the U.S., the money charged for formal instruction. In some schools, tuition is the only expense other than postage. In other schools, there may be fees as well as tuition. In England, tuition refers to the instruction or teaching at a school, such as the tuition offered in history.

tuition waiver: A form of financial assistance in which the school charges little or no tuition.

tutor: See *mentor*. A tutor can also be a hired assistant who helps a student prepare for a given class or examination.

undergraduate: Pertaining to the period of study from the end of high school to the earning of a Bachelor's degree; also to a person in such a course of study. ("Barry is an undergraduate at Reed College, one of the leading undergraduate schools.")

university: An institution that usually comprises one or more undergraduate colleges, one or more graduate schools, and, often, one or more professional schools.

Lesson 9 in Jack's home study course
in entomology was a bit more than
he had bargained for.

Appendix B
Bibliography

"What! Another of those damned, fat, square, thick books!
Always scribble, scribble, scribble, eh, Mr. Gibbon?"
THE DUKE OF GLOUCESTER, GIBBON'S PATRON,
ON BEING PRESENTED WITH VOL. III OF HIS *DECLINE AND FALL OF THE ROMAN EMPIRE*

Most of these books are available in bookstores and libraries. Some, however, are sold only or primarily by mail. In those cases we have given ordering information. In addition, some highly recommended books are now out of print. If you feel from the description that they would be useful in your situation, try your local library or a good second-hand bookstore.

GENERAL REFERENCE BOOKS

The H.E.P. Higher Education Directory (Higher Education Publications, 6400 Arlington Blvd., Suite 648, Falls Church, VA 22042; 703-532-2300) We list this first because it is the one we use the most. Until 1983, the U.S. Department of Education published a comprehensive directory of information on colleges and universities. When President Reagan announced his intention to shut down the Department of Education, their publication was discontinued and H.E.P. began publishing an almost identical directory. It emerges toward the end of each year and gives detailed factual information (no opinions or ratings) on all accredited and a few other schools. They used to list California-approved schools as well, but stopped in 1988. About 620 pages.

Accredited Institutions of Postsecondary Education (Oryx Press). The standard reference book for accredited schools, issued around the middle of each year, it lists every accredited institution and candidate for accreditation. This is the book most people use to determine conclusively whether or not a given American school is accredited.

Barron's Profiles of American Colleges (Barron's Education Series). A massive 1,300-page volume that describes every accredited college and university in America, with lists of majors offered by each school.

Comparative Guide to American Colleges by James Cass and Max Birnbaum (HarperCollins). One of the "standard" directories of traditional schools. Unlike Lovejoy's and Barron's, however, it is both factual and opinionated, a good feature. Over 800 pages of school descriptions and statistical information.

Directory of External Graduate Programs by Mary C. Kahl (Regents College, Cultural Education Center, Albany NY 12230). Twenty-six typewritten pages; a page on each of 20 programs, with a bit more information on each than in this book.

How to Earn a College Degree Without Going to College by James P. Duffy (John Wiley & Sons). Much along the lines of our guide, but describes only Bachelor's programs at accredited schools (fewer than 100 of them) and only wholly nonresident programs.

How to Earn an Advanced Degree Without Going to Graduate School by James P. Duffy (John Wiley & Sons). The graduate-school version of the above book lists 140 accredited nonresidential Master's and doctoral programs.

The Independent Study Catalog (Peterson's Guides). In effect, a master catalog listing all 10,000+ courses offered by the 71 U.S. and Canadian institutions offering correspondence study. Only the course titles are given, so it is still necessary to write to the individual schools for detailed information. Updated periodically, the latest edition is the 6th, for 1995.

International Handbook of Universities (Groves Dictionaries) 1,506 pages and an amazing $215 price tag. Gives detailed information on virtually every college, university, technical institute, and training school in the world, with the exception of the British Commonwealth and the U.S., which are covered in two companion volumes.

Lovejoy's College Guide by Charles T. Straughn & Barbarasue Straughn (Prentice-Hall). Briefer descriptions than other guides. In the past, the usefulness of Lovejoy's has been marred by the listing of some real clinkers: totally phony diploma mills that somehow managed to get past the editors.

Oryx Guide to Distance Learning (Oryx Press). 608 pages for a whopping $89.95. Lists 115 accredited U.S. institutions, focusing on audio, video, and on-line instruction.

Peterson's Guide to Graduate and Professional Programs (Peterson's Guides). Five large books, each describing in detail opportunities for residential graduate study in the U.S. Volumes cover social science and humanities, biological and agricultural sciences, physical sciences, and engineering. There is also a summary volume. The series is updated annually.

Peterson's Guide to Four-Year Colleges (Peterson's Guides). Another massive annual directory (some 2,800 pages), covering traditional accredited schools only.

Campus-Free College Degrees by Marcie K. Thorson (Thorson Guides). This well-done book covers the same territory as ours, but accredited schools only.

Best's External Degree Directory by Thomas J. Lavin. Much more detail than this book on many fewer schools. At $50 for under 300 pages, a bit pricey.

CREDIT FOR LIFE
EXPERIENCE LEARNING

Creditable Portfolios: Dimensions in Diversity (Council for Adult and Experiential Learning [CAEL], 223 W. Jackson Blvd., #510, Chicago, IL 60606, (312) 922-5909. $85 for all seven; $65 for any four). A looseleaf portfolio containing nine actual student portfolios from seven schools, including rationales for the procedures used, and credit awarded.

Earn College Credit for What You Know by Lois Lamdin (CAEL; see above; $8.95). How to put together a life experience portfolio: how to gather the necessary information, document it, and assemble it.

National Guide to Educational Credit for Training Programs and Guide to the Evaluation of Educational Experiences in the Armed Forces (Oryx Press). Many nontraditional programs use these four large volumes to assess credit for non-school learning. They describe and make credit recommendations for hundreds of corporate and military training programs.

Self-Assessment and Planning Manual by Linda Headley-Walker, *et al* (University of the State of New York, 7 Columbia Circle, Albany, NY 12203). While prepared primarily for potential Regents College students, this inexpensive and splendid 72-page manual could benefit anyone uncertain whether to pursue a nontraditional degree, and, if so, how to go about it. Guided exercises help the reader determine if he or she really needs a degree, how to assess prior educational experience, how to plan financially, and so forth.

Using Licenses and Certificates as Evidence of College-Level Learning by Harriet Cabell (CAEL; see above; $3). A five-page summary of Dr. Cabell's doctoral research, examining the practices of schools that award credit based on applicants' licenses and certificates.

The Value of Personal Learning Outside College by Peter Smith (Acropolis Books). Dr. Smith, the founder of Vermont Community College and later the lieutenant governor of Vermont, has written a charming and very useful book on matters related to earning credit for non-school learning (which, he points out, accounts for 90% of what an adult knows). Many inspiring case histories of adults who pursued this path, plus appendices that help one identify and describe out-of-school learning. (Formerly titled *Your Hidden Credentials)*

FOREIGN SCHOOLS

Worldwide Educational Directory by Mohammad S. Mirza (International Educational Services, P.O. Box 10503, Saddar, Karachi 3, Pakistan). Nearly 400 typewritten pages (in English) listing degree and non-degree-granting schools. Most of the data are accurate, but some less-than-wonderful schools are included, without warning, along with the good ones. Lack of index or alphabetized listings makes it very difficult to use.

World-Wide Inventory of Non-Traditional Degree Programs (UNESCO, c/o Unipub, 4611-F Assembly Drive, Lanham, MD 20706-4391). A generally useful United Nations report on what many of the world's nations are doing in the way of nontraditional education. Some helpful school descriptions, and lots of detailed descriptions of evening courses offered by workers' cooperatives in Bulgaria and suchlike.

Guide to Education Abroad by I. B. Chaudhary. Published from a now-closed P.O. Box in Bombay, this is an illegal pirated copy of our book. If anyone ever sees an ad for this dreadful product, please let us know, so we can commence proper legal action. Thank you.

UNISA: Information on the University of South Africa for Prospective American Students by Cameron Nolan ($15 from Nolan & Kennedy, 23400 Covello St., West Hills, CA 91304). UNISA is one of the few major universities in the world offering degrees through the doctoral level entirely by correspondence study. But the process of dealing with them can be extremely complex and frustrating. Ms. Nolan has written a detailed guide to the process of applying to, enrolling in, and working at the University. If you are considering UNISA, her 110-page single-spaced typewritten report may save time and anguish.

World Guide to Higher Education (Bowker Publishing Co.). A comprehensive survey, by the United Nations, of educational systems, degrees, and qualifications, from Afghanistan to Zambia.

MEDICAL SCHOOLS

Foreign Medical Schools for U.S. Citizens by Carlos Pestana, M.D., Ph.D. (P.O. Box 790617, San Antonio, TX 78279-0617). This wonderful book is now back in print in an updated 1995 edition. It gives anecdotal, well-written, and very informative write-ups on the good and less-good best foreign schools for American medical school applicants, as well as application tips and other survival advice. Well worth the $20 (includes shipping by two-day priority mail.)

The Medical School Applicant: advice for premedical students by Carlos Pestana, M.D., Ph.D. (see immediately above; $13). Another wonderful book by Dr. Pestana, bringing his unique perspective to all the usual matters that books on medical schools have, and a great deal more, including a remarkable chapter on "Special angles: the dirty tricks department—a frank analysis of unconventional pathways to a medical education."

FINANCIAL AID

Finding Money for College by John Bear and Mariah Bear (Ten Speed Press). We collected all the information we could find about the nontraditional and unorthodox approaches to getting a share in the billions of dollars that go unclaimed each year, including barter, real estate and tax gambits, negotiation, creative payment plans, obscure scholarships, foundations that make grants to individuals, etc. Any bookstore can supply or order this book, or you can buy it by mail from the distributor of *Bears' Guide*, C & B Publishing, P. O. Box 826, Benicia, CA 94510.

The Scholarship Book by Daniel Cassidy and Michael Alves (Career Press), The Graduate Scholarship Directory by Daniel Cassidy (Career Press), and The International Scholarship Directory by Daniel Cassidy (Career Press). A complete printout of the data banks of information used by Cassidy's National Scholarship Research Service, described in Chapter 8. Tens of thousands of sources are listed for undergraduate and graduate students, for study in the U.S. and overseas.

Leider's Lectures: A Complete Course in Understanding Financial Aid by Robert Leider (Octameron Associates, 1900 Mt. Vernon Ave., Alexandria, VA 22301-1302). Contains an immense amount of useful information and good advice compacted into 40 pages.

Octameron also publishes a series of other helpful books, booklets, and pamphlets on financial aid (and other academic subjects) for $5–$8. For a catalog and price list, write to the above address.

MISCELLANY

Killing the Spirit: Higher Education in America by Page Smith (Viking Penguin). In 1990, one of John's writer-heroes issued this extraordinary book about everything that is wrong in higher education. From page 1: "The major themes might be characterized as the impoverishment of the spirit by 'academic fundamentalism,' the flight from teaching, the meretriciousness of most academic research, the disintegration of the disciplines, the alliance of the universities with the Department of Defense . . . etc., and last but not least, the corruptions incident to 'big time' collegiate sports." Read this wonderful book.

College on Your Own by Gene R. Hawes and Gail Parker (Bantam Books). This remarkable book, now out of print, serves as a syllabus for a great many fields, for people who want to do college-level work at home, with or without the guidance of a college. A brief overview of each field (anthropology, biology, chemistry, history, etc.) and a detailed reading list for learning more about the field. Quite valuable in preparing learning contracts. Why doesn't some shrewd publisher put this fine volume back in print?

The External Degree as a Credential: Graduates' Experiences in Employment and Further Study by Carol Sosdian and Laure Sharp (National Institute of Education). This 1978 report is probably the most often misquoted and misinterpreted educational survey ever published. Many schools (some good, some not) cite the findings (a high satisfaction level of external students and a high acceptance level of external degrees) without mentioning it related only to fully accredited undergraduate degrees, and has little or no relevance to unaccredited graduate degrees.

The Ph.D. Trap by Wilfred Cude (Medicine Label Press, RR2, West Bay, Nova Scotia B0E 3K0 Canada). The author was treated very badly in his own graduate program, which turned him into a reformer. Farley Mowat writes that he is "the kind of reformer this world needs. Humane, literate, reasonable, and utterly implacable, he has just unmasked the gruesome goings on in the academic morgue that deals in doctoral degrees. Any student contemplating the pursuit of a doctorate had better read The Ph.D. Trap as a matter of basic self-preservation...."

This Way Out: A guide to alternatives to traditional college education in the U.S. by John Coyne and Tom Hebert (E. P. Dutton). A delightful, if out-of-date book, now out of print, that describes a small number of alternatives in detail, with inspirational interviews with participants. Includes an intriguing essay on self-education by hiring tutors, and sections as diverse as how to study, how to hitchhike successfully, what to do when revolution breaks out in the country in which you are studying, and how to deal with large universities worldwide.

Winning the Ph.D. Game by Dr. Richard W. Moore (Dodd, Mead & Co.). Now apparently out of print, this is a lighthearted, extremely useful guidebook for current and prospective doctoral students. Covers the entire process, from selecting schools to career planning. Moore's aim is to "describe the folk wisdom passed from one generation of graduate students to the next (in order to) make the whole process less traumatic." He succeeds admirably.

DIPLOMA MILLS

Diploma Mills: Degrees of Fraud by David W. Stewart and Henry A. Spille (Oryx). Originally this book was to provide details on specific operating diploma mills, but sadly, the authors either lost courage or were dissuaded by their attorneys, and it turned out to be only a moderately interesting survey of the history of the problem, with a once useful but now quite dated summary and evaluation of the current school laws in all 50 states.

Diploma Mills: The Paper Merchants by Jerry Seper and Richard Robinson. Reprint of a lengthy series of articles that ran in the Arizona *Republic* newspaper in 1983, describing many institutions they chose to call diploma mills, then operating in Arizona. Many subsequently relocated to other states. The newspaper stopped distributing the booklet; but you can get a photocopy from us for

$10 (including first class postage). This is for historical reference only. Please don't buy this booklet expecting to get the addresses of currently-operating diploma mills; they aren't in here. John & Mariah Bear, P. O. Box 7070, Berkeley, CA 94707.

JOURNALS

Two journals or periodicals that have articles on nontraditional or alternative or external education:

The American Journal of Distance Education, which started in 1987, published by the Office for Distance Education, College of Education, 403 S. Allen St., Suite 206, Pennsylvania State University, University Park, PA 16801-5202.

Distance Education, the journal of ASPESA, the Australian and South Pacific External Studies Association, Deakin University Press, Geelong, Victoria 3217, Australia.

ELECTRONIC BULLETIN BOARDS

There are at least four 'rest stops' along the information superhighway where people gather electronically to discuss issues relating to distance learning and nontraditional higher education. If you have a computer, a modem, and access to the Internet (we use the gateway provided by American OnLine), you are welcome to join in the discussion, or just "lurk" and read the communications without ever identifying yourself.

The only problem with the Internet is the sheer volume of available information. Just these few locations, representing the tiniest fraction of one percent of what is out there, nonetheless account for thousands of pages of information, and hundreds of new messages every week.

A major source of information is Dr. E's Eclectic Compendium of Electronic Resources for Adult/Distance Education. The html version is at this location: http://www.oak-ridge.com/orr.html FTP at host:una.hh.lib.umich.edu Path: /inetdirsstacks Fill: disted:ellsworth (*Note:* if you don't know what all this stuff means, then you must seek outside assistance for getting started on the Internet.)

alt.education.distance Perhaps the most active news group on the Internet discussing nontraditional or alternative education is known as alt.education.distance. It is the one place John checks into regularly to answer questions, make comments, suffer abuse, and gain information. He accesses it through the "Newsgroup" section in the Internet access section of America OnLine, but it can also be reached through any other Internet access service.

DEOS, the Distance Education Online Service, is a service offered by the Center for Distance Learning at Pennsylvania State University. The on-line access is listserv@psuvm.bitnet.psu.edu Leave a message reading: subscribe deos (your name)

AEDNET (Adult Education Network) is a comparable service offered by Nova Southeastern University. To learn more about them on-line, log in to listserv@alpha.acast.nova.edu and leave a message reading: subscribe aednet (your name)

John Bear on line. At press time, John had been offered the opportunity to conduct a nontraditional degree forum on America OnLine, a bulletin board service with over one million members, to begin sometime in 1995. Unlike most other providers, AOL does not charge extra for high-speed connections (9,600 or 14,400 baud), or for Internet connections. AOL can be reached at (800) 827-3338. They generally offer ten free hours of on-line time for newcomers to explore the system. John can be reached, in the meantime, at johnbbear@aol.com

SELF-SERVING BOOKS

Every so often, the owners of less-than-wonderful schools have published entire books solely to be able to give themselves a splendid write-up in the midst of many other reasonably accurate school listings, and, occasionally, to "get even" on us for daring to criticize their "schools."

Directory of United States Traditional and Alternative Colleges and Universities by Dr. Jean-Maximillien De La Croix de Lafayette. This large $30 volume contains much useful information on schools. Universities are rated by number of stars. Among the small number of top-rated schools in the U.S. is Andrew Jackson University, established by Dr. De La Croix de Lafayette.

Guide to Alternative Education by Educational Research Associates. This $35 waste of time claims to be "continuously updated," but the so-called 1994 version we bought not only had hundreds of errors, but it listed schools that went out of business ten or more years ago. We learned about this book when a fictitious name we used in a communication with Century University received a solicitation to buy it. Not surprisingly, the longest and most favorable listing in the entire book is the one for Century University.

How to Earn a University Degree Without Ever Leaving Home by William Ebbs. A 54-page book selling for $20, with an astonishing number of errors of fact. Identifies the University de la Romande as the most outstanding nontraditional school in the world. William Ebbs is the pseudonym of Raymond Seldis, administrator, at the time, of the University de la Romande. What an amazing coincidence! The now-defunct California University for Advanced Studies is identified as the second best school in the world.

How to Obtain a College Degree by Mail by Edward P. Reddeck. Reddeck has been imprisoned at least twice for running phony schools, and once published this entire large book solely to be able to include a section extolling his phony American International University as one of the world's best.

Legal University Degrees by Mail by "Jacques Canburry" or, in another printing, "Herald Crenshaw."

Written and published by Ronald Pellar, the man who runs the diploma mill called Columbia State University from a mail forwarding service in Louisiana. Amazingly, the book chooses Columbia State as the best university in America and refers to this book as a "phony guide," and a "brochure." Despite a cover price of $49.95, the book has been sent free to those who request it. For goodness sake, don't waste any money buying it, but if Pellar will send you a free one, and you enjoy what some have called "educational pornography," then why not. He has used many mail forwarding services. The most recent one we know about is Official University Directory, 15568 Brookhurst, #139, Westminster, CA 92683.

Finally, a word or two about this book, *Bears' Guide*, from John: Over the years, some critics have accused me of writing a self-serving book, because kind words were said about schools with which I had some connection or affiliation. This sort of criticism is, I believe, quite unwarranted. Of course I have said positive things about those five schools with which I have had some connection over the past 21 years; I wouldn't have become involved with them if I didn't think they were good. But in this book, I have been careful to make clear my connection (as, currently, with the MBA of Heriot-Watt University), and I have always treated hundreds of other schools, some of them fierce competitors, very favorably.

Established
June 3, 517

Appendix C
About the Personal
Counseling Services

If you would like personal advice and recommendations, based on your own specific situation, a personal counseling service is available, by mail. John started this service in 1977, at the request of many readers. While John remains a consultant, since 1981, the actual personal evaluations and consulting are done by two colleagues of his, who are leading experts in the field of nontraditional education.

For a modest consulting fee:

1. You will get a long personal letter evaluating your situation, recommending the best degree programs for you (including part-time programs in your area if relevant) and estimating how long it will take and what it will cost you to complete you degree(s).

2. You will get answers to any specific questions you may have, with regard to any programs you may now be considering, institutions you have already dealt with, or other relevant matters.

3. You will get detailed, up-to-the-minute information on institutions and degree programs, equivalency exams, sources of the correspondence courses you may need, career opportunities, resumé writing, sources of financial aid, and other topics, in the form of prepared notes.

4. You will be able to telephone the service, to get as much follow-up counseling as you need for one full year, to keep updated on new programs and other changes, and to use the service as your personal information resource.

If you are interested in personal counseling, please write or call and you will be sent descriptive literature and a counseling questionnaire, without cost or obligation.

Once you have these materials, if you wish counseling, simply fill out the questionnaire and return it, with a letter and resumé if you like, along with the fee, and your personal reply and counseling materials will be prepared and airmailed to you.

For free information about this service, write or telephone:

Degree Consulting Services
P. O. Box 3533
Santa Rosa, California 95402
(707) 539-6466

NOTE: Use the above address only for matters related to the counseling service. For all other matters, write to us at P.O. Box 7070, Berkeley, CA 94707. Thank you.

—*John and Mariah Bear*

Appendix D
Why Religious Schools Are
No Longer Listed, and Where
to Find Out About Them

From a survey of our readers, it became clear that the chapter on Bible and other religious schools was of interest to maybe 3 percent of them, yet it accounted for nearly a third of our mail, two thirds of the complaint letters and hate mail, and about 99 percent of the anonymous letters. It seemed that whatever John said, it annoyed, angered, or infuriated someone. And the problem was compounded because either he had an especially hard time getting the facts straight, or those facts were elusive, or both. So, we gratefully accepted the offer of the Reverend Dr. Josh Walston of Washington state to create a separate book that covered only religious schools, to be published by C & B, the publishers of the book you hold in your hands. In mid 1995, however, Dr. Walston decided that he would like to begin self-publishing said book. This necessarily means an interruption in publication as he tools up for this venture, updates the last edition, and so on. He expects to have the new edition ready sometime in 1996; for more detailed information, you can contact him at P.O. Box 847, Longview, WA 98632, phone: (360) 577-8039. In the interim, he has kindly authorized us to reprint to following listings for interested readers. They represent, in his opinion, the best bets for students interested in such schools.

ACCREDITED SCHOOLS

ICI University   B
6300 North Belt Line Road
Irving, TX 75063
Dr. George M. Flattery, President
Bible, religious education
1967
Nonprofit, church $$$
(800) 444-0424
ICI offers a Bachelor of Arts entirely nonresidentially through regional and national offices in some 120 or more countries worldwide. Accredited by the Distance Education and Training Council (formerly the National Home Study Council).

Moody Bible Institute   B, M
820 North LaSalle Drive
Chicago, IL 60610
Philip Van Wynen, Dean of Enrollment Management
Religion, music, liberal arts
Nonprofit, independent $$
(312) 329-4000, (800) 955-1123
Some of Moody's Bachelor's and Master's degrees can be earned through courses taken in module form over standard school breaks (Christmas, spring, summer), with independent study in between. Moody also offers 24 correspondence courses, including Greek and Hebrew.

Southeastern College of the   B
Assemblies of God
see page 106 of this book

UNACCREDITED SCHOOLS

Bethany Bible College and Seminary   B, M, D
2311 Hodgesville Road, Box 1944
Dothan, AL 36302
Dr. H. D. Shuemake, Chancellor
Religious studies
Nonprofit $$
(205) 793-3189
Offers residential and nonresidential degrees at all levels in religious fields. Credit awarded for full-time ministry experience.

Faraston Theological Seminary   B, M, D
P.O. Box 847
Longview, WA 98632-7521
Dr. Rick Walston, President
Apologetics, Bible, ministry, philosophy, theology
Nonprofit $$
(360) 577-8039 (phone/fax)
In the school Dt. Walston established, each student, rather than following a preset curriculum, chooses a mentor (from Faraston's faculty, or approved others) who works with the student to develop and fulfill a course of study.

Greenwich School of Theology   B, M, D
29 Howbeck Lane, Clarborough, Nr. Retford
Notts. DN22 9LW, U.K.
The Rev. Dr. Byron Evans, Dean of Studies
Religion, theology, related areas
Nonprofit, independent $$
(44-1777) 703-058
Many students are members of the clergy in the U.K., but lay students and those living elsewhere in the world are welcome. Meetings are occasionally held at various U.K. locations, but all work may be done through correspondence study.

Subject Index

For years, our readers have been telling us how nice it would be if *Bears' Guide* had, in addition to a complete index to schools, a complete index to the *subjects* said schools offer. We agree that it would be extremely helpful if a reader interested in, say, an M.S. in financial planning could easily discern all the schools offering that degree, rather than having to skim through the entire book. Improvements have been made with each edition, and the following list *is* the most complete ever. Unfortunately, it's still not as comprehensive as we'd like, for a few reasons: (1) Many schools don't give us full information in the first place, either through oversight or, more likely, because knowing that courses and faculty are subject to change, they use a noncommittal statement like "many arts and science degrees are offered" to avoid error. (2) Some schools (mainly the big state colleges and universities, as well as some ambitious nontraditional institutions) offer so many subjects that it would be ridiculous to list them all.

READ ☞ That's why, in the school listings, you'll often see the notation "many fields" instead of specific subjects.
THIS! *Therefore, it will be necessary for you to review the school listings, looking for those that say "many fields."* This single matter is the cause of most of the *unjustified* complaints we get: "I was looking for a degree in forestry, and I didn't find it in your book." If you write to us thus, we will respond saying, "See the first paragraph at the top of page 313." It is also the case that many unaccredited schools offer independent study in almost any field a student may wish. Accordingly, for the most part, only the more structured single-subject unaccredited programs are listed here. See chapters 19-21 for those unaccredited schools with a wide range of fields.

Finally, bear in mind that many subject areas are so broad ("general studies") or all-inclusive ("social science") that a wide range of things can be done in them. Further, there are "side door" approaches to various fields. If a school offers only "history" and a student wishes to study "technology," it may be possible to do a degree in the history of technology. "Education" is another commonly-used side door.

The following list contains only those programs that require little or no on-campus residency. The reason for this is that there are now so many evening and weekend programs (many of which are in chapters 18 and 21) that offer the basics: business, accounting, management, teacher certification, etc. To list them all would swell this index to epic proportions, while helping very few readers. (How many people, after all, are willing to move cross country to be near the best-sounding night course in accounting!) Those looking for specific residential courses will find it simple to skim the appropriate chapter (18 lists accredited schools; 21 has unaccredited) for nearby resources. (The main index, of course, lists *all* schools, in alphabetical order).

Accounting
Barry University
Bemidji State University
City University
College of Great Falls
Elizabethtown College
Liberty University
Loyola College
Marywood College
Metropolitan State University
Northwood College
Regents College
Roger Williams College
Southwestern Adventist College
St. Mary of the Woods University
Thomas Edison State College
Universidad Autonoma Nacional de Mexico
University of Delaware
University of New England
Upper Iowa University

Acoustics
Heriot-Watt University
Pennsylvania State University

Acquisitions Management
American Graduate University

Acupuncture
California Acupuncture College
South Baylo University
Southwestern Acupuncture College

Addiction Studies
Graceland College

Administration
Athabasca University
Central Michigan University
Lindenwood College
Nova Southeastern University
Pacific States University

Roger Williams University
Southwestern Adventist College
University of New England
Walden University

Administration of Justice
Roger Williams University
University of Wyoming

Administrative Services
Universidad de San Jose

Advertising
Syracuse University

Aeronautics
Embry-Riddle Aeronautical University

African-American Studies
Thomas Edison State College

Agricultural Studies
Charles Sturt University
Iowa State University
Kansas State University
Massey University
National Universities Degree
    Consortium
Universidad Estatal a Distancia
University of London
University of Missouri at Columbia
University of Natal
University of New England
University of Wisconsin—River Falls

American Studies
Trinity College

Applied Science
Darling Downs Institute of
    Advanced Education

Architecture
University of Natal

Art History
Huron University
Trinity College

Art Therapy
Norwich University

Arts (incl. performing and visual)
Atlantic Union College
Brandon University
California State University,
    Dominguez Hills
Calumet College
Charles Sturt University
Darling Downs Institute of
    Advanced Education
FernUniversität
Goddard College
Huron University
Judson College
Norwich University
Open University (UK)
Rochester Institute of Technology
Southern International University
Southern Oregon State College
University of Natal
University of New England
University of South Africa

Asian Studies
University of New England

Aviation Management
City University

Banking
Universidad Mexicana del Noreste

Behavioral Sciences
Lesley College
Universidad de San Jose
University of Maryland
New York Institute of Technology
Atlantic Union College

Biochemistry
Trinity College

Biology
Judson College
Universidad de San Jose

Business (general)
American University in London
Auburn University
Bellarmine College
Boricua College
Darling Downs Institute
Davis and Elkins University
Dyke College
Electronic University Network
Empire State College
Foundation for Economic Education
Goddard College
Holborn College
Huron University
Iowa State University
Judson College
Liberty University
Loyola College
Massey University
Northeastern Illinois University
Nova Southeastern University
Old Dominion University
Ramkhamhaeng University
Southern Oregon State College
Southwestern Adventist College
Universidad Estatal a Distancia
University of Kentucky
University of Maryland
University of Massachusetts at
    Amherst
University of North Dakota
University of Phoenix
University of the State of New York
Webster University

Business Administration, M.B.A.
Athabasca University
Ball State University
Baruch College
Caldwell College
Calumet College
Chadron College
City University
Clarkson University
College of Great Falls
Colorado State University
Columbia Union College
Heriot-Watt University
Institute of Professional Financial
    Managers
International Management Training
    Centres
International School of Informational
    Management
John F. Kennedy University
Mary Washington College
Marywood College
Metropolitan State University
New York Institute of Technology
Oklahoma State University
Oral Roberts University
Portland State University
Regent University
Rensselaer Polytechnic Institute
Roger Williams University
Saint Mary-of-the-Woods
Southwestern Adventist College
Syracuse University
Universidad Autonoma Nacional de
    Mexico
University of Delaware
University of Durham
University of Hull
University of Montana
University of Natal
University of Nebraska, Lincoln
University of Pittsburgh
University of Sarasota
University of South Carolina
University of Wisconsin—Platteville
Uppsala University
Western Graduate College

California Studies
California State University—Chico

Career Development
John F. Kennedy University

Chemistry
Judson College

St. Mary-of-the-Woods
Universidad de San Jose
Universidad Estatial a Distancia
Universidad Nacional Abierta a
Mexico
University of Alaska
University of Calgary
University of Delaware
University of Kentucky
University of Mindanao
University of Natal
University of Nebraska—Lincoln
University of New Brunswick
University of Northern Colorado
University of Santa Barbara
University of Sarasota
University of South Africa
University of Surrey
University of Wyoming
Western Institute for Social Research
Western Michigan University

Educational & Training Systems Design
University of Twente

Educational Administration & Management
Eastern Michigan University
University of La Verne

Electronics & Electrical Engineering
Cooks Institute
FernUniversität
George Washington University
Grantham School of Engineering
Rice University
University of Idaho
World College

Emergency Medical Services
American College of Prehospital
Medicine

Engineering
Arizona State University
Auburn University
California State University—
Northridge
Colorado State University
Darling Downs Institute
Florida Atlantic University
Georgia Institute of Technology
Iowa State University
Mary Washington College
National Technological University

Oklahoma State University
Old Dominion University
Purdue University
Rensselaer Polytechnical Institute
Rochester Institute of technology
Southern Methodist University
Stanford University
Universidad Nacional Abierta
University of Colorado at Boulder
University of Delaware
University of Houston
University of Idaho
University of Illinois at Urbana-
Champaign
University of Kentucky
University of Massachusetts at
Amherst
University of Natal
University of Nebraska, Lincoln
University of North Dakota
University of South Carolina
University of Tennessee, Knoxville
University of Virginia
University of Wisconsin—Madison
Virginia Polytechnical Institute
Western Michigan University

English
Atlantic Union College
Bemidji State University
Caldwell College
Indiana University of Pennsylvania
Judson College
Southwestern Adventist College
St. Mary-of-the-Woods
Universidad Nacional Abierta a
Mexico
University of Delaware
University of East Asia
University of Waterloo
Uppsala University

Entrepreneurial Studies
Open University (Florida)

Environmental Health
Ferris State University

Environmental Studies
Antioch University
California State University—Chico
Lakehead University
Lesley College
University of Environmental Sciences
University of London

European Studies
Huron University

Family & Consumer Sciences
Iowa State University

Family Studies
University of Kentucky

Fashion
Judson College

Feminist Studies
Goddard College (see also, *Women's Studies*)

Film
California State University—
Dominguez Hills

Finance
American College
Barry University

Financial Planning
Asia Pacific International University
College for Financial Planning

Fire Sciences & Administration
California State University—Los
Angeles
City University
Open Learning Fire Service Program
University of Maryland

French
University of London
Uppsala University

General Studies
Athabasca University
Bob Jones University
Brandon University
Calumet College
Capital University
Indiana University
Indiana University Southeast
University of Nevada—Reno
University of Wisconsin—Green Bay
Western Michigan University

Geography
Universidad Nacional de Educacion
"Enrique Guzman y Valle"
University of Waterloo

German
Queens University

Gerontology
Lindenwood University
St. Mary-of-the-Woods College

Gestalt Therapy
Gestalt Institute of New Orleans

Government Contracting
American Graduate University

Hazardous Waste Management
National Technological University

Health Administration
Lindenwood College
St. Joseph's College
Trinity University
University of Colorado—Denver
University of North Carolina—
Chapel Hill

Health Care Management
City University

Health Sciences/Health Studies
Bishop Clarkson College
California College for Health
Sciences
California Institute of Integral
Studies
Charles Sturt University
John F. Kennedy University
University of Massachusetts at
Amherst
Webster University

Herbalism & Herbology
Dominion Herbal College
Emerson College of Herbology
Samra University of Oriental Medicine

Historic Preservation
Roger Williams University

History
Atlantic Union College
Bemidji State University
Caldwell College
California State University—
Dominguez Hills
Eckerd College
Judson College
Southwestern Adventist College

Trinity College
University of Delaware
University of Pittsburgh
University of Waterloo

Holistic & Natural Health
American College of Nutrition
American College of Nutripathy
Bastyr College
Dr. Jay Scherer's Academy of Natural
Healing
Galien College of Natural Healing
International College of Natural
Health Sciences
Pacific School of Nutrition
School of Natural Healing
Wild Rose College of Natural Healing

Home Economics
Judson College
University of Nebraska—Lincoln

Hospitality & Tourism
Lakehead University
Mt. Saint Vincent's University

**Human & Organizational
Development**
Eckerd College
Fielding Institute
Lindenwood College
Saint Mary's College (Minn.)

Human Behavior
See *Psychology*

Human Resource Management
Salve Regina University

Human Services
College of Great Falls
Empire State College
Graduate School of America
Lesley College
Metropolitan State University
New Hampshire College
Prescott College
Walden University
Western Institute for Social Research

Human Sexuality
Institute for the Advanced Study of
Human Sexuality

Humanities
Burlington College

California State University—
Dominguez Hills
Calumet College
Deakin University
Massey University
Open University of Israel
Ramkhamhaeng University
Saint Mary-of-the-Woods College
Southern Methodist University
Southern Oregon State College
Universidad de San Jose
University of Maryland

Hypnotherapy
American Institute of Hypnotherapy
American International University
Heartwood Institute
Southwest University

Independent Studies
Brigham Young University
Murray State University
University of South Florida

Industrial Technology
Universidad Nacional de Educacion
"Enrique Guzman y Valle"

Information Management
International School of Information
Management

Information Systems
New Jersey Institute of Technology

**Instructional & Performance
Technology**
Boise State University

Interdisciplinary Studies
Empire State College
Graduate School of America
New York Institute of Technology

Interior Design
Atlantic Union College
Judson College

International Business & Trade
Asian Pacific International University
Instituto Politinica Nacional

International Relations
Huron University
Open University of Israel
Salve Regina University

Universidad Nacional Abierta a
   Mexico
Uppsala University

Jewish Studies
Open University of Israel

Journalism
Saint Mary-of-the-Woods College
University of Nebraska—Lincoln

Languages
Atlantic Union College
Caldwell College
University of Natal

**Law (non–U.S. Bar qualifying. See
   also *Chapter 23, Nontraditional
   Law Schools*)**
Columbia Pacific University
FernUniversität
Greenwich University
Holborn College
Kensington University
Newport University
Nova Southeastern University
Open University of the Netherlands
Ramkhamhaeng University
Somerset University
Universidad Nacional Abierta a
   Mexico
University of Eastern Asia
University of London
University of South Africa
Uppsala University
Washington School of Law
William Howard Taft University

Leadership
University of New England

Liberal Arts
American University in London
Boricua College
Burlington College
Electronic University Network
Iowa State University
Northeastern Illinois University
Prescott College
Southern Methodist University
University of the State of New York

Liberal Studies
Elizabethtown College
Framingham State College
Graceland College

John F. Kennedy University
Linfield College
Mary Washington College
Northern Arizona University
Norwich University
Nova Southeastern University
Regis University
Salve Regina University
Syracuse University
University of Iowa
University of Northern Iowa
University of Oklahoma

Library Science
Syracuse University
University of South Carolina

Literature
California State University—
   Dominguez Hills
Goddard College
Indiana University of Pennsylvania
Universidad Nacional de Educacion
   "Enrique Guzman"

Management
American College
Asia Pacific International University
Barry University
Bellevue University
Central Michigan University
Clarkson College
College of Saint Scholastica
Colorado State University
Concordia University
Davis & Elkins University
Eckerd College
Heriot-Watt University
Huron University
International Management Training
   Center
Linfield College
Metropolitan State University
National Universities Degree
   Consortium
Northwood University
Open University (UK)
Open University of Israel
Open University of the Netherlands
Prescott College
Purdue University
Regent University
Southwestern College
Sri Lanka Institute of Distance
   Education
Universidad Nacional Abierta

University of Maryland
University of Massachusetts at
   Amherst
University of Phoenix
University of South Africa
Upper Iowa University
Walden University

**Management of Information
   Systems**
Asia Pacific International University
Salve Regina University

Maritime Management
Maine Maritime Academy

Marketing
Barry University
Northwood University
Upper Iowa University

Martial Arts
Eurotechnical Research University
Feather River University

Massage Therapy
Heartwood Institute
Northern Institute of Massage

Mathematics
FernUniversität
Judson College
Open University (UK)
Open University of Israel
Sri Lanka Institute of Distance
   Education
Trinity University
Universidad Nacional Abierta
Universidad National "Enrique
   Guzman"
University of Massachusetts at
   Amherst

Mechanics
University of Illinois at Urbana–
   Champaign

Media Studies
New School for Social Research
Universidad Nacional Abierta

Medical Technology
University of North Dakota

Metaphysics
American International University

Saint John's University
University of Metaphysics

Microcomputer Management
College of Great Falls

Military Science
American Military Academy

Museum Studies
John F. Kennedy University

Music
Brandon University
California State University—
    Dominguez Hills
California State University—
    Sacramento
U.S. College of Music

Naturopathy
Anglo-American Institute of
    Drugless Therapy

Nuclear Science
University of Maryland

Nursing
Athabasca University
Bellarmine College
Bishop Clarkson College
Brandon University
City University
Clarkson College
Corpus Christi University
Florida Atlantic University
Graceland College
Grand Valley State University
Kansas-Newman College
Loyola College
Murray State University
Old Dominion University
Southern Oregon State College
Southwestern Baptist University
Syracuse University
University of Calgary
University of Delaware
University of New Brunswick
University of North Dakota
University of the State of New York

Open Studies
Mankato State University

Operations Research
University of Northern Colorado

Organizational Studies & Administration
Eckerd College
Graduate School of America

Paralegal Studies
College of Great Falls
Saint Mary-of-the-Woods College
University of Maryland

Peace Studies
Antioch University

Pharmacy
Purdue University

Philosophy
Barry University
California Institute of Integral
    Studies
California State University—
    Dominguez Hills
Trinity College
Universidad Nacional Abierta a Mexico
University of Waterloo

Photography
Rochester Institute of Technology

Physical Education
Atlantic Union College
Physics
Universidad Nacional Abierta

Political Science & Studies
Ramkhamhaeng University
Queens University
Uppsala University

Poultry Science
Universidad Nacional Abierta a Mexico

Professional Studies
Bard College
Bellevue College
Elizabethtown College
Troy State University

Psychology & Counseling
Antioch University
Atlantic Union College
Australian College of Applied
    Psychology
Barry University
Caldwell College

California Institute of Integral
    Studies
College of Great Falls
Columbia Union College
Electronic University Network
Fielding Institute
Goddard College
Institute of Imaginal Studies
Institute of Transpersonal Psychology
John F. Kennedy University
Judson College
La Jolla University
Lindenwood College
Nova Southwestern University
Pacific States University
Pacifica Graduate Institute
Prescott College
Queens University
Saint Mary-of-the-Woods College
Saybrook Institute
Sonoma State University
Universidad de San Jose
Universidad Nacional Abierta a
    Mexico
University of Delaware
University of Idaho
University of London
University of Pittsburgh
University of Waterloo
Western Institute for Social Research

Public Administration
College of Great Falls
Saint Mary-of-the-Woods College
University of Maryland

Public Health
Loma Linda University
University of Massachusetts at Amherst
University of North Carolina at
    Chapel Hill

Public Policy Studies
Trinity College

Quality Assurance
California State University—
    Dominguez Hills

Radiology & Radiologic Technology
Bishop Clarkson College
Saint Joseph's College

Regional Studies
Atlantic Union College

Religious & Spiritual Studies
Berean College
Bob Jones University
Caldwell College
California Institute for Integral
  Studies
Columbia Union College
Faith Bible College
Griggs University
Harmony College of Applied Science
Judson College
Liberty University
North Central Bible College
Oklahoma Baptist University
Oral Roberts University
Oxford Graduate School
Princeton Theological Seminary
Saint John's University
Saint Martin's College & Seminary
Saint Mary-of-the-Woods College
Southeastern College of the Assem-
  blies of God
Southwestern Adventist College
University of South Africa
University of Waterloo

Restaurant & Food Service Management
Syracuse University

Rural Development
University of Alaska

Sciences
Boricua College
Charles Sturt University
Eurotechnical Research University
Florida Atlantic University
Goddard College
Massey University
Open University (UK)
Open University of Israel
Open University of the Netherlands
Ramkhamhaeng University
Southern Oregon State College
Sri Lanka Institute of Distance
  Learning
State University College
Universidad de San Jose
Universidad Nacional Abierta
Universidad Nacional de Educacion
  "Enrique Guzman"
University of Massachusetts at
  Amherst
University of Natal
University of New England

World Open University

Security Management
University of Leicester

Social Sciences
California State University—Chico
FernUniversität
Massey University
Open University (UK)
Open University of Israel
Saint Mary-of-the-Woods College
Southern Methodist University
Southern Oregon State College
Southwestern Adventist College
State University College
Syracuse University
Universidad de San Jose
Universidad Estatal a Distancia
Universidad Nacional Abierta
University of Maryland
University of Massachusetts at Amherst
University of Natal
University of Wyoming
Washington State University

Social Studies
Bemidji State University
Calumet College
Deakin University
University of Waterloo

Social Work
California State University—
  Sacramento
New Hampshire College
University of Alaska
University of North Dakota
Western Michigan University

Sociology
Caldwell College
College of Great Falls
Judson College
Universidad Nacional Abierta a Mexico
Wilfrid Laurier University

Software Engineering
National Technological University

Speech & Language
Nova Southeastern University

Speech Pathology
University of Wyoming

Statistics
Colorado State University
University of Massachusetts at
  Amherst

Systems Analysis
Linfield College

Tax Preparation & Law
Washington School of Law
William Howard Taft University

Technology & Technological Studies
American Technological University
Massey University
National Technological University
Open University (UK)
Open University of the Netherlands
Purdue University
Rensselaer Polytechnic Institute
Roger Williams University
Sri Lanka Institute of Distance
  Education
University of the State of New York
West Virginia Institute of
  Technology

Theater Arts
California State University—
  Dominguez Hills
Trinity College

Training & Development
International Management Centers

Transpersonal Studies
Atlantic Union College

Urban & Regional Planning
University of New England

Valuation Sciences
Lindenwood College

Vocational Education
Bemidji State University
Western Michigan University

Women's Studies
Antioch University
Atlantic Union College
Goddard College
Trinity College

School Index

This is an index to all the schools in chapters 16 through 25 and chapter 29. Schools mentioned incidentally in other chapters are not indexed.

California Western University. *See* California Coast University
Calumet College 117
Cambridge College 148
Cambridge Graduate School of Psychology 230
Campbell University 148
Campbellsville College 148
Campus-Free College. *See* Beacon College
Canadian School of Management 206
Canadian Temple College of Life 257
Canisius College 149
Capital City Religious Institute 207
Capital College 257
Capital University 117
Cardinal Publishing Company 257
Cardinal Stritch College 149
Carlton University 257
Carnegie Institute of Engineering 257
Carolina Institute of Human Relations 257
Carroll College 149
Carroll Studios 257
Carson-Newman College 149
Carthage College 288
Castleton State College 149
Cedar Crest College 149
Centenary College (Louisiana) 149
Centenary College (New Jersey) 150
Center for Psychological Studies 230
Center Graduate School 230
Central Board of Higher Education 257
Central California College of Law 241
Central Michigan University 94
Central States Research Center 257
Central Texas College 230
Central University 257
Central Washington University 150
Central Wesleyan College 150
Centre de Télé-Enseignement Universitaire 94
Centro de Estudios Universitarios Xochicalco 288
Century University 207
Chadron State College 95
Chadwick University 207
Chaminade University 150
Chapman College 150
Charles Dederich School of Law 288
Charles Sturt University 118
Charter Oak State College 95
Chartered University of Huron 257

Chase University 288
Chicago City-Wide College 95
Chicago Conservatory College 288
Chicago Medical College 257
Chicago State. *See also* Board of Governors B.A. Degree Program
Chicago State University 118
Chillicothe Business College 258
Chirological College of California 258
Christian College 258
Christian Congregation 288
Christian Fellowship Foundation 258
Christian Learning Institute. *See* University of the Rockies
CIFAS School of Medicine 288
Cincinnati Bible College and Seminary 150
City Business College. *See* International University (Missouri)
City Medical Correspondence College 258
City University 95
City University Los Angeles 207, 240
City University of New York 150, 151
Clark University 151
Clarkson College 95
Clarksville School of Theology 288
Clayton School of Natural Healing *See* American Holistic College
Clayton Theological Institute 258
Clayton University 288
Clemson College 258
Cleveland State University 151
Clinical Hypnosis Center 288
Clinical Psychotherapy Institute 288
Coast University 258
Cogswell College. *See* Open Learning Fire Service
Coker College 151
Colby-Sawyer College 288
Colegio Jacinto Trevino 288
Colgate College 258
College for Financial Planning. 95
College for Human Services 288
College Misericordia 151
College of Life 258
College of Adaptive Education Sciences 288
College of Applied Science 258
College of Clinical Hypnosis 288
College of Divine Metaphysics 258
College of Franklin and Marshall 258
College of Great Falls 96
College of Hard Knocks 258

College of Hilton Head 258
College of Homeopathy 258
College of Journalism 258
College of Life Science. *See* American Health Sciences Institute
College of Mount Saint Joseph 151
College of Mount Saint Vincent 152
College of Natural Therapeutics 258
College of Naturatrics 258
College of New Rochelle 152
College of Nonsense 258
College of Notre Dame of Maryland 152
College of Oriental Studies 288
College of Professional Studies 288
College of Racine 288
College of Saint Catherine 152
College of Saint Francis 152
College of Saint Mary 152
College of Saint Rose 152
College of Saint Scholastica 118, 153
College of Santa Fe 153
College of Southeastern Europe 207
College of Spiritual 258
College of Staten Island 153
College of the Palm Beaches 288
College of Universal Truth 258
Collegii Romanii 258
Collegium Technologicum Sussexensis Britannia 258
Colorado Christian University 153, 258
Colorado Institute of Transpersonal Psychology 289
Colorado State University 96. *See also* Mind Extension University; National Universities Degree Consortium
Colorado Technical College 289
Columbia College 153
Columbia College of Nursing 153
Columbia Pacific University 207, 240
Columbia School 258
Columbia State University 258
Columbia Southern University 208
Columbia Union College 96
Columbia University 118
Commenius International University 289
Commercial University 259
Commonwealth School of Law 259
Commonwealth University 259
Concordia University 153
Concoria Institute 289

*"So many schools. So many schools.
How will I ever decide?"*

rently unaccredited, their literature says the school, "anticipates eventual accreditation." Credit awarded for appropriate, degree-related life-experience learning. Former name: Pacific University of Hawaii.

Liverpool John Moores University (Rodney House, 70 Mount Pleasant, Liverpool, U.K. L3 5UX. Phone: (151) 231-2121, fax: (151) 709-0172): B.A. in health care fields through written "instructional packs" with supporting local tutorials from the former Liverpool Polytechnic.

London University (Anita Pincas, ESOL Dept., Institute of Education, 20 Bedford Way, London U.K. WC1H OAL. Phone: (44-171) 612-6522, fax: (44-171) 612-6534, Email: a.pincas@ioe.ac.uk): M.A. in education available through modules available over the Internet, and on-line interaction, with three weekends per year, in London.

Manchester Metropolitan University (All Saints, Manchester, U.K. M15 6BH. Phone: (161) 247-2000, fax: (161) 236-7383): Bachelor's in retail marketing though distance learning.

Napier University (219 Collington Road, Edinburgh, Scotland EH14 1DJ. Phone: (131) 444-2266, fax: (131) 455-7209): Open-learning M.B.A., as well as a variety of "certificates" in business-related fields.

Oxford Brookes University (Gipsy Lane, Oxford, U.K. OX3 0BP. Phone: (1865) 741 111, fax: (1865) 483-073): Distance-learning M.A. in education, intended for international school teachers.

Permaculture Academy: Bill Mollison, who we are informed by an on-line correspondent is the founder of a degree-granting institution in Australia, is working on founding a U.S. academy that will award diplomas and Bachelor's and graduate degree, probably in New Mexico. Permaculture is the study and practice of agriculture based on natural ecosystems, sustainable farming, renewable resources, etc.

Queens University (Kingston, Ontario, Canada): According to an article in the Chronicle of Higher Education, has begun offering an M.B.A. based on interactive video; a recent teleconference linked weekend executive M.B.A. students across the country.

University of Bath (Claverton Down, Bath, U.K. BA2 7AY. Phone: (1225) 826-826, fax: (1225) 462-508): Civil engineers or "equivalent," whatever that means, may pursue an M.S. in construction management over three to five years through correspondence, workbooks, video- and audiotapes, regular contact with tutors, and an annual ten-day residency in the first two years.

University of Birmingham: According to an on-line correspondent, this British school offers a distance-learning Master of Arts for teachers of linguistics or English (in Linguistics, Translation Studies, and Applied Linguistics) through a partnership with David English House, of Hiroshima. Applicants to this two-year program must have teaching experience and a Bachelor's degree or equivalent.

University of Dundee (Dundee, Scotland DD1 4HN. Phone: (1382) 223-181, fax: (1382) 201-604): Master's in medical education through a distance-learning program based on written materials and assigned textbooks, for people who teach in health-care fields. Also offers distance-learning diplomas in a number of medical-related fields, including rehabilitation technology and advanced nursing studies,

University of Huddersfield (Queensgate, Huddersfield, HD1 3DH U.K. Phone: (1484) 422-288, fax: (1484) 516-151): Offers both a Master's degree and a postgraduate diploma in geographic information systems (GIS).

University of Keele (Staffordshire, U.K. ST5 5BG. Phone: (1484) 621-111, fax: (1484) 613-847): Offers a two-year part-time M.B.A. based on instruction, examination, and a dissertation.